NCERT PHYSICS

REVISION WORK BOOK

Most Effective Revision
& Concept Zipper for >>>>

JEE, NEET & CUET

Vol 1 CLASS XI

NCERT PHYSICS

REVISION WORK BOOK

Most Effective Revision
& Concept Zipper for >>>>

JEE, NEET & CUET

Vol 1 CLASS XI

Authors
Dharmendra Singh *(B.Tech)*
Avinash Kumar *(B.Tech)*

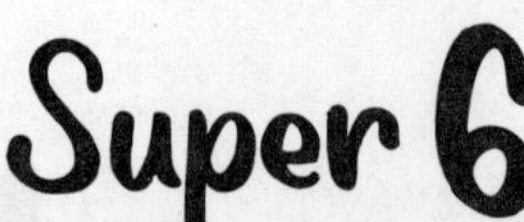

ADVANTAGES OF REVISION WORK BOOKS

1. Learn with fun while practicing with Self Assessment.
2. Different question types are helpful in increasing the learning and understanding about **Core Concepts** and **Conceptual Applications**.
3. Figure based small methodical questions also help in increasing **figure visualisation**.
4. Innovative style of practice in Workbook manner helps in breaking the monotonicity of subject.
5. Complete sync with NCERT along with **Competition Connect** and **Competition Edge Up** helps in building the foundation for the preparation of competitions like JEE, NEET and CUET.
6. Questions with one word or maximum one sentence long answers are very helpful in **Faster Revision** and **Confidence Boost Up**.

ARIHANT PRAKASHAN (SERIES), MEERUT

Administrative & Production Offices

Regd. Office
'Ramchhaya' 4577/15, Agarwal Road, Darya Ganj, New Delhi -110002
Tele: 011- 47630600, 43518550

Head Office
Kalindi, TP Nagar, Meerut (UP) - 250002
Tel: 0121-7156203, 7156204

Sales & Support Offices
Agra, Ahmedabad, Bengaluru, Bareilly, Chennai, Delhi, Guwahati, Hyderabad, Jaipur, Jhansi, Kolkata, Lucknow, Nagpur & Pune.

PRICE ₹310.00

PO No. : TXT-59-T066454-08-25

Published by Arihant Publications (India) Ltd.

For further information about the books published by Arihant, log on to www.arihantbooks.com or e-mail at info@arihantbooks.com

Follow us on   

FAB 4 Features

NCERT Tracker
Every topic is tagged with NCERT page numbers for better syncing with NCERT.

TOPIC 1

The International System of Units

NCERT Pg 1-3

1. Tick (✓/×) for correct/incorrect statement in given boxes.

(i) Unit of measurement is a well defined quantity. ☐

(ii) Unit of measurement must be adopted universally by convention or by law. ☐

(iii) Unit must be easily and accurately reproducible. ☐

(iv) Unit for a measurement must be too large. ☐

***13.** To determine the number of significant figures, the scientific notation is $a \times 10^b$. Here, the exponent b is called ______ (order/magnitude) of ________ (order/magnitude).

14. Tick (✓/×) for correct/incorrect statements in given boxes.

(i) All the non-zero digits are significant. ☐

(ii) All the zero between two non-zero digits are significant. ☐

(iii) The terminal or trailing zero(s) in a number without a decimal point are significant. ☐

Important Concept Tagging
Every question which is based on the important concept from JEE/NEET/CUET point of view is marked with *.

COMPETITION CONNECT

Topic 1. Accuracy, Precision of Instruments and Errors in Measurements [NCERT (Old) Pg. 22-27]

1. Usually there is a difference in true value and measured value of a quantity.

Now, complete following sentences choosing suitable option.

Error is positive, if observed value is ________ (more/less) than true value and is negative, if observed value is ________ (more/less) than true value.

Also, true value of a quantity is obtained by ________ (adding/subtracting) error from observed value.

2. The precision of a measurement is a measure of how close the measured value is to the true value.

True ☐ False ☐

Competition Connect
Supplement containing related portions of old NCERT which are present in NEET/JEE/CUET syllabus but removed from latest NCERT.

COMPETITION EDGE UP

1. *The dimensional formula of latent heat is* **[NCERT Pg. 7, JEE Main 2024]**

(a) $[MLT^{-2}]$ ☐ (b) $[M^0LT^{-2}]$ ☐

(c) $[ML^2T^{-2}]$ ☐ (d) $[M^0L^2T^{-2}]$ ☐

2. *In an expression $a \times 10^b$,* **[NCERT Pg. 4, JEE Main 2024]**

(a) b is order of magnitude for $a \geq 5$ ☐

(b) b is order of magnitude for $a \leq 5$ ☐

(c) a is order of magnitude for $b \leq 5$ ☐

(d) b is order of magnitude for $5 < a \leq 10$ ☐

6. *If mass is written as $m = k\,c^P G^{\frac{-1}{2}} h^{\frac{1}{2}}$, then the value of p will be (constants have their usual meaning with k a dimensionless constant)* **[NCERT Pg. 9, JEE Main 2024]**

(a) $\frac{-1}{3}$ ☐ (b) 2 ☐

(c) $\frac{1}{2}$ ☐ (d) $\frac{1}{3}$ ☐

7. *A force is represented by $F = ax^2 + bt^{1/2}$, where x = distance and t = time. The dimensions of b^2/a are* **[NCERT Pg. 9, JEE Main 2024]**

(a) $[ML^{-1}T^{-1}]$ ☐ (b) $[ML^3T^{-3}]$ ☐

(c) $[ML^2T^{-3}]$ ☐ (d) $[MLT^{-2}]$ ☐

Competition Edge Up
Selected PYQs in Sync with NCERT Chapter.

CONTENTS

Chapter 01

Units and Measurement

Scan and take Chapter Test

TOPIC 1

The International System of Units

1. Tick (✓/×) for correct/incorrect statement in given boxes.

(i) Unit of measurement is a well defined quantity. ☐

(ii) Unit of measurement must be adopted universally by convention or by law. ☐

(iii) Unit must be easily and accurately reproducible. ☐

(iv) Unit for a measurement must be too large. ☐

2. Let x is the numeric value of a physical quantity when it is compared with a unit u, then correct relation is

(a) $\frac{x}{u}$ = constant ☐ (b) $x \cdot u$ = constant ☐

(c) $\frac{x}{u^2}$ = constant ☐ (d) $x^2 \cdot u$ = constant ☐

3. Match the terms in Column I with the terms in Column II.

Column I	Column II
A. Fundamental quantity	1. Derived units
B. Combination of base units	2. System of units
C. Complete set of units	3. Base units

A. ________________ B. ________________ C. ________________

4. The unit of plane angle is __________ with the symbol ________ and the unit of the solid angle is _____________ with the symbol_____________ .

*Concepts of all questions bearing * are important for JEE/NEET/CUET.*

5. Which of the following pair is correctly matched?

I. Plane angle → (figure: O, r, $d\theta$, dS) II. Partial angle → (figure: O, r, $d\Omega$, dA)

____

6. Match the fundamental quantities given in Column I with their units in Column II.

Column I	Column II
A. Length	1. Cd
B. Mass	2. mol
C. Time	3. K
D. Electric current	4. A
E. Temperature	5. s
F. Amount of substance	6. kg
G. Luminous intensity	7. m

A. ______ B. ______ C. ______ D. ______
E. ______ F. ______ G. ______

7. Pick the odd one out from the given terms.

Kilogram, Kelvin, Amount of substance, Candela

____

8. Match the items in Column I with their values in Column II.

Column I	Column II
A. Size of atomic nucleus	1. 9.46×10^{15} m
B. 1 parsec	2. 10^{-14} m
C. 1 light year	3. 3.08×10^{16} m

A. ______ B. ______ C. ______

9. Arrange the following in increasing order of their values in SI unit.

Barn, Hectare, Are

____

10. Pick the odd one out from given terms.

Tonne, Carat, Quintal, Roentgen.

____

11. Match the units given in Column I with their value in Column II.

Column I	Column II
A. Litre	1. $3{\cdot}7\times 10^{-10}\ s^{-1}$
B. Carat	2. $10^{-3}\ m^3$
C. Curie	3. 200 mg
D. Roentgen	4. 2.58×10^{-4} C/kg

A. ________ B. ________ C. ________ D. ________

TOPIC 2

Significant Figures

NCERT Pg. 3-7

12. A choice of change of different ________ (units/number) does not change the ________ (units/number) of significant digits or figures in a measurement.

***13.** To determine the number of significant figures, the scientific notation is $a\times 10^b$. Here, the exponent b is called ______ (order/magnitude) of _______ (order/magnitude).

14. Tick (✓/✗) for correct/incorrect statements in given boxes.

(i) All the non-zero digits are significant. ☐

(ii) All the zero between two non-zero digits are significant. ☐

(iii) The terminal or trailing zero(s) in a number without a decimal point are significant. ☐

(iv) For a number greater than 1, without decimal, the trailing zero(s) are not significant. ☐

(v) For a number with a decimal, the trailing zero(s) are significant. ☐

***15.** State the number of significant figures in the following

I. 0.007 m^2 II. 2.64×10^{24} kg III. 0.2370 g/cm^3

____

16. Pick the odd one out in term of significant figure.

123 m, 12300 cm, 123000 mm, 4.700 m

____

17. Ratio of number of significant figures in 4500 and 0.045 is ________ .

18. Which of the following is correctly matched pair for significant figures?

I. Division or multiplication → Final result has least decimal places

II. Addition or subtraction → Final result has least significant figures

____

19. In an experiment, refractive index of water is found to have values

1.29, 1.33, 1.34, 1.35, 1.32, 1.36, 1.30 and 1.33

Then, mean value of refractive index is _______ and true value of refractive index is _______ .

20. Consider the following points regarding rounding off the uncertain digits and choose correct statement(s).

I. The preceding digit is raised by 1, if the insignificant digit to be dropped is more than 5 and is left unchanged, if it is less than 5.

II. If the preceding digit is odd, the insignificant digit is simply dropped and if it is even, the preceding digit is raised by 1.

____

21. The value of π is 3.1415926... upto 4 significant figures is

(a) 3.142 ☐ (b) 3.141 ☐ (c) 3.143 ☐ (d) 3.144 ☐

***22.** Each side of a cube is measured to be 7.203 m. Find the correct matching pair from given values.

I. Total surface area $\rightarrow$ 311.29 m^2 II. Volume $\rightarrow$ 373.7 m^3

____

23. 5.74 g of a substance occupies 1.2 cm^3. Its density in correct significant figures is

(a) 4.9 g/cm^3 ☐ (b) 5.2 g/cm^3 ☐ (c) 4.8 g/cm^3 ☐ (d) 4.4 g/cm^3 ☐

24. Find the value of 12.9 g – 7.06 g in correct significant digits.

____

***25.** If length l = (16.2 ± 0.1%) cm and breadth b = (10.1 ± 0.1%) cm, then which of the following is the correct matched pair?

I. Area of rectangle $\rightarrow$ (164 ± 3) cm^2 II. Uncertainty in area $\rightarrow$ 3 cm^2

____

26. The temperatures of two bodies measured by a thermometer, are T_1 = (20°C ± 0.5°C) and T_2 = (50°C ± 0.5° C). Calculate the temperature difference with error.

(a) (30 ±0)°C ☐ (b) (33 ± 2)° C ☐ (c) (30 ± 1)°C ☐ (d) (35 ± 2)°C ☐

27. The length and breadth of a rectangular sheet have been measured by a measuring scale to an accuracy of 0.1 cm. If the measured values are 35.2 cm and 21.7 cm respectively, then find the relative error in area of the sheet.

____

***28.** Calculate the relative error in measuring mass (1.02 ± 0.01) g and (9.89 ± 0.01) g.

____

TOPIC 3

Dimensions of Physical Quantities

29. The pairs of physical quantities are given below. Find the odd one out.

(a) Volumetric strain and coefficient of friction ☐

(b) Disintegration constant of a radioactive substance and frequency of light wave ☐

(c) Heat capacity and gravitational potential ☐

(d) Stefan's constant and Wien's constant ☐

30. The dimensional formula for universal gas constant is

(a) $[ML^2T^{-2}mol^{-1}K^{-1}]$ ☐ (b) $[ML^3T^{-3}mol^{-2}K^{-2}]$ ☐

(c) $[M^2LT^{-1}mol^{-1}K^{-1}]$ ☐ (d) $[M^3LT^{-2}mol^{-1}K^{-2}]$ ☐

***31.** Some physical constants are given in Column I and their dimensional formulae are given in Column II. Match the Column I with Column II.

Column I	Column II
A. Planck's constant	1. $[ML^{-1}T^{-2}]$
B. Gravitational constant	2. $[ML^{-1}T^{-1}]$
C. Bulk modulus	3. $[ML^2T^{-1}]$
D. Coefficient of viscosity	4. $[M^{-1}L^3T^{-2}]$

A. ____________ B. ____________ C. ____________ D. ____________

32. Tick (✓/✗) for correct/incorrect statement in given boxes.

(i) An equation obtained by equating a physical quantity with its dimensional formula is called dimensional equation. ☐

(ii) Dimensional equation of speed $[v]$, force $[F]$ may be expressed as $[v] = [M^0LT^{-1}]$ and $[F] = [MLT^{-2}]$. ☐

(iii) Dimensional analysis helps us in deducing certain relation among different physical quantity. ☐

(iv) Dimensional analysis are helpful in checking the derivation, accuracy and dimensional consistency or homogeneity of expressions. ☐

(v) Physical quantities represented by symbols on both sides of a mathematical equation must have the same dimensions. ☐

33. Special functions such as trigonometric, logarithmic and exponential functions are dimensionless.

True ☐ False ☐

TOPIC 4

Dimensional Analysis and its Applications

34. Equation $\frac{1}{2}mv^2 = mgh$ is dimensionally correct, where m is the mass of the body, v is the velocity, g is the acceleration due to gravity and h is the height.

True ☐ False ☐

35. The SI unit of energy is $y = \text{kg-m}^2\text{s}^{-2}$ that of speed v is ms^{-1} and of acceleration a is ms^{-2}. Which of the formulae for kinetic energy K given below is valid? Can you rule out on the basis of dimensional arguments (m stands for mass of body)?

I. $K = m^2v^2$ II. $K = \frac{1}{2}mv^2$ III. $K = ma$ IV. $K = \frac{3}{16}mv^2$

V. $K = \frac{1}{2}mv^2 + ma$

____

36. The period of oscillations of a simple pendulum depends on its length l, mass of the bob m and acceleration due to gravity g. Pick the odd one out from the given expression.

I. $T = 4\pi\sqrt{\frac{g}{l}}$ II. $T = 2\pi\sqrt{\frac{l}{g}}$ III. $T = 2\pi\sqrt{\frac{l^2}{g}}$ IV. $T = 2\pi\sqrt{\frac{l^4}{g}}$

____

37. In a particular system, units of length, mass and time are chosen to be 10 cm, 10 g and 0.1 s, respectively. Unit of force in this system will be ________ N.

***38.** Dimensions of critical velocity v of flow of a liquid through a tube are $[\eta^x \cdot \rho^y \cdot r^z]$, where η = coefficient of viscosity, ρ = density of fluid and r = radius of tube.

Value of product $x \cdot y \cdot z$ = __________ .

***39.** Velocity v of a particle at time t is given by $v = at + \frac{b}{t+c}$, where a, b and c are constants.

Then, dimensions of $[abc]$ = _______ .

COMPETITION CONNECT

Topic 1 Accuracy, Precision of Instruments and Errors in Measurements [NCERT (Old) Pg. 22-27]

1. Usually there is a difference in true value and measured value of a quantity.

Now, complete following sentences choosing suitable option.

Error is positive, if observed value is ________ (more/less) than true value and is negative, if observed value is ________ (more/less) than true value.

Also, true value of a quantity is obtained by ________ (adding/subtracting) error from observed value.

2. The precision of a measurement is a measure of how close the measured value is to the true value.

True ☐ False ☐

3. Two experiments are given below for measuring a value of near to 3.678 cm.

Experiment 1 Using a measuring instrument of resolution 0.1 cm, the measured value is found to be 3.5 cm.

Experiment 2 Using another instrument of resolution 0.01 cm, the value is determined to be 3.38 cm.

Which measurement is more accurate and which is more precise?

(a) Experiment 1 only ☐
(b) Experiment 2 only ☐
(c) Experiment 1 and Experiment 2 respectively ☐
(d) None of the above ☐

4. **Statement I** Every measurement is approximate due to error in the measurement.

Statement II Systematic errors tend to be in the one direction.

Which of the following statement(s) is/are correct?

(a) Only Statement I ☐ (b) Only Statement II ☐
(c) Both statements I and II ☐ (d) Neither statement I nor II ☐

5. Match the types of error in Column I with their cause in Column II.

	Column I		Column II
A.	Instrumental errors	1.	External conditions (like temperature, humidity, etc.)
B.	Imperfection in experimental technique	2.	Individual's carelessness
C.	Personal errors	3.	Only in one direction
D.	Systematic errors	4.	Imperfect design

A. ________ B. ________ C. ________ D. ________

6. Which of the following is incorrect about the reduction of systematic error?

I. By improving experimental techniques
II. Selecting better instruments
III. Taking average of many values

____

7. Random errors arise due to random and unpredictable fluctuations in experimental conditions.

True ☐ False ☐

8. Two clocks are being tested against a standard clock located in a national laboratory. At 12:00:00 noon by the standard clock, the readings of the two clocks are

	Clock 1	**Clock 2**
Monday	12 : 00 : 05	10 : 15 : 06
Tuesday	12 : 01 : 15	10 : 14 : 59
Wednesday	11 : 59 : 08	10 : 15 : 18
Thursday	12 : 01 : 50	10 : 15 : 07
Friday	11 : 59 : 15	10 : 14 : 53
Saturday	12 : 01 : 30	10 :15 : 24
Sunday	12 : 01 : 19	10 : 15 : 11

If you are doing an experiment that requires precision time interval measurements, which of the following statement(s) is/are correct?

(a) The average reading of Clock 1 is closer to standard time. ☐
(b) The average reading of Clock 2 is closer to standard time. ☐
(c) Clock 1 is preferred than Clock 2. ☐
(d) Clock 2 is preferred over Clock 1. ☐

9. We measure the period of oscillation of a simple pendulum. In successive measurements, the readings turn out to be 2.63 s, 2.56 s, 2.42 s, 2.71 s and 2.80 s. Find the following values.

(i) Mean absolute error (ii) Relative error
(iii) Percentage error

---

10. Tick (✓/✗) for correct/incorrect statement in given boxes.

(i) When two quantities are added or subtracted, the absolute error in the final result is the sum of the absolute error in the individual quantities. ☐

(ii) When two quantities are multiplied or divided, the absolute error in the result is the sum of the absolute errors in the multipliers. ☐

11. The resistance $R = \frac{V}{I}$, where $V = (100 \pm 5)$ V and $I = (10 \pm 0.2)$ A. The percentage error in R is ______________ .

12. Two resistors of resistances $R_1 = (100 \pm 3)\Omega$ and $R_2 = (200 \pm 4)\Omega$ are connected (I) in series and (II) in parallel, then which matching pair is correct for the above?

I. $R \longrightarrow (300 \pm 7)\Omega$ II. $R \longrightarrow 66.7 \pm 1.8\Omega$

---

13. Match the operations given in Column I with the error in Column II.

	Column I		Column II
A.	$Z = A + B$	1.	$\frac{\Delta Z}{Z} = \frac{\Delta A}{A} + \frac{\Delta B}{B}$
B.	$Z = \frac{A}{B}$	2.	$\frac{\Delta Z}{Z} = p\frac{\Delta A}{A} + q\frac{\Delta B}{B}$
C.	$Z = A^n$	3.	$\frac{\Delta Z}{Z} = n\frac{\Delta A}{A}$
D.	$Z = A^p \cdot B^q$	4.	$\Delta Z = \Delta A + \Delta B$

A. ____________ B. ____________ C. ____________ D. ____________

14. Find the relative error in Z, if $Z = \frac{A^4 B^{\frac{1}{3}}}{CD^{\frac{3}{2}}}$.

(a) $\frac{4}{5}\left(\frac{\Delta A}{A}\right) + \frac{1}{3}\left(\frac{\Delta B}{B}\right) + \left(\frac{\Delta C}{C}\right) + \frac{3}{2}\left(\frac{\Delta D}{D}\right)$ ☐ (b) $4\left(\frac{\Delta B}{B}\right) + \frac{1}{3}\left(\frac{\Delta A}{A}\right) + \left(\frac{\Delta C}{C}\right) + \frac{2}{3}\left(\frac{\Delta D}{D}\right)$ ☐

(c) $4\left(\frac{\Delta A}{A}\right) + \frac{1}{3}\left(\frac{\Delta B}{B}\right) + \left(\frac{\Delta C}{C}\right) + \frac{3}{2}\left(\frac{\Delta D}{D}\right)$ ☐ (d) $2\left(\frac{\Delta A}{A}\right) + \frac{1}{3}\left(\frac{\Delta B}{B}\right) + \left(\frac{\Delta C}{C}\right) + \frac{3}{2}\left(\frac{\Delta D}{D}\right)$ ☐

15. The period of oscillation of a simple pendulum is $T = 2\pi\sqrt{\frac{L}{g}}$. Measured value of L is 20.0 cm known to 1 mm accuracy and time for 100 oscillations of the pendulum is found to be 90 s using a wrist watch of 1s resolution.

Find the correctly matched pair from given below.

I. Relative error in $g \longrightarrow 0.027$

II. Accuracy in determination of $g \longrightarrow 3\%$

____

16. If error in radius is 3%, then the percentage error in volume of sphere is __________.

17. The resistance of a metallic wire is given by $R = \frac{V}{I}$, where V is the potential difference and I is the current. In a circuit, the potential difference across resistance is $V = (8 \pm 0.8)$ V and current in circuit $I = (4 \pm 0.2)$ A. Which of the following statement is correct for given information?

(a) The value of resistance with percentage error is $(4 \pm 11.25\%)\Omega$. ☐

(b) The percentage error in V is $\pm$ 0.25%. ☐

(c) The percentage error in I is $\pm$ 6%. ☐

(d) The percentage error in R is $\pm$ 15%. ☐

18. The period of oscillation of a simple pendulum is 1.62 s. Of this, the reliable, certain and uncertain digits are respectively

(a) 1, 6, 2 ☐ (b) 1, 2, 6 ☐ (c) 6, 2 ,1 ☐ (d) 1, 2, 6 ☐

Assertion-Reason Questions

Direction (Q. Nos. 1-12) *In the following questions, a statement of Assertion is followed by a corresponding statement of Reason. From the following options, choose the correct one.*

(a) Both Assertion and Reason are correct and Reason is the correct explanation of Assertion.
(b) Both Assertion and Reason are correct but Reason is not the correct explanation of Assertion.
(c) Assertion is correct but Reason is incorrect.
(d) Assertion is incorrect but Reason is correct.

1. **Assertion** (A) A limited number of units are needed to express all physical quantities.
Reason (R) Physical quantities are inter-related with one another.

(a) ☐ (b) ☐ (c) ☐ (d) ☐

2. **Assertion** (A) A caesium atomic clock is used at National Physical Laboratory, New Delhi to maintain the Indian standard of time.
Reason (R) The caesium atomic clocks are very accurate and precise.

(a) ☐ (b) ☐ (c) ☐ (d) ☐

***3.** **Assertion** (A) A digital stopwatch is more precise than an analog stopwatch.
Reason (R) A digital stopwatch measures time in smaller increments, typically to the nearest hundredth of a second, enhancing precision.

(a) ☐ (b) ☐ (c) ☐ (d) ☐

4. **Assertion** (A) When we change the unit of measurement of a quantity, its numerical value changes.
Reason (R) Smaller the unit of measurement, smaller is its numerical value.

(a) ☐ (b) ☐ (c) ☐ (d) ☐

***5.** **Assertion** (A) Out of two measurements, $L = 0.7$ m and $L = 0.70$ m, the second one is more accurate.
Reason (R) In every measurement, the last digit is not accurately known.

(a) ☐ (b) ☐ (c) ☐ (d) ☐

6. **Assertion** (A) The significant figures in a measurement indicate its precision.

Reason (R) The more significant figures implies greater precision in a instrument.

(a) ☐ (b) ☐ (c) ☐ (d) ☐

***7.** **Assertion** (A) The error in the measurement of radius of the sphere is 0.3%. The permissible error in its surface area is 0.6%.

Reason (R) The permissible error is calculated by the formula.

$$\frac{\Delta A}{A} = 4\frac{\Delta r}{r}.$$

(a) ☐ (b) ☐ (c) ☐ (d) ☐

8. **Assertion** (A) L/R and CR both have same dimensions.

Reason (R) L/R and CR both have dimensions of time.

(a) ☐ (b) ☐ (c) ☐ (d) ☐

9. **Assertion** (A) Special functions such as trigonometric, logarithmic and exponential functions are dimensionless.

Reason (R) A pure number, ratio of similar physical quantities, such as angle and refractive index, has no dimensions.

(a) ☐ (b) ☐ (c) ☐ (d) ☐

10. **Assertion** (A) The method of dimensions analysis cannot validate the exact relationship between physical quantities in any equation.

Reason (R) It does not distinguish between the physical quantities having same dimensions.

(a) ☐ (b) ☐ (c) ☐ (d) ☐

11. **Assertion** (A) If $s = ut + \frac{1}{2}at^2 + b$, then dimensions of b must be that of length.

Reason (R) The physical quantities that can be added or subtracted must have same dimensions.

(a) ☐ (b) ☐ (c) ☐ (d) ☐

12. **Assertion** (A) The equation $x = x_0 + v_0t + \frac{1}{2}at^2$ may gives an incorrect value of displacement x, here v_0 is the initial velocity and x_0 is the position of object at $t = 0$.

Reason (R) Dimensionally correct equation need not to be actually an exact (correct) equation.

(a) ☐ (b) ☐ (c) ☐ (d) ☐

Case Based Questions

1. A dimensional equation is an equation that relates the dimensions of different physical quantities. It helps to ensure that both sides of an equation are dimensionally consistent, meaning they have the same dimensions. For example, consider the equation for force $F = ma$. The dimensional equation for this is : $[F] = [m]\,[a] = [M]\,[LT^{-2}] = [MLT^{-2}]$.

(i) The dimensional formula for the gravitational constant G in Newton's law of universal gravitation is

(a) $[ML^2T^{-2}]$ ☐ (b) $[M^{-1}L^3T^{-2}]$ ☐

(c) $[ML^{-1}T^2]$ ☐ (d) $[M^0L^3T^{-1}]$ ☐

(ii) The dimensionally consistent equation is

(a) $v = u + at$ ☐ (b) $F = ma^2$ ☐

(c) $E = mc$ ☐ (d) $p = \frac{F}{A}$ ☐

*(iii) The speed of sound v in a gas depends on the pressure p and density ρ. Using dimensional analysis, the correct relationship is

(a) $V = K\sqrt{\frac{p}{\rho}}$ ☐ (b) $V = Kp\rho$ ☐

(c) $V = K\sqrt{\frac{\rho}{p}}$ ☐ (d) $V = \frac{Kp^2}{\rho}$ ☐

(iv) The dimensional formula of strain is

(a) $[M^0L^0T^0]$ ☐ (b) $[M^1L^{-1}T^{-2}]$ ☐

(c) $[M^0L^0T^{-1}]$ ☐ (d) $[M^1L^1T^1]$ ☐

2. Imagine you are conducting an experiment to determine the density of a substance using a balance and a graduated cylinder. You weight the substance and measure its volume. Both measurements involve the concept of significant figures.

(i) Which of the following measurements has the most significant figures?

(a) 2.0 g ☐ (b) 0.0023 g ☐

(c) 23.0 g ☐ (d) 2000 g ☐

(ii) If a ruler marked in centimeters is used to measure a length as 12.345 cm, the number of significant figures in this measurement is

(a) 2 ☐ (b) 3 ☐

(c) 4 ☐ (d) 5 ☐

(iii) After adding 1.23 g and 4.567 g, the number of significant figures in the result should be

(a) 2 ☐ (b) 3 ☐

(c) 4 ☐ (d) 5 ☐

(iv) The density of a substance is calculated as 0.125 g/mL. If its mass and volume measurements have 3 and 2 significant figures respectively, then the density should be reported as

(a) 0.1 g/mL ☐ (b) 0.12 g/mL ☐

(c) 0.125 g/mL ☐ (d) 0.1250 g/mL ☐

COMPETITION EDGE UP

1. The dimensional formula of latent heat is **[NCERT Pg. 7, JEE Main 2024]**

(a) $[MLT^{-2}]$ ☐ (b) $[M^0LT^{-2}]$ ☐
(c) $[ML^2T^{-2}]$ ☐ (d) $[M^0L^2T^{-2}]$ ☐

2. In an expression $a \times 10^b$, **[NCERT Pg. 4, JEE Main 2024]**

(a) b is order of magnitude for $a \geq 5$ ☐
(b) b is order of magnitude for $a \leq 5$ ☐
(c) a is order of magnitude for $b \leq 5$ ☐
(d) b is order of magnitude for $5 < a \leq 10$ ☐

3. What is the dimensional formula of ab^{-1} in the equation $\left(p + \frac{a}{V^2}\right)(V - b) = RT$, where symbols have their usual meanings. **[NCERT Pg. 8, JEE Main 2024]**

(a) $[M^0L^3T^{-2}]$ ☐ (b) $[ML^2T^{-2}]$ ☐
(c) $[M^{-1}L^5T^3]$ ☐ (d) $[M^6L^7T^4]$ ☐

4. The equation of stationary wave is $y = 2a\sin\left(\frac{2\pi nt}{\lambda}\right)\cos\left(\frac{2\pi x}{\lambda}\right)$.

Which of the following is not correct? **[NCERT Pg. 9, JEE Main 2024]**

(a) The dimension of nt is [L] ☐
(b) The dimension of x is [L] ☐
(c) The dimension of $\frac{n}{\lambda}$ is [T] ☐
(d) The dimension of n are $[LT^{-1}]$ ☐

5. Consider two physical quantities A and B related to each other as $E = \frac{B - x^2}{At}$ where E, x and t have dimensions of energy, length and time, respectively. The dimensions of AB are **[NCERT Pg. 9, JEE Main 2024]**

(a) $[L^{-2}M^1T^0]$ ☐
(b) $[L^2M^{-1}T^1]$ ☐
(c) $[L^0M^{-1}T^1]$ ☐
(d) $[L^{-2}M^{-1}T^1]$ ☐

6. If mass is written as $m = k\,c^P G^{\frac{-1}{2}} h^{\frac{1}{2}}$, then the value of p will be (constants have their usual meaning with k a dimensionless constant) **[NCERT Pg. 9, JEE Main 2024]**

(a) $\frac{-1}{3}$ ☐ (b) 2 ☐
(c) $\frac{1}{2}$ ☐ (d) $\frac{1}{3}$ ☐

7. A force is represented by $F = ax^2 + bt^{1/2}$, where x = distance and t = time. The dimensions of b^2/a are **[NCERT Pg. 9, JEE Main 2024]**

(a) $[ML^{-1}T^{-1}]$ ☐ (b) $[ML^3T^{-3}]$ ☐
(c) $[ML^2T^{-3}]$ ☐ (d) $[MLT^{-2}]$ ☐

8. The quantities which have the same dimensions as those of solid angle are **[NCERT Pg. 7, NEET 2024]**

(a) strain and angle ☐
(b) stress and angle ☐
(c) strain and arc ☐
(d) angular speed and stress ☐

9. A force defined by $F = \alpha t^2 + \beta t$ acts on a particle at a given time t. The factor which is dimensionless, if α and β are constants, is **[NCERT Pg. 8, NEET 2024]**

(a) $\frac{\beta t}{\alpha}$ ☐ (b) $\frac{\alpha t}{\beta}$ ☐
(c) $\alpha\beta t$ ☐ (d) $\frac{\alpha\beta}{t}$ ☐

10. The area of a rectangular field (in m^2) of length 55.3m and breadth 25m after rounding off the value for correct significant digits is **[NCERT Pg. 6, NEET 2022]**

(a) 1382 ☐ (b) 1382.5 ☐
(c) 14×10^2 ☐ (d) 138×10^1 ☐

11. Dimensions of stress are **[NCERT Pg. 7, NEET (Sep.) 2020]**

(a) $[ML^2T^{-2}]$ ☐
(b) $[ML^0T^{-2}]$ ☐
(c) $[ML^{-1}T^{-2}]$ ☐
(d) $[MLT^{-2}]$ ☐

Chapter 02

Motion in a Straight Line

TOPIC 1

Instantaneous Velocity and Speed

1. A car starts at rest from origin O and continues to move till point C as shown in the graph.

Which of the following pair is the correct match?

I. $AB \rightarrow$ Uniform motion

II. At $t = t_2 \rightarrow$ Brakes are applied

III. At $t = t_3 \rightarrow$ Car stops

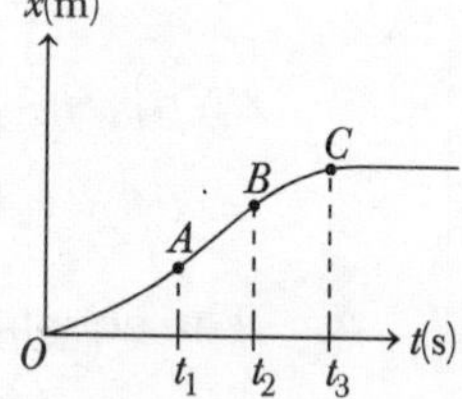

2. Given graph x-t represents the motion of an object, then match the following items given in Column I with those given in Column II.

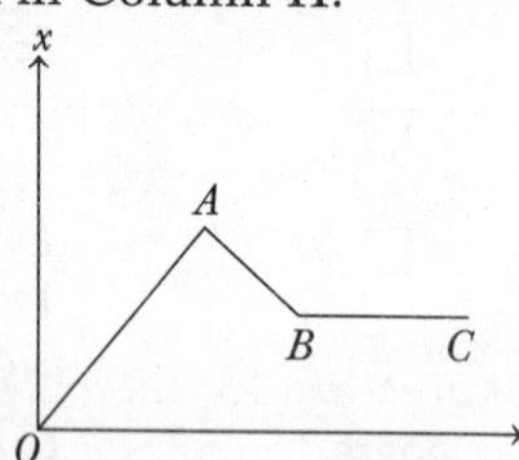

Column I		Column II	
A.	Path OA	1.	Positive velocity
B.	Path AB	2.	Object rest
C.	Path BC	3.	Negative velocity
D.	Point A	4.	Change in direction of motion

A. ____________ B. ____________ C. ____________ D. ____________

*Concepts of all questions bearing * are important for JEE/NEET/CUET.*

3. The following x-t graph given below shows the motion of an object along a straight line, then which of the following statement is correct?

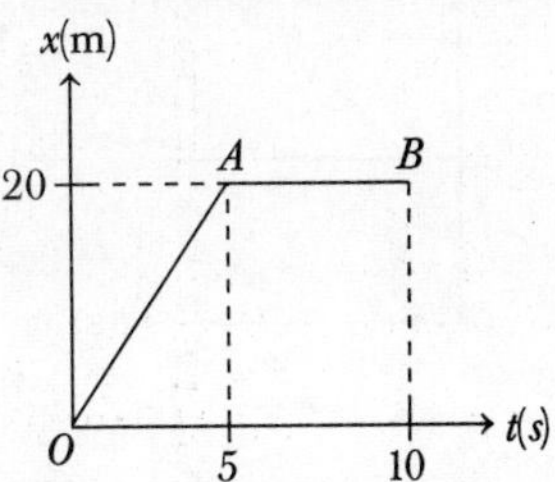

I. Part OA of the graph represents uniform motion.

II. Part AB of the graph represents the object standing still (at rest) at $x = 20$ m.

(a) I only ☐ (b) II only ☐ (c) Both I and II ☐ (d) Neither I nor II ☐

4. A car moves along a straight line according to the x-t graph given below. The instantaneous velocity of the car at $t = t_1$ is ____________ (zero/positive).

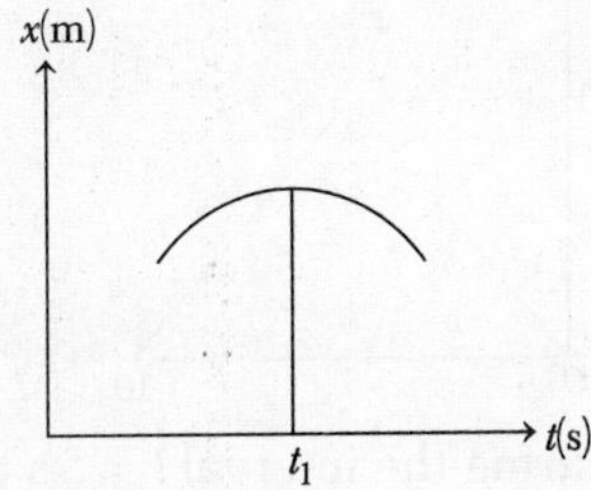

5. Is the graphical method for determination of the instantaneous velocity always a convenient method?

Yes ☐ No ☐

6. In order to calculate the value of velocity at different instants, there can be two different approaches. Which of the statement(s) out of the given statements correctly expresses that approach?

I. With the help of data of position of different instant or exact expression for the position as a function of time, we calculate $\frac{\Delta x}{\Delta t}$, whose limiting value gives velocity at that instant.

II. With the help of the exact expression for the position as a function of time, we use differential calculus for the given expression and calculate $\frac{dx}{dt}$ at different instants of time.

III. With the help of the given x-t graph, we calculate the slope of the tangent drawn at points on the x-t graph at different time instants.

____

7. For the x-t graph given below, the v-t graph is given as

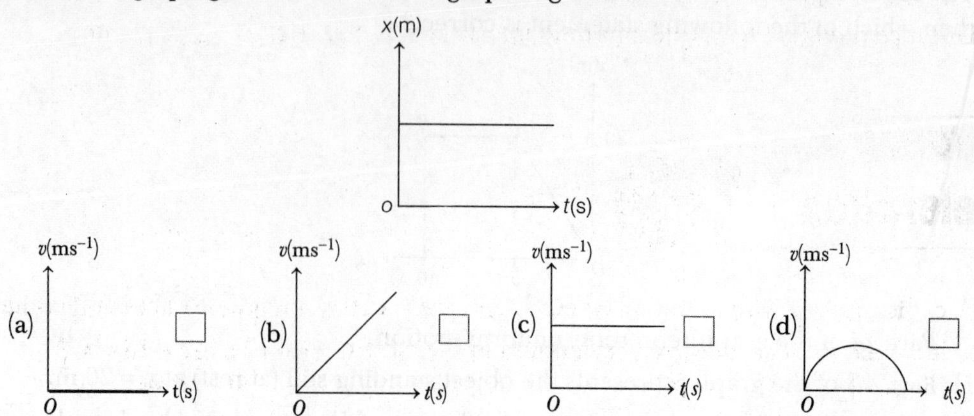

8. The x-t graph for motion of a car is given below. With reference to the graph, which of the given statement(s) is /are correct/incorrect?

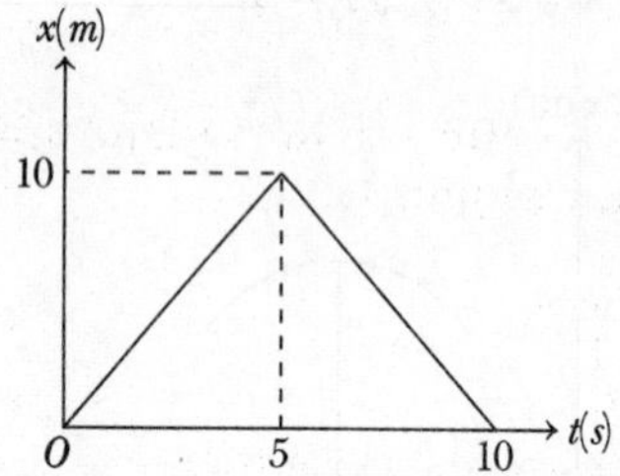

(i) The instantaneous speed during the interval $t = 5$ s to $t = 10$ s is negative for all time instants. ☐

(ii) The velocity and average velocity for the interval $t = 0$ s to $t = 5$ s is equal and positive. ☐

(iii) The car changes its direction of motion at $t = 5$ s. ☐

(iv) The instantaneous speed and the instantaneous velocity is positive at all time instants during the interval $t = 0$ s to $t = 5$ s. ☐

9. The displacement equation for a moving body is given as $s = 9t^2 - t^3$, where s is in metre and t in second, then the body achieves maximum speed along $+x$-direction at a distance of 84 m.

True ☐ False ☐

10. If the distance-time graph of a particle moving in a straight line is given, then how can you find the particle's instantaneous velocity at a specific time?

(a) By finding the area under the graph up to that time ☐

(b) By calculating the slope of the graph at that time ☐

(c) By finding the total displacement divided by the total time ☐

(d) By looking at the intercept of the graph ☐

11. A particle moves along a straight line with an acceleration given by $a(t) = 6t - 4$. If the initial velocity of the particle at $t = 0$ is 2 m/s. What is the velocity of the particle at $t = 2$ s ?

(a) 4 m/s ☐ (b) 6 m/s ☐ (c) 8 m/s ☐ (d) 10 m/s ☐

12. Velocity of a particle is $v = At + Bt^2$, here $A = 3\text{ m/s}^2$ and $B = 4\text{ m/s}^3$. Distance travelled by particle in time interval $t = 1$ to $t = 2$ is ________ m.

TOPIC 2

Acceleration

NCERT Pg 15-17

13. A car is moving with speed of 30 ms^{-1}. At time $t = 10$ s, it applies brakes and comes to rest in next 5s. The average acceleration of the car from $t = 10$ s to $t = 15$ s is

(a) 6 ms^{-2} ☐ (b) -6 ms^{-2} ☐ (c) 3 ms^{-2} ☐ (d) -18 ms^{-2} ☐

---

14. When a particle moving with a speed of 6.25 m/s is accelerated at a rate of $-2.5\sqrt{v}$, (v = instantaneous speed), it comes to rest after ________ s.

15. With reference to the v-t graph shown below, match the following items given in Column I with items given in Column II.

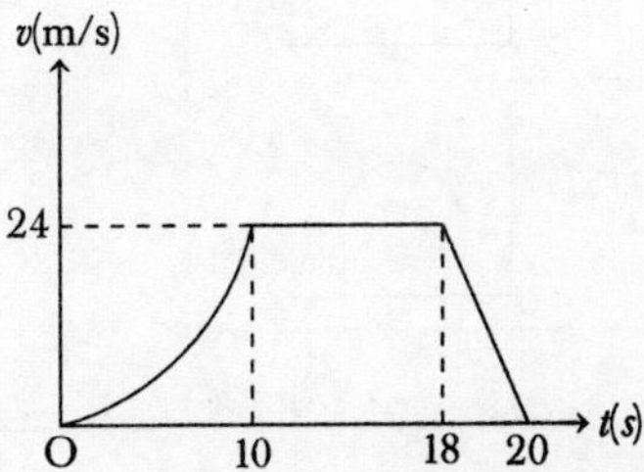

	Column I		Column II
A.	Average acceleration for time interval $t_1 = 0$ to $t_2 = 10$ s	1.	0 ms^{-2}
B.	Average acceleration for time interval $t_1 = 10$ s to $t_2 = 18$ s	2.	-12 ms^{-2}
C.	Average acceleration for time interval $t_1 = 18$ s to $t = 20$ s	3.	2.4 ms^{-2}

A. ________ B. ________ C. ________

16. With reference to the below acceleration-time graph, three pairs are given. Which of the pair is correctly matched?

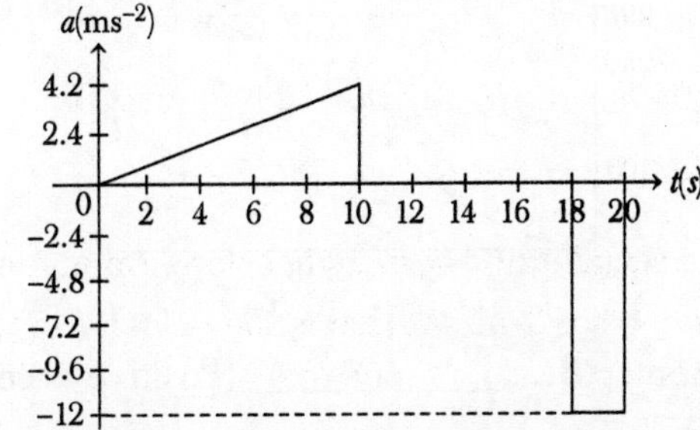

I. $t = 0$ to $t = 10$ s $\rightarrow$ Non-uniform acceleration
II. $t = 10$ s to $t = 18$ s $\rightarrow$ Zero acceleration
III. $t = 18$ s to $t = 20$ s $\rightarrow$ Constant acceleration

---

***17.** The velocity of a particle is given as $v(t) = 3t^3 - 2t^2$. The instantaneous acceleration (in ms^{-2}) of the particle at $t = 1$ s is ____________.

18. When the acceleration is uniform, it equals to the average acceleration over that period.
True ☐ False ☐

19. Match the following items given in Column I with items x-t graph in Column II.

Column I	Column II
A. Positive acceleration	1.
B. Negative acceleration	2.
C. Zero acceleration	3.

A. ____________ B. ____________ C. ____________

20. The motion of a particle is represented by the x-t graph shown below. Which of the following pair(s) is/are correctly matched?

I. Positive acceleration $\rightarrow 0$ to t_1
II. Negative acceleration $\rightarrow t_2$ to t_3
III. Zero acceleration $\rightarrow t_1$ to t_2

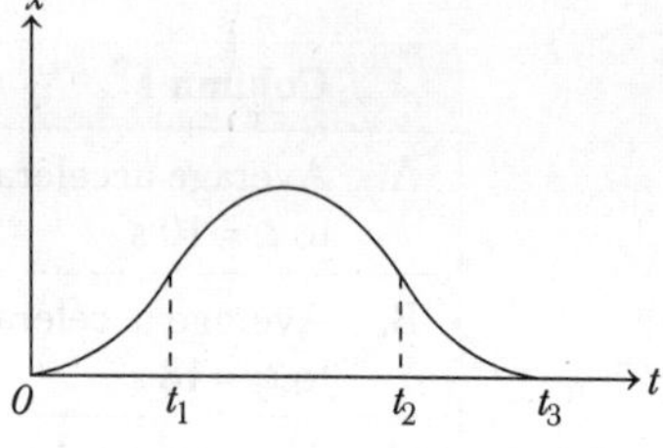

---

21. The motion of a car moving in a straight line is shown by x-t graph below. Complete the given analogy for given graph.

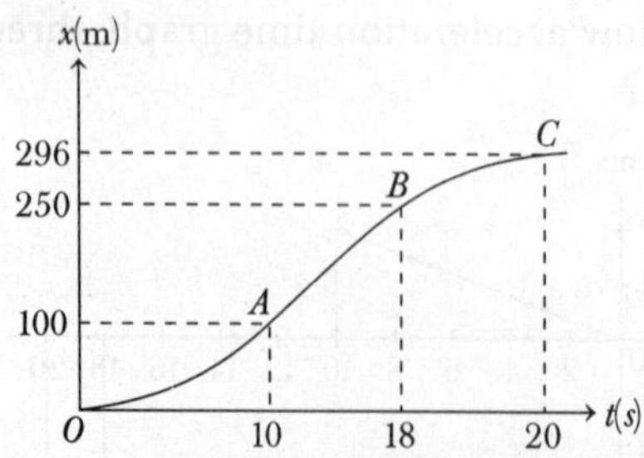

AB : Positive acceleration : : BC : ____________ (Positive acceleration/Negative acceleration)

22. The velocity-time graph for motion of an object moving in positive direction with a constant negative acceleration is

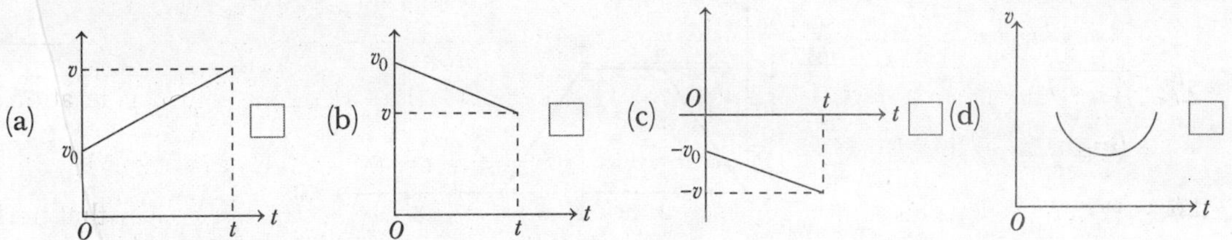

23. Two cars A and B are moving along straight line with constant acceleration as shown in the velocity-time graph. Which of the car has greater acceleration?

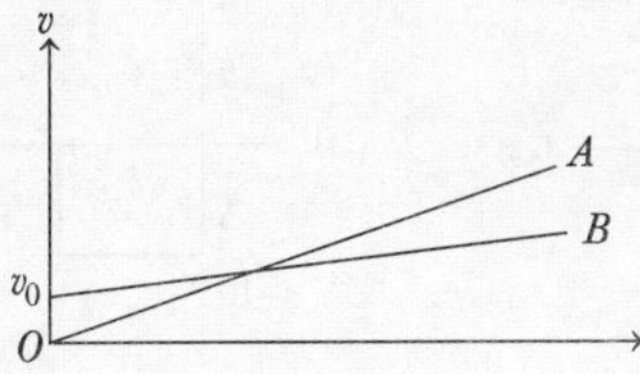

---

24. The x-t, v-t and a-t graphs have sharp kinks at same points implying that the functions are differentiable at these points.

True ☐ False ☐

25. For motion of an object under free fall, match the following items given in Column I with the graphs given in Column II.

Column I	Column II
A. Variation of acceleration with time	1. O t(s)
B. Variation of velocity with time	2. O t(s)
C. Variation of distance with time	3. O t(s)

A. ________ B. ________ C. ________

26. A particle moves along a straight line such that its displacement at any time t is given by

$$s = t^3 - 9t^2 + 6t + 2$$

The velocity, when its acceleration is zero is

(a) -15 ms^{-1} ☐ (b) -21 ms^{-1} ☐ (c) 24 ms^{-1} ☐ (d) 18 ms^{-1} ☐

***27.** The velocity-time graph for a vehicle is shown in figure. Draw acceleration-time graph from it.

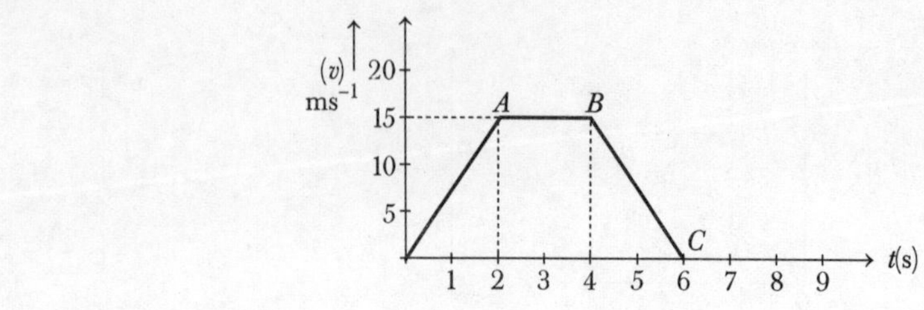

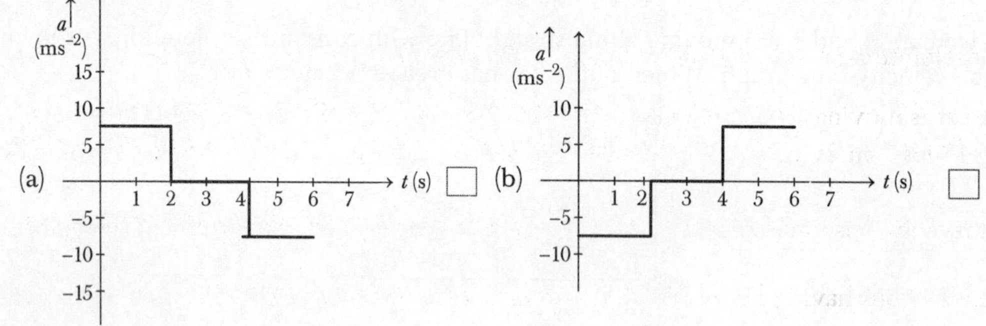

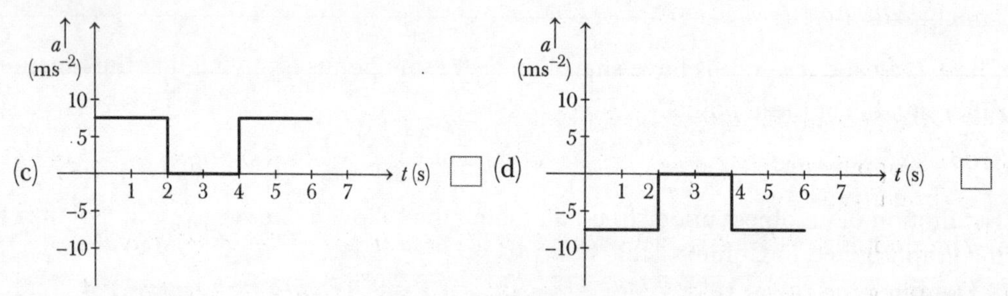

TOPIC 3

Kinematic Equations for Uniformly Accelerated Motion

28. The relation $v = v_0 + at$ can be graphically represented as

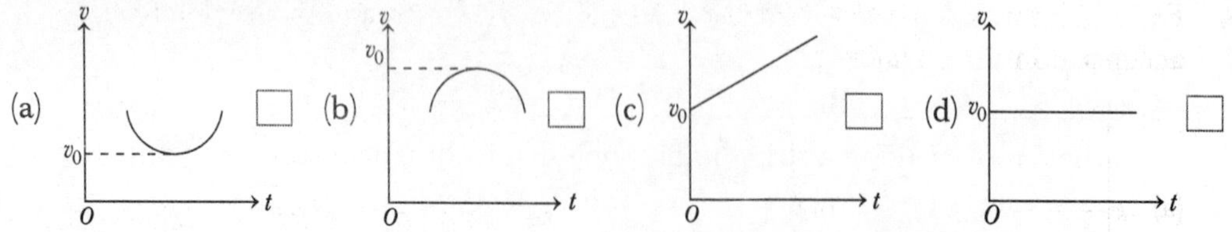

29. The relation $\bar{v} = \dfrac{v + v_0}{2}$ is valid for __________ (constant/variable) acceleration only.

30. For a particle, v^2 *versus* x graph is

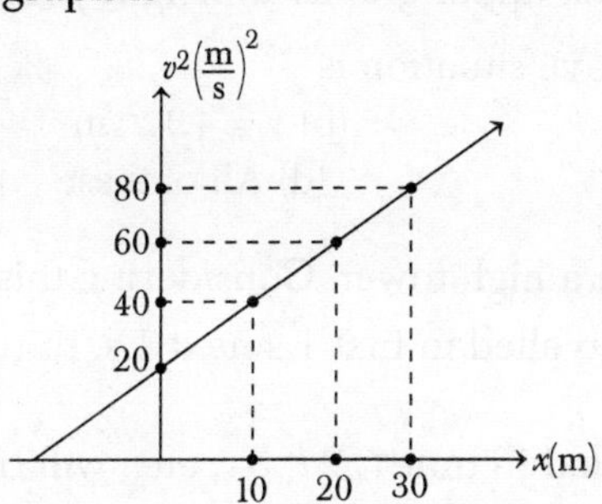

Acceleration of particle will be __________ ms^{-2}.

31. A car is moving with a velocity of 30 ms^{-1}, on applying the brakes the velocity decreases to 15 ms^{-1} in 2s. The acceleration of the car is __________. (+ 7.5 ms^{-2}/– 7.5 ms^{-2})

***32.** A moving bus having initial speed $\frac{100}{9}$ m/s can be stopped after 2m by applying brakes. If another bus having initial speed of $\frac{200}{9}$ m/s stops after a distance of x metre by applying same brakes, then find the value of x.

____

33. Tick (✓/✕) for correct/incorrect statement in given boxes.

(i) The stopping distance is an important factor for road safety and depends only on initial velocity. ☐

(ii) The stopping distance is proportional to the square of the initial velocity. ☐

(iii) Doubling the initial velocity increases the stopping distance by a factor of 4 (for the same deceleration). ☐

***34.** A ball is thrown vertically upwards with a velocity of 20 ms^{-1} from the top of a multistorey building. The height of the point from where the ball is thrown is 25.0 m from the ground. Find the correct match of given information.

I. Maximum height attained → 20 m above building

II. Ball hit ground in time → 5 s

____

35. For a ball thrown upwards from a tower of height h with an initial velocity v, the acceleration-time graph is

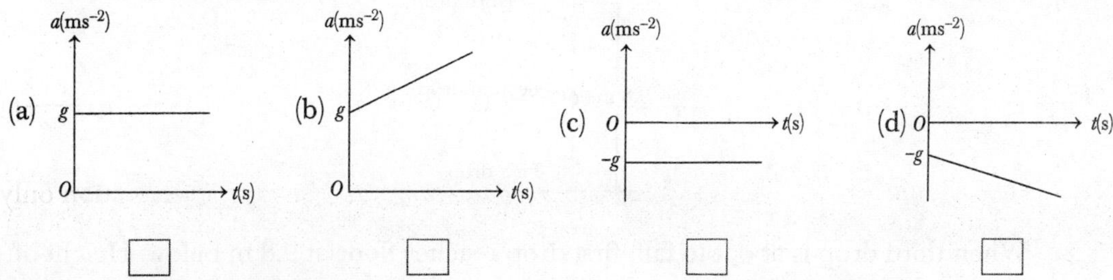

☐ ☐ ☐ ☐

36. An object released from rest under gravity at height y. The equation of motion which correctly expresses the above situation is

(a) $v = 9.8\,t\ \text{ms}^{-1}$ ☐ (b) $y = 4.9\,t^2$ m ☐
(c) $v^2 = 19.6\,y\ \text{m}^2\ \text{s}^{-2}$ ☐ (d) All of these ☐

***37.** An object is dropped from a high tower. Considering this, fill the following sentences.

(i) The ratio of distance travelled in first 1 s next 1 s, third 1 s, etc., will be __________ (1 : 3 : 5 / 1 : 2 : 3).

(ii) Ratio of distance travelled in time t, $2t$, $3t$, etc., will be _______ $(1 : 3 : 5 / 1^2 : 2^2 : 3^2)$.

(iii) Ratio of time intervals to cover successive 1 m distances is ______ $(1^3, 2^3, 3^3 / \sqrt{1} : (\sqrt{2} - \sqrt{1}) : (\sqrt{3} - \sqrt{2})$.

38. The table given below shows the motion of an object under the free fall. The position of the object after the different time intervals of 0, τ, 2τ, 3τ, are given in the second column. With reference to object after this table, find values of entries A and B shown in columns.

t	y	y in terms of $y_0 \left(= -\frac{1}{2}g\tau^2\right)$	Distance traversed in successive intervals	Ratio of distances traversed
0	0	0		
τ	$-\frac{1}{2}g\tau^2$	y_0	y_0	1
2τ	$-4\left(\frac{1}{2}\right)g\tau^2$	$4y_0$	$3y_0$	3
3τ	$-9\left(\frac{1}{2}\right)g\tau^2$	(A)	$5y_0$	5
4τ	$-16\left(\frac{1}{2}\right)g\tau^2$	$16\,y_0$	$7y_0$	7
5τ	$-25\left(\frac{1}{2}\right)g\tau^2$	$25\,y_0$	$9y_0$	9
6τ	$-36\left(\frac{1}{2}\right)g\tau^2$	$36\,y_0$	(B)	11

____

***39.** A dripping tap is shown below

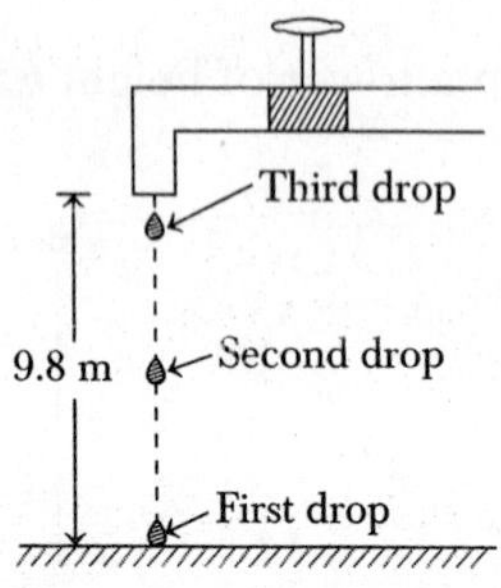

When third drop is about to fall, first drop reaches floor at 9.8 m below. Height of second drop at this instant (from ground) will be __________ m.

40. A tennis ball is released from height h, it bounces on floor and reaches at height $\frac{h}{2}$. Draw its velocity (v) *versus* height (h) graph.

____

***41.** A body covers 15 m in 2nds and 25 m in 4th s. How much distance will it cover in 4 s after the 5th second ?

(a) 150 m ☐ (b) 170 m ☐
(c) 175 m ☐ (d) 180 m ☐

42. An object is moving with uniform acceleration. Its velocity after 4 s is 20 m/s and after 8th second is 32 m/s. Find the distance travelled by the object in 12th second.

(a) 40 m ☐ (b) 42.5 m ☐
(c) 44.5 m ☐ (d) 46 m ☐

43. The time a person takes to observe, think and act in particular situation which demands immediate action is _________ (action/reaction) time.

44. Two persons A and B conduct an experiment to measure the reaction time of A. B drops a ruler vertically through the gap between A's thumb and forefinger. After A catches it, the distance d travelled by the ruler is $d = 21.0$ cm. The reaction time for this particular case is

(a) 0.2 s ☐ (b) 0.3 s ☐ (c) 0.4 s ☐ (d) 0.1 s ☐

COMPETITION CONNECT

Topic 1. Position, Path Length and Displacement [NCERT (Old) Pg. 39-42]

1. Tick (✓/✗) for correct/incorrect statement in given boxes.

(i) If one or more coordinates of an object change with time, we say that the object is in motion with respect to the given reference frame. ☐

(ii) If none of the coordinates of an object change with respect to the given reference frame, the object is at rest. ☐

(iii) If a person says that a car is moving on a road, then the description of this event is with respect to a frame of reference attached either to the person or to the ground. ☐

2. Which of the following statement is true for a car moving on the road?

(a) With respect to the frame of reference attached to the ground, the car is at rest. ☐

(b) With respect to the frame of reference attached to the person sitting in the car, the car is at rest. ☐

(c) With respect to the frame of reference attached to the person outside the car, the car is at rest. ☐

(d) None of the above ☐

Topic 2. Average Velocity and Average Speed [NCERT (Old) Pg. 42-43]

3. In the following figure, displacement-time graph is given. The average velocity between time $t = 5$ s and $t = 7$ s is ______________ .

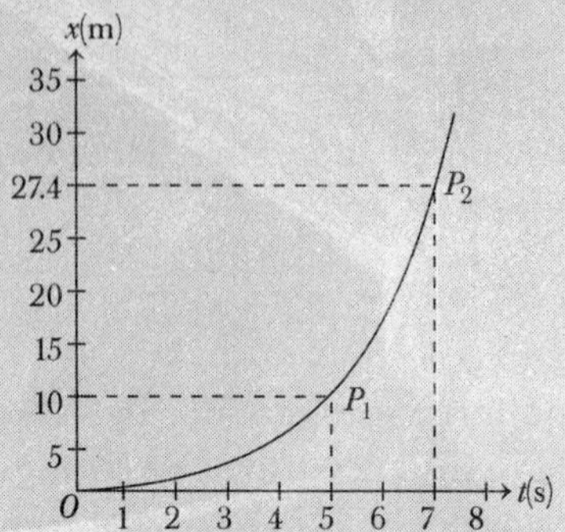

4. From the given position-time graph, the average velocity of the object will be __________ .

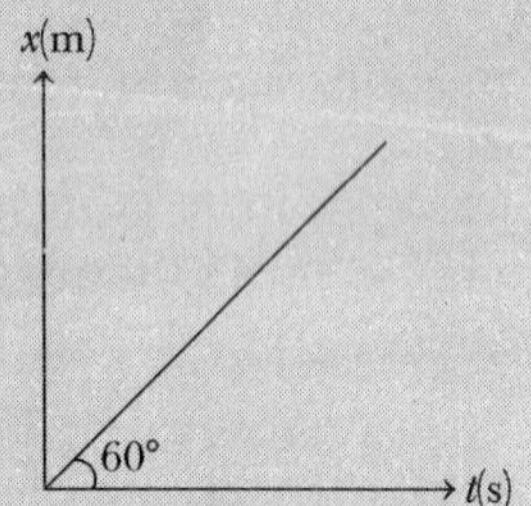

5. Answer the following questions in Yes or No.

(i) Will average velocity be zero, if the displacement of object is zero? ☐

(ii) Will instantaneous velocity be zero, if average velocity is zero ? ☐

6. A particle moving in a straight line covers half distance with speed of 3 m/s. Other half is covered in two equal time intervals with speed of 4.5 m/s and 7.5 m/s.
Average speed of the particle for entire journey = _____ m/s.

7. A car is moving along a straight line, say OP as shown in figure. It moves from O to P in 18 s and return from P to Q in 6 s.

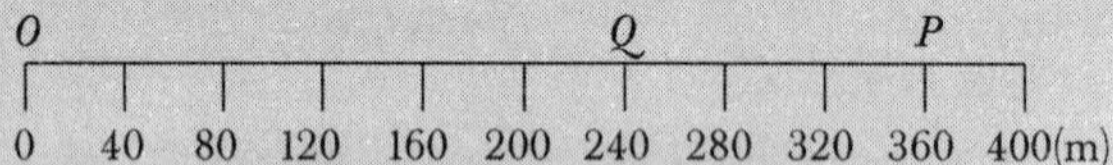

Which of the following match is correct?

I. Average velocity $(O \rightarrow P) \rightarrow 20\ ms^{-1}$

II. Average speed $(O \rightarrow P) \rightarrow 20\ ms^{-1}$

III. Average speed $(O \rightarrow P \rightarrow Q) \rightarrow 20\ ms^{-1}$

8. A body moves from A to B with a constant speed of 20 km/h and B to A with constant speed of 30 km/h. There is a point C mid-way between A and B.

Now, fill the following blanks.

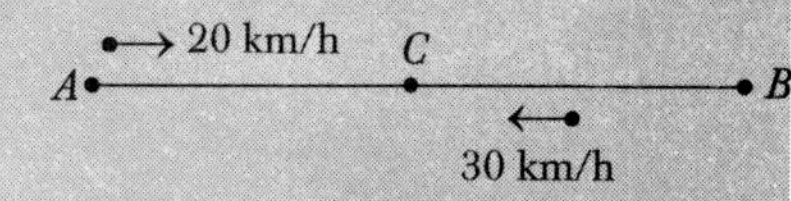

I. Ratio of instantaneous speeds at C while going from A to B and while going from B to A is ________ .

II. Average speed of complete trip is _____ km/h.

9. The expression for motion of an object is given as $x(t) = 0.08t^3$. Find the correct match for given expression.

I. Instantaneous velocity at $t = 3$ s $\rightarrow 2.5$ ms^{-1}

II. Instantaneous velocity at $t = 5$ s $\rightarrow 6$ ms^{-1}

III. Average velocity between ($t = 3$ to 5 s) $\rightarrow 3.92$ ms^{-1}

---

10. The x-t graph represents the motion of a car at different time instants. With reference to the graph given below, which of the following statement(s) is/are correct?

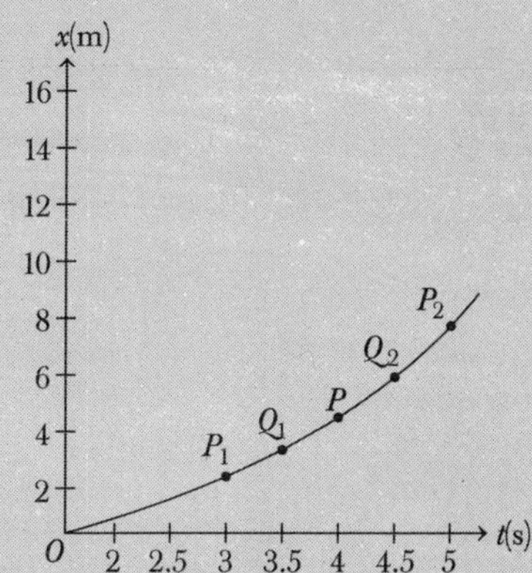

I. For the time interval $t = 3.5$ s to $t = 4.5$ s, the value of average velocity is given by the slope of the line Q_1Q_2.

II. The slope of the tangent at point P gives the instantaneous velocity of the car.

---

11. The position of an object moving along X-axis is given by $x = a - bt^2$, where $a = 8.5$ m, $b = 2.5$ ms^{-2} and t is measured in seconds. For the given situation, match terms in Column I with the values in Column II.

	Column I		Column II
A.	Velocity at $t = 2$ s	1.	-15 ms^{-1}
B.	Velocity at $t = 0$ s	2.	-10 ms^{-1}
C.	Instantaneous speed at $t = 2$ s	3.	0 ms^{-1}
D.	Average velocity between $t = 2$ s and $t = 4$ s	4.	10 ms^{-1}

A. ____________ B. ____________ C. ____________ D. ____________

12. Tick (✓/×) for correct/incorrect statement in given boxes.

(i) Average speed over a finite interval of time is greater or equal to the magnitude of the average velocity. ☐

(ii) The instantaneous speed at an instant is equal to the magnitude of the instantaneous velocity at that instant. ☐

(iii) The rate of change of velocity is a constant for all objects in free fall. ☐

(iv) The rate of change of displacement is a constant for all objects in free fall. ☐

(v) The change in velocity with distance is not a constant for all objects in free fall, it decreases with the increasing distance of fall. ☐

13. If the average velocities v_A and v_B of two objects moving along X-axis is same, then which of the given statements can be correct?

I. The value of $v_B - v_A$ is zero.

II. The two objects are at a certain distance of $[x_B(0) - x_A(0)]$, where $x_A(0)$ and $x_B(0)$ are initial positions.

III. The magnitude of relative velocity v_{AB} is zero but v_{BA} is non-zero.

____

Topic 3. Relative Velocity [NCERT (Old) Pg. 51-53]

14. The relation for relative velocities between two objects A and B is given by

$$v_{BA} = -v_{AB}$$

The equation is valid, if v_A and v_B are velocities of A and B with respect to________________, respectively.

15. Match the following items given in Column I with those given in Column II.

	Column I		Column II
A.	Position-time graph of two objects having equal velocities.	1.	x(m), O, t(s)
B.	Position-time graph of two objects having unequal velocities but in same direction.	2.	x(m), O, t(s)
C.	Position-time graph of two objects having velocities in opposite direction.	3.	x(m), O, t(s)

A. ______________ B. ______________ C. ______________

16. Two parallel rail tracks run north-south. Train A moves north with a speed of 54 km/h and train B moves south with a speed of 90 km/h. Which of the following pair is correctly matched?

I. v_B (w.r.t. A) $\rightarrow$ 40 ms^{-1} towards south

II. v_{ground} (w.r.t. B) $\rightarrow$ 25 ms^{-1} towards north

---

17. A person is moving with a velocity of 10 ms^{-1} towards north. A car moving with a velocity of 20 ms^{-1} towards south crosses the person. The magnitude of velocity of car relative to the person is x ms^{-1}. Find the value of x.

---

18. From two bus depots, buses travel from A to B and B to A. Time interval between any 2 buses (in same direction) leaving any depot is T h.

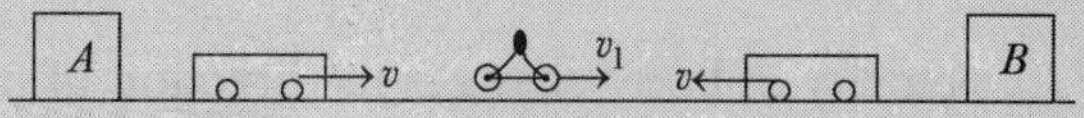

A cyclist cycling from A to B with speed of 30 km/h notices time interval between 2 buses from A to B is 20 min and from B to A is 5 min.

Now, complete following blanks.

A. Speed of bus from A to B relative to cyclist = __________ km/h.

B. Speed of bus from B to A relative to cyclist = __________ km/h.

C. Speed of bus relative to ground = __________ km/h.

D. Distance between two buses = __________ km.

E. Time, T = __________ h.

Assertion-Reason Questions

Direction (Q. Nos. 1-10) *In the following questions, a statement of Assertion is followed by a corresponding statement of Reason. From the following options, choose the correct one.*

(a) Both Assertion and Reason are correct and Reason is the correct explanation of Assertion.
(b) Both Assertion and Reason are correct but Reason is not the correct explanation of Assertion.
(c) Assertion is correct but Reason is incorrect.
(d) Assertion is incorrect but Reason is correct.

***1. Assertion** (A) For motion along a straight line and in the same direction, the magnitude of average velocity is equal to the average speed.
Reason (R) For motion along a straight line and in the same direction, the magnitude of displacement is equal to the path length.

(a) ☐ (b) ☐ (c) ☐ (d) ☐

***2.** **Assertion** (A) For uniform motion, velocity is the same as the average velocity at all instants.

Reason (R) In uniform motion along a straight line, the object covers equal distances in equal intervals of time.

(a) ☐ (b) ☐ (c) ☐ (d) ☐

3. **Assertion** (A) In the *s-t* diagram as shown in figure, the body starts moving in positive direction but not from $s = 0$.

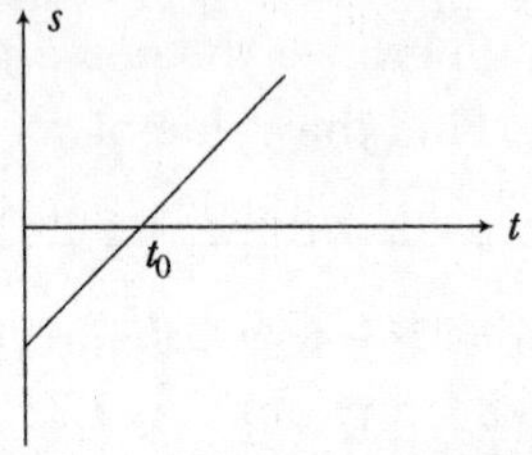

Reason (R) At $t = t_0$, velocity of body changes its direction of motion.

(a) ☐ (b) ☐ (c) ☐ (d) ☐

***4.** **Assertion** (A) In the *v-t* diagram as shown in figure, average velocity between the interval $t = 0$ and $t = t_0$ is independent of t_0.

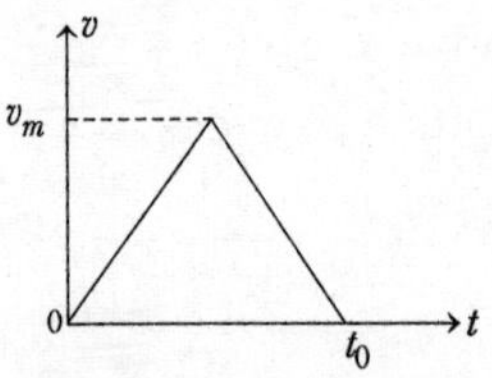

Reason (R) Average velocity in the given interval is $\frac{1}{2} v_m$.

(a) ☐ (b) ☐ (c) ☐ (d) ☐

5. **Assertion** (A) A body cannot be accelerated, when it is moving uniformly.

Reason (R) When direction of motion of the body changes, then body may have acceleration.

(a) ☐ (b) ☐ (c) ☐ (d) ☐

6. **Assertion** (A) A body is momentarily at rest at the instant, if it reverse the direction.
Reason (R) A body cannot have acceleration, if its velocity is zero at a given instant of time.

(a) ☐ (b) ☐ (c) ☐ (d) ☐

7. **Assertion** (A) If acceleration of a particle moving in a straight line varies as $a \propto t^n$, then $s \propto t^{n+2}$

Reason (R) If *a-t* graph is a straight line,then *s-t* graph may be a parabola.

(a) ☐ (b) ☐ (c) ☐ (d) ☐

8. **Assertion** (A) In realistic situation, the x-t, v-t and a-t graphs will be smooth. This means physically that acceleration and velocity cannot change values abruptly at an instant.
Reason (R) Changes are always continuous.
(a) ☐ (b) ☐ (c) ☐ (d) ☐

9. **Assertion** (A) The value of acceleration in free fall is taken as $a = -g = -9.8 \text{ ms}^{-2}$, if upward direction is taken as positive.
Reason (R) The accel ration due to gravity is always directed downward, which is taken as positive, if upwar rection is taken as positive.
(a) ☐ (b) ☐ (c) ☐ (d) ☐

***10.** As tion (A) Particle A is moving Eastwards and particle B Northwards with same speed. The velocity of A with respect to B is in South-East direction.

Reason (R) Relative velocity between them is zero as their speeds are same.
(a) ☐ (b) ☐ (c) ☐ (d) ☐

Case Based Questions

1. In the study of motion in one dimension, consider a car moving along a straight road. The car's position as a function of time is given by the equation $x(t) = 4t^2 - 2t + 3$, where x is the position in metres and t is the time in seconds. The initial position of the car at $t = 0$ is 3 m. The car starts with an initial velocity and accelerates uniformly.

(i) The initial velocity of the car at $t = 0$, is
(a) 2 m/s ☐ (b) – 2 m/s ☐
(c) 0 m/s ☐ (d) 4 m/s ☐

(ii) At what time t will the car be at rest momentarily?
(a) 0.25 s ☐ (b) 0.5 s ☐ (c) 1 s ☐ (d) 2 s ☐

(iii) For a rectilinear motion displacement can be
(a) positive only ☐ (b) negative only ☐
(c) zero ☐ (d) All of these ☐

(iv) In which of the following case, the motion is in a straight line ?
(a) A kite flying on a windy day ☐
(b) Speeding train on straight railway track ☐
(c) Carrom coin rebounding from the side of the board ☐
(d) None of the above ☐

2. James is an engineer, testing a prototype of a new electric car on a straight test track. The car starts from rest from the starting line (position $x = 0$) and accelerates uniformly down the track. James measures the car's acceleration to be 2 m/s^2. He records the car's velocity and position at various time intervals. After 5 s, he notes that the car has reached at velocity 10 m/s.
Using the kinematic equations for uniformly accelerated motion, James wants to predict

the car's position and velocity at different points in time.
(Given, $u = 0$ m/s and $a = 2$ m/s^2)

(i) Consider the car moving along a straight line with its velocity-time graph given by a straight line, that slopes downward. The statement that correctly explains about car's motion is

(a) The car is moving with constant acceleration. ☐
(b) The car is decelerating uniformly. ☐
(c) The car's acceleration is increasing. ☐
(d) The car's displacement is constant. ☐

(ii) The car starts from rest and accelerates uniformly. The graphs correctly represents the relation between displacement(s) and time (t) is

(a) A straight line passing through the origin. ☐
(b) A parabola opening upwards ☐
(c) A parabola opening downwards ☐
(d) A hyperbola. ☐

(iii) After 4 s, distance travelled by the car is

(a) 8 m ☐ (b) 12 m ☐ (c) 16 m ☐ (d) 32 m ☐

(iv) The car's velocity when it has travelled 25 meters, is

(a) 5 m/s ☐ (b) 10 m/s ☐ (c) 12 m/s ☐ (d) 15 m/s ☐

COMPETITION EDGE UP

1. Two cars are travelling towards each other at speed of 20 ms^{-1} each. When the cars are 300 m apart, both the drivers apply brakes and the cars retard at the rate of 2 ms^{-2}. The distance between them when they come to rest is **[NCERT Pg. 20, JEE Main 2024]**

(a) 25 m ☐ (b) 200 m ☐
(c) 100 m ☐ (d) 50 m ☐

2. A body travels 102.5 m in nth second and 115.0 m in $(n + 2)$th second. The acceleration is **[NCERT Pg. 18, JEE Main 2024]**

(a) 5 m / s^2 ☐ (b) 9 m / s^2 ☐
(c) 6.25 m / s^2 ☐ (d) 12.5 m / s^2 ☐

3. A particle initially at rest starts moving from reference point $x = 0$ along X-axis, with velocity v that varies as, $v = 4\sqrt{x}$ m/s. The acceleration of the particle is .... ms^{-2}. **[NCERT Pg. 16, JEE Main 2024]**

4. The relation between time t and distance x is $t = \alpha x^2 + \beta x$, where α and β are constants. The relation between acceleration a and velocity v is **[NCERT Pg. 18, JEE Main 2024]**

(a) $a = -5\alpha v^5$ ☐
(b) $a = -2\alpha v^3$ ☐
(c) $a = -3\alpha v^2$ ☐
(d) $a = -4\alpha v^4$ ☐

5. The displacement and the increase in velocity of a moving particle in the time interval of t to $(t + 1)$ s are 125 m and 50 m/s, respectively. The distance travelled by the particle in $(t + 2)$th s is .... m. **[NCERT Pg. 15, JEE Main 2024]**

6. The velocity (v)-time (t) plot of the motion of a body is shown below **[NCERT Pg. 16, NEET 2024]**

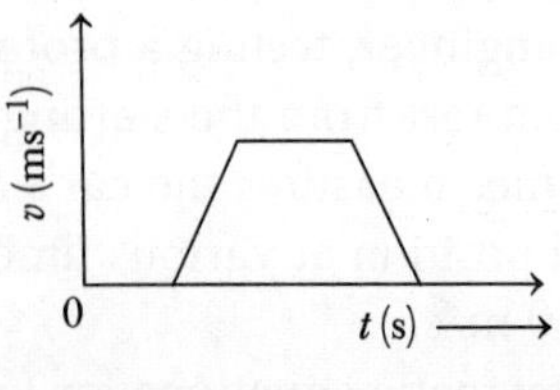

The acceleration (a)- time (t) graph that best suits this motion is

(a) 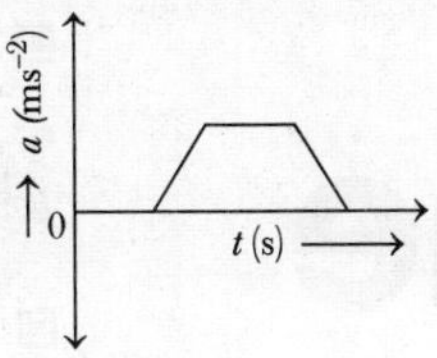 ☐

(b) 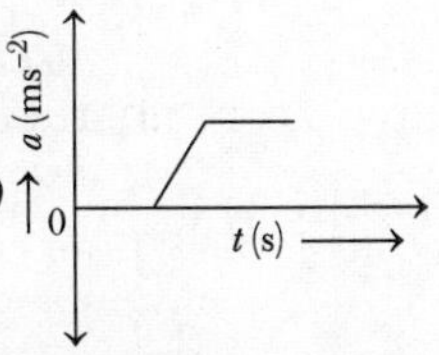 ☐

(c) 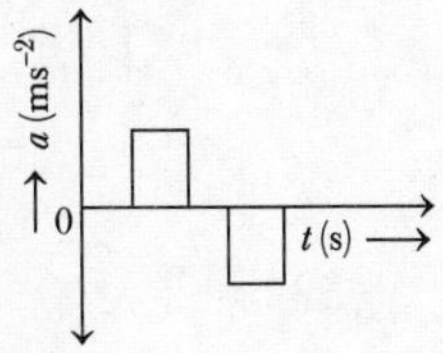 ☐

(d) 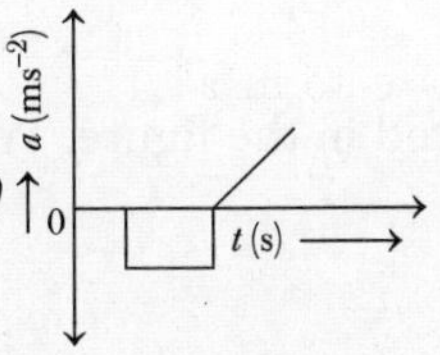 ☐

7. A horizontal bridge is built across a river. A student standing on the bridge throws a small ball vertically upwards with a velocity 4 m s^{-1}. The ball strikes the water surface after 4 s. The height of bridge above water surface is (Take, $g = 10 \text{ m s}^{-2}$).
[NCERT Pg 18, NEET 2023]

(a) 60 m ☐ (b) 64 m ☐

(c) 68 m ☐ (d) 56 m ☐

8. The ratio of the distances travelled by a freely falling body in the 1st, 2nd, 3rd and 4th second **[NCERT Pg. 20, NEET 2022]**

(a) 1 : 4 : 9 : 16 ☐

(b) 1 : 3 : 5 : 7 ☐

(c) 1 : 1 : 1 : 1 ☐

(d) 1 : 2 : 3 : 4 ☐

9. A car starts from rest and accelerates at 5 m/s^2. At $t = 4$ s, a ball is dropped out of a window by a person sitting in the car. What is the velocity and acceleration of the ball at $t = 6$ s? (Take, $g = 10 \, m/s^2$)
[NCERT Pg. 17, NEET 2021]

(a) 20 m/s, 5 m/s^2 ☐

(b) 20 m/s, 0 ☐

(c) $20\sqrt{2}$ m/s, 0 ☐

(d) $20\sqrt{2}$ m/s, 10 m/s^2 ☐

10. A small block slides down on a smooth inclined plane, starting from rest at time $t = 0$. Let s_n be the distance travelled by the block in the interval $t = n - 1$ to $t = n$. Then, the ratio $\frac{s_n}{s_{n+1}}$ is **[NCERT Pg. 20, NEET 2021]**

(a) $\frac{2n-1}{2n}$ ☐ (b) $\frac{2n-1}{2n+1}$ ☐

(c) $\frac{2n+1}{2n-1}$ ☐ (d) $\frac{2n}{2n-1}$ ☐

11. A person sitting in the ground floor of a building notices through the window of height 1.5 m, a ball dropped from the roof of the building crosses the window in 0.1 s. What is the velocity of the ball when it is at the topmost point of the window? ($g = 10 \, m/s^2$)
[NCERT Pg. 20, NEET (Oct.) 2020]

(a) 15.5 m/s ☐ (b) 14.5 m/s ☐

(c) 4.5 m/s ☐ (d) 20 m/s ☐

12. A ball is thrown vertically downward with a velocity of 20 m/s from the top of a tower. It hits the ground after some time with a velocity of 80 m/s. The height of the tower is ($g = 10 \, m/s^2$)
[NCERT Pg. 18, NEET (Sep.) 2020]

(a) 340 m ☐ (b) 320 m ☐

(c) 300 m ☐ (d) 360 m ☐

Chapter 03

Motion in a Plane

Scan and take Chapter Test

TOPIC 1

Addition and Subtraction of Vectors-Graphical Method

NCERT Pg 29-31

***1.** Six vectors **a** to **f** have the magnitudes and directions indicated in the figure. Which of the following option(s) is true?

(a) **b** + **c** = **c** ☐
(b) **d** + **c** = **f** ☐
(c) **d** + **e** = **f** ☐
(d) **b** + **e** = **f** ☐

2. Consider the following figure.

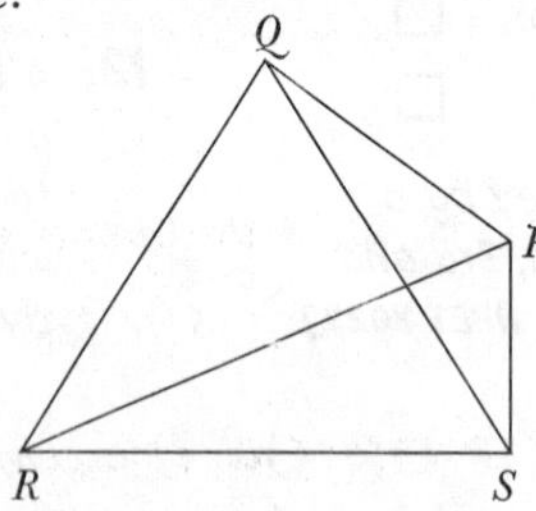

Give a single vector which is equivalent to the combination of given vectors.

A. **PQ** + **QR** = ______________________________

B. **RS** + **SP** + **PQ** = ______________________________

C. **QS** − **PS** = ______________________________

*Concepts of all questions bearing * are important for JEE/NEET/CUET.*

3. Match the Column I with Column II.

	Column I		Column II
A.	$\mathbf{C}-\mathbf{A}-\mathbf{B}=0$	1.	
B.	$\mathbf{A}-\mathbf{C}-\mathbf{B}=0$	2.	
C.	$\mathbf{B}-\mathbf{A}-\mathbf{C}=0$	3.	
D.	$\mathbf{A}+\mathbf{B}=-\mathbf{C}$	4.	

A____________ B____________ C____________ D____________

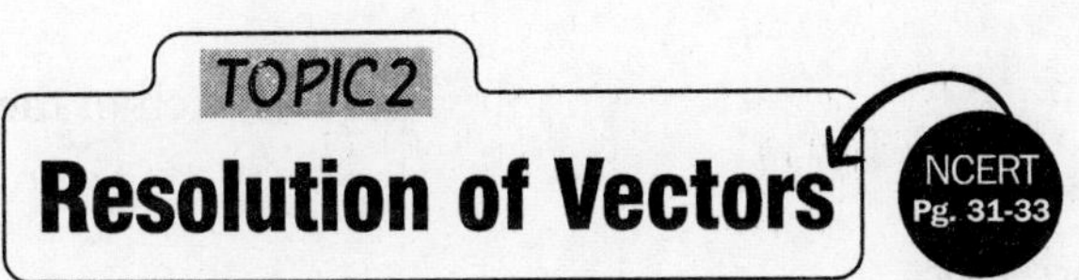

TOPIC 2 Resolution of Vectors

NCERT Pg. 31-33

4. Consider vector **OA**, where coordinates of *A* are (2, 2).

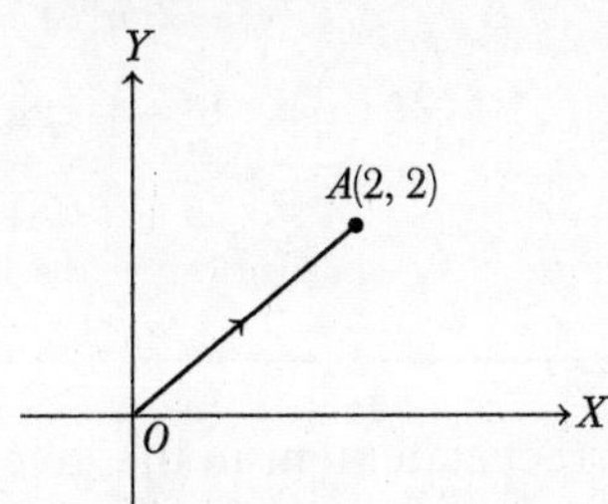

Vector obtained by rotating **OA** by 45° anti-clockwise is

(a) $2\sqrt{2}\hat{\mathbf{j}}$ ☐ (b) $2\hat{\mathbf{j}}$ ☐ (c) $2\hat{\mathbf{i}}$ ☐ (d) $2\sqrt{2}\hat{\mathbf{i}}$ ☐

5. The resultant of these forces **OP**, **OQ**, **OR**, **OS** and **OT** is approximately (in N) (Take, $\sqrt{3}=1.7$, $\sqrt{2}=1.4$ and given $\hat{\mathbf{i}}$ and $\hat{\mathbf{j}}$ are unit vectors along *X*, *Y*-axes)

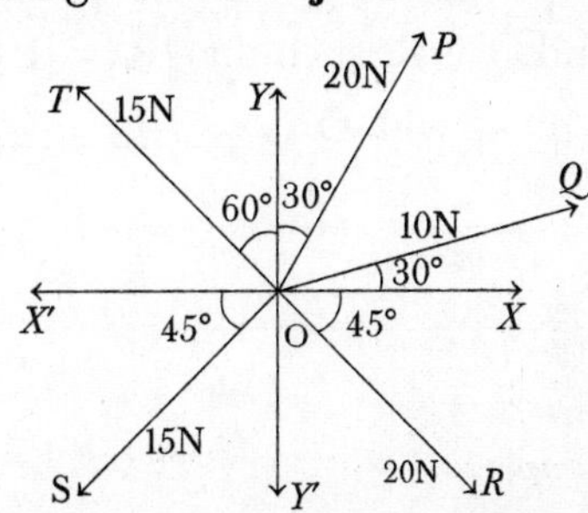

(a) $9.25\hat{\mathbf{i}} + 5\hat{\mathbf{j}}$ ☐ (b) $3\hat{\mathbf{i}} + 15\hat{\mathbf{j}}$ ☐

(c) $2.5\hat{\mathbf{i}} - 14.5\hat{\mathbf{j}}$ ☐ (d) $-1.5\hat{\mathbf{i}} - 15.5\hat{\mathbf{j}}$ ☐

6. Consider two vectors **a** and **b** with an angle θ between them, such that $|\mathbf{a}| = |\mathbf{b}| = 3$ units.
Let $\mathbf{R} = \mathbf{a} + \mathbf{b}$, now choose correctly matched pair from the given below.
I. $|\mathbf{R}| = 3 \rightarrow \theta = 120°$ II. $|\mathbf{R}| = 3\sqrt{2} \rightarrow \theta = 60°$

____

TOPIC 3

Vector Addition-Analytical Method

7. If $\mathbf{A} = 2\hat{\mathbf{i}} + 4\hat{\mathbf{j}} - 3\hat{\mathbf{k}}$ and $\mathbf{B} = 3\hat{\mathbf{i}} + \hat{\mathbf{j}} - 2\hat{\mathbf{k}}$, then a unit vector in direction of $\mathbf{A} + \mathbf{B}$ is $\frac{1}{\sqrt{3}}(\hat{\mathbf{i}} + \hat{\mathbf{j}} + \hat{\mathbf{k}})$.

True ☐ False ☐

8. Given, $\mathbf{a} = 4\hat{\mathbf{i}} + 3\hat{\mathbf{k}}$ and $\mathbf{b} = -2\hat{\mathbf{i}} + \hat{\mathbf{j}} + 5\hat{\mathbf{k}}$

Now, match Column I with Column II correctly.

Column I	Column II
A. $\mathbf{a} + \mathbf{b}$	1. $-2\hat{\mathbf{i}} + 5\hat{\mathbf{j}} + 31\hat{\mathbf{k}}$
B. $\mathbf{a} - \mathbf{b}$	2. $6\hat{\mathbf{i}} - \hat{\mathbf{j}} - 2\hat{\mathbf{k}}$
C. $2\mathbf{a} + 5\mathbf{b}$	3. $2\hat{\mathbf{i}} + \hat{\mathbf{j}} + 8\hat{\mathbf{k}}$

A__________ B__________ C__________

9. Tick (✓/✗) for correct/incorrect statement in the given boxes.

(i) Vector sum of three non-parallel vectors will be a zero vector if and only if three vectors form a cyclic triangle. ☐

(ii) Resultant of three coplanar forces of magnitude 4, 8 and 3 units acting on a particle can be zero. ☐

(iii) If $|\mathbf{P} - \mathbf{Q}| = |\mathbf{P} + \mathbf{Q}|$, then **P** and **Q** are perpendicular vectors. ☐

10. The sum of two forces **P** and **Q** is **R**, such that $|\mathbf{R}| = |\mathbf{P}|$. The angle θ (in degrees) that the resultant of 2**P** and **Q** will make with **Q** is __________ .

TOPIC 4

Motion in a Plane

NCERT Pg 34-38

11. An object starts moving from origin such that its velocity at any instant is given by $v = (2\hat{i} + 3\hat{j})$ m/s. Coordinates of particle after 10 s are

$x =$ ____________ m, $y =$ ____________ m

12. Coordinates of a particle (in metres) moving over a curve are given as $x = t^3$ and $y = t^4$, where t = time in seconds.

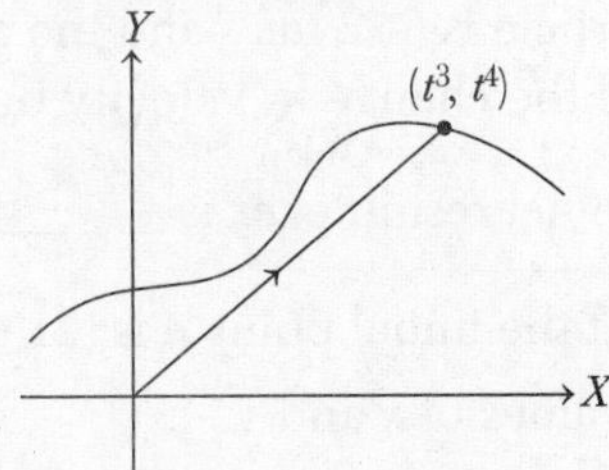

Speed of particle at $t = 1$ s is ____________ m/s.

13. A particle is moving in XY-plane according to the equation $x = pt, y = pt(1 - qt)$, where p and q are positive constants and t is time. When the velocity vector makes an angle of 45° with acceleration vector, then

I. $t = \frac{1}{p}$ II. $t = \frac{1}{q}$

Choose the correct one.

____

14. A particle is moving in XY-plane. At certain instant of time, the components of its velocity and acceleration are as follows. $v_x = 6$ m/s, $v_y = 8$ m/s, $a_x = 24$ m/s^2 and $a_y = 12$ m/s^2. The rate of change of speed of the particle is found to be x m/s^2. The value of x is ____________.

15. An object starts from origin at $t = 0$ s. Its acceleration along X and Y-axes are 6 m/s^2 and 8 m/s^2, respectively. Its distance from origin at $t = 4$ s is ____________ m.

16. A particle has initial velocity $(3\hat{i} + 4\hat{j})$ and has acceleration $(0.4\,\hat{i} + 0.3\,\hat{j})$. Its speed after 10 s is ____________ unit.

TOPIC 5

Projectile Motion

NCERT Pg 38-40

17. The projectile motion of a particle of mass 5 g is shown in the figure.

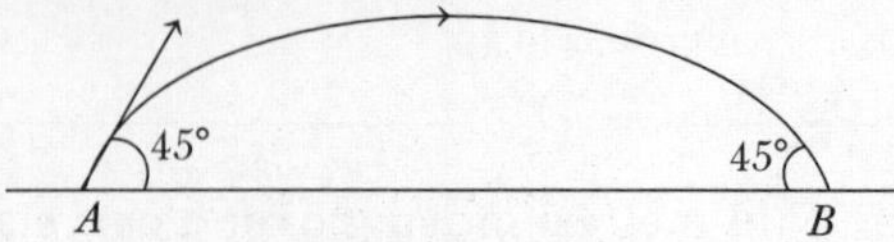

The initial velocity of the particle is $5\sqrt{2}$ ms^{-1} and the air resistance is assumed to be negligible. The magnitude of the change in velocity between the points A and B is x ms^{-1}. The value of x to the nearest integer is ____________ .

18. The velocity of a projectile at the initial point A is $(2\hat{\mathbf{i}} + 3\hat{\mathbf{j}})$ m/s. Its velocity (in m/s) at point B is $x\hat{\mathbf{i}} + y\hat{\mathbf{j}}$. Find the values of x and y.

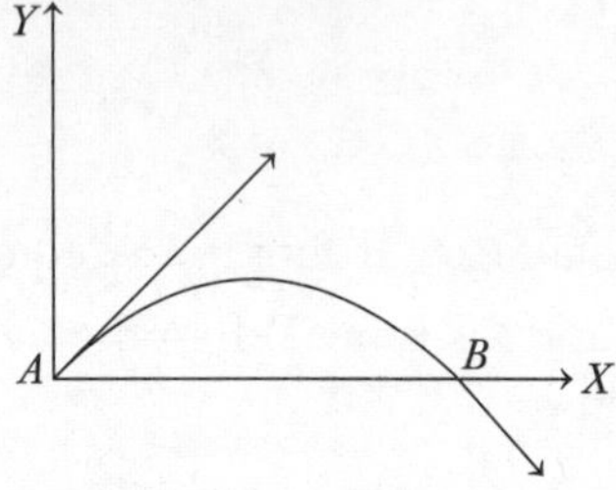

---

19. Trajectory of a particle, is given by $y = \sqrt{3}x - \frac{gx^2}{2}$, its angle of projection with vertical direction is 60°. (Take, $g = 10$ m/s^2)

True ☐ False ☐

20. A particle moves along parabola $y = \sqrt{3}x - \frac{1}{2}x^2$. Initial speed of particle is ________ m/s.

21. A particle is projected from the ground at an angle of 45° with the horizontal at speed $u = 10$ m/s. The radius of curvature of the path of the particle when its velocity makes an angle of 30° is $\frac{40}{\sqrt{3}x}$. Find the value of x.

---

22. For any projectile, ratio of maximum height and square of time of flight is a constant.

True ☐ False ☐

***23.** A projectile is thrown at an angle θ and 90° − θ with horizontal. Let h_1, h_2 and t_1, t_2 indicates maximum heights and time of flights in two cases.

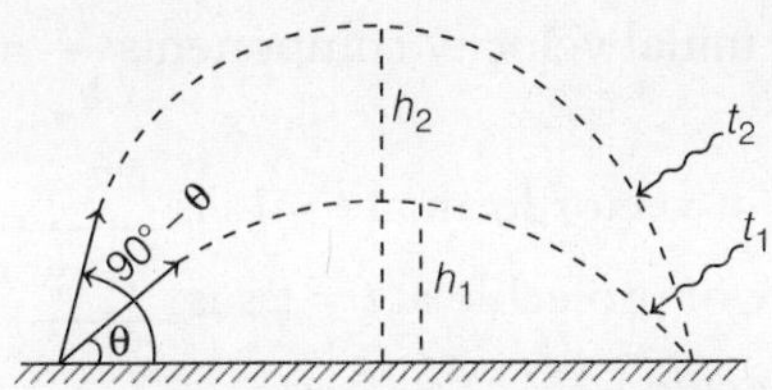

It covers a range of 400 m. Now, choose correctly matched pairs.

I. $\sqrt{h_1 h_2} \rightarrow 100$ m II. $t_1 t_2 \rightarrow 40$ m

---

***24.** The horizontal range and the maximum height of a projectile are equal. Find the angle of projection of the projectile.

---

25. A missile is fired for maximum range with an initial velocity of 20 m/s. If $g = 10 \text{ m/s}^2$, the range of the missile will be __________ m .

***26.** A boy can throw a ball to a maximum possible distance of 100 m. Its speed of throw is __________ m/s.

27. A projectile is thrown to achieve maximum possible range which is R metres. Coordinates of point when this projectile is moving with slowest speed is __________ .

***28.** Ratio of ranges of a projectile at $\theta = 30°$ and $\theta = 60°$ is __________ .

29. Two particles are projected with same initial velocities at an angle 30° and 60° with the horizontal, then their

(a) heights will be equal ☐ (b) ranges will be equal ☐
(c) time of flights will be equal ☐ (d) ranges will be different ☐

30. A player kicks a football with an initial speed of 25 ms^{-1} at an angle of 45° from the ground. What are the maximum height and the time taken by the football to reach at the highest point during motion? (Take, $g = 10 \text{ ms}^{-2}$)

(a) $h_{max} = 10$ m, $T = 2.5$ s ☐ (b) $h_{max} = 15.625$ m, $T = 3.54$ s ☐
(c) $h_{max} = 15.625$ m, $T = 1.77$ s ☐ (d) $h_{max} = 3.54$ m, $T = 0.125$ s ☐

31. Consider following projection of particle from origin at $t = 0$ s.

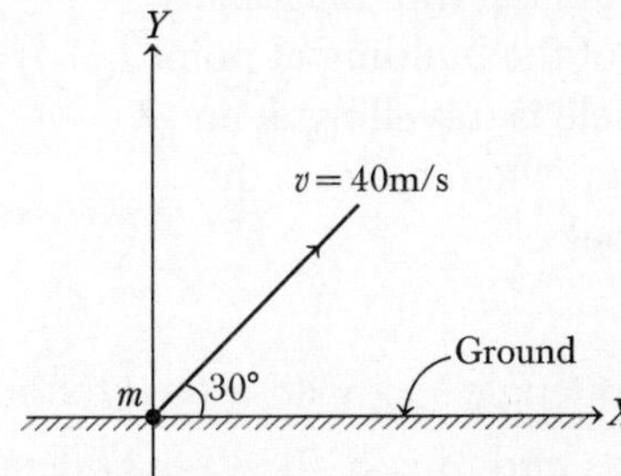

I. Ratio of magnitudes, initial velocity components $\frac{v_x}{v_y}$ = __________ .

II. Velocity of projectile in vector form at $t = 1$ s is __________ m/s.

III. Magnitude of velocity of projectile at $t = 2$ s is __________ m/s.

IV. Time of flight of projectile is __________ s.

V. Ratio of range and maximum height of projectile is __________ .

32. Two particles P and Q are thrown from the same point in the same vertical plane as shown in figure simultaneously.

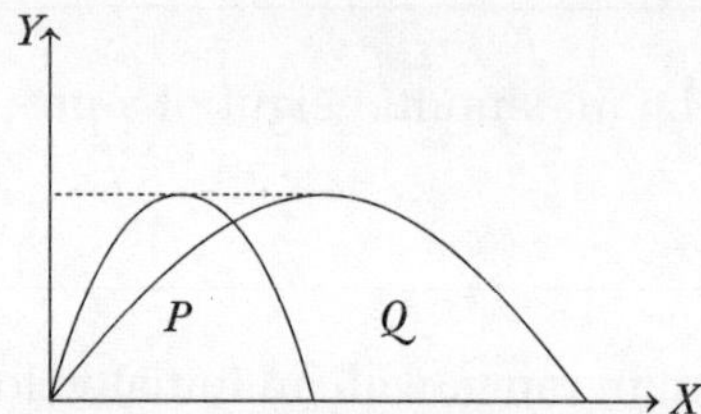

Then, choose the correct statements given below.

I. Projection speed of particle P is greater than that of Q.

II. Horizontal component of velocity for particle Q is greater than that of P.

III. The vertical component of velocities of both P and Q are always equal throughout the duration for which both the particles in air.

IV. Time of flight of particles P is less than that of particle Q.

***33.** A shell is fired from a fixed artillery gun with an initial speed u, such that it hits the target on the ground at a distance R from it. If t_1 and t_2 are the values of the time taken by it to hit the target in two possible ways, the product $t_1 t_2$ is

(a) $\frac{R}{4g}$ ☐ (b) $\frac{R}{g}$ ☐

(c) $\frac{R}{2g}$ ☐ (d) $\frac{2R}{g}$ ☐

34. A particle is fired from point P in the diagonal plane of building of dimensions 20 m (length) ×15 m (breadth) × 12.5 m (height) as shown in figure. The particle just clears the roof diagonally and falls on the other side of the building at point Q. It is found that the particle is travelling at an angle 45° with the horizontal when it clears the edge A and B of the diagonal

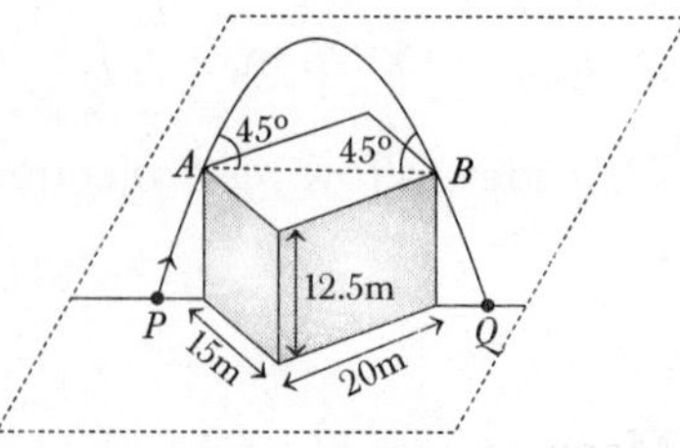

Take, $g = 10 \text{ m/s}^2$). Match the Column I with Column II.

	Column I		Column II
A.	The speed (in m/s) of the particle at point A	1.	60
B.	The speed (in m/s) of projection at point P	2.	$10\sqrt{5}$
C.	The speed (in m/s) of particle at the top of the trajectory	3.	$25\sqrt{3}$
D.	Range (PQ) of the particle (in m)	4.	$5\sqrt{10}$
E.	Angle of projection at point P (in degrees)	5.	$5\sqrt{5}$
F.	Time of flight of particle is (in s)	6.	$\sqrt{15}$

A __________ B __________ C __________
D __________ E __________ F __________

TOPIC 6

Uniform Circular Motion

NCERT Pg 40-42

35. Instantaneous acceleration for uniform circular motion is always directed towards __________ of the circle.

36. Match the items in Column I with values in Column II for the uniform circular motion.

	Column I		Column II
A.	Speed	1.	Constant
B.	Velocity	2.	Variable
C.	Magnitude of acceleration	3.	Zero
D.	Acceleration		

A__________B__________C__________D__________

37. A particle is moving with a constant speed v over circumference of a circle of radius r.

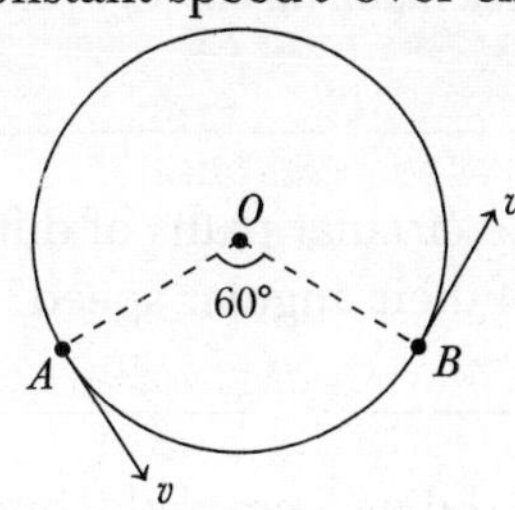

Magnitude of change in velocity is __________ unit.

38. Which of the following statement(s) is/are false for a particle moving in a circle with a constant angular speed?

(a) The velocity vector is tangent to the circle. ☐
(b) The acceleration vector is tangent to the circle. ☐
(c) The acceleration vector point towards the centre of the circle. ☐
(d) The velocity and acceleration vectors are perpendicular to each other. ☐

39. Two cars A and B move along a concentric circular path of radius r_A and r_B with velocities v_A and v_B maintaining constant distance, then $v_A : v_B$ is equal to ______________.

40. A cyclist starts from centre of a circular park of radius 1 km and moves along a path *OPRQO* as shown in figure. If he maintains constant speed of 10 m/s, what is his acceleration at point R in magnitude?

Q R O P

(a) 0.1 ms^{-2} ☐ (b) 0.3 ms^{-2} ☐ (c) 0.2 ms^{-2} ☐ (d) 0.4 ms^{-2} ☐

41. A particle is moving with a constant speed v in a circle. What is the magnitude of average velocity after half rotation?

____

***42.** A wheel completes 2000 revolutions to cover the 9.5 km distance, then the diameter of the wheel is ____________ m.

43. An insect is trapped in a circular groove of radius 12 cm moves along the groove steadily and completes 7 revolutions in 100 s.

Match the quantity given in Column I with their respective units in Column II for the above information.

Column I	Column II
A. Angular speed (in rad/s)	1. 2.3
B. Linear speed (in cm/s)	2. 5.3
C. Magnitude of acceleration (in cm/s^2)	3. 0.44

A____________ B____________ C____________

44. Two balls are moving along the circular paths of different radii with same time period of revolution. What is the ratio of their angular speed?

____

45. A particle moves in a circle of radius 5 cm with constant speed and time period 0.2π s. The acceleration of the particle is ______________ m/s^2.

46. A particle moves, such that its position vector $\mathbf{r}(t) = \cos \omega t\,\hat{\mathbf{i}} + \sin \omega t\,\hat{\mathbf{j}}$, where ω is a constant and t is time. Then, which of the following statement(s) is/are correct for the velocity $\mathbf{v}(t)$ and acceleration $\mathbf{a}(t)$ of the particle?

(a) **v** and **a** both are parallel to **r**. ☐

(b) **v** is perpendicular to **r** and **a** is directed away from the origin. ☐

(c) **v** and **a** both are perpendicular to **r**. ☐

(d) **v** is perpendicular to **r** and **a** is directed towards the origin. ☐

47. Two cars of masses m_1 and m_2 are moving in circles of radii r_1 and r_2, respectively. Speed of the cars are such that they make complete circles in the same time t, then find the ratio of their speed. What is the ratio of their centripetal acceleration?

____

48. For a particle in uniform circular motion, the acceleration **a** at a point $P(R, \theta)$ on the circle of radius R is (here, θ is measured from the X-axis) given by

I. $-\frac{v^2}{R}\cos\theta\,\hat{\mathbf{i}} - \frac{v^2}{R}\sin\theta\,\hat{\mathbf{j}}$ ☐ II. $-\frac{v^2}{R}\sin\theta\,\hat{\mathbf{i}} + \frac{v^2}{R}\cos\theta\,\hat{\mathbf{j}}$ ☐

COMPETITION CONNECT

Topic Relative Velocity in Two Dimensions [NCERT (Old) Pg. 76-77]

1. Two cars A and B start simultaneously with accelerations

$$a_A = (3\hat{\mathbf{i}} - 2\hat{\mathbf{j}})\ \text{m/s}^2,\ a_B = (\hat{\mathbf{i}} + 3\hat{\mathbf{j}})\ \text{m/s}^2$$

After a time interval of 5 s,

I. Relative velocity of A with respect to B is _______________ m/s.

II. A and B are _______________ m apart.

III. Acceleration of A relative to B is _______________ m/s^2.

2. Points A and B are moving, such that B always remains in North of A (i.e. AB is a line parallel to Y-axis).

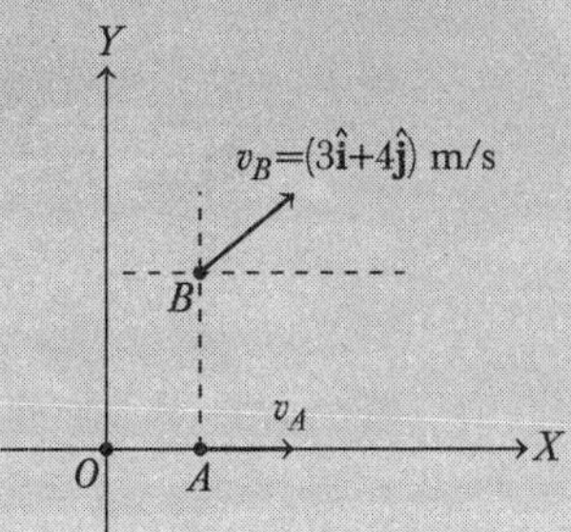

Velocity of A with respect to XOY frame will be _______________ m/s.

3. A and B are two moving particles. Positions of A and B are shown with respect to a fixed point O.

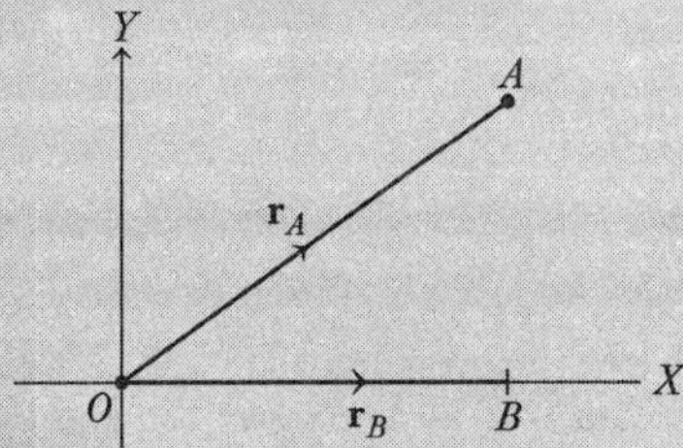

Now, complete these sentences.

I. Vector $\mathbf{r}_{AB}$ = ______________ $(\mathbf{r}_A - \mathbf{r}_B / \mathbf{r}_B - \mathbf{r}_A)$

II. Let $\mathbf{r}_A = 3t\,\hat{\mathbf{i}} + 4t\,\hat{\mathbf{j}}(\text{m})$ and $\mathbf{r}_B = 2t\,\hat{\mathbf{i}}(\text{m})$, here t = time in seconds, then velocity of A with respect to B at $t = 2\,\text{s}$ is ______________ m/s.

III. Velocity of B with respect to A at $t = 3\,\text{s}$ is ______________ m/s.

4. Two particles A and B move with constant velocities $\mathbf{v}_1$ and $\mathbf{v}_2$. At the initial moment, their position vectors are $\mathbf{r}_1$ and $\mathbf{r}_2$, respectively. The condition for particles A and B for their collision is

(a) $\dfrac{\mathbf{r}_1 - \mathbf{r}_2}{|\mathbf{r}_1 - \mathbf{r}_2|} = \dfrac{\mathbf{v}_1 - \mathbf{v}_2}{|\mathbf{v}_2 - \mathbf{v}_1|}$ ☐ (b) $\mathbf{r}_1 \cdot \mathbf{v}_1 = \mathbf{r}_2 \cdot \mathbf{v}_2$ ☐

(c) $\mathbf{r}_1 \times \mathbf{v}_1 = \mathbf{r}_2 \times \mathbf{v}_2$ ☐ (d) $\mathbf{r}_1 - \mathbf{r}_2 = \mathbf{v}_1 - \mathbf{v}_2$ ☐

5. Two particles A and B are moving on two concentric circles of radii R_1 and R_2 with equal angular speed ω. At $t = 0$, their positions and direction of motion are shown in the figure.

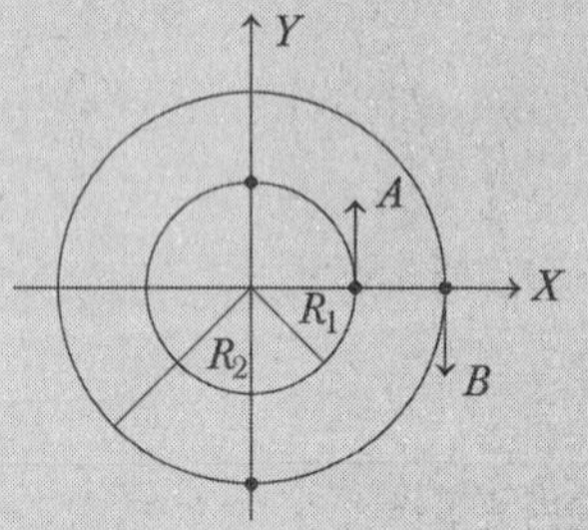

The relative velocity $\mathbf{v}_A - \mathbf{v}_B$ at $t = \dfrac{\pi}{2\omega}$ is given by ____________.

6. Rain is falling vertically with speed of 4 m/s, a man is cycling along North with speed of 3 m/s. Velocity of rain with respect to man has a magnitude ______________ m/s and it is inclined at an angle of ______________ degrees with North direction.

7. A swimmer can swim in river at the speed of 5 km/h and water is flowing in river at the speed of 3 km/h. River width is 0.5 km.

Now, match entries of Column I and Column II.

	Column I		Column II
A.	Resultant speed of man while crossing river along shortest path	1.	6 min
B.	Time to cross river along shortest path	2.	$\sqrt{34}$ km/h
C.	Shortest time in which river can be crossed	3.	7.5 min
D.	Speed of man when river is crossed in shortest time	4.	4 km/h

A______________ B______________ C______________ D______________

8. The speed of a swimmer in still water is 20 m/s. The speed of river water is 10 m/s and is flowing due to East. If he is standing on the South bank and wishes to cross the river along the shortest path, the angle (in degree) at which he should make his strokes with respect to North is given by __________.

9. A person swims in a river aiming to reach exactly opposite point on the bank of a river. His speed of swimming is 0.5 m/s at an angle 120° with direction of flow of water. Find the speed of water in stream.

---

10. The speed of a boat is 5 km/h in still water. It crosses a river of width 1.0 km along the shortest possible path in 15 min. The velocity of the river water is (in km/h) __________ .

11. A person is swimming with a speed of 10 m/s at an angle of 120° with the flow and reaches to a point directly opposite on the other side of the river. The speed of the flow is x m/s. The value of x to the nearest integer is __________ .

12. A swimmer can swim with velocity of 12 km/h in still water. Water flowing in a river has velocity 6 km/h. The direction with respect to the direction of flow of river water, he should swim in order to reach the point on the other bank just opposite to his starting point is __________ (in degree). (Round off to the nearest integer)

Assertion-Reason Questions

Direction (Q. Nos. 1-10) *In the following questions, a statement of Assertion is followed by a corresponding statement of Reason. From the following options, choose the correct one.*

(a) Both Assertion and Reason are correct and Reason is the correct explanation of Assertion.
(b) Both Assertion and Reason are correct but Reason is not the correct explanation of Assertion.
(c) Assertion is correct but Reason is incorrect.
(d) Assertion is incorrect but Reason is correct.

1. Assertion (A) If A, B, C and D are four points on a semi-circular arc with centre at O, such that $|\mathbf{AB}| = |\mathbf{BC}| = |\mathbf{CD}|$, then $\mathbf{AB} + \mathbf{AC} + \mathbf{AD} = 4\mathbf{AO} + \mathbf{OB} + \mathbf{OC}$.

O, A, D, B, C

Reason (R) Polygon law of vector addition yields

$$\mathbf{AB} + \mathbf{BC} + \mathbf{CD} + \mathbf{AD} = 2\mathbf{AO}$$

(a) ☐ (b) ☐ (c) ☐ (d) ☐

2. Assertion (A) Particle-1 is dropped from a tower and particle-2 is projected horizontal from the same tower, then both the particles reach the ground simultaneously.
Reason (R) Both the particles strike the ground with different speeds.

(a) ☐ (b) ☐ (c) ☐ (d) ☐

3. Assertion (A) Magnitude of resultant of two vectors may be less than the magnitude of either vector.
Reason (R) Vector addition is commutative.

(a) ☐ (b) ☐ (c) ☐ (d) ☐

4. **Assertion** (A) A particle in *XY*-plane is governed by $x = a \sin \omega t$ and $y = a \cos \omega t$, where a as well as ω are constants, then the particle will have parabolic motion.
Reason (R) A particle under the influence of mutually perpendicular velocities has curvilinear motion.

(a) ☐ (b) ☐ (c) ☐ (d) ☐

5. **Assertion** (A) In case of projectile motion, the magnitude of rate of change in velocity is variable.
Reason (R) In projectile motion, magnitude of velocity first decreases and then increases during the motion.

(a) ☐ (b) ☐ (c) ☐ (d) ☐

6. **Assertion** (A) If a particle is projected vertically upwards with velocity u, the maximum height attained by the particle is h_1. The same particle is projected at angle 30° from horizontal with the same speed u. Now, the maximum height is h_2. Thus, $h_1 = 4h_2$
Reason (R) In first case, $v = 0$ at highest point and in second case, $v \neq 0$ at highest point.

(a) ☐ (b) ☐ (c) ☐ (d) ☐

7. **Assertion** (A) If a particle is projected horizontally from a certain height, its time of flight depends on its horizontal speed.
Reason (R) The time of flight depends on the vertical components of motion only.

(a) ☐ (b) ☐ (c) ☐ (d) ☐

8. **Assertion** (A) Sum of maximum height for angles α and $90° - \alpha$ is independent of the angle of projection.

Reason (R) For angles α and $90° - \alpha$, the horizontal range R is same.

(a) ☐ (b) ☐ (c) ☐ (d) ☐

9. **Assertion** (A) The maximum height of projectile is always 25% of the maximum range.
Reason (R) For maximum range, projectile should be projected at 90°.

(a) ☐ (b) ☐ (c) ☐ (d) ☐

10. **Assertion** (A) The acceleration vector in a non-uniform circular motion has both radial and tangential components.
Reason (R) Non-uniform circular motion involves changing speed and changing direction of motion.

(a) ☐ (b) ☐ (c) ☐ (d) ☐

Case Based Questions

1. A ball A is projected with speed 50 ms^{-1} at an angle 37° with horizontal. At the same time, a second ball B is projected in a direction as shown in the figure with speed 60 ms^{-1} from a point 91 m from A. Both balls collide in air.

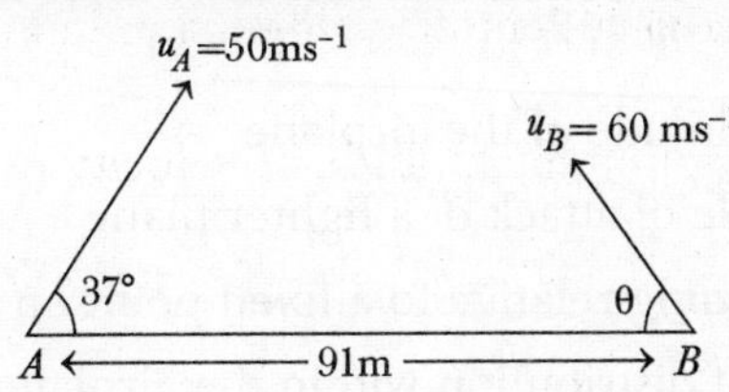

(i) The value of θ is

(a) 53° ☐ (b) 37° ☐

(c) 30° ☐ (d) 60° ☐

(ii) The time when collision takes place is

(a) 2 s ☐ (b) 1 s ☐

(c) 4 s ☐ (d) 1.7 s ☐

(iii) Height of point of collision is

(a) 25.1 m ☐ (b) 30 m ☐

(c) 28.3 m ☐ (d) 15 m ☐

(iv) The path traced by a projectile in space is

(a) coral ☐ (b) orbit ☐

(c) track ☐ (d) trajectory ☐

2. When an airplane flies, its actual velocity is given by

$v_a = v_{aw} + v_w$

Here, v_a = the velocity of airplane with respect to ground,
v_{aw} = the velocity of airplane with respect to wind blow velocity, it is also known as air velocity of airplane and v_w = velocity of wind.
Consider an airplane whose magnitude of velocity is 100 ms^{-1}. To reach its destination, the airplane must fly east. The heading of a plane is the direction in which v_{aw} is directed.

(i) If the plane has an eastward heading while a 20 ms^{-1} wind blows northward, the plane velocity is deflected from due east by angle α. The value of tan α is

(a) 0.2 ☐ (b) 0.8 ☐

(c) 1.2 ☐ (d) 5 ☐

(ii) The pilot maintains an eastward heading while wind blows northward. The magnitude of velocity (in ms^{-1}) with respect to ground is

(a) $26\sqrt{20}$ ☐ (b) $\frac{20}{\sqrt{26}}$ ☐

(c) $20\sqrt{26}$ ☐ (d) 20 ☐

(iii) Relative motion refers to the airplane's speed relative to

(a) a stationary observer on the ground ☐

(b) the surrounding air ☐

(c) the rotational speed of the earth ☐

(d) its own previous position in space ☐

(iv) The significance of the direction of a velocity vector in the context of airplane navigation is that

(a) it determines the altitude of the airplane ☐

(b) it specifies the angle of attack of a fighter plane ☐

(c) it indicates the heading relative to a fixed point on the ground ☐

(d) it affects the weight distribution within the airplane ☐

COMPETITION EDGE UP

1. *The resultant of two vectors* A *and* B *is perpendicular to* A *and its magnitude is half that of* B. *The angle (in degree) between vectors* A *and* B *is ....*

[NCERT Pg. 32, JEE Main 2024]

2. *A body of mass M thrown horizontally with velocity v from the top of the tower of height H touches the ground at a distance of 100 m from the foot of the tower. A body of mass 2M thrown at a velocity $\frac{v}{2}$ from the top of the tower of height 4H will touch the ground at a distance of ...... m.*

[NCERT Pg. 39, JEE Main 2024]

3. *The angle of projection for a projectile to have same horizontal range and maximum height is* **[NCERT Pg. 40, JEE Main 2024]**

(a) $\tan^{-1}\left(\frac{1}{2}\right)$ ☐

(b) $\tan^{-1}\left(\frac{1}{4}\right)$ ☐

(c) $\tan^{-1}(2)$ ☐

(d) $\tan^{-1}(4)$ ☐

4. *Three vectors* OP, OQ *and* OR *each of magnitude A are acting as shown in figure. The resultant of the three vectors is $A\sqrt{x}$. The value of x is ....*

[NCERT Pg. 34, JEE Main 2024]

Q, O, 45°, P, R

5. *The maximum height reached by a projectile is 64 m. If the initial velocity is halved, the new maximum height of the projectile is .... m.*

[NCERT Pg. 39, JEE Main 2024]

6. *A vector has magnitude same as that of* $A = 3\hat{i} + 4\hat{j}$ *and is parallel to* $B = 4\hat{i} + 3\hat{j}$. *The x and y-components of this vector in first quadrant are x and 3 respectively, where x = ...* **[NCERT Pg. 32, JEE Main 2024]**

7. *Projectiles A and B are thrown at angles of 45° and 60° with vertical, respectively from top of a 400 m high tower. If their ranges and times of flight are same, the ratio of their speeds of projection $v_A : v_B$ is [Take, $g = 10\ ms^{-2}$]*

[NCERT Pg. 39, JEE Main 2024]

(a) $\sqrt{2} : 1$ ☐ (b) $1 : 2$ ☐

(c) $1 : \sqrt{3}$ ☐ (d) $1 : \sqrt{2}$ ☐

8. A particle moving with uniform speed in a circular path maintains
[NCERT Pg. 40, NEET 2024]

(a) constant velocity ☐
(b) constant acceleration ☐
(c) constant velocity but varying acceleration ☐
(d) varying velocity and varying acceleration ☐

9. The angular acceleration of a body, moving along the circumference of a circle, is
[NCERT Pg. 40, NEET 2023]

(a) along the radius towards the centre ☐
(b) along the tangent to its position ☐
(c) along the axis of rotation ☐
(d) along the radius, away from centre ☐

10. A bullet is fired from a gun at the speed of 280 m s^{-1} in the direction 30° above the horizontal. The maximum height attained by the bullet is ($g = 9.8$ m s^{-2}, sin 30° = 0.5)
[NCERT Pg. 39, NEET 2023]

(a) 2000 m ☐
(b) 1000 m ☐
(c) 3000 m ☐
(d) 2800 m ☐

11. A car starts from rest and accelerates at 5 m/s^2. At $t = 4$ s, a ball is dropped out of a window by a person sitting in the car. What is the velocity and acceleration of the ball at $t = 6$ s? (Take $g = 10$ m/s^2)
[NCERT Pg. 39, NEET 2021]

(a) $20\sqrt{2}$ m/s, 10 m/s^2 ☐
(b) 20 m/s, 5 m/s^2 ☐
(c) 20 m/s, 0 ☐
(d) $20\sqrt{2}$ m/s, 0 ☐

12. A particle moving in a circle of radius R with a uniform speed takes a time T to complete one revolution. If this particle were projected with the same speed at an angle θ to the horizontal, the maximum height attained by it equals 4R. The angle of projection θ is then given by
[NCERT Pg. 42, NEET 2021]

(a) $\theta = \cos^{-1}\left(\frac{gT^2}{\pi^2 R}\right)^{1/2}$ ☐
(b) $\theta = \cos^{-1}\left(\frac{\pi^2 R}{gT^2}\right)^{1/2}$ ☐
(c) $\theta = \sin^{-1}\left(\frac{\pi^2 R}{gT^2}\right)^{1/2}$ ☐
(d) $\theta = \sin^{-1}\left(\frac{2gT^2}{\pi^2 R}\right)^{1/2}$ ☐

Chapter 04

Laws of Motion

Scan and take Chapter Test

TOPIC 1

The Law of Inertia and Newton's First Law of Motion

NCERT Pg. 50-53

1. A boy sitting on the topmost berth of a train compartment drops an apple into the open hand of his friend (sitting directly below his hand at a distance of 0.7 m). The apple falls exactly into the hand of his friend. This occurs due to ________________ (inertia of rest/ inertia of motion).

2. If we were to imagine a world without any frictional force, then no external force would be required to keep a body moving uniformly along a straight line.

True ☐ False ☐

3. A ball released from rest on a smooth inclined plane rolls down as shown below.

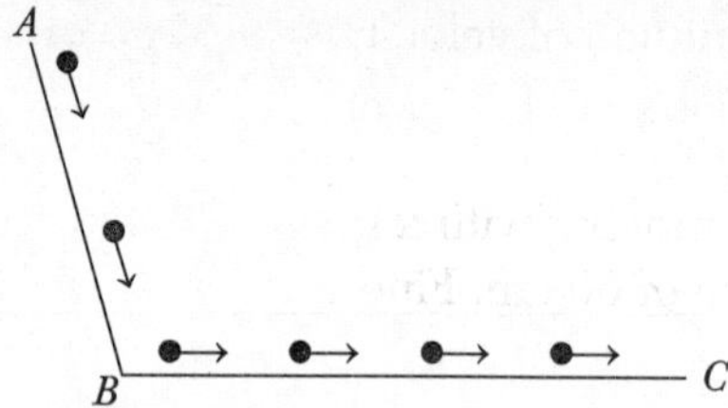

In ideal situation (when there is no friction), the distance travelled by the ball on the surface BC will be ________________ (finite/infinite).

4. An astronaut accidently gets separated out of his spaceship travelling in interstellar space at a constant velocity of 50 m/s, then velocity of astronaut at the instant when he is outside the spaceship will be ______________ .

5. The state of rest or of uniform linear motion both imply zero acceleration.

Yes ☐ No ☐

*Concepts of all questions bearing * are important for JEE/NEET/CUET.*

6. Consider the motion of a vehicle starting from rest, picking up speed and then moving on a smooth straight road with uniform speed (shown in the following figure) when the vehicle is stationary, there is no net force acting on it. During pick-up, it accelerates. This happens due to

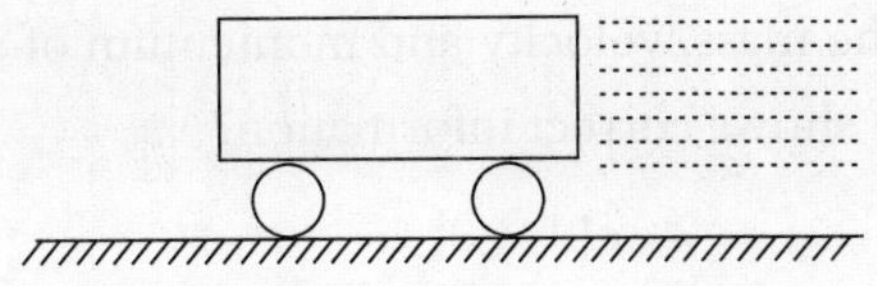

(a) net internal force □ (b) net external force □
(c) sum of net internal and external forces □ (d) None of these □

TOPIC 2

Netwon's Second and Third Law of Motion

7. If various forces are acting on a body, then only resultant force can produce net acceleration in the body.

True □ False □

8. A car of mass 10^3 kg is moving with a velocity of 108 km/h on a level road. The momentum of the car is 1.08×10^5 kg-m/s.

True □ False □

9. A body under the action of a force $F = (3\hat{\mathbf{i}} + 4\hat{\mathbf{j}} - 5\hat{\mathbf{k}})$ N acquires an acceleration of $\sqrt{2}$ m/s^2. The mass of the body is ________kg.

10. A time dependent force $\mathbf{F} = (6t^2\hat{\mathbf{i}} + 4t\,\hat{\mathbf{j}})$ N is applied on a body of mass 3 kg which is initially at rest. The magnitude of velocity at the end of 3 s will be

(a) $6\sqrt{10}$ m/s □ (b) $5\sqrt{2}$ m/s □ (c) $3\sqrt{41}$ m/s □ (d) $7\sqrt{5}$ m/s □

11. A bullet of mass 0.04 kg moving with a speed of 90 m/s enters a heavy wooden block and is stopped after a distance of 60 cm. Find the average resistive force exerted by the block on the bullet.

____

12. The motion of a particle of mass m is described by $y = ut + \frac{1}{2}gt^2$. The force acting on the particle is __________ (mg/9.8 N).

13. A particle moving with velocity **v** is acted by three forces shown by the vector triangle PQR. The velocity of the particle will

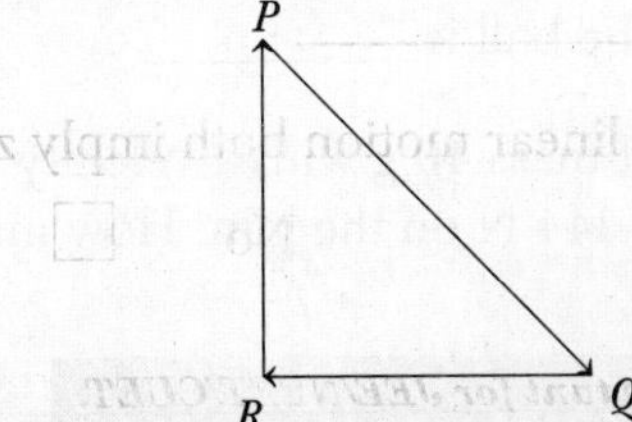

(a) decrease
(b) remain constant
(c) change according to the smallest force QR
(d) increase

14. If m, v and p denote the mass, velocity and momentum of a moving body, then which of the following graph(s) shows correct information?

I. p vs v: m = constant

II. p vs m: v = constant

III. v vs m: p = constant

15. I. When mass and velocity of a moving body, both are increased to double, the momentum will be ____________ .

II. When mass of a moving body is increased to double, whereas its velocity is decreased to half, momentum will be ____________ .

16. A car and a loaded truck are parked on a horizontal road. Choose correct statements.

I. A much greater force is needed to push the truck than the car to bring them to the same speed in same time.

II. A greater opposing force is needed to stop a loaded truck than a car in same time.

17. If two stones, one light and the other heavy, are dropped from the top of a building, a person on the ground will find it easier to catch the light stone than the heavy stone.

True ☐ False ☐

18. Tick (✓/×) for correct/incorrect statement in given boxes.

(i) A bullet fired by a gun can easily pierce human tissue before it stops, resulting in grave injury. ☐

(ii) For a given mass, greater is the speed, greater is the opposing force needed to stop the body in a certain time. ☐

(iii) Force not only depends on the change in momentum, but also on how fast the change is brought about. ☐

(iv) If a force is not parallel to the velocity of the body, then it changes only the component of velocity along the direction of force. ☐

19. A ball of mass 1.5 kg drops vertically on a floor hitting with a speed of 25 ms^{-1}. It rebounds with an initial speed of 15 ms^{-1}. If the ball was in contact for only 0.03 s, then force exerted on the floor by the ball is ____________ .

20. A machine gun fires a bullet of mass 40 g with a velocity 1.2 km/s. The man holding it, can exert a maximum force of 144 N on the gun. How many bullets can be fired per second at the most?

21. A force F acting on a particle of mass m is indicated by the force-time graph shown below. The change in momentum of the particle in 0 to 12 s is found to be $x \times 10^2$ N-s, then find the value of x here.

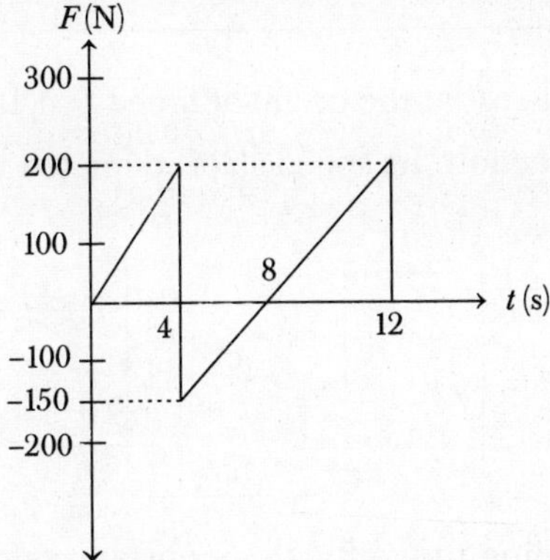

***22.** A player takes 0.1 s to catch a ball of mass 150 g moving with velocity of 20 m/s. The force imparted by the ball on the hands of the player is ________ .

23. The initial mass of a rocket is 1000 kg. Calculate at what rate the fuel should be burnt, so that the rocket is given an acceleration of 20 ms^{-1}. The gases come out at a relative speed of 500 ms^{-1} with respect to the rocket (Take, $g = 10\ m/s^2$)

24. A particle of mass M originally at rest is subjected to a force whose direction is constant but magnitude varies with time according to the relation $F = F_0\left[1 - \left(\frac{t-T}{T}\right)^2\right]$,

where F_0 and T are constants. The force acts only for the time interval $2T$. The velocity v of the particle after time $2T$ is ________ $\left(\frac{4F_0T}{3M} / \frac{F_0T}{2M}\right)$.

25. A force $\mathbf{F} = (40\hat{\mathbf{i}} + 10\hat{\mathbf{j}})$ N acts on a body of mass 5 kg. If the body starts from rest, its position vector $\mathbf{r}$ at time $t = 10$ s will be ________ .

26. A boy pushes a box of mass 2 kg with a force $\mathbf{F} = (20\hat{\mathbf{i}} + 10\hat{\mathbf{j}})$ N on a frictionless surface. If the box was initially at rest, then ________ m is displacement along the X-axis after 10 s.

27. A body of mass 2 kg moves under a force of $(2\hat{\mathbf{i}} + 3\hat{\mathbf{j}} + 5\hat{\mathbf{k}})$N. It starts from rest and was at the origin initially. After 4 s, its new coordinates are (8, b, 20). Find the value of b. (Round off to the nearest integer)

***28.** A bullet of mass 20 g has an initial speed of 1 ms^{-1} just before it starts penetrating a mud wall of thickness 20 cm. If the wall offers a mean resistance of 2.5×10^{-2}N, the speed of the bullet after emerging from the other side of the wall is close to ________ .

29. An impulsive forces act on bodies for ________ (short/long) duration of time and does not remain ________ (constant/variable)with time.

30. A balloon with mass m is descending down with an acceleration a (where, $a < g$). How much mass should be removed from it, so that it starts moving up with an acceleration a?

31. A particle of mass m is at rest at the origin at time $t = 0$. It is subjected to a force $F(t) = F_0 e^{-bt}$ in the x-direction. Its speed $v(t)$ is depicted by which of the following curves?

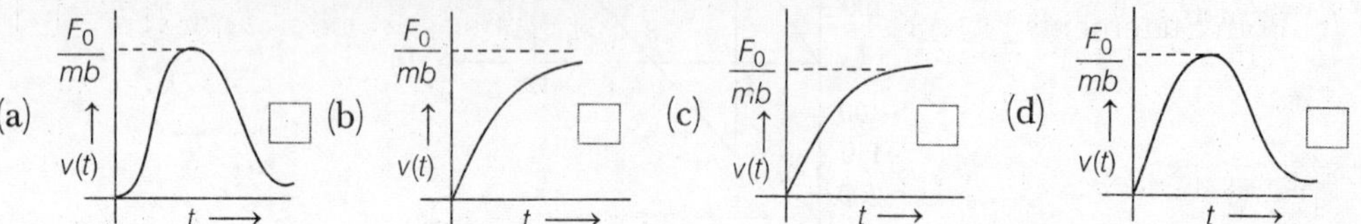

32. An object of mass m is being moved with a constant velocity under the action of an applied force of 2 N along a frictionless surface as shown in the following figure.

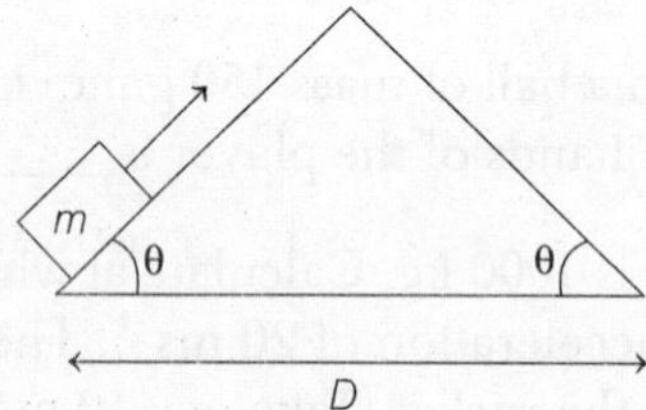

Draw the correct graph between applied force *versus* distance for the above condition.

***33.** A batsman hits back a ball straight in the direction of the bowler without changing its initial speed of 12 ms^{-1}. If the mass of the ball is 0.15 kg, then impulse imparted to the ball is (Take, $g = 10\ m/s^2$)

(a) 1.8 N-s ☐ (b) 3.6 N-s ☐

(c) 5.4 N-s ☐ (d) 7.2 N-s ☐

34. Two identical balls strike a rigid wall with the same speed but at different angles (Case A and Case B) and get reflected without any change in speed as shown in figure. What is the ratio of the magnitudes of impulses imparted to the balls by the wall in both the cases?

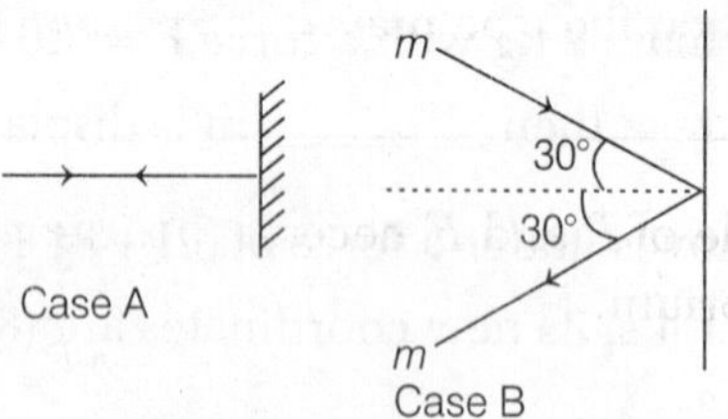

35. A bullet of mass 0.1 kg is fired on a wooden block to pierce through it, but it stops after moving a distance of 50 cm into it. If the velocity of bullet before hitting the wood is 10 m/s and it slows down with uniform deceleration, then the magnitude of effective retarding force on the bullet is x N. Find the value of x to the nearest integer.

36. **Statement I** Action-reaction pair consists of mutual forces which are always equal and opposite between two bodies.

Statement II Two forces on the same body which happen to be equal and opposite can never constitute an action-reaction pair.

Which of the above statement(s) is/are correct?

(a) Only Statement I ☐ (b) Only Statement II ☐

(c) Both Statements I and II ☐ (d) Neither Statement I nor II ☐

TOPIC 3

Conservation of Momentum and Equilibrium of a Particle

37. Two spheres A and B of masses m_1 and m_2 respectively, collide. A is at rest initially and B is moving with velocity v along X-axis. After collision, B has a velocity $\frac{v}{2}$ in a direction perpendicular to the original direction. The mass A moves after collision in the direction ________ $\left[\theta = \tan^{-1}\left(\frac{1}{2}\right) \text{ to the } X\text{-axis} / \theta = \tan^{-1}\left(\frac{-1}{2}\right) \text{ to the } X\text{-axis}\right]$.

38. A particle of mass 1 kg is thrown vertically upwards with speed 100 m/s. After 5 s, it explodes into two parts. One part of mass 400 g comes back with speed 25 m/s, what is the speed of other part just after explosion?

____

39. A bullet of mass 20 g is fired from a gun of mass 2 kg. If the recoil velocity of gun is 10 m/s, then velocity of the muzzle is ________.

40. On a mine site, a rock is exploded. On explosion, rock breaks into three parts. Two parts go off at right angles to each other. These two are : 1 kg first part moving with a velocity of 12 ms^{-1} and 2 kg second part moving with a velocity of 8 ms^{-1}. If the third part flies off with a velocity 4 ms^{-1}, then find the mass of third part.

____

41. Determine the magnitude of P and F necessary to keep the concurrent force system (shown below) in equilibrium.

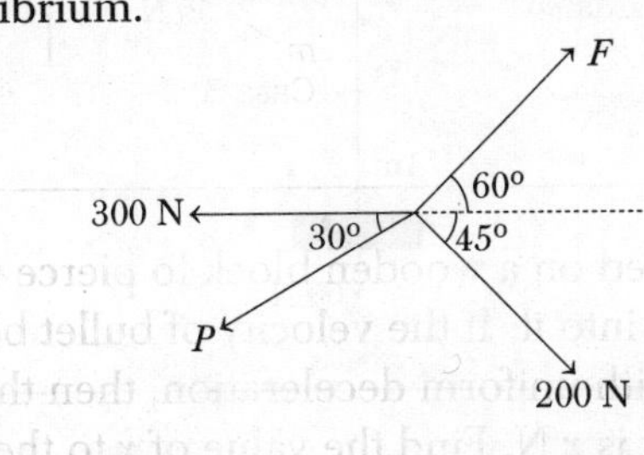

____

42. If body is in equilibrium, then which of the following statement is correct?

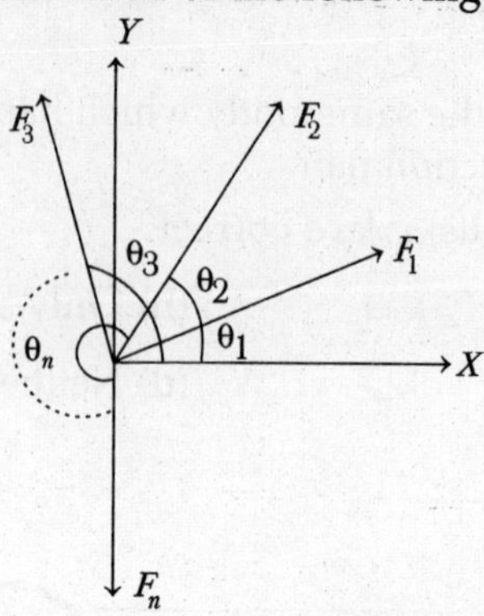

I. $\Sigma F_x = 0$ and $\Sigma F_y = 0$ II. $\Sigma F_x \neq 0$ and $\Sigma F_y \neq 0$

43. A body is under the action of two mutual forces of 8 N and 6 N. For equilibrium, magnitude of resultant force must be of 14 N.

Yes ☐ No ☐

44. Two equal forces are acting on a body at an angle of 60° between them. If the resultant force on the body is equal to $40\sqrt{3}$ N, then magnitude of each force is found to be 4×10^x dyne. Find the value of x.

45. If three forces of equal magnitudes are acting on a body in such a way that body is in equilibrium, then each pair of forces will be inclined at an angle of 120°.

True ☐ False ☐

46. A mass of 6 kg is suspended by a rope of length 2 m from the ceiling. A force of 50 N in the horizontal direction is applied at the mid-point P of the rope, as shown in the following figure. What is the angle that the rope makes with the vertical in equilibrium? (Take, $g = 10 \text{ ms}^{-2}$). Neglect the mass of the rope.

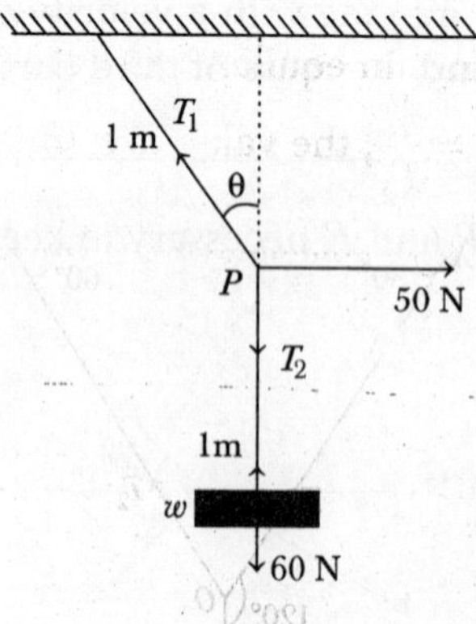

47. Four forces are acting on a body as shown below. If the bodies are in equilibrium, then find the value of $(F_2 - F_1)$ in newton.

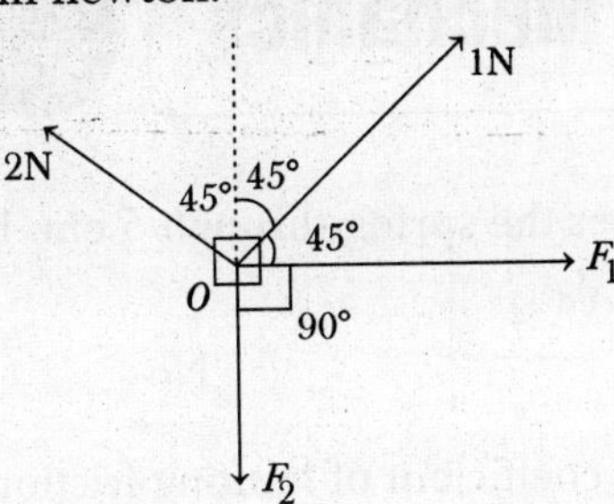

48. Two forces $\mathbf{F}_1 = (8\hat{\mathbf{i}} - 4\hat{\mathbf{j}})$ N and $\mathbf{F}_2 = (-3\hat{\mathbf{i}} + 3\hat{\mathbf{j}})$ N are acting upon a body of mass 10 kg. A third force $\mathbf{F}_3$ acts on the body in such a way that body becomes stable. The magnitude of force F_3 is

(a) $\sqrt{29}$ N ☐ (b) $\sqrt{26}$ N ☐
(c) $\sqrt{41}$ N ☐ (d) $\sqrt{52}$ N ☐

49. As shown in the following figure, one end of string of length 50 cm is fixed to a point P and the other end is fastened to a small object of mass 800 g. The object is pulled aside by a horizontal force F, until it is 30 cm from the vertical through P. Then,

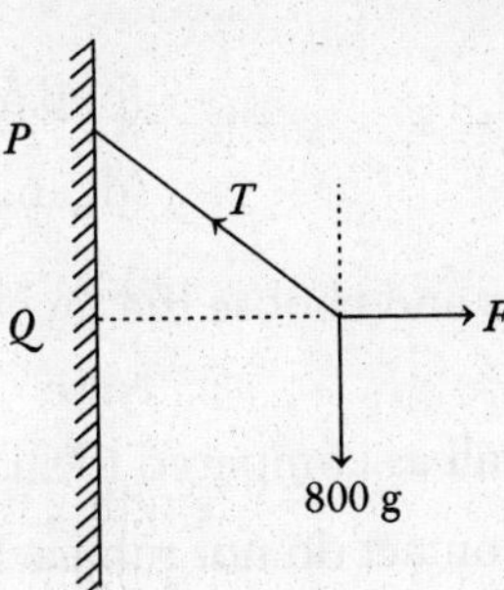

$T =$ ________ N $F =$ ________ N

50. An object of weight 10 N hangs in equilibrium from two strings OX and OY as shown in the following figure. If $\tan \alpha = \frac{T_1}{T_2}$, the value of α (in degree) is __________.

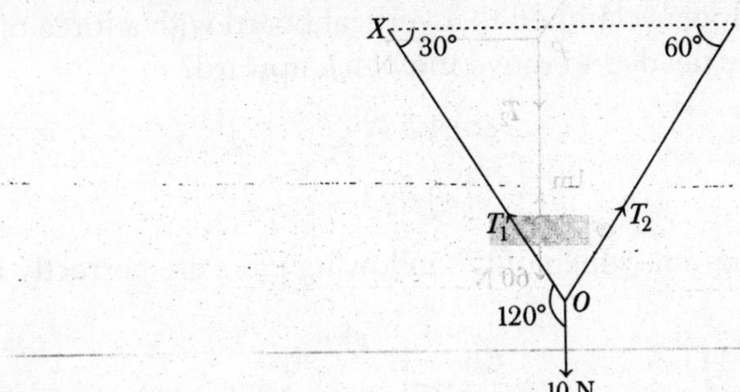

TOPIC 4

Common Forces in Mechanics

NCERT Pg 59-62

51. A force of 50 N compresses the spring through 5 cm. Force constant of the spring will be 10^x N/m. Here, x refers to 3.

Yes ☐ No ☐

52. On an inclined plane, the coefficient of limiting friction between any two surfaces in contact is equal to the X of the angle of Y.

Here, X and Y refer to ____________ .

53. A block of mass 0.5 kg is pushed against a vertical wall by a force of 12 N. The coefficient of friction between the wall and block is 0.6. The magnitude of the force exerted by the wall on the block is

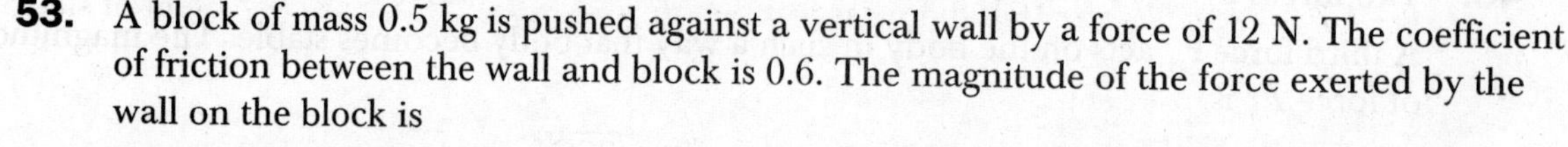

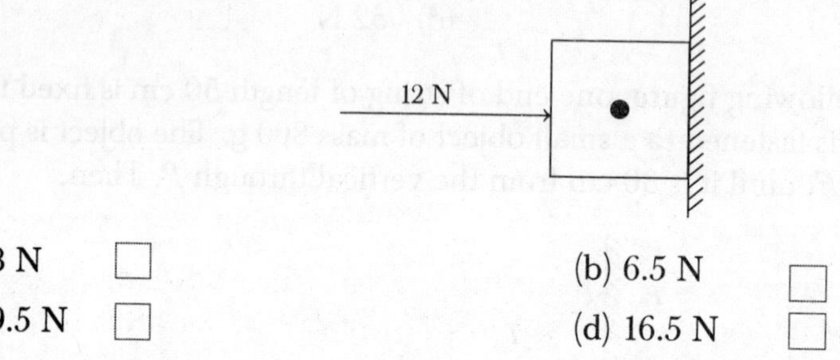

(a) 13 N ☐ (b) 6.5 N ☐
(c) 19.5 N ☐ (d) 16.5 N ☐

54. Read the following statements and choose the incorrect statements in the code given below.

I. Rolling friction is quite small as compared to sliding friction.
II. In rolling, the surfaces at contact do not rub each other.
III. For a rolling body, the velocity of point of contact with respect to the surface remains zero all the times although the centre of the wheel moves forward.
IV. On an ordinary road, the friction between the tyres and the road provides the necessary external force to accelerate the car.

____

55. A block of wood with mass 1 kg is clamped to a vertical board with a force of 10 N. What is the minimum vertical force needed to move the block upward?

(a) 11.5 N ☐ (b) 1.5 N ☐
(c) 5.0 N ☐ (d) 8.5 N ☐

56. With respect to following diagram, which of the following pairs are correctly matched?

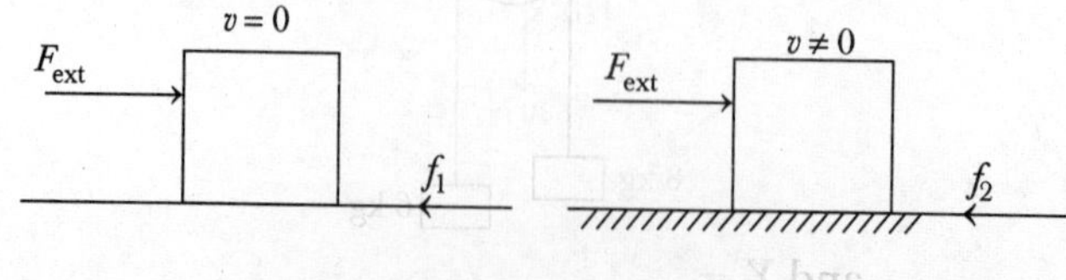

(i) $f_1 \rightarrow$ Static friction (ii) $f_2 \rightarrow$ Dynamic friction

---

57. Tick (✓/×) for correct/incorrect statement in given boxes.

(i) A body moving with uniform velocity does not need any force on smooth surface. ☐

(ii) If a body is moving with uniform velocity on a rough surface, then applied external force is used to overcome the frictional force. ☐

(iii) The coefficient of static friction between the box and the surface of train is 0.15. The maximum acceleration of the train in which a box lying on its surface remain stationary will be 1.5 m/s^2. ☐

***58.** A mass of 4 kg rests on a horizontal plane. The plane is gradually inclined until at an angle $\theta = 15°$ with the horizontal, the mass just begins to slide. What is the coefficient of static friction between the block and the surface?

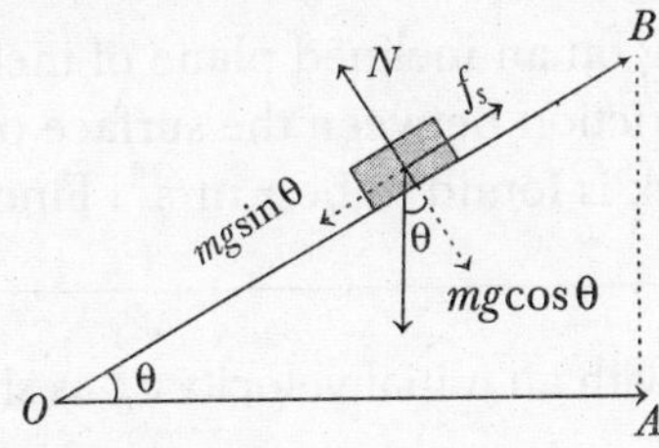

***59.** In the figure shown below, the coefficient of kinetic friction between the trolley and the surface is 0.04. The acceleration of the block and tension in the string respectively, are (Take, $g = 10$ m/s^2 and mass of the string is negligible)

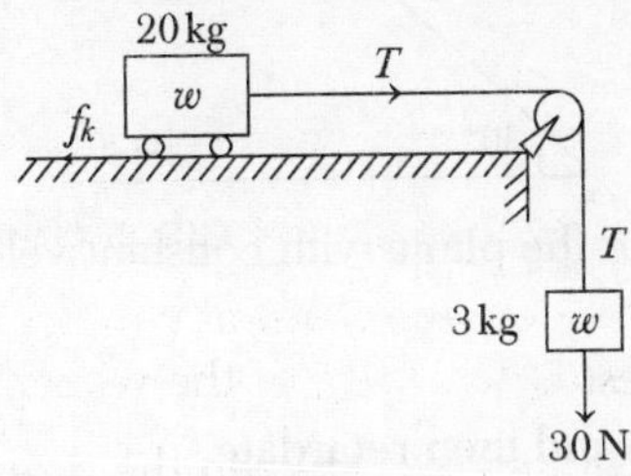

(a) 0.96 m/s^2, 22.1 N ☐ (b) 0.56 m/s^2, 27.1 N ☐
(c) 0.96 m/s^2, 27.1 N ☐ (d) 0.88 m/s^2, 22.1 N ☐

60. In the following figure, 8 kg and 6 kg are hanging stationary from a rough pulley and are about to move. They are stationary due to roughness of the pulley. The force of friction acting on the rope is X and coefficient of friction of the pulley is Y, then

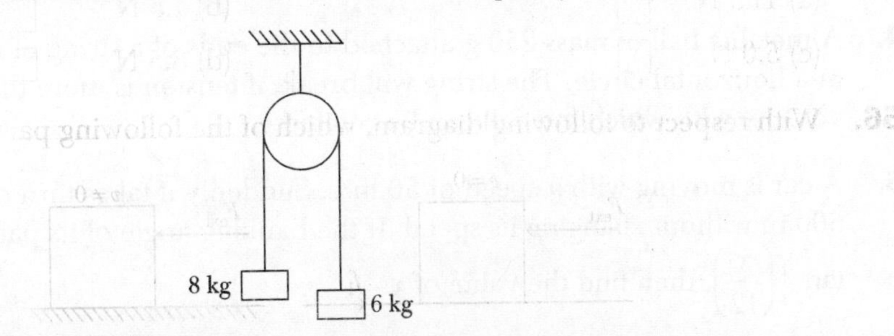

X = ________________ and Y = ________________

61. A body of small mass slides down on an inclined plane of inclination α with the horizontal. The coefficient of friction between the body and surface is given as $\mu = \mu_0 x$, where x is the distance through which mass slides down and μ_0 is a constant. Considering this fact, match the items of Column I with the items of Column II.

Column I	Column II
A. The speed of body is maximum after covering a distance of	1. $\sqrt{\dfrac{g}{\mu_0 \operatorname{cosec}^2\alpha \cos\alpha}}$
B. Distance of the body from its initial point, where it will come to rest is	2. $\dfrac{1}{\mu \cot\alpha}$
C. The maximum speed of the body is	3. $\dfrac{2}{\mu_0 \cot\alpha}$

A__________ B__________ C__________

62. A block of mass 2 kg resting on an inclined plane of inclination 30°, just start moving down. If the coefficient of friction between the surface of block and inclined plane is 0.2, acceleration of the block is found to be x m/s^2. Find the value of x.

____

63. A metallic block is moving with an initial velocity u_0 as shown in the following figure. The block will

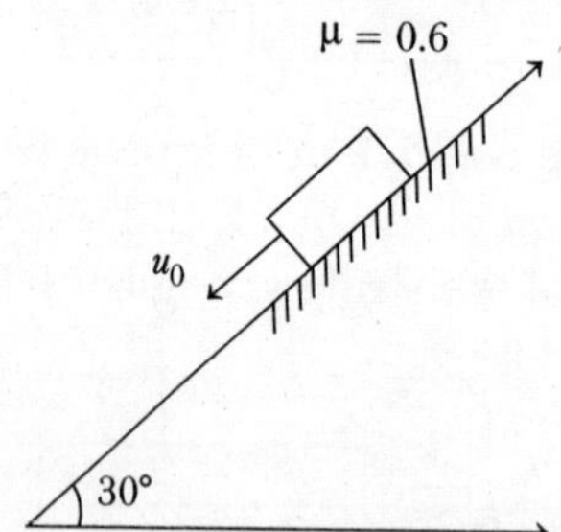

(a) continue to move down on the plane with constant velocity u_0

(b) accelerated down

(c) slow down and come to rest

(d) first accelerate downward and then retardate

TOPIC 5 Circular Motion

64. A metallic ball of mass 250 g attached to the ends of a string of length 196 cm is rotating in a horizontal circle. The string will break, if tension is more than 25 N. The maximum velocity with which the ball can be rotated is ________ (14/18) m/s.

65. A car is moving with a speed of 50 m/s. Suddenly it takes turn on a banked road of radius 600 m without changing its speed. If the banking angle of its path is found to be $\tan^{-1}\left(\dfrac{x}{12}\right)$, then find the value of x.

____

66. If the coefficient of friction between the tyres of car and road is 0.1, then maximum speed of the car at the turn of the level road of radius 100 m will be

(a) 100 m/s ☐ (b) 10 m/s ☐

(c) 75 m/s ☐ (d) 25 m/s ☐

67. A cyclist speeding at 18 km/h on a level road takes a sharp circular turn of radius 3 m without reducing the speed. The coefficient of static friction between the tyres and the road is 0.1, then

(a) the cyclist will not slip while taking the turn ☐

(b) the cyclist will slip while taking the turn ☐

(c) Cannot decide the slipping condition of cyclist due to absence of some data ☐

(d) None of the above ☐

68. A circular race track of radius 300 m is banked at an angle of 15°, if the coefficient of friction between the wheels off a race car and the road is 0.2.
The optimum speed of the race car to avoid wear and tear on its tyres is x ms^{-1} and the maximum permissible speed to avoid slipping is y m/s, then find the value of $(y - x)$.

---

69. A car turns on a banked road without slipping as shown in the following figure. Which of the following pairs are correctly matched?

N θ $N\cos\theta$
$a = v^2/R$
f mg
$f\sin\theta$
θ

I. $N\sin\theta + f\cos\theta \rightarrow \dfrac{mv^2}{R}$ II. $mg + f\sin\theta \rightarrow N\cos\theta$

---

70. Tick (✓/×) for correct/incorrect statement in given boxes.

(i) A car is negotiating a curved road of radius R. The road is banked at angle θ. The coefficient of friction between the tyres of the car and the road is μ_s. The maximum safe velocity on this road will be $\sqrt{gR\left(\dfrac{\mu_s + \tan\theta}{1-\mu_s\tan\theta}\right)}$. ☐

(ii) A car of mass 1000 kg negotiates a banked curve of radius 90 m on a frictionless road. If the banking angle is 45°, the speed of the car is x ms^{-1}. Here, x refers to 30 ms^{-1}. ☐

TOPIC 6

Solving Problems in Mechanics

NCERT Pg. 64-66

***71.** In the following figure, if all the surfaces are assumed to be frictionless ($\mu = 0$), then net force on the 2 kg block by 1 kg block is

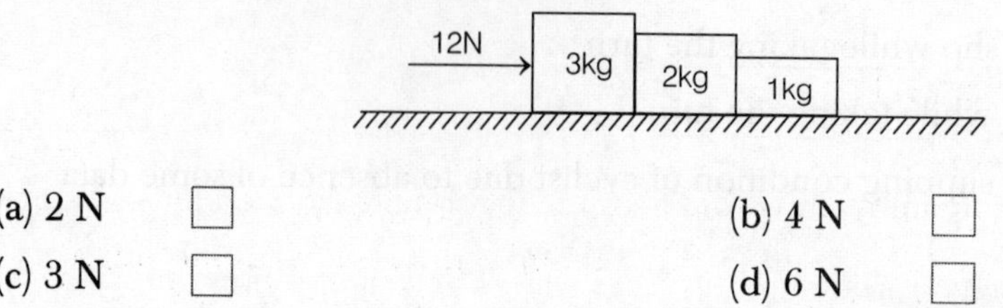

(a) 2 N ☐ (b) 4 N ☐

(c) 3 N ☐ (d) 6 N ☐

***72.** Consider the following diagram shown below. A wooden block of mass 2 kg rests on a solid horizontal floor. When an iron cylinder of mass 25 kg is placed on top of the block, the floor yields steadily and the block and the cylinder together go down with an acceleration of 0.1 m/s^2. The action of the block on the floor before and after the floor yields are respectively ________________ .

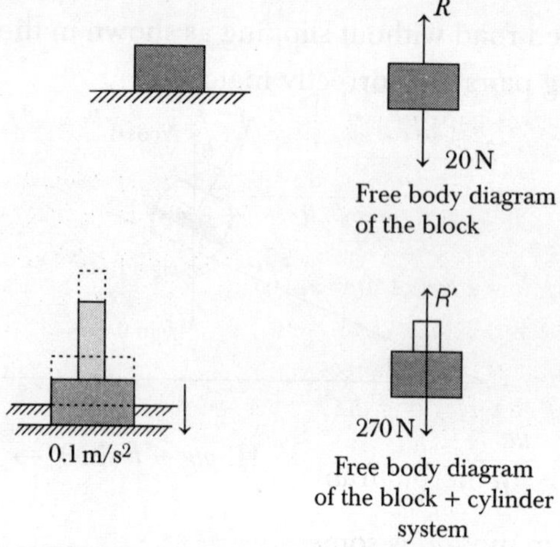

73. A steel block of 10 kg rests on a horizontal floor as shown. When three iron cylinders are placed on it as shown, the block and cylinders go down with an acceleration 0.2 m/ ^2. The normal reaction R by the floor, if mass of the iron cylinders are equal and of 20 kg each, is __________ N. (Take, $g = 10 \text{ m/s}^2$ and $\mu_s = 0.2$)

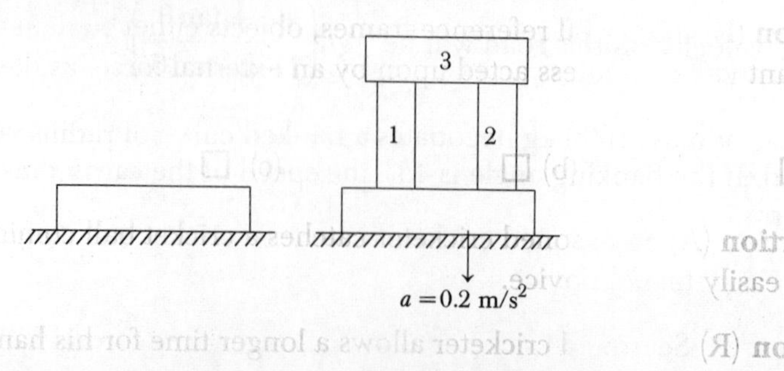

74. A block of mass $\sqrt{3}$ kg is kept on a horizontal rough surface of coefficient of friction $1/3\sqrt{3}$. The critical force to be applied on the vertical surface as shown at an angle 60° with horizontal such that it does not move, will be $3x$. Find the value of x.

(Take, $g = 10\ \text{ms}^{-2}$, $\sin 60° = \frac{\sqrt{3}}{2}$, $\cos 60° = \frac{1}{2}$)

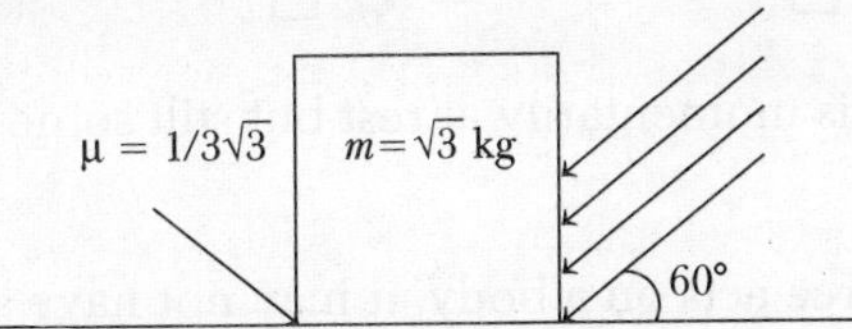

75. A block starts moving up an inclined plane of inclination 30° with an initial velocity of v_0. It comes back to its initial position with velocity $\frac{v_0}{2}$. The value of the coefficient of kinetic friction between the block and the inclined plane is close to $\frac{I}{1000}$, calculate the nearest integer to I.

Assertion-Reason Questions

Direction (Q. Nos. 1-10) *In the following questions, a statement of Assertion is followed by a corresponding statement of Reason. From the following options, choose the correct one.*

(a) Both Assertion and Reason are correct and Reason is the correct explanation of Assertion.
(b) Both Assertion and Reason are correct but Reason is not the correct explanation of Assertion.
(c) Assertion is correct but Reason is incorrect.
(d) Assertion is incorrect but Reason is correct.

1. **Assertion** (A) Earth is an inertial frame.

Reason (R) A frame in motion is sometimes an inertial frame and sometimes a non-inertial.

(a) ☐ (b) ☐ (c) ☐ (d) ☐

2. **Assertion** (A) Newton's law of motion apply only in inertial reference frames.

Reason (R) In inertial reference frames, objects either remain at rest or move with constant velocity unless acted upon by an external force, as described by Newton's first law.

(a) ☐ (b) ☐ (c) ☐ (d) ☐

3. **Assertion** (A) A seasoned cricketer catches a cricket ball coming in with great speed far more easily than a novice.

Reason (R) Seasoned cricketer allows a longer time for his hands to stop the ball.

(a) ☐ (b) ☐ (c) ☐ (d) ☐

4. **Assertion** (A) Product of mass and velocity (i.e. momentum) is basic to the effect of force on motion.

Reason (R) Same force for same time causes the same change in momentum for different bodies.

(a) ☐ (b) ☐ (c) ☐ (d) ☐

5. **Assertion** (A) A body is momentarily at rest but still some force is acting on it at that time.

Reason (R) When a force acts on a body, it may not have some acceleration.

(a) ☐ (b) ☐ (c) ☐ (d) ☐

6. **Assertion** (A) If force is not parallel to the velocity of the body, but makes some angle with it, it changes the component of velocity along the direction of force.

Reason (R) The component of velocity normal to the force remains unchanged.

(a) ☐ (b) ☐ (c) ☐ (d) ☐

7. **Assertion** (A) Newton's third law of motion is applicable only when bodies are in motion.

Reason (R) Newton's third law applies to all types of forces, e.g. gravitational, electric or magnetic forces, etc.

(a) ☐ (b) ☐ (c) ☐ (d) ☐

8. **Assertion** (A) Friction opposes motion of a body.

Reason (R) Static friction is self adjusting while kinetic friction is constant.

(a) ☐ (b) ☐ (c) ☐ (d) ☐

9. **Assertion** (A) A string has a mass *m*. If it is accelerated, tension is non-uniform and if it is not accelerated, tension is uniform.

Reason (R) Tension force is an electromagnetic force.

(a) ☐ (b) ☐ (c) ☐ (d) ☐

10. **Assertion** (A) In the system of two blocks of equal masses as shown, the coefficient of friction between the blocks (μ_2) is less than coefficient of friction (μ_1) between lower block and ground.

μ_2 m $\rightarrow F$

m μ_1

For all values of force F applied on upper block, lower block remains at rest.

Reason (R) Frictional force on lower block due to upper block is not sufficient to overcome the frictional force on lower block due to ground.

(a) ☐ (b) ☐ (c) ☐ (d) ☐

Case Based Questions

1. According to Newton's second law of motion, $F = ma$, where F is force, a is acceleration and m is mass of the body. If $a = 0$, then $F = 0$ means no force is required to move an object in a straight line with uniform velocity. If a force acts on a body for a short duration of time t, then efect of force is measured by impulse.

$$\text{Impulse} = F \times t = \text{Change in momentum}$$

(i) A cricket ball of mass 130 g is moving with velocity 14 m/s and hit by a person so that the ball turned back with velocity 26 m/s. If duration of contact between ball and bat is 0.02 s then the impulse is

(a) 6.3 N-s ☐ (b) 5.2 N-s ☐

(c) 4.3 N-s ☐ (d) 1.2 N-s ☐

(ii) Average force exerted by the bat is

(a) 52 N ☐ (b) 20 N ☐

(c) 26 N ☐ (d) 150 N ☐

(iii) The acceleration of ball is

(a) 200 m/s^2 ☐ (b) 2000 m/s^2 ☐

(c) 250 m/s^2 ☐ (d) 700 m/s^2 ☐

(iv) In cricket, the distance a ball travels after beigh hit by a batsman is primarily influenced by

(a) The elasticity of the cricket bat ☐

(b) The spin imparted on the ball by the bowler ☐

(c) The weight of the ball ☐

(d) The initial velocity and angle of projection imparted by the batsman. ☐

Or

A heavier cricket bat requires more force from the batsman to achieve the same acceleration as a lighter bar. This phenomenon can be explained by

(a) Newton's first law of motion ☐ (b) Newton's second law of motion ☐

(c) Newton's third law of motion ☐ (d) Conservation of mechanical energy ☐

2. In mechanics, we encounter several kinds of forces. Except gravitational force, all common forces in mechanics are contact forces.

Some examples of contact forces are given below

When bodies are in contact (i.e. book resting on a table, a system of rigid bodies connected by rods, hinges and other type of supports), there are mutual contact forces (for each pair of bodies) satisfying the third law.

When a spring is compressed or extented by an external force, a restoring force is generated. This force is usually proportional to compression or elongation (for small displacements).

The spring force F is written as $F = -kx$, where x is the displacement and k is the force constant.

(i) Three blocks A, B and C of masses 4 kg, 2 kg and 1 kg respectively, are in contact on a frictionless surfaces, as shown in the figure. A 12 N force is applied on the 4 kg block. The force between A and B is

(a) 10 N ☐ (b) $\frac{48}{7}$ N ☐

(c) $\frac{40}{9}$ N ☐ (d) $\frac{36}{7}$ N ☐

(ii) Normal reaction on a block kept on a horizontal ground

(a) is always mg ☐

(b) may be equal to mg ☐

(c) is always greater than mg ☐

(d) is always less than mg ☐

Or

Take a rectangular block A. Make one surface of A smooth and well polished and the opposite surface of A very rough. While finding the force of limiting friction by putting weight when (i) rough surface is in contact with the table and (ii) when smooth surface is in contact with table we observe that more weight is required in case (i) than in case (ii) This suggests that

(a) Force of friction is directly proportional to the area of contact. ☐

(b) Force of friction is always equal to applied force. ☐

(c) Force of friction is independent of nature of surface. ☐

(d) Force of friction is more between rough surfaces. Than between smooth surfaces. ☐

(iii) A vertical spring with a spring constant of 500 N/m is stretched by 0.25 m, if a 2 kg mass is attached to the spring, the total force exerted by the spring is

(a) –105.4 N ☐ (b) 105.4 N ☐

(c) –125.0 N ☐ (d) 125.0 N ☐

(iv) When a person stands on a bathroom scale, the reading on the scale represents

(a) person's mass ☐

(b) force exerted by the person on the scale ☐

(c) normal reaction force exerted by the scale on the person ☐

(d) the gravitational force acting on the person ☐

COMPETITION EDGE UP

1. A player caught a cricket ball of mass 150 g moving at a speed of 20 m/s. If the catching process is completed in 0.1 s. The magnitude of force exerted by the ball on the hand of the player is

[NCERT Pg. 54, JEE Main 2024]

(a) 150 N ☐ (b) 30 N ☐
(c) 3 N ☐ (d) 300 N ☐

2. A body of weight 200 N is suspended from a tree branch through a chain of mass 10 kg. The branch pulls the chain by a force equal to (if $g = 10\,m/s^2$)

[NCERT Pg. 65, JEE Main 2024]

(a) 100 N ☐ (b) 150 N ☐
(c) 200 N ☐ (d) 300 N ☐

3. A 2 kg brick begins to slide over a surface which is inclined at an angle of 45° with respect to horizontal axis. The coefficient of static friction between their surfaces is

[NCERT Pg. 61, JEE Main 2024]

(a) 1.7 ☐ (b) 1 ☐
(c) 0.5 ☐ (d) $\frac{1}{\sqrt{3}}$ ☐

4. A coin is placed on a disc. The coefficient of friction between the coin and the disc is μ. If the distance of the coin from the centre of the disc is r, the maximum angular velocity which can be given to the disc, so that the coin does not slip away, is

[NCERT Pg. 63, JEE Main 2024]

(a) $\sqrt{r/\mu g}$ ☐ (b) $\mu/\sqrt{rg}$ ☐
(c) $\mu g/r$ ☐ (d) $\sqrt{\mu g/r}$ ☐

5. Three blocks A, B and C are pulled on a horizontal smooth surface by a force of 80 N as shown in figure.

[NCERT Pg. 65, JEE Main 2024]

A 5 kg —T_1— B 3 kg —T_2— C 2 kg → F = 80 N

The tensions T_1 and T_2 in the string are respectively

(a) 60 N, 80 N ☐ (b) 88 N, 96 N ☐
(c) 40 N, 64 N ☐ (d) 80 N, 100 N ☐

6. A train is moving with a speed of 12 m/s on rails which are 1.5 m apart. To negotiate a curve of radius 400 m, the height by which the outer rail should be raised with respect to the inner rail is (Given, $g = 10\,m/s^2$)

[NCERT Pg. 63, JEE Main 2024]

(a) 4.8 cm ☐ (b) 5.4 cm ☐
(c) 6.0 cm ☐ (d) 4.2 cm ☐

7. A bob is whirled in a horizontal plane by means of a string with an initial speed of ω rpm. The tension in the string is T. If speed becomes 2ω while keeping the same radius, the tension in the string becomes

[NCERT Pg. 63, NEET 2024]

(a) T ☐ (b) 4T ☐
(c) T / 4 ☐ (d) $\sqrt{2}T$ ☐

8. A horizontal force 10 N is applied to a block A as shown in figure. The mass of blocks A and B are 2 kg and 3 kg, respectively. The blocks slide over a frictionless surface. The force exerted by block A on block B is

[NCERT Pg. 65, NEET 2024]

F = 10 N → A 2 kg | B 3 kg

(a) zero ☐
(b) 4 N ☐
(c) 6 N ☐
(d) 10 N ☐

9. Calculate the maximum acceleration of a moving car so that a body lying on the floor of the car remains stationary. The coefficient of static friction between the body and the floor is 0.15 ($g = 10\ m\ s^{-2}$).

[NCERT Pg. 61, NEET 2023]

(a) 150 ms^{-2} ☐ (b) 1.5 ms^{-2} ☐
(c) 50 ms^{-2} ☐ (d) 1.2 ms^{-2} ☐

10. A ball of mass 0.15 kg is dropped from a height 10 m, strikes the ground and rebounds to the same height. The magnitude of impulse imparted to the ball is nearly ($g = 10\,m/s^2$)

[NCERT Pg. 56, NEET 2021]

(a) 0 ☐
(b) 4.2 kg-m/s ☐
(c) 2.1 kg-m/s ☐
(d) 1.4 kg-m/s ☐

Chapter 05

Work, Energy and Power

TOPIC 1

Scalar Product, Notion of Work and Kinetic Energy : Work-Energy Theorem

1. If $\mathbf{A} \cdot \mathbf{B} = \lambda |\mathbf{A}|^2$, where λ is a constant, then $\mathbf{A} \parallel \mathbf{B}$.

Yes ☐ No ☐

2. If $\mathbf{A} \cdot \mathbf{B} = 0$, then

(a) $\mathbf{A} = \mathbf{0}$ ☐ (b) $\mathbf{B} = \mathbf{0}$ ☐

(c) **A** is perpendicular to **B** ☐ (d) All are correct ☐

3. Moving object of mass 2 kg has a speed of 2 m/s at point A and 4 m/s at point B. Total work done on the object as it moves from point A to point B is ________ J.

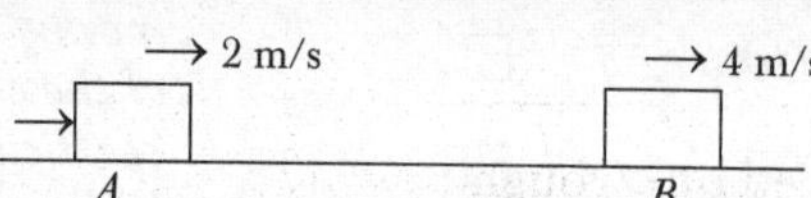

4. A ball of mass 10 g falling from a tower of height of 2 km hits ground with speed of 100 m/s. Find the work done by resistive force (in joules).

____

5. A raindrop of mass 1 g falling from a height of 10^3 m. It hits the ground with a speed of 50 ms^{-1}. Choose the correct statement.

I. Work done by gravitation force is 20 J.

II. Work done by resistive force of air on the raindrop is -8.75 J.

____

*Concepts of all questions bearing * are important for JEE/NEET/CUET.*

6. An object of mass 20 kg is at rest. If we apply 5 N force on it, then work done in first second is ________ J.

7. A particle of mass m is thrown vertically upwards with a speed of u m/s, so the work done by the force of gravity during time particle goes up is ________ .

8. Work done by a force on a moving object is 100 J. It was travelling at a speed of 2 ms^{-1}. Find the new speed of the object, if the mass of the object is 2 kg.

____

TOPIC 2

Work & Kinetic Energy

NCERT Pg 73-75

9. If force is given $\mathbf{F} = \hat{\mathbf{i}} + 2\hat{\mathbf{j}} - \hat{\mathbf{k}}$ and displacement is $\mathbf{d} = \hat{\mathbf{i}} + 2\hat{\mathbf{j}} + \hat{\mathbf{k}}$, then angle between force and displacement is ________ .

10. A particle moves from a point $(-2\hat{\mathbf{i}} + 5\hat{\mathbf{j}})$ to $(4\hat{\mathbf{i}} + 3\hat{\mathbf{k}})$ when a force of $(4\hat{\mathbf{i}} + 3\hat{\mathbf{j}})$ N is applied. How much work has been done by the force?

(a) 9 J ☐ (b) 11 J ☐

(c) 5 J ☐ (d) 2 J ☐

11. In effect of a constant force, a particle's position and time are related as $x = (t-3)^2$, where x is in metre and time is in seconds, then work done by force in first 6 s is found to be x J. Find the value of x.

____

12. An object is displaced from point P(2m, 3m, 4m) to a point Q(1m, 2m, 3m) under a constant force $\mathbf{F} = (2\hat{\mathbf{i}} + 3\hat{\mathbf{j}} + 4\hat{\mathbf{k}})$ N. The work done by this force in this process is found to be $x \times 10^7$ erg. Find the value of x.

____

13. A body of mass 1 kg is placed on a rough horizontal surface having coefficient of friction equal to 0.2. When a force of 20 N is applied on the body, then work done by applied force on the body in 4 s is found to be ________ kJ.

14. Two bodies of masses 4 kg and 5 kg are moving with equal momentum, then ratio of their respective kinetic energy is ________ .

15. Draw the graph between $\sqrt{E_K}$ *versus* $\frac{1}{p}$,

where E_K = kinetic energy and p = momentum.

____

16. If a gun moves backward when we fire a bullet from gun, then kinetic energy of gun will be less than the kinetic energy of bullet.

True ☐ False ☐

17. When speed of a vehicle is increased by 2 m/s, then its kinetic energy becomes double. Choose the correct statement.

I. Original speed of the vehicle is $2(\sqrt{2}+1)$ m/s.

II. Original speed of the car is $(2\sqrt{2}+1)$ m/s.

---

18. If we increase momentum of an object by 100%, then kinetic energy of object will increase by ________ %.

19. If a car is moving with twice of its initial speed, then its new kinetic energy will be quadrupled.

True ☐ False ☐

20. Two objects of masses m_1 and m_2 have velocities v_1 and v_2. Both objects have same momentum but kinetic energies of these objects are E_1 and E_2. If mass $m_1 > m_2$, then ________ $(E_1 < E_2 / E_1 > E_2)$.

TOPIC 3

Work done by a Variable Force

NCERT Pg 75-76

21. A graph between force and displacement is given below.

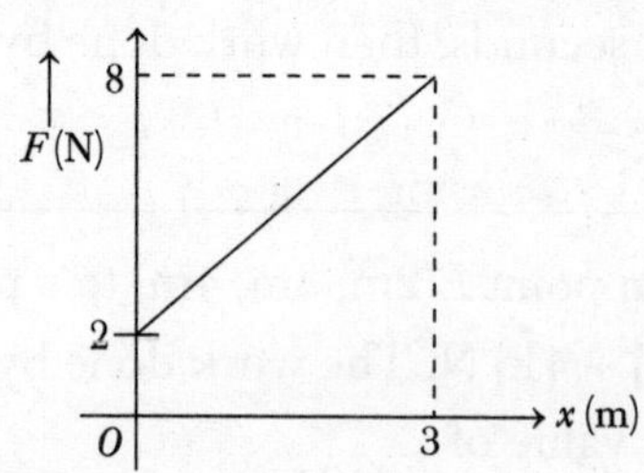

Work done by force is ________ J.

22. Force F on a particle moving in a straight line varies with distance d as shown in the following figure. The work done on the particle during its displacement of 12 m is

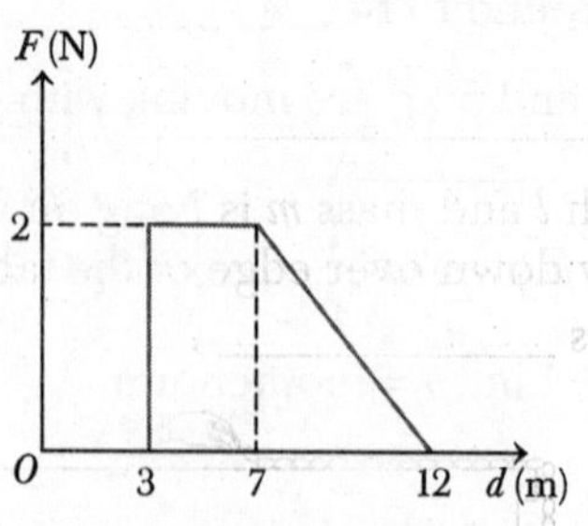

(a) 21 J ☐ (b) 19 J ☐ (c) 13 J ☐ (d) 18 J ☐

23. A particle moves in one-dimension from rest under the influence of a force that varies with the distance travelled by the particle as shown in the following figure. The kinetic energy of the particle after it has travelled 3 m is

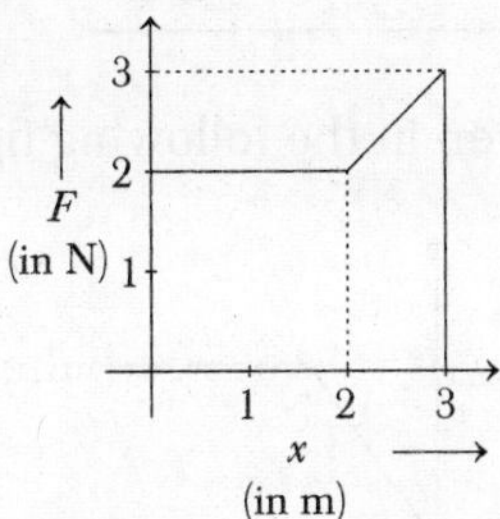

(a) 4 J ☐ (b) 2.5 J ☐ (c) 6.5 J ☐ (d) 5 J ☐

24. A position dependent force $F = (7 - 2x + 3x^2)$, acts on a small body of mass 2 kg and displaces it from $x = 0$ to 5 m. Calculate the work done (in J).

____

TOPIC 4

The Work-Energy Theorem for a Variable Force

NCERT Pg 76-77

25. A block of mass 10 kg moving x-direction with a constant speed of 10 ms^{-1}, is subjected to a retarding force $F = 0.1\, x \text{ J/m}$ during its travel from $x = 20$ m to 30 m. Its final KE will be

(a) 475 J ☐ (b) 450 J ☐

(c) 275 J ☐ (d) 250 J ☐

26. A block of mass 1 kg moving on a horizontal surface with speed of 2 m/s enters a rough patch ranging from $x = 0.10$ m to 2.01 m. The retarding force F on the block in this range is inversely proportional to x as $F_r = \frac{-k}{x}$ for $0.1 < x < 2.01$ m and $F_r = 0$ for $x < 0.1$ m and $x > 2.01$ m. If $k = 0.5$ J, then final speed of the block as it crosses this patch is x m/s. Find the value of x.

____

27. If a uniform chain of length l and mass m is lying on a smooth table and one-fifth of its length is hanging vertically down over edge of the table, then work required to pull hanging part on the table is ____________ .

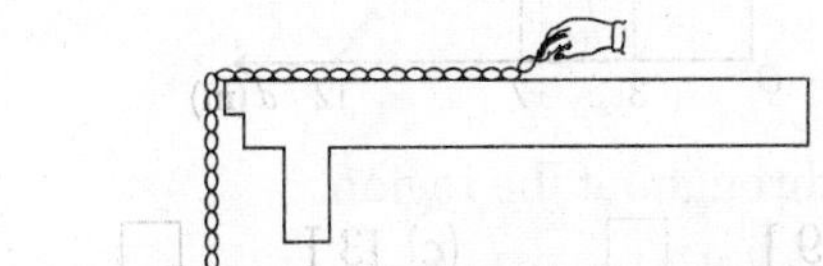

TOPIC 5

The Concept of Potential Energy

NCERT Pg 77-78

28. A graph between $U(x)$ and x given in the following figure. The corresponding force *versus* position graph is

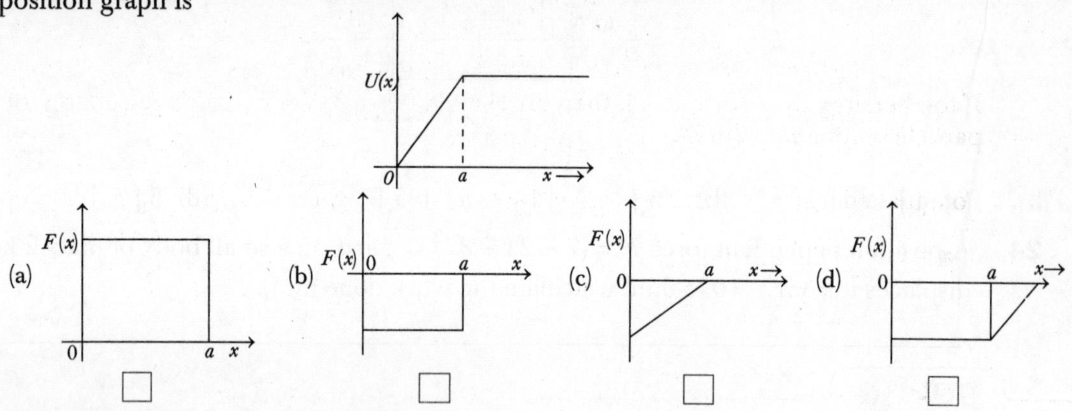

29. Potential energy U *versus* position x graph of a particle is shown below. E indicates total energy line of particle ($E = 10$ J).

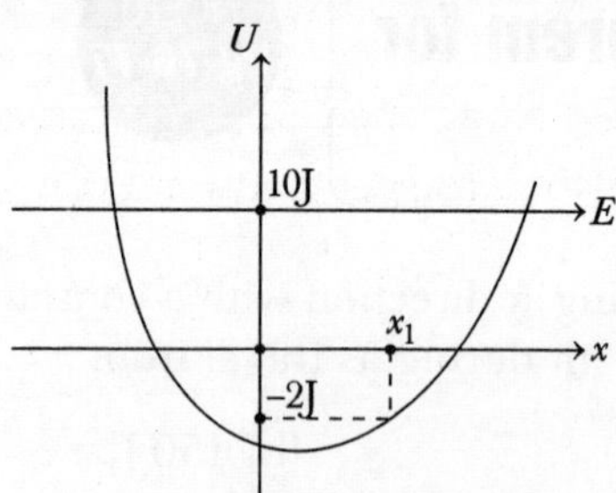

At position $x = x_1$, potential energy of particle is $U(x_1) = -2$ J. If mass of particle is 0.5 kg, then velocity of particle at $x = x_1$ will be______ m/s.

30. Given below is the plot of a potential energy function $U(x)$ for a system, in which a particle is in one-dimensional motion, while a conservative force $F(x)$ acts on it. Suppose that E_{mech} = 8 J. Which one of the following statements is incorrect for this system ?

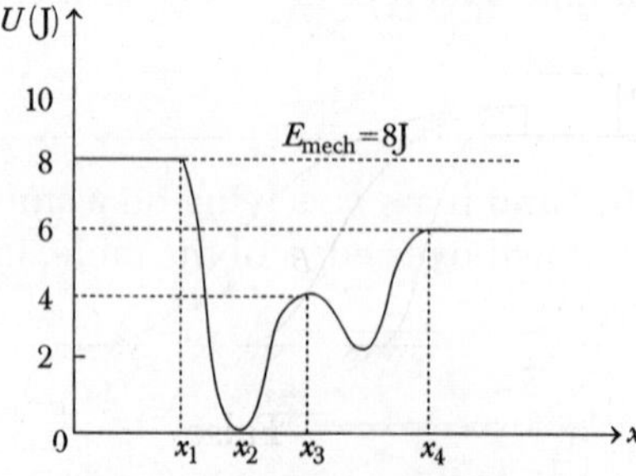

(a) At $x > x_4$, KE is constant throughout the region.

(b) At $x < x_1$, KE is smallest and the particle is moving at the slowest speed.

(c) At $x = x_2$, KE is greatest and the particle is moving at the fastest speed.

(d) At $x = x_3$, KE = 4 J.

31. PE *versus* position(x) graph of a moving particle is shown below.

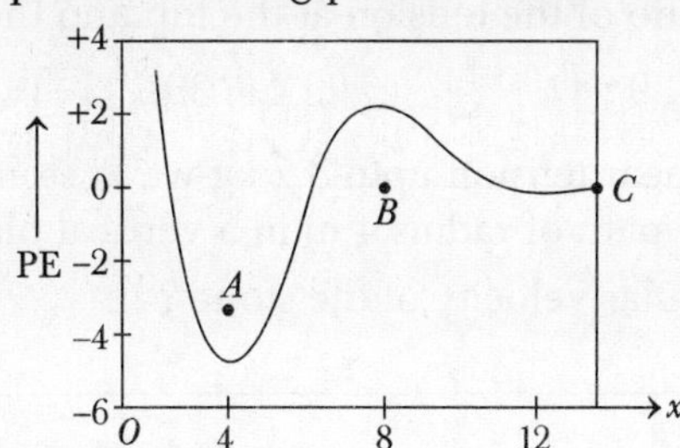

If total energy of particle is 2 J, then on point ________ $(A/B/C)$, kinetic energy of particle will be maximum.

32. Potential energy of a particle is given by $U(x) = \frac{kx^2}{2}$, where $k = 0.5$ N/m. Force on particle at $x = 1$ m is ________________ N.

TOPIC 6

The Conservation of Mechanical Energy

33. A block of mass $m = 1$ kg slides along a frictionless surface as shown in figure. If it is released from rest at point A, then its speed at point B is ____________m/s.

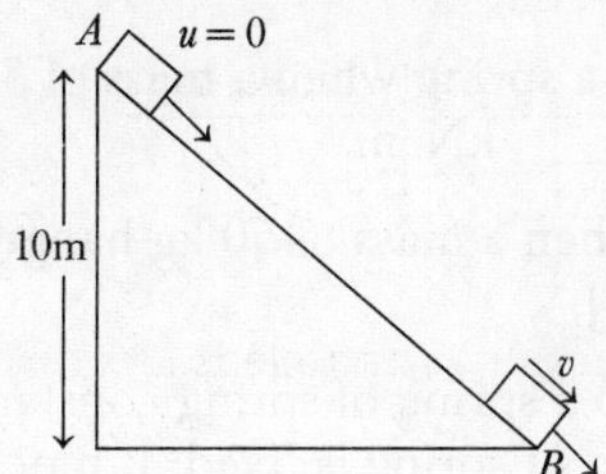

34. A block P is slipping on three inclined frictionless surface. If block weight is mg and work done by it on three given surfaces A, B and C is W_A, W_B and W_C respectively, then $W_A = W_B = W_C$.

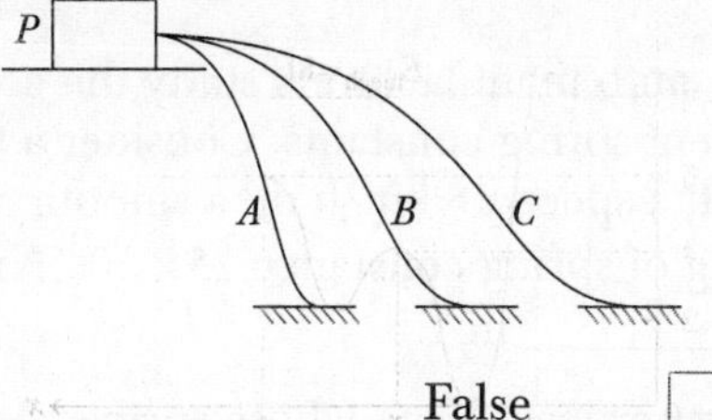

True ☐ False ☐

35. If a body loses half of its velocity on penetrating 3 cm in a wooden block, then how much will it penetrate more before coming to rest?

____

36. A stone of mass 1 kg is tied to a string 4 m long and is rotated at constant speed of 40 ms^{-1} in a vertical circle. The ratio of the tension at the top and the bottom is

(a) 11:12 ☐ (b) 39 : 41 ☐ (c) 41: 39 ☐ (d) 12:11 ☐

37. A weightless thread can bear tension upto 3.7 kg-wt. A stone of mass 500 g is tied to it and revolved in a circular path of radius 4 m in a vertical plane. If $g = 10\ ms^{-2}$, then what will be the maximum angular velocity of the stone ?

______

38. A particle suspended with a string is given an initial velocity u. If string gets slack at topmost point C, then ratio of KE of body at points A and C is ______.

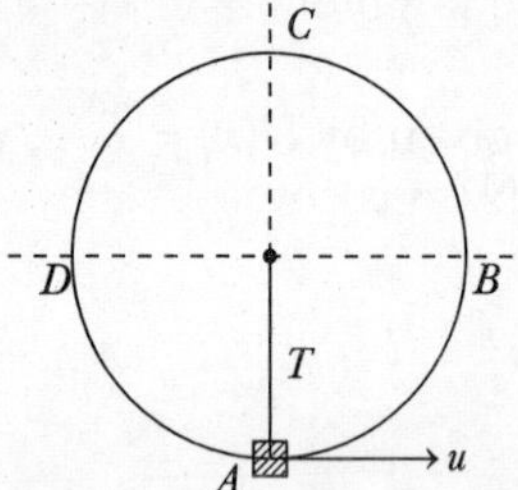

TOPIC 7

The Potential Energy of a Spring

NCERT Pg 80-83

39. Extension of 20 cm occurs in a spring when a mass of 50 kg is hanged from it. Spring constant of spring is ______ kN/m.

***40.** A spring extends by 20 cm when a mass of 50 kg hanged on it. Potential energy stored by spring will be ______ J.

41. A block of mass m attached to a spring of spring constant k oscillates on a smooth horizontal table and other end of spring is fixed. If block has a speed v when spring is at its natural length, then how far the block will move on table before coming to instantaneous rest ?

(a) $v\sqrt{\frac{m}{k}}$ ☐ (b) $\frac{mv}{k}$ ☐ (c) $\sqrt{\frac{mv}{k}}$ ☐ (d) $\frac{mv}{\sqrt{k}}$ ☐

42. To simulate car accidents, auto manufacturers study the collisions for moving cars with mounted springs of different spring constants. Consider a typical simulation with a car of mass 1000 kg moving with a speed 18 km/h on a smooth road and colliding with a horizontal mounted spring of spring constant $6.25 \times 10^3\ Nm^{-1}$. Maximum compression of the spring is ______ m.

43. A block of mass m falls on vertical spring whose spring constant is k. Block decrease spring length by x. If the block velocity is v when it comes in contact with spring, then which one of the following relations is correct for the given system ?

I. $\frac{1}{2}mv^2 = \frac{1}{2}kx^2 - mgx$ II. $\frac{1}{2}mv^2 + \frac{1}{2}kx^2 = mgx$

______

44. If two springs S_1 and S_2 of force constants k_1 and k_2 respectively are stretched by the same force, it is found that the more work is done on spring S_1 than on spring S_2.

True ☐ False ☐

45. An engine is attached to a wagon through a shock absorber of length 1.5 m. The system with a total mass of 40000 kg is moving with a speed of 72 kmh^{-1} when the brakes are applied to bring it to rest. In the process of the system being brought to rest, the spring of the shock absorber gets compressed by 1.0 m. If 90% of energy of the wagon is lost due to friction, the spring constant is ________ $\times 10^5$ N/m.

46. Potential energy of a spring is increased by 20 J when it is stretched by 4 cm. If it is stretched by 5 cm, then increase in potential energy is found to be 31.25 J.

True ☐ False ☐

47. A spring of force constant 980 N/m is compressed by 10 cm, if a block is dropped on it from a height of 0.4 m. Which of the following statement is true ?

I. Mass of block is less than 2 kg.

II. Mass of the block is more than 2 kg.

---

48. Total mechanical energy of the system is conserved, if the forces doing work on it are

(a) conservative ☐ (b) non-conservative ☐
(c) Both (a) and (b) ☐ (d) Neither (a) nor (b) ☐

TOPIC 8
Power

NCERT Pg 83

49. Water is falling on blades of a turbine at a rate of 100 kg/s from a certain spring. If the height of spring is 100 m, then power transferred to turbine will be 100 kW.

True ☐ False ☐

50. A force applied by engine of a train of mass 2.05×10^6 kg changes its velocity from 5 m/s to 25 m/s in 5 min. The power of engine is ________ MW.

***51.** An elevator can carry a maximum load of 1200 kg is moving up with a constant speed of 2 m/s. The frictional force opposing motion is 2000 N. Determine minimum power delivered by motor to elevator (in W).

---

52. An engine pumps water continuously through a hose. Water leaves the hose with a velocity v and m is the mass per unit length of the water jet. What is the rate at which kinetic energy is imparted to water ?

(a) $\frac{1}{2}mv^3$ ☐ (b) mv^3 ☐
(c) $\frac{1}{2}mv^2$ ☐ (d) $\frac{1}{2}m^2v^2$ ☐

53. An automobile of mass m accelerates starting from origin and initially at rest, while the engine supplies constant power P. The position is given as a function of time by

(a) $\left(\frac{9P}{8m}\right)^{\frac{1}{2}} \cdot t^{\frac{3}{2}}$ ☐ (b) $\left(\frac{8P}{9m}\right)^{\frac{1}{2}} \cdot t^{\frac{2}{3}}$ ☐ (c) $\left(\frac{9m}{8P}\right)^{\frac{1}{2}} \cdot t^{\frac{3}{2}}$ ☐ (d) $\left(\frac{8P}{9m}\right)^{\frac{1}{2}} \cdot t^{\frac{3}{2}}$ ☐

***54.** An elevator can carry a maximum load of 1800 kg. (Elevator + passenger) is moving up with a constant speed of 2 m/s. The friction force opposing the motion is 4000 N. Choose the correct statement.

I. The minimum power delivered by the motor to elevator is 59 HP.

II. The net downward force on the elevator is 22000 N.

55. Two particles moving in same direction do not lose all their energy in completely inelastic collision.

True ☐ False ☐

56. Tick (✓/✗) for correct/incorrect statement in given boxes.

I. Linear momentum remains conserved in elastic collision as well as in inelastic collision. ☐

II. Kinetic energy remains conserved only in an elastic collision. ☐

57. Which of these is not a collision?

I. Change in path of a comet as it approaches a solar system.

II. Scattering of α-particles in Rutherford's experiment.

III. Blast of a projectile in its path.

IV. A duster slides over classroom table and strike a chalk piece.

58. A bullet of mass m travelling with a speed v hits a block of mass M initially at rest gets embedded in it. The combined system is free to move and there is no other force acting on the system. The heat generated in the process will be ____________.

59. A 2 kg mass moving on a smooth frictionless surface with velocity of 10 m/s hits another 2 kg mass kept at rest, in a perfectly inelastic collision. After collision, they move with a speed of __________ m/s.

60. If a shell fired from a cannon explodes in mid-air, then its total kinetic energy increases.

True ☐ False ☐

61. A alpha particle of mass m suffers elastic collision with a nucleus at rest of unknown mass. It is scattered directly backwards losing 64% of its initial kinetic energy, the mass of nucleus is ____________ $(4m/2m)$.

62. Body A of mass $4m$ moving with speed u collides with another body B of mass $2m$ at rest. Collision is head-on and elastic in nature. After the collision, the fraction of energy lost by colliding body A is $\left(\frac{1}{9}\right)$.

True ☐ False ☐

***63.** Two identical balls A and B having velocities of 0.5 m/s and – 0.3 m/s respectively, collide elastically in one-dimension. The velocities of B and A after the collision respectively, will be

(a) 0.3 m/s and 0.5 m/s ☐
(b) – 0.5 m/s and 0.3 m/s ☐
(c) 0.5 m/s and – 0.3 m/s ☐
(d) – 0.3 m/s and 0.5 m/s ☐

64. A body of mass m_1 moving with a velocity u collides elastically with another body of mass m_2 at rest, then tick (✓/✗) for correct/incorrect statement in given boxes.

(i) The fraction of kinetic energy transferred to second body is $\frac{4m_1m_2}{(m_1+m_2)^2}$. ☐

(ii) The fraction of energy retained by the first body is $\left(\frac{m_1-m_2}{m_1+m_2}\right)^2$. ☐

(iii) If $m_1 = m_2$, then energy transferred is 100%. ☐

(iv) The energy lost during collision is found as heat. ☐

65. A neutron collides, head-on with a deuterium at rest elastically. What fraction of the neutron's energy would be transferred to the deuterium?

____

66. Two masses m_a and m_b moving with velocities v_a and v_b in opposite direction collide elastically and after collision, m_a and m_b move with velocity v_b and v_a respectively, then ratio m_a / m_b is __________.

***67.** Two perfectly elastic objects A and B of identical mass are moving with velocities 15 ms^{-1} and 10 ms^{-1} respectively, collide along the direction of line joining them. Their velocities of collision are respectively

(a) 10 ms^{-1}, 15 ms^{-1} ☐
(b) 20 ms^{-1}, 5 ms^{-1} ☐
(c) 0 ms^{-1}, 25 ms^{-1} ☐
(d) 5 ms^{-1}, 20 ms^{-1} ☐

***68.** A metal ball of mass 2 kg moving with a velocity of 36 km/h has a head-on collision with a stationary ball of mass 3 kg. If after the collision, the two balls move together, then what will be the loss in kinetic energy due to collision?

____

69. A bullet of 10 g moving with velocity v, collides head-on with the stationary bob of a pendulum and recoils with velocity 100 m/s. The length of the pendulum is 0.5 m and mass of the bob is 1 kg. The minimum value of v __________ m/s, so that the pendulum describes a circle. (Assume, the string to be inextensible and $g = 10$ m/s^2)

0.5 m
v
10 g 1 kg

70. Three objects A, B and C are kept in a straight line on a frictionless horizontal surface. The masses of A, B and C are m, $2m$ and $2m$, respectively. The object A moves towards B with a speed of 9 m/s and makes an elastic collision with it. Thereafter, B makes a completely inelastic collision with C. All motions occur along same straight line. The final speed of object C is

A	B	C
m	$2m$	$2m$

(a) 6 m/s ☐ (b) 9 m/s ☐ (c) 4 m/s ☐ (d) 3 m/s ☐

71. An object flying in air with velocity $(20\hat{\mathbf{i}} + 25\hat{\mathbf{j}} - 12\hat{\mathbf{k}})$ suddenly breaks in two pieces whose masses are in the ratio 1: 5. The smaller mass flies off with a velocity $(100\hat{\mathbf{i}} + 35\hat{\mathbf{j}} + 8\hat{\mathbf{k}})$. The velocity of the larger piece will be

(a) $4\hat{\mathbf{i}} + 23\hat{\mathbf{j}} - 16\hat{\mathbf{k}}$ ☐ (b) $-100\hat{\mathbf{i}} - 35\hat{\mathbf{j}} - 8\hat{\mathbf{k}}$ ☐

(c) $20\hat{\mathbf{i}} + 15\hat{\mathbf{j}} - 80\hat{\mathbf{k}}$ ☐ (d) $-20\hat{\mathbf{i}} - 15\hat{\mathbf{j}} - 80\hat{\mathbf{k}}$ ☐

72. A particle of mass $5m$ at rest suddenly breaks on its own into three fragments. Two fragments of mass m each move along mutually perpendicular direction with each speed v. The energy released during the process is $x\ mv^2$. Find the value of x.

Assertion-Reason Questions

Direction (Q. Nos. 1-10) *In the following questions, a statement of Assertion is followed by a corresponding statement of Reason. From the following options, choose the correct one.*

(a) Both Assertion and Reason are correct and Reason is the correct explanation of Assertion.
(b) Both Assertion and Reason are correct but Reason is not the correct explanation of Assertion.
(c) Assertion is correct but Reason is incorrect.
(d) Assertion is incorrect but Reason is correct.

1. **Assertion** (A) The work done in moving a body over a closed circular loop is zero for every force in nature.
Reason (R) Work done depends on nature of force.

(a) ☐ (b) ☐ (c) ☐ (d) ☐

2. **Assertion** (A) If a force is applied on a rigid body. Body is in motion but point of application of force is stationary. Then, work done by the force is zero.
Reason (R) If body is moving, then point of application of force should also move.

(a) ☐ (b) ☐ (c) ☐ (d) ☐

3. **Assertion** (A) Stopping distance $= \dfrac{\text{Kinetic energy}}{\text{Stopping force}}$

Reason (R) Work done in stopping a body is equal to change in kinetic energy of the body.

(a) ☐ (b) ☐ (c) ☐ (d) ☐

4. **Assertion** (A) The work done in bringing a body down from the top to the base along a frictionless inclined plane is the same as the work done in bringing it down from the vertical side.
Reason (R) The gravitational force on the body along the inclined plane is the same as that along the vertical side.

(a) ☐ (b) ☐ (c) ☐ (d) ☐

5. **Assertion** (A) The two objects A and B will reach at the ground with same speed, if inclined plane is frictionless. The two objects as shown in figure during their motion to the ground level will be travelling at equal speeds.

Reason (R) Net force on both the objects during their motion is same.

(a) ☐ (b) ☐ (c) ☐ (d) ☐

6. **Assertion** (A) In the principle of conservation of energy, we include mass into total energy, because mass can be converted into energy.
Reason (R) The coefficient of friction between the block and the surface decreases with the increase in the angle of inclination.

(a) ☐ (b) ☐ (c) ☐ (d) ☐

7. **Assertion** (A) Two springs of force constants k_1 and k_2 are stretched by the same force. If $k_1 > k_2$, then work done in stretching the first (W_1) is less than work done in stretching the second (W_2).
Reason (R) Spring force, $F = k_1x_1 = k_2x_2$

(a) ☐ (b) ☐ (c) ☐ (d) ☐

8. **Assertion** (A) Friction is a non-conservative force.
Reason (R) This is because work done against friction, in moving a body over a closed path is never zero.

(a) ☐ (b) ☐ (c) ☐ (d) ☐

9. **Assertion** (A) Decrease in mechanical energy is more in case of an object sliding up a relatively less inclined plane due to friction.
Reason (R) The coefficient of friction between the block and the surface decreases with the increase in the angle of inclination.

(a) ☐ (b) ☐ (c) ☐ (d) ☐

10. **Assertion** (A) If the surface between the blocks A and B is rough, then work done by friction on block B is always negative.

Smooth

Reason (R) Total work done by friction in both the blocks is always zero.

(a) ☐ (b) ☐ (c) ☐ (d) ☐

Case Based Questions

1. Work done by a constant force acting on a body in any direction is calculated by using $W = \mathbf{F} \cdot \mathbf{s}$. Now consider a force which acts always in one direction whose magnitude may keep on varying.

Let us assume that the magnitude of the force is also a function of x or say $F(x)$ is known to us. Now, work done by this force in moving a body from x_1 to x_2 is given as

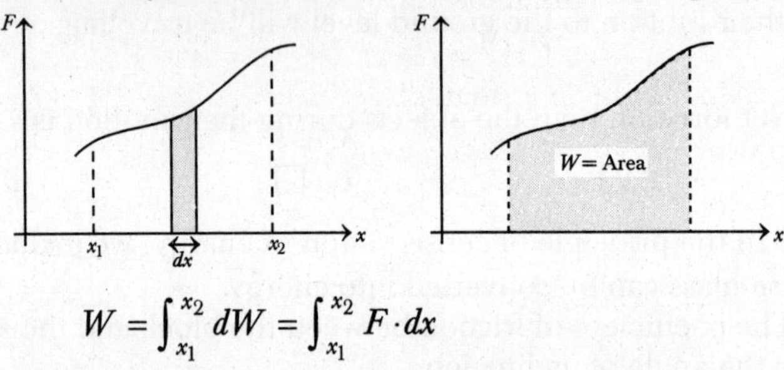

$$W = \int_{x_1}^{x_2} dW = \int_{x_1}^{x_2} F \cdot dx$$

It is important to note that $\int_{x_1}^{x_2} F \cdot dx$ is also the area under F-x graph between $x = x_1$ to $x = x_2$.

For some type of forces, work done may be path dependent or path independent.

(i) Viscous force and gravitational force are, respectively

(a) conservative, non-conservative ☐

(b) non-conservative, conservative ☐

(c) conservative, conservative ☐

(d) non-conservative, non-conservative ☐

(ii) Which of the following statements is incorrect ?

(a) Work done may be negative or zero. ☐

(b) Work depends on frame of reference. ☐

(c) If work done by the conservative force is positive, then potential energy of the system will increase. ☐

(d) Change in potential energy is equal to the negative of work done by conservative force. ☐

(iii) A block of mass $m = 2$ kg is pulled by a force $F = 40$ N upwards through a height $h = 2$ m. The work done on the block by the applied force F is. ($g = 10$ m/s^2)

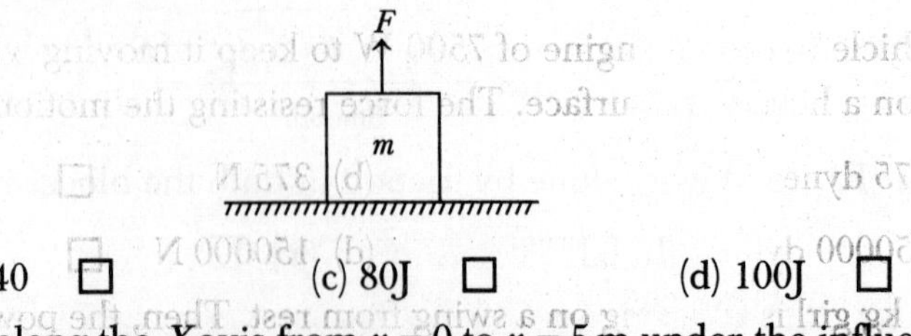

(a) 60J ☐ (b) 40 ☐ (c) 80J ☐ (d) 100J ☐

(iv) A particle moves along the X-axis from $x = 0$ to $x = 5$ m under the influence of a force given by $F = 7 - 2x + 3x^2$. Work done in the process is

(a) 70 ☐ (b) 270 ☐ (c) 35 ☐ (d) 135 ☐

Or

Work done by a force $\mathbf{F} = (\hat{\mathbf{i}} + 2\hat{\mathbf{j}} + 3\hat{\mathbf{k}})$ N acting on a particle in displacing it from the point $\mathbf{r}_1 = \hat{\mathbf{i}} + \hat{\mathbf{j}} + \hat{\mathbf{k}}$ to the point $\mathbf{r}_2 = \hat{\mathbf{i}} - \hat{\mathbf{j}} + 2\hat{\mathbf{k}}$ is

(a) 3 J ☐ (b) −1 J ☐ (c) zero ☐ (d) 2 J ☐

2. Power is the rate at which a force does work. If a force does 20 J of work in 10 s, the average rate at which it is working is 2 J/s or the average power is 2 W.
Power is also measured in horse power (HP). It is a unit of power that compares the power of a machine to the muscle power of the horse.

$$1 \text{ HP} = 746 \text{ W}$$

The work done by a force **F** in a small displacement $d\mathbf{r}$ is $dW = \mathbf{F} \cdot d\mathbf{r}$. Thus, the instantaneous power delivered by the force is $P = \frac{dW}{dt} = \mathbf{F} \cdot \frac{d\mathbf{r}}{dt} = \mathbf{F} \cdot \mathbf{v} = Fv \cos \theta$

Thus, power is equal to the scalar product of force with velocity.

(i) A force F acting on a particle varies with the position x as shown in the figure. Power required for displacing the particle in 1 second from $x = 0$ to 2m is

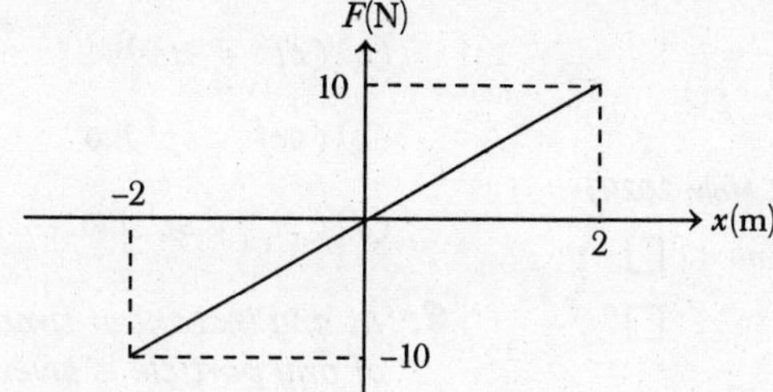

(a) 10 W ☐ (b) 20 W ☐ (c) 5 W ☐ (d) 15 W ☐

(ii) Which of the following statements is incorrect for a body performing uniform circular motion ?

(a) Power of centripetal force will be zero ☐

(b) Power of centripetal force will never be zero. ☐

(c) Work done by the centripetal force will be always zero. ☐

(d) Power is equal to scalar product of force with velocity. ☐

(iii) An engine develops 10 kW of power. How much time will it take to lift a mass of 200 kg to a height of 40 m? ($g = 10 \text{ ms}^{-2}$)

(a) 4 s ☐ (b) 5 s ☐ (c) 8 s ☐ (d) 10 s ☐

Or

A vehicle needs an engine of 7500 W to keep it moving with a constant velocity of 20 m/s on a horizontal surface. The force resisting the motion is

(a) 375 dyne ☐ (b) 375 N ☐

(c) 150000 dyne ☐ (d) 150000 N ☐

(iv) A 50 kg girl is swinging on a swing from rest. Then, the power delivered when moving with a velocity of 2 m/s upwards in a direction making an angle 60° with the verticle is

(a) 980 W ☐ (b) 490 W ☐ (c) $490\sqrt{3}$ W ☐ (d) 245 W ☐

COMPETITION EDGE UP

1. A particle of mass m moves on a straight line with its velocity increasing with distance according to the equation $v = \alpha\sqrt{x}$, where α is a constant. The total work done by all the forces applied on the particle during its displacement from x = 0 to x = d, will be **[NCERT Pg. 73, JEE Main 2024]**

(a) $\frac{m\alpha^2 d}{2}$ ☐ (b) $2m\alpha^2 d$ ☐

(c) $\frac{m}{2\alpha^2 d}$ ☐ (d) $\frac{md}{2\alpha^2}$ ☐

2. A block is simply released from the top of an inclined plane as shown in the figure below. The maximum compression in the spring when the block hits the spring is

5kg, μ=0, 10m, 30°, 2m, k=100 N/m, μ=0.5

[NCERT Pg. 80, JEE Main 2024]

(a) 1 m ☐ (b) $\sqrt{5}$ m ☐

(c) $\sqrt{6}$ m ☐ (d) 2 m ☐

3. Three bodies A, B and C have equal kinetic energies and their masses are 400 kg, 1.2 kg and 1.6 kg respectively. The ratio of their linear momenta is

[NCERT Pg. 75, JEE Main 2024]

(a) $1 : \sqrt{3} : \sqrt{2}$ ☐

(b) $\sqrt{2} : \sqrt{3} : 1$ ☐

(c) $1 : \sqrt{3} : 2$ ☐

(d) $\sqrt{3} : \sqrt{2} : 1$ ☐

4. A bullet of mass 50 g is fired with a speed 100 m/s on a plywood and emerges with 40 m/s. The percentage loss of kinetic energy is **[NCERT Pg. 75, JEE Main 2024]**

(a) 44% ☐ (b) 84% ☐

(c) 32% ☐ (d) 16% ☐

5. Four particles A, B, C, D of mass $\frac{m}{2}$, m, 2m, 4m, have same momentum, respectively. The particle with maximum kinetic energy is **[NCERT Pg. 75, JEE Main 2024]**

(a) A ☐ (b) C ☐

(c) D ☐ (d) B ☐

6. A body is moving unidirectionally under the influence of a constant power source. Its displacement in time t is proportional to

[NCERT Pg. 83, JEE Main 2024]

(a) t ☐ (b) $t^{\frac{2}{3}}$ ☐

(c) t^2 ☐ (d) $t^{\frac{3}{2}}$ ☐

7. A body of mass 2 kg begins to move under the action of a time dependent force given by $\mathbf{F} = (6t\hat{i} + 6t^2\hat{j})$ N. The power developed by the force at the time t is given by **[NCERT Pg. 83, JEE Main 2024]**

(a) $(9t^5 + 6t^3)$ W ☐

(b) $(6t^4 + 9t^5)$ W ☐

(c) $(9t^3 + 6t^5)$ W ☐

(d) $(3t^3 + 6t^5)$ W ☐

8. At any instant of time t, the displacement of any particle is given by 2t – 1 (SI unit) under the influence of force of 5 N. The value of instantaneous power is (in SI unit)

[NCERT Pg. 83, NEET 2024]

(a) 10 ☐ (b) 5 ☐

(c) 7 ☐ (d) 6 ☐

9. Two bodies A and B of same mass undergo completely inelastic one dimensional collision. The body A moves with velocity v_1 while body B is at rest before collision. The velocity of the system after collision is v_2. The ratio $v_1 : v_2$ is **[NCERT Pg. 84, NEET 2024]**

(a) 1 : 2 ☐ (b) 2 : 1 ☐

(c) 4 : 1 ☐ (d) 1 : 4 ☐

10. The potential energy of a long spring when stretched by 2 cm is U. If the spring is stretched by 8 cm, potential energy stored in it will be **[NCERT Pg. 81 NEET 2023]**

(a) 4 U ☐ (b) 8U ☐

(c) 16 U ☐ (d) 2U ☐

Chapter 06

System of Particles and Rotational Motion

Scan and take Chapter Test

1. For a rotating rigid body, particles may exist in different rotational plane which are parallel to each other and perpendicular to the rotational axis.

True  False □

2. Consider the following statements and choose the correct one.

I. If the line joining any two internal points does not remain parallel to itself, then body is in rotation.

II. The motion of a rigid body which is not pivoted or fixed is either a pure translational motion or a combination of translational and rotational motion.

____

3. Study the figure given below.

Which point is having only one type of motion? Also, write the name of that motion.

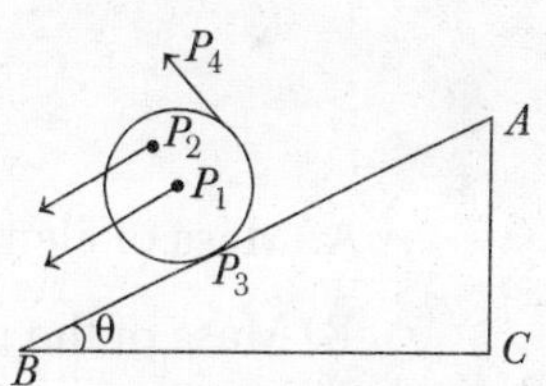

____

4. In the following diagram, $OA = OB = AB = 1\,\text{m}$.

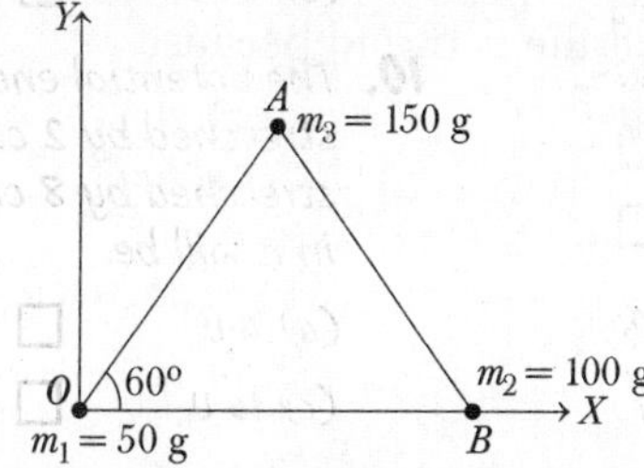

If X_{CM}, Y_{CM} be the position of centre of mass, then

X_{CM} = ____________, Y_{CM} = ____________

*Concepts of all questions bearing * are important for JEE/NEET/CUET.*

5. What will be the coordinate for centre of mass, if two equal point masses are placed at (– 4, 0) and (4, 0), respectively?

____

***6.** The coordinates of centre of mass of particles of mass 10 g, 20 g and 30 g are (1, 1, 1) m. The position of the coordinate of mass 40 g which when added to the system, if position of combined centre of mass becomes origin will be __________ .

***7.** Let four masses 2*m*, 2*m*, 3*m* and 5*m* are placed at the vertices of a 1 m length square. What will be the coordinates of centre of mass, if masses 2 *m* and 5*m* are placed at origin and *Y*-axis, respectively?

____

8. Three particles of respective masses $m_1 = 12\,\text{kg}$, $m_2 = 25\,\text{kg}$ and $m_3 = 38$ kg form an equilateral triangle of side length $a = 1.4$ m. We locate m_1 at the origin on the *XY*-plane and put m_2 to the right of m_1 on the *X*-axis.

Tick (✓/✗) for correct/incorrect statement in given boxes.

(i) The *x*-coordinate of centre of mass is 97.3 cm. ☐

(ii) The *y*-coordinate of centre of mass is 37 cm. ☐

(iii) The *x*-coordinate of centre of mass is 82.1 cm. ☐

(iv) The *y*-coordinate of centre of mass is 61.3 cm. ☐

9. Linear mass density of a rod of length 3 m is $\lambda(x) = 4x^2\,\text{kg m}$,
here, x = distance from origin along *X*-axis.

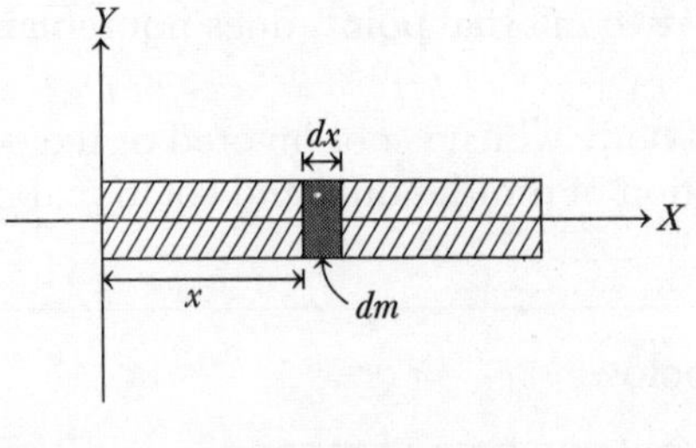

Y
dx
X
x
dm

A. Mass of element of length *dx* is $dm =$ ☐

B. Mass of the rod, $m = \int_0^2 dm =$ ☐ kg.

C. Centre of mass of rod is located at $X_{CM} =$ ☐ m and $Y_{CM} =$ ☐ m.

Fill above boxes with appropriate answer.

10. Three masses *m*, 2*m* and 3*m* are placed at the vertices of an equilateral triangle. The centre of mass will not be exactly at the centroid because

(a) position vector is unspecified ☐

(b) masses are not equal ☐

(c) point of symmetry is not valid ☐

(d) All of the above ☐

11. Consider the following figure.

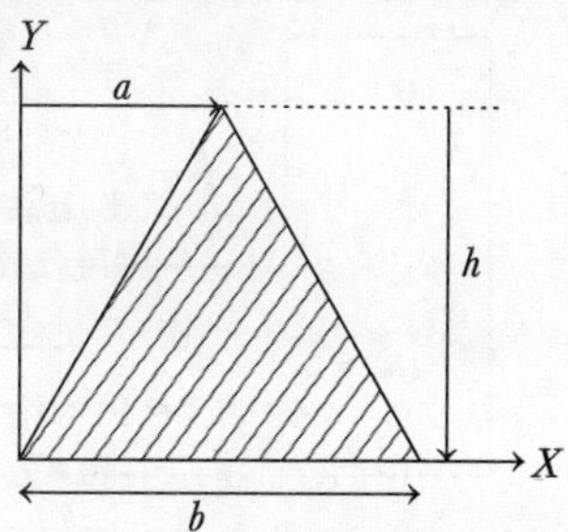

Coordinates of centre of mass of above triangular lamina are

X_{CM} = ________________ and Y_{CM} = ________________ .

12. Match the objects shown in Column I with their respective position of centre of mass listed in Column II.

Column I	Column II
A. R	1. $\dfrac{R}{4}$
B. R, R	2. $\dfrac{2R}{\pi}$
C. R	3. $\dfrac{R}{3}$
D. R	4. $\dfrac{R}{2}$

A. ________________ B. ________________ C. ________________ D. ________________

13. Which of the following is an incorrect matching pair?

Object		Centre of mass
I. Semi-circular ring	$\rightarrow$	$\dfrac{2R}{\pi}$
II. Semi-circular disc	$\rightarrow$	$\dfrac{2R}{3\pi}$
III. Semi-hollow sphere	$\rightarrow$	$\dfrac{R}{2}$
IV. Semi-solid sphere	$\rightarrow$	$\dfrac{3R}{8}$

Here, R = radius of solid.

____

14. If a cone is formed due to rotation of a triangular plate, then the centre of mass coincides at the same point for both triangular plate and hollow cone.

Yes ☐ No ☐

15. Which point represents the centre of mass of an L-shaped lamina given below?

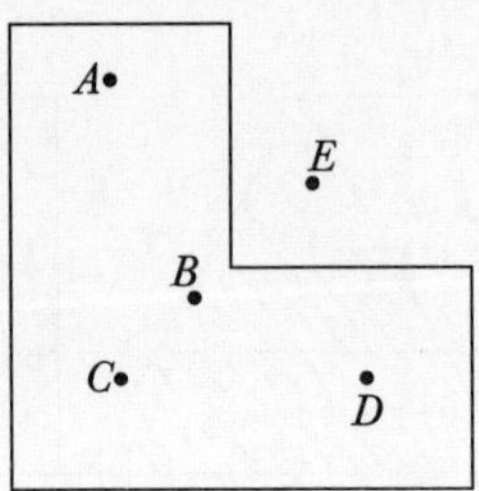

____

TOPIC 3

Motion of Centre of Mass

NCERT Pg 99-100

16. A projectile of mass 5 kg explodes in its course. One fragment of mass 3 kg falls at three-fourth of the range R of the projectile. The other fragment will fall at ____ $\left(\frac{11}{8}/\frac{3}{8}\right)R$.

17. Two particles of equal mass have velocities $\mathbf{v}_1 = 4\hat{\mathbf{i}}$ m/s and $\mathbf{v}_2 = 4\hat{\mathbf{j}}$ m/s. First particle has an acceleration $\mathbf{a}_1 = (2\hat{\mathbf{i}} + 2\hat{\mathbf{j}})$ m/s^2, while the acceleration of the other particle is zero. Then,

(i) $\mathbf{v}_{CM}$ = ☐ m/s

(ii) $\mathbf{a}_{CM}$ = ☐ m/s^2

(iii) The centre of mass of the two particles moves in a ________ path.

18. A system consisting of two objects has total momentum of $18\hat{\mathbf{i}}$ kg ms^{-1} and its centre of mass has velocity $3\hat{\mathbf{i}}$ ms^{-1}. One of the object has the mass 4 kg and velocity $1.5\hat{\mathbf{i}}$ ms^{-1}. The mass and velocity of other object is 2 kg and $6\hat{\mathbf{i}}$ ms^{-1}.

Yes ☐ No ☐

19. Two bodies A and B initially at rest move towards each other under a mutual force of attraction. No other force acts on them. At an instant, when the speed of A is v and the speed of B is $2v$, the speed of centre of mass is found to be nv. Find the value of n here.

____

20. Four particles A, B, C and D are kept at the corners of a square as shown below. Then, choose the correct statement(s).

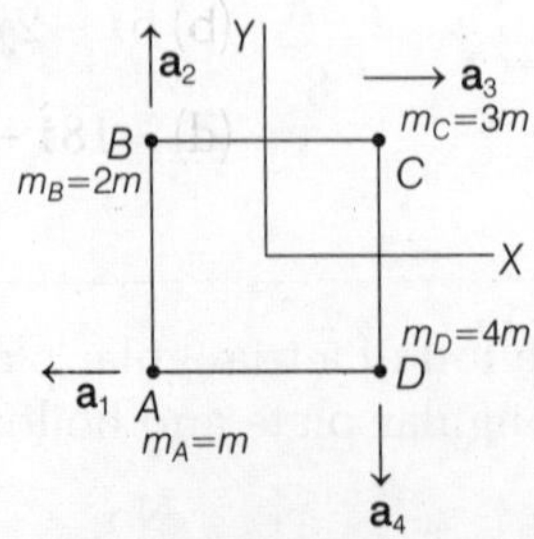

I. The acceleration of the centre of mass of the particle is $\frac{a}{5}(\hat{\mathbf{i}} - \hat{\mathbf{j}})$ m/s^2.

II. The acceleration of the centre of mass of the particle is $\frac{a}{5}(\hat{\mathbf{i}} - \hat{\mathbf{j}})$ m/s^2 only if $|\mathbf{a}_1| = |\mathbf{a}_2| = |\mathbf{a}_3| = |\mathbf{a}_4|$.

TOPIC 4

Momentum and Vector Product of two Vectors

21. What will be the magnitude of vector product of two vectors $\mathbf{a} = (3\hat{\mathbf{i}} - 4\hat{\mathbf{j}} + 5\hat{\mathbf{k}})$ and $\mathbf{b} = (-2\hat{\mathbf{i}} + \hat{\mathbf{j}} - 3\hat{\mathbf{k}})$?

---

22. A mass m_1 constrained to move in horizontal direction is allowed to collide with another mass m_2. Given, $m_1 = 85$ g, $m_2 = 200$ g, $v_1 = 6.4\,\hat{\mathbf{i}}$ cm s^{-1} and $v_2 = (-6.7\hat{\mathbf{i}} - 2\hat{\mathbf{j}})$ cm s^{-1}.

Which of the following statement(s) is/are correct/incorrect ?

(i) Velocity of centre of mass is $(-2.3\hat{\mathbf{i}} - 1.4\hat{\mathbf{j}})$ cm s^{-1}. ☐

(ii) Linear momentum of the system is $(-796\hat{\mathbf{i}} - 400\hat{\mathbf{j}})$ g cm s^{-1}. ☐

(iii) If centre of mass is taken as frame of reference, then velocity of m_1 is $(9.2\hat{\mathbf{i}} - 1.4\hat{\mathbf{j}})$ cm s^{-1}. ☐

23. Vector product of two vectors is given by $(x\,\hat{\mathbf{i}} + y\,\hat{\mathbf{j}} + z\,\hat{\mathbf{k}})$. If two vectors are $\mathbf{a} = (3\hat{\mathbf{i}} - 2\hat{\mathbf{j}} + 2\hat{\mathbf{k}})$ and $\mathbf{b} = (2\hat{\mathbf{i}} + 2\hat{\mathbf{j}} + 3\hat{\mathbf{k}})$, then (x, y, z) is __________.

24. The area of a parallelogram formed by the vectors $\mathbf{A} = \hat{\mathbf{i}} - 2\hat{\mathbf{j}} + 3\hat{\mathbf{k}}$ and $\mathbf{B} = 3\hat{\mathbf{i}} - 2\hat{\mathbf{j}} + \hat{\mathbf{k}}$ as its adjacent sides, is

(a) $8\sqrt{3}$ units ☐ (b) 64 units ☐

(c) 32 units ☐ (d) $4\sqrt{6}$ units ☐

25. If $\mathbf{A} = \hat{\mathbf{i}} + 2\hat{\mathbf{k}}$ and $\mathbf{B} = \hat{\mathbf{j}} - \hat{\mathbf{k}}$ then, $\mathbf{A} \times \mathbf{B}$ eaual to

---

26. What is the values of linear velocity, if $\omega = 3\hat{\mathbf{i}} - 4\hat{\mathbf{j}} + \hat{\mathbf{k}}$ and $\mathbf{r} = 5\hat{\mathbf{i}} - 6\hat{\mathbf{j}} + 6\hat{\mathbf{k}}$?

(a) $6\hat{\mathbf{i}} - 2\hat{\mathbf{j}} + 3\hat{\mathbf{k}}$ ☐ (b) $6\hat{\mathbf{i}} - 2\hat{\mathbf{j}} + 8\hat{\mathbf{k}}$ ☐

(c) $4\hat{\mathbf{i}} - 13\hat{\mathbf{j}} + 6\hat{\mathbf{k}}$ ☐ (d) $-18\hat{\mathbf{i}} - 13\hat{\mathbf{j}} + 2\hat{\mathbf{k}}$ ☐

TOPIC 5

Angular Velocity and its Relation with Linear Velocity

27. A cylinder of radius 20 cm along the surface with a constant speed of 80 cm/s. Then, answer the following questions.

(a) What is the rotational speed of cylinder about its axis?

____

(b) What is the magnitude and direction of acceleration of the points on its surface?

____

(c) What is the velocity of the point at the top of the cylinder at any moment ?

____

(d) What is the velocity of the point of the cylinder which is in contact with floor at any moment?

____

28. Two particles moving in concentric circles of radii 4 m and 6 m, respectively. If both have same linear speed, then what is the ratio of angular speed?

____

29. Let $\frac{OP_1}{OP_2} = 2$.

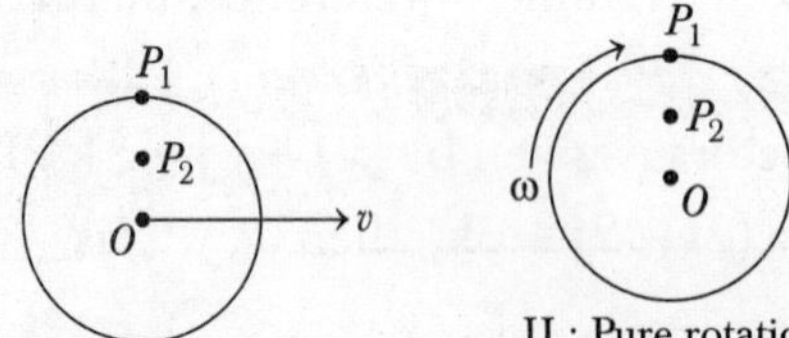

I : Pure translation

II : Pure rotation about axis through O

Case I Ratio of speeds of P_1 and P_2; $\frac{v_{P_1}}{v_{P_2}}$ = ______________ (less than 1/more than 1/equals to 1).

Case II Ratio of linear speeds of P_1 and P_2; $\frac{v_{P_1}}{v_{P_2}}$ = ______________ (more than 1 /less than 1/equals to 1).

30. Study the diagram given below and mark correct statements.

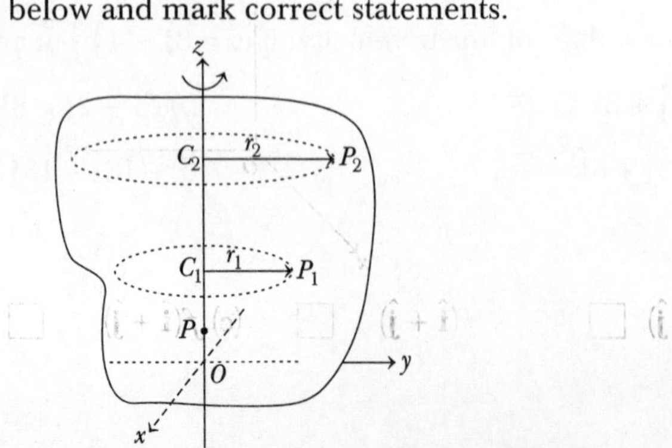

Statement I Linear velocity of particle P_1 is less than that of particle P_2.

Statement II Angular velocity of particle P_1 is same as angular velocity of particle P_2.

Statement III Particles at point P will always remain stationary.

31. A disc lies in YZ-plane and rotates uniformly about its axis in this plane. The direction of angular velocity will be ________ (X-axis/Z-axis).

32. Consider a disc rotating as shown. Tick (✓/×) on correct/incorrect expressions.

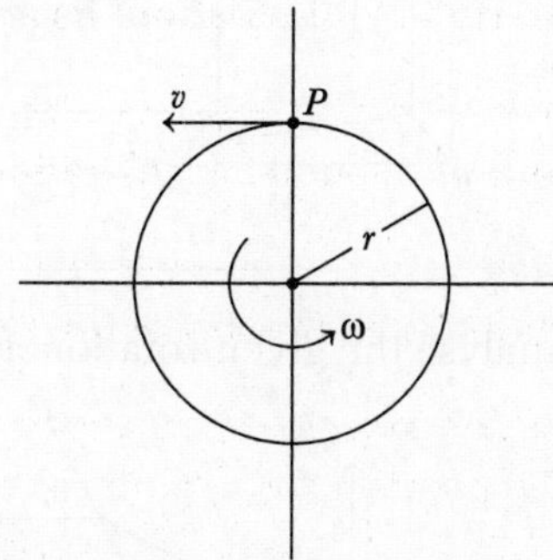

A. Tangential acceleration of point P, $a_t = \frac{dv}{dt}$. ☐

B. $a_t = \frac{dv}{dt} = \frac{d}{dt}(r\omega) = r\frac{d\omega}{dt} = r\alpha$ (where, α = angular acceleration). ☐

TOPIC 6

Torque and Angular Momentum

33. A torque of 2.5 N-m is acting on a particle of mass 1 kg about the origin. If $F = 1\,\text{N}$ and distance of particle from the origin is 5 m, then the angle between force and position vector is ________ $\left(\frac{\pi}{3}/\frac{\pi}{6}\right)$.

34. A force of $-f\hat{\mathbf{k}}$ acts on O (the origin of the coordinate system). The torque about $(1, -1)$ is

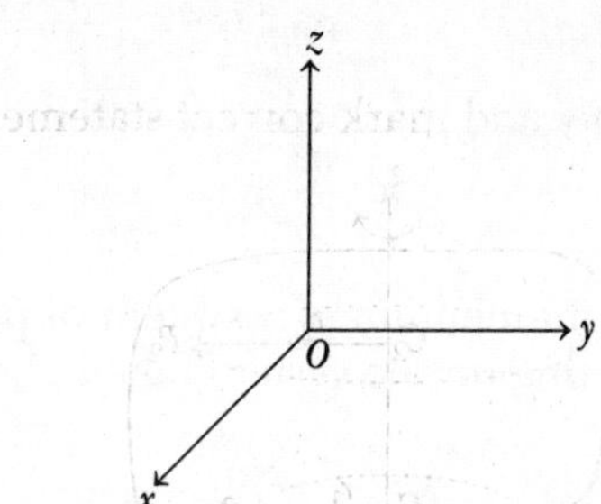

(a) $f(\hat{\mathbf{i}} - \hat{\mathbf{j}})$ ☐ (b) $-f(\hat{\mathbf{i}} + \hat{\mathbf{j}})$ ☐ (c) $f(\hat{\mathbf{i}} + \hat{\mathbf{j}})$ ☐ (d) $-f(\hat{\mathbf{i}} - \hat{\mathbf{j}})$ ☐

***35.** A force of $(4\hat{\mathbf{i}} - 3\hat{\mathbf{j}} + 5\hat{\mathbf{k}})$ N is applied at point whose position vector is $(7\hat{\mathbf{i}} + 4\hat{\mathbf{j}} - 2\hat{\mathbf{k}})$ m. The torque of force about the origin is ________ .

36. A door is fixed with the wall with the help of frictionless hinges, as shown in the figure below. At which point, the applied force will not be able to rotate the door?

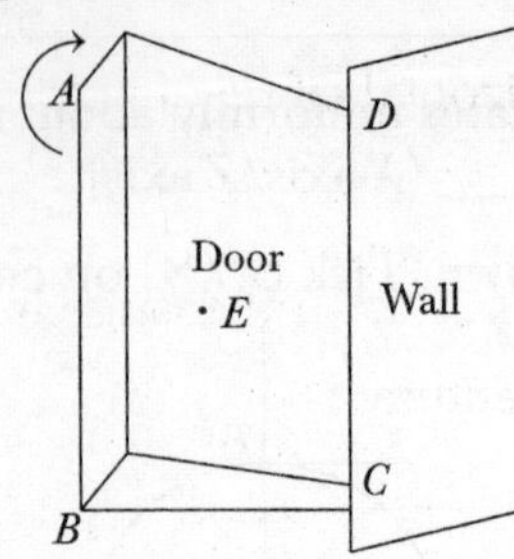

____

37. A diagram is given below. Analyse the given rotation and find the direction of torque.

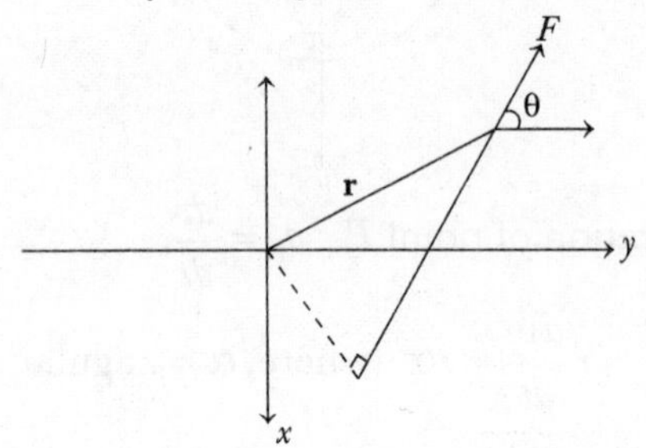

____

38. Tick (✓/×) for correct/incorrect statement in given boxes.

(i) In rotational equilibrium, torque is independent of the origin about which force is applied. ☐

(ii) If the translational equilibrium condition holds for a rigid body, then shift of a origin does not matter. ☐

(iii) The moment of a couple does not depend on the point about which you take the moments. ☐

39. A particle is moving with uniform velocity v as given in the figure.

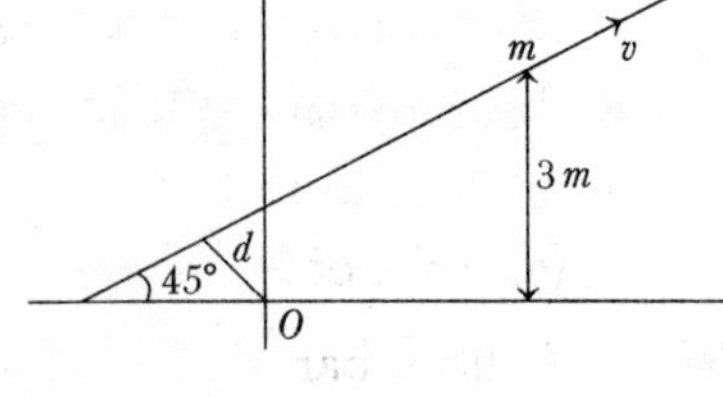

The angular momentum about O is given by

(a) $\frac{3mv}{\sqrt{2}}$ ☐ (b) $\frac{8mv}{3}$ ☐

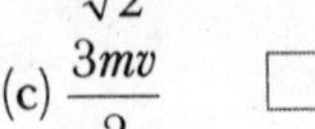

(c) $\frac{3mv}{2}$ ☐ (d) $\frac{mv}{3}$ ☐

40. The time rate of total angular momentum of a system of particles about a point is equal to the sum of external torques acting on the system taken about the same point.

Yes ☐ No ☐

41. A particle of mass m is thrown with speed v at an angle 30° with horizontal. Tick (✓/×) for correct/incorrect statement.

(i) The maximum height is $\frac{v^2}{8g}$. ☐

(ii) Linear momentum is $\frac{\sqrt{3}}{2}mv$. ☐

(iii) Angular momentum is $\frac{\sqrt{3}}{16}\frac{mv^2}{g}$, at maximum height . ☐

42. A block of mass m moves in horizontal circle of radius r with velocity v. If the radius is reduced to $\frac{r}{2}$, then find

(i) new velocity (ii) change in kinetic energy

(iii) initial and final angular momentum

---

43. Two solid spheres (shown) initially at rest are rotated by applying same torque.

Ratio of their angular speeds $\frac{\omega'}{\omega}$ after t seconds will be__________.

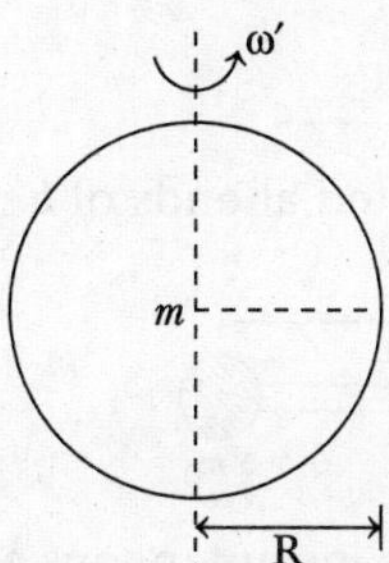

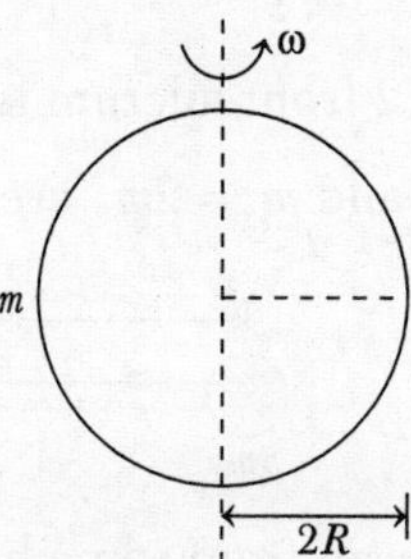

TOPIC 7

Equilibrium of a Rigid Body

44. Which of the following are examples of couple?

(a) A bar magnet hanging in North-South direction. ☐

(b) Our finger trying to open or close a lid. ☐

(c) Both (a) and (b) ☐

(d) None of the above ☐

***45.** A metal bar of 70 cm long and 4 kg in mass is supported on two knife edges placed 10 cm from each end. A 6 kg load is suspended at 30 cm from one end.

Consider the above condition and tick (✓/×) on correct/incorrect statements.

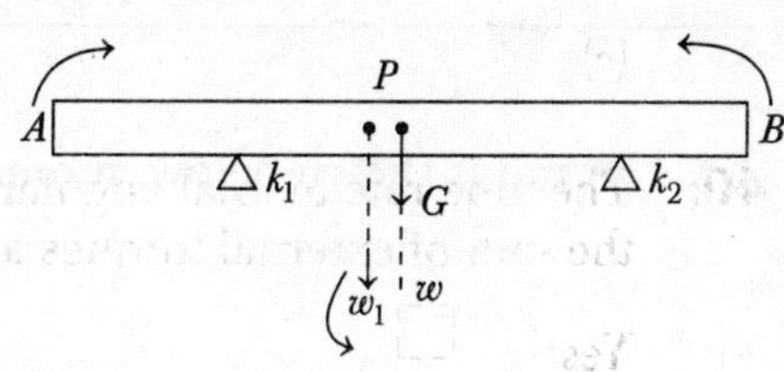

(i) Normal reaction at k_1 is 55 N. ☐

(ii) Normal reaction at k_2 is 43 N. ☐

(iii) Normal reaction at k_1 is 50 N. ☐

(iv) Normal reaction at k_2 is 39 N. ☐

46. A 3 m long ladder of 20 kg mass is inclined to a frictionless wall. Its feet is 1 m away from the wall on the floor. Reaction force of the floor is _____________ .

***47.** Write the translation equilibrium condition for the lever given below.

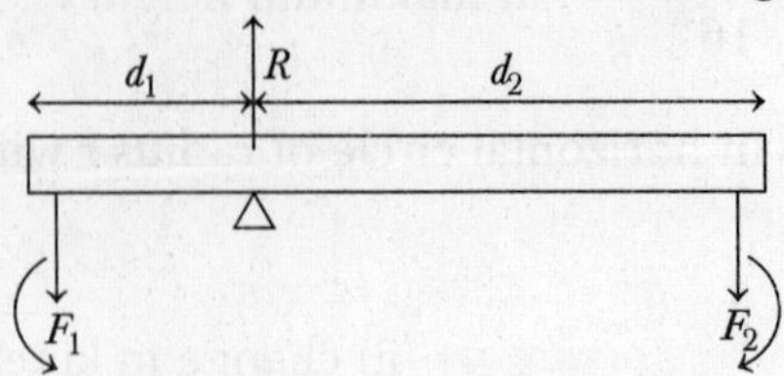

____

***48.** Two babies are playing on a modified see-saw, as given below. Baby 1 is 15 kg and Baby 2 is 25 kg.

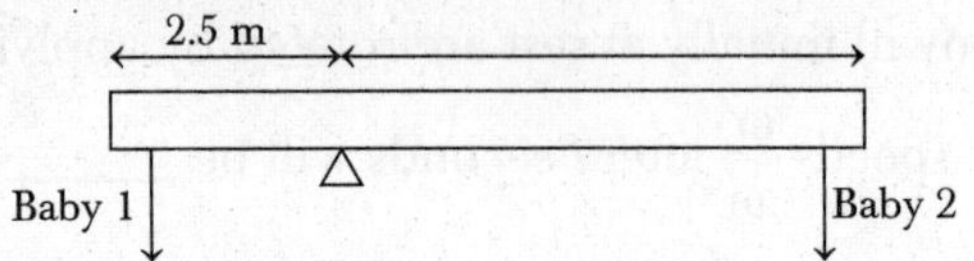

The distance of Baby 2 from fulcrum is __________ .

***49.** Two masses $m_1 = 5m_0$ and $m_2 = 2m_0$ are connected at ends of a rigid massless rod of length 3 m.

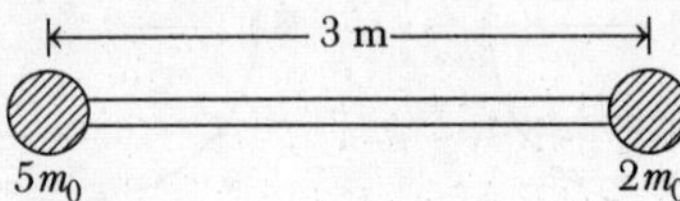

When this rod is released from some height, its instantaneous angular acceleration α will be _______ rad/s^2.

50. Two rods are given below. Point C is not fixed .

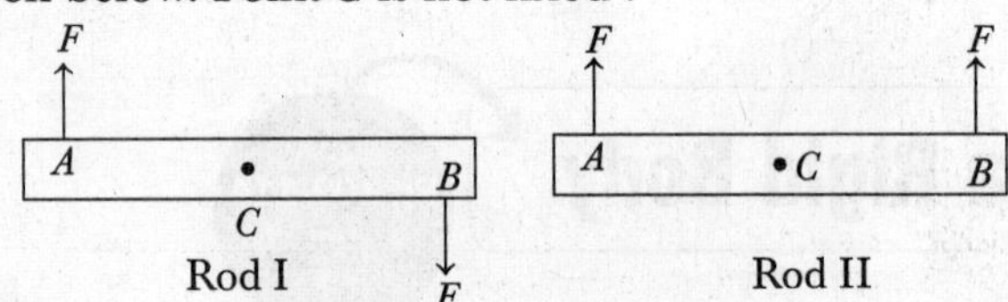

Which rod is in rotation and which of these in translation?

____

TOPIC 8

Moment of Inertia

NCERT Pg 114-116

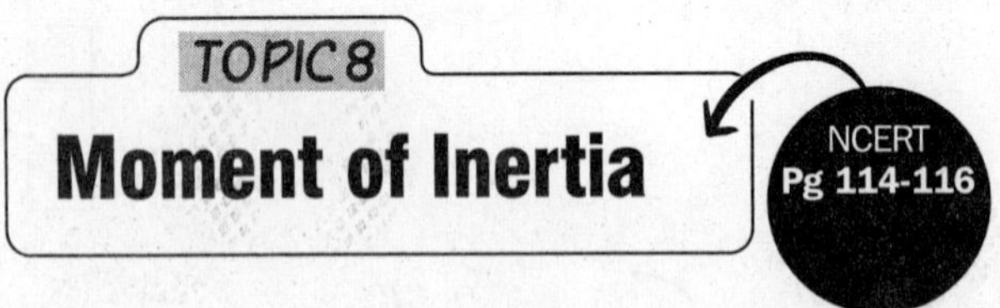

51. A rod is shown below, moment of inertia for the rod of mass m is given by

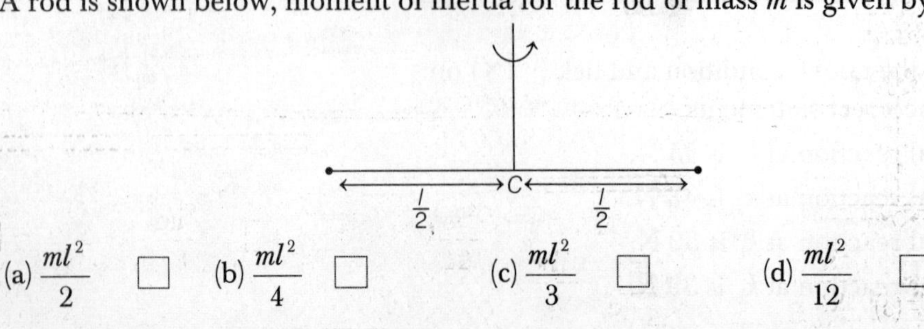

(a) $\frac{ml^2}{2}$ ☐ (b) $\frac{ml^2}{4}$ ☐ (c) $\frac{ml^2}{3}$ ☐ (d) $\frac{ml^2}{12}$ ☐

52. What is the radius of gyration (K) of a circular disc rotating perpendicular to its plane from the centre?

---

53. Identify the wrong matching pair in regards to the value of moment of inertia.

Object		Moment of Inertia
A. Circular disc	→	$\frac{mR^2}{4}$
B. Hollow cylinder	→	mR^2
C. Solid sphere	→	$\frac{mR^2}{5}$
D. Ring	→	mR^2

---

54. As we move away from the centre of mass, the radius of gyration ________ (increases/decreases).

55. Match the objects of Column I with their respective moment of inertia in Column II.

Column I	Column II
A. l	1. $\frac{ml^2}{2}$
B. l	2. $\frac{2}{5}ml^2$
C. l	3. $\frac{2}{3}ml^2$
D. z, l	4. $\frac{ml^2}{3}$

A. ____________ B. ____________ C. ____________ D. ____________

56. What will be the moment of inertia of thin uniform square plate about its diagonal, having mass m and length L?

____

57. The radius of gyration of a thin uniform rod about its one end is $\frac{L}{\sqrt{3}}$.

True ☐ False ☐

***58.** Three identical thin rods each of the length l and mass M are joined together to form a ladder H. What is the moment of inertia of the system about one of the sides of H?

(a) $\frac{Ml^2}{4}$ ☐ (b) $\frac{Ml^2}{3}$ ☐ (c) $\frac{2Ml^2}{3}$ ☐ (d) $\frac{4Ml^2}{3}$ ☐

59. Column I represents objects and Column II represents ratio $\frac{K^2}{R^2}$, where K is radius of gyration. Match the Column I with Column II.

Column I	Column II
A. Uniform solid sphere	1. 1
B. Solid circular disc	2. 0.4
C. Hollow sphere	3. 0.67
D. Uniform ring	4. 0.5

A. ________ B. ________ C. ________ D. ________

TOPIC 9

Kinematics of Rotational Motion about a Fixed Axis

60. When a ceiling fan is switched OFF, its angular velocity becomes half while it makes 36 rotations. How many more rotations will it make before coming to rest?

____

61. The linear motion and rotational motion are analogous to each other. Complete the formulae.

$$v = u_0 + at : \omega = \omega_0 + \alpha t, \; x = x_0 + v \cdot t + \frac{1}{2} at^2 : \theta = \theta_0 + \_\_\_\_\_\_$$

$$v^2 = v_0^2 + 2ax : \omega^2 = \omega_0^2 + 2\alpha(\theta - \theta_0)$$

62. A wheel of car is rotating at the rate of 20 rev/s. On pressing the accelerator for 10 s, it starts rotating at 75 rev/s. The angular acceleration of the wheel is $p\pi$ rad/s^2. Find the value of p.

____

63. The angular speed of a motor wheel is increased from 1200 rpm to 3120 rpm in 16 s. Find

(i) initial angular velocity, (ii) final angular velocity,

(iii) angular acceleration and (iv) number of revolutions.

____

64. A rigid body rotates about a fixed axis with variable angular velocity equal to $\alpha - \beta t$, at the time t, where α, β are constants. The angle through which it rotates before its stops

(a) $\frac{\alpha^2}{2\beta}$ ☐ (b) $\frac{\alpha^2 - \beta^2}{2\alpha}$ ☐ (c) $\frac{\alpha^2 - \beta^2}{2\beta}$ ☐ (d) $\frac{(\alpha - \beta)\alpha}{2}$ ☐

65. The motor of an engine is rotating about axis with an angular velocity of 100 rpm. It comes to rest in 15 s, after being switched off. Assuming constant angular deceleration. What are the number of revolutions made by it before coming to rest?

____

TOPIC 10

Dynamics and Angular Momentum in Case of Rotation about a Fixed Axis

66. A rod of length 50 cm is released when it is making angle of 30° with horizontal.

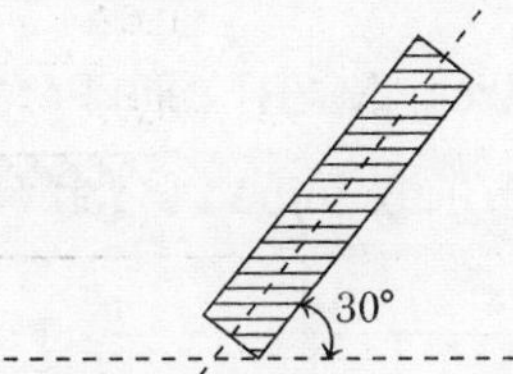

Its angular speed when it is again horizontal will be __________ rad/s.

***67.** Two discs with moment of inertia I_1 and I_2 and angular speeds ω_1 and ω_2 respectively, are brought in contact as shown below.

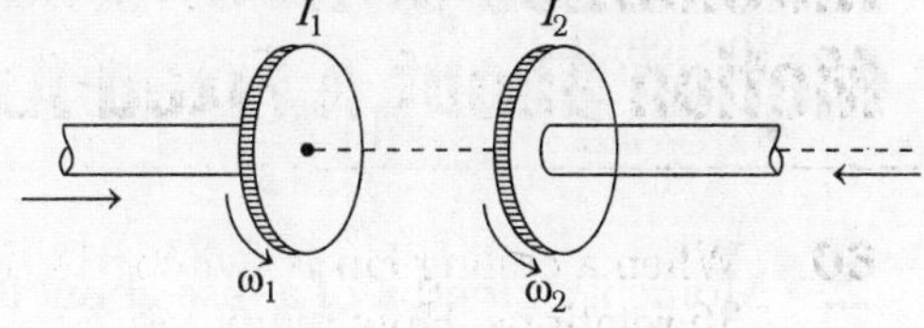

There is no external torque on system also, $I_1 = I$ and $I_2 = 2I$ and $\omega_2 = 3\omega$, $\omega_1 = \omega$.
Now, complete the following sentences.

A. Final angular speed of system = __________ .

B. Percentage loss of kinetic energy of system in this process = __________ .

68. Two stones of masses m and $2m$ are attached with ends of a massless string. The string is made to rotate with angular speed ω about an axis passing through the centre of mass of the system and perpendicular to the plane. The angular momentum of the system about the axis of rotation is

(a) $\frac{2m\omega L}{5}$ ☐ (b) $\frac{4m\omega L^2}{9}$ ☐ (c) $\frac{m\omega L^2}{3}$ ☐ (d) $\frac{3m\omega L^2}{2}$ ☐

69. A flywheel of mass 20 kg and radius 20 cm is pulled with the help of a cord with a force of 25 N. If 2 m of the cord is unwound, the gain in the kinetic energy will be 50 J.

Yes ☐ No ☐

70. ________ rad/s^2 will be the net acceleration on the body shown in the figure about O.

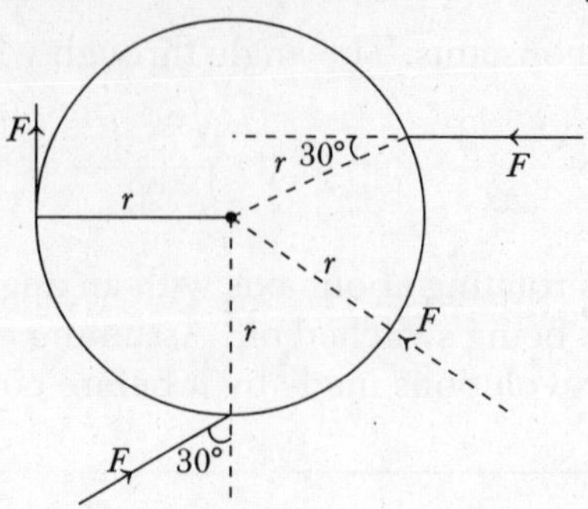

71. A student is sitting on a swivel chair with her arms folded. If she is spinning with angular velocity ω, then after stretching her arms,

(a) angular velocity increases ☐ (b) angular velocity decreases ☐
(c) angular velocity becomes zero ☐ (d) None of the above ☐

COMPETITION CONNECT

Topic 1. Theorems of Perpendicular and Parellel Axes [NCERT (Old) Pg. 164-167]

1. Two uniform rods $P(m, L)$ and $Q(3m, 3L)$ are joined together as shown figure given below.

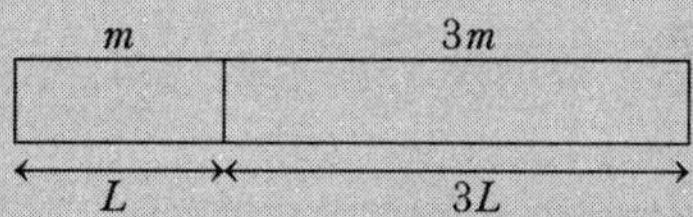

The moment of inertia through the centre of mass of system of rods and perpendicular to the length is

(a) $\frac{16}{3}mL^2$ ☐ (b) $\frac{mL^2}{15}$ ☐ (c) $\frac{3}{15}mL^2$ ☐ (d) $\frac{2}{15}mL^2$ ☐

2. Moment of inertia of a disc about its diameter is given by $\frac{mR^2}{4}$. The moment of inertia about perpendicular axis passing through centre is given by

(a) $\frac{mR^2}{4}$ ☐ (b) $\frac{mR^2}{2}$ ☐ (c) mR^2 ☐ (d) $2mR^2$ ☐

3. The moment of inertia of a ring about a tangent to the circle of the ring will be xMR^2. What is the value of x?

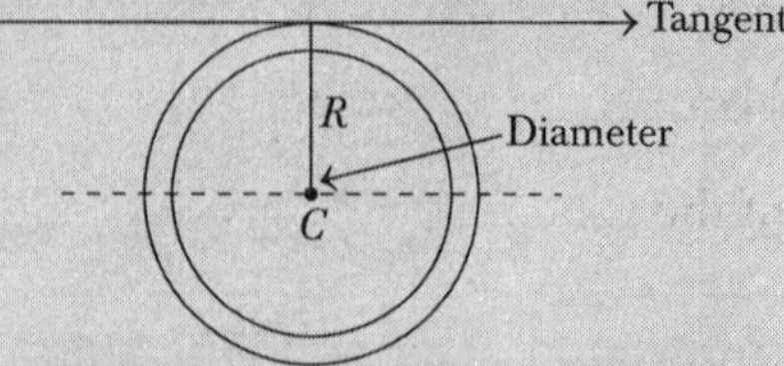

Topic 2. Rolling Motion [NCERT (Old) Pg. 173-175]

4. A solid cylinder and a sphere of same mass and same radius are rolling without slipping. If kinetic energy of cylinder is 75 J, then sphere has 70 J kinetic energy.

Yes ☐ No ☐

5. A solid cylinder is pulled with force F on a rough horizontal surface as shown in the following figure.

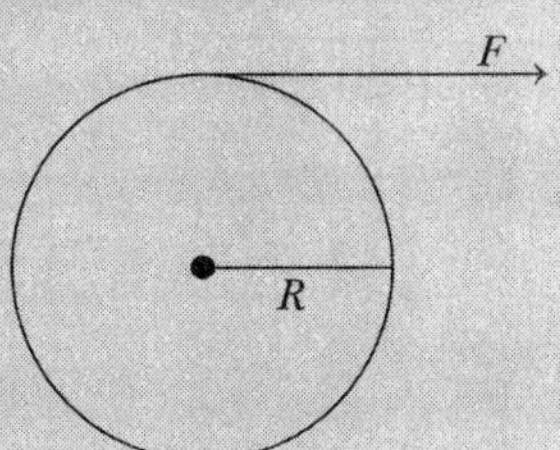

The acceleration of the centre of mass of the cylinder is ________ $\left(\frac{4}{3} / \frac{3}{4}\right)\frac{F}{m}$.

6. Ratio of speeds (v_2 / v_1) of points P_1 and P_2 of a rolling wheel as shown in figure is ________.

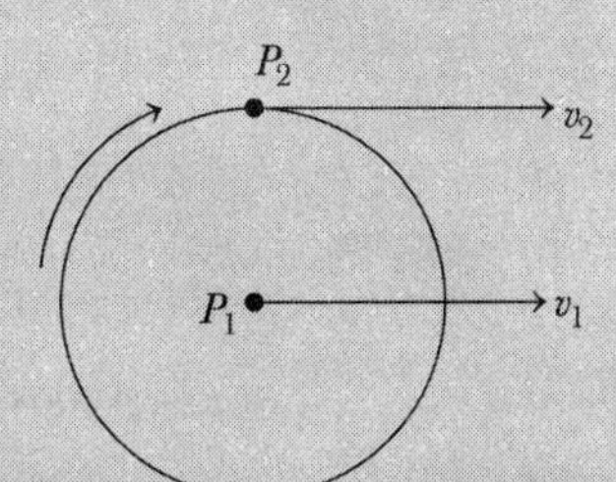

7. A hollow sphere is made to climb an inclined surface as shown in the following figure. The maximum height attained by the hollow sphere is

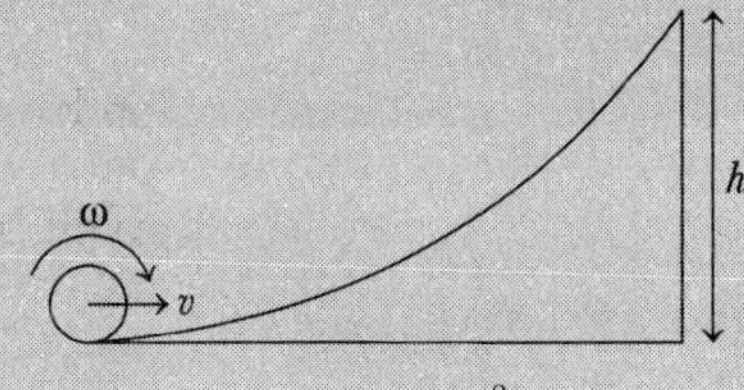

(a) $\frac{5}{8}\frac{v^2}{g}$ ☐ (b) $\frac{5}{6}\frac{v^2}{g}$ ☐ (c) $\frac{2}{3}\frac{v^2}{g}$ ☐ (d) $\frac{v^2}{2g}$ ☐

8. If a solid sphere of mass m rolls without slipping such that $v = v_0$, then the ratio of rotational KE to total KE is ________ (5 : 2/2 : 7).

9. The total kinetic energy of the rolling body is given by $K = \frac{1}{2}I\omega^2 + \frac{1}{2}mv_{CM}^2$.

True ☐ False ☐

10. What will be the shape of the body, if its KE of rotation is 40% of the KE in translatory motion, while rolling down in inclined plane?

____

11. A wheel of mass 8 kg and radius 40 cm is rolling on a horizontal road with angular velocity of 15 rad s^{-1}. The moment of inertia of the wheel about the axis is 0.64 kgm^{-2}. What is the total kinetic energy of the wheel?

____

12. What will be the angular momentum of a solid sphere of mass m and radius R rolling on a horizontal sphere with a uniform speed v?

____

13. An inclined plane is given below.

If a ring, a solid disc and solid sphere is allowed to roll down under the influence of gravity, then

(a) $v_{ring} < v_{disc} < v_{sphere}$ ☐ (b) $v_{ring} = v_{disc} < v_{sphere}$ ☐

(c) $v_{ring} > v_{disc} < v_{sphere}$ ☐ (d) $v_{ring} > v_{disc} > v_{sphere}$ ☐

Assertion-Reason Questions

Direction (Q. Nos. 1-10) *In the following questions, a statement of Assertion is followed by a corresponding statement of Reason. From the following options, choose the correct one.*

(a) Both Assertion and Reason are correct and Reason is the correct explanation of Assertion.

(b) Both Assertion and Reason are correct but Reason is not the correct explanation of Assertion.

(c) Assertion is correct but Reason is incorrect.

(d) Assertion is incorrect but Reason is correct.

1. Assertion (A) The centre of mass of exploding projectile will always follow parabolic path.

Reason (R) The sum of internal forces is necessarily zero, which means the centre of mass is unaffected in absence of external forces.

(a) ☐ (b) ☐ (c) ☐ (d) ☐

2. Assertion (A) The position of centre of mass of body depend upon shape and size of the body.

Reason (R) Centre of mass of a body lies always at the centre of the body.

(a) ☐ (b) ☐ (c) ☐ (d) ☐

3. Assertion (A) If no external force acts on a system of particles, then the centre of mass will not move in any direction.

Reason (R) If net external force is zero, then the linear momentum of the system remains constant.

(a) ☐ (b) ☐ (c) ☐ (d) ☐

4. **Assertion** (A) If a particle moves with a constant velocity, then angular momentum of this particle about any point remains constant.

Reason (R) Angular momentum is a vector quantity.

(a) ☐ (b) ☐ (c) ☐ (d) ☐

5. **Assertion** (A) If a particle is rotating in a circle, then angular momentum about centre is mvR.

Reason (R) In circular motion, angular momentum about centre is always constant.

(a) ☐ (b) ☐ (c) ☐ (d) ☐

6. **Assertion** (A) A body is moving along a circle with a constant speed. Its angular momentum about the centre of the circle remains constant.

Reason (R) In this situation, a constant non-zero torque acts on the body.

(a) ☐ (b) ☐ (c) ☐ (d) ☐

7. **Assertion** (A) Moment of inertia of a particle is same, whatever be the axis of rotation.

Reason (R) Moment of inertia depends on mass and distance of the particles.

(a) ☐ (b) ☐ (c) ☐ (d) ☐

8. **Assertion** (A) Unlike mass, moment of inertia is not a fixed quantity.

Reason (R) Moment of inertia depends on distribution of mass about the axis of rotation, the orientation and position of the axis of rotation with respect to the body.

(a) ☐ (b) ☐ (c) ☐ (d) ☐

***9.** **Assertion** (A) A rolling cylinder does not exhibit pure translational motion.

Reason (R) A motion of cylinder is also constrained about an axis in rotational motion.

(a) ☐ (b) ☐ (c) ☐ (d) ☐

***10.** **Assertion** (A) Total kinetic energy of a rolling body is dependent of the radius of gyration and velocity of centre of mass.

Reason (R) Total kinetic energy of a rolling body is equal to sum of its rotational and translational kinetic energy.

(a) ☐ (b) ☐ (c) ☐ (d) ☐

Case Based Questions

1. The centre of mass of a body or a system of body is the point which moves as though all of the mass were concentrated there and all external forces were applied to it. Hence, a point at which the entire mass of the body or system of bodies is supposed to be concentrated is known as the centre of mass.

If a system consists of more than one particle (or bodies) and net external force on the system is zero with centre of mass at rest. Then, the centre of mass will not move along that direction. Even though some particles of the system may move along that direction. Answer the following questions.

(i) Two bodies of masses 1 kg and 2 kg are lying in x-y plane at (–1, 2) and (2, 4), respectively. The co-ordinates of the centre of mass is

(a) $\left(1, \frac{10}{3}\right)$ ☐ (b) (1, 0) ☐ (c) (0, 1) ☐ (d) None of these ☐

(ii) All the particles of a body are situated at a distance R from the origin. The distance of centre of mass of the body from the origin is

(a) $= R$ ☐ (b) $\leq R$ ☐ (c) $> R$ ☐ (d) $\geq R$ ☐

(iii) Two balls of same masses start moving towards each other due to gravitational attraction, if the initial distance between them is L. Then, they meet at a distance of .... from the first ball.

M M F F L

(a) $\frac{L}{2}$ ☐ (b) L ☐

(c) $\frac{L}{3}$ ☐ (d) $\frac{L}{4}$ ☐

(iv) In a system of two identical particles, one particle is at rest and other has acceleration a. What is the acceleration of the centre of mass?

(a) a ☐ (b) $a/2$ ☐ (c) $2a$ ☐ (d) zero ☐

2. Torque is a quantity which measures the capability of a force to rotate a body. Torque due to a force is also known as the moment of a force. Torque is the rotational analogue of force of linear motion. It is defined as the product of the force and the perpendicular distance between the line of action of the force and the axis of rotation. This perpendicular distance is known as the force arm.

O r F θ A $r_\perp$

Torque = Force × Force arm

$\tau = \mathbf{r} \times \mathbf{F}$

$\tau = rF \sin\theta$ (where, θ is the angle between **r** and **F**)

The SI unit of torque is N-m. Its dimensions are $[ML^2T^{-2}]$.

Answer the following questions.

(i) A force of $10(-\hat{\mathbf{k}})$ N acts on the origin of the coordinate system. The torque about the point $(1m, -1m, 0m)$ is

(a) $10(\hat{\mathbf{i}} + \hat{\mathbf{j}})$ N-m ☐ (b) $5(\hat{\mathbf{i}} + \hat{\mathbf{j}})$ N-m ☐

(c) $10(\hat{\mathbf{i}} + \hat{\mathbf{k}})$ N-m ☐ (d) $5(\hat{\mathbf{i}} + \hat{\mathbf{k}})$ N-m ☐

(ii) The dimensions of torque are

(a) $[ML^2T^{-1}]$ ☐ (b) $[ML^2T^{-2}]$ ☐ (c) $[ML^{-2}T^{-2}]$ ☐ (d) $[ML^{-2}T^2]$ ☐

(iii) The value of torque of a force $\mathbf{F} = (\hat{\mathbf{i}} + 2\hat{\mathbf{j}} - 3\hat{\mathbf{k}})$ N about a point O if the position vector of point of application of force about O is $\mathbf{r} = (2\hat{\mathbf{i}} + 3\hat{\mathbf{j}} - 3\hat{\mathbf{k}})$ m is

(a) $(7\hat{\mathbf{i}} + 5\hat{\mathbf{j}} - \hat{\mathbf{k}})$ N-m ☐ (b) $(7\hat{\mathbf{i}} - 5\hat{\mathbf{j}} - \hat{\mathbf{k}})$ N-m ☐

(c) $(7\hat{\mathbf{i}} + 5\hat{\mathbf{j}} + \hat{\mathbf{k}})$ N-m ☐ (d) $(-7\hat{\mathbf{i}} + 5\hat{\mathbf{j}} + \hat{\mathbf{k}})$ N-m ☐

(iv) If a force $\mathbf{F} = (5\hat{\mathbf{i}} - 3\hat{\mathbf{j}} + 8\hat{\mathbf{k}})$ N acts on a point at position vector $\mathbf{r} = (2\hat{\mathbf{i}} + \hat{\mathbf{j}} + \hat{\mathbf{k}})$ m, what is the forque about the origin?

(a) $(-3\hat{\mathbf{i}} + 8\hat{\mathbf{j}} - 13\hat{\mathbf{k}})$Nm ☐ (b) $(11\hat{\mathbf{i}} + 6\hat{\mathbf{j}} - 7\hat{\mathbf{k}})$ Nm ☐

(c) $(7\hat{\mathbf{i}} - 14\hat{\mathbf{j}} + 8\hat{\mathbf{k}})$ Nm ☐ (d) $(7\hat{\mathbf{i}} - 3\hat{\mathbf{j}} - 11\hat{\mathbf{k}})$ Nm ☐

COMPETITION EDGE UP

1. A string is wrapped around the rim of a wheel of moment of inertia 0.40 kg-m^2 and radius 10 cm. The wheel is free to rotate about its axis. Initially the wheel is at rest. The string is now pulled by a force of 40 N. The angular velocity of the wheel after 10 s is x rad/s, where x is

[NCERT Pg. 120, JEE Main 2024]

2. A uniform thin metal plate of mass 10 kg with dimensions is shown. The ratio of x and y-coordinates of centre of mass of plate is n / 9. The value of n is ....

[NCERT Pg. 96, JEE Main 2024]

(0, 2) (1, 2) (2, 2) (3, 2) (1, 1) (0, 0) (3, 0)

3. The identical spheres each of mass 2m are placed at the corners of a right angled triangle with mutually perpendicular sides equal to 4 m each. Taking point of intersection of these two sides as origin, the magnitude of position vector of the centre of mass of the system is $\frac{4\sqrt{2}}{x}$, where the value of x is ....

[NCERT Pg. 96, JEE Main 2024]

4. A body of mass 5 kg moving with a uniform speed $3\sqrt{2}$ ms^{-1} in XY-plane along the line $y = x - 4$. The angular momentum of the particle about the origin will be .... kg m^2 s^{-1}. **[NCERT Pg. 106, JEE Main 2024]**

5. The moment of inertia of a thin rod about an axis passing through its mid-point and perpendicular to the rod is 2400 g cm^2. The length of the 400 g rod is nearly

[NCERT Pg. 116, NEET 2024]

(a) 8.5 cm ☐ (b) 17.5 cm ☐
(c) 20.7 cm ☐ (d) 72.0 cm ☐

6. The square of ratio of radius of gyration of a solid sphere of mass M and radius R about its own axis to the radius of gyration of the thin hollow sphere of same mass and radius about its axis is

[NCERT Pg. 115, NEET 2023]

(a) 5 : 3 ☐ (b) 2 : 5 ☐
(c) 5 : 2 ☐ (d) 3 : 5 ☐

7. Two objects of mass 10 kg and 20 kg respectively, are connected to the two ends of a rigid rod of length 10 m with negligible mass. The distance of the centre of mass of the system from the 10 kg mass is

[NCERT Pg. 97, NEET 2022]

(a) $\frac{20}{3}$ m ☐ (b) 10 m ☐
(c) 5 m ☐ (d) $\frac{10}{3}$ m ☐

8. The angular speed of a fly wheel moving with uniform angular acceleration changes from 1200 rpm to 3120 rpm in 16 seconds. The angular acceleration in rad/s^2 is

[NCERT Pg. 117, NEET 2022]

(a) 4π ☐ (b) 12π ☐
(c) 104π ☐ (d) 2π ☐

9. From a circular ring of mass M and radius R, an arc corresponding to a 90° sector is removed. The moment of inertia of the remaining part of the ring about an axis passing through the centre of the ring and perpendicular to the plane of the ring is K times MR^2. Then, the value of K is

[NCERT Pg. 114, NEET 2021]

(a) $\frac{3}{4}$ ☐ (b) $\frac{7}{8}$ ☐
(c) $\frac{1}{4}$ ☐ (d) $\frac{1}{8}$ ☐

10. The angular speed of the wheel of a vehicle is increased from 360 rpm to 1200 rpm in 14 s. Its angular acceleration is

[NCERT Pg. 117, NEET (Oct.)2020]

(a) 2π rad/s^2 ☐
(b) 28π rad/s^2 ☐
(c) 120π rad/s^2 ☐
(d) 1 rad/s^2 ☐

11. Two particles of mass 5 kg and 10 kg respectively, are attached to the two ends of a rigid rod of length 1 m with negligible mass.
The centre of mass of the system from the 5 kg particle is nearly at a distance of

[NCERT Pg. 97, NEET (Sep.) 2020]

(a) 50 cm ☐ (b) 67 cm ☐
(c) 80 cm ☐ (d) 33 cm ☐

Chapter 07

Gravitation

1. Study the diagram and mark aphelion and perihelion points for the planet.

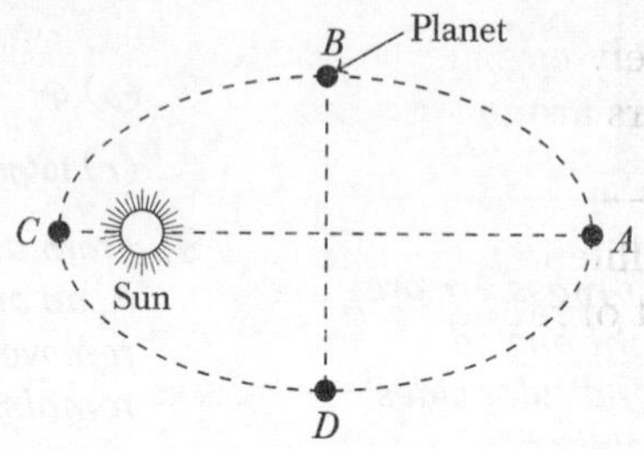

2. For a planet, its perihelion distance from its star is 0.3 AU. If the major axis of this planet is 27 AU, then the distance of aphelion is ________

3. A planet is revolving around the sun. What will the relation for speeds v_A, v_B and v_C for the given figure?

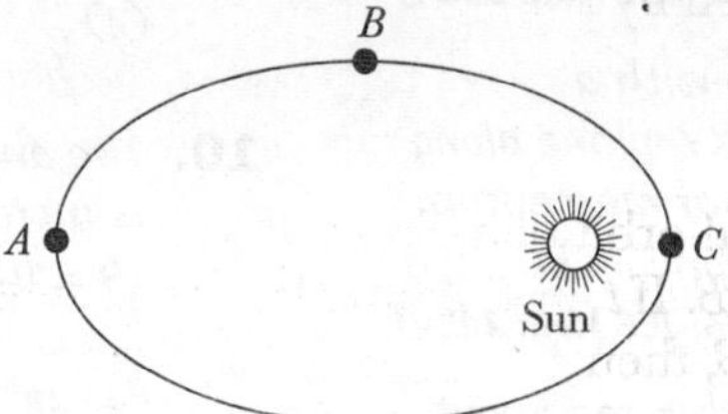

(a) $v_A > v_B > v_C$ ☐ (b) $v_A < v_B < v_C$ ☐

(c) $v_A = v_B = v_C$ ☐ (d) $v_A < v_B > v_C$ ☐

4. The maximum and minimum velocities of a planet are 3×10^4 ms^{-1} and 1×10^3 ms^{-1}, respectively. If its maximum distance from sun is 4×10^4 km, then calculate the minimum distance of planet from sun.

5. Let area swept by the line joining mars and the sun during month of January be A. The area swept by the same line during second week of that month is ________ $\left(\frac{9A}{31}/\frac{7A}{31}\right)$.

*Concepts of all questions bearing * are important for JEE/NEET/CUET.*

6. Mercury, venus and saturn revolve around the sun in time t_m, t_v and t_s, respectively. Which of the following is correct increasing order of time period?

(a) $t_m < t_s < t_v$ ☐ (b) $t_s < t_m < t_v$ ☐ (c) $t_m < t_v < t_s$ ☐ (d) $t_s < t_v < t_m$ ☐

7. If the radius of earth's orbit is made (1/4)th, then duration of an year will become

(a) 8 times ☐ (b) 4 times ☐

(c) (1/8) times ☐ (d) (1/4) tim s ☐

8. A binary star system of two stars A and B having time p riod T_A and T_B respectively, revolve around each other. If radii and masses are R_A, R . and M_A, M_B respectively, is given for both stars, so

(a) $T_A > T_B$, then $R_A > R_B$ ☐ (b) $T_A > T_B$, then $M_A > M_B$ ☐

(c) $\left(\frac{T_A}{T_B}\right) = \left(\frac{R_A}{R_B}\right)^3$ ☐ (d) $T_A = T_B$ ☐

9. If the distance between earth and sun is reduced to half, then number of days in a year would become ________ .

10. Mars orbit is approximately circular with radius 1.52 AU. What will be time period (in days) of revolution of mars around the sun?

____

11. The time period of a satellite in a circular orbit of radius R is T. The period of another satellite in a circular orbit of radius $9R$ is $27T$.

True ☐ False ☐

12. What will be the area enclosed by earth's orbit, if ratio of earth's orbital angular momentum to its mass is 4.4×10^{15} m^2/s?

____

13. If the areal velocity of a planet is v and position vector from the sun is **r**, then area swept by the planet in Δt is given by $\Delta A = \frac{1}{2}(\mathbf{r} \times \mathbf{v}\, \Delta t)$.

Yes ☐ No ☐

14. The figure shows elliptical orbit of a planet m about the sun S. The shaded area SCD is twice the shaded area SAB. If t_1 is the time for the planet to move from C to D and t_2 is the time to move from A to B, then ________ ($t_1 = 4t_2/t_1 = 2t_2$).

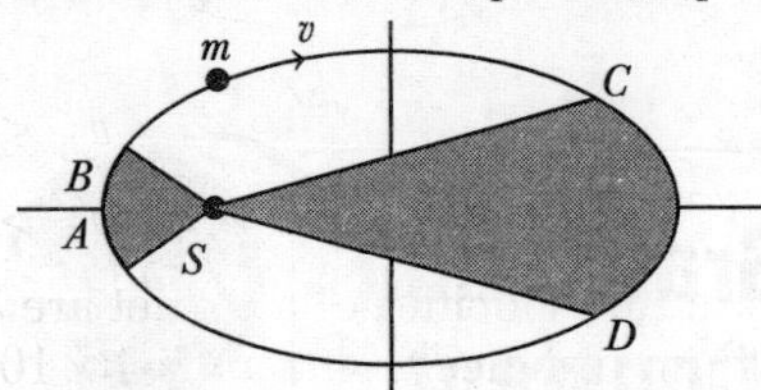

15. A planet revolving in elliptical orbit has

I. a constant velocity of revolution.

II. the least velocity when it is nearest to the sun.

III. its areal velocity is directly proportional to its velocity.

IV. areal velocity is inversely proportional to its velocity.

V. to follow a trajectory, such that the areal velocity is constant.

Choose the correct answer from the options given below.

(a) Only I ☐ (b) Only IV ☐

(c) Only III ☐ (d) Only V ☐

***16.** For a planet given in figure at location P, the distance and velocity is given by r_P and v_P, and at A velocity is given by r_A and v_A, respectively.

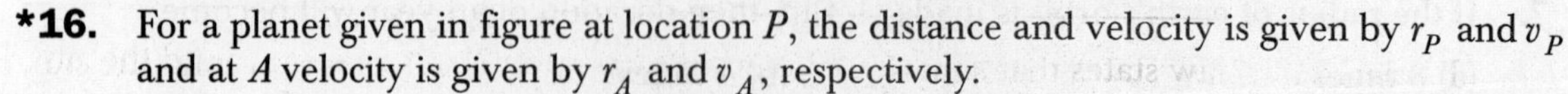

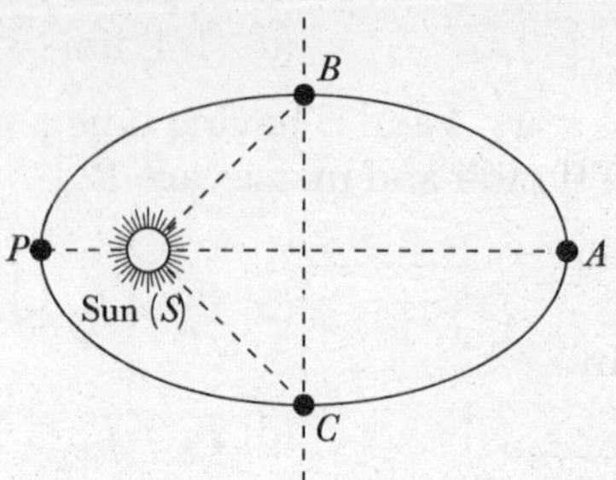

The time taken to sweep area BAC is equal to the time taken to sweep area CPB.

True ☐ False ☐

17. If mass of a planet is 2% of mass of earth. The ratio of gravitational pull of earth on the planet and that of planet on the earth will be same.

True ☐ False ☐

18. The kinetic energies of a planet in an elliptical orbit about the sun at positions A, B and C are K_A, K_B and K_C, respectively. AC is the major axis and SB is perpendicular to AC at the position of the sun S as shown in the figure, then

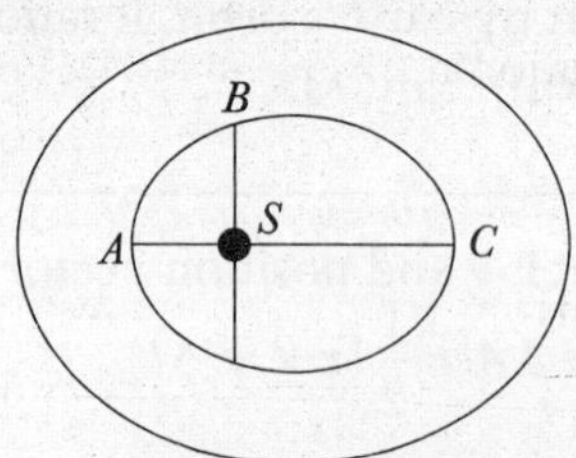

(a) $K_B < K_A < K_C$ ☐ (b) $K_A > K_B > K_C$ ☐

(c) $K_A < K_B < K_C$ ☐ (d) $K_B > K_A > K_C$ ☐

TOPIC 2

Universal Law of Gravitation and Gravitational Constant

19. A particle follows Kepler's law of planetary motion. If the semi-major axis is given by R and central force is inversely proportional to R^n, then the period of revolution will be

(a) $T \propto R^{\frac{n+1}{2}}$ ☐ (b) $T^2 \propto R^3$ ☐

(c) $T \propto R^{-\frac{n}{2}}$ ☐ (d) $T \propto R$ ☐

20. A certain mass point revolves around a heavier mass in circular orbit of radius R with time period of revolution T. If central force is inversely proportional to R^6, then time period is proportional to R^n. Find the value of n.

____

21. Kepler's third law states that square of period of revolution T of a planet around the sun, is proportional to third power of average distance r between the sun and planet, i.e. $T^2 = kr^3$, here k is constant.

If the masses of the sun and planet are M and m respectively, then as per Newton's law of gravitation force of attraction between them is $F = \frac{GMm}{r^2}$, here G is gravitational constant.

The relation between G and k is described as

____

22. Two spherical bodies of mass 1 kg and 5 kg and radii 2 m and 4 m are released in free space with initial separation between their centres equal to 24 m. If they attract each other due to gravitational force only, then distance covered by smaller body before collision is __________ m.

23. A rocket is fired from the earth towards the sun. At what distance from earth's centre, the gravitational force on rocket is zero?

(Take, $M_s = 2 \times 10^{30}$ kg, $M_e = 6.0 \times 10^{24}$ kg and orbital radius $= 1.5 \times 10^{11}$ m)

____

24. Three uniform point masses of mass m each are placed on the vertices of an equilateral triangle of side l. The gravitational force on one point mass due to other two is $\frac{\sqrt{3}Gm^2}{l^2}$.

Yes ☐ No ☐

25. For which of the following arrangements, gravitational force at m is maximum?

I. M ← r → $2M$ ← r → m

II. Right triangle with M at top, m at the right angle, $64M$ at the other vertex; sides $6r$ and $8r$

III.

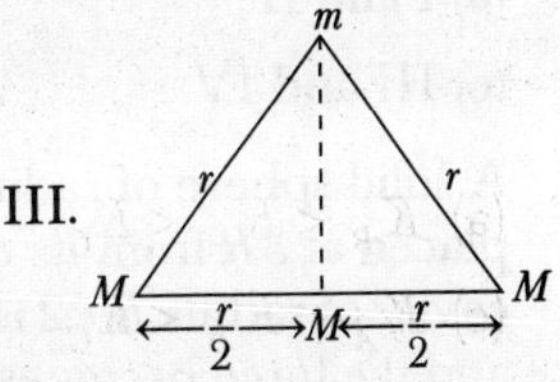

____

26. What will be the speed of individual particle, if all the particles move in the circular path under their mutual gravitational force of attraction as shown below?

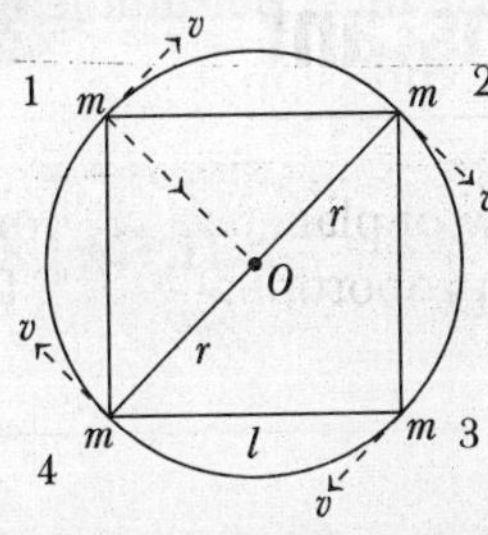

____

27. The force of attraction due to a hollow spherical shell of uniform density and a point mass situated outside is just as if the entire mass of the shell is concentrated at the centre of the shell.

True ☐ False ☐

28. The magnitude of force of attraction due to a hollow spherical shell of uniform density on a point mass situated inside it is zero?

Yes ☐ No ☐

29. Find the gravitational force of attraction between the ring and sphere as shown in the figure, where the plane of the ring is perpendicular to the line joining the centres. If $\sqrt{8}\ R$ is the distance between the centres of a ring (of mass m) and a sphere (of mass M), where both have equal radius R.

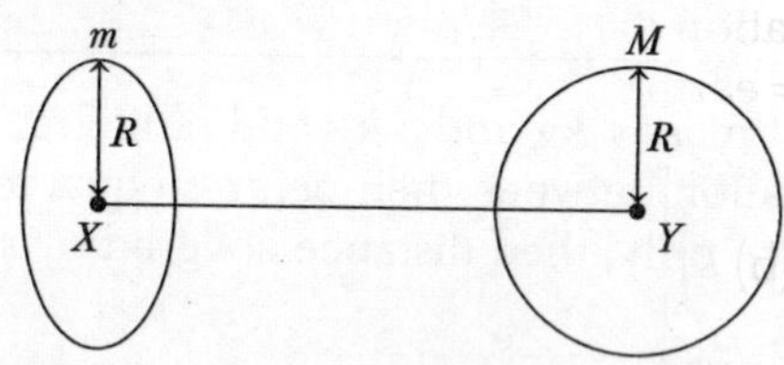

30. The magnitudes of gravitational field at distance r_1 and r_2 from the centre of a uniform sphere of radius R and mass M are F_1 and F_2, respectively.

I. $\frac{F_1}{F_2} = \frac{r_1}{r_2}$, if $r_1 < R$ and $r_2 < R$.

II. $\frac{F_1}{F_2} = \frac{r_2^2}{r_1^2}$, if $r_1 > R$ and $r_2 > R$.

III. $\frac{F_1}{F_2} = \frac{r_1}{r_2}$, if $r_1 > R$ and $r_2 > R$.

IV. $\frac{F_1}{F_2} = \frac{r_1^2}{r_2^2}$, if $r_1 < R$ and $r_2 > R$.

Which of the above statements are correct?

(a) I and II ☐ (b) II and III ☐

(c) III and IV ☐ (d) I and IV ☐

31. A solid sphere of radius R gravitationally attracts a particle placed at $3R$ from its centre with a force F_1. Now, a spherical cavity of radius $R/2$ is made in the sphere (as shown in figure) and the force becomes F_2. The value of $F_1 : F_2$ is

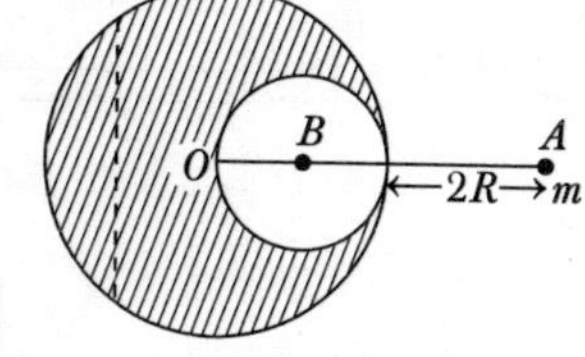

(a) 25 : 36 ☐ (b) 36 : 25 ☐

(c) 50 : 41 ☐ (d) 41 : 50 ☐

32. A straight rod of length L extends from $x = a$ to $x = L + a$. The gravitational force, it exerts on a point mass m at $x = 0$, if the mass per unit length of the rod is $A + Bx^2$ given by one of the following. Choose that expression.

I. $Gm\left[A\left(\frac{1}{a} - \frac{1}{a+L}\right) + BL\right]$

II. $Gm\left[A\left(\frac{1}{a} - \frac{1}{a+L}\right) - BL\right]$

TOPIC 3

Acceleration Due to Gravity and Gravitational Potential Energy

33. The value of acceleration due to gravity at earth's surface is 9.8 ms^{-2}. At $x \times 10^6$ m above surface of earth, the value of g becomes 4.9 ms^{-2}. Then, x will be ______.

34. A rock weighs 200 kg on the surface of earth. Its weight at half-way down to the centre of the earth will be ______ (1000 N/400 N).

35. The variation of acceleration due to gravity g with distance d from the centre of earth is best represented by (R = earth's radius)

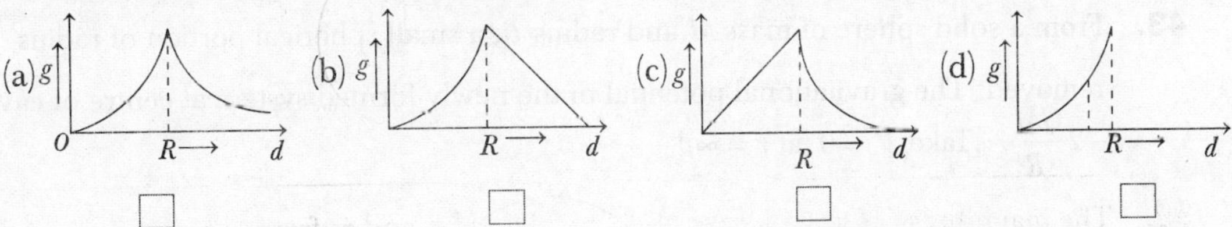

36. The acceleration due to gravity at height 1 km above the earth is same as at a depth x km below the surface of earth. What will be the value of x?

______

37. The weight of a body on the surface of earth is 40 kg. The gravitational force on it due to the earth at a height equal to the half of radius of earth is 30 kg-wt.

Yes ☐ No ☐

38. As we move away from the centre of the solid sphere,

(a) gravitational potential energy decreases ☐

(b) gravitational force decreases ☐

(c) acceleration due to gravity decreases ☐

(d) All of the above ☐

39. What will be mean distance between the earth and moon, if gravitational potential energy of the system is -7.79×10^{28} J?

(Take, $G = 6.67 \times 10^{-11}$ N-m^2 kg^{-2}, $M_e = 6 \times 10^{24}$ kg, $M_m = 7.4 \times 10^{22}$ kg)

______

40. At what height from the surface of earth, the gravitational and potential and the value of g are -5.4×10^7 J kg^{-2} and 6.0 ms^{-2}, respectively? (Take, the radius of earth as 6400 km.)

______

41. Infinite number of bodies, each of mass 2 kg are situated on X-axis at distances 1 m, 2 m, 4 m and 8 m respectively, from the origin. The resulting gravitational potential due to this system at the origin will be

(a) $-G$ ☐ (b) $-\frac{8}{3}G$ ☐

(c) $-\frac{4}{3}G$ ☐ (d) $-4G$ ☐

42. A particle of mass M is situated at the centre of a spherical shell of same mass and radius a. The gravitational potential at a point situated at $a/2$ distance from the centre will be $-x\frac{GM}{a}$. Find the value of x.

---

43. From a solid sphere of mass M and radius R, a small spherical portion of radius $\frac{R}{2}$ is removed. The gravitational potential of the newly formed system at centre of cavity is $-2\frac{GM}{R}$. [Take, $V = 0$ (at $r = \infty$)]

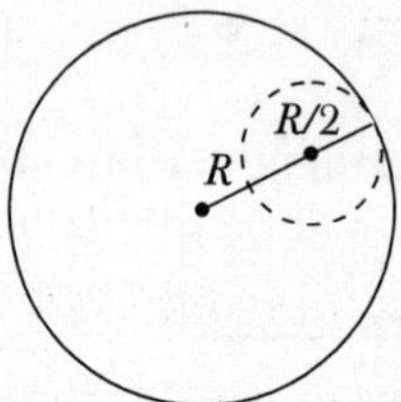

Yes ☐ No ☐

44. At a specific height, the gravitational potential and acceleration due to gravity are -9.4×10^7 J kg^{-2} and 4.0 ms^{-2}, respectively. The height will be __________ km.

45. Two point masses m_1 and m_2 are separated by a distance 6 m and gravitational potential energy of the system is U_1. The new distance of separation is 12 m, if m_2 is moved away from m_1 and in this case, gravitational potential becomes U_2.

The ratio $\frac{U_1}{U_2}$ is $\frac{1}{x}$. Find the value of x.

---

46. For the given arrangement in figure shown below, gravitational potential energy at centre O is

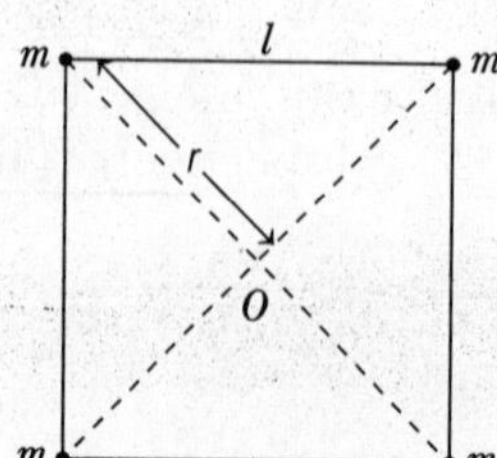

(a) $-4\sqrt{2}\dfrac{Gm}{l}$ ☐ (b) $4\sqrt{2}\dfrac{Gm}{l^2}$ ☐

(c) $-2\sqrt{2}\dfrac{Gm^2}{l}$ ☐ (d) $-2\sqrt{2}\dfrac{Gm}{l}$ ☐

47. The gravitation field in a region is given by $\mathbf{E} = (5\hat{\mathbf{i}} + 12\hat{\mathbf{j}})$ N/kg. What will be the change in potential energy of a mass of 2 kg when it is moved from point (0, 0) to (12, 5) ?

____

48. Match the following arrangements of masses in given Column I with their corresponding expression of gravitational potential at point in Column II.

Column I	Column II
A. M• ——— •P (distance r)	1. $-\dfrac{3GM}{2R}$
B. Sphere of mass M, radius R, point P at distance r from centre O	2. $-\dfrac{GM}{r}$
C. Ring of radius R, centre O, point P on axis at distance r	3. $-\dfrac{GM}{\sqrt{R^2 + r^2}}$

A. __________ B. __________ C. __________

49. Assuming that the gravitational potential energy of an object at infinity is zero, the change in potential energy of an object of mass m when taken to a height h from the surface of earth (of radius R and mass M) is given by ________.

50. A body of mass $2M$ splits into four masses (m, $M - m$, m, $M - m$), which are rearranged to form a square as shown in the figure. The ratio of $\dfrac{M}{m}$ for which the gravitational potential energy of the system becomes maximum is $x : 1$. Find the value of x.

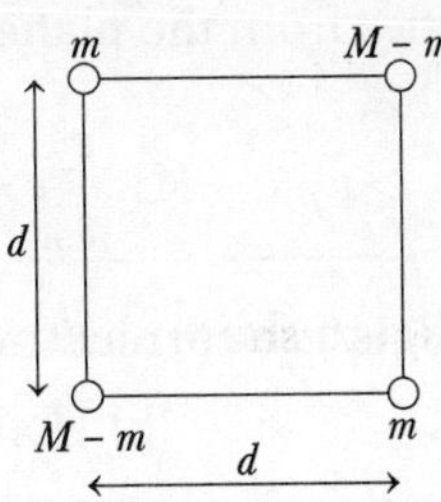

____

TOPIC 4 Escape Speed

NCERT Pg 135-137

51. A body is projected vertically upwards from the surface of earth with a velocity sufficient enough to carry it to infinity. The time taken by it to reach height h is

(a) $\sqrt{\frac{R_e}{2g}}\left[\left(1+\frac{h}{R_e}\right)^{3/2}-1\right]$ s ☐ (b) $\sqrt{\frac{2R_e}{g}}\left[\left(1+\frac{h}{R_e}\right)^{3/2}-1\right]$ s ☐

(c) $\frac{1}{3}\sqrt{\frac{R_e}{2g}}\left[\left(1+\frac{h}{R_e}\right)^{3/2}-1\right]$ s ☐ (d) $\frac{1}{3}\sqrt{\frac{2R_e}{g}}\left[\left(1+\frac{h}{R_e}\right)^{3/2}-1\right]$ s ☐

***52.** Three spheres each of radius R have masses m_A, m_B and m_C, such that $m_A > m_B > m_C$. The relation for the escape speed for these three masses will be ________ .

53. If radius of the earth is reduced keeping the mass constant, then escape velocity will ________ (increase/decrease/remain same) .

54. The ratio of masses of sun and earth is 3×10^5 and the ratio of radii of sun and earth is 108. The ratio of escape velocities on the surface of sun and earth is ________ .

55. Tick (✓/✗) for correct/incorrect statement in given boxes.

(i) Escape velocity is the independent of the mass of the object. ☐

(ii) If velocity v is greater than escape velocity v_e $(v > v_e)$, then the object will move in inter-planetary distance. ☐

(iii) For a planet having an atmosphere, the escape velocity v_e should be lesser than v_{rms}. ☐

(iv) A particle is fired with velocity v_0 in upward direction, then $\sqrt{v^2 - gR_e^2}$ will be its velocity at distance of $2R_e$ from centre of earth. ☐

56. Two spherical planets P and Q have the same density ρ, masses M_P and M_Q and surface area A and $4A$, respectively. A spherical planet R also has same density and having mass $(M_P + M_Q)$. The escape velocities from the planets P, Q and R are v_P, v_Q and v_R, respectively. Then,

I. $v_Q > v_R > v_P$ II. $v_R > v_Q > v_P$ III. $\frac{v_R}{v_P} = 3$ IV. $\frac{v_P}{v_Q} = \frac{1}{2}$

Which of the above statement(s) is/are correct?

(a) I and II ☐ (b) II and III ☐

(c) II and IV ☐ (d) I and IV ☐

***57.** The value of gravitational acceleration at a planet is $\frac{\sqrt{6}}{11}g$. The average mass density of the planet is $\frac{1}{3}$ times that of the earth. If the escape speed on the surface of the earth is taken to be 11 kms^{-1}, the escape speed on this planet will be approximately________ km/s.

58. Suppose two planets (spherical in shape) of radii R and $2R$ but masses M and $9M$ respectively have a centre-to-centre separation $8R$ as shown in the figure.

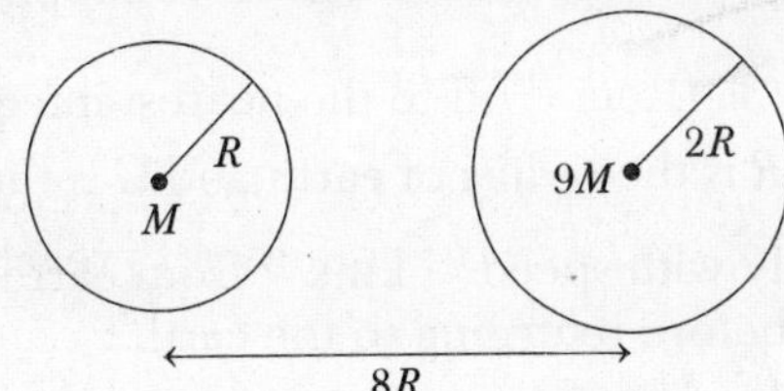

A satellite of mass m is projected from the surface of the planet of mass M directly towards the centre of the second planet. The minimum speed v required for the satellite to reach the surface of the second planet is $\sqrt{\frac{a}{7}\frac{GM}{R}}$, then the value of a is

[Take, the two planets are fixed in their position]

____

***59.** The escape velocity from the earth's surface is v. The escape velocity from the surface of another planet having a radius four times that of earth and same mass density is ______ $(4v/2v)$.

60. The ratio of escape velocity at earth v_e to the escape velocity at a planet v_p, whose radius and mean density are twice as that of earth is $1 : 2\sqrt{2}$.

True ☐ False ☐

61. A black hole is an object whose gravitational field is so strong that even light cannot escape from it. To what approximate radius would earth (mass $= 5.98 \times 10^{24}$ kg) have to be compressed to be a black hole?

____

62. The radius (in km) to which the present radius of earth ($R = 6400$ km) to be compressed, so that the escape velocity is increased 10 times, is 64.

True ☐ False ☐

63. Two solid spheres of radius R and masses M and $4M$ are separated by $6R$ distance apart. A projectile of mass m is launched from surface of sphere having M. The minimum speed v for which projectile reaches the surface of second sphere will be $\sqrt{\frac{8}{5}\frac{GM}{R}}$.

True ☐ False ☐

64. The earth is assumed to be a sphere of radius R. A platform is arranged at a height R from the surface of the earth. The escape velocity of a body from this platform is fv_e, where v_e is its escape velocity from the surface of the earth. Find the value of f.

____

65. The initial velocity v_i required to project a body vertically upward from the surface of the earth to reach a height of $10R$, where R is the radius of the earth may be described in terms of escape velocity v_e, such that $v_i = \sqrt{\frac{x}{y}} \times v_e$. The value of x will be ______.

66. If one wants to remove all the mass of the earth to infinity in order to break it up completely. The amount of energy that needs to be supplied will be $\frac{x}{5}\frac{GM^2}{R}$, where x is __________ (6/3). (Round off to the nearest integer)
(M is the mass of earth, R is the radius of earth and G is the gravitational constant)

67. A rocket is fired vertically with speed 5 kms^{-1} from earth surface. The rocket will travel __________ m distance before returning to the earth.

68. A particle is projected vertically upwards from the earth's surface with kinetic energy equal to half of the minimum value needed for it to escape.
What is the ratio of height to which it rises above the surface of earth and radius of earth?

____

69. A particle of mass m is projected with a velocity $v = kv_e (k < 1)$ from the surface of the earth, where v_e = escape velocity. The maximum height above the surface reached by the particle is

(a) $R\left(\frac{k}{1-k}\right)^2$ ☐ (b) $R\left(\frac{k}{1+k}\right)^2$ ☐

(c) $\frac{R^2 k}{1+k}$ ☐ (d) $\frac{Rk^2}{1-k^2}$ ☐

TOPIC 5

Earth Satellites & Energy of an Orbiting Satellite

NCERT Pg 137-139

***70.** Two satellites A and B have masses m and $2m$, respectively. If ratio of their orbital radii is $\frac{1}{2}$, then ratio of their time periods will be __________.

71. A satellite of mass 1000 kg is supported in an orbit around the earth at 2×10^6 m above the earth's surface. The orbital speed is

(a) 6.9×10^3 m/s ☐ (b) 7.2×10^3 m/s ☐

(c) 8×10^3 m/s ☐ (d) 10×10^3 m/s ☐

72. An artificial satellite maintaining its speed exactly half of the escape velocity is at the height of 7600 km.

True ☐ False ☐

73. The mass density of a spherical galaxy varies as $\frac{k}{r}$ over a large distance r from its centre. In that region, a small star is in a circular orbit of radius R. Then, the period of revolution T depends on R as

(a) $T \propto R$ ☐ (b) $T^2 \propto R^3$ ☐

(c) $T^2 \propto R$ ☐ (d) $T^2 \propto \frac{1}{R^3}$ ☐

74. Calculate the energy supplied by thrower to throw the mass 9000 kg into an orbit of 400 km above earth surface.

____

75. The ratio of total energy to the potential energy of satellite in an orbit is $\frac{3}{4}$.

True ☐ False ☐

76. A satellite is transferred from an orbit of radius $2R_e$ to $4R_e$. If the mass of the satellite is 400 kg, then the energy required for this transfer is ________ J.

77. Two satellites of the earth S_1 and S_2 are moving in the same orbit. The mass of S_1 is four times the mass of S_2, then tick (✓/✗) on correct/incorrect statement in given boxes.

(i) The time period of S_1 is four times that of S_2. ☐

(ii) The potential energies of the earth and satellite in the two cases are equal. ☐

(iii) S_1 and S_2 are moving with the same speed. ☐

(iv) The kinetic energies of the two satellites are equal. ☐

78. The satellite of mass m is orbiting around the earth in a circular orbit with a velocity v and its total energy will be mv^2.

Yes ☐ No ☐

79. A satellite is moving in a low nearly circular orbit around the earth. Its radius is roughly equal to that of the earth's radius R_e. By firing rockets attached to it, its speed is instantaneously increased in the direction of its motion, so that it becomes $\sqrt{\frac{3}{2}}$ times larger.

Due to this, the farthest distance from the centre of the earth that the satellite reaches is R. What is the value of R?

____

Assertion-Reason Questions

Direction (Q. Nos. 1-10) *In the following questions, a statement of Assertion is followed by a corresponding statement of Reason. From the following options, choose the correct one.*

(a) Both Assertion and Reason are correct and Reason is the correct explanation of Assertion.
(b) Both Assertion and Reason are correct but Reason is not the correct explanation of Assertion.
(c) Assertion is correct but Reason is incorrect.
(d) Assertion is incorrect but Reason is correct.

1. **Assertion** (A) Areal velocity of a planet around sun will become two times if mass of planet is halved.

Reason (R) Areal velocity $= \frac{L}{2m}$. Where L is angular momentum of planet about centre of sun.

(a) ☐ (b) ☐ (c) ☐ (d) ☐

2. **Assertion** (A) A planet having longer distance from the sun takes longer time to revolve around it.

Reason (R) The acceleration due to earth's gravity is given by $a = \frac{4\pi^2 R}{T^2}$.

(a) ☐ (b) ☐ (c) ☐ (d) ☐

3. **Assertion** (A) Angular momentum of a planet is constant about any point.

Reason (R) Force acting on the planet is a central force.

(a) ☐ (b) ☐ (c) ☐ (d) ☐

4. **Assertion** (A) Four point masses each of mass m are placed at points 1, 2, 3 and 6 of a regular hexagon of side a. Then, the gravitational field at the centre of hexagon is $\frac{Gm}{a^2}$.

5 4
6 3
1 2

Reason (R) The field strength due to masses at 3 and 6 are cancelled out.

(a) ☐ (b) ☐ (c) ☐ (d) ☐

5. **Assertion** (A) The force of attraction between a hollow spherical shell of uniform density and a point mass situated outside is just as if the entire mass of the shell is concentrated at the centre of the shell.

Reason (R) Gravitational force caused by various regions of the shell have components along the line joining the point mass to the centre as well as along a direction perpendicular to this line.

(a) ☐ (b) ☐ (c) ☐ (d) ☐

6. **Assertion** (A) The principle of superposition is not valid for gravitational forces.

Reason (R) Gravitational force is a central force.

(a) ☐ (b) ☐ (c) ☐ (d) ☐

7. **Assertion** (A) An object can have different potential energy depending on its location.

Reason (R) Gravitational potential energy is dependent on the reference point. It is taken zero at infinity.

(a) ☐ (b) ☐ (c) ☐ (d) ☐

8. **Assertion** (A) There is no atmosphere on the surface of moon.

Reason (R) The escape velocity of moon's surface is greater than root mean square velocity of the gas molecules..

(a) ☐ (b) ☐ (c) ☐ (d) ☐

9. **Assertion** (A) When an artificial satellite moves around the earth in a circular orbit with a constant speed, its velocity is not constant because the direction of motion of the satellite is changing continuously.

Reason (R) The force of gravity of earth keeps the satellite in circular orbit around it.

(a) ☐ (b) ☐ (c) ☐ (d) ☐

10. **Assertion** (A) Let W_1 be the work done in taking away a satellite from the surface of earth to its orbit and then W_2 the work done in rotating the satellite in circular orbit there. Then, $W_1 = W_2$

Reason (R) $W_2 = \frac{GMm}{4R}$

(a) ☐ (b) ☐ (c) ☐ (d) ☐

Case Based Questions

1. We know that the earth attracts every object with a certain force and this force depends on the mass (m) of the object and the acceleration due to the gravity (g). The weight of an object is the force with which it is attracted towards the earth. Mathematically where, w = weight of object, m = mass of object
and g = acceleration due to the gravitational force
As the weight of an object is the force with which it is attracted towards the earth, the SI unit of weight is the same as that of force, i.e. newton (N). The weight is a force acting vertically downwards, it has both magnitude and direction. The value of g is constant at a given place. Therefore, the weight of an object is directly proportional to the mass say m, of the object. Weight of an object varies when its position changes with respect to earth's surface.

(i) Dimensions of acceleration due to gravity are

(a) $[ML^1T^{-2}]$ ☐ (b) $[ML^{-1}T^{-2}]$ ☐

(c) $[ML^1T^{-3}]$ ☐ (d) None of these ☐

(ii) The weight of an object on earth with a mass of 25 kg is ....
(Given, $g = 9.8 \text{ m/s}^2$)

(a) 290 N ☐ (b) 245 N ☐

(c) 280 N ☐ (d) 275 N ☐

(iii) The weight of a body on moon is 500 N, then it's mass is ....
(Given, $g = 1.62 \text{ m/s}^2$)

(a) 3086.4 kg ☐ (b) 30.864 kg ☐

(c) 308.64 kg ☐ (d) 3.0864 kg ☐

(iv) Weight of a body at height $3R$ from the surface of earth will be [Take, weight of object on the surface of earth = w]

(a) $\frac{w}{8}$ ☐ (b) $\frac{w}{16}$ ☐ (c) $\frac{w}{4}$ ☐ (d) $\frac{w}{2}$ ☐

Or

Weight of a body increases

(a) on going above the earth's surface ☐

(b) on going below the earth's surface ☐

(c) on going from equator to pole ☐

(d) All of the above ☐

2. The gravitational potential energy of two particles of masses m_1 and m_2 separated by a distance r is given by

m_1 •-------- r --------• m_2

$$U = -\frac{Gm_1 m_2}{r}$$

This is actually the negative of work done in bringing these masses from infinity to a distance r, by the gravitational forces between them.

$$\text{Gravitational potential energy} = \left(-\frac{Gm_1}{r}\right) \times m_2$$

∴ Gravitational potential energy = Gravitational potential × Mass of the body

Gravitational potential energy is a scalar quantity. Its SI unit is joule.

Answer the following questions.

(i) Three particles of masses m, $2m$ and $4m$ are placed at the corner of an equilateral triangle of side a, then the potential energy of the system is

(a) $\frac{-14Gm^2}{a}$ ☐ (b) $\frac{-7Gm^2}{a}$ ☐

(c) $\frac{+14Gm^2}{a}$ ☐ (d) $\frac{+7Gm^2}{a}$ ☐

(ii) The resulting gravitational potential due to the system of infinite number of bodies, each of mass 2 kg are situated on X-axis at distance m, $2m$, $4m$ and $8m$ respectively, from the origin is

(a) $-4G$ ☐ (b) $4G$ ☐

(c) $8G$ ☐ (d) $16G$ ☐

(iii) Dimensions of gravitational potential energy are

(a) $[ML^{-2}T^{-2}]$ ☐ (b) $[ML^2T^{-2}]$ ☐

(c) $[ML^1T^{-1}]$ ☐ (d) $[ML^{-2}T^2]$ ☐

(iv) The gravitational potential energy is actually the negative of

(a) Work done in bringing the masses together from infinity. ☐

(b) Kinetic energy of the masses. ☐

(c) The force between the masses ☐

(d) The energy of infinity potential ☐

Or

The gravitational potential energy of a system of particles is maximum when

(a) the distance between the particle is zero. ☐

(b) the distance between the particles is infinite ☐

(c) the masses are zero ☐

(d) the gravitational constant is zero ☐

COMPETITION EDGE UP

1. An astronaut takes a ball of mass m from earth to space. He throws the ball into a circular orbit about earth at an altitude of 318.5 km. From earth's surface to the orbit, the change in total mechanical energy of the ball is $x\frac{GM_e m}{21R_e}$. The value of x is (Take, $R_e = 6370$ km)

[NCERT Pg. 134, JEE Main 2024]

(a) 9 ☐ (b) 11 ☐

(c) 10 ☐ (d) 12 ☐

2. Two satellite A and B go round a planet in circular orbits having radii 4R and R respectively. If the speed of A is 3v, the speed of B will be

[NCERT Pg. 136, JEE Main 2024]

(a) 12v ☐ (b) 3v ☐

(c) 6v ☐ (d) $\frac{4}{3}$v ☐

3. Assuming the earth to be a sphere of uniform mass density, a body weighed 300 N on the surface of earth. How much it would weight at R/4 depth under surface of earth ? **[NCERT Pg. 134, JEE Main 2024]**

(a) 225 N ☐ (b) 375 N ☐

(c) 300 N ☐ (d) 75 N ☐

4. To project a body of mass m from earth's surface to infinity, the required kinetic energy is (assume, the radius of earth is R_E, g = acceleration due to gravity on the surface of earth)

[NCERT Pg. 135, JEE Main 2024]

(a) $\frac{1}{2}mgR_E$ ☐ (b) mgR_E ☐

(c) $4mgR_E$ ☐ (d) $2mgR_E$ ☐

5. A satellite revolving around a planet in stationary orbit has time period 6 h. The mass of planet is one-fourth the mass of earth. The radius of orbit planet is (Given, radius of geostationary orbit for earth is 4.2×10^4 km) **[NCERT Pg. 137, JEE Main 2024]**

(a) 8.4×10^4 km ☐

(b) 1.4×10^4 km ☐

(c) 1.68×10^5 km ☐

(d) 1.05×10^4 km ☐

6. The mass of a planet is 1/10 th that of the earth and its diameter is half that of the earth. The acceleration due to gravity on that planet is **[NCERT Pg. 133, JEE Main 2024]**

(a) 19.6 ms^{-2} ☐

(b) 9.8 ms^{-2} ☐

(c) 4.9 ms^{-2} ☐

(d) 3.92 ms^{-2} ☐

7. Two bodies of mass m and 9m are placed at a distance R. The gravitational potential on the line joining the bodies where the gravitational field equals zero, will be (G = gravitational constant)

[NCERT Pg. 135, NEET 2023]

(a) $-\frac{12\ Gm}{R}$ ☐ (b) $-\frac{16\ Gm}{R}$ ☐

(c) $-\frac{20\ Gm}{R}$ ☐ (d) $-\frac{8\ Gm}{R}$ ☐

8. A body of mass 60 g experiences a gravitational force of 3.0 N, when placed at a particular point. The magnitude of the gravitational field intensity at that point is

[NCERT Pg. 133, NEET 2022]

(a) 50 N/kg ☐ (b) 20 N/kg ☐

(c) 180 N/kg ☐ (d) 0.05 N/kg ☐

9. The escape velocity from the earth's surface is v. The escape velocity from the surface of another planet having a radius, four times that of earth and same mass density is **[NCERT Pg. 136, NEET 2021]**

(a) v ☐

(b) 2 v ☐

(c) 3 v ☐

(d) 4 v ☐

10. What is the depth at which the value of acceleration due to gravity becomes 1/n times the value that the surface of earth? (Radius of earth = R)

[NCERT Pg. 134, NEET (Oct.) 2020]

(a) R/n^2 ☐

(b) $R(n-1)/n$ ☐

(c) $Rn/(n-1)$ ☐

(d) R/n ☐

Chapter 08

Mechanical Properties of Solids

Scan and take Chapter Test

1. Read the following statements and choose the correct statement(s).

I. Putty or mud behaves like an elastic material.

II. In solids, interatomic forces are totally attractive.

III. Elasticity is shown by materials because interatomic or intermolecular forces become non-zero when a body is deformed.

____

2. Intermolecular forces are repulsive when a specimen is under ________ (tension/compression) and are attractive when a specimen is under ________ (tension/compression).

3. For an elastic solid, force F *versus* mean separation r between two molecules is plotted below.

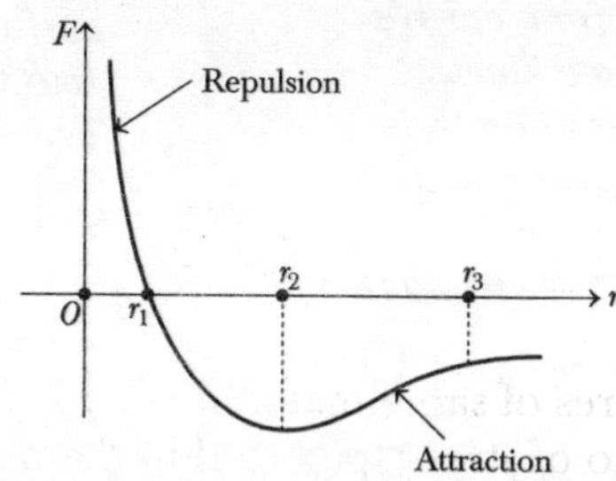

In undeformed condition, molecular separation is ________ ($r_1 / r_2 / r_3$).

4. A steel wire is stretched slightly and hold in stretched position. Ratio of external and internal deforming forces is ________ (less than/more than/equal to) unity.

5. On suspending a weight of 5 kg, the elastic wire of length 2 cm having area of cross-section 0.5 m^2, becomes double of its initial length. The instantaneous stress on the wire is

(a) 10 Pa ☐ (b) 20 Pa ☐

(c) 30 Pa ☐ (d) 40 Pa ☐

*Concepts of all questions bearing * are important for JEE/NEET/CUET.*

6. Match different objects given in Column I with the respective tangential force (acting on them) given in Column II.

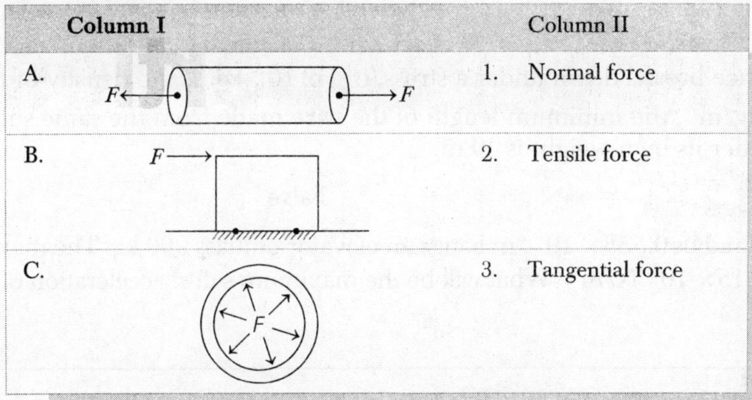

Column I	Column II
A.	1. Normal force
B.	2. Tensile force
C.	3. Tangential force

A. ____________ B. ____________ C. ____________

7. A wire is stretched to double of its length. The strain is

(a) 2 ☐ (b) 1 ☐

(c) 3 ☐ (d) $\frac{1}{2}$ ☐

***8.** A wire of radius 2.0×10^{-3}m carries a load 4 kg. The tensile stress developed due to this load in the wire is $x\times 10^{6}\,\text{Nm}^{-2}$. Find the value of x.

____

***9.** One end of a uniform wire of length L and weight w is attached to a point of roof and weight w_1 is suspended to its power end. If A is the area of cross-section of the wire, the stress in the wire at height $\frac{3L}{4}$ from its lower end is

(a) $\frac{A}{3w_1}$ ☐ (b) $\frac{3}{4}\frac{A}{w_1}$ ☐

(c) $\frac{3}{4}\left(\frac{w_1+w}{A}\right)$ ☐ (d) $\frac{w_1+\frac{3}{4}w}{A}$ ☐

10. The ratio of radii of two wires of same material is 2 : 1. If these wires are stretched by equal force, what is the ratio of stress produced in them?

____

11. A rectangular frame is to be suspended symmetrically by two strings of equal length on two supports as shown in following figures. It can be done in one of the three ways. Which figure represents the strings in least stress?

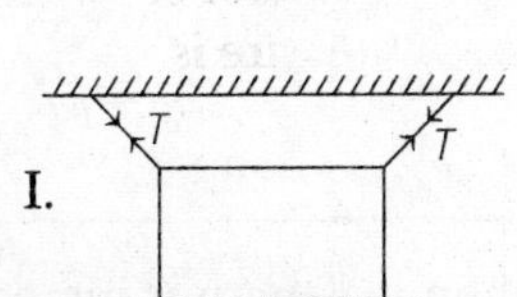

I.

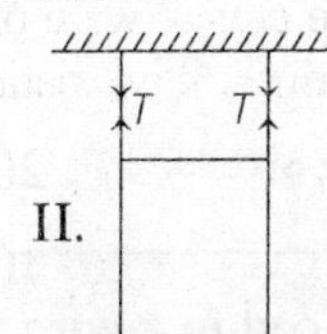

II.

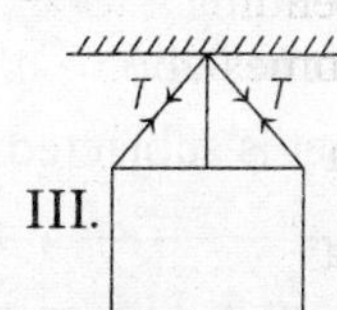

III.

____

12. A cable can support 800 N load. It is cut into two halves. The maximum load that each half can support is 3200 N.

Yes ☐ No ☐

13. A substance breaks down under a stress (σ_u) of 10^5 Pa. If the density of the substance is 2×10^3 kg/m^3, the minimum length of the wire made from the same substance which will break under its own weight is 10 m.

True ☐ False ☐

***14.** A wire of radius 0.535×10^{-2} m hangs an elevator of mass 900 kg. The maximum allowed stress is 1.15×10^8 N/m^2. What will be the maximum safest acceleration of this lift in upward motion?

____

15. A force 20 N is needed to break a wire of radius 0.01 m. The force needs to break the wire of radius 0.02 m of same length will be ______________

***16.** A cube of aluminium of side 0.1 m is subjected to a shearing force of 100 N. The top face of the cube is displaced by 0.02 cm w.r.t. the bottom face. The shearing strain would be

(a) 0.002 ☐ (b) 0.001 ☐ (c) 0.02 ☐ (d) 0.01 ☐

***17.** A bar of cross-section A is subjected to equal and opposite tensile forces at its ends. Consider a plane section of the bar, whose normal makes an angle θ with the axis of the bar.

θ

Match the different types of stress listed in Column I with their respective values listed in Column II.

Column I	Column II
A. Tensile stress on this plane	1. 0
B. Shearing stress on this plane	2. $\left(\frac{F}{A}\right)\cos^2\theta$
C. Tensile stress will be maximum for the value of θ as	3. $\frac{F}{2A}\sin 2\theta$
D. The shearing stress will be maximum for the value of θ as	4. 45°

A. ______________ B. ______________ C. ______________ D. ______________

18. An object of volume 1000 mL is taken 5 km below the surface of Indian Ocean and its volume is found to be 996 mL. Now, choose the correct statements.

I. Change in volume is 4 mL.

II. Strain in 0.4%

III. Object is subjected to shearing stress.

____

19. **Statement I** Linear strain produced in a wire will be 0.01 when its length is increased by 1% on hanging 2 kg-wt through it.

Statement II If each side of a uniform metallic cube is decreased by 1%, then under volumetric compression, bulk strain will be 0.03.

Which of the following statement(s) is/are correct?

(a) Only statement I (b) Only statement II

(c) Both statements I and II (d) Neither statement I nor II

20. A 1 m rod is elongated by 1.59 mm under stress of $3.18 \times 10^{8}\ Nm^{-2}$. The percentage volumetric strain produced is __________ .

TOPIC 2

Hooke's Law and Stress-Strain Curve

21. Hooke's law is not valid for gases. Which one of the following statements explain this statement?

(a) Small forces causes very small change in gas molecules.

(b) Small forces causes large deformation in the gases.

(c) Gases do not have definite shape to study elasticity.

(d) All of the above

22. In given graph, stress and strain are directly proportional upto point __________ $(A/B/C)$.

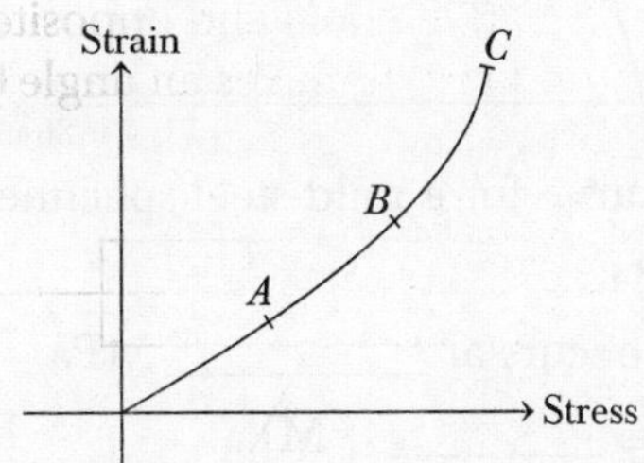

23. Stress-strain graph of a specimen is shown below.

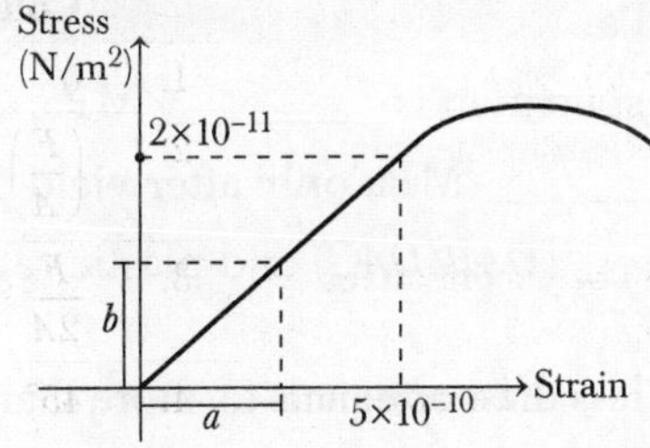

Ratio, $\frac{a}{b}$ = __________ m^2/N.

24. When the force is removed after the yield point of a material, the material returns to its __________ .

25. The stress-strain graph of a material is given below.

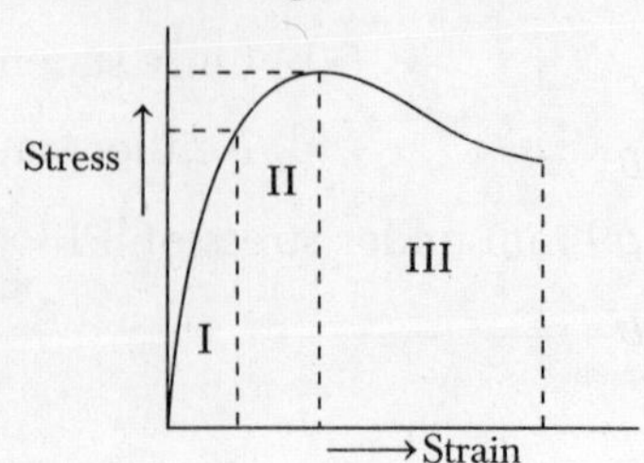

Which region corresponds to the very small increment in strain?

26.

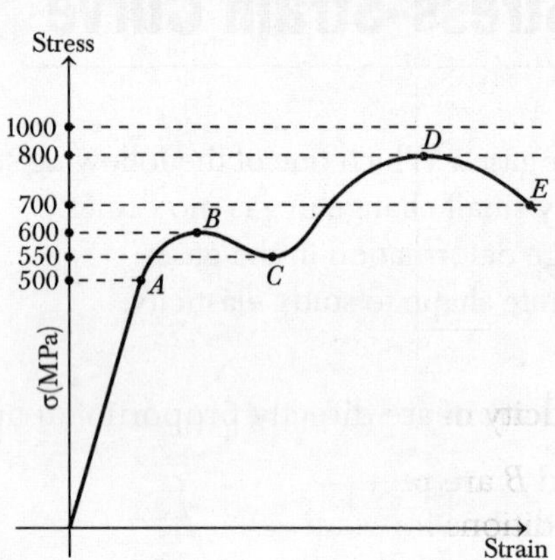

Here is shown stress-strain curve for a mild-steel specimen.
Now, fill the following blanks.

(i) Elastic limit of specimen occurs at __________ MPa.

(ii) Upper yield stress value is __________ MPa.

(iii) Lower yield stress value is __________ MPa.

(iv) Material specimen regains its shape after point __________ (*A*/*B*/*C*/*D*) and its elastic limit is at __________ MPa.

(v) Ultimate stress value for specimen is __________ MPa.

(vi) Specimen breaks at __________ MPa only after yield point.

(vii) Elastic region is __________ (*OAB*/ *OAC*) and plastic region is __________ (*ABD*/ *BCD*/ *BCE*).

(viii) Yield stress is __________ (less than or equals to/more than or equals to/equal to) 600 MPa.

(ix) Elastic limit value is __________ (less than or equals to/more than or equals to/ equals to) 600 MPa.

27. Match the Column I listed with different curves (shown in the following stress-strain graph) with the respective characteristic material (exhibited by them) listed in Column II.

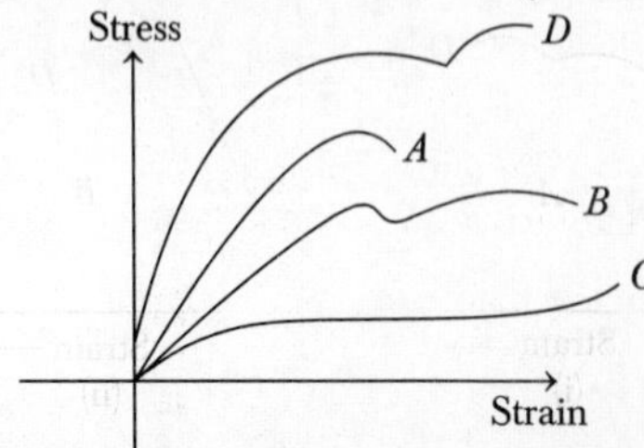

Column I	Column II
A. Curve *A*	1. Elastomer
B. Curve *B*	2. Brittle material
C. Curve *C*	3. Metal
D. Curve *D*	4. Ductile material

A. ________ B. ________ C. ________ D. ________

28. Following plot is obtained using an alloy steel and hard steel sample.

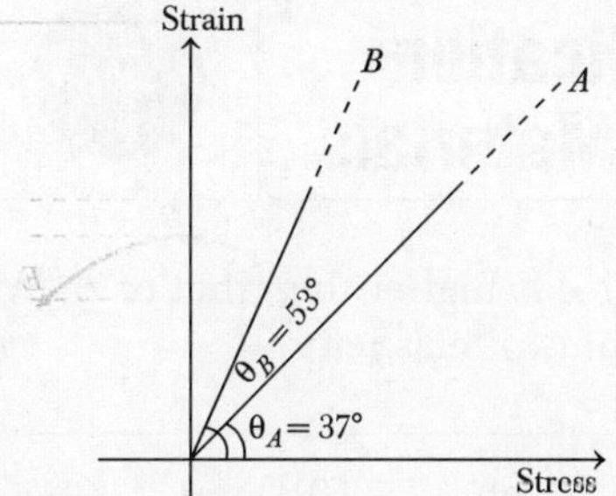

Ratio of modulus of elasticity of sample *A* with that of sample *B* will be ________ .

29. Stress-strain graphs *A* and *B* are prepared by a student (as shown below) but he forgets to specify, what are the conditions for *A* and *B*? Choose the correct statement.

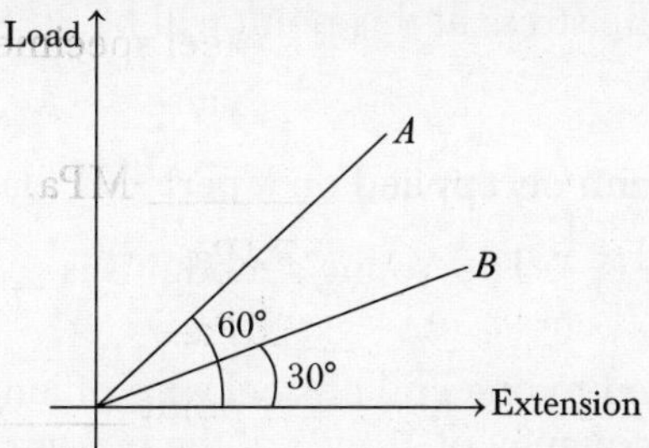

I. If *A* and *B* are made for two different wires of identical dimensions, then $Y_A : Y_B = 3:1$.

II. If *A* and *B* are made for two different wires of equal length and of same material, then wire *A* is more thicker than *B*.

III. If *A* and *B* are drawn for same wire at two different temperatures, then $T_A > T_B$.

IV. If *A* and *B* are drawn for wires of same material and same area but of different lengths, then $l_A > l_B$.

---

30. The stress-strain graphs for materials *A* and *B* are shown in Figs. (i) and (ii) (given, $\theta < \alpha$).

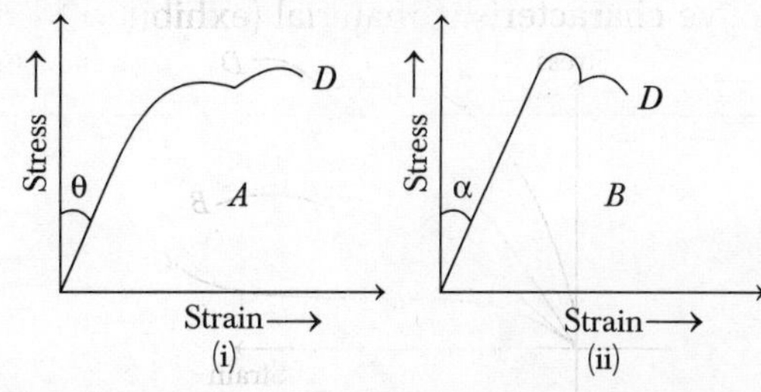

The graphs are drawn to the same scale.

I. Which of the materials has greater Young's modulus ?

______

II. Which of the two is the stronger material?

______

TOPIC 3

Elastic Moduli and Application of Elastic Behaviour of Materials

NCERT Pg 170-176

31. Given that density of material A is higher than that of B. Which material will possess higher value of Young's modulus of elasticity?

______

32. The Young's modulus of a steel rod is 2×10^{11} Nm^{-2}. Over the rod, stress of 3.18×10^{8} Nm^{-2} is applied. If initial length is 1 m, then elongated length will be______ mm.

33. For steel, the Young's modulus and the strain at breaking point is given as 2×10^{10} Nm^{-2} and 0.15, respectively. The stress at this point will be 30×10^{10} Nm^{-2}.

True ☐ False ☐

34. The stress of 20×10^{8} Nm^{-2} is applied on a perfectly elastic wire. The ratio of initial length to the final length is $\frac{1}{2}$. The Young's modulus is ______ N/m^{2}.

35. A mass of 14.5 kg fastened to one end of steel wire of length 1 m, is whirled in a vertical circle with an angular frequency of 1 rev/s at the bottom of the circle. If the elongation produced in the wire be 1.87 mm, then cross-sectional area of the wire is 6.5×10^{-x} m^{2}. Find the value of x.

______

36. A cylinder made up of same material have area of cross-section 1.26×10^{-3} m^{2} and length 0.5 m. If a force of 1078 N is applied on it, then what will be the fractional decrease in its length? (Take, $Y = 9.4 \times 10^{9}$ Nm^{-2})

______

***37.** A copper wire of length 2.2 m and steel wire of length 1.6 m having radius 1.5 mm are connected together. If a load of x N is applied, then the elongation is found to be 0.70 mm, find the value of x.

______

38. Consider a heavy wire hanging from a rigid support.

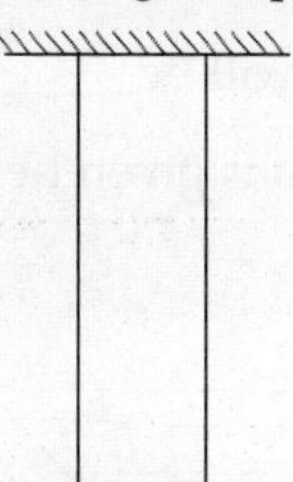

Weight of wire = 10 N, area of wire = 100 cm^2, length of wire = 20 cm and Young's modulus of wire = 2×10^{11} N/m^2.

For above parameters, elongation of wire due to weight is __________ m.

39. A space probe of mass 10 kg is attached to one end of a wire of length 0.3 m. It is rotated along with a space station as shown in the following figure.

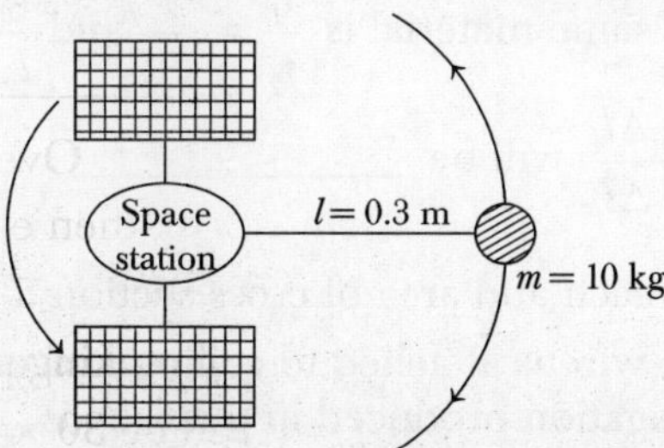

Breaking stress of wire is 4.8×10^7 Nm^{-2} and area of cross-section of wire is 10^{-2} cm^2. Maximum permissible angular speed of rotation of probe will be __________ rad/s.

40. Two wires of same length, same radius and made of different material are joined and loaded as shown in the following figure.

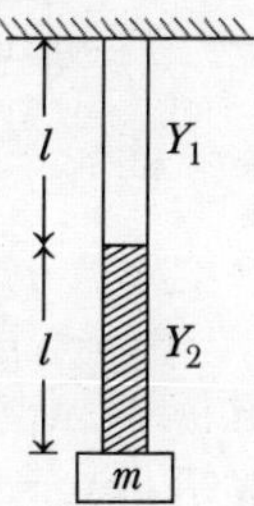

If Y_1 and Y_2 are the Young modulii of respective wires, then Young's modulus of combination will be harmonic mean of Y_1 and Y_2.

Yes ☐ No ☐

41. Two blocks are connected as shown below.

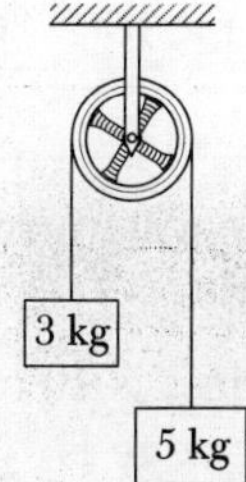

Pulley and string are ideal. If breaking stress for wire (string) is $\frac{24}{\pi} \times 10^2$ N/m^2, then minimum radius of wire required will be ________ cm.

42. The graph of the stress *versus* strain is given below. The Young's modulus of the material is ______________ N/m^2.

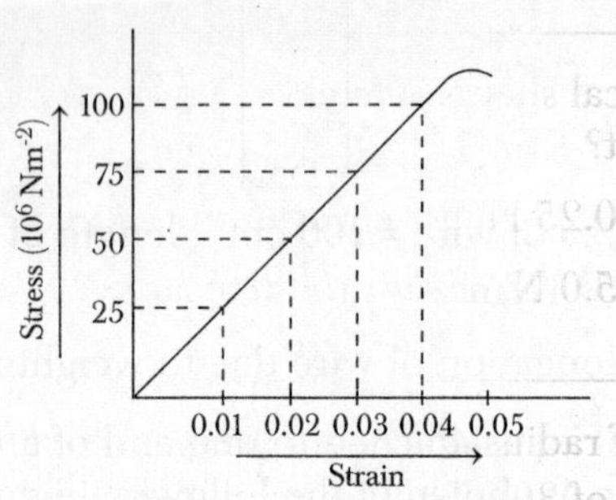

43. The data of two wires of same material is $\frac{r_1}{r_2} = \frac{1}{\sqrt{2}}$ and $\frac{l_1}{l_2} = \frac{1}{2}$. If they are stretched by equal forces, the ratio of $\frac{\Delta l_1}{\Delta l_2}$ will be ______________.

***44.** Two wires of length 1 m each and area of cross-section 1×10^{-6} m^2 each are joined together. One end of the wire is attached to ceiling and other end is subjected to a stress of 8×10^6 Nm^{-2}. The elongation produced in this way is _______ $\times 10^{-3}$ m.

(Take, $Y_1 = 120 \times 10^9$ Nm^{-2}, $Y_2 = 60 \times 10^9$ Nm^{-2})

45. A rod of length L is subjected to a temperature rise of ΔT. Let α be the coefficient of linear expansion of rod. Rod is heated in two different ways as shown below.

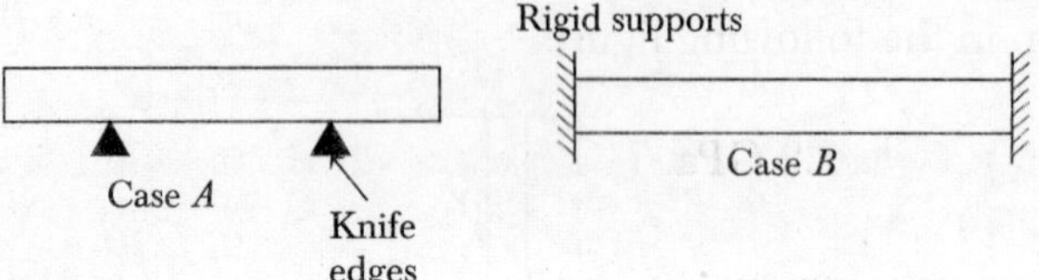

Now, fill these blanks.

I. Change of length in Case $A =$ ________ and in Case $B =$ ________ .

II. Thermal strain in Case $A =$ ________ and in Case $B =$ ________ .

III. Thermal stress in Case $A =$ ________ and in Case $B =$ ________

(where, Y = Young's modulus of material)

46. Calculate the pressure which required to prevent expansion of a steel wire of length 10 cm when it temperature is raised by 100°C.

(Take, $Y = 2 \times 10^{11}$ N/m^2 and $\alpha = 1.1 \times 10^{-5}$ °C^{-1})

***47.** A square lead slab experienced a shearing force of 9.0×10^4 N as shown in the given figure alongside.

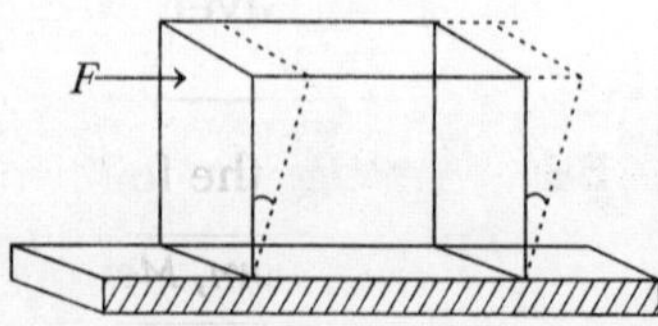

The box is 50 cm long and its thickness is 10 cm. The displacement produced in the upper edge is ____________ mm. (0.16/0.32) (Take, shear modulus, $G = 5.6 \times 10^9$ N/m^2)

48. The area of upper face of a rectangular block is 0.5 m × 0.5 m and the lower face is fixed. The height of the block is 1 cm. A shearing force applied to the upper face produces a displacement of 0.015 mm. (Take, $\eta = 4.5 \times 10^{10}$ N/m^2)

Find

(i) shearing strain, (ii) shear stress (iii) and shearing force.

---

49. The upper face of a cubical shape of length 5 cm is displaced by 0.65 cm. Which of the given statement is correct?

I. For a tangential force 0.25 N, the shear modulus is 770 N/m^2.

II. For a tangential force 5.0 N, shear modulus is 800 N/m^2.

---

50. The upper end of wire of radius 4 mm and length 10 cm is clamped and its other end is twisted through an angle of 30°. The angle of shear is ________ .

51. Bulk modulus of a ball is ________ N/m^2, if a pressure increase of 100 atm (1 atm ≈ 10^5 Pa) is required to obtain a strain of 0.01%.

52. Ethanol can be pressurised easily, whereas mercury cannot, because

(a) density of ethanol is higher than the mercury ☐

(b) the bulk modulus of mercury is higher than ethanol ☐

(c) ethanol is an organic compound ☐

(d) All of the above ☐

53. Fractional compression at 2000 m below sea level is C_1 and fractional compression at 4000 m is C_2. The relation between C_1 and C_2 is

(a) $C_1 = C_2$ ☐ (b) $C_1 > C_2$ ☐

(c) $C_2 > C_1$ ☐ (d) None of these ☐

54. Bulk modulus of water is 2.2 GPa. The fractional compression $\left(\frac{\Delta V}{V}\right)$ at 3000 m below the Indian ocean is ________ .

55. A solid sphere of radius 1 cm made of soft material of bulk modulus 12 GPa is surrounded by a liquid in a cylindrical container of area of cross-section 1.0×10^{-2} m^2. When a force of 50 N is applied to compress the liquid in the container, the fractional decrement is found to be 13.88×10^{-9}.

True ☐ False ☐

56. Two litres of water when subjected to a pressure of 10 atm, it gets compressed by 1.013 cc. Then, find

(i) bulk modulus of water (ii) and compressibility of water.

---

57. Determine the increase in pressure required to decrease the volume of a water sample by 0.01%. Given that the bulk modulus of water is 2.2×10^9 Pa.

---

58. Arrange the following in increasing order of their bulk modulus.

Aluminium, Mercury, Air at STP

---

59. What will be the bulk modulus for rubber ball whose volume is reduced to 14.5% under uniform stress of 1.45×10^4 N/m^2?

____

60. Match type of force given in Column I with suitable entries of Column II and Column III.

Column I	Column II	Column III
A. Longitudinal force	1. Shear strain	P. Bulk modulus
B. Tangential force	2. Volumetric strain	Q. Rigidity modulus
C. Normal force	3. Tensile strain	R. Young's modulus

A. ____________ B. ____________ C. ____________

61. Read the following statements and choose the correct statements.

I. The strain parallel to the applied force is termed as lateral strain.

II. Poisson's ratio is dimensionless.

III. The value of Poisson's rate for steel is less than 0.5, whereas for aluminium, it is greater than 0.5.

____

62. Due to action of deformation force, separation of atoms or molecules either increases or decreases. This causes an ____________ (increase/decrease) of potential energy.

63. Let a rod of cross-sectional area A, length L is stretched by an amount l due to an applying force F as shown below.

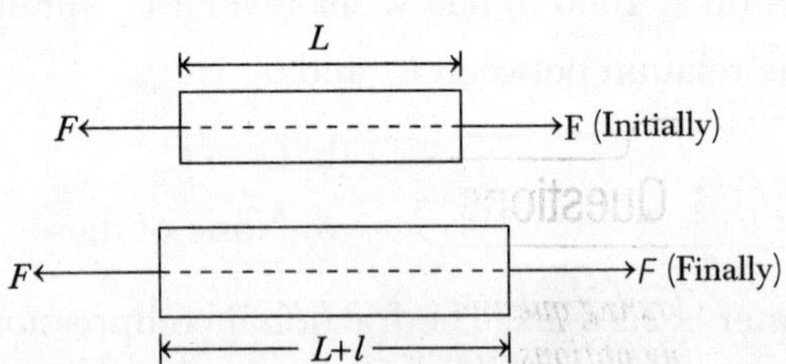

Now, complete following blanks. (Y = Young's modulus of material)

A. For some stretch x, Y = ____________

B. Work done by force to stretch rod from elongation x to $x + dx$ is dW = ____________

C. Total work done in stretching rod, so that its final length is $L + l$, is

$$W = \int_0^l dW = [\_\_\_\_\_\_\_\_]_0^l$$

D. Work done over rod is stored in form of ____________ energy.

E. Energy stored in stretched rod is U_X = ____________ joules.

F. Energy density of stretched rod is U_X = ____________.

64. A spring with spring constant of 5 N/m is stretched for an extra 10 cm. How much extra energy is stored in the elastic potential energy of the spring by this extension?

____

65. Two thin wires of same material having same length are subjected to same load. Energy stored per unit volume in wires are in ratio $\frac{u_A}{u_B} = \frac{1}{4}$, then ratio of their diameters will be ________ .

A B m m

66. Area of cross-section of a railway track is 0.01 m^2. The temperature of track raised by 10°C due to passing of train. Energy stored per metre of track is x J/m. Find the value of x.
(Take, $\alpha = 10^{-5}\ ^\circ C^{-1}$ and $Y = 10^{11}\ Nm^{-2}$)

---

67. If shear modulus of a wire material is 5.9×10^{11} dyne/cm^2, then potential energy of wire of 4×10^{-3} cm in diameter and 5 cm long twisted through an angle of 10′, is

(a) 1.253×10^{-11} J ☐ (b) 1.35×10^{-12} J ☐
(c) 1.42×10^{-12} J ☐ (d) 1.123×10^{-12} J ☐

68. Two wires of same material having radius in ratio 1 : 2 and length in ratio 2 : 1 will require the energy in ratio $E_1 : E_2$ in order to stretch them by 1 mm. What is the ratio of $E_1 : E_2$?

---

69. Force on a wire when increased from F_1 to F_2, its length increases by l. Energy stored in wire is $U = \frac{1}{2}\left(\frac{F_1 + F_2}{2}\right) \cdot l$.

True ☐ False ☐

Assertion-Reason Questions

Direction (Q. Nos. 1-10) *In the following questions, a statement of Assertion is followed by a corresponding statement of Reason. From the following options, choose the correct one.*
(a) Both Assertion and Reason are correct and Reason is the correct explanation of Assertion.
(b) Both Assertion and Reason are correct but Reason is not the correct explanation of Assertion.
(c) Assertion is correct but Reason is incorrect.
(d) Assertion is incorrect but Reason is correct.

1. **Assertion** (A) For rubber, strain is more as compared to steel.
Reason (R) Rubber is less elastic than steel.

(a) ☐ (b) ☐ (c) ☐ (d) ☐

2. **Assertion** (A) Strain is a unitless quantity.
Reason (R) Strain is equivalent to force.

(a) ☐ (b) ☐ (c) ☐ (d) ☐

***3.** **Assertion** (A) Upto elastic limit of a stress-strain curve, the steel wire tends to regain its original shape when stress is removed.
Reason (R) Within elastic limit, the wire follows Hooke's law.

(a) ☐ (b) ☐ (c) ☐ (d) ☐

4. **Assertion** (A) Spring balance shows incorrect readings after using it for a long time.
Reason (R) Spring in the spring balance loses its elastic strength over the period of time.

(a) ☐ (b) ☐ (c) ☐ (d) ☐

***5.** **Assertion** (A) The elongation produced in the copper will be greater than aluminium w.r.t. their corresponding breaking point.
Reason (R) Young's modulus of elasticity for copper is higher than that for aluminium.

(a) ☐ (b) ☐ (c) ☐ (d) ☐

6. **Assertion** (A) Solid, liquid and gas, all possess same value of bulk modulus of rigidity.
Reason (R) Bulk modulus of elasticity corresponds to fractional change in volume.

(a) ☐ (b) ☐ (c) ☐ (d) ☐

7. **Assertion** (A) Incompressible liquids have finite value of bulk modulus of elasticity.
Reason (R) Compressibility is inverse of bulk modulus of elasticity.

(a) ☐ (b) ☐ (c) ☐ (d) ☐

8. **Assertion** (A) If a wire is stretched, only half of the work done in stretching the wire remains stored as elastic potential energy.
Reason (R) Potential energy stored in the wire is 1/2 (stress) × (strain).

(a) ☐ (b) ☐ (c) ☐ (d) ☐

9. **Assertion** (A) Young's modulus for a perfectly plastic body is zero.
Reason (R) For a perfectly plastic body, restoring force is zero.

(a) ☐ (b) ☐ (c) ☐ (d) ☐

10. **Assertion** (A) When a solid sphere is placed in the fluid under high pressure, then it is compressed uniformly on all sides.
Reason (R) The force applied by fluid acts in perpendicular direction at each point of surface.

(a) ☐ (b) ☐ (c) ☐ (d) ☐

Case Based Questions

1. The relation between the stress and the strain for a given material under tensile stress can be found experimentally. In a standard test of tensile properties, a wire is stretched by an applied force. The fractional change in length and the applied force need to cause the strain are recorded. The applied force is gradually increased in steps and the change in length is noted. A graph is plotted between the stress (which is equal in magnitude to the applied force per unit area) and the strain produced. A typical graph for a metal is shown below.

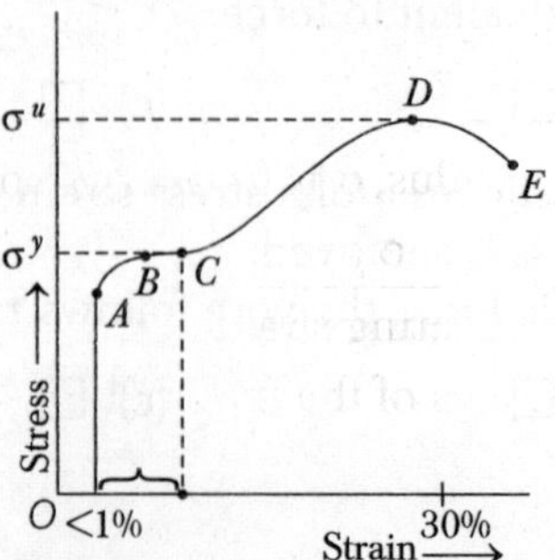

Answer the following questions

(i) Which point on the stress-strain curve occurs after the proportionality limit?

(a) Upper yield point ☐ (b) Lower yield point ☐

(c) Elastic limit ☐ (d) Ultimate point ☐

(ii) The slope of the stress-strain curve in the elastic deformation region is

(a) elastic modulus ☐ (b) plastic modulus ☐

(c) poisson's ratio ☐ (d) None of these ☐

(iii) Which of the following four stress-strain graphs represent a ductile material and a brittle material?

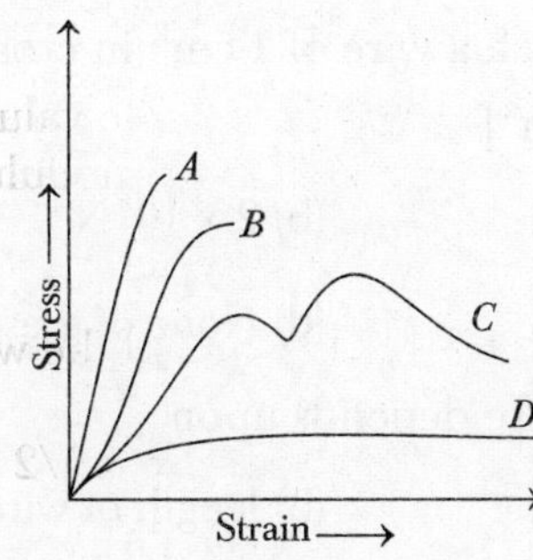

(a) *A* is for a brittle material, *B* is for a ductile material ☐

(b) *A* is for a brittle material, *D* is for a ductile material ☐

(c) *A* is for a brittle material, *C* is for a ductile material ☐

(d) *C* is for a brittle material, *A* is for a ductile material ☐

(iv) Aluminium is a .... material.

(a) brittle ☐ (b) plastic ☐

(c) ductile ☐ (d) Both (b) and (c) ☐

Or

Ceramic is a .... material.

(a) brittle ☐ (b) plastic ☐

(c) ductile ☐ (d) Both (a) and (c) ☐

2. The proportional region within the elastic limit of the stress-strain curve is of great importance for structural and manufacturing engineering designs. The ratio of stress and strain, called modulus of elasticity, is found to be a characteristic of the material. Modulus of elasticity can be divided into three categories.

I. Young modulus : $Y = \frac{\sigma}{\varepsilon}$

where, Y, is Young modulus, σ is tensile (or compressive) stress, ε is longitudinal strain.

II. Shear modulus : $G = \frac{\sigma_S}{\text{Shearing strain}}$

where, G = shear modulus of the material, σ_S = shearing stress.

III. Bulk modulus : $K = \dfrac{-p}{\dfrac{\Delta V}{V}}$

where, K = bulk modulus, p = hydraulic stress, $\dfrac{\Delta V}{V}$ = hydraulic strain.

Answer the following questions

(i) Choose the correct relation from the given options.

(a) $Y = \dfrac{9KG}{2G + 3K}$ N/m ☐ (b) $Y = \dfrac{9KG}{3K - G}$ N/m ☐

(c) $K = \dfrac{YG}{9G - 3Y}$ N/m ☐ (d) $G = \dfrac{3YK}{9K + Y}$ N/m ☐

(ii) The force required to stretch a wire of 1 cm^2 in cross-section to double its length is [Given, $Y = 2 \times 10^{11}\ N/m^2$]

(a) 2×10^7 N ☐ (b) 2×10^8 N ☐

(c) 2×10^{11} N ☐ (d) None of these ☐

(iii) The breaking stress of a wire depends upon

(a) material of wire ☐ (b) length of wire ☐

(c) radius of wire ☐ (d) shape of cross-section ☐

Or

Young's modulus of a body does not depend on

(a) material of the body ☐ (b) the way of deformation of body ☐

(c) length of wire ☐ (d) None of these ☐

(iv) If the Young's modulus of a metal wire of cross-section area 4 mm^2, experiencing 10^8 N of force is $10^{15}\ N/m^2$, then the value of strain is

(a) 0.25 ☐ (b) 0.05 ☐

(c) 0.025 ☐ (d) 0.005 ☐

COMPETITION EDGE UP

1. *Two persons pull a wire towards themselves. Each person exerts a force of 200 N on the wire. Young's modulus of the material of wire is 1×10^{11} Nm^{-2}. Original length of the wire is 2 m and the area of cross-section is 2 cm^2. The wire will extend in length by .... μm.*

[NCERT Pg. 170, JEE Main 2024]

2. *Young's modulus is determined by the equation given by $Y = 49000 \dfrac{M}{l} \dfrac{dyne}{m^2}$, where M is the mass and l is the extension of wire used in the experiment. Now, error in Young's modulus Y is estimated by taking data from M-l plot is graph paper. The smallest scale division are 5 g and 0.02 cm along load axis and extension axis, respectively. If the value of M and l are 500 g and 2 cm respectively, then percentage error of Y is* **[NCERT Pg. 170, JEE Main 2024]**

(a) 0.5% ☐ (b) 0.2% ☐

(c) 2% ☐ (d) 0.02% ☐

3. *The density and breaking stress of a wire are 6×10^4 kg/m^3 and 1.2×10^8 N/m^2 respectively. The wire is suspended from a* rigid support on a planet, where acceleration due to gravity is 1/3rd of the value on the surface of earth. The maximum length of the wire with breaking is .... m. (Take, $g = 10\,m/s^2$)

[NCERT Pg. 168, JEE Main 2024]

4. One end of a metal wire is fixed to a ceiling and a load of 2 kg hangs from the other end. A similar wire is attached to the bottom of the load and another load of 1 kg hangs from this lower wire. Then, the ratio of longitudinal strain of upper wire to that of the lower wire will be .... [Area of cross-section of wire $= 0.005\ cm^2$, $Y = 2 \times 10^{11}\ Nm^{-2}$ and $g = 10\ ms^{-2}$]

[NCERT Pg. 170, JEE Main 2024]

5. With rise in temperature, the Young's modulus of elasticity

[NCERT Pg. 170, JEE Main 2024]

(a) remains unchanged ☐
(b) changes erratically ☐
(c) decreases ☐
(d) increases ☐

6. Young's modulus of material of a wire of length L and cross-sectional area A is Y. If the length of the wire is doubled and cross-sectional area is halved, then Young's modulus will be

[NCERT Pg. 170, JEE Main 2024]

(a) 4Y ☐ (b) Y ☐
(c) 2Y ☐ (d) $\frac{Y}{4}$ ☐

7. Two metallic wires P and Q have same volume and are made up of same material. If their area of cross-sections are in the ratio 4 : 1 and force F_1 is applied to P, an extension of Δl is produced. The force which is required to produce same extension in Q is F_2. The value of $\frac{F_1}{F_2}$ is ....

[NCERT Pg. 170, JEE Main 2024]

8. A wire of length L and radius r is clamped at one end. If its other end is pulled by a force F, its length increases by l. If the radius of the wire and the applied force both are reduced to half of their original values keeping original length constant, the increase in length will become

[NCERT Pg. 171, JEE Main 2024]

(a) 3/2 times ☐ (b) 4 times ☐
(c) 2 times ☐ (d) 3 times ☐

9. The maximum elongation of a steel wire of 1 m length, if the elastic limit of steel and its Young's modulus respectively are 8×10^8 Nm^{-2} and $2 \times 10^{11}\ Nm^{-2}$, is

[NCERT Pg. 170, NEET 2024]

(a) 4 mm ☐
(b) 0.4 mm ☐
(c) 40 mm ☐
(d) 8 mm ☐

10. A metallic bar of Young's modulus 0.5×10^{11} $N\,m^{-2}$ and coefficient of linear thermal expansion $10^{-5}\ °C^{-1}$, length 1 m and area of cross-section $10^{-3}\ m^2$ is heated from 0°C to 100°C without expansion or bending. The compressive force developed in it is

[NCERT Pg. 170, NEET 2024]

(a) 5×10^3 N ☐ (b) 50×10^3 N ☐
(c) 100×10^3 N ☐ (d) 2×10^3 N ☐

11. Let a wire be suspended from the ceiling (rigid support) and stretched by a weight w attached at its free end. The longitudinal stress at any point of cross-sectional area A of the wire is **[NCERT Pg. 168, NEET 2023]**

(a) w / A ☐ (b) w / 2A ☐
(c) zero ☐ (d) 2w / A ☐

12. A wire of length L, area of cross-section A is hanging from a fixed support. The length of the wire changes to L_1 when mass M is suspended from its free end. The expression for Young's modulus is

[NCERT (New) Pg. 170, NEET 2020]

(a) $\frac{Mg(L_1 - L)}{AL}$ ☐ (b) $\frac{MgL}{AL_1}$ ☐
(c) $\frac{MgL}{A(L_1 - L)}$ ☐ (d) $\frac{MgL_1}{AL}$ ☐

Chapter 9

Mechanical Properties of Fluids

1. Average pressure on a thigh bone of human (mass of upper body = 40 kg, area of cross-section of bone = 10 cm^2) is ____________.

2. Figure given alongside shows an element in the interior of a fluid at rest. This elemental volume is in the shape of a right-angled prism. Let the elemental volume be small enough that we can ignore the effect of gravity, but it is drawn in an enlarged scale for the sake of clarity.

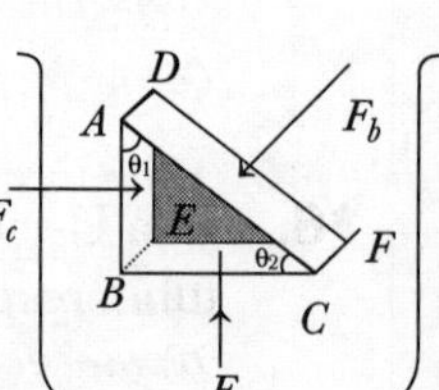

Choose the correct statement.

I. At equilibrium, $F_c = F_b \sin\theta$ and $F_a = F_b \cos\theta$

II. $\dfrac{F_b}{A_b} = \dfrac{F_c}{A_c} = \dfrac{F_a}{A_a}$

---

3. Consider a fluid volume in a beaker. If p_1 and p_2 are pressures on top and bottom of volume considered, then $(p_1 - p_2)$ is equals to

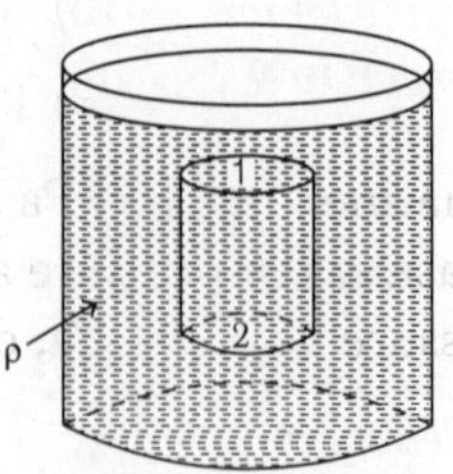

(a) weight of fluid

(b) weight of fluid per unit volume

(c) weight of fluid per unit area

(d) Both (b) and (c)

Concepts of all questions bearing * are important for JEE/NEET/CUET.

4. Four different beakers contains fluid upto same level and their bottoms are not interconnected. Ratio of volumes in beakers is 1 : 2: 3: 1.5.

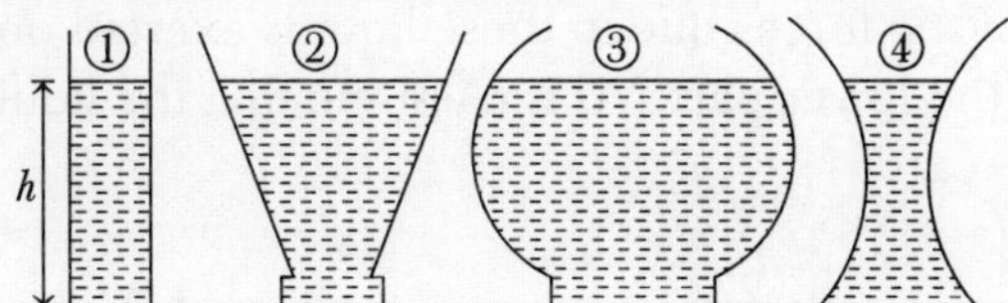

Ratio of pressure at bottom of beakers will be______________ .

5.

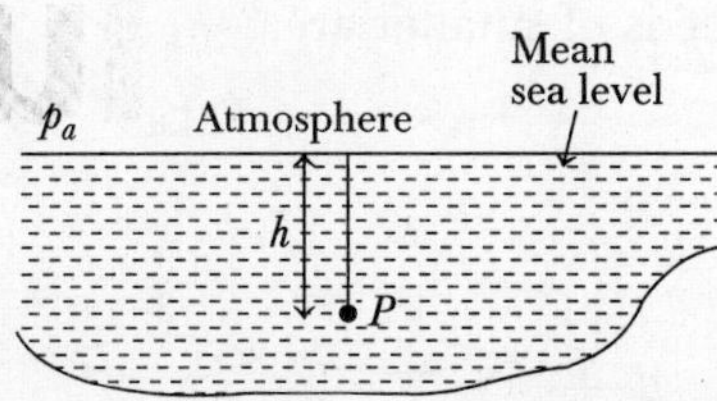

A point P, gauge pressure is ______________ and absolute pressure is ______________ .

6. At a depth of 1000 m in an ocean, ratio of absolute and gauge pressure is nearly ___________ .

7. A barometer is constructed using a liquid (density = 760 kg/m^3). What would be the height of the liquid column when a mercury barometer reads 76 cm? (Take, density of mercury = 13600 kg/m^3)

____

***8.** In a U-tube as shown in the figure, water and oil are in the left side and right side of the tube, respectively. The heights from the bottom for water and oil columns are 15 cm and 20 cm, respectively. The density of the oil is [Take, $\rho_{water} = 1000$ kg/m^3]

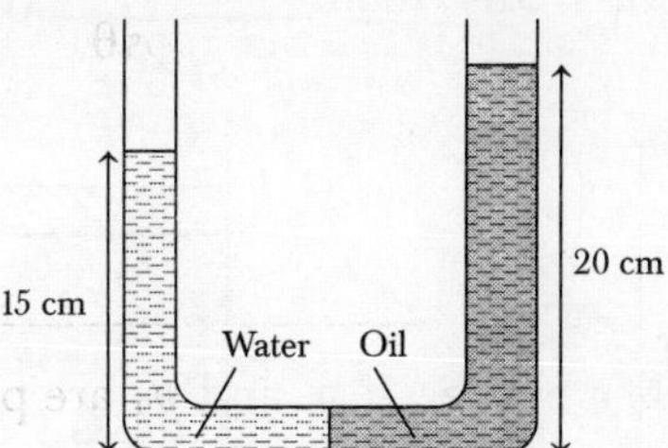

(a) 1200 kg/m^3 ☐ (b) 750 kg/m^3 ☐
(c) 1000 kg/m^3 ☐ (d) 1333 kg/m^3 ☐

***9.** The pressure acting on a submarine is 3×10^5 Pa at a certain depth. If the depth is doubled, the percentage increase in the pressure acting on the submarine would be (Assume that atmospheric pressure is 1×10^5 Pa, density of water is 10^3 kg m^{-3}, $g = 10$ ms^{-2})

(a) $\frac{200}{3}$% ☐ (b) $\frac{200}{5}$% ☐ (c) $\frac{5}{200}$% ☐ (d) $\frac{3}{200}$% ☐

***10.** Two liquids of densities ρ_1 and ρ_2 $(\rho_2 = 2\rho_1)$ are filled up behind a square wall of side 10 m as shown in figure. Each liquid has a height of 5 m. The ratio of the forces due to these liquids exerted on upper part *MN* to that at the lower part *NO* is (Assume that the liquids are not mixing)

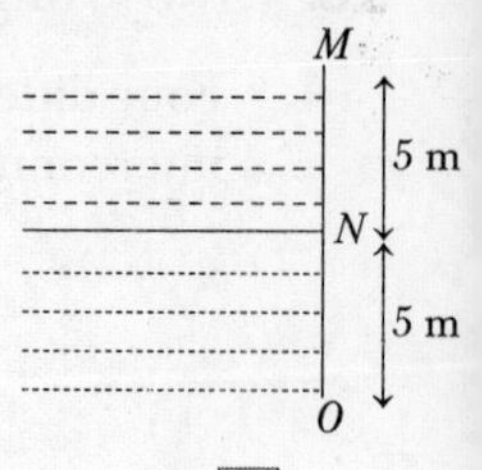

(a) 1/2 ☐ (b) 2/3 ☐ (c) 1/4 ☐ (d) 1/3 ☐

11. In a car brake system, piston connected with brake padel is larger, whereas piston connected with brake shoe is of smaller area.

True ☐ False ☐

12. Consider following device,

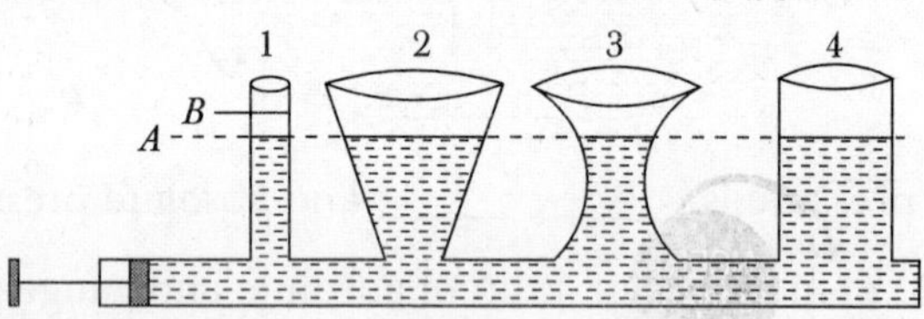

When piston is pushed in, water level reaches upto point *B* in vessel 1.
Now, choose correct statement.

I. Final level in vessel 2 < level in vessel 4 < level in vessel 3.

II. Final level in vessels 2, 3 and 4 is same but it is less than *B*.

III. Final level in vessels 2, 3 and 4 is more than *B*.

IV. Final level in vessels 1, 2, 3 and 4 is upto *B*.

---

13. In given arrangement, if $A_1 = 3A_2$, then __________ $(F_1 = 3F_2 \,/\, F_2 = 3F_1)$.

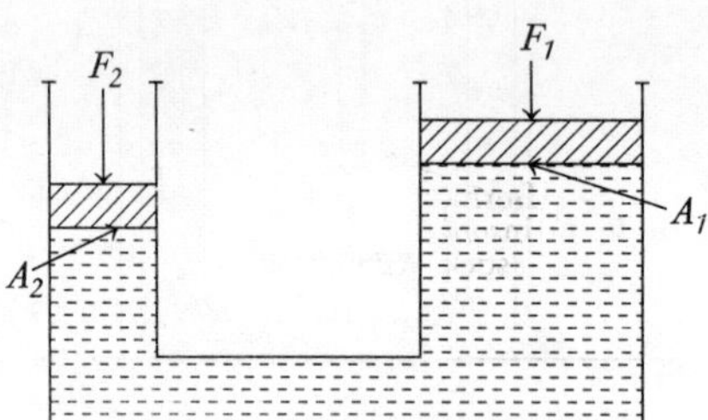

14. In given arrangement, $A_1 = 3A_2$

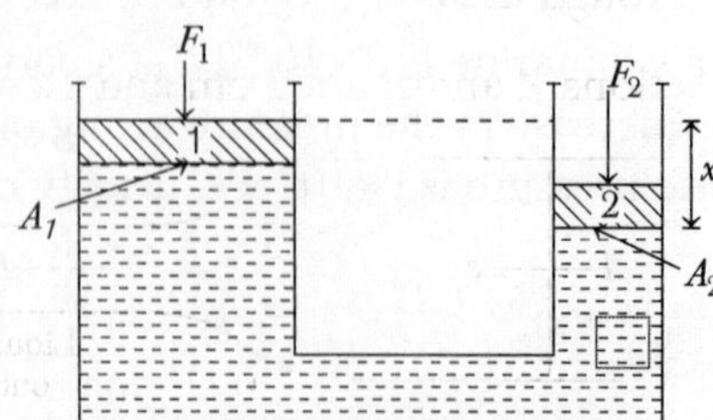

(i) If piston 2 moves through a distance of 30 cm, then distance moved by piston 1 will be __________ cm.

(ii) If work done by piston 2 is 20 J, then work done by piston 1 will be __________ J.

15. Two syringes are connected as shown below.

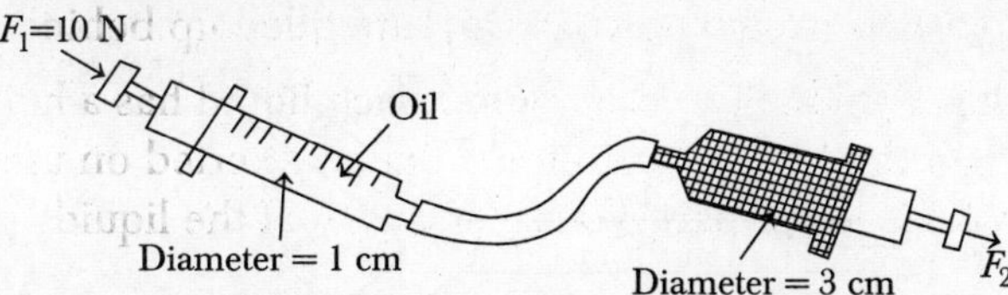

First syringe is pushed with a force $F_1 = 10$ N, then calculate the force F_2 on piston of second syringe.

____

16. A hydraulic press can lift 100 kg when a mass m is placed on the smaller piston. It can lift ______kg when the diameter of the larger piston is increased by 4 times and that of the smaller piston is decreased by 4 times keeping the same mass m on the smaller piston.

17. A burning insence stick is shown below. Label the type of flow in each of following case.

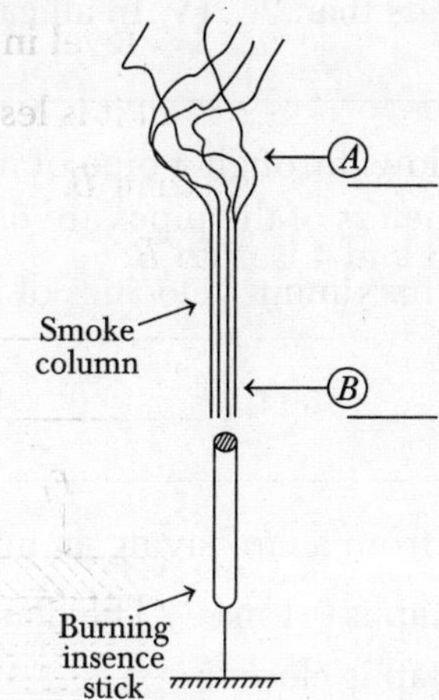

____

18. Consider a tube of varying cross-section area.
If $A_3 > A_2 > A_1$, then fluid velocities are in order of ____________.
Also, volume flow rates through areas A_1, A_2 and A_3 are in order of ____________.

19. In a tube, diameters of sections A and B are 2 cm and 4 cm, respectively.

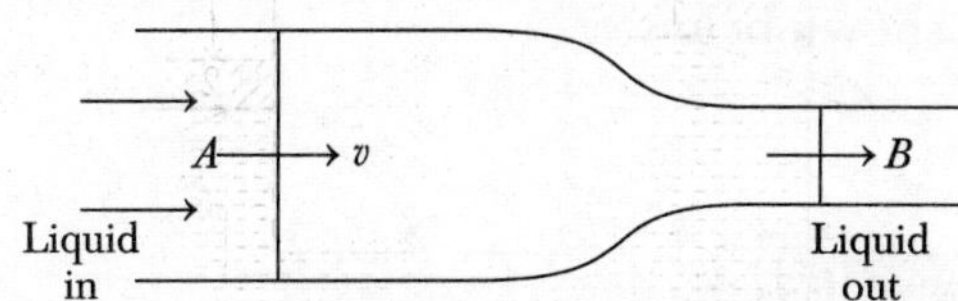

Ratio of water speeds at A and B will be ____________ $\left(4 / \frac{1}{4}\right)$.

20. Outlet velocity through section C is ______________ m/s. Areas and velocities are marked in each section.

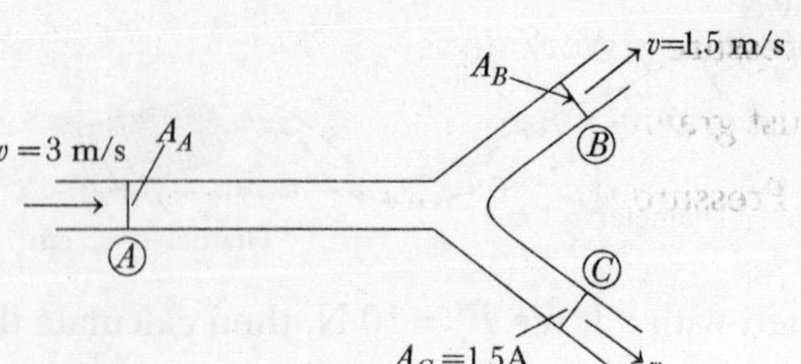

21. Consider tapering tube, ratio of areas of cross-section is 2.

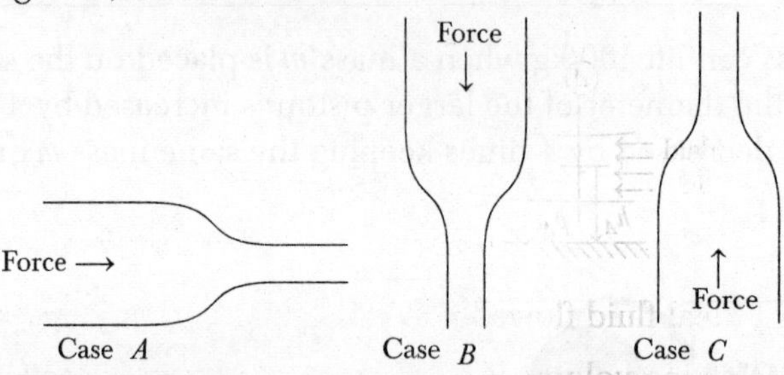

Now, choose correct statements.

I. In case A, velocity ratio is 2.
II. In case B, velocity ratio is more than 2.
III. In case C, velocity ratio is less than 2.
IV. In all cases, velocity ratio is 2.

---

22. An ideal fluid flows (laminar flow) through a pipe of non-uniform diameter. The maximum and minimum diameters of the pipes are 6.4 cm and 4.8 cm, respectively. The ratio of the minimum and the maximum velocities of fluid in this pipe is $\frac{x}{y}$. Find the values of x and y.

***23.** Water is flowing continuously from a tap having an internal diameter 8×10^{-3} m. The water velocity as it leaves the tap is $0.4\ \text{ms}^{-1}$. The diameter of the water stream at a distance 2×10^{-1}m below the tap is close to ______________ m.

TOPIC 3 Bernoulli's Principle

NCERT Pg 187-190

24. For flow of ideal fluid shown below.

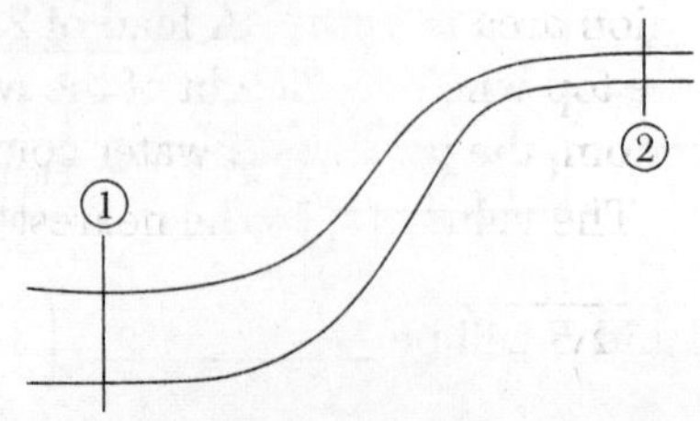

For flow from selection 1 to 2, which of these is true?

(a) Work done by pressure = Work done against gravity + Change in KE

(b) Work done against gravity = Pressure work + Change in KE

(c) Change in KE = Pressure work + Work against gravity

(d) All are correct

25. 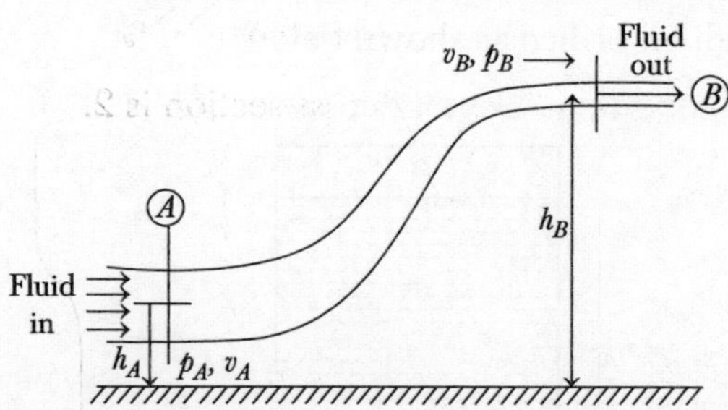

Let V = volume of ideal fluid flowed into tube in a short time interval, then

I. Work done in pushing volume V from point A to B against pressure difference = ____________ .

II. Change in potential energy of fluid (density ρ) as it moves from A to B = ____________ .

III. Change in kinetic energy of flow from A to B = ____________ .

26. A plane speeded on runway, air speed relative to wing is 120 ms^{-1} over top surface and 80 ms^{-1} over bottom surface.

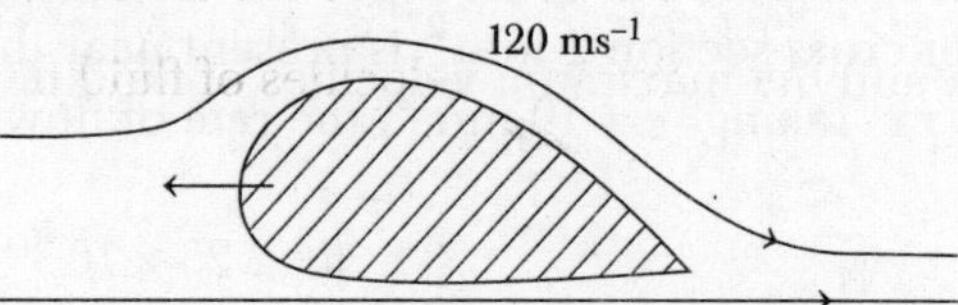

Air density is 1.2 kg m^{-3}. Pressure difference on two sides of wing is

(a) 4800 Pa

(b) 9600 Pa

(c) 4090 Pa

(d) 9500 Pa

27. A wind with speed 40 m/s blows parallel to the roof of a house. The area of the roof is 250 m^2. Assuming that the pressure inside the house is atmospheric pressure, the force exerted by the wind on the roof and the direction of the force will be ____________ and ____________, respectively (Take, $\rho_{air} = 1.2 \text{ kg/m}^3$).

28. Consider a water tank as shown in the following figure. Its cross-sectional area is 0.4 m^2. The tank has an opening B near the bottom whose cross-section area is 1 cm^2. A load of 24 kg is applied on the water at the top when the height of the water level is 40 cm above the bottom, the velocity of water coming out the opening B is $v \text{ ms}^{-1}$. The value of v, to the nearest integer, is ____________ .

(Take, value of g to be 10 ms^{-2})

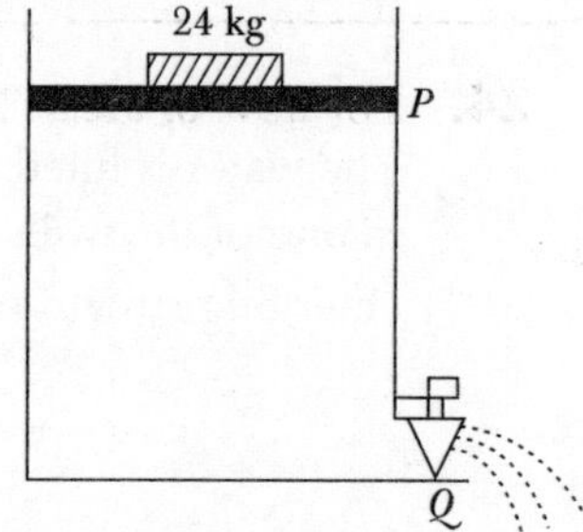

29. Water flows in a horizontal tube (see figure alongside). The pressure of water changes by 700 Nm^{-2} between P and Q, where the area of cross-sections are 40 cm^2 and 20 cm^2, respectively. Find the rate of flow of water through the tube. (Take, density of water = 1000 kgm^{-3})

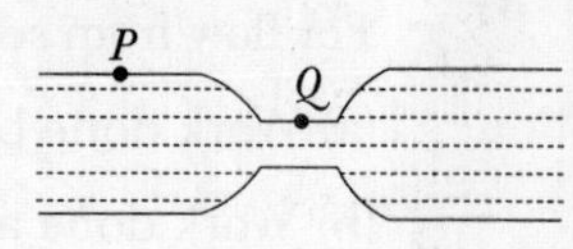

---

30. Consider flow through an orifice as shown below.

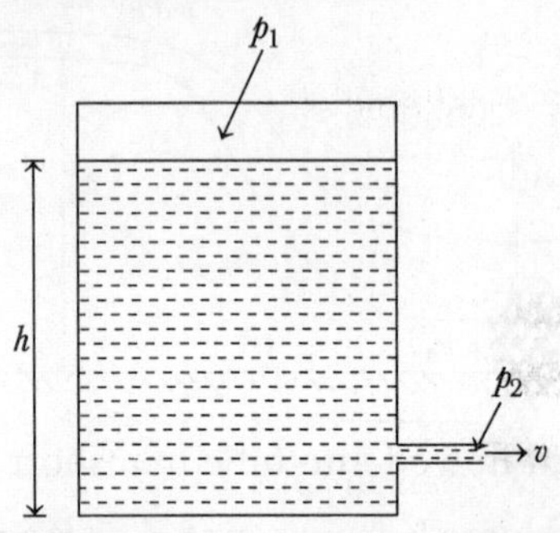

Now, choose correctly matched pair.

I. $v \approx \sqrt{2gh}$, if $p_1 = p_2$

II. $v \approx \dfrac{2\sqrt{p_1 - p_2}}{h}$, if $p_1 >> p_2$

---

31. Velocity of efflux through an open tank is nearly equal to velocity of free fall.

True ☐ False ☐

32. A small hole of area of cross-section 2 mm^2 is present near the bottom of a fully filled open tank of height 2 m. Taking $g = 10\ m/s^2$, the rate of flow of water through the open hole would be nearly

(a) $8.9 \times 10^{-6} m^3/s$ ☐
(b) $2.23 \times 10^{-6}\ m^3/s$ ☐
(c) $6.4 \times 10^{-6}\ m^3/s$ ☐
(d) $12.6 \times 10^{-6}\ m^3/s$ ☐

33. Given vessel takes 10 min to get emptied through hole at bottom.

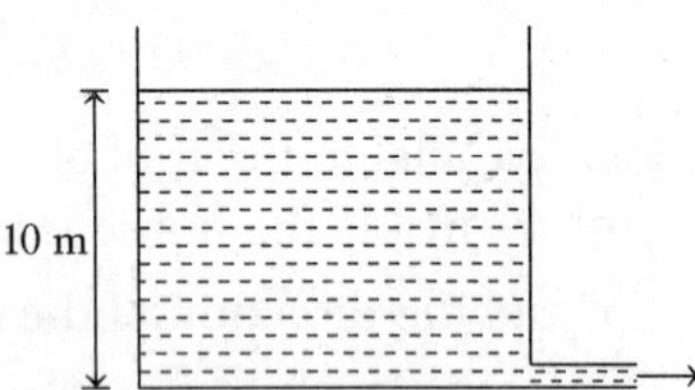

If it is half filled, then time to get empty (from same hole) will be x min. What is the value of x?

---

34. The water is filled upto height of 12 m in a tank having vertical sidewalls. A hole is made in one of the walls at a depth h below the water level. The value of h for which the emerging stream of water strikes the ground at the maximum range is ____________ m.

35. Consider laminar flow in a tube as shown below.

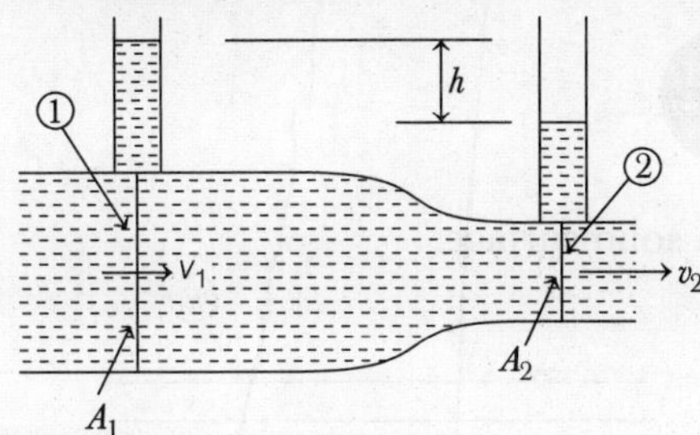

Now, choose incorrect statement.

I. Volume flow per unit time is $A_1 v_1$. II. $v_2 - v_1 = \sqrt{2gh}$ III $v_2^2 - v_1^2 = 2gh$

***36.**

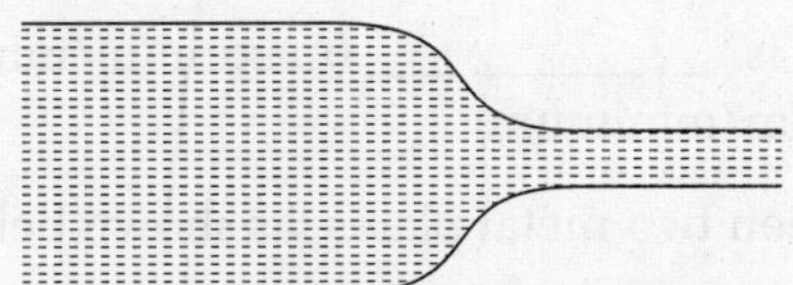

Water is flowing through the tube shown above. Pressure along axis of tube varies as

(a) 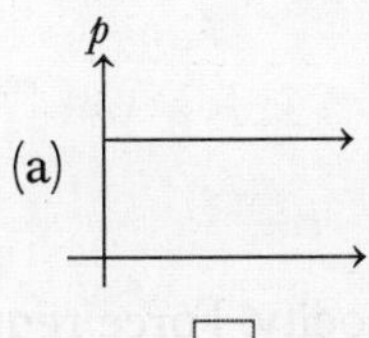 ☐ (b) 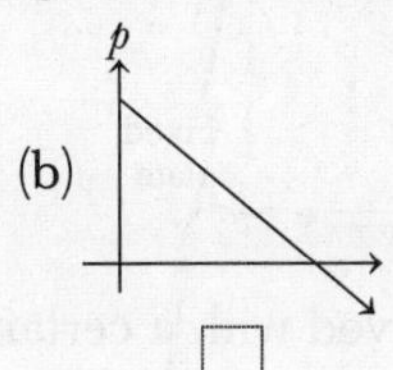 ☐ (c) 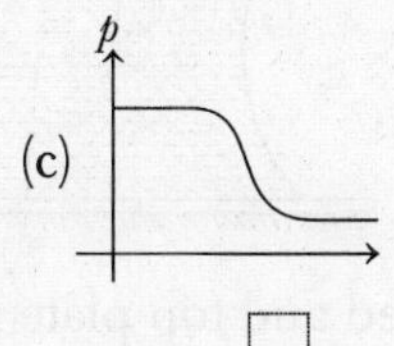 ☐ (d) 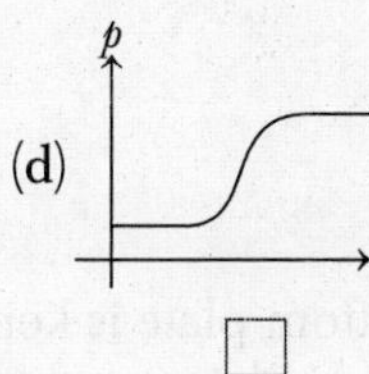 ☐

37. Consider cross-section of airplane wing moving from left to right. In which case, there is an upward force on wing?

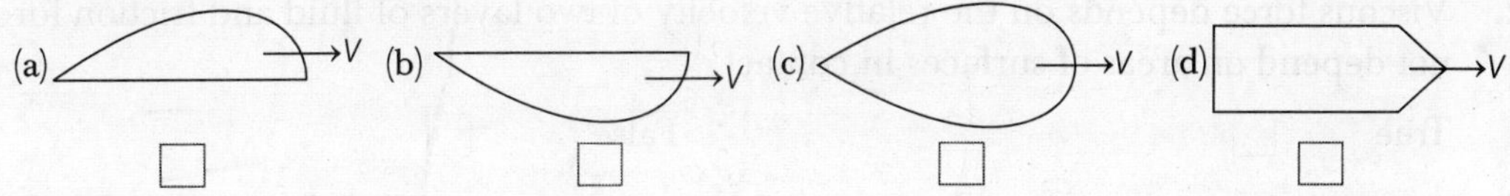

☐ ☐ ☐ ☐

38. Pressure reading of above manometer is $3.5 \times 10^5\ \text{N/m}^2$. When valve is opened, pressure falls to $3 \times 10^5\ \text{N/m}^2$, what will be the velocity of flow through tube?

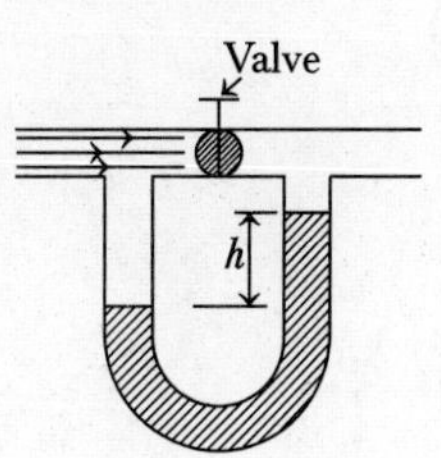

39. In which of these cases, ball will rise upward? (Ball is thrown horizontally in still air.)

(a) ω → v ☐ (b) ω → v ☐ (c) → v ☐ (d) ω ☐

40. A fluid is flowing over a solid surface.

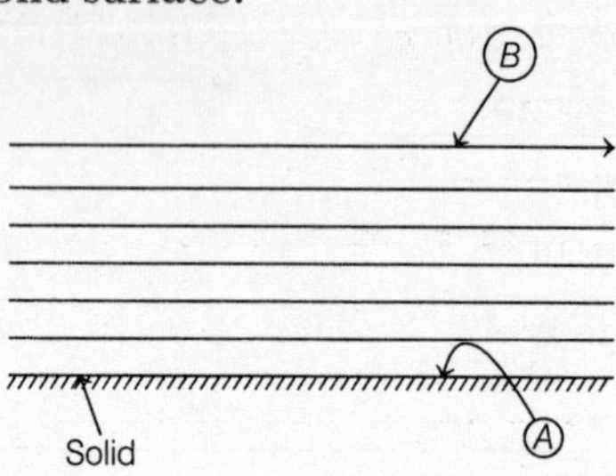

Then, velocity of layer A is ____________ (maximum/minimum) and layer B is ____________ (maximum/minimum).

41. A fluid mass exists between two metal plates (as shown below).

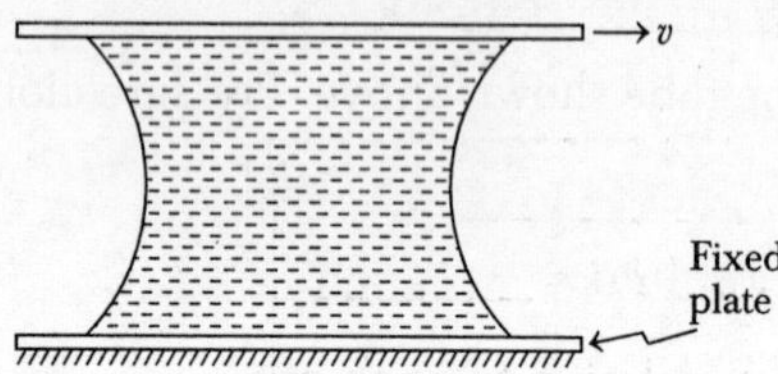

Bottom plate is kept fixed and top plate is moved with a certain velocity. Force required to move plate is proportional to

(a) density of fluid ☐ (b) volume of fluid ☐
(c) viscosity of fluid ☐ (d) surface tension of fluid ☐

42. Viscous force depends on the relative velocity of two layers of fluid and friction force does not depend on areas of surfaces in contact.

True ☐ False ☐

43.

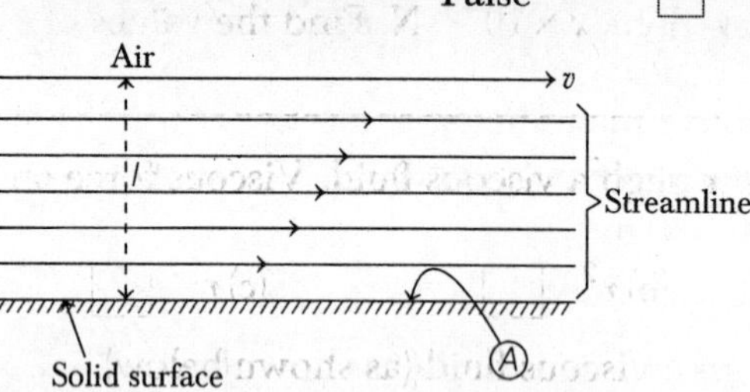

Consider a fluid flow (depth l and velocity of topmost layer v) as shown above. Now, complete the following.

A. In time interval Δt, shear strain developed in fluid volume is ____________ .

B. Strain rate of flow is ____________ .

C. Shearing stress is ____________ .

D. Coefficient of viscosity is ____________ .

44. A spinning ball is dropped in a fluid volume. It comes to rest after sometime. Arrange these fluids in increasing order of time taken by ball to comes to rest.

Blood, Glycerine, Honey, Machine oil

---

45. In following arrangement, $m_1 = 0.01$ kg, $m_2 = 0.01$ kg and area of block (mass m_1) = 0.1 m^2. Film thickness of liquid = 0.3 mm.

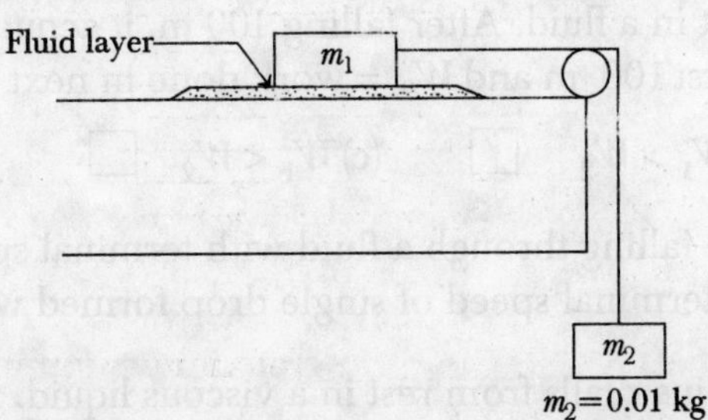

On releasing m_2, m_1 started moving with a constant speed of 0.085 ms^{-1}. Now, complete the following.

A. Shear stress on fluid = ____________

B. Strain rate of fluid = ____________

C. Coefficient of viscosity of fluid = ____________

46. Two fluid layers are moving relative to each other at a speed of 0.1 ms^{-1} and distance between these layers is 5×10^{-4} m.

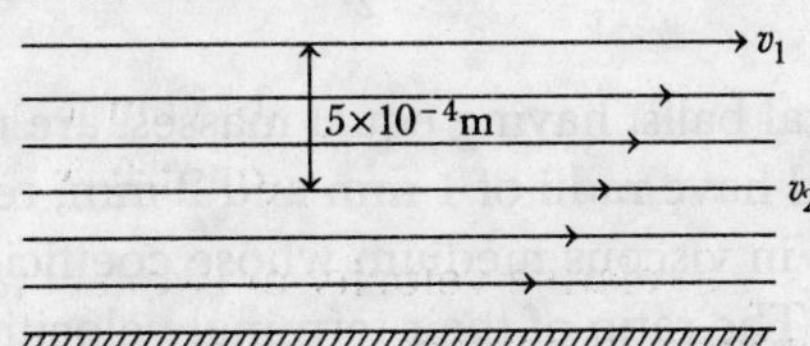

If area of flowing fluid is 1×10^{-2} m^2 and viscosity of fluid is 1×10^{-3} Pa-s, then viscous forces between layers will be $x \times 10^{-y}$ N. Find the values of x and y.

---

47. A spherical ball falls through a viscous fluid. Viscous force on ball is proportional to (r = radius of ball)

(a) r^{-1} ☐ (b) r^2 ☐ (c) r ☐ (d) r^{-2} ☐

48. A ball is falling through a viscous fluid (as shown below).

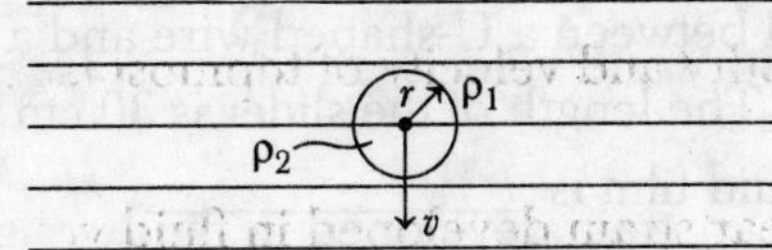

(Take, ρ_1 = density of fluid; ρ_2 = density of ball and η = density of fluid, v = velocity of ball, r = radius of ball)

Now, complete the following.

A. Force of gravity on ball = ____________

B. Upward force of buoyancy = ____________

C. Viscous force due to motion of ball = ____________

***49.** An object falls through a viscous fluid, its speed varies with time as

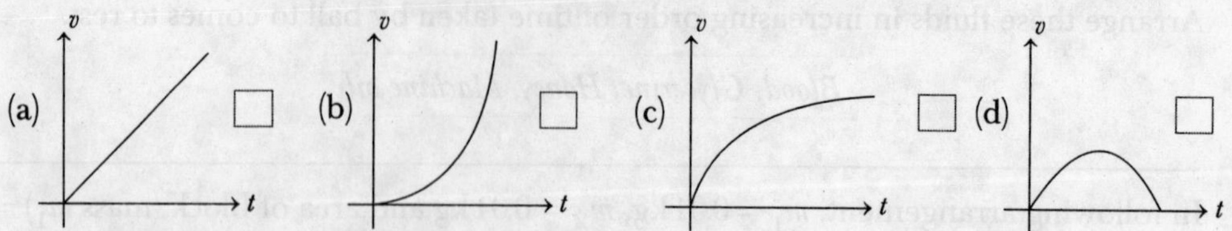

50. A body falls from rest in a fluid. After falling 100 m, it acquires terminal speed. If W_1 = work done in first 100 m and W_2 = work done in next 100 m, then

(a) $W_1 = W_2$ ☐ (b) $W_1 > W_2$ ☐ (c) $W_1 < W_2$ ☐ (d) $W_1 \approx 0$ ☐

51. Two drops of rain are falling through a fluid with terminal speed of 5 cms^{-1}. If they coalesce in path, the terminal speed of single drop formed will be ____________.

52. A small sphere of radius r falls from rest in a viscous liquid. As a result, heat is produced due to viscous force. The rate of production of heat when the sphere attains its terminal velocity, is proportional to r^4.

True ☐ False ☐

53. The velocity of a small ball of mass m and density d when dropped in a container filled with glycerine becomes constant after some time. If the density of glycerine is $d/2$, then the viscous force acting on the ball will be

(a) $\frac{mg}{2}$ ☐ (b) mg ☐ (c) $\frac{3}{2}mg$ ☐ (d) $2\,mg$ ☐

54. Two small spherical metal balls, having equal masses, are made from materials of densities ρ_1 and ρ_2 ($\rho_1 = 8\rho_2$) and have radii of 1 mm and 2 mm, respectively. They are made to fall vertically (from rest) in viscous medium whose coefficient of viscosity equals η and whose density is 0.1 ρ_2. The ratio of their terminal velocities would be ____________ $\left(\frac{79}{36} / \frac{19}{36}\right)$.

TOPIC 5 Surface Tension

55. A thin liquid film formed between a U-shaped wire and a light slider supports a weight of 1.5×10^{-2} N (see figure). The length of the slider is 30 cm and its weight is negligible. The surface tension of the liquid film is ____________.

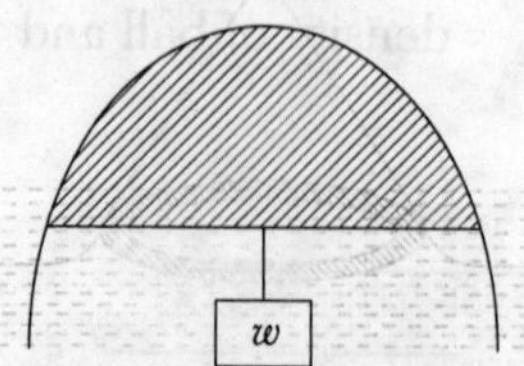

56. Consider a thin film of a liquid over a U-shaped rail and a slider.

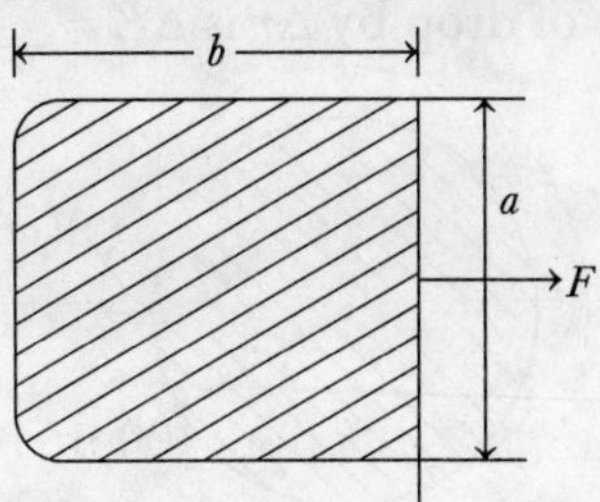

Let force F is applied slowly (not to break the liquid film) to extend area of liquid film. Let slider moves by a distance x, so the work done on slider = ____________

Surface tension of liquid = ____________

57. Tick (✓/×) for correct/incorrect statement in given boxes.

I. Force required to pull a square plate (S = surface tension of water) of side a which is floating over water is $4aS$. ☐

II. A needle of length l is floating over water (surface tension S). Mass of needle is $\frac{Sl}{2g}$. ☐

58. Consider following experiment in which a soap film is formed between a wire frame and a light slider is supporting a weight.

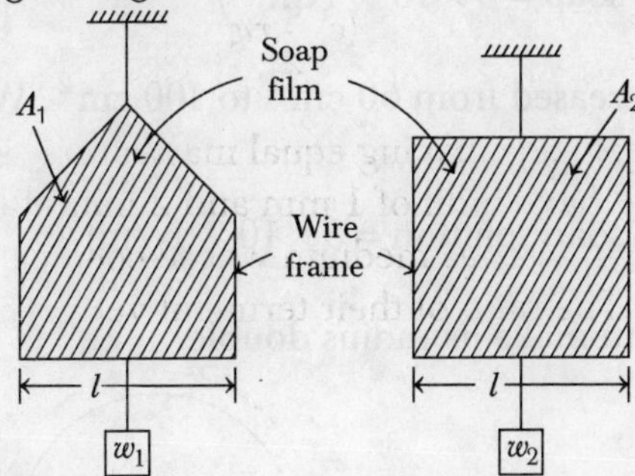

If area A_2 is twice of A_1, then

(a) $w_1 = 2w_2$ ☐

(b) $w_2 = 2w_1$ ☐

(c) $w_2 = w_1$ ☐

(d) no relation exists between w_1 and w_2 ☐

59. A ring of mass m with internal and external radii r_1 and r_2 respectively, is being lifted from the surface of a liquid of surface tension S.

Force F required to lift the ring will be given by F = ____________.

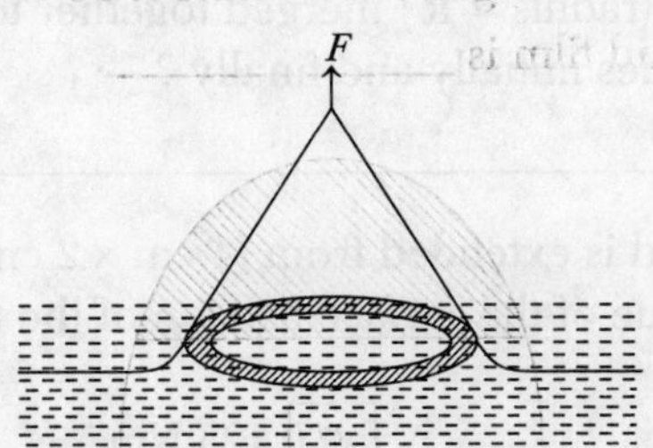

60. Consider a drop of radius r and surface tension of liquid is S. The extra surface energy needed to increase the radius of drop by Δr is $\Delta E =$ ________.

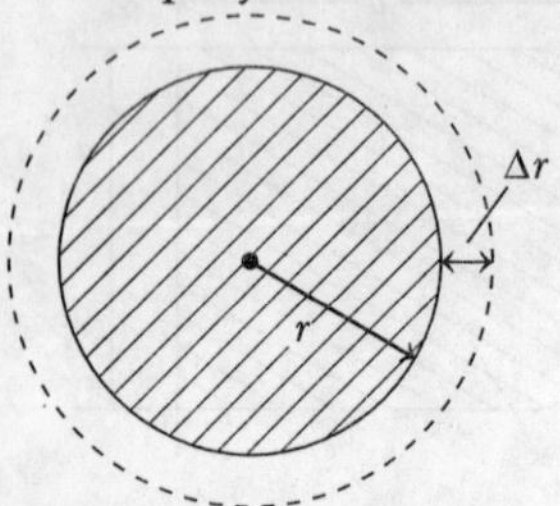

61. Work done by excess pressure Δp, inside drop in extending radius by Δr is given by $W =$ ________.

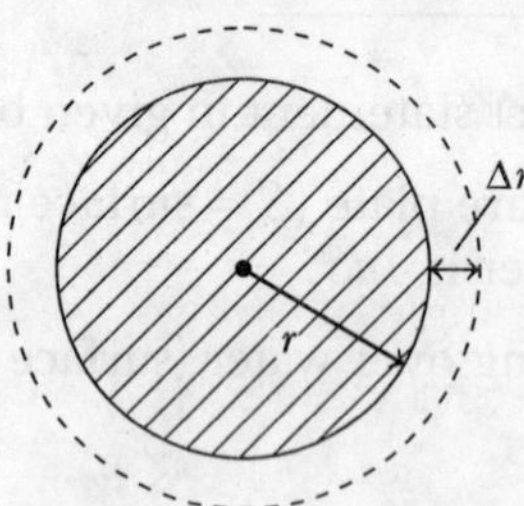

62. Work done in blowing a soap bubble of radius 10 cm is ________ J.

(Take, surface tension of soap $= 3 \times 10^{-2}$ Nm^{-1})

63. Area of a soap film is increased from 60 cm^2 to 100 cm^2. Work done in this process will be ________.

(Take, surface tension of soap solution $= 3 \times 10^{-2}$ N/m)

64. A soap bubble is blown to make its radius double.

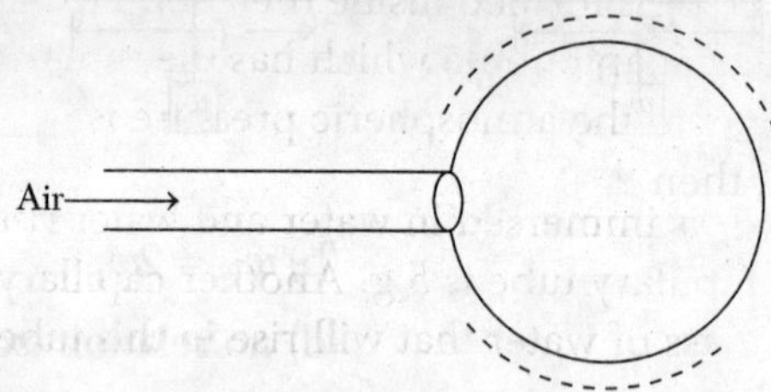

Energy required in this process is ________ $(24\pi r^2 S / 4\pi r^2 S)$.
(Take, S = surface tension of soap solution and r = initial radius of bubble)

65. Two small mercury drops (radius $= R$) merged together to form a single drop. What is the ratio of total surface energies initially and finally ?

***66.** A rectangular film of liquid is extended from (4 cm × 2 cm) to (5 cm× 4 cm). If the work done is 3×10^{-4} J, the value of the surface tension of the liquid is x Nm^{-1}. Find the value of x.

(a) 0.250 Nm^{-1} ☐ (b) 0.125 Nm^{-1} ☐
(c) 0.2 Nm^{-1} ☐ (d) 8.0 Nm^{-1} ☐

67. Two mercury drops (each of radius r) merge to form a bigger drop. The surface energy of the bigger drop, if T is the surface tension, is $2^{x/y}\pi r^2 T$. Find the value of x/y.

---

68. A liquid drop is placed on a solid surface as shown in the following figure.

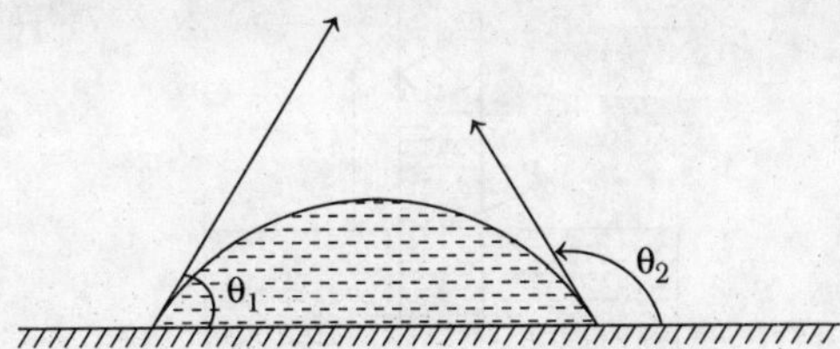

Here, angle of contact is θ_2.

Yes ☐ No ☐

69. If a liquid wets the surface, then angle of contact is __________ (acute/obtuse). Also, if a liquid does not wet the surface, then angle of contact is ________ (acute/obtuse).

70. Angle of contact for water with any solid surface is always less than 90°.

True ☐ False ☐

71. Soaps and detergents are added to __________ (increase/decrease) the angle of contact and water proofing agents are added to ____________ (increase/decrease) the angle of contact.

72. In a soap bubble excess of pressure $(p_{in} - p_{out})$ is $\frac{3S}{R}$.

True ☐ False ☐

73. A soap bubble of radius 3 cm is formed inside the another soap bubble of radius 6 cm. The radius of an equivalent soap bubble which has the same excess pressure as inside the smaller bubble with respect to the atmospheric pressure is _______ cm.

74. A capillary tube of radius r is immersed in water and water rises in it to a height h. The mass of the water in the capillary tube is 5 g. Another capillary tube of radius $2r$ is immersed in water. The mass of water that will rise in this tube is ____________ .

75. Tick (✓/×) for correct/incorrect statement in given boxes.

(i) Pressure inside two soap bubbles is 1.01 atm and 1.02 atm, respectively. Ratio of their volumes will be 8 : 1. ☐

(ii) A small soap bubble is connected with a large bubble, then air flow occurs from B to A. ☐

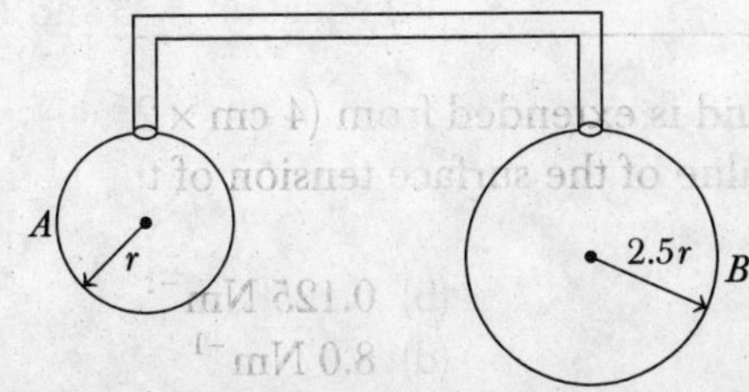

(iii) If meniscus is concave, then liquid rises in capillary. ☐

(iv) Pressure at a point just below the meniscus is low than atmospheric pressure. ☐

(v) For the capillary shown at point P, pressure due to liquid column = pressure due to surface tension. ☐

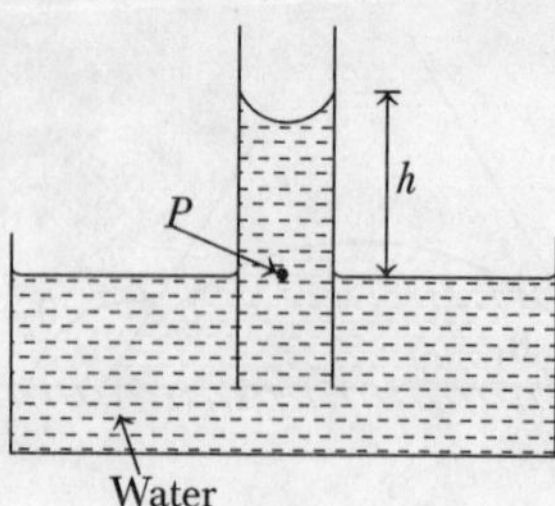

76. Two liquids with relative densities 0.8 and 0.6 have surface tensions 60 dyne/cm and 50 dyne/cm, respectively. What is the ratio of heights of liquid columns is capillary of radius r?

____

***77.** Three liquids of densities ρ_1, ρ_2 and ρ_3 (with $\rho_1 > \rho_2 > \rho_3$), having the same value of surface tension T, rise to the same height in three identical capillaries. The angles of contact θ_1, θ_2 and θ_3 obey

(a) $\frac{\pi}{2} > \theta_1 > \theta_2 > \theta_3 \geq 0$ ☐
(b) $0 \leq \theta_1 < \theta_2 < \theta_3 < \frac{\pi}{2}$ ☐
(c) $\frac{\pi}{2} < \theta_1 < \theta_2 < \theta_3 < \pi$ ☐
(d) $\pi > \theta_1 > \theta_2 > \theta_3 > \frac{\pi}{2}$ ☐

COMPETITION CONNECT

Topic Pressure [NCERT (Old) Pg. 246-252]

1. In given experiment, all three blocks have same volume.

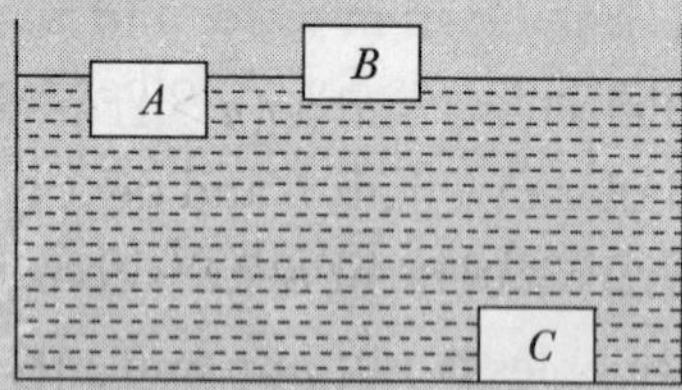

Maximum buoyant force acts on

(a) block A ☐
(b) block B ☐
(c) block C ☐
(d) equal on A, B and C ☐

2. Consider the given figure and arrange the densities of blocks A, B and C in correct order.

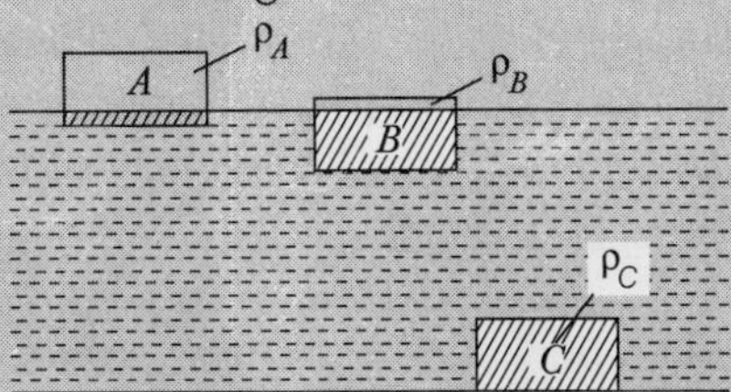

---

3. An object of mass m and density d_1 floats half submerged in a liquid of density d_2, then upward force acting on body is $\frac{mgd_2}{2d_1}$ and weight of body is mg.

True ☐ False ☐

4. Consider a solid cylinder of length L, cross-sectional area A. If floats in a beaker containing two immiscible liquids as shown below.

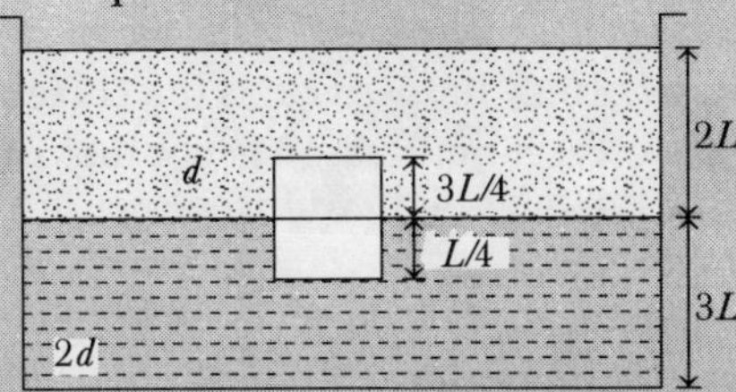

Densities of fluids are d and $2d$ and density of solid cylinder is D. Find the ratio of $\frac{D}{d}$.

---

5. Percentage of iceberg in sea water is around ____________ percent.

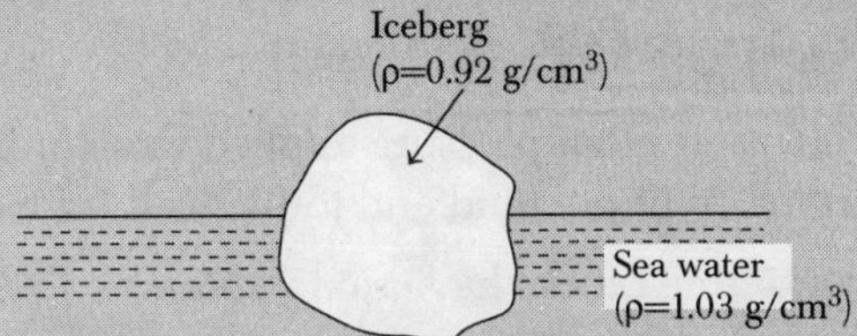

6. Two non-mixing liquids of densities ρ and $n\rho (n > 1)$ are put in a container. The height of each liquid is h. A solid cylinder of length L and density d is put in this container. The cylinder floats with its axis vertical and length pL ($p < 1$) in the denser liquid. The density d is equal to

(a) $\{2 + (n + 1)p\}\rho$ ☐ (b) $\{2 + (n - 1)p\}\rho$ ☐
(c) $\{1 + (n - 1)p\}\rho$ ☐ (d) $\{1 + (n + 1)p\}\rho$ ☐

7. A hollow spherical shell at outer radius R floats just submerged under the water surface. The inner radius of the shell is r. If the specific gravity of the shell material is $\frac{27}{8}$ with respect to water, then the value of inner radius r is found to be $\left(\frac{x}{27}\right)^{1/3} R$. Find the value of x.

---

8. A leak proof cylinder of length 1 m, made of a metal which has very low coefficient of expansion is floating vertically in water at 0 °C such that its height above the water surface is 20 cm. When the temperature of water is increased to 4°C, the height of the cylinder above the water surface becomes 21 cm. The density of water at $T = 4$ °C, relative to the density at $T = 0$ °C is close to ______________ .

9. A wooden block floating in a bucket of water has $\frac{4}{5}$ of its volume submerged. When certain amount of an oil is poured into the bucket, it is found that the block is just under the oil surface with half of its volume under water and half in oil. The density of oil relative to that of water is ______________ .

Assertion-Reason Questions

Direction (Q. Nos. 1-10) *In the following questions, a statement of Assertion is followed by a corresponding statement of Reason. From the following options, choose the correct one.*

(a) Both Assertion and Reason are correct and Reason is the correct explanation of Assertion.
(b) Both Assertion and Reason are correct but Reason is not the correct explanation of Assertion.
(c) Assertion is correct but Reason is incorrect.
(d) Assertion is incorrect but Reason is correct.

1. **Assertion** (A) Fluid pressure increases with depth in a static fluid.

Reason (R) The weight of the fluid above a point at a depth creates an additional pressure due to gravity.

(a) ☐ (b) ☐ (c) ☐ (d) ☐

2. **Assertion** (A) Pascal's law applies to both liquids and gases.

Reason (R) Pascal's law states that pressure applied to a confined fluid is transmitted undiminished to every point of the fluid and to the walls of the container.

(a) ☐ (b) ☐ (c) ☐ (d) ☐

3. **Assertion** (A) If a fluid at rest, the pressure at a point is the same in all directions.

Reason (R) Pressure is a scalar quantity and does not have a directional component.

(a) ☐ (b) ☐ (c) ☐ (d) ☐

***4.** **Assertion** (A) In a streamline flow, the velocity of fluid particles passing through a particular point remains constant over time.

Reason (R) Streamline flow is characterised by layers of fluid that move parallel to each other without mixing.

(a) ☐ (b) ☐ (c) ☐ (d) ☐

***5.** **Assertion** (A) In laminar flow, fluid particles move in random and chaotic paths.

Reason (R) Laminar flow is characterised by smooth and orderly fluid motion.

(a) ☐ (b) ☐ (c) ☐ (d) ☐

6. **Assertion** (A) Area of water stream from a tap becomes narrower as it falls.

Reason (R) Area × Velocity = A constant for a laminar flow.

(a) ☐ (b) ☐ (c) ☐ (d) ☐

7. **Assertion** (A) The viscosity of gases increases with increase the temperature.

Reason (R) With increase in temperature, gas molecu attain more kinetic energy and the rate of collision is more.

(a) ☐ (b) ☐ (c) ☐ (d) ☐

8. **Assertion** (A) Viscosity of liquid decreases with an incre e in temperature.

Reason (R) Viscosity is a measure of fluid's resistance to flow.

(a) ☐ (b) ☐ (c) ☐ (d) ☐

***9.** **Assertion** (A) Adding salt to water increases its surface tension.

Reason (R) Salt ions disrupts the cohesive forces between water molecules, reducing surface tension.

(a) ☐ (b) ☐ (c) ☐ (d) ☐

10. **Assertion** (A) Surface energy is a measure of the stability of a liquid interface.

Reason (R) Higher surface energy indicates a more stable liquid interface.

(a) ☐ (b) ☐ (c) ☐ (d) ☐

Case Based Questions

1. A hydraulic lift is a crucial piece of equipment in various industries, including automotive repair, manufacturing and construction. It uses Pascal's law to lift heavy object with minimal effort. Consider a car repair shop where a hydraulic lift is used to raise cars for maintenance and repairs. The lift consists of two pistons connected by a tube filled with hydraulic fluid. The small piston has a cross-sectional area of 0.02 m^2 and the large piston has a cross-sectional area of 1 m^2. When a force (200 N) applied to the small piston, it creates pressure in the hydraulic fluid, which is then transferred to the large piston, allowing it to lift the car.

Based on the given case study, answer the following questions.

(i) What is the pressure generated in the hydraulic fluid when a force of 200 N is applied to the small piston?

(a) 10 Pa ☐ (b) 1000 Pa ☐
(c) 5000 Pa ☐ (d) 10000 Pa ☐

(ii) What is the force exerted by the large piston when a force of 200 N is applied to the small piston?

(a) 2000 N ☐ (b) 10000 N ☐
(c) 50000 N ☐ (d) 100000 N ☐

(iii) If the large piston lifts a car to a height of 0.5 m, what is the work done by hydraulic lift?

(a) 1000 J ☐ (b) 5000 J ☐
(c) 2500 J ☐ (d) 50000 J ☐

(iv) If the volume of hydraulic fluid displaced by the small piston is 0.01 m^3, what is corresponding displacement volume for the large piston?

(a) 0.02 m^3 ☐ (b) 0.5 m^3 ☐
(c) 0.01 m^3 ☐ (d) 1 m^3 ☐

Or

If the efficiency of the hydraulic lift is 80%. What is the actual work output when the input work is 25000 J?

(a) 10000 J ☐ (b) 15000 J ☐
(c) 20000 J ☐ (d) 25000 J ☐

2. Consider a scenerio in a greenhouse where plants are watered through a system that uses capillary action. The system involves thin tubes that draw water from a reservoir into the soil, ensuring that the plants receive a steady supply of water without over-watering.

Take : The radius of capillary tube (r) = 0.5 mm

Surface tension of water (T) = 0.0728 N/m

Contact angle of water with the tube = 0° (ideal wetting)

Based in the given case study, answer the following questions.

(i) What is the pressure difference inside and outside the water column in the capillary tube?

(a) 108.2 Pa ☐ (b) 145.6 Pa ☐
(c) 194.8 Pa ☐ (d) 291.2 Pa ☐

(ii) How much surface energy is required to raise the water column in the capillary tube?

(a) 4 μJ ☐ (b) 6 μJ ☐
(c) 7 μJ ☐ (d) 10 μJ ☐

(iii) What is the total work done by the surface tension in lifting the water column in the capillary tube?

(a) 10×10^{-6} J ☐ (b) 7×10^{-6} J ☐
(c) 70×10^{6} J ☐ (d) 10×10^{6} J ☐

(iv) At what height upto water rises in capillary tube?

(a) 0.03 m ☐ (b) 0.6 m ☐
(c) 0.15 m ☐ (d) 0.2 m ☐

Or

How would the capillary rise change, if the radius of the tube were doubled?

(a) It would remain the same ☐ (b) It would double ☐
(c) It would be halved ☐ (d) It would be quartered. ☐

COMPETITION EDGE UP

1. A spherical ball of radius 1×10^{-4} m and density 10^5 kg / m^3 falls freely under gravity through a distance h before entering a tank of water. If after entering in water the velocity of the ball does not change, then the value of h is approximately (The coefficient of viscosity of water is 9.8×10^{-6} N s/m^2)

[NCERT Pg. 192, JEE Main 2024]

(a) 2296 m ☐ (b) 2518 m ☐

(c) 2396 m ☐ (d) 2249 m ☐

2. Pressure inside a soap bubble is greater than the pressure outside by an amount (Given, R = Radius of bubble, S = Surface tension of bubble)

[NCERT Pg. 192, JEE Main 2024]

(a) $\frac{4R}{S}$ ☐

(b) $\frac{2S}{R}$ ☐

(c) $\frac{4S}{R}$ ☐

(d) $\frac{S}{R}$ ☐

3. A small ball of mass m and density ρ is dropped in a viscous liquid of density ρ_0. After sometime the ball falls with constant velocity. The viscous force on the ball is

[NCERT Pg. 192, JEE Main 2024]

(a) $mg\left(\frac{\rho_0}{\rho} - 1\right)$ ☐

(b) $mg\left(1 - \frac{\rho_0}{\rho}\right)$ ☐

(c) $mg(1 - \rho\rho_0)$ ☐

(d) $mg\left(1 + \frac{\rho}{\rho_0}\right)$ ☐

4. Mercury is filled in a tube of radius 2 cm up to a height of 30 cm. The force exerted by mercury on the bottom of the tube is...... N.

(Given, atmospheric pressure = 10^5 Nm^{-2}, density of mercury = 1.36×10^4 kg m^{-3}, $g = 10$ ms^{-2}, $\pi = \frac{22}{7}$)

[NCERT Pg. 183, JEE Main 2024]

5. Given below are two statements.

Statement I Viscosity of gases is greater than that of liquids.

Statement II Surface tension of a liquid decreases due to the presence of insoluble impurities.

In the light of the above statements, choose the most appropriate answer from the options given below

[NCERT Pg. 190, 192, JEE Main 2024]

(a) Both Statement I and Statement II are correct. ☐

(b) Statement I is incorrect but Statement II is correct. ☐

(c) Both Statement I and Statement II are incorrect. ☐

(d) Statement I is correct but Statement II is incorrect. ☐

6. A sphere of relative density σ and diameter D has concentric cavity of diameter d. The ratio of D/d, if it just floats on water in a tank is **[NCERT Pg. 183, JEE Main 2024]**

(a) $\left(\frac{\sigma + 1}{\sigma - 1}\right)^{1/3}$ ☐

(b) $\left(\frac{\sigma - 1}{\sigma}\right)^{1/3}$ ☐

(c) $\left(\frac{\sigma}{\sigma - 1}\right)^{1/3}$ ☐

(d) $\left(\frac{\sigma - 2}{\sigma + 2}\right)^{1/3}$ ☐

7. Small water droplets of radius 0.01 mm are formed in the upper atmosphere and falling with a terminal velocity of 10 cm/s. Due to condensation, if 8 such droplets are coalesced and formed a larger drop, the new terminal velocity will be....... cm/s.

[NCERT Pg. 187, JEE Main 2024]

8.

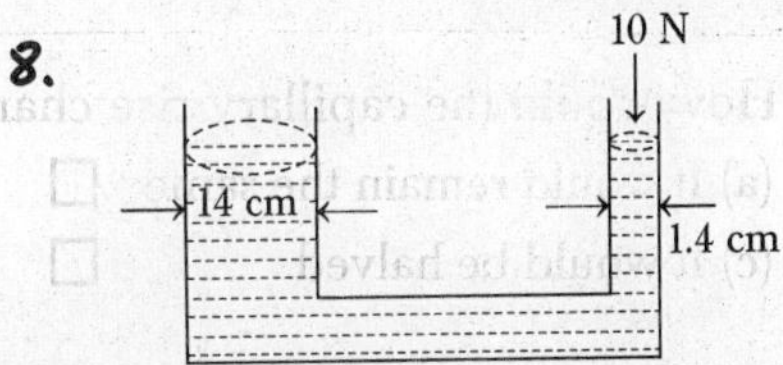

A hydraulic press containing water has two arms with diameters as mentioned in the figure. A force of 10 N is applied on the surface of water in the thinner arm. The force required to be applied on the surface of water in the thicker arm to maintain equilibrium of water is .... N.

[NCERT Pg. 185, JEE Main 2024]

9. A thin flat circular disc of radius 4.5 cm is placed gently over the surface of water. If surface tension of water is 0.07 N-m^{-1}, then the excess force required to take it away from the surface is

[NCERT Pg. 194, NEET 2024]

(a) 19.8 mN ☐
(b) 198 N ☐
(c) 1.98 mN ☐
(d) 99 N ☐

10. The venturimeter works on

[NCERT Pg. 187, NEET 2023]

(a) Bernoulli's principle ☐
(b) the principle of parallel axes ☐
(c) the principle of perpendicular axes ☐
(d) Huygen's principle ☐

11. The amount of energy required to form a soap bubble of radius 2 cm from a soap solution is nearly (surface tension of soap solution = 0.03 N m^{-1})

[NCERT Pg. 196, NEET 2023]

(a) 5.06×10^{-4} J ☐
(b) 3.01×10^{-4} J ☐
(c) 50.1×10^{-4} J ☐
(d) 30.16×10^{-4} J ☐

12. If a soap bubble expands, the pressure inside the bubble **[NCERT Pg. 196, NEET 2022]**

(a) increases ☐
(b) remains the same ☐
(c) is equal to the atmospheric pressure ☐
(d) decreases. ☐

13. A spherical ball is dropped in a long column of a highly viscous liquid. The curve in the graph shown, which represents the speed of the ball (v) as a function of time (t) is

[NCERT Pg. 192, NEET 2022]

(a) B ☐ (b) C ☐
(c) D ☐ (d) A ☐

14. A capillary tube of radius r is immersed in water and water rises in it to a height h. The mass of the water in the capillary tube is 5 g. Another capillary tube of radius 2r is immersed in water. The mass of water that will rise in this tube is

[NCERT Pg. 197, NEET (Sep.) 2020]

(a) 5.0 g ☐ (b) 10.0 g ☐
(c) 20.0 g ☐ (d) 2.5 g ☐

15. A liquid does not wet the solid surface if angle of contact is

[NCERT Pg. 195, NEET (Oct.) 2020]

(a) equal to 45° ☐
(b) equal to 60° ☐
(c) greater than 90° ☐
(d) zero ☐

16. A barometer is constructed using a liquid (density = 760 kg/m^3). What would be the height of the liquid column, when a mercury barometer reads 76 cm? (Density of mercury = 13600 kg/m^3)

[NCERT Pg. 184, NEET (Oct.) 2020]

(a) 1.36 m ☐ (b) 13.6 m ☐
(c) 136 m ☐ (d) 0.76 m ☐

Chapter 10

Thermal Properties of Matter

Scan and take Chapter Test

TOPIC 1

Temperature and Heat

NCERT Pg 202-203

1. What does a hot utensil indicate?

(a) Low temperature ☐ (b) High temperature ☐

(c) Constant temperature ☐ (d) None of these ☐

2. Name the unit in which heat energy transferred is measured.

____

3. Fill in the blank.

Heat is the (form of energy/temperature difference) _________ transferred between systems by virtue of temperature difference.

4. Match the following columns.

Column I	Column II
A. Icecold water warms up	1. Heat transfer from the environment to the object
B. Hot tea cools down	2. Heat transfer from the object to the environment
C. Heat flows from the environment	3. Temperature difference between system and surroundings
D. Heat flows to the environment	4. Temperature perception by touch.

A. _________ B. _________ C. _________ D. _________

5. Temperature is a direct measure of hotness or coldness.

True ☐ False ☐

6. We can rely on our sense of touch to accurately measure temperature for scientific purposes.

True ☐ False ☐

*Concepts of all questions bearing * are important for JEE/NEET/CUET.*

TOPIC 2

Measurement of Temperature, Ideal Gas Equation and Absolute Temperature

***7.** Fill the blank spaces for given temperature in other units.
$-40°F =$ ________ °C = ________ K

8. A graph of two temperature scales *A* and *B* is as shown in figure given alongside. Between lower and upper fixed points, there are 150 divisions on scale *A* and 100 divisions on scale *B*. Find the relation between *A* and *B*.

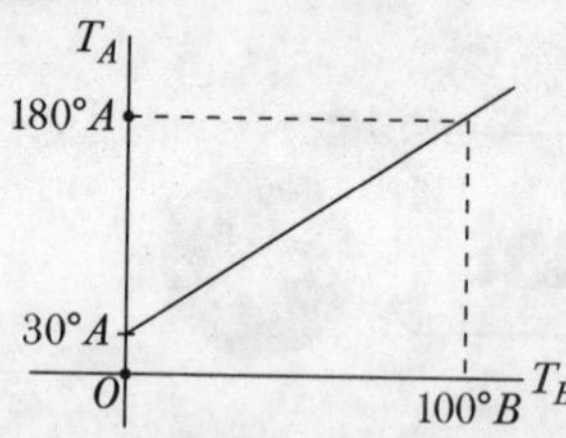

____

9. A thermometer has incorrect calibrations. It reads melting point of ice as – 10° C and 60°C temperature as 50°C, so the boiling point of water noted by this thermometer will be ________.

10. On a new scale of temperature (which is linear) and called the W scale, the freezing and boiling points of water are 39°W and 239°W, respectively. What will be the temperature on the new scale, corresponding to a temperature of 39°C on the Celsius scale ?

____

11. A thermometer graduated according to a linear scale reads a value x_0 when in contact with boiling water and $x_0/3$ when in contact with ice. What is the temperature of an object in °C, if this thermometer in the contact with the object reads $x_0/2$?

(a) 35 ☐ (b) 60 ☐ (c) 40 ☐ (d) 25 ☐

12. Consider relation of pressure variation and volume variation of a gas

$$p_T = p_0(1 + \alpha T) \text{ and } V_T = V_0(1 + \beta T)$$

Ratio of constants α and β for low density gases will be ________ (less than 1/more than 1/equal to 1).

13. *p*-*T* graph of a gas at constant volume is as shown below.

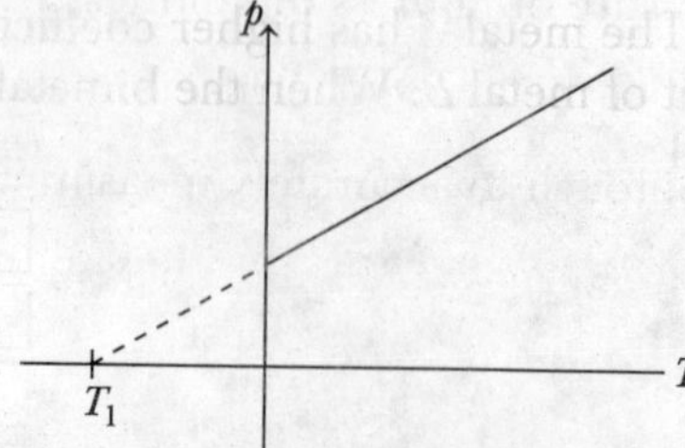

Temperature T_1 is nearly ________ °C.

14. Which of these statement(s) is/are correct regarding p-T graphs of low density gases?

I. Slope of all graphs is constant.

II. y-intercept of all graphs is same.

III. All graphs are parabolic.

IV. All graphs have same x-intercept.

TOPIC 3 Thermal Expansion

15. Amount of contraction of metal and glass is different for same reduction of temperature.

True ☐ False ☐

16. Coefficient of linear expansion for a solid is a constant that does not change with temperature.

True ☐ False ☐

17. Correct variation of coefficient of expansion with temperature is

(a)
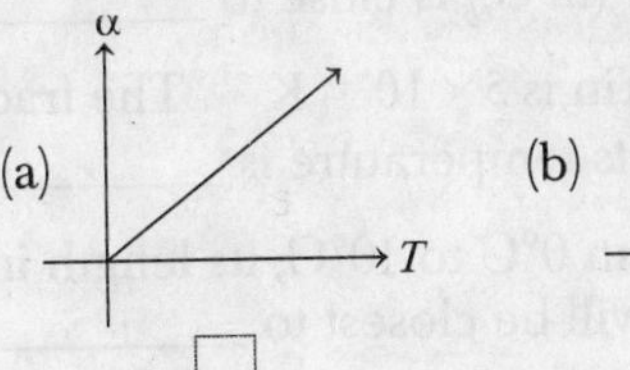

(b)
α
T

(c)
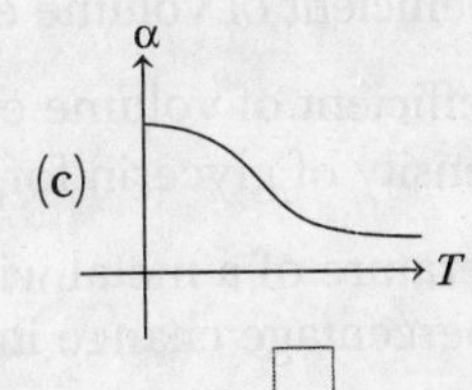

(d)
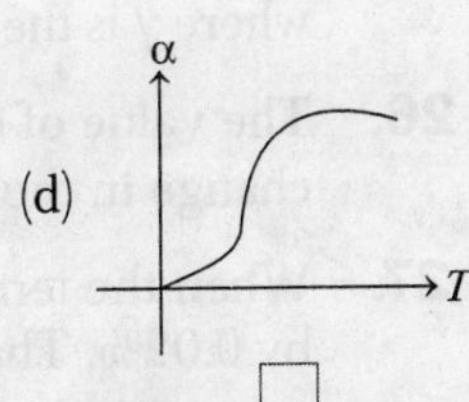

18. Coefficient of linear expansion of brass and steel rods are α_1 and α_2 and lengths of brass and steel rods are l_1 and l_2, respectively. If $(l_2 - l_1)$ is maintained same at all temperatures, which one of the following relation holds good ?

(a) $\alpha_1 l_2^2 = \alpha_2 l_1^2$ ☐ (b) $\alpha_1^2 l_2 = \alpha_2^2 l_1$ ☐

(c) $\alpha_1 l_1 = \alpha_2 l_2$ ☐ (d) $\alpha_1 l_2 = \alpha_2 l_1$ ☐

19. A copper rod of 88 cm and an aluminium rod of unknown length have their increase in length independent of increase in temperature. Find the length of aluminium rod in metre. (Take, $\alpha_{Cu} = 1.7 \times 10^{-5} K^{-1}, \alpha_{Al} = 2.2 \times 10^{-5} K^{-1}$)

20. A bimetallic strip consists of metals A and B. It is mounted rigidly as shown in figure alongside. The metal A has higher coefficient of expansion compared to that of metal B. When the bimetallic strip is placed in a cold bath, it will

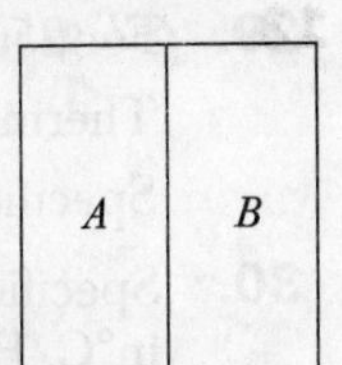

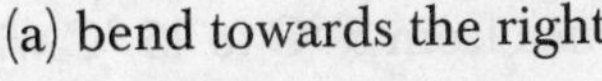

(a) bend towards the right ☐

(b) not bend but shrink ☐

(c) Neither bend nor shrink ☐

(d) bend towards the left ☐

21. Consider a cube of side length l and coefficient of linear expansion α. Now, complete following, taking length $l = 2$ m. (Here, Δl, ΔA and ΔV indicates change in length, change of area and change of volume for same increase of temperature)
$\Delta l : \Delta A : \Delta V ::$ ____________

22. A uniform solid brass sphere is freely spinning about its diameter with angular speed ω_0. What is its angular speed when temperature is increased by 100 °C?
(Take, $\alpha_{brass} = 2 \times 10^{-5}$ °C^{-1})

____

23. Each side of a box made of metal sheet in cubic shape is a at room temperature T, the coefficient of linear expansion of the metal sheet is α. The metal sheet is heated uniformly by a small temperature ΔT, so that its new temperature is $T + \Delta T$. Calculate the increase in the volume of the metal box.

____

24. A glass beaker of one litre volume is full of mercury at 0°C. Temperature is then raised to 100° C. Amount of mercury spilled out is nearly____________ cc.
(Take, $\gamma_{mercury} = 1.82 \times 10^{-4}$ °C^{-1} and $\alpha_{glass} = 0.1 \times 10^{-4}$ °C^{-1})

25. A bakelite beaker has volume capacity of 500 cc at 30°C. When it is partially filled with V_m volume (at 30°C) of mercury, it is found that the unfilled volume of the beaker remains constant as temperature is varied. If $\gamma_{(beaker)} = 6 \times 10^{-6}$ °C^{-1} and $\gamma_{(mercury)} = 1.5 \times 10^{-4}$ °C^{-1}, where γ is the coefficient of volume expansion, then V_m (in cc) is close to ____________.

26. The value of coefficient of volume expansion of glycerin is 5×10^{-4} K^{-1}. The fractional change in the density of glycerin for a rise of 40°C in its temperature is ____________.

27. When the temperature of a metal wire is increased from 0°C to 10°C, its length increases by 0.02%. The percentage change in its mass density will be closest to ____________.

TOPIC 4

Specific Heat Capacity

NCERT Pg 208-209

28. Water (mass = 5 g) requires 500 cal of heat to raise its temperature from 0°C to 100°C.
Heat capacity of water = ____________ cal/°C and
specific heat capacity of water = ____________ cal/g°C.

29. For 25 g sample of a metal, 300 J of heat rises temperature from 25°C to 45°C.
Thermal capacity of sample is ____________ J/°C.
Specific heat of sample is ____________ J/kg°C.

30. Specific heat of a substance $C = 0.2 + 0.14\,t + 0.023t^2$ cal/g °C, where t = temperature in°C. Heat required to raise temperature of 2 g of substance from 5 °C to 15 °C will be x cal, what is the value of x?

____

31. Two different metal bodies *A* and *B* of equal mass are heated at a uniform rate under similar conditions. The variation of temperature of the bodies is graphically represented as shown in the following figure. The ratio of specific heat capacities is ______ $\left(\frac{3}{8}/\frac{3}{4}\right)$.

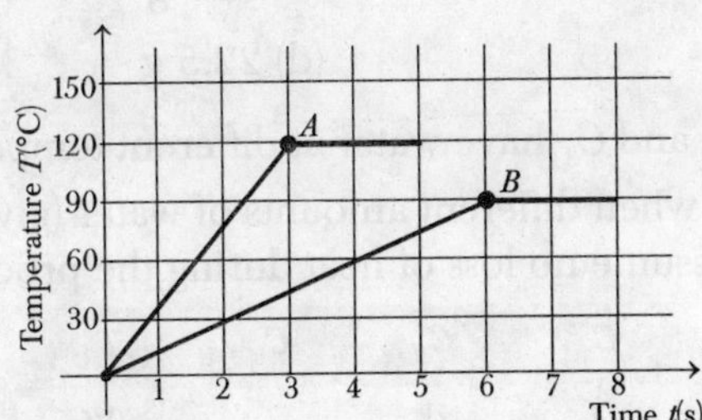

32. A bullet of mass 5 g, travelling with a speed of 210 m/s, strikes a fixed wooden target. One-half of its kinetic energy is converted into heat in the bullet while the other half is converted into heat in the wood. The rise of temperature of the bullet, if the specific heat of its material is 0.030 cal $g^{-1}°C^{-1}$, is close to

(a) 87.5°C ☐ (b) 83.3°C ☐

(c) 119.2°C ☐ (d) 38.4°C ☐

33. Two bodies attain thermal equilibrium at temperature T, then
$m_1 s_1 \cdot (T - T_1) = m_2 s_2 \cdot (T - T_2)$

True ☐ False ☐

34. Equal masses of two liquids at temperatures 30°C and 20°C respectively, are mixed together. Equilibrium temperature of mixture is found to be nearly 26 °C. What is the ratio of specific heat of liquids?

______

35. Two identical bodies are made of a material for which the heat capacity increases with temperature. One of these is at 100°C, while the other one is at 0°C. If the two bodies are brought into contact, then assuming no heat loss, the final common temperature is

(a) 50°C ☐

(b) more than 50°C ☐

(c) less than 50°C but greater than 0°C ☐

(d) 0°C ☐

***36.** To cool 250 g of cola at 25 °C, a person uses ice from a freezer at – 20 °C. Specific heat of ice used is 2000 J $kg^{-1}K^{-1}$, latent heat of ice is 3.34×10^5 J kg^{-1} and specific heat of cola is 4160 J $kg^{-1}K^{-1}$. If final mixture temperature is 0 °C, then amount of ice added is nearly ______.

37. Steam at 100°C is passed into 20 g of water at 10°C. When water acquires a temperature of 80°C, the mass of water present will be x g. Find the value of x. (Take, specific heat of water = 1 cal $g^{-1} \, °C^{-1}$ and latent heat of steam = 540 cal g^{-1})

(a) 24 g ☐ (b) 31.5 g ☐
(c) 42.5 g ☐ (d) 22.5 g ☐

38. Three containers C_1, C_2 and C_3 have water at different temperatures. The table below shows the final temperature T when different amounts of water (given in litres) are taken from each container and mixed (assume no loss of heat during the process)

C_1	C_2	C_3	T
1L	2L	–	60°C
–	1L	2L	30°C
2L	–	1L	60°C
1L	1L	1L	θ

The value of θ (in °C to the nearest integer) is ________.

***39.** Ice is heated and following graph is obtained.

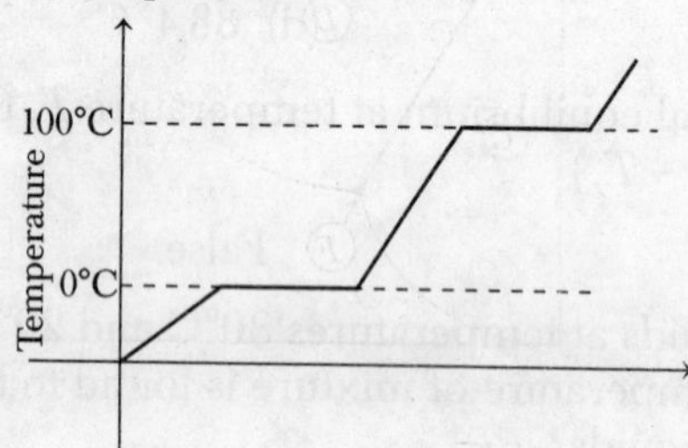

Here, variable on X-axis is ________ (heat quantity/time).

***40.** Heating curve for water is as shown below.

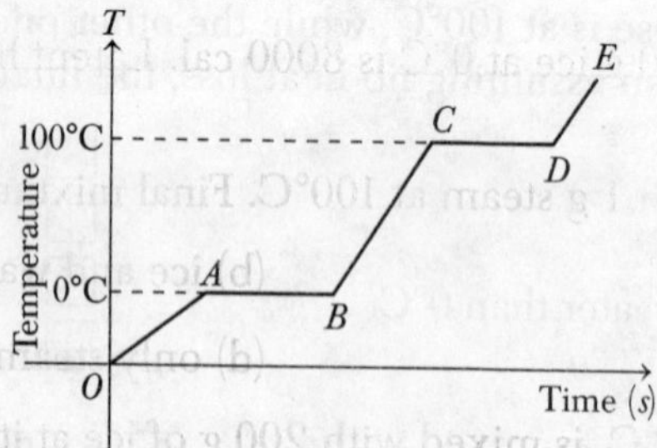

Tick (✓/✗) for correct/incorrect statement in given boxes.

(i) $OA \rightarrow$ Heating of solid ice ☐
(ii) $AB \rightarrow$ Melting of solid ice ☐
(iii) $BC \rightarrow$ Ice-water mixture is being heated ☐
(iv) $CD \rightarrow$ Boiling of water ☐

***41.** Heating curve for dry ice (solid CO_2) will be

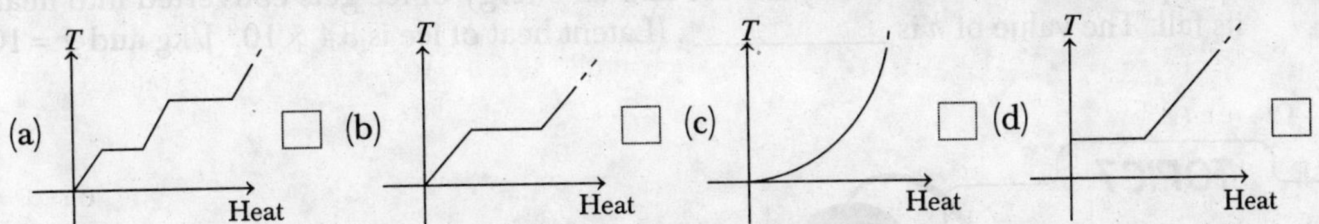

***42.** Liquid oxygen at 50 K is heated to 300 K at constant pressure of 1 atm. The rate of heating is constant. Which one of the following graphs represents the variation of temperature with time?

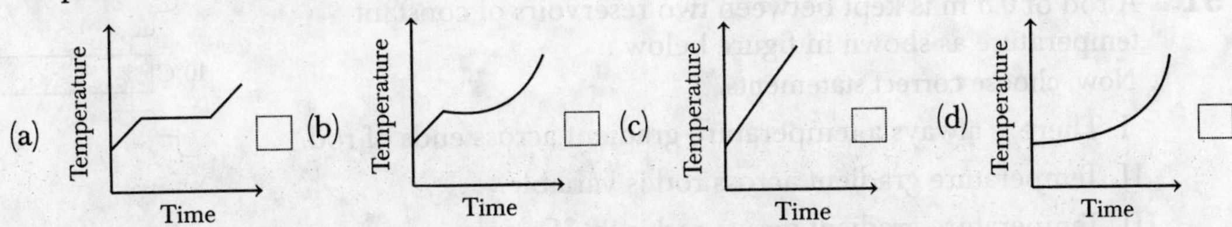

43. Regelation occurs due to __________ (lowering/elevation) of melting point of water.

44. During sublimation process, solid and vapour states of substance are not in thermal equilibrium.

Yes ☐ No ☐

45. Phase diagram for water is shown below. Name the region marked in it.

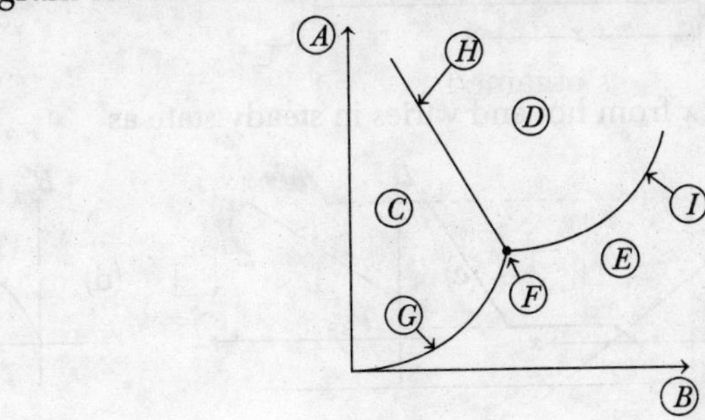

A = __________ B = __________ C = __________

D = __________ E = __________ F = __________

G = __________ H = __________ and I = __________

46. Heat required to melt 100 g ice at 0°C is 8000 cal. Latent heat of fusion for water will be __________ .

47. 5 g ice at 0° is mixed with 1 g steam at 100°C. Final mixture contains

(a) only water ☐ (b) ice and water ☐

(c) water and steam ☐ (d) only steam ☐

48. M grams of steam at 100°C is mixed with 200 g of ice at its melting point in a thermally insulated container. If it produces liquid water at 40°C (heat of vaporisation of water is 540 cal/g and heat of fusion of ice is 80 cal/g), the value of M is __________ .

49. 5g ice at 0°C is mixed with 1 kg steam at 100 °C. Final temperature of mixture after equilibrium will be __________ °C.

50. A piece of ice falls from a height h, so that it melts completely. Only one-quarter of the heat produced is absorbed by the ice and all energy of ice gets converted into heat during its fall. The value of h is ________. (Latent heat of ice is 3.4×10^5 J/kg and $g = 10$ N/kg)

51. A rod of 0.5 m is kept between two reservoirs of constant temperature as shown in figure below.
Now, choose correct statements.

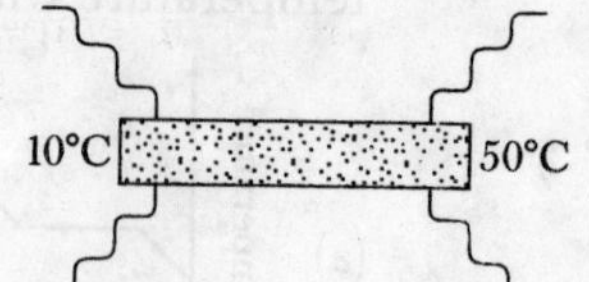

I. There is always a temperature gradient across ends of rod.
II. Temperature gradient across rod is variable.
III. Temperature gradient across rod is 80 °C m^{-1}.
IV. Temperature gradient depends on material of rod.

52.

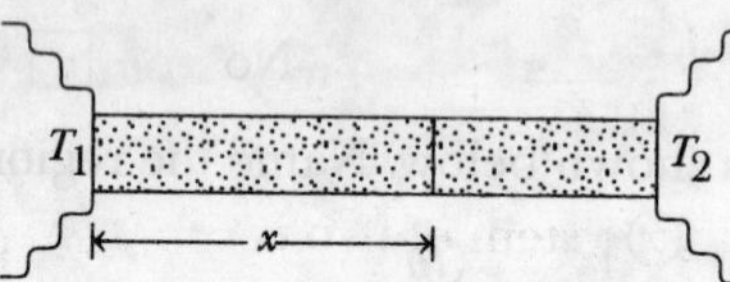

Heat flow rate H at a distance x from hot end varies in steady state as

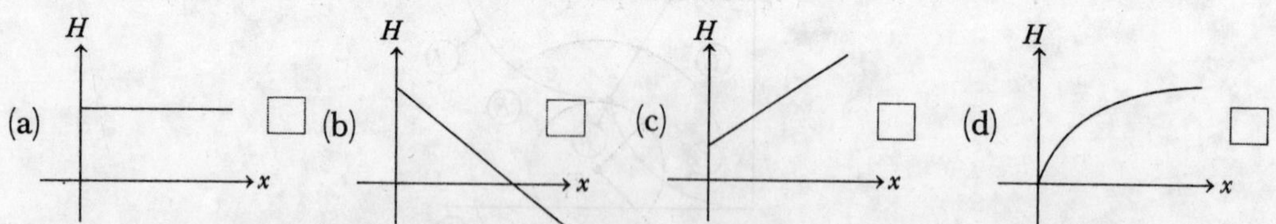

53. A thermocol wall (area = 400 cm^2, thickness 4 cm, thermal conductivity $= 2 \times 10^{-4}$ cal s^{-1} cm^{-1}°C^{-1}) separates region of temperatures 0°C and 100°C. Heat flow through it in 1 day will be around x kcal. What is the value of x?

54. Three ends of identical rods are kept at 0°C, 60°C and 60°C. Other three ends are joined together.

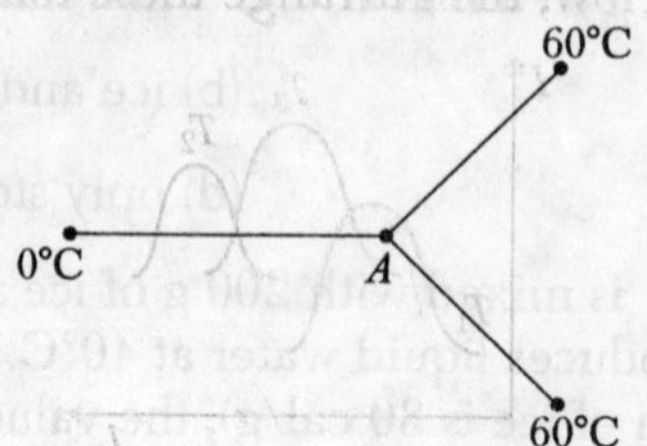

What is the value of temperature of joint A in steady state condition?

55. Four identical rods are joined as shown in the following figure.

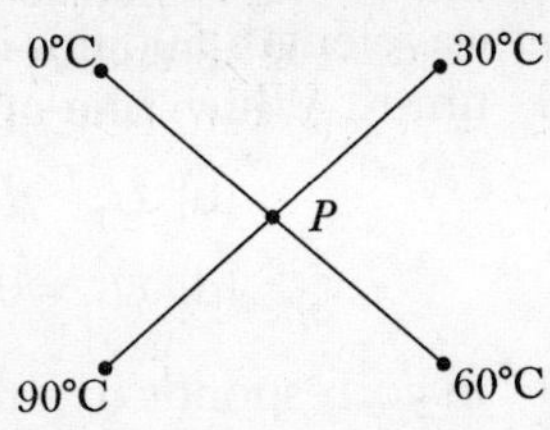

Temperature of junction P will be __________ °C.

56. In given arrangement, ratio of conductivities is $K_A : K_B : K_C :: 2 : 4 : 3$. Ratio of temperatures T_1 and T_2 is around __________.

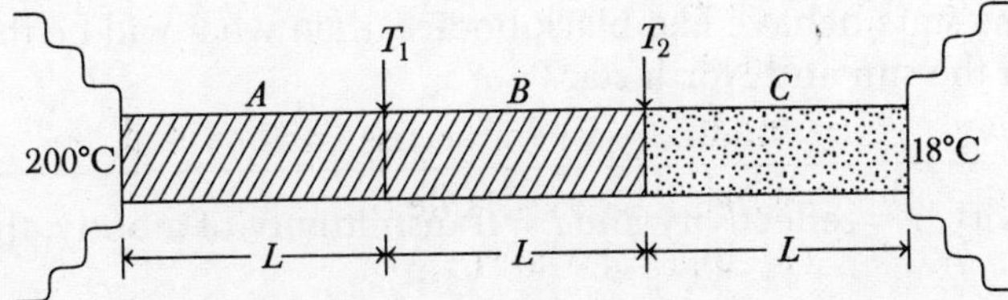

57. Two identical metal wires of thermal conductivities K_1 and K_2 respectively, are connected in series. The effective thermal conductivity of the combination is

(a) $\dfrac{2K_1 K_2}{K_1 + K_2}$ ☐ (b) $\dfrac{K_1 + K_2}{2K_1 K_2}$ ☐ (c) $\dfrac{K_1 + K_2}{K_1 K_2}$ ☐ (d) $\dfrac{K_1 K_2}{K_1 + K_2}$ ☐

58. The following figure shows a system of two concentric spheres of radii r_1 and r_2 and kept at temperatures T_1 and T_2, respectively. The radial rate of flow of heat in a substance between the two concentric spheres, is proportional to __________.

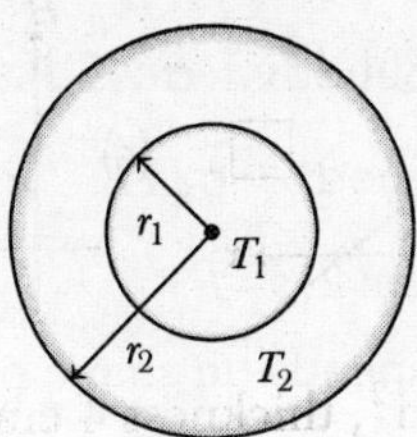

59. Heat radiations are produced by molecules or atoms by virtue of oscillations of charged particles.

Yes ☐ No ☐

60. The plots of intensity of radiation *versus* wavelength of three black bodies at temperatures T_1, T_2 and T_3 are shown below, then arrange these temperatures in increasing order.

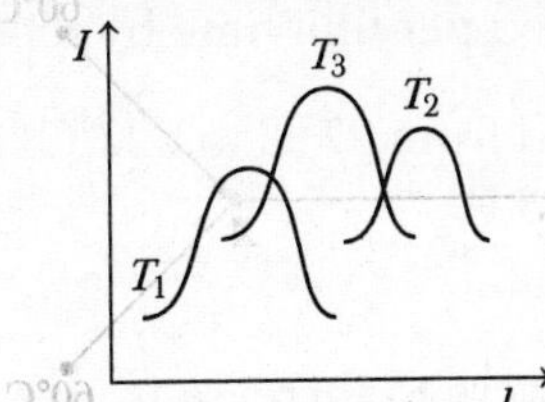

61. A black body is at a temperature of 5760 K. The energy of radiation emitted by the body at wavelength 250 nm is U_1, at wavelength 500 nm is U_2 and that at 1000 nm is U_3 and Wien's constant, $b = 2.88 \times 10^6$ nm-K. Which one of the following is correct?

(a) $U_3 = 0$ ☐ (b) $U_1 > U_2$ ☐
(c) $U_2 > U_1$ ☐ (d) $U_1 = 0$ ☐

62. The wavelength $\lambda_m = 5.5 \times 10^{-7}$ m corresponds to a temperature of the sun of 5500 K. If the furnace has wavelength λ_m equal to 11×10^{-7} m, then find the temperature of furnace.

____

63. The intensity of radiation emitted by the sun has its maximum value at a wavelength of 510 nm and that emitted by the North star has the maximum value at wavelength of 350 nm. If these stars behave like black bodies, then what will be the ratio of surface temperature of the sun and North star?

____

64. If a = absorptivity, r = reflectivity and t = transmittivity of a body, then $a + r + t =$ ______________.

65. Transmission and reflective powers of a coated surface are $\frac{1}{6}$ and $\frac{1}{3}$ respectively, then ratio of its absorptive and reflective powers is __________ $\left(\frac{2}{3}/\frac{3}{2}\right)$.

66. Ratio of emissivity and absorptivity of most of real bodies is __________ (1/less than 1/more than 1).

67. A body at a temperature T(K) is placed in an atmospheres of T_0 (K).

Now, choose incorrect statement.

I. The rate of heat absorption of body $= \sigma eAT_0^4$.

II. The rate of heat emission by body $= \sigma eAT^4$.

III. No net heat is exchanged when $T_0 = T$.

IV. Rate of heat emission also depends on shape of body.

T_0(K)

____

68. Consider two copper spheres of radius 4 m at 2000 K and radius 1m at 4000 K. What is the ratio of energy radiated per unit time?

____

69. A sphere and a cube of same material and same volume are heated at same temperature. Ratio of amount of heat radiated per unit time by them is ______________.

70. Temperature of a body is raised from 27°C to 227°C. Factor by which rate of radiation increases is __________ $\left(\frac{625}{81}/\frac{732}{34}\right)$.

71. If the temperature of the sun were to increase from T to $2T$ and its radius from R to $2R$, then the ratio of the radiant energy received on earth to what it was previously, will be __________ (32/64).

TOPIC 8

Newton's Law of Cooling

72. Let a body cool down from temperature θ_1 to temperature θ_2 when it is placed in a room of temperature θ_0. Then, $\frac{\theta_1 - \theta_2}{t}$ is proportional to ________ .

73. A body cools from 52.5°C to 47.5°C in 5 min and to 42.5°C in 7.5 min. Temperature of surroundings will be ________ °C.

74. Temperature of a hot water bottle falls from 90°C to 80°C in time t_1, from 80°C to 70°C in time t_2 and from 70°C to 60°C in time t_3. Then, correct relation is

(a) $t_1 = t_2 = t_3$ ☐ (b) $t_1 > t_2 > t_3$ ☐ (c) $t_1 < t_2 < t_3$ ☐ (d) $t_1 + t_2 = t_3$ ☐

75. A bowl of a liquid cools from 60°C to 50°C in 10 min and to 42°C in next 10 min. Surrounding temperature is ________ .

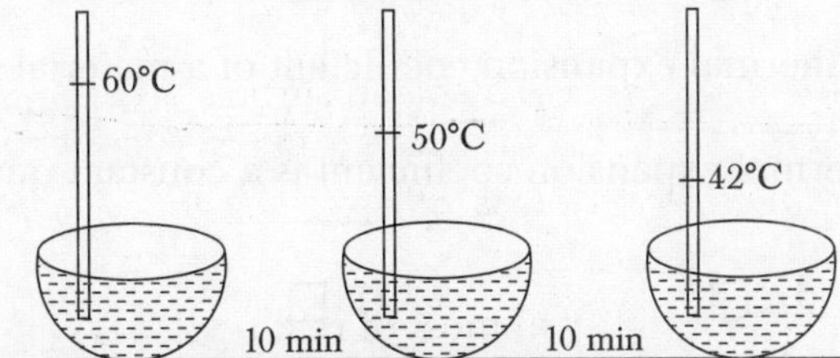

76. A metal sphere cools from 62°C to 61°C in 2 min with surrounding temperature of 30°C. Time taken by sphere to cool from 46°C to 45.5°C in ________ min.

77. An object kept in a large room having air temperature of 25°C takes 12 min to cool from 80°C to 70°C. The time taken to cool for the same object from 70°C to 60°C would be nearly ________ .

78. A body takes 4 min to cool from 61° C to 59°C. If the temperature of the surroundings is 30°C, then what is the time taken by the body to cool from 51°C to 49° C?

____

79. In 5 min, a body cools from 75°C to 65°C at room temperature of 25°C. The temperature of body at the end of next 5 min is ________ °C.

Assertion-Reason Questions

Direction (Q. Nos. 1-10) *In the following questions, a statement of Assertion is followed by a corresponding statement of Reason. From the following options, choose the correct one.*

(a) Both Assertion and Reason are correct and Reason is the correct explanation of Assertion.

(b) Both Assertion and Reason are correct but Reason is not the correct explanation of Assertion.

(c) Assertion is correct but Reason is incorrect.

(d) Assertion is incorrect but Reason is correct.

1. Assertion (A) Heat is the form of energy transferred between systems due to temperature difference.

Reason (R) Heat occurs only when there is no temperature difference.

(a) ☐ (b) ☐ (c) ☐ (d) ☐

2. **Assertion** (A) Temperature can be perceived by touch.
Reason (R) Our temperature sense is reliable and accurate for scientific purposes.

(a) ☐ (b) ☐ (c) ☐ (d) ☐

3. **Assertion** (A) The Celsius scale is more commonly used for scientific temperature measurements than the Fahrenheit scale.
Reason (R) The Celsius scale is more practical for everyday use.

(a) ☐ (b) ☐ (c) ☐ (d) ☐

4. **Assertion (A)** All gases at low densities exhibit the same expansion behaviour.
Reason (R) The behaviour of gases at low densities can be described by the ideal gas law.

(a) ☐ (b) ☐ (c) ☐ (d) ☐

5. **Assertion** (A) The kelvin scale is based on the concept of absolute zero.
Reason (R) Absolute zero is the temperature at which the volume of an ideal gas becomes zero.

(a) ☐ (b) ☐ (c) ☐ (d) ☐

6. **Assertion** (A) The thermal expansion coefficient of a material is dependent of its temperature.
Reason (R) The thermal expansion coefficient is a constant quantity for a specific material.

(a) ☐ (b) ☐ (c) ☐ (d) ☐

7. **Assertion** (A) If a metal bar is heated and its length increases, its density decreases.
Reason (R) The mass of the bar increases with increase in temperature.

(a) ☐ (b) ☐ (c) ☐ (d) ☐

8. **Assertion** (A) Metals generally have higher specific heat capacities compared to non-metals.
Reason (R) Specific heat capacity is lower in materials with strong intermolecular forces.

(a) ☐ (b) ☐ (c) ☐ (d) ☐

9. **Assertion** (A) Calorimeters must be perfectly insulated to ensure accurate heat measurements.
Reason (R) Insulation prevents heat loss to the surroundings, ensuring that all heat measured is from the reaction.

(a) ☐ (b) ☐ (c) ☐ (d) ☐

10. **Assertion (A)** Newton's law of cooling can be used to determine the time required for an object to reach a specific temperature.
Reason (R) The law provides a relationship between the temperature difference and the rate of cooling.

(a) ☐ (b) ☐ (c) ☐ (d) ☐

Case Based Questions

1. Railway tracks in India are subjected to diverse climatic conditions, which significantly affect their dimensions due to thermal expansion and contraction. Consider a railway track made of steel with a coefficient of linear thermal expansion of 11×10^{-6} per °C. The track is installed at a temperature of 30°C and can experience variations from 0°C to 45°C.

Answer the following questions

(i) During a hot summer day, the temperature rises to 40°C. The change in length of a 1 km long railway track due to thermal expansion.

(a) 100 mm ☐ (b) 110 mm ☐

(c) 120 mm ☐ (d) 130 mm ☐

(ii) The railway tracks are often laid with small gaps between section

(a) to reduce maintenance costs ☐

(b) to allow for thermal expansion and contraction ☐

(c) to increase train speed ☐

(d) to prevent rusting ☐

(iii) Choose the correct statement for choosing steel as railway tracks.

(a) Higher coefficient reduces maintenance frequency. ☐

(b) Lower coefficient increases safety. ☐

(c) Higher coefficient requires more careful design. ☐

(d) High tensile and high thermal coefficient is best suited for longer operation. ☐

(iv) Which of the following is correct in terms of railway tracks maintenance during monsoon?

(a) increased temperature fluctuations ☐

(b) heavy rainfall and humility ☐

(c) decreased track stability ☐

(d) improved maintenance efficiency ☐

Or

If a railway track in India experiences a temperature drop to 5°C. Calculate the contraction in length of the track.

(a) 250 mm ☐ (b) 275 mm ☐

(c) 300 mm ☐ (d) 325 mm ☐

2. Imagine you are responsible for cooling a hot beverage. You have a cup containing 200 g of hot coffee at 90°C and you decide to add ice cubes to cool it down. Each ice cube has mass of 20 g and is initially at 0°C. Assume the specific heat capacity of water is 4.18 J/g °C and the latent heat of fusion for ice is 334 J/g.

Answer the following questions based on the case study.

(i) The amount of heat required to melt one ice cube of 20 g initially at 0°C.

(a) 6680 J ☐ (b) 3340 J ☐

(c) 4180 J ☐ (d) 8360 J ☐

(ii) How much heat will the melted ice (water at 0°C) absorb to reach the final temperature of T (assume $T = 90°$ C) is the equilibrium temperature?

(a) 8361 J ☐ (b) 7524 J ☐

(c) 4180 J ☐ (d) 3340 J ☐

(iii) The equilibrium temperature T after adding two ice cubes, assuming all heat exchange happens between the coffee and the ice.

(a) 15°C ☐ (b) 68°C ☐

(c) 45°C ☐ (d) 60°C ☐

(iv) If no ice is added and the coffee is allowed to cool naturally to room temperature (25°C), how much heat is lost by the coffee?

(a) 54340 J ☐ (b) 54100 cal ☐

(c) 83600 J ☐ (d) 16720 cal ☐

Or

If the coffee was initially at 80°C instead of 90°C, how many ice cubes (each 20g) would be needed to reach an equilibrium temperature of 30°C?

(a) 2 ☐ (b) 3 ☐

(c) 4 ☐ (d) 5 ☐

COMPETITION EDGE UP

1. *On celsius scale, the temperature of body increases by 40°C. The increase in temperature on fahrenheit scale is*

[NCERT Pg. 203, JEE Main 2024]

(a) 72°F ☐ (b) 75°F ☐

(c) 70°F ☐ (d) 68°F ☐

2. *A block of ice at −10°C is slowly heated and converted to steam at 100°C. Which of the following curves represent the phenomenon qualitatively?*

[NCERT Pg. 210, JEE Main 2024]

(a) Temperature → / Heat supplied → ☐

(b) Temperature → / Heat supplied → ☐

(c) Temperature→ Heat supplied→ ☐

(d) Temperature→ Heat supplied→ ☐

3. 0.08 kg air is heated at constant volume through 5°C. The specific heat of air at constant volume is 0.17 kcal/kg°C and J = 4.18 J/cal. The change in its internal energy is approximately.

[NCERT Pg. 208, JEE Main 2024]

(a) 318 J ☐

(b) 142 J ☐

(c) 298 J ☐

(d) 284 J ☐

4. A metallic bar of Young's modulus, 0.5×10^{11} N-m^{-2} and coefficient of linear thermal expansion 10^{-5} °C^{-1}, length 1 m and area of cross-section 10^{-3} m^2 is heated from 0°C to 100°C without expansion or bending. The compressive force developed in it is **[NCERT Pg. 207, NEET 2024]**

(a) 5×10^3 N ☐

(b) 50×10^3 N ☐

(c) 100×10^3 N ☐

(d) 2×10^3 N ☐

5. A cup of coffee cools from 90°C to 80°C in t minutes, when the room temperature is 20°C. The time taken by a similar cup of coffee to cool from 80°C to 60°C at a room temperature same at 20°C, is

[NCERT Pg. 220, NEET 2021]

(a) $\frac{13}{10}t$ ☐ (b) $\frac{13}{5}t$ ☐

(c) $\frac{10}{13}t$ ☐ (d) $\frac{5}{13}t$ ☐

6. Three stars A, B and C have surface temperatures T_A, T_B, T_C, respectively. Star A appears bluish, star B appears reddish and star C yellowish.

Hence, **[NCERT Pg. 218, NEET (Oct.) 2020]**

(a) $T_A > T_B > T_C$ ☐

(b) $T_B > T_C > T_A$ ☐

(c) $T_C > T_B > T_A$ ☐

(d) $T_A > T_C > T_B$ ☐

7. The quantities of heat required to raise the temperature of two solid copper spheres of radii r_1 and r_2 ($r_1 = 1.5\ r_2$) through 1 K are in the ratio **[NCERT Pg. 208, NEET (Sep.) 2020]**

(a) $\frac{9}{4}$ ☐ (b) $\frac{3}{2}$ ☐

(c) $\frac{5}{3}$ ☐ (d) $\frac{27}{8}$ ☐

Chapter 11

Thermodynamics

Scan and take Chapter Test

TOPIC 1

Thermal Equilibrium and Zeroth Law of Thermodynamics

1. In the figure given below, two systems A and B are separated by an insulating fixed wall (adiabatic wall) and also insulated from surroundings by insulated wall.

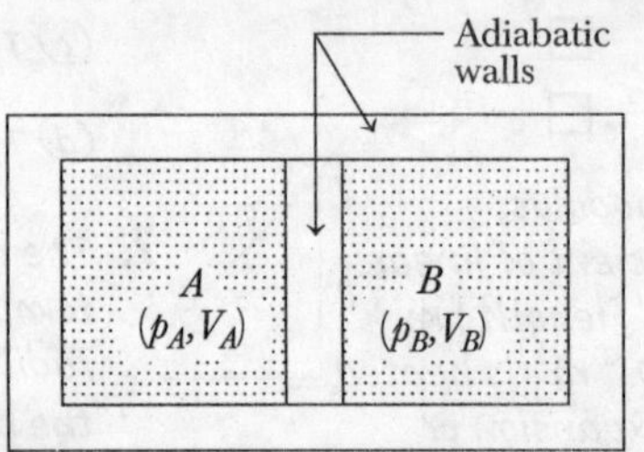

Choose the correct option regarding above information.

(a) The pressures of A and B will change with time.
(b) The temperatures of A and B will change with time.
(c) The thermodynamic states of A and B will not change with time.
(d) None of the above

2. Three systems 1, 2 and 3 are having pressure and volume (p_1, V_1), (p_2, V_2) and (p_3, V_3). Systems 1 and 3 are in thermal equilibrium and equation $p_1V_1 - nbp_1 - p_3V_3 = 0$ holds true. Systems 2 and 3 are in thermal equilibrium and equation $p_2V_2 - p_3V_3 + \frac{nb' p_3V_3}{V_2} = 0$ holds true. Relation which express the thermal equilibrium between systems 1 and 2 is ________.

3. Three thermodynamic systems are at a temperature of 60°C. What can be concluded about them?

(a) No heat flow occurs between the three systems
(b) The three systems are in thermal equilibrium with each other
(c) They obey zeroth law of thermodynamics
(d) All of the above

Concepts of all questions bearing * are important for JEE/NEET/CUET.

TOPIC 2

Heat, Internal Energy, Work and First Law of Thermodynamics

4. Tick (✓/×) for correct/incorrect statement in given boxes.

(i) Internal energy of a given mass of gas depends on state described by pressure, volume and temperature. ☐

(ii) Internal energy also depend on how the state of gas is achieved. ☐

(iii) Pressure, volume, temperature and internal energy are thermodynamic state variable of the system. ☐

(iv) Internal energy of a real gas is sum of the kinetic and potential energies of its molecules. ☐

(v) Internal energy of an ideal gas is the sum of kinetic energies of its molecules. ☐

(vi) Heat and work are two different modes of altering state of a thermodynamic system without changing its internal energy. ☐

5. An ideal monoatomic gas is taken from A to B by the following three ways p, q and r as shown in the given p-V curve.

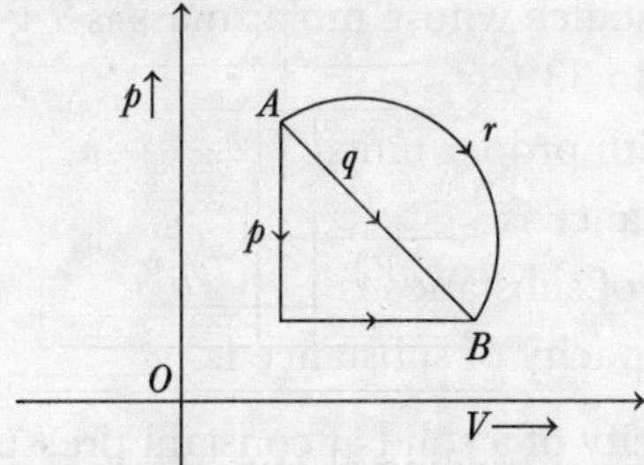

Then, amongst which of these ways, the internal energy would be same?

____

6. In changing the state of thermodynamics from A to B, the heat required is Q and the work done by the system is W. The change in internal energy is ________.

7. Heat given to a system is 35 J and work done by the system is 15 J. The change in the internal energy of the system will be ________ (20/30) J.

8. A system is given 300 cal of heat and it does 600 J of work. Change in internal energy of system in the process is ________ J.

9. If 110 J of heat is added to a gaseous system, whose internal energy change is 40 J, then amount of external work done is 150 J.

True ☐ False ☐

10. When the amount of work done is 333 cal and change in internal energy is 167 cal, the heat supplied is ________ cal.

11. If we had a system on which 10 J of work is done and change in internal energy of system is 3.5 J, calculate the amount of heat loss/gain by system.

____

12. Consider a system taken from state a to state b.

Let 80 J of heat flows into system and system does 30 J of work.

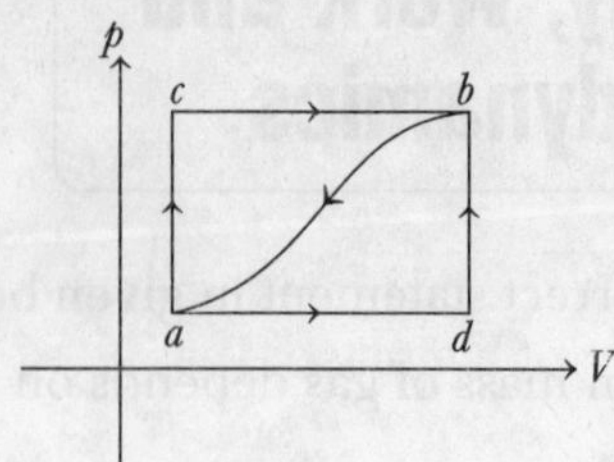

Now, fill following blanks.

I. For path $a \to c \to b$, $\Delta U =$ ________ J

II. For path $a \to d \to b$, if $\Delta W = 10$ J, then $\Delta Q =$ ________ J

III. For path $b \to a$, $\Delta W =$ ________ $\Delta U =$ ________, $\Delta Q =$ ________

TOPIC 3

Specific Heat Capacity

NCERT Pg 231-232

13. Let 20 g sample of a substance whose molar mass is 2 g requires 40 J of heat to raise its temperature from 23 °C to 33°C.

Now, fill these blanks (with proper units).

I. Heat capacity of substance is ________ .

II. Specific heat capacity of substance is ________ .

III. Molar specific heat capacity of substance is ________ .

14. Molar specific heat capacity of a solid at constant pressure is $3R$.

True ☐ False ☐

15. For an ideal gas, molar specific heat capacity at constant volume is $\frac{3}{2}R$. Find its molar specific heat capacity at constant pressure.

____

16. The amount of heat needed to raise the temperature of 2 moles of an ideal monoatomic gas from 273 K to 373 K, when no work is done will be ________ (R = Universal gas constant).

***17.** Which of the following graph represents the correct for variation of specific heat capacity of water with temperature?

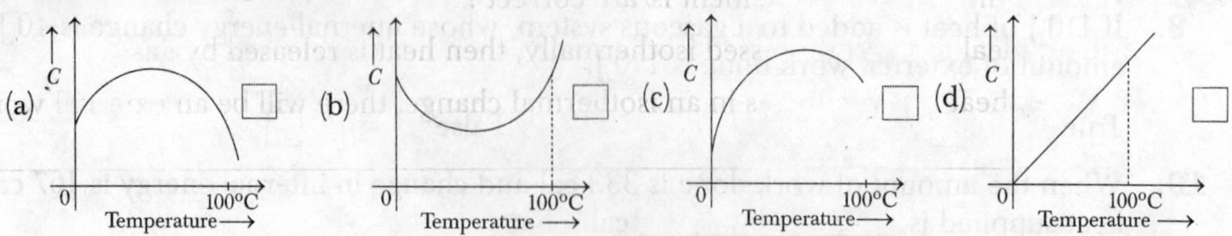

TOPIC 4

Thermodynamic State Variables, Equation of State and Thermodynamic Processes

18. The change in internal energy of the mass of gas when the volume changes from V to $2V$ at constant pressure will be $\frac{pV}{\gamma - 1}$.

True ☐ False ☐

19. Which of the following statement is/are correct ?

I. A quasi-static process is a hypothetical construct.

II. In isothermal process, heat transferred from the reservoir to system does affect the temperature of the reservoir.

III. In practice, processes are slow and do not involve large temperature gradient are reasonably approximation to an ideal quasi-static process.

---

20. A 0.5 mole of gas at temperature 300 K expands isothermally from an initial volume of 2 L to 6 L, then work done by gas is ________ J.

***21.** The following p-V curve shows two isothermal process for two different temperatures. Identify the higher temperature.

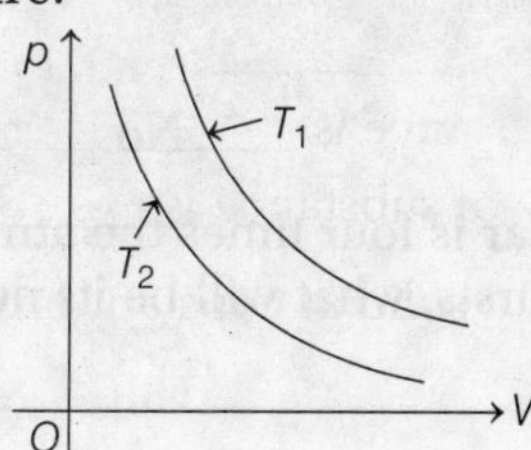

(a) $T_1 > T_2$ ☐ (b) $T_1 < T_2$ ☐

(c) $T_1 = T_2$ ☐ (d) None of these ☐

22. In an isothermal reversible expansion, if the volume of 96 g of oxygen at 27°C is increased from 70 L to 140 L, then work done by gas will be ________.

23. In an isothermal process, if the volume of an ideal gas is halved, then work done by a gas is ________ (positive/negative).

24. Which of the following statement is/are correct ?

I. If an ideal gas is compressed isothermally, then heat is released by gas.

II. When heat is given to gas in an isothermal change, there will be an external work done.

---

25. Consider p-V graph given

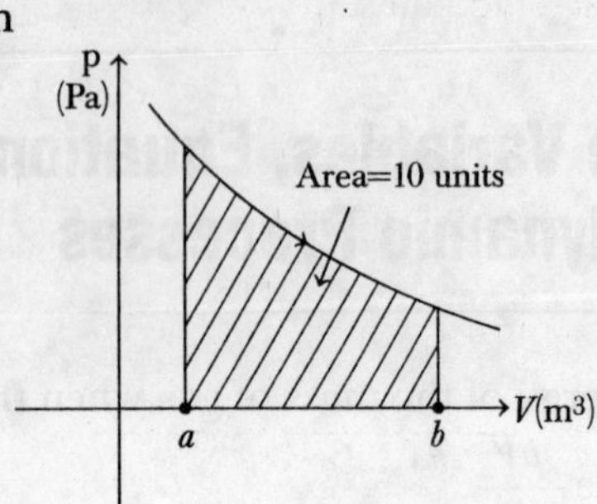

Work done in above process = ________ (+10 J/– 10 J).

26. p-V curves of an ideal gas for two adiabatic processes are shown in the following figure, then processes (b) and (d) are ____________.

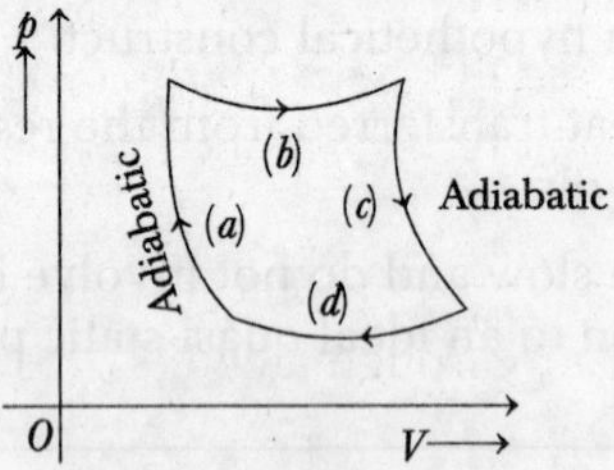

27. If an ideal gas undergoes a change in its state adiabatically from (p_1V_1) to (p_2V_2), then work done will be ________ .

28. In an adiabatic process, the state of gas is changed from $(p_1V_1T_1)$ to $(p_2V_2T_2)$. So, $T_1V_1^{\gamma-1} = T_2V_2^{\gamma-1}$.

Yes ☐ No ☐

29. The pressure in the tyre of a car is four times the atmospheric pressure at 300 K. If this tyre suddenly bursts, what will be its new temperature (Take, $\gamma = 1.4$)?

____

30. During the adiabatic process, 1g mol of a diatomic gas ($\gamma = 1.4$) is compressed adiabatically. So, its temperature rise is from 27°C to 127°C, the work done will be ________ J.

31. The slopes of isothermal and adiabatic curves are related as ____________ .

32. Which of these pairs is/are correctly matched for an adiabatic process?

I. $W > 0 \rightarrow T_2 < T_1$ II. $W < 0 \rightarrow T_1 > T_2$ III. $\Delta U + \Delta W = 0$

____

***33.** A gas is compressed isothermally to half of its initial volume. The same gas is compressed separately through an adiabatic process until its volume is again reduced to half, then

(a) compressing the gas through adiabatic process will require more work to be done. ☐

(b) compressing the gas isothermally or adiabatically will require the same amount of work ☐

(c) the case (whether compression through isothermal or through adiabatic process) which of requires more work will depend upon the atomicity of the gas ☐

(d) compressing the gas isothermally will require more work to be done ☐

***34.** Thermodynamic processes are indicated in the following diagram.

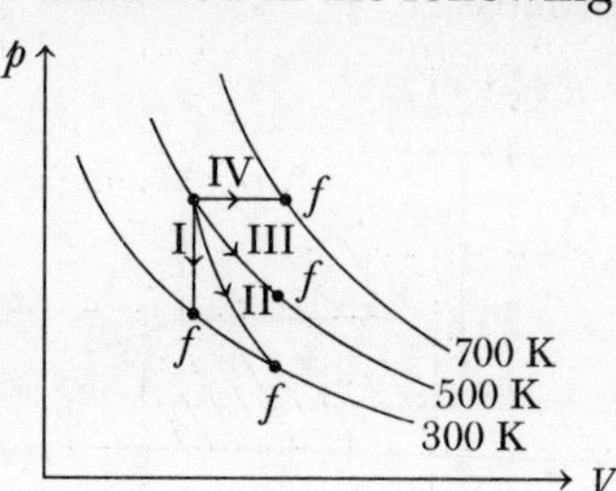

Match the Column (process number) with Column II (process name).

Column I	Column II
A. Process I	1. Adiabatic
B. Process II	2. Isobaric
C. Process III	3. Isochoric
D. Process IV	4. Isothermal

A. ____________ B. ____________ C. ____________ D. ____________

35. A sample of ideal gas is carried through a cyclic process *BAC*, here *CB* is an isothermal process.

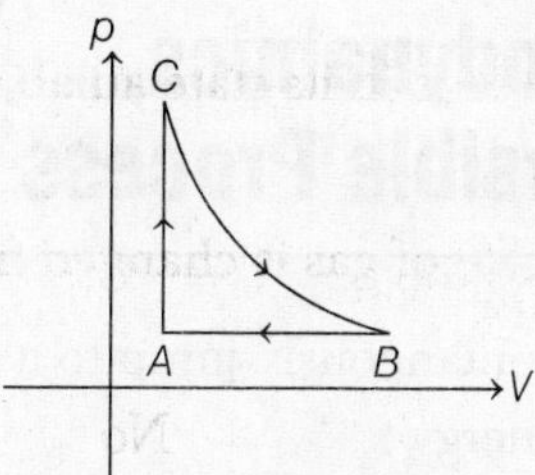

Fill the following table with (+) or (−) or 0 to indicate increase, decrease or no change in various quantities.

Path	dp	dV	dT	dU	dQ	dW
BA						
AC						
CB						

36. A container having 1 mol of a gas at a temperature 27°C has movable piston which maintains constant pressure of 1 atm in container. The gas is compressed until temperature becomes 127°C. Find the work done in the process. (C_p for gas is 7.03 cal/mol-K)

***37.** In an isobaric process, the work done by a diatomic gas is 10 J. The heat given to the gas will be [C_p for diatomic gas $= \frac{7}{2}R$]

(a) 35 J ☐ (b) 30 J ☐

(c) 45 J ☐ (d) 60 J ☐

***38.** Consider the given cyclic process.

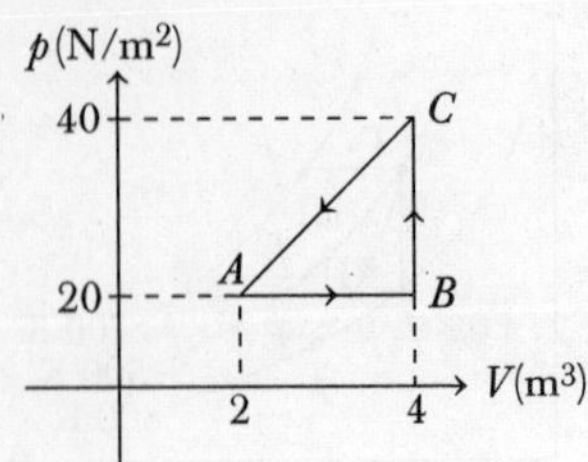

Now, choose correct statements.

I. Work done in complete cycle is positive.

II. Change in internal energy in complete cycle is positive.

III. Work done in cyclic process is – 20 J.

IV. Change in internal energy is positive for *AB* process.

TOPIC 5

Second Law of Thermodynamics, Reversible and Irreversible Process

39. A book on a table cannot spontaneously jump to a height *h* because

(a) the table cannot transfer energy

(b) the second law of thermodynamics is violated

(c) the first law of thermodynamics is violated

(d) the books are too heavy

40. The second law of thermodynamics introduces the concept of ______ (enthalpy/entropy) to explain why certain process do not occur spontaneously.

41. All thermodynamics processes are reversible in nature.

True ☐ False ☐

42. Why can't the diffusion of cooking gas back into the cylinder be reversed spontaneously?

(a) Due to the first law of thermodynamics.

(b) Due to presence of friction and viscosity.

(c) Because of irreversible process governed by the second law of thermodynamics.

(d) Because of the conservation of energy.

43. Which of these pairs are correctly matched ?

I. The combustion reaction of mixture of petrol and air → Reversible process

II. Cooking gas leaking from a gas cylinder in the kitchen → Irreversible process

III. The stirring of a liquid in thermal contact with a reservoir will increase the internal energy of reservoir → Reversible process

44. Which one of the following figures represents Carnot cycle with an ideal gas as working substance?

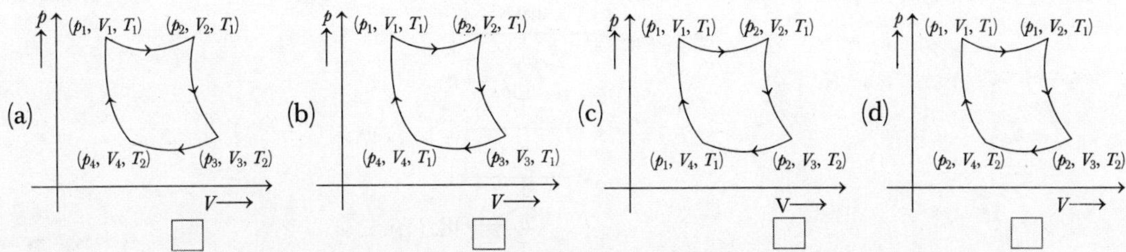

45. In Carnot engine, total work done by the gas in one complete cycle is

(a) $\mu RT_1 \ln\left(\frac{V_1}{V_2}\right) - \mu RT_2 \ln\left(\frac{V_4}{V_3}\right)$ ☐ (b) $\mu RT_1 \ln\left(\frac{V_2}{V_1}\right) - \mu RT_2 \ln\left(\frac{V_3}{V_4}\right)$ ☐

(c) $\mu RT_1 \ln\left(\frac{V_1}{V_2}\right) - \mu RT_1 \ln\left(\frac{V_4}{V_3}\right)$ ☐ (d) $\mu RT_1 \ln\left(\frac{V_2}{V_1}\right) - \mu RT_1 \ln\left(\frac{V_3}{V_4}\right)$ ☐

46. The temperature of reservoir of Carnot engine operating with an efficiency of 70% is 1000 K. The temperature of its sink is 27°C.

True ☐ False ☐

47. In a Carnot engine, when $T_2 = 0°C$ and $T_1 = 200°C$, its efficiency is η_1 and when $T_1 = 0°C$ and $T_2 = -200°C$, its efficiency is η_2. Find the ratio of $\frac{\eta_1}{\eta_2}$.

____

48. The efficiency of Carnot engine operating between reservoirs maintained at temperatures 27°C and – 123°C is __________ (40%/50%).

49. A Carnot engine operates between 227°C and 27°C. What is the efficiency of the engine?

____

50. If an engine is working between two given temperatures T_1 and T_2 of the hot and cold reservoirs respectively, then no engine can have efficiency more than that of Carnot engine.

True ☐ False ☐

51. Efficiency of a Carnot engine working between 125°C and 15°C is ________ %.

52. In a Carnot engine, heat absorbed is 200 J and released isothermally. The hot reservoir temperature is 500 K and cold reservoir temperature is 300 K, then released heat will be x J. What is the value of x?

____

53. Two Carnot engines A and B working between temperatures $A \rightarrow$ 1000 K and 500 K and $B \rightarrow x$ K and 1000 K have same efficiency. Value of x is ____________ .

54. A reversible engine converts (1/6)th of heat into work. When temperature of sink is lowered by 82°C, its efficiency is doubled. Its source temperature is ____________ °C and sink temperature is ____________ °C.

55. Two Carnot engines work as shown below.

900 K → E_1 → W_1 → T → E_2 → W_2 → 400 K

Now, fill these blanks.

I. If $W_1 = W_2$, then T = ____________ K

II. If $\eta_1 = \eta_2$, then T = ____________ K

Assertion-Reason Questions

Direction (Q. Nos. 1-10) *In the following questions, a statement of Assertion is followed by a corresponding statement of Reason. From the following options, choose the correct one.*

(a) Both Assertion and Reason are correct and Reason is the correct explanation of Assertion.
(b) Both Assertion and Reason are correct but Reason is not the correct explanation of Assertion.
(c) Assertion is correct but Reason is incorrect.
(d) Assertion is incorrect but Reason is correct.

***1.** **Assertion** (A) Thermal equilibrium is a state where there is no net flow of heat between two systems in contact.
Reason (R) In thermal equilibrium, the temperatures of the two systems are equal and no further changes occur spontaneously w.r.t. heat flow.

(a) ☐ (b) ☐ (c) ☐ (d) ☐

2. **Assertion** (A) Heat is a form of energy that can be completely converted into work.
Reason (R) According to first law of thermodynamics, energy cannot be created or destroyed, only converted from one form to another.

(a) ☐ (b) ☐ (c) ☐ (d) ☐

3. **Assertion** (A) First law of thermodynamics does not forbid flow of heat from lower temperature to higher temperature.
Reason (R) Heat supplied to a system always equal to the increase in its internal energy.

(a) ☐ (b) ☐ (c) ☐ (d) ☐

***4. Assertion** (A) In isothermal process for an ideal gas, pressure of a given mass of gas varies inversely as its volume.
Reason (R) In isothermal process for an ideal gas, temperature is fixed, so pV = constant.

(a) ☐ (b) ☐ (c) ☐ (d) ☐

5. Assertion (A) In quasi-static process, system changes its variable slowly, so that it remains in thermal and mechanical equilibrium with its surroundings.
Reason (R) In quasi-static process, difference in the pressure of the system and external pressure is not small.

(a) ☐ (b) ☐ (c) ☐ (d) ☐

6. Assertion (A) In an isochoric process, heat absorbed by the gas goes entirely to change its internal energy and its temperature.
Reason (R) In isochoric process, no work is done on or by the gas.

(a) ☐ (b) ☐ (c) ☐ (d) ☐

***7. Assertion** (A) A quasi-static isothermal expansion of an ideal gas in a cylinder fitted with a frictionless movable piston is a reversible process.
Reason (R) A process is reversible only if a system is in equilibrium with the surroundings at every stage.

(a) ☐ (b) ☐ (c) ☐ (d) ☐

8. Assertion (A) In an isolated system, the entropy increases.
Reason (R) The processes in an isolated system are adiabatic.

(a) ☐ (b) ☐ (c) ☐ (d) ☐

9. Assertion (A) Thermodynamic processes in nature are irreversible.
Reason (R) Dissipative effects cannot be eliminated.

(a) ☐ (b) ☐ (c) ☐ (d) ☐

10. Assertion (A) The efficiency of a Carnot engine depends only on the temperature of the hot and cold reservoirs.
Reason (R) The Carnot cycle is reversible and operates between two thermal reservoirs.

(a) ☐ (b) ☐ (c) ☐ (d) ☐

Case Based Questions

1. Consider a system consisting 1 mol of an ideal gas undergoing various thermodynamic processes. The initial state of the gas is at temperature $T_1 = 300$ K and volume $V_1 = 2\ \text{m}^3$. The gas undergoes the following processes.
(A) Isothermal expansion to $V_2 = 4\ \text{m}^3$
(B) Adiabatic compression back to the original volume, $V_1 = 2\ \text{m}^3$
(C) Isochoric heating to a final temperature, $T_2 = 600$ K.
Now, answer the following questions based on the paragraph.

(i) The change in entropy during isothermal expansion is

(a) positive ☐ (b) negative ☐
(c) zero ☐ (d) Cannot be said ☐

(ii) The change in entropy during isochoric heating

(a) zero ☐ (b) positive ☐

(c) negative ☐ (d) unity ☐

(iii) Work done by the gas during isothermal expansion is

(a) 1 kJ ☐ (b) 1.7 kJ ☐

(c) 2.7 kJ ☐ (d) 2.5 kJ ☐

(iv) What is the change in internal energy during the adiabatic compression?

(a) 0 J ☐ (b) $\Delta U = -Q$ ☐

(c) $\Delta U = W$ ☐ (d) $\Delta U = Q - W$ ☐

Or

How much heat is added to the gas during the isochoric heating?

(a) 3.7 kJ ☐ (b) 4.2 kJ ☐

(c) 5.2 kJ ☐ (d) 8.6 kJ ☐

2. A 2 kg block of copper is initially at a temperature of 300 K. The specific heat capacity of copper is 385 J/kg-K. The block is heated in two stages
A. first at constant pressure upto 350 K.
B. then at constant volume upto 400 K.
Based on the given paragraph answer the following questions.

(i) The heat added during first process

(a) 38.5 kJ ☐ (b) 77.0 kJ ☐

(c) 192.5 kJ ☐ (d) 385.0 kJ ☐

(ii) Change in internal energy of copper block in first process

(a) 38.5 kJ ☐ (b) 77.0 kJ ☐

(c) 192.5 kJ ☐ (d) 385.0 kJ ☐

(iii) How much heat is added to copper during second process?

(a) 38.5 kJ ☐ (b) 77.0 kJ ☐

(c) 192.5 kJ ☐ (d) 385.0 kJ ☐

(iv) What is the total change in internal energy after both processes?

(a) 38.5 kJ ☐ (b) 77.0 kJ ☐

(c) 192.5 kJ ☐ (d) 385.0 kJ ☐

Or

Total heat added to the copper block will be

(a) 38.5 kJ ☐ (b) 77.0 kJ ☐

(c) 192.5 kJ ☐ (d) 385.0 kJ ☐

COMPETITION EDGE UP

1. A real gas within a closed chamber at 27°C undergoes the cyclic process as shown in figure. The gas obeys $pV^3 = RT$ equation for the path A to B. The net work done in the complete cycle is (assuming $R = 8$ J/mol K) **[NCERT Pg. 235, JEE Main 2024]**

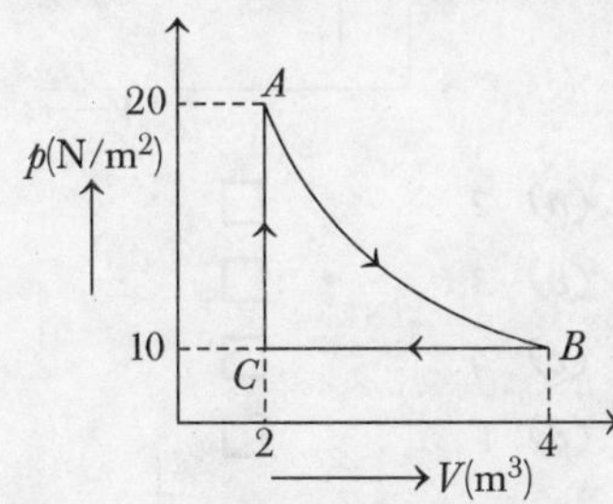

(a) − 20 J ☐ (b) 20 J ☐
(c) 205 J ☐ (d) 225 J ☐

2. The volume of an ideal gas ($\gamma = 1.5$) is changed adiabatically from 5 L to 4 L. The ratio of initial pressure to final pressure is **[NCERT Pg. 235, JEE Main 2024]**

(a) $\frac{8}{5\sqrt{5}}$ ☐ (b) $\frac{16}{25}$ ☐
(c) $\frac{4}{5}$ ☐ (d) $\frac{2}{\sqrt{5}}$ ☐

3. A sample of 1 mole gas at temperature T is adiabatically expanded to double its volume. If adiabatic constant for the gas is $\gamma = \frac{3}{2}$, then the work done by the gas in the process is **[NCERT Pg. 235, JEE Main 2024]**

(a) $\frac{R}{T}[2 - \sqrt{2}]$ ☐
(b) $RT[2 + \sqrt{2}]$ ☐
(c) $\frac{T}{R}[2 + \sqrt{2}]$ ☐
(d) $RT[2 - \sqrt{2}]$ ☐

4. A total 48 J heat is given to one mole of helium kept in a cylinder. The temperature of helium increases by 2° C. The work done by the gas is (Given, $R = 8.3\ J\ K^{-1}\ mol^{-1}$) **[NCERT Pg. 230, JEE Main 2024]**

(a) 24.9 J ☐
(b) 72.9 J ☐
(c) 23.1 J ☐
(d) 48 J ☐

5. The heat absorbed by a system in going through the given cyclic process is **[NCERT Pg. 235, JEE Main 2024]**

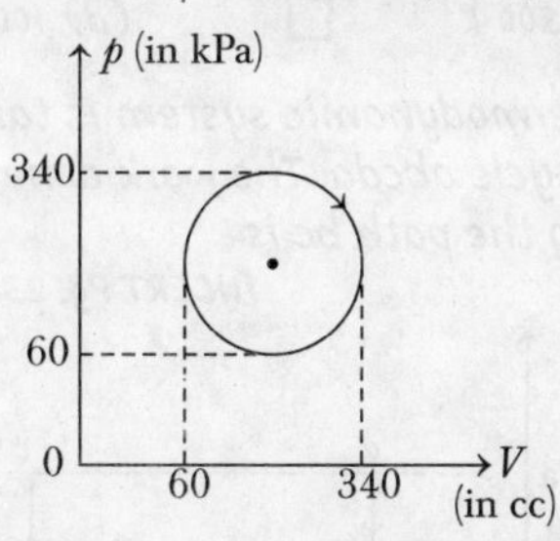

(a) 616 J ☐
(b) 431.2 J ☐
(c) 19.6 J ☐
(d) 61.6 J ☐

6. The given figure represents two isobaric processes for the same mass of an ideal gas, then **[NCERT Pg. 235, JEE Main 2024]**

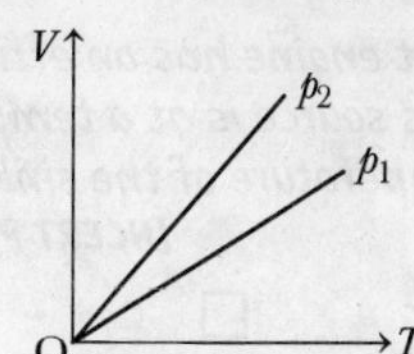

(a) $p_2 > p_1$ ☐ (b) $p_2 \geq p_1$ ☐
(c) $p_1 = p_2$ ☐ (d) $p_1 > p_2$ ☐

7. Two thermodynamical processes are shown in the figure. The molar heat capacity for process A and B are C_A and C_B. The molar heat capacity at constant pressure and constant volume are represented by C_p and C_V, respectively. Choose the correct statement. **[NCERT Pg. 235, JEE Main 2024]**

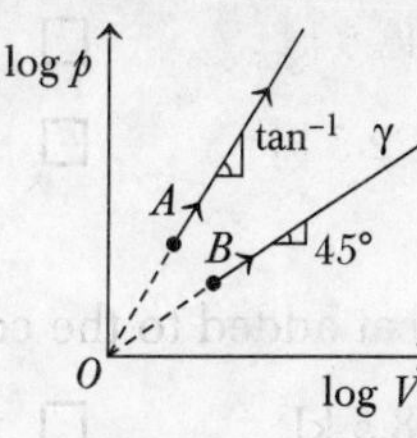

(a) $C_A > C_P > C_V$ ☐
(b) $C_A = 0$ and $C_B = \infty$ ☐
(c) $C_B = \infty$ and $C_A = 0$ ☐
(d) $C_P > C_V > C_A = C_B$ ☐

8. The temperature of a gas having 2.0×10^{25} molecules per cubic metre at 1.38 atm (Given, $k = 1.38 \times 10^{-23}\ JK^{-1}$) is

[NCERT Pg. 235, JEE Main 2024]

(a) 300 K ☐ (b) 200 K ☐

(c) 500 K ☐ (d) 100 K ☐

9. A thermodynamic system is taken through the cycle abcda. The work done by the gas along the path bc is

[NCERT Pg. 235, NEET 2024]

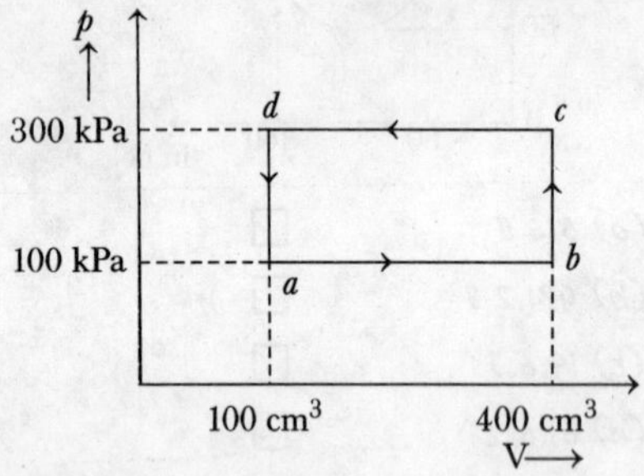

(a) zero ☐ (b) 30 J ☐

(c) −90 J ☐ (d) −60 J ☐

10. A Carnot engine has an efficiency of 50% when its source is at a temperature 327°C. The temperature of the sink is

[NCERT Pg. 237, NEET 2023]

(a) 15°C ☐

(b) 100°C ☐

(c) 200°C ☐

(d) 27°C ☐

11. An ideal gas undergoes four different processes from the same initial state as shown in the figure below. Those processes are adiabatic, isothermal, isobaric and isochoric. The curve which represents the adiabatic process among 1, 2, 3 and 4 is

[NCERT Pg. 235, NEET 2022]

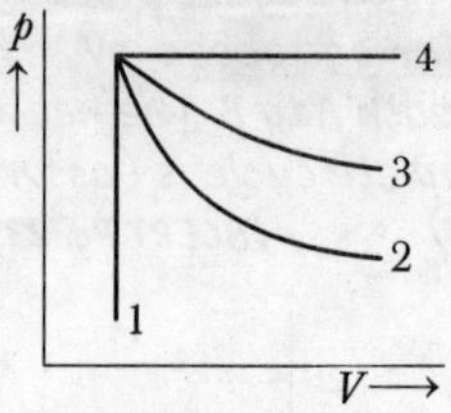

(a) 2 ☐

(b) 3 ☐

(c) 4 ☐

(d) 1 ☐

12. The p-V diagram for an ideal gas in a piston cylinder assembly undergoing a thermodynamic process is shown in the figure. The process is

[NCERT Pg. 235, NEET (Oct.) 2020]

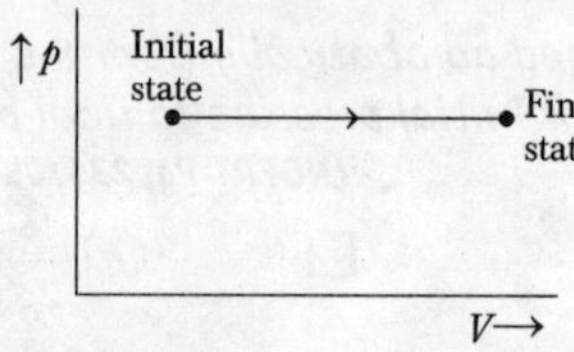

(a) adiabatic ☐

(b) isochoric ☐

(c) isobaric ☐

(d) isothermal ☐

Chapter 12

Kinetic Theory

Scan and take Chapter Test

TOPIC 1

Molecular Nature of Matter and Behaviour of Gases

1. According to the Atomic hypothesis, atoms

(a) only attract each other

(b) only repel each other

(c) attract and repel each other based on distance

(d) Neither attract nor repel

2. Write down the size of atom in metre.

______

3. John Dalton proposed the atomic theory to explain the laws of (definite/indefinite) ______ and (multiple/double) ______ proportions.

4. A chamber with a gas is maintained at a pressure of 8.31×10^{-10} N/m^2 and temperature 100 K. Number of molecules of gas in each 1 cm^3 volume is ______.

5. We have two identical vessels, A filled with hydrogen and B with equal mass of helium. They are kept in same room.
Choose incorrectly matched pair.

I. Ratio of pressures $\frac{p_A}{p_B} \rightarrow 2$

II. Ratio of number of moles $\frac{\mu_A}{\mu_B} \rightarrow \frac{1}{2}$

______

*Concepts of all questions bearing * are important for JEE/NEET/CUET.*

6. Given graph indicates, which of the following?

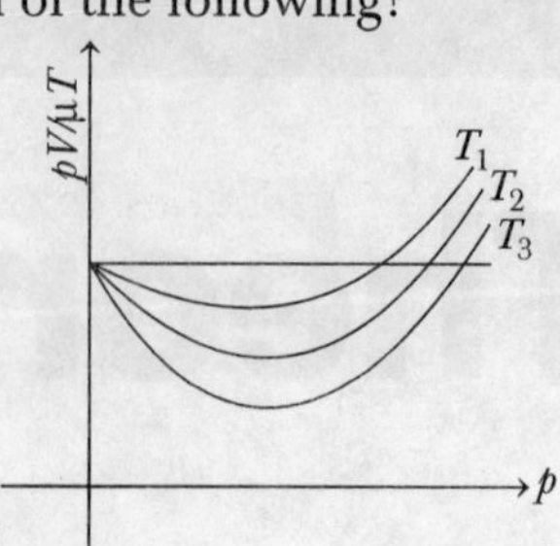

(a) $T_3 > T_2 > T_1$ ☐

(b) $\dfrac{pV}{\mu T}$ value for a real gas is constant. ☐

(c) All real gases approach ideal behaviour with increase of pressure. ☐

(d) All real gases show identical ideal behaviour at high temperatures and low pressures. ☐

7. Given figure shows the plot of $\dfrac{pV}{nT}$ *versus* p for oxygen gas at two different temperatures.

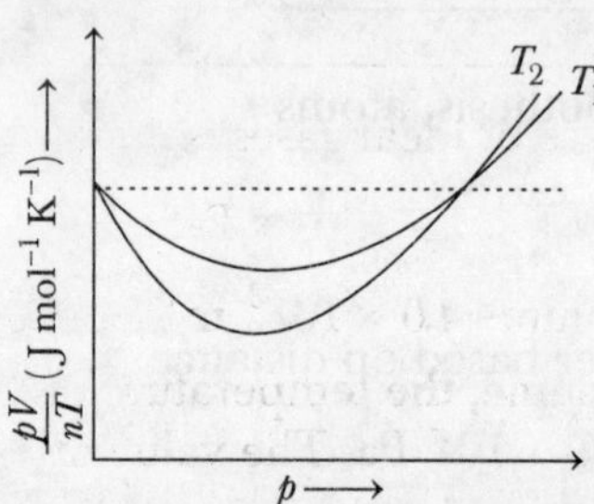

Read the following statements concerning the above curves and choose the correct statements.

I. The dotted line corresponds to the ideal behaviour.

II. $T_1 > T_2$

III. The value of $\dfrac{pV}{nT}$ at the point, where the curves meet the Y-axis is the same for all gases.

8. The p-V graph of two different gases of massess m_1 and m_2 are drawn at constant temperature T. Choose the correct option.

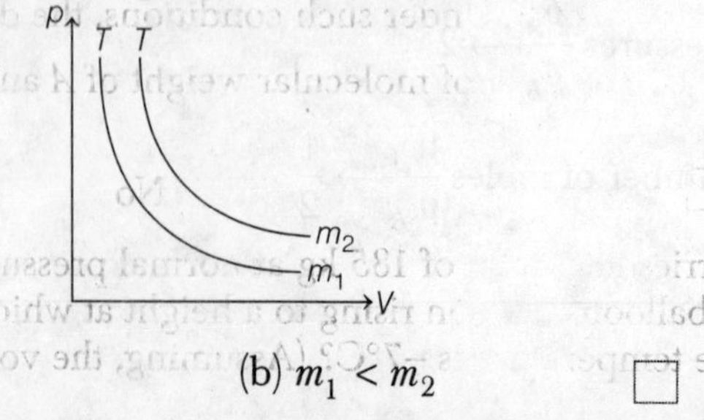

(a) $m_1 > m_2$ ☐ (b) $m_1 < m_2$ ☐

(c) $m_1 = m_2$ ☐ (d) None of these ☐

9. At constant pressure, if 8 mol of an ideal gas at 273 K is heated to double its volume, calculate the new temperature.

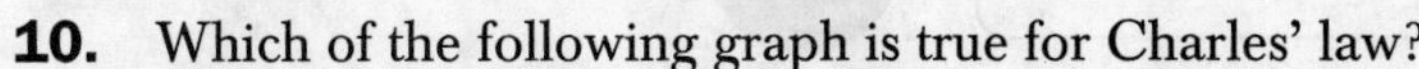

10. Which of the following graph is true for Charles' law?

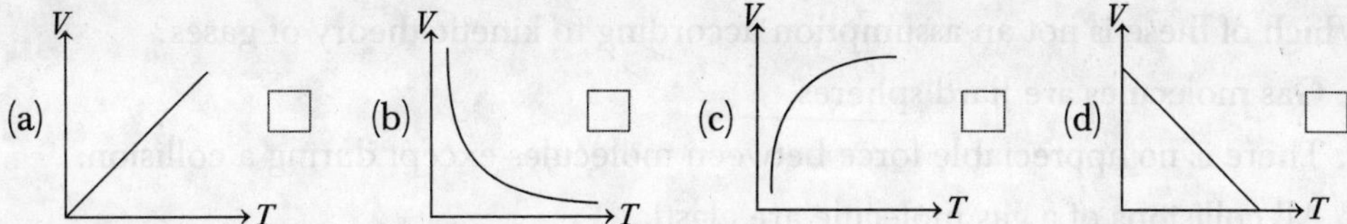

11. Arrange the values of pressures in order of their increasing values from given T-V curve.

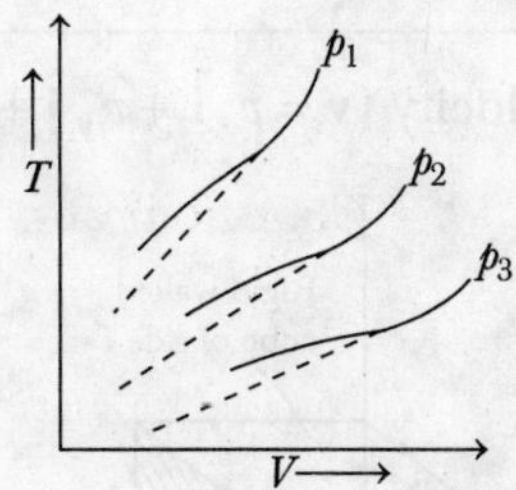

____

12. The total pressure of a mixture of ideal gases is equals to the sum of their partial pressures.

True ☐ False ☐

13. A cylindrical container of volume 4.0×10^{-3} m^3 contains one mole of hydrogen and two moles of carbon dioxide. Assume, the temperature of the mixture is 400 K. The pressure of the mixture of gases is 24.9×10^x Pa. The value of x is ______.
(Take, gas constant, $R = 8.3\,\text{J mol}^{-1}\text{K}^{-1}$)

14. A cylinder contains hydrogen gas at pressure of 249 kPa and temperature 27°C. Its density is (Take, gas constant, $R = 8.3\,\text{J mol}^{-1}\,\text{K}^{-1}$) ______.

15. A given sample of an ideal gas occupies a volume V at a pressure p and absolute temperature T. The mass of each molecule of the gas is m. Which of the following gives the density of the gas?

(a) p/kT ☐ (b) pm/kT ☐
(c) p/kTV ☐ (d) mkT ☐

16. Two vessels separately contain two ideal gases A and B at the same temperature, the pressure of A being twice that of B. Under such conditions, the density of A is found to be 1.5 times the density of B. The ratio of molecular weight of A and B is $\frac{x}{y}$. Is $\frac{x}{y}$ here denote $\frac{3}{4}$?

Yes ☐ No ☐

17. A balloon carries total load of 185 kg at normal pressure and temperature of 27°C. What load will the balloon carry on rising to a height at which the barometric pressure is 45 cm of Hg and the temperature is −7°C? (Assuming, the volume constant)

____

TOPIC 2

Kinetic Theory of an Ideal Gas

NCERT Pg 248-252

18. Which of these is not an assumption according to kinetic theory of gases?

I. Gas molecules are hard spheres.

II. There is no appreciable force between molecules except during a collision.

III. All collisions of a gas molecule are elastic.

IV. Time for a collision is comparable to time elapsed between any two collisions.

19. A gas molecule mass m and velocity $(\mathbf{v} = v_x\hat{\mathbf{i}} + v_y\hat{\mathbf{j}} + v_z\hat{\mathbf{k}})$ hits the shaded wall.

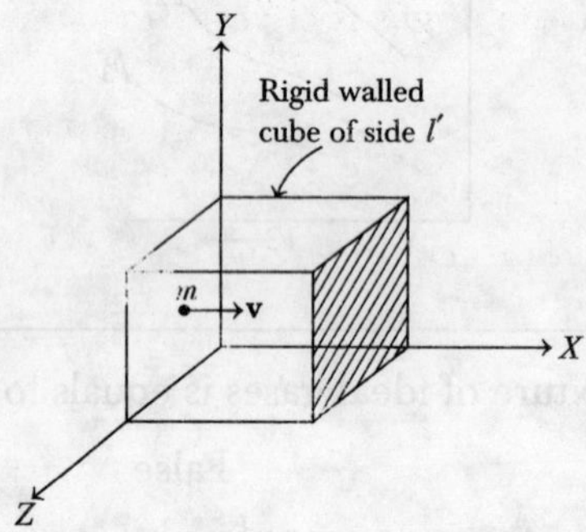

Now, choose correct statement.

I. If collision is inelastic, then velocity after collision is $\mathbf{v}' = -v_x\hat{\mathbf{i}} + v_y\hat{\mathbf{j}} + v_z\hat{\mathbf{k}}$.

II. Momentum imparted to wall in 1 collision is $2mv_x$.

III. Number of molecules hitting shaded wall in time Δt is $\frac{1}{2} \cdot l^2 v_x \Delta tx$.

(where, n = number of molecules per unit volume)

20. A gas molecule with velocity $v = (2\hat{\mathbf{i}} - 2\hat{\mathbf{j}} - 2\hat{\mathbf{k}})$ m/s elastically hits a wall (perpendicular to X-axis), then it rebounds with velocity v' = ______ m/s.

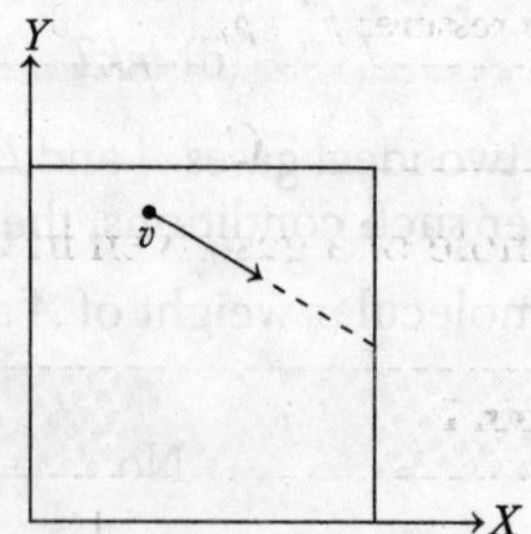

21. During a hailstorm, which lasts about 30 s, around 200 hailstones hits a window (area = $0.5\ \text{m}^2$) at an angle of 60° with surface of window. Mass of a hailstone is 5 g and it is moving with a speed of 6 m/s. Pressure over window pane is around ______ Pa.

22. A scaled cubical container (volume V) contains 20 particles each of mass m. Speed and number of particles are as

Speed	Number of particles
v	2
$2v$	3
$3v$	5
$4v$	4
$5v$	3
$6v$	2
$7v$	1

If pressure in container is p, then product $pV = xmv^2$. Value of x is ________ .

23. In isobaric condition, if volume of gas is changed, its kinetic energy will remain same.

True ☐ False ☐

24. A given sample of an ideal gas occupies a volume V at a pressure p and absolute temperature T. The mass of each molecule of the gas is m, then choose the correct statements.

I. $\rho \propto p$ II. $\rho \propto \frac{1}{T}$

(where, ρ is the density of gas)

____

25. At a temperature of ________ K, kinetic energy of an ideal gas molecule is 1 eV. (Take, $1 \text{ eV} = 1.6 \times 10^{-19}$ J, $k_B = 1.38 \times 10^{-23}$ J/mol-K)

26. A gas mixture contains two non-reacting gases A and B in a container. Molar mass of gas A is greater than that of B. Now, match the ratios of quantities listed in Column I with their respective values listed in Column II.

	Column I		Column II
A.	Ratio of rms speeds $v_A : v_B$	1.	equal to 1
B.	Ratio of KE $E_A : E_B$	2.	less than 1
C.	Ratio of partial pressures $p_A : p_B$	3.	more than 1

A________________ B________________ C________________

27. Match the kinetic energy of 1 mole of a gas given in Column I with atomicity of gas in Column II.

	Column I		Column II
A.	$3\,RT$	1.	one
B.	$\frac{5}{2}RT$	2.	two
C.	$\frac{3}{2}RT$	3.	three

A________________ B________________ C________________

28. At constant volume, if temperature of gas molecules are doubled, the new kinetic energy will be _______________ (doubled/tripled).

29. Increase in temperature of a gas filled in a container would lead to

(a) increase in its kinetic energy ☐

(b) decrease in its pressure ☐

(c) decrease in intermolecular distance ☐

(d) increase in its mass ☐

30. The number of molecules in 1L of an ideal gas at 300 K and 2 atm pressure with mean kinetic energy 2×10^{-9} J per molecule is

(a) 0.75×10^{11} ☐ (b) 3×10^{11} ☐

(c) 1.5×10^{11} ☐ (d) 6×10^{11} ☐

31. At what temperature will the rms speed of oxygen molecules become just sufficient for escaping from the earth's atmosphere?
(Take, mass of oxygen molecule, $m = 2.6 \times 10^{-26}$ kg and Boltzmann's constant, $k_B = 1.38 \times 10^{-23}\ \text{JK}^{-1}$)

____

32. Match the different velocities of gaseous molecules given in Column I with their respective values given in Column II.

Column I	Column II
A. v_{rms}	1. $\sqrt{\frac{8k_BT}{\pi m}}$
B. v_{av}	2. $\frac{k_BT}{m}$
C. v_{mp}	3. $\sqrt{\frac{3k_BT}{m}}$

A_________ B_________ C_________

33. Arrange the following (at constant temperature T) in increasing order : v_{av}, v_{rms} and v_{mp}.

____

34. Calculate the ratio of v_{rms} of argon (Ar) to chlorine (Cl_2) at same temperature.

____

35. Find the ratio of root mean square speed of any gas at temperatures T and $2T$.

____

36. There are 12 molecules in a chamber (size 1 cm × 1 cm × 1cm) having speeds (in cm/s) 6, 2, 4, 6, 6, 4, 1, 8, 5, 3, 7 and 8, respectively.

(a) Mean speed of molecules is ______ cm/s.

(b) RMS speed of molecules is ______ cm/s.

(c) Most probable speed of molecules is _____ cm/s.

(d) Number of back and forth round trips per second = ______.

37. In following plot of Maxwell's distribution of molecular speeds.

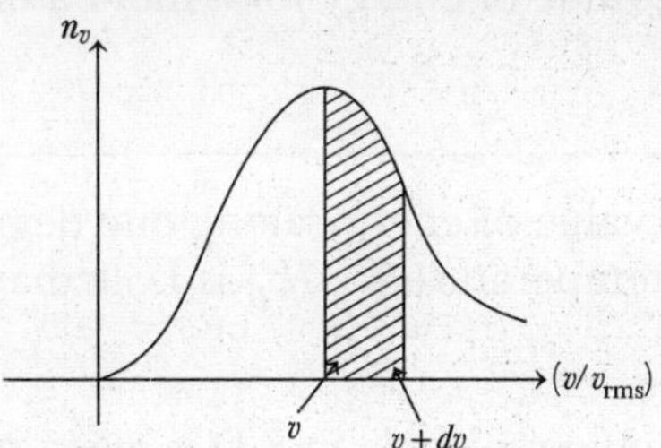

Area of strip (shown here) indicates ______________________ .

38. If the rms speed of oxygen molecules at 0°C is 160 m/s, find the rms speed of hydrogen molecules at 0°C.

____

39. Consider a mixture of gas molecule of types *A*, *B* and *C* having masses $m_A < m_B < m_C$. The ratio of their root-mean-square speeds at normal temperature and pressure is

(a) $v_A = v_B = v_C = 0$ ☐ (b) $\frac{1}{v_A} > \frac{1}{v_B} > \frac{1}{v_C}$ ☐ (c) $v_A = v_B \neq v_C$ ☐ (d) $\frac{1}{v_A} < \frac{1}{v_B} < \frac{1}{v_C}$ ☐

40. The root-mean-square speed of molecules of a given mass of a gas at 27°C and 1 atm pressure is 200 ms^{-1}. The root-mean-square speed of molecules of the gas at 127°C and 2 atm pressure is $\frac{x}{\sqrt{3}}$ ms^{-1}. The value of *x* will be______________ .

41. Consider a sample of oxygen behaving like an ideal gas. At 300 K, the ratio of root-mean-square (rms) velocity to the average velocity of gas molecule would be __________ $\left(\sqrt{\frac{3\pi}{8}}/\sqrt{\frac{8}{3}}\right)$. (Molecular weight of oxygen is 32 g/mol and $R = 8.3\,JK^{-1}$ mol^{-1})

42. The temperature of a gas is raised from 27°C to 927°C. The root-mean-square speed

(a) is $\sqrt{\left(\frac{927}{27}\right)}$ times the earlier value ☐ (b) remains the same ☐

(c) gets halved ☐ (d) gets doubled ☐

TOPIC 3

Law of Equipartition of Energy

43. Match the type of gas given in Column I with its respective ratio of translational to rotational degrees of freedom given in Column II.

	Column I		Column II
A	Monoatomic	1.	1.5
B.	Diatomic	2.	1.0
C.	Triatomic (non-linear)	3.	Infinity

A______________ B______________ C______________

44. What will be the average value of energy for a monoatomic gas in thermal equilibrium at temperature T?

____

45. What will be the average value of energy along one degree of freedom for an ideal gas in thermal equilibrium at a temperature T ? (k_B is Boltzmann constant)

____

46. The kinetic energy of a single molecule in 3-D is given by

(a) $E_t = \frac{1}{2}mv_x^2$ ☐ (b) $E_t = \frac{1}{2}mv_x^2 + \frac{1}{2}mv_y^2$ ☐

(c) $E_t = \frac{3}{2}k_BT$ ☐ (d) $E_t = \frac{1}{2}m(v_x^2 + v_y^2 + v_z^2)$ ☐

47. In thermal equilibrium each translational degree of freedom contributes $\frac{1}{2}K_BT$ to the total energy.

True ☐ False 

48. How many degree of freedom does a diatomic molecules have if it can rotate about its centre of mass?

____

49. Match the different quantities listed in Column I with their respective values listed in Column II.

Column I		Column II
A. Root-mean-square of gas molecules	1.	$\frac{1}{3}nm\bar{v}^2$
B. Pressure exerted by ideal gas	2.	$\sqrt{\frac{3RT}{M}}$
C. Average kinetic energy of a molecule	3.	$\frac{5}{2}RT$
D. Total internal energy of 1 mole of a diatomic gas	4.	$\frac{3}{2}k_BT$

A ____________ B ____________ C ____________ D ____________

TOPIC 4

Specific Heat Capacity

NCERT Pg 253-254

50. Let $\gamma = \frac{C_p}{C_V}$ for a gas, then choose correctly matched pair.

I. Fraction of heat that increases internal energy $\rightarrow \frac{1}{\gamma}$

II. Fraction of heat that can be converted into work $\rightarrow 1 + \frac{1}{\gamma}$

____

51. A gas has 6 degrees of freedom. This gas does 25 J of piston work when it is given a total heat of ____________ J.

52. Match values of KE per mole of gas (Column I) with molar specific heat at constant pressure (Column II) and ratio of C_p and C_V (Column III).

Column I	Column II	Column III
A. $\frac{3}{2}RT$	1. $4R$	P. $\frac{7}{5}$
B. $\frac{5}{2}RT$	2. $\frac{5}{2}R$	Q. $\frac{5}{3}$
C. $3RT$	3. $\frac{7}{2}R$	R. $\frac{4}{3}$

A____________ B____________ C____________

53. Tick (✓/✗) for correct/incorrect statement in given boxes.

(i) In Mayer's formula, i.e. $C_p - C_V = R$ is valid for all types of gases, i.e. monoatomic, diatomic and polyatomic gases. ☐

(ii) Molar specific heat capacity at constant pressure and volume for monoatomic gas are $\frac{5}{2}R$ and $\frac{1}{2}R$, respectively. ☐

(iii) $\frac{7}{2}R$ and $\frac{5}{2}R$ are the values of C_p and C_V of diatomic gases. ☐

(iv) Mean energy per molecules of polyatomic molecule having n degree of freedom is $\frac{7n}{5}kT$. ☐

54. If one mole of the polyatomic gas is having two vibrational modes and β is the ratio of molar specific heats for polyatomic gas $\left(\beta = \frac{C_p}{C_V}\right)$, then the value of β is ____________.

55. The temperature of 3.00 mol of an ideal diatomic gas is increased by 40.0°C without changing the pressure of the gas. The molecules in the gas rotate but do not oscillate. If the ratio of change in internal energy of the gas to the amount of work done by the gas is $x/10$, then the value of x (round off to the nearest integer) is ____________.
(Take, $R = 8.31\,\text{J mol}^{-1}\,\text{K}^{-1}$)

56. The correct relation between the degrees of freedom f and the ratio of specific heat γ is

(a) $f = \frac{2}{\gamma - 1}$ ☐ (b) $f = \frac{2}{\gamma + 1}$ ☐ (c) $f = \frac{\gamma + 1}{2}$ ☐ (d) $f = \frac{1}{\gamma + 1}$ ☐

57. A gas mixture consists of 3 mol of oxygen and 5 mol of argon at temperature T. Assuming the gases to be ideal and the oxygen bond to be rigid, the total internal energy (in units of RT) of the mixture is ____________ (13/15).

58. To raise the temperature of a certain mass of gas by 50°C at a constant pressure, 160 cal of heat is required. When the same mass of gas is cooled by 100°C at constant volume, 240 cal of heat is released. How many degrees of freedom does each molecule of this gas have (assume gas to be ideal)?

____

59. The value of $\gamma\left(=\frac{C_p}{C_V}\right)$, for hydrogen, helium and another ideal diatomic gas X (whose molecules are not rigid but have an additional vibrational mode) are respectively, equal to

(a) $\frac{7}{5}, \frac{5}{3}, \frac{9}{7}$ ☐
(b) $\frac{5}{3}, \frac{7}{5}, \frac{9}{7}$ ☐
(c) $\frac{5}{3}, \frac{7}{5}, \frac{7}{5}$ ☐
(d) $\frac{7}{5}, \frac{5}{3}, \frac{7}{5}$ ☐

60. A gas mixture consists of 2 mol of O_2 and 4 mol of Ar at temperature T. Neglecting all vibrational modes, the total internal energy of the system is nRT. Here, n refers to ______ .

61. Tick (✓/✗) for correct/incorrect statement in given boxes.

(i) The equivalent heat capacity of n_1 mole of gas having specific heat capacity at constant volume C_{V_1} with n_2 mole having heat capacity C_{V_2} is $\frac{n_1 C_{V_1} + n_2 C_{V_2}}{n_1 + n_2}$. ☐

(ii) n_1 mole of gas having degree of freedom f_1 mixed with n_2 mole of gas having degree of freedom f_2, then the equivalent degree of freedom of mixture of gases will be $f_{mix} = n_1 f_1 + n_2 f_2$. ☐

62. Two ideal polyatomic gases at temperatures T_1 and T_2 are mixed, so that there is no loss of energy. If f_1 and f_2, m_1 and m_2, n_1 and n_2 be the degrees of freedom, masses, number of molecules of the first and second gas respectively, the temperature of mixture of these two gases is

(a) $\frac{n_1 T_1 + n_2 T_2}{n_1 + n_2}$ ☐
(b) $\frac{n_1 f_1 T_1 + n_2 f_2 T_2}{n_1 f_1 + n_2 f_2}$ ☐
(c) $\frac{n_1 f_1 T_1 + n_2 f_2 T_2}{f_1 + f_2}$ ☐
(d) $\frac{n_1 f_1 T_1 + n_2 f_2 T_2}{n_1 + n_2}$ ☐

63. Two moles of an ideal gas with $\frac{C_p}{C_V} = \frac{5}{3}$ are mixed with 3 mol of another ideal gas with $\frac{C_p}{C_V} = \frac{4}{3}$. The value of $\frac{C_p}{C_V}$ for the mixture is 1.42.

True ☐ False ☐

64. Three perfect gases at absolute temperatures T_1, T_2 and T_3 are mixed. The masses of molecules are m_1, m_2 and m_3 and the number of molecules are n_1, n_2 and n_3, respectively. Assuming no loss of energy, the final temperature of the mixture is ______________ .

65. Assume a gas molecule is moving with speed v through a gas volume having n molecules per unit volume as shown below.

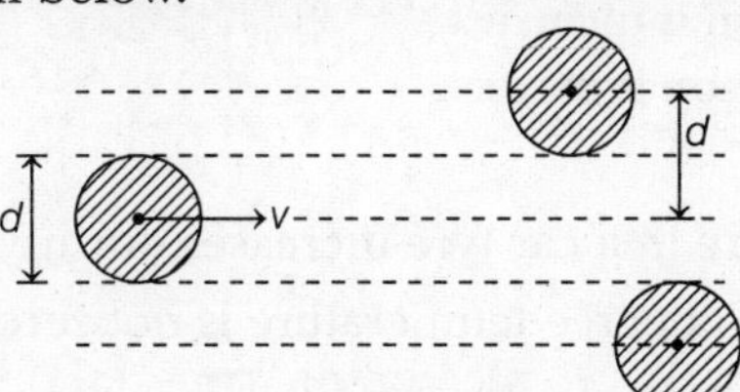

Distance moved by molecule in time interval Δt = ________.
Number of collisions made by molecule in time interval Δt = ________.
Mean free path (average distance between two successive collision) is ________.

66. Ratio of mean free path length of a gas at temperature T_1 (= 200 K) and at temperature T_2 (= 400 K) under constant pressure and volume conditions is ________.

67. The mean free path λ for a gas molecule depends upon diameter d of the molecule as

(a) $\lambda \propto \frac{1}{d^2}$ ☐ (b) $\lambda \propto d$ ☐ (c) $\lambda \propto d^2$ ☐ (d) $\lambda \propto \frac{1}{d}$ ☐

68. Calculate the value of mean free path λ for oxygen molecules at temperature 27°C and pressure 1.01×10^5 Pa. Assume, the molecular diameter is 0.3 nm and the gas is ideal. (Take, $k_B = 1.38 \times 10^{-23}$ JK^{-1})

____

69. A system consists of two types of gas molecules A and B having same number density $2 \times 10^{25}/\text{m}^3$. The diameter of A and B are 10 Å and 5 Å, respectively. They suffer collision at room temperature. The ratio of average distance covered by the molecule A to that of B between two successive collisions is ________ $\times 10^{-2}$.

70. Two gases argon (atomic radius 0.07 nm, atomic weight 40) and xenon (atomic radius 0.1 nm, atomic weight 140) have the same number density and are at the same temperature. The ratio of their respective mean free times is closest to

(a) 4.67 ☐ (b) 2.3 ☐ (c) 3.67 ☐ (d) 1.83 ☐

71. Under an adiabatic process, the volume of an ideal gas gets doubled. Consequently, the mean collision time between the gas molecule changes from τ_1 to τ_2. If $\frac{C_p}{C_V} = \gamma$ for this gas, then a good estimate for $\frac{\tau_2}{\tau_1}$ is given by ________.

72. Draw the graph that depicts the behaviour of the mean free time τ (time between two successive collisions) for the molecules of an ideal gas, as a function of temperature $\frac{1}{\sqrt{T}}$, qualitatively (graphs are schematic and not drawn to scale).

____

Assertion-Reason Questions

Direction (Q. Nos. 1-10) *In the following questions, a statement of Assertion is followed by a corresponding statement of Reason. From the following options, choose the correct one.*

(a) Both Assertion and Reason are correct and Reason is the correct explanation of Assertion.
(b) Both Assertion and Reason are correct but Reason is not the correct explanation of Assertion.
(c) Assertion is correct but Reason is incorrect.
(d) Assertion is incorrect but Reason is correct.

1. **Assertion** (A) Air pressure in a car tyre increases during driving.
Reason (R) Absolute zero degree temperature is not zero energy temperature.
(a) ☐ (b) ☐ (c) ☐ (d) ☐

2. **Assertion** (A) If a gas container in motion is suddenly stopped, the temperature of the gas rises.
Reason (R) The kinetic energy of ordered mechanical motion is converted into the kinetic energy of random motion of gas molecules.
(a) ☐ (b) ☐ (c) ☐ (d) ☐

3. **Assertion** (A) In a mixture of gases at a fixed temperature, the heavier molecule has the lower average speed.
Reason (R) Temperature of a gas is a measure of the average kinetic energy of a molecule.
(a) ☐ (b) ☐ (c) ☐ (d) ☐

4. **Assertion** (A) In case of collision of gas molecules in a given amount of gas, total kinetic energy is conserved.
Reason (R) All collisions of the gas molecule in a given amount of gas are elastic.
(a) ☐ (b) ☐ (c) ☐ (d) ☐

5. **Assertion** (A) The rms speed and most probable speeds of the molecules in a gas are same.
Reason (R) The maxwell distribution curve for the speed of the molecules in a gas is not symmetrical.
(a) ☐ (b) ☐ (c) ☐ (d) ☐

6. **Assertion** (A) Each vibrational mode gives two degrees of freedom.
Reason (R) By law of equipartition of energy, the energy for each degree of freedom in thermal equilibrium is $2k_BT$.
(a) ☐ (b) ☐ (c) ☐ (d) ☐

7. **Assertion** (A) The number of degree of freedom of a linear triatomic molecules is 7.
Reason (R) The number of degree of freedom depends on number of particle in the system.
(a) ☐ (b) ☐ (c) ☐ (d) ☐

8. **Assertion** (A) $C_p > C_v$
Reason (R) At constant pressure, some heat is spent in the expansion of the gas.
(a) ☐ (b) ☐ (c) ☐ (d) ☐

9. **Assertion** (A) The ratio of $\frac{C_p}{C_v}$ for a diatomic gas is more then that for a monoatomic gas.

Reason (R) The molecules of a monoatomic gas have less degrees of freedom than those of a diatomic gas.

(a) ☐ (b) ☐ (c) ☐ (d) ☐

10. **Assertion** (A) A gas can transmit only those sound waves whose wavelength is more than mean free path length.

Reason (R) If mean free path is greater than the wavelength, the molecules cannot oscillate because they will move through a large distance.

(a) ☐ (b) ☐ (c) ☐ (d) ☐

Case Based Questions

1. In a closed container, gas molecules move randomly with high velocities. The kinetic theory of gases explains that the pressure exerted by a gas is due to collisions of molecules with the walls of the container. According to the kinetic theory, the average kinetic energy of gas molecules is directly proportional to the absolute temperature of the gas. This relationship is given by the equation

$$\text{Average kinetic energy} = \frac{3}{2} k_B T$$

where k_B is the Boltzmann constant and T is the absolute temperature. Additionally, the kinetic theory describes that the root mean square (rms) speed of gas molecules is given by

$$V_{\text{rms}} = \sqrt{\frac{3k_B T}{m}}$$

where m is the mass of a gas molecule.

(i) Given that the average kinetic energy of gas molecules is directly proportional to temperature, which of the following statement is correct if the temperature of a gas is doubled?

(a) The average kinetic energy of the molecules is halved. ☐

(b) The average kinetic energy of the molecules remains the same. ☐

(c) The average kinetic energy of the molecules doubles. ☐

(d) The average kinetic energy of the molecules ☐

(ii) If root mean square (rms) speed of gas molecule at temperature T is V_{rms}. What will be the rms speed if the temperature is increased to $4T$?

(a) $2\,V_{\text{rms}}$ ☐ (b) $\sqrt{2}\,V_{\text{rms}}$ ☐

(c) $4\,V_{\text{rms}}$ ☐ (d) V_{rms} ☐

(iii) Considering two containers of the same volume, one containing gas A with molar mass M_A and other containing gas B with molar mass M_B. If both gases are at the same temperature. Which of the following statement is correct regarding their $V_{\text{rms},\,A}$ and $V_{\text{rms},\,B}$?

(a) $V_{\text{rms}, A} = V_{\text{rms}, B}$ ☐

(b) $V_{\text{rms}, A} \cdot M_A = V_{\text{rms}, B} \cdot M_B$ ☐

(c) $V_{\text{rms}, A} \cdot \sqrt{M_A} = V_{\text{rms}, B} \cdot \sqrt{M_B}$ ☐

(d) $V_{\text{rms}, A}\ M_A^2 = V_{\text{rms}, A}\ M_B^2$ ☐

(iv) According to the kinetic theory, which of the following best explains why gas pressure increases when the volume of a gas is decreased at constant temperature?

(a) Molecules move faster. ☐

(b) Molecules collide with the walls more frequently. ☐

(c) Molecules increase in mass. ☐

(d) Molecules expand in size. ☐

Or

For an ideal gas in a container with a fixed volume, if the number of gas molecules is doubled while keeping the temperature constant, what happens to the pressure exerted by the gas?

(a) The pressure is halved. ☐ (b) The pressure remains the same. ☐

(c) The pressure doubles. ☐ (d) The pressure quadruples. ☐

2. A company that manufactures high performance air conditioning systems for industrial use is exploring ways to improve the efficiency and reliability of their products. The systems operate by circulating a refrigerant gas, which undergoes various processes including compression, expansion, and heat exchange. The company's engineers are particularly interested in understanding the specific heat capacities and mean free paths of the refrigerant gases they use, as these properties are crucial for optimizing the thermal performance and ensuring the durability of the system components.

The engineers consider two refrigerant gases, Gas A and Gas B. Gas A is a monatomic gas with a molar mass of 40 g/mol, while Gas B is a diatomic gas with a molar mass of 28 g/mol. Both gases are used under similar conditions, but they exhibit different behaviors due to their molecular structures.

The specific heat capacities at constant volume C_v and constant pressure C_p for these gases are essential for determining the amount of energy required for heating and cooling.

(i) The heat capacity of Gas A at constant volume (monoatomic) is $\frac{3}{2}$ R. The C_p will be

(a) $\frac{3}{2}R$ ☐ (b) $\frac{5}{2}R$ ☐

(c) $2R$ ☐ (d) $\frac{7}{2}R$ ☐

(ii) The heat capacity for Gas B (diatomic) at constant volume (C_v) is $\frac{5}{2}$ R. The C_p will be

(a) $\frac{5}{2}R$ ☐ (b) $\frac{3}{2}R$ ☐

(c) $2R$ ☐ (d) $\frac{7}{2}R$ ☐

(iii) The engineer's are analysing the mean free path of Gas A molecules at a specific temperature and pressure. If the diameter of the gas molecules is doubled while maintaining the same temperature and pressure, what happens to the mean free path?

(a) It doubles ☐ (b) It remains the same ☐

(c) It is halved ☐ (d) It is reduced to one-fourth ☐

(iv) In one of their tests, the engineers observed that the pressure inside the air conditioning system doubled while the temperature remained constant. How does this change in pressure affect the mean free path of the gas molecules?

(a) It remains the same ☐ (b) It is halved ☐

(c) It doubles ☐ (d) It quadruples ☐

Or

Considering the specific heat capacities, which gas (A or B) would require more energy to raise the temperature of a given mass of gas by one degree Celsius at constant pressure, assuming equal masses of the gases are used?

(a) Gas A ☐

(b) Gas B ☐

(c) Both require the same amount of energy ☐

(d) Cannot be determined without additional information ☐

COMPETITION EDGE UP

1. *A mixture of one mole of monoatomic gas and one mole of a diatomic gas (rigid) are kept at room temperature 27°C. The ratio of specific heat of gases at constant volume respectively is* **[NCERT Pg. 309, JEE Main, 2024]**

(a) $\frac{3}{2}$ ☐ (b) $\frac{3}{5}$ ☐

(c) $\frac{5}{3}$ ☐ (d) $\frac{7}{5}$ ☐

2. *Energy of 10 non-rigid diatomic molecules at temperature T is* **[NCERT Pg. 253, JEE Main 2024]**

(a) $70\,k_BT$ ☐ (b) $\frac{7}{2}RT$ ☐

(c) $35k_BT$ ☐ (d) $35RT$ ☐

3. *A sample contains mixture of helium and oxygen gas. The ratio of root mean square speed of helium and oxygen in the sample is* **[NCERT Pg. 250, JEE Main 2024]**

(a) $\frac{1}{4}$ ☐ (b) $\frac{2\sqrt{2}}{1}$ ☐

(c) $\frac{1}{2\sqrt{2}}$ ☐ (d) $\frac{1}{32}$ ☐

4. *The translational degree of freedom (f_t) and rotational degree of freedom (f_r) of CH_4 molecule are* **[NCERT Pg. 252, JEE Main 2024]**

(a) $f_t = 3$ and $f_r = 2$ ☐

(b) $f_t = 2$ and $f_r = 3$ ☐

(c) $f_t = 3$ and $f_r = 3$ ☐

(d) $f_t = 2$ and $f_r = 2$ ☐

5. *A gas mixture consists of 8 moles of argon and 6 moles of oxygen at temperature T. Neglecting all vibrational modes, the total internal energy of the system is* **[NCERT Pg. 253, JEE Main, 2024]**

(a) 21 RT ☐ (b) 29 RT ☐

(c) 27 RT ☐ (d) 20 RT ☐

6. *If three moles of monoatomic gas ($\gamma = 5/3$) is mixed with two moles of a diatomic gas ($\gamma = 7/5$), the value of adiabatic exponent γ for the mixture is* **[NCERT Pg. 253, JEE Main, 2024]**

(a) 1.75 ☐ (b) 1.52 ☐

(c) 1.40 ☐ (d) 1.35 ☐

7. The average kinetic energy of a monoatomic molecule is 0.414 eV at temperature.
(Use $k_B = 1.38 \times 10^{-23}$ J/mol-K)
[NCERT Pg. 253, JEE Main, 2024]

(a) 1600 K ☐ (b) 3000 K ☐

(c) 1500 K ☐ (d) 3200 K ☐

8. The following graph represents the T-V curves of an ideal gas (where T is the temperature and V the volume) at three pressures p_1, p_2 and p_3 compared with those of Charles's law represented as dotted lines. **NCERT Pg. 247, NEET 2024**

Then the correct relation is.

(a) $p_3 > p_2 > p_1$ ☐

(b) $p_1 > p_3 > p_2$ ☐

(c) $p_2 > p_1 > p_3$ ☐

(d) $p_1 > p_2 > p_3$ ☐

9. Match Column I with Column II and choose the correct match from the given choices.
[NCERT Pg. 250, NEET 2021]

	Column I		Column II
A.	Root mean square of gas molecules	1.	$\frac{1}{3}nm\bar{v}^2$
B.	Pressure exerted by ideal gas	2.	$\sqrt{\frac{3RT}{M}}$
C.	Average kinetic energy of a molecule	3.	$\frac{5}{2}RT$
D.	Total internal energy of 1 mole of a diatomic gas	4.	$\frac{3}{2}k_BT$

Codes

	A	B	C	D	
(a)	3	1	4	2	☐
(b)	2	3	4	1	☐
(c)	2	1	4	3	☐
(d)	3	2	1	4	☐

10. A cylinder contains hydrogen gas at pressure of 249 kPa and temperature 27°C. Its density is ($R = 8.3$ J mol^{-1} K^{-1})
[NCERT Pg. 246, NEET (Sep.) 2020]

(a) 0.2 kg/m^3 ☐

(b) 0.1 kg/m^3 ☐

(c) 0.02 kg/m^3 ☐

(d) 0.5 kg/m^3 ☐

11. The average thermal energy for a monoatomic gas is (where, k_B is Boltzmann constant and T is absolute temperature.)
[NCERT Pg. 250, NEET (Sep.) 2020]

(a) $\frac{3}{2}k_BT$ ☐ (b) $\frac{5}{2}k_BT$ ☐

(c) $\frac{7}{2}k_BT$ ☐ (d) $\frac{1}{2}k_BT$ ☐

12. The mean free path λ for a gas, with molecular diameter d and number density n can be expressed as
[NCERT Pg. 255, NEET (Sep.) 2020]

(a) $\frac{1}{\sqrt{2}\, n\pi d^2}$ ☐

(b) $\frac{1}{\sqrt{2}\, n^2\pi d^2}$ ☐

(c) $\frac{1}{\sqrt{2}\, n^2\pi^2 d^2}$ ☐

(d) $\frac{1}{\sqrt{2}\, n\pi d}$ ☐

13. The mean free path l for a gas molecule depends upon diameter, d of the molecule as **[NCERT Pg. 255, NEET (Oct.) 2020]**

(a) $l \propto \frac{1}{d^2}$ ☐ (b) $l \propto d$ ☐

(c) $l \propto d^2$ ☐ (d) $l \propto \frac{1}{d}$ ☐

Chapter 13

Oscillations

Scan and take Chapter Test

TOPIC 1

Periodic and Oscillatory Motion

1. The rotation of earth about its axis is
(a) periodic motion
(b) simple harmonic motion
(c) non-periodic motion
(d) None of the above

2 The periodic function $f(t) = A \sin \omega t$ repeats itself after
(a) 2π (b) 3π (c) π (d) $\pi/2$

3. The function $\log \omega t$
(a) is a periodic function
(b) is a non-periodic function
(c) could represents oscillatory motion
(d) can represents circular motion

4. Choose the periodic function from the following.
(a) $A \sin^3 (\omega t)^2$ (b) $\sin \omega t + \cos \omega t$
(c) $\tan(\omega t)^3$ (d) $e^{\omega t}$

5. Figures depict four *x*-*t* plots for linear motion of a particle. Which of the plots represent a non-periodic motion?

(a)
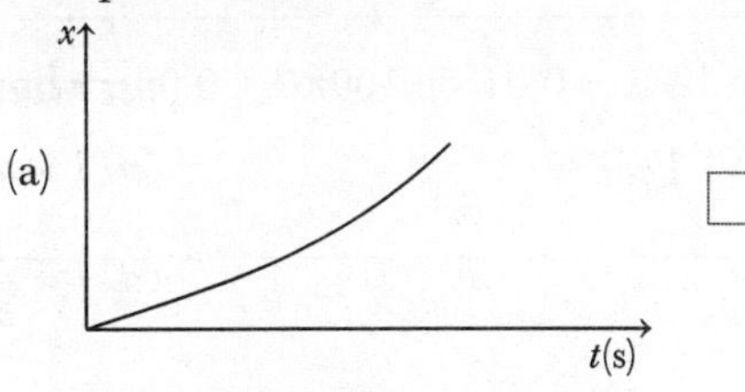

(b)
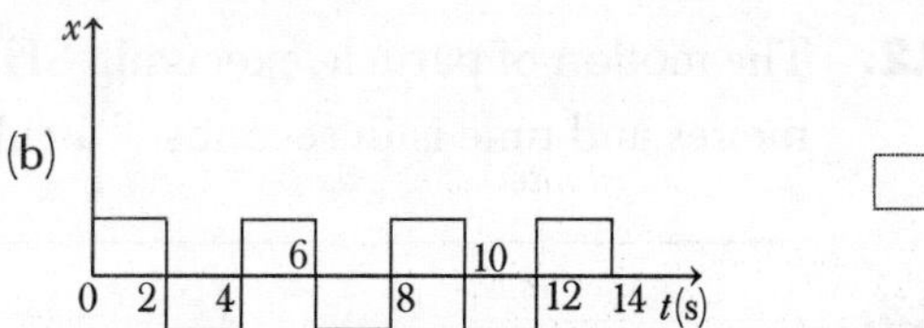

(c)
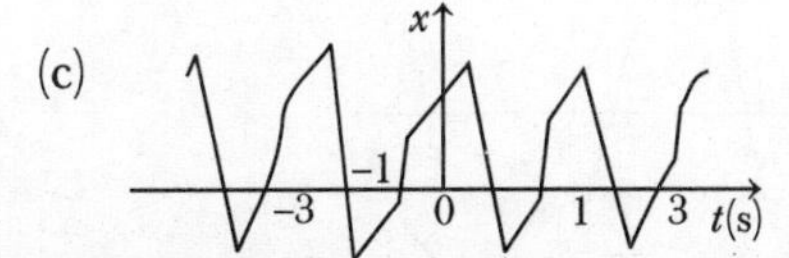

(d)
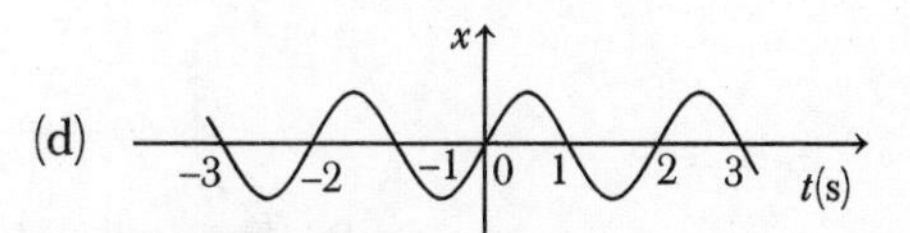

Concepts of all questions bearing * are important for JEE/NEET/CUET.

6. Which of the following graph is of periodic motion?

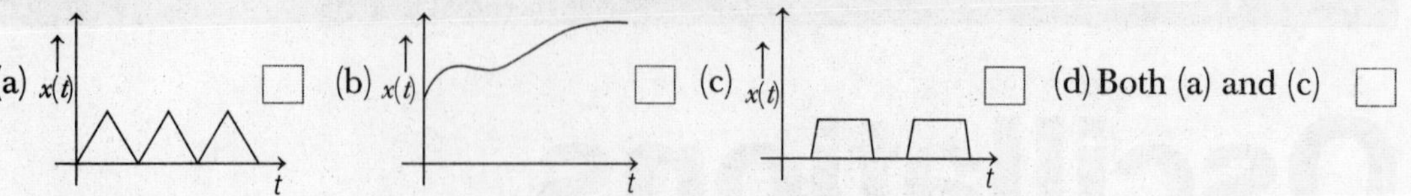

TOPIC 2

Simple Harmonic Motion and Uniform Circular Motion

7. Simple harmonic motion is any periodic motion in which displacement is a sinusoidal function of time.

Yes  No ☐

8. The oscillatory motion will be simple harmonic motion, if displacement x of the particle from the origin varies with time as $x(t) =$ ______________.

9. In SHM, graph of x *versus* t is correctly represented by

I. II.

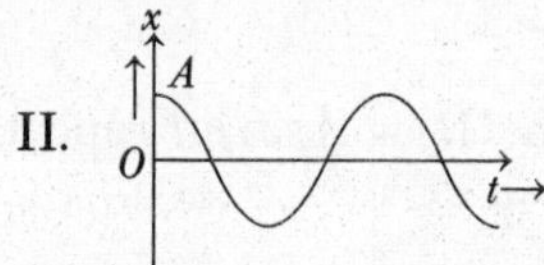

____

10. Write a function of time representing a simple harmonic motion with a period of $\frac{\pi}{\omega}$.

____

***11.** Out of the following functions representing motion of a particle, which one represents SHM?

I. $y = \sin \omega t - \cos \omega t$

II. $y = \sin^3 \omega t$

III. $y = 5\cos\left(\frac{3\pi}{4} - 3\,\omega t\right)$

IV. $y = 1 + \omega t + \omega^2 t^2$

____

12. The motion of particle executing SHM is given by $x = 0.01 \sin 100\pi(t + 0.05)$, where x is in metres and time is in seconds. Calculate the time period.

____

13.

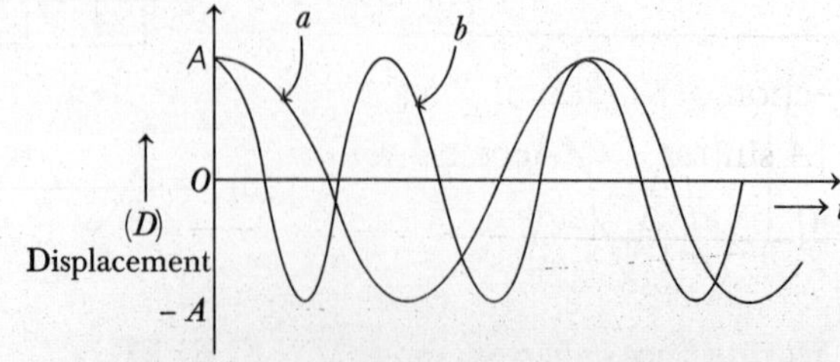

In above plot, curve b has period and frequency __________ (half and twice /twice and twice) of curve a.

14. Two equations of displacement in SHM are given by

$$x(t) = A\cos(\omega t + \phi)$$
$$y(t) = A\sin(\omega t + \phi)$$

I. then phase difference between both of them is $\frac{\pi}{2}$.

II. both equations have same amplitude.

Choose the correct statements.

____

15. Two simple harmonic motions are represented by the equations $y_1 = 10\sin\left(3\pi t + \frac{\pi}{3}\right)$ and $y_2 = 5(\sin 3\pi t + \sqrt{3}\cos 3\pi t)$.

Ratio of amplitude of y_1 to $y_2 = x : 1$. The value of x is __________.

16. A particle performs simple harmonic motion with a period of 2 s. The time taken by the particle to cover a displacement equal to half of its amplitude from the mean position is 5 s.

Yes ☐ No ☐

17. $y = A\sin(\omega t + \phi_0)$ is the time-displacement equation of SHM. At $t = 0$, the displacement of the particle is $y = \frac{A}{2}$ and it is moving along negative x-direction. Find the initial phase angle ϕ_0.

____

18. A simple harmonic motion is represented by $y = 5(\sin 3\pi t + \sqrt{3}\cos 3\pi t)$ cm. The amplitude and time period of the motion are 10 cm and (2/3) s.

True ☐ False ☐

***19.** The displacement of a particle varies according to the relation $x = 4(\cos \pi t + \sin \pi t)$. The amplitude of the particle is

(a) -4 ☐ (b) 4 ☐ (c) $4\sqrt{2}$ ☐ (d) 8 ☐

20. The displacement of a particle executing simple harmonic motion is given by __________

$$y = A_0 + A\sin\omega t + B\cos\omega t$$

Then, the amplitude of its oscillation is given by __________.

21. When two displacements represented by $y_1 = a\sin\omega t$ and $y_2 = b\cos\omega t$ are superimposed, the motion is

I. simple harmonic with amplitude $\frac{a}{b}$

II. simple harmonic with amplitude $\sqrt{a^2 + b^2}$

____

22. If we take projection of motion of P on Y-axis diameter of circle, then displacement $y(t)$ is __________ [$A\sin(\omega t + \phi)$/$A\cos(\omega t + \phi)$].

***23.** The radius of circle, the period of revolution, initial position and sense of revolution are indicated in the below figure.

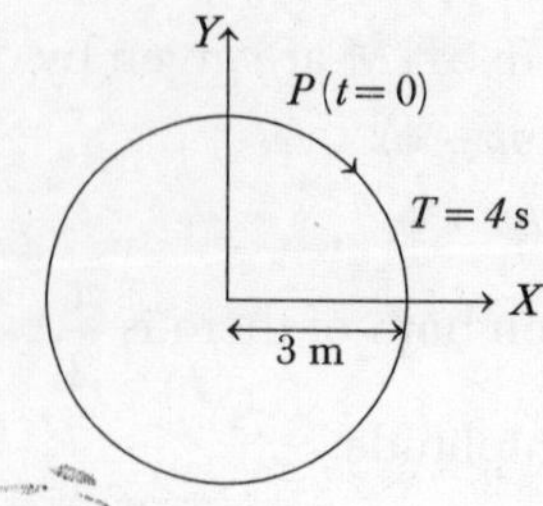

y-projection of the radius vector of rotating particle P is

(a) $y(t) = 4\sin\left(\frac{\pi t}{2}\right)$, where y in m ☐ (b) $y(t) = 3\cos\left(\frac{3\pi t}{2}\right)$, where y in m ☐

(c) $y(t) = 3\cos\left(\frac{\pi t}{2}\right)$, where y in m ☐ (d) $y(t) = -3\cos 2\pi t$, where y in m ☐

TOPIC 3

Velocity and Acceleration in SHM

***24.** The point A moves with a uniform speed along the circumference of a circle of radius 0.36 m and covers 30° in 0.1 s, then the perpendicular projection P from A on the diameter MN represents the simple harmonic motion of P. The restoration force per unit mass when P touches M will be

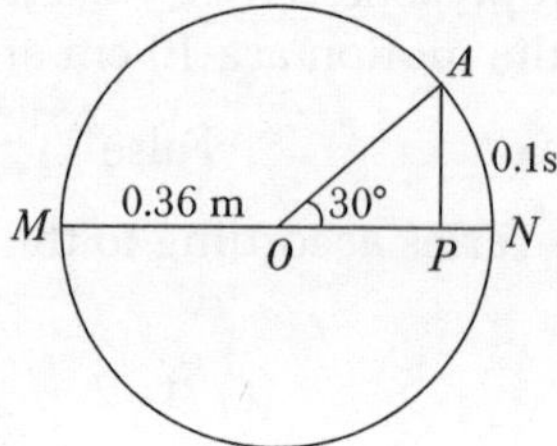

(a) 100 N ☐ (b) 9.87 N ☐ (c) 50 N ☐ (d) 0.49 N ☐

25. Identify which equation of motion represents simple harmonic motion.

I. Acceleration $= -k_0x + k_1x^2$

II. Acceleration $= -k(x + a)$

III. Acceleration $= k(x + a)$

where, k, k_0, k_1 and a are all positive constants.

---

26. The displacement function of a particle in SHM is described by

$$x = A\cos(\omega t + \phi),\ \omega = 2\pi/T$$

If the initial ($t = 0$) position of the particle is 1 cm and its initial velocity is π cm s^{-1}, what is the initial phase angle? (The angular frequency of particle is π s^{-1}).

---

27. The displacement of a particle along the X-axis is given by $x = a \sin^2 \omega t$. The motion of the particle corresponds to

(a) simple harmonic motion of frequency ω/π

(b) simple harmonic motion of frequency $3\omega/2\pi$

(c) non-simple harmonic motion

(d) simple harmonic motion of frequency $\omega/2\pi$

28. A particle executes SHM in a line 4 cm long, its velocity when passing through the centre of line is 12 cm/s, the time period will be ____________ s.

29. A particle executing simple harmonic motion of amplitude 5 cm has frequency of oscillation is 1 Hz. Find the maximum speed.

____

30. The displacement x (in m) of a particle in simple harmonic motion is related to time t (in s) as $x = 0.01 \cos\left(\pi t + \frac{\pi}{4}\right)$, then maximum velocity of the motion will be 0.1π.

True ☐ False ☐

31. A particle executes simple harmonic motion represented by displacement function as

$$x(t) = A \sin(\omega t + \phi)$$

If the position and velocity of the particle at $t = 0$ s are 2 cm and 2ω cms^{-1} respectively, then find the amplitude of the simple harmonic motion.

____

32. A particle is making simple harmonic motion along the X-axis. If at a distances x_1 and x_2 from the mean position, the velocities of the particle are v_1 and v_2 respectively, then calculate time period of its oscillation.

____

33. A particle executes SHM, the graph of velocity as a function of displacement is an ellipse.

True ☐ False ☐

34. A particle executes SHM with amplitude A and time period T. The displacement of the particle when its speed is half of maximum speed is $\frac{\sqrt{x}A}{2}$. The value of x is ____________ .

35. The displacement of an object attached to a spring and executing simple harmonic motion is given by $x = 2 \times 10^{-2} \cos \pi t$ m. The time at which the maximum speed first occurs is ____________ s (0.5/0.7).

36. Two simple harmonic motions are represented by the equations $y_1 = 0.1 \sin\left(100\pi t + \frac{\pi}{3}\right)$ and $y_2 = 0.1 \cos 100\pi t$. The phase difference of the velocity of particle 1 with respect to the velocity of particle 2 is $\frac{\pi}{3}$.

Yes ☐ No ☐

37. A point performs simple harmonic oscillation of period T and the equation of motion is given by $x = a \sin\left(\omega t + \frac{\pi}{6}\right)$. After the elapse of what fraction of the time period, the velocity of the point will be equal to half of its maximum velocity?

____

38. Which of these pairs are correctly matched in SHM?

I. Phase difference between displacement and velocity $\rightarrow \frac{\pi}{2}$

II. Phase difference between displacement and acceleration $\rightarrow \pi$

____

39. Speed v and the acceleration α of a particle executing simple harmonic motion at $x = 0$ will satisfy the condition

(a) v_{min}, α_{min} ☐ (b) $v_{max}, \alpha = 0$ ☐ (c) v_{max}, α_{max} ☐ (d) None of these ☐

40. The acceleration of a particle performing SHM is 12 cm/s^2 at a distance of 3 cm from the mean position. Find its time period.

____

41. If a simple harmonic wave having an amplitude and a time period T is represented by the equation $y = 5 \sin \pi(t + 4)$ m, then acceleration of wave in SHM is $-a\pi^2 \sin(\pi t + b\pi)$. Here, a and b refer to

____

42. If a simple harmonic oscillator has got a displacement of 0.02 m and acceleration equal to 2.0 m/s^2 at any time, then the angular frequency of the oscillator is equal to 100 rad/s.

True ☐ False ☐

43. A particle executes simple harmonic motion with an amplitude of 5 cm. When the particle is at 4 cm from the mean position, the magnitude of its velocity in SI units is equal to that of its acceleration. Then, find its periodic time (in s).

____

44. Two simple harmonic motions of angular frequency 100 rad s^{-1} and 1000 rad s^{-1} have the same displacement amplitude. Find the ratio of their maximum accelerations.

____

45. The phase difference between displacement and acceleration of a particle in a simple harmonic motion is $\frac{3\pi}{2}$ rad.

True ☐ False ☐

46. A particle executes linear simple harmonic motion with an amplitude of 3 cm. When the particle is at 2 cm from the mean position, the magnitude of its velocity is equal to that of its acceleration. Then, calculate its time period (in second).

____

47. A particle is executing a simple harmonic motion. If its maximum acceleration is α and maximum velocity is β, then its time period of vibration will be $2\pi \frac{x}{y}$. Find the value of $\frac{x}{y}$.

____

TOPIC 4

Force Law for Simple Harmonic Motion

48. Two identical springs of spring constant $2k$ are attached to a block of mass $2m$ and to fixed supports as shown in the following figure. When mass is displaced from its equilibrium position on either side, it executes a simple harmonic motion, so time period of oscillations of this system is ______________ .

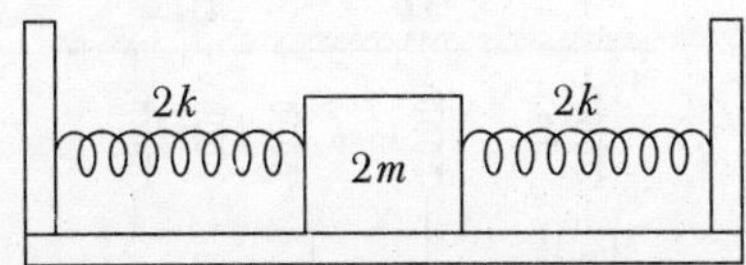

49. A 10 kg collar is attached to a spring of spring constant 400 Nm^{-1}. It slides without friction over a horizontal rod. The collar is displaced from its equilibrium position 10 cm and released the maximum speed of collar is ___________ .

50. The time period of a body suspended by a spring is T. If spring is cut into two equal parts and suspended by both parts in parallel, then new time period will be $\frac{T}{\sqrt{2}}$.

True ☐ False ☐

51. I. Let x_1 and x_2 are the extensions in springs when a force F is applied as shown in the following figure, then $x_1 + x_2 = F\left(\frac{1}{k_1} + \frac{1}{k_2}\right)$.

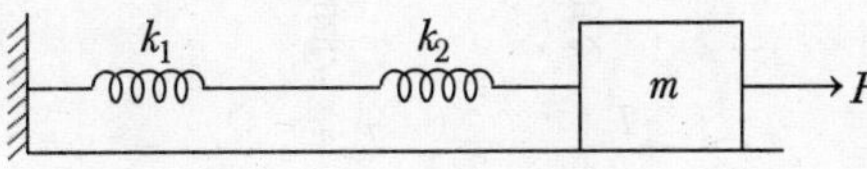

True ☐ False ☐

II. Let x = displacement of mass when force F is applied, so $F = -(k_1 + k_2) \cdot x$

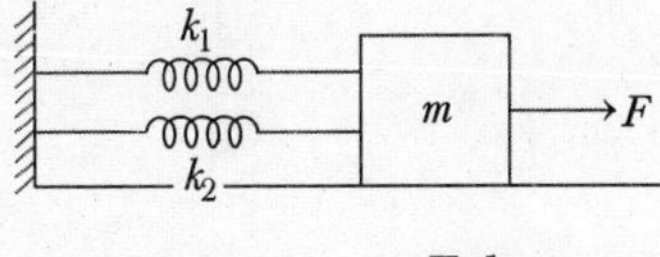

True ☐ False ☐

52. A spring is stretched by 5 cm by a force of 10 N. What is the time period of the oscillations when a mass of 2 kg is suspended by it?

____

53. A body of mass m is attached to the lower end of a spring whose upper end is fixed. The spring has negligible mass. When the mass m is slightly pulled down and released, it oscillates with a time period of 3 s. When the mass m is increased by 1 kg, the time period of oscillations becomes 5 s. Find the value of mass (in kg).

____

54. When mass m is suspended from two light springs separately, time periods are found 3 s and 4 s, respectively.

Now, choose correctly matched pair.

I. Springs are in series $\rightarrow$ Time period $\frac{7}{5}$ s

II. Springs are in parallel $\rightarrow$ Time period $\frac{12}{5}$ s

---

55. Consider following systems.

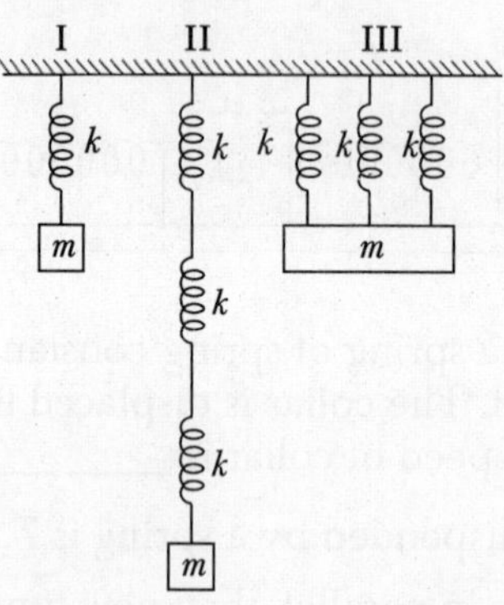

Ratio of time periods of system will be ____________.

***56.** Consider two identical springs each of spring constant k and negligible mass compared to the mass M as shown below. Fig.1 shows one of them and Fig.2 shows their series combination. Find the ratios of time period of oscillation of the two SHM.

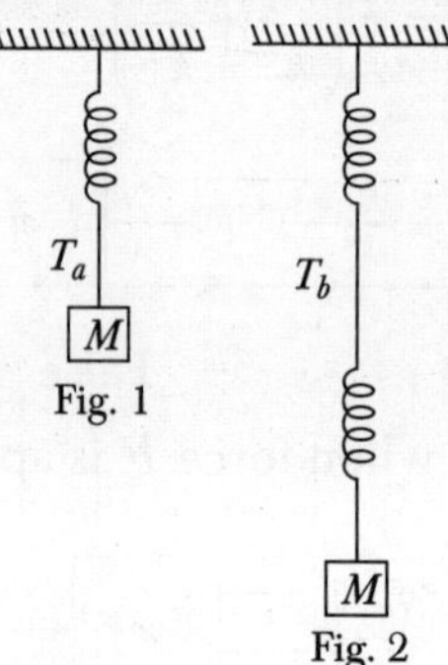

Fig. 1

Fig. 2

***57.** Two identical springs of spring constant 2 N/m are attached to a block of mass 400 kg and to fixed support (see figure). When the mass is displaced from equilibrium position on either side, it executes simple harmonic motion. The time period of oscillations of this system is

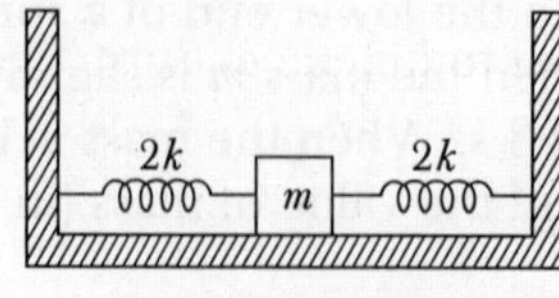

(a) 2π ☐ (b) 4π ☐ (c) 20π ☐ (d) $\pi/10$ ☐

*58. In the given figure, a body of mass m is held between two massless springs, on a smooth inclined plane. The free ends of the springs are attached to firm supports. If each spring has spring constant k, then the frequency of oscillation of given body is ________ .

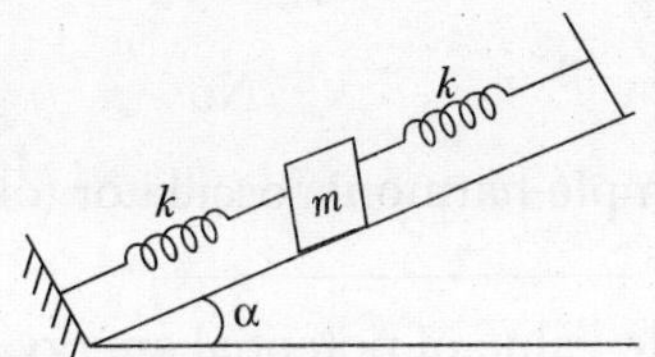

59. In the reported figure, two bodies A and B of masses 200 g and 800 g are attached with the system of springs. Springs are kept in a stretched position with some extension when the system is released. The horizontal surface is assumed to be frictionless. The angular frequency will be ________ rads^{-1}, when k = 20 N/m.

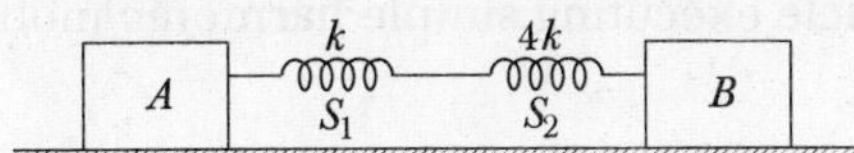

60. The displacement-time graph of a particle executing SHM is given in the following figure (sketch is schematic and not to scale).

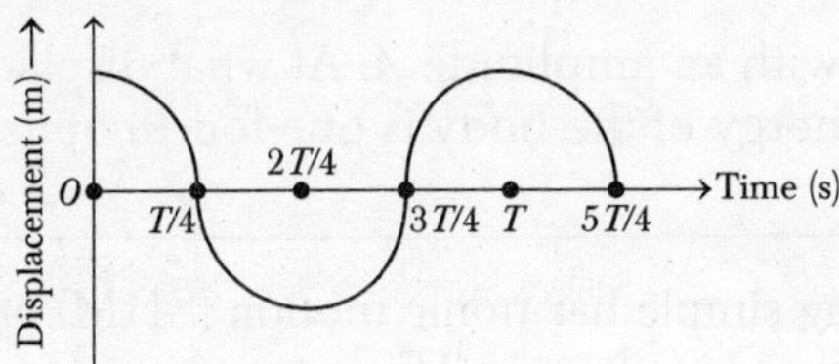

Which of the following statement(s) is/are true for this motion? Tick (✓/✗) on correct/incorrect statement.

A. The force is zero at $t = \frac{3T}{4}$. ☐

B. The acceleration is maximum at $t = T$. ☐

C. The speed is maximum at $t = \frac{T}{4}$. ☐

D. The potential energy is equal to kinetic energy of the oscillation at $t = \frac{T}{2}$. ☐

61. The kinetic energy of a particle executing SHM is 16 J when it is in its mean position. If the amplitude of oscillation is 25 cm and the mass of the particle is 5.12 kg, the time period of its oscillation is $\frac{\pi}{5}$ s.

Yes ☐ No ☐

62. The potential energy of a simple harmonic oscillator (of total energy E), when the particle is half way to its end point is ________________ .

Fill above blank with suitable value of potential energy in term of total energy E.

63. A body executes simple harmonic motion. The potential energy (PE), the kinetic energy (KE) and total energy (TE) are measured as a function of displacement x. Then,

(a) PE is maximum when $x = 0$ ☐
(b) KE is maximum when $x = 0$ ☐
(c) TE is zero when $x = 0$ ☐
(d) KE is maximum when x is maximum ☐

64. The total energy of particle executing simple harmonic motion is dependent of displacement (x).

True ☐ False ☐

65. A particle executes simple harmonic motion along a straight line with an amplitude A. The potential energy is maximum when the displacement is $\pm\frac{A}{2}$.

Yes ☐ No ☐

66. A particle of mass m executes simple harmonic motion with amplitude A and frequency ν. The average kinetic energy during its motion from the position of equilibrium to the end is $4\pi^2 mA^2\nu^2$.

True ☐ False ☐

67. A body executes SHM with an amplitude A. At what displacement from the mean position, the potential energy of the body is one-fourth of its total energy ?

____

68. A particle starts executing simple harmonic motion (SHM) of amplitude A and total energy E. At any instant, if its kinetic energy is $\frac{3E}{4}$, then its displacement y is given by $\frac{A\sqrt{3}}{2}$.

True ☐ False ☐

69. In a simple harmonic oscillation, what fraction of total mechanical energy is in the form of kinetic energy when the particle is mid-way between mean and extreme positions?

____

70. The kinetic energy and potential energy of a simple harmonic oscillation become equal at $x = \pm\frac{A}{\sqrt{2}}$.

Yes ☐ No ☐

71. A particle undergoing simple harmonic motion has time dependent displacement given by $x(t) = A\sin\frac{\pi t}{90}$. The ratio of kinetic to potential energy of this particle at $t = 210$ s will be $\frac{x}{y}$.

Find the values of x and y.

____

***72.** An object of mass 0.2 kg executes simple harmonic oscillations along the X-axis with a frequency of $\frac{25}{\pi}$ Hz. At the position $x = 0.04$ m, the object has the kinetic energy of 0.5 J and potential energy of 0.4 J. The amplitude of oscillations is ________.

73. If a body having mass m and performing SHM with amplitude A with a restoring force $F = -kx$, where x is the displacement, then the total energy of body depends on amplitude and time period.

True ☐ False ☐

***74.** Variations of potential and kinetic energies of a simple harmonic oscillator are shown in following figure, then which of the figure is correct?

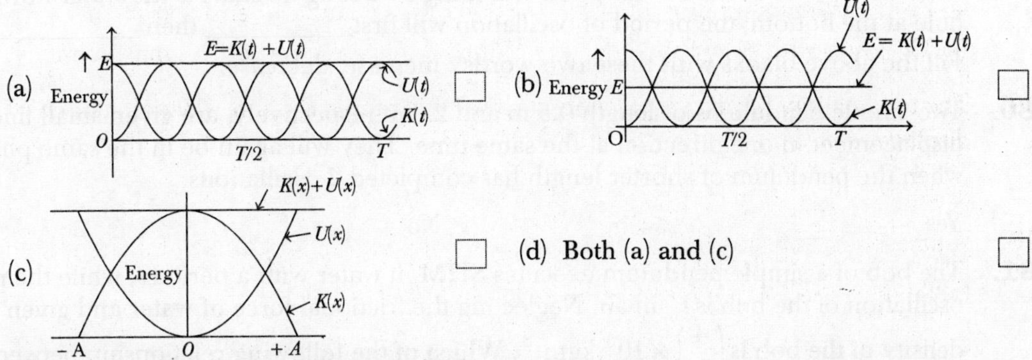

75. The variation of displacement with time of a particle executing free simple harmonic motion is shown in the following figure.

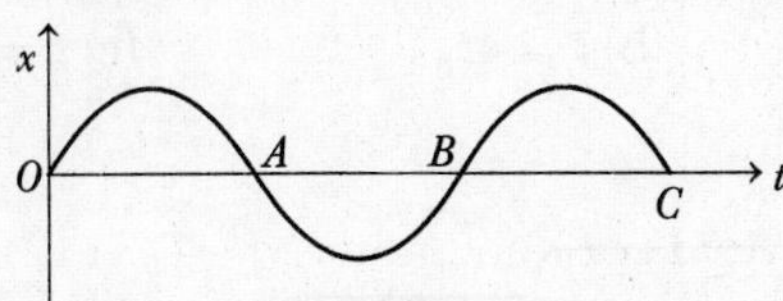

Plot the potential energy $U(x)$ *versus* time (t) graph of the particle.

____

***76.** A block whose mass is 1 kg is fastened to spring. The spring has a spring constant of 50 Nm^{-1}. The block is pulled to a distance $x = 10$ cm from its equilibrium position on a frictionless surface from rest at $t = 0$. Calculate total energies of block when it is 5 cm away from the mean position.

____

77. A particle is executing simple harmonic motion with a time period T. At time $t = 0$, it is at its position of equilibrium. Draw the kinetic energy *versus* time graph of the particle.

____

***78.** An ideal pendulum is hung from the roof of a sufficiently high building and is moving freely to and fro. The acceleration of the bob of the pendulum is 20 ms^{-2} at a distance of 5 m from the mean position. The time period of oscillation is x s.
Here, x refers to ____________.

79. A hollow sphere is filled with water. It is hung by a long thread. As the water flows out of a hole at the bottom, the period of oscillation will first __________ then __________.
Fill the above blanks with these two words : increase, decrease.

80. Two simple pendulums of length 0.5 m and 2.0 m respectively, are given small linear displacement in one direction at the same time. They will again be in the same phase when the pendulum of shorter length has completed 2 oscillations.

Yes ☐ No ☐

***81.** The bob of a simple pendulum executes SHM in water with a period t, while the period of oscillation of the bob is t_0 in air. Neglecting the frictional force of water and given that the density of the bob is $\left(\frac{4}{3}\right) \times 10^3$ kgm^{-3}. Which of the following relationship between t and t_0 is correct?

(a) $t = t_0$ ☐ (b) $t = 4t_0$ ☐ (c) $t = 2t_0$ ☐ (d) $t = \frac{t_0}{2}$ ☐

Assertion-Reason Questions

Direction (Q. Nos. 1-9) *In the following questions, a statement of Assertion is followed by a corresponding statement of Reason. From the following options, choose the correct one.*
(a) Both Assertion and Reason are correct and Reason is the correct explanation of Assertion.
(b) Both Assertion and Reason are correct but Reason is not the correct explanation of Assertion.
(c) Assertion is correct but Reason is incorrect.
(d) Assertion is incorrect but Reason is correct.

***1. Assertion** (A) Acceleration of a particle in SHM is zero at mean position.
Reason (R) Two SHMs must have same phase, if amplitude is same.

(a) ☐ (b) ☐ (c) ☐ (d) ☐

2. Assertion (A) In SHM, the motion is to and fro and periodic.

Reason (R) In SHM, the particle's velocity is $v = \omega\sqrt{A^2 - x^2}$ (where, x is displacement of particle)

(a) ☐ (b) ☐ (c) ☐ (d) ☐

3. **Assertion** (A) The graph between velocity and displacement for SHM is an ellipse.
Reason (R) Velocity does not change uniformly with displacement in SHM.

(a) ☐ (b) ☐ (c) ☐ (d) ☐

4. **Assertion** (A) The time period of a pendulum, on a satellite orbiting the earth is infinity.
Reason (R) The time period of a pendulum is inversely proportional to $\sqrt{g}$.

(a) ☐ (b) ☐ (c) ☐ (d) ☐

***5.** **Assertion** (A) When a girl sitting on a swing stands up, the periodic time of swing decreases.
Reason (R) When a girl stands up, more weight is felt on the string of the swing.

(a) ☐ (b) ☐ (c) ☐ (d) ☐

***6.** **Assertion** (A) The graph of potential energy and kinetic energy of a particle in SHM with respect to pesition a parabola.
Reason (R) PE and KE do not vary linearly with position.

(a) ☐ (b) ☐ (c) ☐ (d) ☐

***7.** **Assertion** (A) Both KE and PE in SHM are always positive.
Reason (R) Both KE and PE peak once, during each period of simple harmonic motion.

(a) ☐ (b) ☐ (c) ☐ (d) ☐

8. **Assertion** (A) In SHM, kinetic energy varies between zero and maximum values.
Reason (R) In SHM, velocity of particle is a periodic function of time.

(a) ☐ (b) ☐ (c) ☐ (d) ☐

***9.** **Assertion** (A) If a pendulum is suspended in a lift and lift is falling, freely, then its time period becomes infinite.
Reason (R) Free falling body has acceleration equal to acceleration due to gravity.

(a) ☐ (b) ☐ (c) ☐ (d) ☐

Case Based Questions

1. Simple harmonic motion is the simplest form of oscillation. A particular type of periodic motion in which a particle moves to and fro repeatedly about a mean position under the influence of a restoring force is termed simple harmonic motion (SHM). A body is undergoing simple harmonic motion if it has an acceleration that is directed towards a fixed point and proportional to the displacement of the body from that point.
Acceleration, $a \propto -x$

$$\Rightarrow \quad a = -kx \text{ or } \frac{d^2x}{dt^2} = -kx$$

where, x = displacement at any instant t.

(i) Which of the following is not a characteristic of simple harmonic motion?

(a) The motion is periodic ☐

(b) The motion is along a straight line about the mean position. ☐

(c) The oscillations are responsible for the energy conversion. ☐

(d) The acceleration of the particle is directed towards the extreme position. ☐

(ii) The equation of motion of a simple harmonic motion is

(a) $\frac{d^2x}{dt^2} = -\omega^2 x$ ☐ (b) $\frac{d^2x}{dt^2} = -\omega^2 t$ ☐

(c) $\frac{d^2x}{dt^2} = -\omega x$ ☐ (d) $\frac{d^2x}{dt^2} = -\omega t$ ☐

(iii) Which of the following expressions does not represent simple harmonic motion?

(a) $x = A(\cos \omega t + \sin \omega t)$ ☐ (b) $x = A\cos(\omega t + \phi)$ ☐

(c) $x = \sin(\omega t + \phi)$ ☐ (d) $x = A \sin \omega t \cos^2 \omega t$ ☐

(iv) The time period of simple harmonic motion depends upon

(a) amplitude ☐ (b) energy ☐

(c) phase constant ☐ (d) mass ☐

Or

The value of ω is

(a) $\sqrt{\frac{k}{m}}$ ☐ (b) $\sqrt{\frac{m}{k}}$ ☐ (c) $\frac{k}{m}$ ☐ (d) $\frac{m}{k}$ ☐

2. The energy of a harmonic oscillation is partly kinetic and partly potential. when a body is displaced from its equilibrium position by doing work upon it, it acquires potential energy. When the body is released, it begins to move back with a velocity, thus acquiring kinetic energy. The total mechanical energy of a harmonic oscillator are independent of time or displacement. Hence, in the absence of any friction force, the total energy of a harmonic oscillator is conserved.

(i) The particle executing simple harmonic motion has a kinetic energy $K_0 \cos^2 \omega t$. The maximum values of potential energy and total energy are respectively,

(a) $\frac{K_0}{2}$ and K_0 ☐ (b) K_0 and $2K_0$ ☐

(c) K_0 and K_0 ☐ (d) 0 and $2K_0$ ☐

(ii) Displacement between maximum potential energy and maximum kinetic energy, position for a particle executing SHM is

(a) $\pm \frac{a}{2}$ ☐ (b) $+a$ ☐ (c) $\pm a$ ☐ (d) –1 ☐

(iii) The total energy of particle performing SHM depends on

(a) K, A, m ☐ (b) K, A ☐ (c) K, A, x ☐ (d) K, x ☐

(iv) In an SHM, when displacement is one-half of the amplitude what fraction of total energy is kinetic?

(a) $\frac{1}{2}$ ☐ (b) $\frac{3}{4}$ ☐ (c) Zero ☐ (d) $\frac{1}{4}$ ☐

Or

At which point both, kinetic and potential energy is equal?

(a) $\frac{A}{2}$ ☐ (b) $\pm \frac{A}{2}$ ☐ (c) $-\frac{A}{\sqrt{2}}$ ☐ (d) $\pm \frac{A}{\sqrt{2}}$ ☐

COMPETITION EDGE UP

1. A particle of mass 0.50 kg executes simple harmonic motion under force $F = -50x\ Nm^{-1}$. The time period of oscillation is $\frac{x}{35}$ s. The value of x is .... (Given, $\pi = \frac{22}{7}$)

[NCERT Pg. 268, JEE Main 2024]

2. The position, velocity and acceleration of a particle executing simple harmonic motion are found to have magnitudes of 4 m, 2 ms $^{-1}$ and 16 ms^{-2} at a certain instant. The amplitude of the motion is $\sqrt{x}$, m where x is ....

[NCERT Pg. 266, JEE Main 2024]

3. A simple pendulum doing small oscillations at a place R height above earth surface has time period of $T_1 = 4$ s. T_2 would be it's time period if it is brought to a point which is at a height 2R from earth surface. Choose the correct relation [R = radius of earth]

[NCERT Pg. 271, JEE Main 2024]

(a) $2T_1 = T_2$ ☐ (b) $T_1 = T_2$ ☐
(c) $2T_1 = 3T_2$ ☐ (d) $3T_1 = 2T_2$ ☐

4. In simple harmonic motion, the total mechanical energy of given system is E. If mass of oscillating particle P is doubled then the new energy of the system for same amplitude is

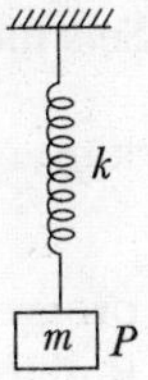

[NCERT Pg. 268, JEE Main 2024]

(a) $\frac{E}{\sqrt{2}}$ ☐ (b) $E\sqrt{2}$ ☐
(c) 2E ☐ (d) E ☐

5. A mass m is suspended from a spring of negligible mass and the system oscillates with a frequency f_1. The frequency of oscillations if a mass 9 m is suspended from the same spring is f_2. The value of f_1/f_2 is .... **[NCERT Pg. 268, JEE Main 2024]**

6. The time period of simple harmonic motion of mass M in the given figure is $\pi\sqrt{\frac{\alpha M}{5k}}$, where the value of α is ....

[NCERT Pg. 268, JEE Main 2024]

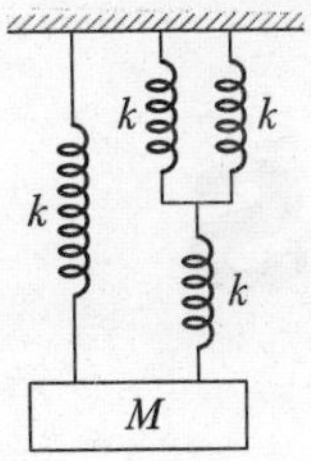

7. If $x = 5 \sin\left(\pi t + \frac{\pi}{3}\right)$ m represents the motion of a particle executing simple harmonic motion, the amplitude and time period of motion respectively, are

[NCERT Pg. 262, NEET 2024]

(a) 5 cm, 2 s ☐ (b) 5 m, 2 s ☐
(c) 5 cm, 1 s ☐ (d) 5 m, 1 s ☐

8. If the mass of the bob in a simple pendulum is increased to thrice its original mass and its length is made half its original length, then the new time period of oscillation is x / 2 times its original time period. Then, the value of x is

[NCERT Pg. 270, NEET 2024]

(a) $\sqrt{3}$ ☐ (b) $\sqrt{2}$ ☐
(c) $2\sqrt{3}$ ☐ (d) 4 ☐

9. Two pendulums of length 121 cm and 100 cm start vibrating in phase. At some instant, the two are at their mean position in the same phase. The minimum number of vibrations of the shorter pendulum after which the two are again in phase at the mean position is **[NCERT Pg. 271, NEET 2022]**

(a) 9 ☐ (b) 10 ☐
(c) 8 ☐ (d) 11 ☐

10. A body is executing simple harmonic motion with frequency n, the frequency of its potential energy is

[NCERT Pg. 268, NEET 2021]

(a) n ☐ (b) 2n ☐
(c) 3n ☐ (d) 4n ☐

11. The phase difference between displacement and acceleration of a particle in a simple harmonic motion is

[NCERT Pg. 266, NEET (Sep.) 2020]

(a) $\frac{3\pi}{2}$ rad ☐ (b) $\frac{\pi}{2}$ rad ☐
(c) zero ☐ (d) π rad ☐

Chapter 14

Waves

Scan and take Chapter Test

TOPIC 1

Transverse and Longitudinal Waves

1. The correct possible order of interconversion of waves when our sound is transferred to the receiver *via* a mobile phone is

(a) sound waves $\rightarrow$ electric current signal $\rightarrow$ electromagnetic waves (radio waves) ☐
(b) sound waves $\rightarrow$ electromagnetic waves $\rightarrow$ electric current signal ☐
(c) sound waves $\rightarrow$ electric current signal $\rightarrow$ sound wave ☐
(d) None of the above ☐

2. Which of the following waves require a medium for their propagation?

(a) Light waves ☐
(b) Radiowaves ☐
(c) X-rays ☐
(d) Seismic waves ☐

3. The wave generated from up and down jerk given to the string or by up and down motion of the piston at end of the pipe is

(a) transverse or longitudinal ☐
(b) progressive ☐
(c) standing ☐
(d) Both (a) and (b) ☐

4. In which of the following cases, the material medium as a whole does not move?

(a) A stream ☐
(b) A wind ☐
(c) Water wave ☐
(d) Both (a) and (c) ☐

5. Which of these pairs are correctly matched? (Here, $\mathbf{y}$ = displacement of particle and $\mathbf{v}$ = wave velocity)

I. Transverse waves : $\mathbf{y} \cdot \mathbf{v} = 0$

II. Longitudinal waves : $\mathbf{y} \times \mathbf{v} \leq 1$

*Concepts of all questions bearing * are important for JEE/NEET/CUET.*

TOPIC 2

Displacement Relation in a Progressive Wave

6. Which of these represents a travelling wave?

I. $y = a\sin\left\{\omega\left(t - \frac{x}{v}\right)\right\}$ II. $y = a\sin\left\{\omega\left(\frac{t}{T} - \frac{x}{\lambda}\right)\right\}$

III. $y = a\sin\left\{\omega\left(\frac{t}{T} + \frac{x}{\lambda}\right)\right\}$ IV. $y = a\sin\left\{\omega\left(t + \frac{x}{v}\right)\right\}$

____

7.

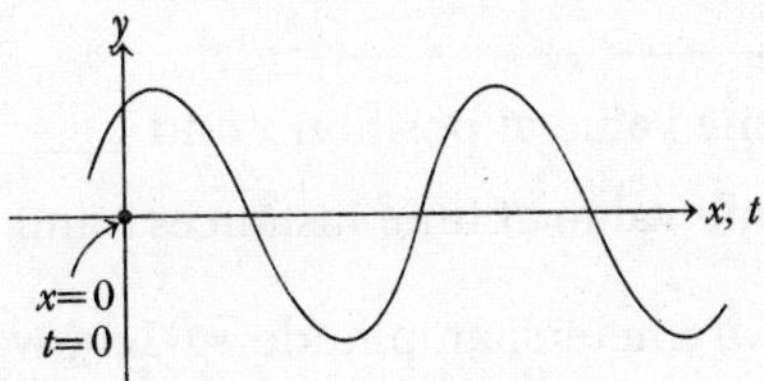

For above wave, displacement y can be expressed as ________ [$y = A\sin(kx - \omega t)$/ $y = A\sin(kx - \omega t + \phi)$].

8.

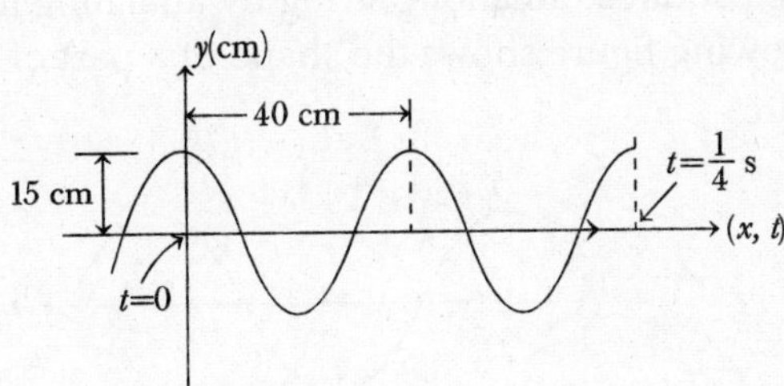

For the wave shown in the given figure, displacement function y can be expressed as

$$y = 15\cos\left(\frac{2\pi}{40}x - 16\pi t\right)$$

Yes  No 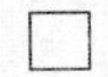

9. The equation of a wave is $y = 4\sin\left[\frac{\pi}{2}\left(2t + \frac{x}{8}\right)\right]$ where, y, x are in cm and time in second.

The displacement y of the wave at distance of $x = 8$ cm and $t = 1$ s is x cm. Here, x refers to ___________.

10. Write the wave equation for given conditions.

I. A sound source of frequency 50 Hz is producing longitudinal waves in air. The amplitude of vibration of air particle is 2 mm and speed of wave is 300 m/s.

____

II. A wave travelling in the positive x-direction have displacement along y-direction as 1 m, wavelength 2π m and frequency of $\frac{1}{\pi}$ Hz.

III. A wave in a string has an amplitude of 2 cm. The wave travels in the positive direction of X-axis with a speed of 128 ms^{-1} and it is noted that 5 complete waves fit in 4 m length of the string.

IV. A wave of amplitude $a = 0.2$ m, velocity $v = 360$ m/s and wavelength 60 m is travelling along positive X-axis.

11. Let a travelling wave is $y = A\sin\left[2\pi\left(\frac{x}{\lambda} - \frac{t}{T}\right)\right]$, then

A. angular frequency of wave is ω = __________.

B. number of complete wavelengths that occur in a unit length in direction of travel of wave is k = __________.

C. displacement y has same value at position x and __________.

D. displacement y has same value at time instances t and __________.

12. A sinusoidal wave with parameters; amplitude = 0.1 m, wavelength = 2 m and speed = 1 m/s. This wave travels over a string towards right with left end of string at origin initially. Equation of motion of left hand of string is __________.

13. Transverse waves are produced in a long string by attaching its free end to a vibrating tuning fork. The following figure shows the shape of a part of the string.
The points in phase are

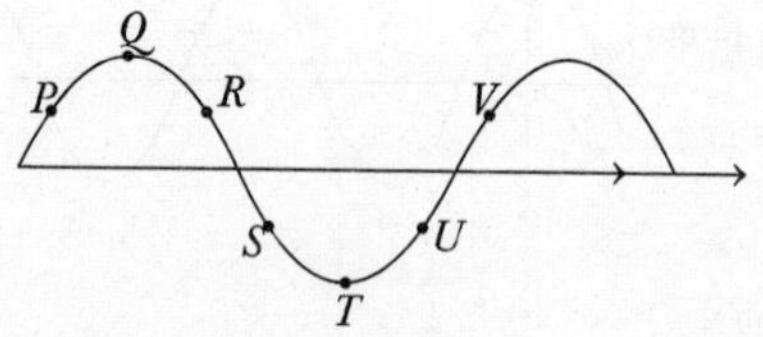

P Q R S T U V

(a) R and U ☐ (b) P and V ☐
(c) P and S ☐ (d) Q and T ☐

14. When a progressive wave is propagating in a medium, at a given instant, two particles which are separated by 5 wavelengths will have

(a) same displacement in opposite direction ☐
(b) same displacement in same direction ☐
(c) different displacement in opposite direction ☐
(d) different displacement in same direction ☐

15. Two waves are represented by the equations $y_1 = a\sin(\omega t + kx + 0.57)$ m and $y_2 = a\cos(\omega t + kx)$ m, where x is in metre and t in second. The phase difference between them is __________.

16. The equation of a transverse wave is $y = 20\sin\pi(0.02x - 2t)$, where y and x are in centimetre and t is in second. The wavelength (in cm) will be __________.

17. A wave travelling along a string is described by $y(x, t) = 0.00327 \sin(72.1\,x - 2.72\,t)$ in which the numerical constants are in SI units. The amplitude and wave number of this wave is given by

(a) 0.00327 mm and 2.72 rad/s ☐ (b) 0.00327 m and 72.1 rad/s ☐

(c) 3.27 mm and 2.72 rad/s ☐ (d) 3.27 mm and 72.1 rad/m ☐

18. A sound wave of frequency 245 Hz travels with the speed of 300 ms^{-1} along the positive X-axis. Each point of the wave moves to and fro through a total distance of 6 cm. What will be the mathematical expression of this travelling wave?

____

19. At a point in a medium, 3600 waves pass in 1 min at a speed of 960 m/s. Wavelength of each wave is __________ m.

TOPIC 3

Speed of a Travelling Wave

NCERT Pg 284-287

20. A transverse wave over a string is described by the wave function

$$y = 0.1 \sin\left(\frac{\pi}{8}x + 4\pi t\right)$$

Consider a particle at $x = 1.6$ m and fill these blanks.

A. Maximum displacement of this particle occurs at $t =$ ________ s.

B. Particle speed at $t = 0.2$ s is ________ m/s.

C. Acceleration of particle at 0.2 s is ______ m/s^2.

21. Consider wave

$$y = 0.25 \sin(0.3x - 40t)$$

(Here, all values are in SI units).

Now, match the Column I with Column II.

Column I		Column II	
A.	Angular frequency (rad/s)	1.	133
B.	Angular wave number (rad/m)	2.	20.9
C.	Wave speed (m/s)	3.	0.3
D.	Wavelength (m)	4.	40

A__________ B__________ C__________ D__________

22. The equation of a wave is given by $y = a \sin\left(100t - \frac{x}{10}\right)$, where x and y are in metre and t in second, then velocity of wave is

(a) 0.1 m/s ☐ (b) 10 m/s ☐

(c) 100 m/s ☐ (d) 1000 m/s. ☐

23. For given wave, $y = 0.2\sin(1.5x + 60\,t)$, where y and x are in metre and t in second. The velocity of the wave is ___________.

24. A travelling wave is represented by $y(x, t) = 0.002 \sin[(0.2 \text{ m}^{-1})x - (0.4 \text{ s}^{-1})\,t]$, where x and t are in metre and seconds, respectively. The speed of propagation of wave is ___________.

25. A wave equation is $y = 0.001\sin(60t + 2x)$, where x and y are in metre and t is in seconds. Now, choose correct statements.

I. The wave travels with a velocity of 30 m/s in the positive direction of the X-axis.

____

II. The wave travels with a velocity of 30 m/s in the negative direction of the X-axis.

____

III. Frequency of wave is $(30 / \pi)$ Hz.

____

IV. Frequency of wave is $(\pi / 30)$ Hz.

____

26. A transverse wave is represented by $y = A \sin(\omega t - kx)$. For what value of the wavelength is the wave velocity equal to the maximum particle velocity?

____

27. A transverse wave is represented by the equation $y = y_0 \sin \frac{2\pi}{\lambda}(vt - x)$.

For what value of λ is the maximum particle velocity equal to two times the wave velocity?

____

28. A transverse wave propagating along X-axis is represented by

$y(x, t) = 8 \sin\left(0.5\pi x - 4\pi t - \frac{\pi}{4}\right)$, where x is in metre and t is in second.

The speed of the wave is

(a) 4π m/s ☐ (b) 0.5π m/s ☐

(c) $\frac{\pi}{4}$ m/s ☐ (d) 8 m/s ☐

29. The speed of transverse wave in a rope of length 10 m and mass 80 g under a tension of 80 N is ___________ m/s.

30. The mass per unit length of a uniform wire is 0.135 g/cm. A transverse wave of the form $y = -0.21 \sin(x + 30\,t)$ is produced in it, where x is in metre and t is in second. Then, the expected value of tension in the wire is $x \times 10^{-2}$ N. Value of x is ___________. (Round off to the nearest integer)

31. Let T = tension, μ = mass per unit length, η = modulus of rigidity, ρ = density, Y = Young's modulus, K = bulk modulus.

Now, match Column I with Column II.

Column I	Column II
A. Speed of sound in a solid metallic rod	1. $\sqrt{\frac{\eta}{\rho}}$
B. Speed of wave over a string	2. $\sqrt{\frac{K}{\rho}}$
C. Speed of wave in a fluid	3. $\sqrt{\frac{T}{\mu}}$
D. Speed of wave in a solid body	4. $\sqrt{\frac{Y}{\rho}}$

A__________ B__________ C__________ D__________

32. A steel wire of length 0.72 m has a mass of 5.0×10^{-3} kg. The speed of transverse waves on the wire is 93 m/s. The tension in the steel wire is __________ N.

33. Young's modulus for steel is 3×10^{10} N/m^2 and its density is 1.2×10^3 kg/m^3. The speed of longitudinal wave in steel __________ .

34. Arrange the following medium in ascending order of speed of sound.

Water, Rubber, Aluminium, Hydrogen

____

35. At 10^5 N/m^2 atmospheric pressure, the density of air is 1.29 kg/m^3. If $\gamma = 1.41$ for air, then find the speed of sound in air.

____

36. The speed of sound in air at NTP is 332 m/s. If $\gamma = 1.40$ and density of air is 1.293 kg/m^3, then the difference of speed of sound by Newton's formula and Laplace modified Newton's formula is nearly __________ m/s

TOPIC 4

Principle of Superposition of Waves

37. Two wave pulses moving over a string are approaching each other (at $t = 0$) as shown in the following figure.

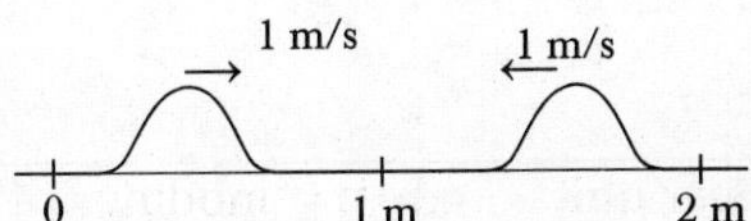

What will be oscillating pattern of string after some time interval t?

---

38. Two wave pulses are moving over a string at $t = 0$ s as shown in the following figure.

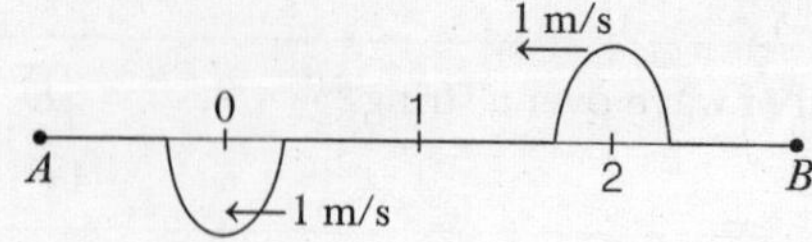

Now, choose correctly matched pair.

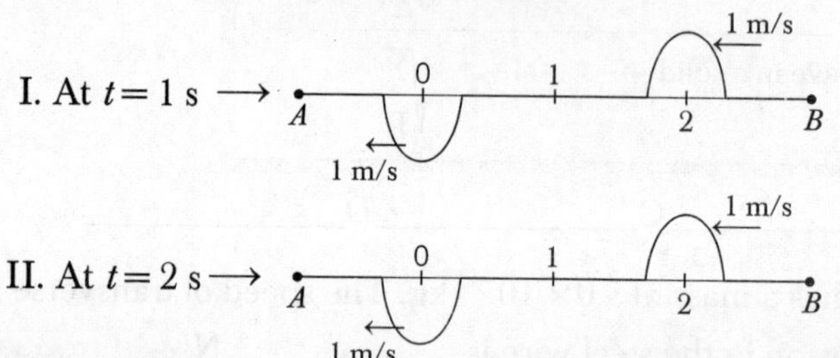

39. Two waves of same frequency and intensity superimpose on each other in opposite phases. After the superposition, the intensity and frequency of waves will ________ .

40. A sound wave is made incident over a medium interface (as shown in the following figure).
I. Incident wave II. Reflected wave III. Transmitted wave

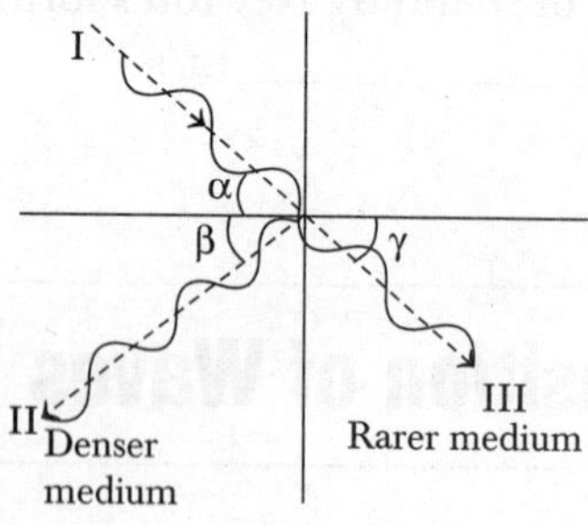

Now, choose correct statements.

A. $f_{I} = f_{II} > f_{III}$, where f = frequency of wave.

B. $\alpha = \beta$ and $\beta < \gamma$.

---

41. Which of these are correctly matched?

I. Incident wave $y = A\sin(kx - \omega t) \rightarrow$ Wave reflected from a hard boundary
$y = -A\sin(kx - \omega t)$

II. Incident wave $y = A\sin(kx - \omega t) \rightarrow$ Wave reflected from soft boundary
$y = A\sin(kx - \omega t)$

____

42. A pulse in a rope approaches a solid wall and it gets reflected from it.

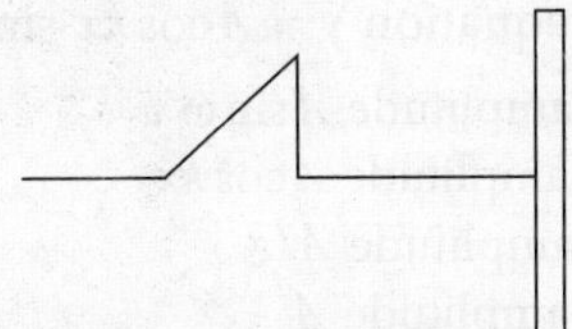

The wave pulse after reflection is best represented by

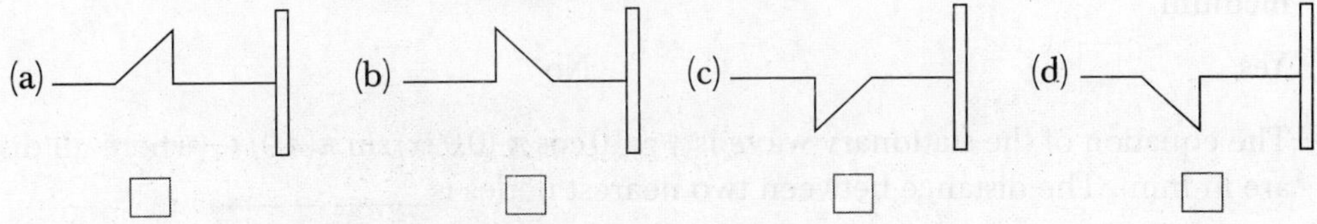

43. The equation of a transverse wave travelling along a string is

$$y(x, t) = 0.3\sin(200x - 0.5\,t)$$

The equations of the reflected wave when reflected by a rigid boundary and when reflected by a free end respectively, is given by

____

44. Two progressive waves moving in opposite directions with same frequency and same amplitude, superpose.

Now, choose incorrect statement.

I. Resultant wave is non-progressive.
II. All particles are at mean position simultaneously.
II. At nodes, energy is only potential.
IV. Energy at anti-nodes is only kinetic.

____

45. Match the following columns.

	Column I		Column II
A.	At node points	1.	Amplitude is maximum
B.	At anti-node points	2.	Amplitude is minimum
		3.	Pressure and density both are high
		4.	Pressure and density both are low

A_____________ B_____________

46. In a stationary wave, the distance (in terms of wavelength) between a node and nearest anti-node is__________ $\left(\frac{\lambda}{4}/\frac{\lambda}{3}\right)$ and between two successive anti-node is $\left(\frac{\lambda}{4}/\frac{\lambda}{2}\right)$ __________.

47. A wave $y = a \sin(\omega t - kx)$ on a string meets with another wave producing a node at $x = 0$, then the equation of the unknown wave will be $y = -a \sin(\omega t + kx)$.

Yes ☐ No ☐

48. A wave is represented by an equation $y = A \cos kx \sin \omega t$, then

(a) it is a stationary wave with amplitude $A \sin \omega t$ ☐
(b) it is a stationary wave with amplitude $A \cos kx$ ☐
(c) it is a stationary wave with amplitude A/z ☐
(d) it is a stationary wave with amplitude A ☐

49. In a stationary wave, there is continuous transfer of energy across any section of the medium.

Yes ☐ No ☐

50. The equation of the stationary wave is $y = 10 \cos \pi\ (0.02x) \sin \pi(4.0)\ t$, (where all distances are in mm). The distance between two nearest nodes is __________ .

51. Standing waves are produced in a 10 m long stretched string. If the string vibrates in 5 segments and the wave velocity is 20 m/s, calculate the frequency.

____

52. A standing wave having 3 nodes and 2 anti-nodes is formed between two atoms having a distance 1.21 Å between them. The wavelength of the standing wave is $x.2x$ Å. What is the value of x?

____

53. When some water is poured in empty vessel, its frequency __________ (increases/decreases).

54. The musical sound produced by close organ pipe is richer than musical sound produced by open organ pipe.

True ☐ False ☐

55. A cylindrical resonance tube open at both ends has a fundamental frequency ν in air. If half of the length is dipped vertically in water, the fundamental frequency of air column will be

(a) ν ☐ (b) 3ν / 2 ☐
(c) ν / 2 ☐ (d) 4ν ☐

56. The fundamental frequency in an open organ pipe is equal to the third harmonic of a closed organ pipe. If the length of the closed organ pipe is 20 cm, the length of the open organ pipe is __________ cm.

57. An air column, closed at one end and open at the other, resonates with a tuning fork when the smallest length of the column is 50 cm. The next larger length with the same tuning fork is

(a) 100 cm ☐ (b) 150 cm ☐

(c) 200 cm ☐ (d) 66.7 cm ☐

58. The fundamental frequency of a closed organ pipe is 125 Hz. If the velocity of sound at 0°C is 332 m/s, then the length of the closed organ pipe is ________ cm.

59. The second overton the open organ pipe is in unison with the second overtone of closed organ pipe. The ratio of lengths of closed organ pipe and open organ pipe is given by $\frac{x}{y}$. Here, x and y refer to ________________, respectively .

60. Tick (✓/×) for correct/incorrect statement in given boxes.

(i) The fundamental frequency of string is 220 cycle per second. Its fifth harmonic frequency is 1100 Hz . ☐

(ii) The fundamental frequency of a pipe with open ends is 200 Hz. If one of the open end is closed, then the fundamental frequency will be 200 Hz. ☐

(iii) An organ pipe blown forcefully, its first overtone of 384 Hz is emitted. It is an open organ pipe emit fundamental note of frequency 128 Hz. ☐

61. The two vibrating air columns are shown in the following figure. The ratio of frequency in the two cases is ______________ .

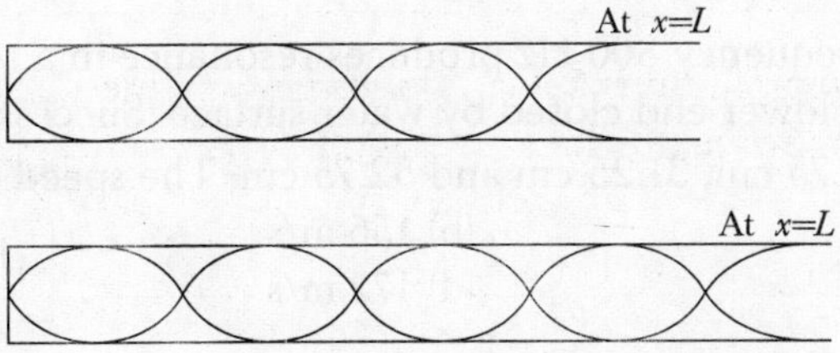

At $x=L$

At $x=L$

62. The fundamental frequency of an open organ pipe is 300 Hz. The first overtone of this organ pipe is in unison with first overtone of closed organ pipe. If the speed of sound is 300 m/s, then what is length of closed organ pipe?

____

63. The vibration of three air columns are represented in the following figure. The ratio of frequencies $f_A : f_B : f_C$ is ______________ .

Ⓐ

Ⓑ

Ⓒ

64. The sum of frequencies of first overtone of a closed pipe and the second overtone of an open pipe of the same length is 180 Hz. The ratio of fundamental frequencies of closed and open pipes is given by ______________ .

65. In a closed organ pipe, the second overtone is produced. In this closed organ pipe, we observe ____________ nodes and ____________ anti-nodes.

66. In case of closed organ pipe which harmonic Pth overtone will be?

(a) $P+1$ ☐ (b) $2P-1$ ☐
(c) $2P+1$ ☐ (d) $P-1$ ☐

67. A pipe closed at one end has a length of 2 m. Velocity of sound in air is 320 m/s, the air column in the pipe can resonate for tuning fork of frequency ____________ Hz. (Choose from given values)

I. 40 II. 60 III. 200 IV. 180

68. The length of an organ pipe is 0.5 m. The velocity of sound in air be 350 m/s. The fundamental frequency of an open organ pipe and close organ pipe will be 350 Hz, 175 Hz.

Yes ☐ No ☐

69. The fundamental standing wave is formed in a cardboard tube of length $L = 67$ cm with two open ends. The speed of sound in air within the cardboard tube is 343 m/s. If you jam your ear against one end of the tube, then the fundamental frequency you hear from the tube is __________ Hz.

70. A tuning fork with frequency 800 Hz produces resonance in a resonance column tube with upper end open and lower end closed by water surface. Successive resonance are observed at length 9.75 cm, 31.25 cm and 52.75 cm. The speed of sound in air is

(a) 500 m/s ☐ (b) 156 m/s ☐
(c) 344 m/s ☐ (d) 172 m/s ☐

71. A one metre long (both ends open) organ pipe is kept in a gas that has double the density of air at STP. Assuming the speed of sound in air at STP is 300 m/s, the frequency difference between the fundamental and second harmonic of this pipe is ________ Hz.

72. A tuning fork of frequency 480 Hz is used in an experiment for measuring speed of sound v in air by resonance tube method. Resonance is observed to occur at two successive lengths of the air column $l_1 = 30$ cm and $l_2 = 70$ cm, then v is equal to __________ .

TOPIC 6 Beats

NCERT Pg 293-294

73. Tick (✓/×) for correct/incorrect statement in given boxes.

(i) An open pipe and a closed pipe are in resonance with each other with their first overtones. The ratio of their lengths are 4/3. ☐

(ii) If two sources have the same frequency, they are said to be in unison and hence, no beats are produced. ☐

(iii) Two waves of slightly different frequencies moving in opposite direction produce beats. ☐

(iv) The number of beats heard per second is numerically equal to the sum of frequencies of the two sound. ☐

(v) Two waves of slightly different frequencies moving in the same direction produce beats. ☐

74. When the two tuning forks of nearly same frequency are vibrated to produce beats, the velocity of propagation of beat will be _____________ (less than /equal to/more than) that of sound.

75. The correct figure that shows schematically, the wave pattern produced by superposition of two waves of frequencies 9 Hz and 11 Hz, is

(a) [graph: y vs t(s), marks 1, 2] ☐ (b) [graph: y vs t(s), marks 1, 2] ☐

(c) [graph: y vs t(s), marks 1, 2] ☐ (d) [graph: y vs t(s), marks 1, 2] ☐

76. A tuning fork produces 4 beats/s when sounded together with a fork of frequency 364 Hz. When the first fork is loaded with little wax, then the number of beats obtained is 2/s. The frequency of the first fork is ________ .

77. Find the beat frequency for following conditions.

I. When two waves of frequency 452 Hz and 458 Hz are superposed.

____

II. Velocity of sound in a medium is 440 m/s. Two waves of wavelength 88 cm and 100 cm are superposed.

____

III. The lengths of two open organ pipes are x and $x + \Delta x$ $(\Delta x << x)$. The speed of sound is v.

____

IV. Three sources of equal intensities and frequencies 411 Hz, 412 Hz and 413 Hz are sounded simultaneously.

____

V. The two sound waves $y_1 = a\sin(326\,\pi\,t)$ and $y_2 = a\sin(330\,\pi\,t)$ are superposed.

____

78. Two waves of frequencies 502 Hz and 507 Hz are produced simultaneously. Find the time interval between successive maximas.

(a) 0.2 s ☐ (b) 0. 5 s ☐
(c) 0.1 s ☐ (d) 0.02 s ☐

79. When arms of one of the tuning forks are filled, its frequency ________ (increases/decreases).

80. Two organ pipes 81 cm and 82 cm long found to give 28 beats in 10 s when each is sounding its fundamental note. The velocity of sound in air is ________ m/s.

81. Tick (✓/×) for correct/incorrect statement in given boxes.

I. Two sound waves with wavelength 500 cm and 550 cm respectively, each propagate in a gas with velocity 330 m/s. The number of beats per second is 6. ☐

II. The two waves of same frequency moving in the same direction give rise to beats. ☐

III. The source of frequency f gives 5 beats/s when sounded with another source of frequency 255/s. The second harmonic $2f$ of first source gives 10 beats/s when sounded with a source of frequency 510/s, then frequency f is equal to 250 per second. ☐

82. Three sound waves of equal amplitudes have frequencies $(v-1)$, v and $(v+1)$. They superpose to give beat. The number of beats produced per second will be ________ (3/2).

83. A tuning fork A of unknown frequency produces 5 beats/s with a fork of known frequency 340 Hz. When fork A is filled, the beat frequency decreases to 2 beats/s. What is the frequency of fork A?

____

Assertion-Reason Questions

Direction (Q. Nos. 1-10) *In the following questions, a statement of Assertion is followed by a corresponding statement of Reason. From the following options, choose the correct one.*

(a) Both Assertion and Reason are correct and Reason is the correct explanation of Assertion.
(b) Both Assertion and Reason are correct but Reason is not the correct explanation of Assertion.
(c) Assertion is correct but Reason is incorrect.
(d) Assertion is incorrect but Reason is correct.

1. Assertion (A) Speed of wave $= \dfrac{\text{Wavelength}}{\text{Time period}}$.

Reason (R) Wavelength is distance between two nearest particles vibrating in phase.

(a) ☐ (b) ☐ (c) ☐ (d) ☐

2. Assertion (A) Transverse waves are not produced in liquids and gases.
Reason (R) Light waves are transverse waves.

(a) ☐ (b) ☐ (c) ☐ (d) ☐

3. **Assertion** (A) In a stationary wave, there is no transfer of energy.

Reason (R) The distance between two consecutive nodes or anti-nodes is $\frac{\lambda}{\sqrt{2}}$.

(a) ☐ (b) ☐ (c) ☐ (d) ☐

4. **Assertion** (A) In the equation of a plane progressive wave $y = r \sin\left(\frac{2\pi}{T}\right)\cdot\left[t - \frac{x}{v}\right]$, wavelength of wave $\lambda = vt$.

Reason (R) Wavelength depends on time.

(a) ☐ (b) ☐ (c) ☐ (d) ☐

5. **Assertion** (A) A vibrating tuning fork sounds louder which its stem is pressed against a desk top.

Reason (R) When a wave reaches another denser medium, part of the wave is reflected.

(a) ☐ (b) ☐ (c) ☐ (d) ☐

6. **Assertion** (A) In case of stationary wave, a person hears a loud sound at the nodes as compared to the anti-nodes.

Reason (R) In a stationary wave, all the particles of the medium vibrate in phase.

(a) ☐ (b) ☐ (c) ☐ (d) ☐

7. **Assertion** (A) Particle velocity and wave velocity both are independent of time.

Reason (R) For propagation of wave motion, the medium must have properties of elasticity and inertia.

(a) ☐ (b) ☐ (c) ☐ (d) ☐

8. **Assertion** (A) In the nth normal mode of vibration of a string, there are $(n + 1)$ nodes and n anti-nodes.

Reason (R) This is because both the ends of the string are fixed and from nodes.

(a) ☐ (b) ☐ (c) ☐ (d) ☐

9. **Assertion** (A) Two tuning forks having frequencies 510 Hz and 524 Hz are kept close and made to vibrate. Beats will not be heard.

Reason (R) Beat is a phenomenon of periodic change in the intensity of sound when two waves of same frequencies travelling in same direction superpose with each other.

(a) ☐ (b) ☐ (c) ☐ (d) ☐

10. **Assertion** (A) To hear distinct beats, difference in frequencies of two sources should be less than 10.

Reason (R) More the number of beats/s, more is the confusion.

(a) ☐ (b) ☐ (c) ☐ (d) ☐

Case Based Questions

1. A wave that travels from one point of medium to another is called a progressive wave. A progressive wave may be transverse or longitudinal. During the propagation of a wave through a medium, if the particles of medium vibrate simple harmonically about their mean positions, then wave is said to be plane progressive harmonic wave.

(i) A wave travelling in the positive x-direction having displacement along y-direction as 1 m, wavelength 2π m and frequency of $\frac{1}{\pi}$ Hz is represented by

(a) $y = \sin(2\pi x + 2\pi t)$ ☐ (b) $y = \sin(x - 2t)$ ☐
(c) $y = \sin(2\pi x - 2\pi t)$ ☐ (d) $y = \sin(10\pi x - 20\pi t)$ ☐

(ii) The equation of harmonic wave is given by $y = 3\sin\frac{\pi}{2}(50t - x)$. The ratio of maximum particle to wave velocity is

(a) 2π ☐ (b) $\frac{3\pi}{2}$ ☐
(c) 3π ☐ (d) $\frac{2}{3\pi}$ ☐

(iii) Two waves are represented by $y_1 = a\sin(\omega t + kx + 0.57)$ and $y_2 = a\cos(\omega t + kx)$ m. The phase difference between them is

(a) 1 rad ☐ (b) 1.25 rad ☐
(c) 1.57 rad ☐ (d) 0.57 rad ☐

(iv) A transverse wave propagating along x-axis is $y(x, t) = 8\sin\left(0.5\pi x - 4\pi t - \frac{\pi}{4}\right)$. Speed of wave is

(a) 8 m/s ☐ (b) 4π m/s ☐
(c) 0.5π m/s ☐ (d) $\frac{\pi}{4}$ m/s ☐

Or

Velocity of wave does not depend upon

(a) amplitude ☐ (b) temperature ☐
(c) medium ☐ (d) All of these ☐

2. When two sound waves of slightly different frequencies travelling along same path in same direction in a medium superimpose upon each other, the velocity of the resultant sound at any point in the medium rises and falls alternatively with time. These are known as beats.

(i) Three sound waves of equal amplitudes have frequencies $(n - 1)$, n and $(n + 1)$. They superimpose to give beats. The number of beats produced per second will be

(a) 3 ☐ (b) 2 ☐
(c) 1 ☐ (d) 4 ☐

(ii) Two second waves with wavelengths 5 m and 5.5 m respectively each propagate in a gas with velocity 330 m/s. We expect following number of beats per second.

(a) 12 ☐ (b) 0 ☐

(c) 3 ☐ (d) 6 ☐

(iii) Two vibrating tuning forks produce waves given by $y_1 = 4 \sin 500\pi t$ and $y_2 = 2 \sin 506\pi t$. Number of beats produced per min is

(a) 360 ☐ (b) 180 ☐

(c) 60 ☐ (d) 3 ☐

(iv) Wave has SHM whose period is 4 s while another wave which also possesses SHM has its period 3 s. If both are combined, then resultant wave will have period equal to

(a) 4 s ☐ (b) 5 s ☐

(c) 12 s ☐ (d) 3 s ☐

Or

Two tuning forks, A and B produce notes of frequencies f and 260 Hz. If number of beats heard by a person is 8. What can be the possible value of f?

(a) 268 Hz ☐ (b) 252 Hz ☐

(c) Both (a) and (b) ☐ (d) Neither (a) nor (b) ☐

COMPETITION EDGE UP

1. *A sonometer wire of resonating length 90 cm has a fundamental frequency of 400 Hz when kept under some tension. The resonating length of the wire with fundamental frequency of 600 Hz under same tension .... cm.*

[NCERT Pg. 285, JEE Main 2024]

2. *A tuning fork resonates with a sonometer wire of length 1 m stretched with a tension of 6 N. When the tension in the wire is changed to 54 N, the same tuning fork produces 12 beats per second with it. The frequency of the tuning fork is .... Hz.*

[NCERT Pg. 293, JEE Main 2024]

3. *In a closed organ pipe, the frequency of fundamental note is 30 Hz. A certain amount of water is now poured in the organ pipe, so that the fundamental frequency is increased to 110 Hz. If the organ pipe has a cross-sectional area of 2 cm^2, the amount of water poured to the organ tube is .... g. (Take, speed of sound in air is 330 m/s)*

[NCERT Pg. 292, JEE Main 2024]

4. *A point source is emitting sound waves of intensity 16×10^{-8} Wm^{-2} at the origin. The difference in intensity (magnitude only) at two points located at a distances of 2 m and 4 m from the origin respectively will be .... $\times 10^{-8}$ Wm^{-2}.*

[NCERT Pg. 288, JEE Main 2024]

5. *A closed and an open organ pipe have same lengths. If the ratio of frequencies of their seventh overtones is $(a - 1/a)$, then the value of a is ....*

[NCERT Pg. 292, JEE Main 2024]

6. *Two open organ pipes of lengths 60 cm and 90 cm resonate at 6th and 5th harmonics respectively. The difference of frequencies for the given modes is .... Hz. (Velocity of sound in air = 333 m/s)*

[NCERT Pg. 292, JEE Main 2024]

7. If the initial tension on a stretched string is doubled, then the ratio of the initial and final speeds of a transverse wave along the string is [NCERT Pg. 285, NEET 2022]

(a) $\sqrt{2}:1$ ☐ (b) $1:\sqrt{2}$ ☐

(c) $1:2$ ☐ (d) $1:1$ ☐

8. The length of the string of a musical instrument is 90 cm and has a fundamental frequency of 120 Hz. Where should it be pressed to produce fundamental frequency of 180 Hz? [NCERT Pg. 290, NEET (Oct.) 2020]

(a) 75 cm ☐

(b) 60 cm ☐

(c) 45 cm ☐

(d) 80 cm ☐

9. In a guitar, two strings A and B made of same material are slightly out of tune and produce beats of frequency 6 Hz. When tension in B is slightly decreased, the beat frequency increases to 7 Hz. If the frequency of A is 530 Hz, the original frequency of B will be [NCERT Pg. 293, NEET (Sep.) 2020]

(a) 524 Hz ☐

(b) 536 Hz ☐

(c) 537 Hz ☐

(d) 523 Hz ☐

10. A tuning fork with frequency 800 Hz produces resonance in a resonance column tube with upper end open and lower end closed by water surface. Successive resonance are observed at lengths 9.75 cm, 31.25 cm and 52.75 cm. The speed of sound in air is [NCERT Pg. 292, NEET (Odisha) 2019]

(a) 500 m/s ☐

(b) 156 m/s ☐

(c) 344 m/s ☐

(d) 172 m/s ☐

Hints & Solutions

Chapter-1

Units and Measurment

1. (i) ✓ (ii) ✓ (iii) ✓ (iv) ×
2. (*b*)
3. A → 3, B → 1, C → 2
4. radian, rad, steradian, sr
5. I
6. A → 7, B → 6, C → 5, D → 4, E → 3, F → 2, G → 1
7. Amount of substance
8. A → 2, B → 3, C → 1
9. Barn < Are < Hectare
10. Roentgen
11. A → 2, B → 3, C → 1, D → 4
12. units, number
13. order, magnitude
14. (i) ✓ (ii) ✓ (iii) × (iv) ✓ (v) ✓
15. I. 0.007 m^2 → significant digit 7

    Number of significant figures is 1.

    II. 2.64×10^{24} kg → significant digits 2, 6, 4

    Number of significant figures is 3.

    III. 0.2370 g / cm^3 → significant digits, 2, 3, 7 and zero to the right of decimal point.

    Number of significant figures is 4.
16. 4.700 m
17. Number of significant figures in 4500 = 2

    Number of significant figures in 0.045 = 2

    So, ratio $= \frac{2}{2} = 1$
18. None is correctly matched
19. Mean value =

    $$\frac{1.29 + 1.33 + 1.34 + 1.35 + 1.32 + 1.36 + 1.30 + 1.33}{8} = 1.33$$

    True value = Mean value = 1.33
20. I
21. (*a*) π has infinite significant figures.

    The value of pie (π) upto 4 significant figures is 3.142
22. (II)

    Surface area $= 6a^2 = 6 \times (7.203)^2 = 311.3\ m^2$

    Volume $= a^3 = (7.203)^3 = 373.7\ m^3$
23. (*c*) Density, $\rho = \frac{\text{Mass}}{\text{Volume}}$

    $$= \frac{5.74}{1.2}\ g\ cm^{-3} = 4.78\ g\ cm^{-3} \simeq 4.8\ gcm^{-3}$$
24. (5.8 g);

    12.9 g − 7.06 g = 5.84 g ≃ 5.8 g

    Smallest number of decimal places to be retained.
25. (I, II)

    Area of rectangle

    $$= l \times b = 16.2 \times 10.1 = 163.62 \approx 164\ cm^2$$

    Uncertainty of area

    $$(\Delta A) = \left(\frac{\Delta l}{l} + \frac{\Delta b}{b}\right) \times A$$

    $$= \left(\frac{0.1}{16.2} + \frac{0.1}{10.1}\right) \times 164 = 3\,cm^2$$
26. (*c*) $T' = T_2 - T_1$

    $$= (50°\,C \pm 0.5°\,C) - (20°\,C \pm 0.5°\,C) = (30 \pm 1)°\,C$$
27. Relative error, $\frac{\Delta A}{A} = \left(\frac{\Delta l}{l} + \frac{\Delta b}{b}\right)$

    $$= \left(\frac{0.1}{35.2} + \frac{0.1}{21.7}\right) = 0.0074$$
28. For $m_1 = (1.02 \pm 0.01)$g

    Relative error $= \frac{\Delta m_1}{m_1}$

    $$= \frac{0.01}{1.02} = 0.0098$$

    For $m_2 = (9.89 \pm 0.01)$g

    Relative error =

    $$\frac{\Delta m_2}{m_2} = \left[\frac{0.01}{9.89}\right] = 0.001$$
29. (*c, d*)
30. (*a*)
31. A → 3, B → 4, C → 1, D → 2
32. (i) ✓ (ii) ✓ (iii) ✓ (iv) ✓ (v) ✓
33. True
34. True
35. II, IV
36. II
37. (0.1);

    $1\ N = 1\ kg\text{-}ms^{-2}$

    $1\ kg = 10^3 g$ and $1m = 10^2$ cm

    $$\therefore 1\ N = \frac{(10^3 g)(10^2 cm)}{s^2}$$

    $$\Rightarrow 1N = \frac{100 \times (10g) \times 10 \times (10\,cm)}{100 \times (0.1\,s)^2}$$

    $$= \frac{10 \times (10g)(10\,cm)}{(0.1\,s)^2}$$

    1N = 10 × New unit of force

    Thus, new unit $= \frac{1}{10} = 0.1$ N
38. (1); $v_C = \frac{k\eta}{\rho r} = \eta^1 \rho^{-1} r^{-1}$

    ⇒ Product $x \cdot y \cdot z = 1$
39. $[L^2T^{-1}]$;

    Given, $v = at + \frac{b}{t + c}$

    Dimensions of acceleration

    $a = [LT^{-2}]$

    Dimensions of c = Time [T]

    Dimensions of b = Distance = [L]

    Therefore, dimensions of $[abc]$ $= [L^2T^{-1}]$

Competition Connect

1. more, less, subtracting
2. False
3. (*b*)
4. (*c*)
5. A–4, B–1, C–2, D–3
6. III
7. True
8. (*a, d*) The range of variation over the seven days of observations is 162 s for Clock 1 and 31s for Clock 2. The average reading of Clock 1 is much closer to standard time than the average reading of Clock 2.

   The important point is that a zero error is not as significant for precision work as its variation because a zero error can always be easily corrected. Hence, Clock 2 is to be preferred over Clock 1.

9. (i) 0.11s;

T_{mean}

$= \frac{2.63 + 2.56 + 2.42 + 2.71 + 2.80}{5}$

$= 262$ s

$\Delta T_{mean} = \frac{[|2.63 - 2.62| + |2.56 - 2.62| + |2.42 - 2.62| + |2.71 - 2.62| + |2.80 - 2.62|]}{5}$

$= 0.11$ s

(ii) 0.04

Relative error $= \frac{\Delta T_{mean}}{T_{mean}}$

$= \frac{0.11}{2.62} = 0.04$

(iii) 4%

Percentage error

$=$ Relative error $\times 100\%$

$= 0.04 \times 100\%$

$= 4\%$

10. (i) ✓, (ii) ×

11. 7%;

Percentage error in V,

$\frac{\Delta V}{V} \times 100 = \frac{5}{100} \times 100 = 5\%$

Percentage error in I,

$\frac{\Delta I}{I} \times 100 = \frac{0.2}{10} \times 100 = 2\%$

Percentage error in

$R = 5\% + 2\% = 7\%$

12. (I, II);

The equivalent resistance of series combination,

$R = R_1 + R_2$

$= (100 \pm 3)\Omega + (200 \pm 4)\Omega$

$= (300 \pm 7)\Omega$

The equivalent resistance of parallel combination,

$R' = \frac{R_1 R_2}{R_1 + R_2}$

$\Rightarrow R' = \frac{100 \times 200}{100 + 200} = \frac{200}{3} = 66.7\Omega$

As, $\frac{1}{R'} = \frac{1}{R_1} + \frac{1}{R_2}$

$\frac{\Delta R'}{R'^2} = \frac{\Delta R_1}{R_1^2} + \frac{\Delta R_2}{R_2^2}$

$\Rightarrow \Delta R' = \frac{\Delta R_1}{R_1^2} \times R'^2 + \frac{\Delta R_2}{R_2^2} \times R'^2$

$\Rightarrow \Delta R' = \frac{R'^2}{R_1^2} \times \Delta R_1 + \frac{R'^2}{R_2^2} \times \Delta R_2$

$\Rightarrow \Delta R' = \left(\frac{66.7}{100}\right)^2 \times 3 + \left(\frac{66.7}{200}\right)^2 \times 4$

$\Delta R' = \pm 1.8\Omega$

Then, $R' = (66.7 \pm 1.8)\Omega$

13. A–4, B–1, C–3, D–2

14. (*c*)

15. (I,II);

$\because g = \frac{4\pi^2 L}{T^2}$

Relative error $= \frac{\Delta L}{L} + 2\left(\frac{\Delta T}{T}\right)$

$= \frac{0.1}{20.0} + 2 \times \left(\frac{1}{90}\right) = 0.027$

= Percentage error = Relative error × 100%

$= 0.027 \times 100\% \approx 3\%$

16. (*a*); Volume $= \frac{4}{3}\pi r^3$

% error in volume

$= 3 \times \frac{\Delta r}{r} \times 100\%$

$3 \times 3 = 9\%$

17. (*d*); Percentage error in I

$= \frac{\Delta I}{I} \times 100\%$

$= \frac{0.2}{4} \times 100\% = 5\%$

Percentage error in V

$= \frac{\Delta V}{V} \times 100\%$

$= \frac{0.8}{8} \times 100\% = 10\%$

Percentage error in resistance

$= \left(\frac{\Delta V}{V} + \frac{\Delta I}{I}\right) \times 100\%$

$= 10 + 5 = 15\%$

18. (*a*) Time period = 1.62s

1 and 6 are reliable and 2 is uncertain.

Assertion-Reason Questions

1. (*a*)

2. (*a*)

3. (*a*); A digital stopwatch is more precise than an analog stopwatch because it measures time in smaller increments, typically to the nearest hundredth of a second while analog stopwatch measures time nearest to the $\frac{1}{100}$th of a second.

4. (*c*); Changing the unit of measurement change the numerical value of a quantity due to the different scales or magnitudes represented by each unit. Smaller units do not always result in smaller numerical values, it depends on the specific conversion between units.

5. (*b*); The second measurement, $L = 0.70$ m includes an additional significant digit compared to $L = 0.7$ m. Having an additional digit implies a higher precision and more accurate measurement.

The last digit in any measurements is uncertain that's why the last digit is not accurately known.

6. (*a*)

7. (*c*); $A = 4\pi r^2$

$\frac{\Delta A}{A} \times 100 = 2\frac{\Delta r}{r} \times 100$

$\Rightarrow \quad 2(0.3)\% = 0.6\%$

8. (*a*); Dimensions of inductance,

$L = [L^2MT^{-2}I^{-2}]$

Dimensions of capacitance,

$L = [L^{-2}M^{-1}T^4I^2]$

and dimensions of resistance,

$R = [L^2MT^{-3}I^{-2}]$

So, $\frac{L}{R} = \frac{[MT^{-2}I^{-2}L^2]}{[L^2MT^{-3}I^{-2}]} = [T]$

$CR = [L^{-2}M^{-1}T^4I^{+2}][L^2MT^{-3}I^{-2}]$

$= [T]$

9. (*b*)

10. (*b*)

11. (*a*)

12. (*d*) A is incorrect but R is correct. The dimensions of each term of the given equation,

$x = x_0 + u_0 t + \frac{1}{2}at^2$ may be written as

$[x] = [L], [x_0] = [L]$,

$[u_0 t] = [LT^{-1}][T]$,

$[at^2] = [LT^{-2}][T^2]$

As each term on the right hand side of this equation has same dimension as left hand side of the equation. Hence, this equation is dimensionally correct. The reason is true because if an equation is dimensionally correct, it does not need to be actually an exact equation.

Case Based Questions

1. (i) (*b*) $F = G\dfrac{m_1 m_2}{r^2}$

$$[G] = \frac{[F][r^2]}{[m_1 m_2]} = \frac{[MLT^{-2}][L^2]}{[M^2]}$$

$$[G] = [M^{-1}L^3T^{-2}]$$

(ii) (*a*) v = Final velocity which has the dimensional formula $[LT^{-1}]$

u = Initial velocity which has the dimensional formula $[LT^{-1}]$

For at,

dimensional formula of acceleration $a = [LT^{-2}]$

dimensional formula of time, $t = [T]$

So, $at = [LT^{-2}][T] = [LT^{-1}]$

Hence, equation (a) is dimensionally consistent.

(iii) (*a*) We know that, dimension of $v = [LT^{-1}]$, $p = [ML^{-1}T^{-2}]$ and $\rho = [ML^{-3}]$

According to question,

$$V \propto p^a \rho^b \quad \ldots(i)$$

$$[LT^{-1}] = [ML^{-1}T^{-2}]^a [ML^{-3}]^b$$

$$[LT^{-1}] = [M^{a+b}L^{-a-3b}T^{-2a}]$$

For the dimensions to be consistent, the exponents of M, L and T must same on both sides of the equation

So, $a + b = 0 \quad \ldots(ii)$

$-a - 3b = 1 \quad \ldots(iii)$

$-2a = -1$

$a = \dfrac{1}{2} \quad \ldots(iv)$

Substitute Eq. (i) in Eq. (ii), we get

$+\dfrac{1}{2} + b = 0$

$b = \dfrac{-1}{2}$

Now, put the value of a and b in Eq. (i)

$$v \propto p^{\frac{1}{2}}\rho^{\frac{-1}{2}}$$

$$v \propto \sqrt{\frac{p}{\rho}}$$

$$v = K\sqrt{\frac{p}{\rho}}$$

(iv) (*a*) Strain is the ratio of two like quantities it has no unit and no dimension.

2. (i) (*c*); 23.0 g (It has 3 significant figures).

(ii) (*d*); 12.345 cm has 5 significant figures.

(iii) (*b*); The sum is 5.797, which should be rounded to the least number of decimal places present in original numbers, yielding 5.80. Therefore, the number of significant figures in the result is three.

(iv) (*b*); 0.12 g/mL (reported with 2 significant figures, matching the least precise measurement).

Competition Edge Up

1. (*d*) Specific heat,

$$Q = ML$$

$$L = \frac{Q}{M} = \frac{[ML^2T^{-2}]}{[M]}$$

$$L = [M^0L^2T^{-2}]$$

2. (*b*) In scientific notation of a physical quanity is given as $a \times 10^b$ and $a \le 5$, then b is order of magnitude of the quantity.

3. (*b*) $\left(p + \dfrac{a}{V^2}\right)(V - b) = RT$

Dimensional formula of $b = [V]$

$\Rightarrow \quad [b] = [L^3]$

$\therefore \quad [b^{-1}] = [L^{-3}]$

$$\left[\frac{a}{V^2}\right] = [p] = [ML^{-1}T^{-2}]$$

$\therefore \quad [a] = [ML^{-1}T^{-2}][L^6]$

$= [ML^5T^{-2}]$

$\therefore \quad [ab^{-1}] = [ML^5T^{-2}][L^{-3}]$

$= [ML^2T^{-2}]$

4. (*c*) Compare the given equation with standard equation of standing wave

$y = A \sin \omega t \cos kx$,

thus $\omega = \dfrac{2\pi n}{\lambda}$, $k = \dfrac{2\pi}{\lambda}$ and 2π is dimensionless.

$$[\omega] = T^{-1} = \left[\frac{n}{\lambda}\right]$$

$$[nT] = [\lambda] = [L]$$

$$[n] = \left[\frac{\lambda}{T}\right] = [\lambda\omega]$$

$$[n] = [LT^{-1}]$$

$$\Rightarrow \left[\frac{n}{\lambda}\right] = [T^{-1}]$$

5. (*b*) Given, $E = \dfrac{B - x^2}{At}$

E = Energy, x = length

t = time

Dimensions of B and x^2 must be same.

Also dimensions of EAt must be same as that of x^2.

$\therefore \quad EAt = B - x^2$

So, $\quad [B] = [x^2] = [L^2]$

Also, $\quad [E][A][t] = [x^2]$

$[ML^2T^{-2}][A][T] = [L^2]$

$\therefore \quad [A] = \dfrac{[L^2]}{[ML^2T^{-1}]}$

$\Rightarrow \quad [A] = [M^{-1}T^1]$

So, dimension of AB is,

$[A][B] = [M^{-1}T^1][L^2] = [M^{-1}L^2T^1]$

6. (*c*) Given,

$$m = k\,c^p \cdot G^{-1/2} \cdot h^{1/2}$$

Substituting dimensions of different quantities on both sides we get,

$$[M] = [L^pT^{-p}][M^{-1}L^3T^{-2}]^{\frac{-1}{2}}[ML^2T^{-1}]^{1/2}$$

$$\Rightarrow \quad [M] = [M]\left[L^{p-\frac{1}{2}}\right].\left[T^{\frac{1}{2}-p}\right]$$

Equating dimensions of length on both sides, we get

$$p - \frac{1}{2} = 0 \text{ or } p = \frac{1}{2}$$

7. (*b*) Given force, $F = ax^2 + bt^{1/2}$

x = distance and t = time

Clearly, dimensions of ax^2 and $bt^{1/2}$ must be that of force.

So, $\quad [ax^2] = [MLT^{-2}]$

$\Rightarrow \quad [a][L^2] = [MLT^{-2}]$

or $\quad [a] = [ML^{-1}T^{-2}]$

Also, $\quad [bt^{1/2}] = [MLT^{-2}]$

$[b][T^{1/2}] = [MLT^{-2}]$

$[b] = [MLT^{-5/2}]$

So, $\left[\dfrac{b^2}{a}\right] = \left[\dfrac{M^2L^2T^{-5}}{ML^{-1}T^{-2}}\right]$

$= [ML^3T^{-3}]$

8. (*a*) Strain and angle are dimensionless quantities as solid angle.
Arc has dimension of length.
Stress has dimension of pressure.

9. (*b*) Given, $F = \alpha t^2 + \beta t$

We know that dimensions on the both sides will be the same, i.e.

$[F] = [\alpha t^2] = [\beta t]$

$\Rightarrow [\alpha][T^2] = [ML^1T^{-2}]$

$\Rightarrow \quad \alpha = [M^1L^1T^{-4}]$

and $[\beta][T] = [M^1LT^{-2}]$

$\Rightarrow \quad \beta = [M^1L^1T^{-3}]$

(a) $\dfrac{[\beta t]}{[\alpha]} = \dfrac{[M^1L^1T^{-2}]}{[M^1L^1T^{-4}]} = [T^2]$

(b) $\dfrac{[\alpha t]}{[\beta]} = \dfrac{[M^1L^1T^{-4}][T]}{[M^1L^1T^{-3}]}$

$= [M^0L^0T^0]$

10. (*c*); Area = Length × Breadth

$= 5503 \times 25 = 1382.5\,\text{m}^2$

Rounding 1382.5 to 2 significant figures, we get

$= 1400\,\text{m}^2 = 14 \times 10^2$

11. (*c*) $\because$ Stress $= \dfrac{\text{Force}}{\text{Area}}$

$\therefore$ Dimensions of

stress $= \dfrac{[MLT^{-2}]}{[L^2]} = [ML^{-1}T^{-2}]$

Chapter-2

Motion in a Straight Line

1. I, II, III

2. A → 1, B → 3, C → 2, D → 4

3. (*c*)

4. zero

5. No

6. I, II, III

7. (*a*); The *x*- *t* graph shown is parallel to time axis. This means that the object is at rest. Hence, the velocity of the object is zero for all time instants. Hence, *u-t* graph coincides with the time axis as shown in graph (a).

8. (i), (ii), (iii), (iv) all are correct.

9. False;

$\because \quad s = 9t^2 - t^3$

Velocity of the body,

$v = \dfrac{ds}{dt} = \dfrac{d}{dt}(9t^2 - t^3)$

$\Rightarrow \quad v = 18t - 3t^2$

$\therefore$ Acceleration,

$a = \dfrac{dv}{dt} = \dfrac{d}{dt}(18t - 3t^2)$

$\Rightarrow \quad a = 18 - 6t$

When speed of the body is maximum, then $a = 0$

i.e. $18 - 6t = 0 \Rightarrow t = 3\,\text{s}$

$\therefore$ Displacement of body at

$t = 3\,\text{s},\ s = 9t^2 - t^3$

$= 9(3^2) - 3^3 = 54\,\text{m}$

10. (*b*)

11. (*b*); The velocity is the integral of the acceleration

$v(t) = \int a(t)\,dt$

$= \int (6t - 4)\,dt$

$= 3t^2 - 4t + C$

Given, $v = 2$ m/s at $t = 0$

$2 = 3(0)^2 - 4(0) + C$

$C = 2$

So, the velocity function is,

$v(t) = 3t^2 - 4t + 2$

at $\quad t = 2\,\text{s}$

$v(2) = 3 \times (2)^2 - 4(2) + 2$

$= 12 - 8 + 2 = 6\,\text{m/s}$

12. $\left(\dfrac{83}{6}\right)$;

Distance travelled $= \int v\,dt$

$= \int (At + Bt^2)\,dt$

$= \left.\dfrac{At^2}{2} + \dfrac{Bt^3}{3}\right|_1^2 = \dfrac{9}{2} + \dfrac{28}{3} = \dfrac{83}{6}\,\text{m}$

13. (*b*); From first equation of motion,

$v = u + at$

According to question,

$0 = 30 + a \times 5$

$\Rightarrow \quad a = -6\,\text{ms}^{-2}$

14. (2); The acceleration of the particle is given as $\dfrac{dv}{dt} = -2.5\sqrt{v}$

$\Rightarrow \quad \dfrac{dv}{\sqrt{v}} = -2.5\,dt$

Particle comes to rest from 6.25 m/s to 0 m/s.

Therefore,

$\therefore \quad \int_{6.25}^{0} v^{-\frac{1}{2}}\,dv = -2.5\int_0^t dt$

$\Rightarrow \quad \left[2v^{\frac{1}{2}}\right]_{6.25}^{0} = -2.5[t]_0^t$

$\Rightarrow \quad t = 2\,\text{s}$

15. A → 3, B → 1, C → 2;

A. Average acceleration from $t_1 = 0$ to $t_2 = 10$ s,

$a = \left.\dfrac{dv}{dt}\right|_0^{10} = \dfrac{24}{10} = 2.4\,\text{ms}^{-2}$

B. Average acceleration from $t_1 = 10$ s to $t_2 = 18$ s,

$a = \left.\dfrac{dv}{dt}\right|_{10}^{18} = \dfrac{0}{8} = 0$

C. Average acceleration from $t_1 = 18$ s to $t = 20$ s,

$a = \left.\dfrac{dv}{dt}\right|_{18}^{20} = -\dfrac{24}{2} = -12\,\text{ms}^{-2}$

16. I, II, III;

I. From 0-10 s, acceleration is changing non-uniformly from 0 – 4.2 m/s^2 as seen from graph.

II. From 10-18 s, its zero.

III. From 18-20 s, its constant at $-12\,\text{m/s}^2$.

17. (5);

Acceleration $= \dfrac{dv}{dt} = \dfrac{d}{dt}(3t^3 - 2t^2)$

$= (9t^2 - 4t)$

The instantaneous acceleration of the particle at $t = 1$ s,

$a_{\text{ins}} = [9(1)^2 - 4(1)] = 5\,\text{ms}^{-2}$

18. True

19. A → 1, B → 3, C → 2

20. I, II;

From $0 \to t_1$, *x-t* graph open upwards and parabolic, so acceleration is positive. From $t_1 \to t_2$ its downwards and parabolic, so acceleration is negative.

From t_2 to t_3, acceleration is negative which is represented by a crest.

21. Negative acceleration

22. (*b*)

23. *A*

24. False

25. A $\to$ 1, B $\to$ 2, C $\to$ 3

26. (*b*); $s = t^3 - 9t^2 + 6t + 2$

Velocity, $v = \frac{ds}{dt} = 3t^2 - 18t + 6$

Acceleration, $a = \frac{dv}{dt} = 6t - 18$

Acceleration is zero at time t given by $6t - 18 = 0$

$t = 3\,\text{s}$

So, velocity v at $t = 3\,\text{s}$ is

$v = 3t^2 - 18t + 6 = 27 - 54 + 6$

$v = -21\,\text{m/s}$

27. (*a*); In the time 0 to 2 s, acceleration of the vehicle

$$a = \frac{15 - 0}{2 - 0} = 7.5\,\text{m/s}^2$$

In time 2 to 4 s. Velocity of the vehicle is uniform. So, acceleration = 0

In time 4 to 6 s, acceleration of the vehicle

$$a = \frac{0 - 15}{6 - 4} = -\frac{15}{2}$$

$$= -7.5\,\text{ms}^{-2}$$

28. (*c*)

29. constant

30. (1); Let (v^2-x) graph be represented as $v^2 = \lambda_0 + \lambda x$, where λ is slope of straight line.

Differentiating both sides w.r.t. x,

$$2v\frac{dv}{dx} = \lambda \Rightarrow \frac{vdv}{dx} = \frac{\lambda}{2}$$

$$\because a = \frac{vdv}{dx} = \frac{\lambda}{2} = \frac{60 - 40}{2(20 - 10)} = 1\,\text{ms}^{-2}$$

31. ($-$ 7.5 m/s^2)

Final velocity, $v = u + at$

$15 = 30 + a \times 2$

$\Rightarrow \quad a = -7.5\,\text{ms}^{-2}$

32. (8); By using third equation of motion for first bus,

$v^2 = u^2 - 2as$

$\Rightarrow \quad a = \frac{2500}{81}\,\text{m/s}^2$

Similarly, if second bus stops at a distance x metre, then

$v^2 = u^2 - 2ax$

$$\Rightarrow \quad 0 = \left(\frac{200}{9}\right)^2 - 2 \times \frac{2500}{81} \times x$$

$\Rightarrow \quad x = 8\,\text{m}$

33. (i) ✓, (ii) ✓, (iii) ✓

34. (I, II);

I. Maximum height

$$= \frac{u^2}{2g} = \frac{400}{20} = 20\,\text{m}$$

II. Total time = Time of ascent (t_1) + Time of fall (t_2)

Therefore, for t_1, we can apply first equation of motion as $v = u + at$

$\Rightarrow \quad 0 = 20 - 10t$

$\Rightarrow \quad t = 2\,\text{s}$

For time of fall t_2, we can use second equation of motion as

$$s = ut + \frac{1}{2}at^2$$

($s = h$ + maximum height $= 20 + 25 = 45\,\text{m}$)

$$\Rightarrow \quad 45 = 0 + \frac{10}{2}(t)^2$$

$\Rightarrow \quad t^2 = 9$ or $t = 3\,\text{s}$

Total time, $T = t_1 + t_2$
$= 2 + 3 = 5\,\text{s}$

35. (*c*)

36. (*d*); For the motion under free fall, we have

$u = 0, a = g$

Thus, equation of motion becomes

$v = u + at \longrightarrow 9.8\,t\,\text{ms}^{-1}$

$y = ut + \frac{1}{2}at^2 \longrightarrow 4.9t^2\,\text{m}$

$v^2 = u^2 + 2as \longrightarrow 19.6y\,\text{m}^2\text{s}^{-2}$

37. (i) 1 : 3: 5;

Distance travelled in 1st second

$$= \frac{1}{2}gt^2 = \frac{1}{2}(9.8)\,\text{m}$$

Distance travelled in 2nd second

$$= \frac{1}{2} \times 9.8 \times 2^2 - \frac{1}{2} \times 9.8$$

$$= 3 \times \frac{1}{2} \times 9.8\,\text{m}$$

Distance travelled in 3rd second

$$= \frac{1}{2} \times 9.8 \times 3^2 - \frac{1}{2} \times 9.8 \times 2^2$$

$$= 5 \times \frac{1}{2} \times 9.8\,\text{m}$$

Therefore, the ratio of distance travelled in first 1 s, next 1s, third 1s is 1 : 3 : 5.

(ii) $1^2 : 2^2 : 3^2$;

As, $s_1 = -\frac{1}{2}gt^2$

$$s_2 = -4\left(\frac{1}{2}\right)gt^2$$

$$s_3 = -9\left(\frac{1}{2}\right)gt^2$$

(iii) $\sqrt{1} : (\sqrt{2} - \sqrt{1}) : (\sqrt{3} - \sqrt{2})$;

Time taken to cover first 1 m distance,

$$h = 0 + \frac{1}{2}gt_1^2$$

$$\Rightarrow \quad t_1 = \sqrt{\frac{2h}{g}} = \sqrt{\frac{2}{g}}$$

$(\because h = 1\,\text{m})$

Time taken to cover 2m distance be t_2, then

$$t_2 = \sqrt{\frac{2h'}{g}} = \sqrt{\frac{2 \times 2}{g}}$$

$\therefore$ Time taken to cover next 1 m distance.

$$t' = t_2 - t_1$$

$$= \sqrt{\frac{2 \times 2}{g}} - \sqrt{\frac{2}{g}}$$

$$= \sqrt{\frac{2}{g}}(\sqrt{2} - \sqrt{1})$$

Similarly, time taken to cover next 1 m distance,

$$t'' = \sqrt{\frac{2}{g}}(\sqrt{3} - \sqrt{2})$$

$$\therefore \quad t_1 : t' : t'' = \sqrt{1} : (\sqrt{2} - \sqrt{1}) : (\sqrt{3} - \sqrt{2})$$

38. $A = 9y_0, B = 11y_0$;

From the table, we have

$$y_0 = -\frac{1}{2}g\tau^2$$

For A, $t = 3\tau$

$$= -\frac{1}{2}g(3\tau)^2$$

$$= -9 \times \frac{1}{2}g\tau^2 = 9y_0$$

For B, distance travelled 6th second

$$= y_6 - y_5$$
$$= 36y_0 - 25y_0 = 11y_0$$

39. (7.35) Time taken by second drop

$= \frac{1}{2} \times$ Time taken by first drop

Time taken by the first drop;

$$9.8 = \frac{1}{2} \times 9.8t^2 \Rightarrow t = \sqrt{2} \text{ s}$$

For second drop, height,

$$h = \frac{1}{2} \times 9.8 \times \left(\frac{\sqrt{2}}{2}\right)^2$$

$\Rightarrow h = 2.45$ m

Therefore, height of the second drop at this instant of time $= 9.8 - 2.45 = 7.35$ m.

40.

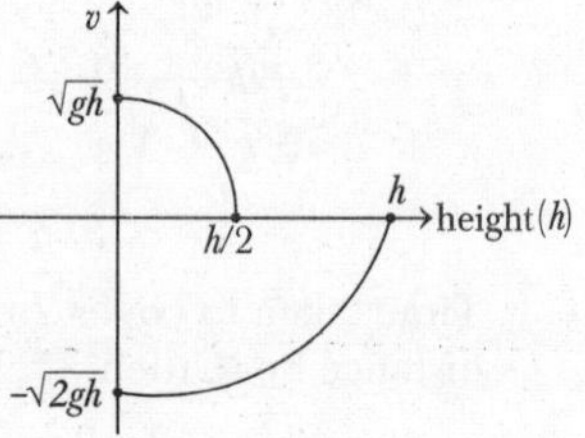

41. (b); Here, $s_{2nd} = 15$ m

$$s_{4th} = 25 \text{ m}$$

As $s_{nth} = u + \frac{a}{2}(2n-1)$

$$s_{2nd} = u + \frac{a}{2}(2\times2-1) = 15$$

$$u + \frac{3a}{2} = 15 \quad \ldots\text{(i)}$$

Also, $s_{4th} = u + \frac{7a}{2} = 25 \quad \ldots$(ii)

Subtracting, Eq. (i) from Eq. (ii)

$a = 5 \text{ m/s}^2$

From (i) $u + \frac{3}{2} \times 5 = 15$

$$u = 15/2 \text{ m/s}$$

Distance covered in 4s after 5th second

$$= s_9 - s_5$$

$$= \left(\frac{15}{2} \times 9 + \frac{1}{2} \times 5 \times 9^2\right) - \left(\frac{15}{2} \times 5 + \frac{1}{2} \times 5 \times 5^2\right)$$

$$= 270 - 100 = 170 \text{ m}$$

42. (b) $v = u + at$

$\therefore$ In first case, $20 = u + 4a \quad \ldots$(i)

In second case, $32 = u + 8a \ldots$(ii)

On solving Eq. (i) and (ii), we get

$$4a = 12$$

$a = 3 \text{ m/s}^2$

So, from Eq. (i)

$$u = 20 - 4 \times 3 = 8 \text{ m/s}$$

$$s_{12th} = 8 + \frac{3}{2}(2\times12-1) = 10 + \frac{69}{2}$$

$$s_{12} = 42.5 \text{ m}$$

43. reaction

44. (a); The ruler drops under free fall, therefore $v_0 = 0$

and $a = g = 9.8 \text{ m/s}^2$

The distance travelled d and reaction time t_r are related as

$$d = \frac{1}{2}gt_r^2$$

$$\Rightarrow t_r = \sqrt{\frac{2d}{g}} = \sqrt{\frac{2\times0.21}{9.8}} \simeq 0.2 \text{ s}$$

Competition Connect

1. (i) ✓, (ii) ✓, (iii) ✓

2. (b);

3. (8.7 m/s);

Average velocity

$$= \frac{\text{Total path length}}{\text{Total time}}$$

$$= \frac{27.4 - 10}{7 - 5} = \frac{17.4}{2} = 8.7 \text{ m/s}$$

4. $\sqrt{3}$ m/s

5. (i) Yes (ii) No

6. (4);

Let x be the total distance.

According to the question, time taken to cover half distance,

$$t_1 = \frac{\text{distance}}{\text{speed}} = \frac{x}{2} \times \frac{1}{3} = \frac{x}{6} \text{ s}$$

For other half, the body covers it in two intervals, $t_2 = t_3$ with different speed.

Thus, distance $\left(\frac{x}{2}\right) =$ speed $\times$ time

$$= 4.5 \times t_2 + 7.5 \times t_3$$

$$\frac{x}{2} = 12t_2 \qquad (\because t_2 = t_3)$$

$$\Rightarrow t_2 = \frac{x}{24}$$

Average speed

$$= \frac{\text{Total path}}{\text{Total time}}$$

$$= \frac{x}{\frac{x}{6} + \frac{x}{24} + \frac{x}{24}}$$

$$v_{avg} = 4 \text{ m/s}$$

7. (I, II, III);

Average velocity from O to P

$$= \frac{\text{Total displacement}}{\text{Total time}}$$

$$= \frac{360}{18} = 20 \text{ ms}^{-1}$$

Average speed from O to P

$$= \frac{\text{Total distance}}{\text{Total time}}$$

$$= \frac{360}{18} = 20 \text{ ms}^{-1}$$

Average speed from O to P to Q

$$= \frac{\text{Total distance}}{\text{Total time}} = \frac{360 + 120}{18 + 6}$$

$$= \frac{480}{24} = 20 \text{ ms}^{-1}$$

8. I. (2/3);

Instantaneous speed at C from A to B = 20 km/h.

Instantaneous speed at C from B to A = 30 km/h.

$$\text{Ratio} = \frac{20}{30} = \frac{2}{3}$$

II. (24)

Time taken by the body to cover distance AB going from A to B,

$$t_1 = \frac{AB}{20} \text{ h}$$

Time taken by the body to cover distance AB going from B to A,

$$t_2 = \frac{AB}{30} \text{ h}$$

$$v_{avg} = \frac{2AB}{t_1 + t_2} = \frac{2AB}{\frac{AB}{20} + \frac{AB}{30}}$$

$$= 24 \text{ km/h}$$

9. (II, III);

I. Instantaneous velocity

$$= \frac{dx}{dt} = \frac{d}{dt}(0.08t^3)$$

$$= 3(0.08)t^2$$

At $t = 3$ s, instantaneous velocity

$$= \left.\frac{dx}{dt}\right|_{t=3} = 0.24 \times (3)^2$$

$$= 2.16 \text{ ms}^{-1}$$

II. Instantaneous velocity at $t = 5$ s

$$= \left.\frac{dx}{dt}\right|_{t=5} = 0.24 \times (5)^2$$

$$= 6 \text{ ms}^{-1}$$

III. Average velocity $= \frac{\Delta x}{\Delta t}$

$$= \frac{x_f - x_i}{t_f - t_i}$$

$$= \frac{x(t = 5\text{ s}) - x(t = 3\text{ s})}{2\text{s}}$$

$$= \left(\frac{10 - 2.16}{2}\right) = 3.92 \text{ ms}^{-1}$$

10. (I, II);

Average velocity is given by the slope of the line (chord) Q_1Q_2

The slope of the x-t graph gives velocity at any time t.

11. A → 2, B → 3, C → 4, D → 1;

Given, $x = a - bt^2$

A. Velocity at $t = 2$ s is given by

$$\left.\frac{dx}{dt}\right|_{t=2\text{s}} = \frac{d}{dt}(a - bt^2)$$

$$= -2bt\Big|_{t=2\text{s}}$$

$$= -2(2.5) \times 2$$

$$= -10 \text{ ms}^{-1}$$

B. Velocity at $t = 0$ s is given by

$$\left.\frac{dx}{dt}\right|_{t=0} = \frac{d}{dt}(a - bt^2) = 0 \text{ ms}^{-1}$$

C. Instantaneous speed at $t = 2$ s is given as

$$\left.\frac{dx}{dt}\right|_{t=2\text{s}} = -2bt\Big|_{t=2\text{s}} = 10 \text{ ms}^{-1}$$

D. Average velocity

$$= \frac{\text{Total displacement}}{\text{Total time}}$$

$$= \frac{1}{2}\left| a - bt^2 \right|_{t=2\text{s}}^{t=4\text{s}}$$

$$= \frac{a - 16b - a + 4b}{2} = -6 \times b$$

$$= -15 \text{ ms}^{-1}$$

12. (i) ✓ (ii) ✓ (iii) ✓ (iv) × (v) ×

13. I, II

14. Ground or any common reference frame.

15. A → 2, B → 1, C → 3

16. I, II;

Consider north as +ve direction

$$v_A = 54 \text{ km/h}$$

$$= 54 \times \frac{5}{18} = 15 \text{ m/s}$$

$$v_B = 90 \text{ km/h}$$

$$= 90 \times \frac{5}{18} = -25 \text{ m/s}$$

Velocity of train B w.r.t. A

$$= v_B - v_A = -25 - 15$$

$$= -40 \text{ m/s}$$

Velocity of ground w.r.t. B

$$= v_g - v_B = 0 - (-25)$$

$$= +25 \text{ m/s}$$

$$= 25 \text{ m/s towards North}$$

17. 30

18. A → 20, B → 80, C → 50, D → 400, E → 8

Assertion-Reason Questions

1. (*a*); For motion in a straight line and in the same direction,

Displacement = Total path length

⇒ Average velocity = Average speed

2. (*b*)

3. (*c*); Slope of s-t graph = velocity = positive

At $t = 0$, $s \neq 0$. Further at $t = t_0 : s = 0, v \neq 0$.

Hence, velocity does not change direction at $t = t_0$.

4. (*a*); Average velocity

$$= \frac{\text{Displacement}}{\text{Time}}$$

$$= \frac{\text{Area of } v\text{-}t \text{ graph}}{\text{Time}}$$

$$= \frac{(1/2)\, v_m\, t_0}{t_0} = \frac{1}{2} v_m$$

It is independent of t_0.

5. (*d*); The uniform motion of a body means that the body is moving with constant velocity. But if the direction of motion is changing (such as in uniform circular motion), its velocity changes and thus acceleration is produced in a body moving uniformly.

6. (*c*); If a particle is released from rest position under gravity, then $v = 0$ but $a \neq 0$

7. (*b*); By integrating a-t equation two times, we will get s-t equation.

8. (*a*); The continuity in graphs is because physical systems cannot change velocity and acceleration instantaneously.

9. (*c*) If upward direction is taken as positive, then downward acceleration due to gravity will be negative (-9.8 m/s^2).

10. (*c*); Relative velocity between particle A and B is not zero because they are moving in different directions.

Case Based Questions

1. (i) (*b*); Given, $x(t) = 4t^2 - 2t + 3$

$$v(t) = \frac{dx}{dt}(t)$$

$$v(t) = \frac{d}{dt}(4t^2 - 2t + 3)$$

$$v(t) = 8t - 2$$

$$v(0) = 8 \times 0 - 2$$

$$v(0) = -2 \text{ m/s}$$

(ii) (*a*); The car is momentarily at rest when its velocity is zero.

$$v(t) = 8t - 2$$

$$0 = 8t - 2$$

$$\Rightarrow 8t = 2 \Rightarrow t = 0.25 \text{ s}$$

(iii) (*d*)

(iv) (*b*)

2. (i) (*b*); A downward sloping straight line in a velocity-time graph indicates uniform deceleration.

(ii) (*b*); For uniformly accelerated motion starting from rest, the displacement-time graph is a parabola opening upwards because $s \propto t^2$.

(iii) (*c*); Using Eq, $s = ut + \frac{1}{2}at^2$

at $t = 4$ s,

$$s = 0 + \frac{1}{2} \times 2 \times (4)^2$$
$$s = 16 \text{ m}$$

(iv) (*b*); Using Eq. $v^2 = u^2 + 2as$

$$v^2 = 0^2 + 2 \times 2 \times 25$$
$$v^2 = 100$$
$$v = \sqrt{100}$$
$$v = 10 \text{ m/s}$$

Competition Edge Up

1. (*c*); Given, relative speed between cars,

$v_2 = 20$ m/s

A ⟶ ⟵ B

$v_1 = 20$ m/s

⟵ 300 m ⟶

$$v_r = 40 \text{ ms}^{-1}$$

Relative retardation, $a_r = 4 \text{ ms}^{-2}$

We know that, $v^2 - u^2 = 2as$

$$0 - (40)^2 = 2 \times (-4) \times s$$
$$\Rightarrow \quad -1600 = -8s \Rightarrow s = 200 \text{ m}$$

Distance between them
$$= 300 - 200 = 100 \text{ m}$$

2. (*c*); Using the formula of *n*th second distance travel,

$$d = u + \frac{a}{2}(2n - 1)$$
$$102.5 = u + \frac{a}{2}(2n - 1) \quad \text{...(i)}$$
$$115 = u + \frac{a}{2}[2(n + 2) - 1]$$
$$115 = u + \frac{a}{2}[2n + 3] \quad \text{...(ii)}$$

Now, Eqs. (ii) – (i), we get
$$12.5 = 2a \Rightarrow a = 6.25 \text{ m/s}^2$$

3. (8); Velocity of particle is given,
$$v = 4\sqrt{x} \text{ m/s}$$
$$\Rightarrow \quad v = \frac{dx}{dt} = 4\sqrt{x}$$
$$\Rightarrow \quad \frac{dx}{\sqrt{x}} = 4dt$$

Integrating we have,
$$\int_0^x \frac{dx}{\sqrt{x}} = 4\int_0^t dt$$
$$2\sqrt{x} = 4t \Rightarrow 4x = 16t^2$$

So, position of the particle is
$$\Rightarrow \quad x = 4t^2$$
$$\Rightarrow \text{Velocity, } v = \frac{dx}{dt} = 4 \times 2t$$

Acceleration, $a = \frac{dv}{dt} = 8 \text{ m/s}^2$

4. (*b*); Since, $t = \alpha x^2 + \beta x$
$$\Rightarrow \quad \frac{dt}{dt} = 2\alpha xv + \beta v \quad \left(\because \frac{dx}{dt} = v\right)$$
$$\Rightarrow \quad 1 = 2\alpha xv + \beta v$$
$$\text{or} \quad v = \frac{1}{2\alpha x + \beta}$$

Now, differentiating with respect to *x*,
$$\frac{dv}{dx} = \frac{-2\alpha}{(2\alpha x + \beta)^2} = -2\alpha v^2$$

Acceleration is, $a = v\frac{dv}{dx} = -2\alpha v^3$

5. (175); Let *u* is initial speed

⟵ 125 ⟶⟵ *x* ⟶

t   *t*+1   *t*+2

u   *u*+50

I   II

For region I,
$$s = ut + \frac{1}{2}at^2 \quad \text{(Time = 1 s)}$$
$$125 = u \times 1 + \frac{1}{2} \times 50 \times 1$$

($a = 50 \text{ m/s}^2$ because time is 1s)

$u = 100$ m/s

Now,

⟵ *x* ⟶

t+1   *t*+2

u =150m/s   II

(*u*+50)

Using equation of motion
$$s = ut + \frac{1}{2}at^2$$
$$x = 150 \times 1 + \frac{1}{2} \times 50 \times 1$$
$$x = 175 \text{ m}$$

6. (*c*) We know that,
$$a = \frac{dv}{dt}$$

For v = constant, $a = 0$

Thus, for v - t graph when v is positive and linearly increasing a will be positive constant and if v is decreasing linearly a will be negative constant.

Hence, option (c) is correct.

7. (*b*); Maximum height attain by the ball, $h' = \frac{v^2}{2g} = \frac{4^2}{2 \times 10} = 0.8$ m

Time of flight from bridge to bridge
$$t_1 = \frac{2v}{g} = \frac{2 \times 4}{10} = 0.8 \text{ s}$$

Time taken by the ball to reach at the surface of water from highest point,
$$t_2 = 4 - \frac{t_1}{2} = 4 - \frac{0.8}{2} = 3.6 \text{ s}$$
$$\therefore \quad h = 0 \times t_2 + \frac{1}{2}gt_2^2$$
$$h = \frac{1}{2} \times 10 \times (3.6)^2 = 64.8 \text{ m}$$

∴ Now, height of bridge above water surface
$$H = h - h' = 64.8 - 0.8 = 64 \text{ m}$$

8. (*b*); Distance travelled by freely falling body in *n*th second
$$s_n = u + \frac{1}{2}g(2n - 1)$$
$$= 0 + \frac{1}{2}g(2n - 1)$$
$$s_n = \frac{1}{2}g(2n - 1)$$

Distance travelled by body in first second ($n = 1$ s)
$$s_1 = \frac{1}{2}g(2 \times 1 - 1) = \frac{g}{2}$$

Distance travelled by body in 2nd second ($n = 2$ s)
$$s_2 = \frac{1}{2}g(2 \times 2 - 1) = \frac{3g}{2}$$

Distance travelled by body in 3rd second ($n = 3$ s)
$$s_3 = \frac{1}{2}g(2 \times 3 - 1) = \frac{5g}{2}$$

Distance travelled by body in 4th second ($n = 4$ s)

$$s_4 = \frac{1}{2}g(2\times4-1) = \frac{7g}{2}$$

$$\therefore\ s_1 : s_2 : s_3 : s_4 = \frac{g}{2} : \frac{3g}{2} : \frac{5g}{2} : \frac{7g}{2}$$

$$= 1:3:5:7$$

9. (*d*); At $t = 4$ s, $v = u + at$

$$\Rightarrow v = 0 + (5)4 \Rightarrow v = 20 \text{ m/s}$$

At $t = 4$ s, the ball is dropped out of a window by a person sitting in the car.

The velocity of the ball in the x-direction,

$$v_x = 20 \text{ m/s (due to the car)}$$

Therefore, in the y-direction,

$$a_y = g = 10 \text{ m/s}^2$$

$$\therefore\ v_y = u + a_y t$$

$$\Rightarrow v_y = 0 + 10\times2$$

$$\Rightarrow v_y = 20 \text{ m/s}$$

The net velocity at $t = 6$s,

$$v = \sqrt{v_x^2 + v_y^2}$$

$$\Rightarrow v = \sqrt{(20)^2 + (20)^2}$$

$$\Rightarrow v = 20\sqrt{2} \text{ m/s}$$

Thus, the velocity of the ball at $t = 6$ s is $20\sqrt{2}$ m/s.

and there is no acceleration in the x-direction, $a_x = 0 \text{ ms}^{-2}$

In y-direction, $a_y = 10 \text{ ms}^{-2}$

Now, we shall determine the net acceleration at $t = 6$ s,

$$a = \sqrt{a_x^2 + a_y^2}$$

$$\Rightarrow a = \sqrt{(0) + (10)^2} \Rightarrow a = 10 \text{ ms}^{-2}$$

10. (*b*); Distance covered in nth seconds,

$$s_n = u + \frac{a}{2}(2n-1)$$

$$\Rightarrow s_n = 0 + \frac{a}{2}(2n-1)$$

$$\Rightarrow s_n = \frac{a}{2}(2n-1) \quad \text{...(i)}$$

Distance cover in $(n+1)$th seconds,

$$s_{n+1} = u + \frac{a}{2}[2(n+1)-1]$$

$$\Rightarrow s_{n+1} = 0 + \frac{a}{2}(2n+2-1)$$

$$\Rightarrow s_{n+1} = \frac{a}{2}(2n+1) \quad \text{...(ii)}$$

On dividing Eq. (i) by Eq. (ii), we get

$$\frac{s_n}{s_{n+1}} = \frac{\frac{a}{2}(2n-1)}{\frac{a}{2}(2n+1)}$$

$$\Rightarrow \frac{s_n}{s_{n+1}} = \frac{(2n-1)}{(2n+1)}$$

11. (*b*); According to question, time taken by the ball to cross the window,

$$t = 0.1\text{s}$$

$$h = 1.5 \text{ m}$$

If u be the velocity at the top most point of the window,

$$h = ut + \frac{1}{2}gt^2$$

$$\Rightarrow 1.5 = u\times0.1 + \frac{1}{2}\times10\times(0.1)^2$$

$$= 14.5 \text{ m/s}$$

12. (*c*); Given, $u = 20$ m/s, $v = 80$ m/s and $h = ?$

From kinematic equation of motion,

$$v^2 = u^2 + 2gh$$

$$\Rightarrow h = \frac{v^2 - u^2}{2g} = \frac{(80)^2 - (20)^2}{2\times10}$$

$$(\because \text{ given, } g = 10 \text{ m/s}^2)$$

$$= 300 \text{ m}$$

Chapter-3

Motion in a Plane

1. (*c*); $\therefore$ $\mathbf{d} + \mathbf{e} = \mathbf{f}$

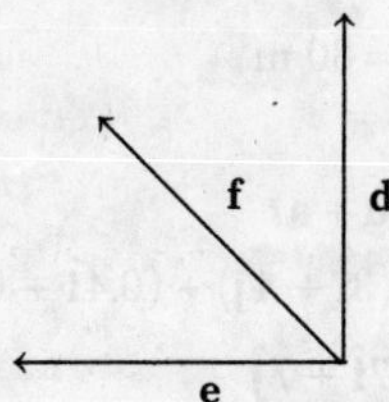

2. (A) **PR** (B) **RQ** (C) **QP**

3. A→4, B→3, C→1, D→2

4. (*a*); According to the question,

$$\mathbf{OA} = 2\hat{\mathbf{i}} + 2\hat{\mathbf{j}}$$

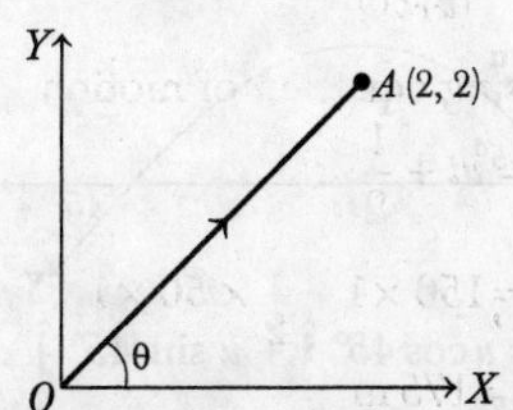

Let θ be an angle made by OA with X-axis, then

$$\tan\theta = \frac{Y}{X} = \frac{2}{2} = 1 \Rightarrow \theta = 45°$$

After the rotation by 45°, **OA** makes an angle 90° with the X-axis, then

$$|\mathbf{OA}| = \sqrt{(2)^2 + (2)^2} = 2\sqrt{2}$$

Hence, the new vector,

$$\mathbf{OA} = 0\hat{\mathbf{i}} + 2\sqrt{2}\hat{\mathbf{j}} = 2\sqrt{2}\hat{\mathbf{j}}$$

5. (*a*);

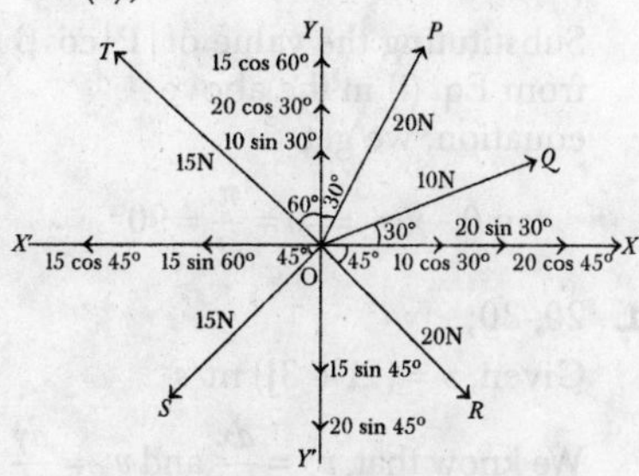

The resultant of these forces is given as

$$\mathbf{F} = \mathbf{OP} + \mathbf{OQ} + \mathbf{OR} + \mathbf{OS} + \mathbf{OT}$$

$$\mathbf{F} = [(10\hat{\mathbf{i}} + 17.32\hat{\mathbf{j}}) + (8.66\hat{\mathbf{i}} + 5\hat{\mathbf{j}}) + (14.14\hat{\mathbf{i}} - 14.14\hat{\mathbf{j}}) + (-10.60\hat{\mathbf{i}} - 10.60\hat{\mathbf{j}}) + (-12.99\hat{\mathbf{i}} + 7.5\hat{\mathbf{j}})]$$

$$\mathbf{F} = (9.21\,\hat{\mathbf{i}} + 5.08\hat{\mathbf{j}}) \text{ N}$$

$$\mathbf{F} \approx (9.25\hat{\mathbf{i}} + 5\hat{\mathbf{j}}) \text{ N}$$

Thus, the resultant force is

$$\mathbf{F} \approx (9.25\hat{\mathbf{i}} + 5\hat{\mathbf{j}}) \text{ N}$$

6. I

7. False;

The unit vector in the direction of **A** + **B** is given by

$$= \frac{\mathbf{A} + \mathbf{B}}{|\mathbf{A} + \mathbf{B}|} = \frac{5\hat{\mathbf{i}} + 5\hat{\mathbf{j}} - 5\hat{\mathbf{k}}}{5\sqrt{3}}$$

$$= \frac{1}{\sqrt{3}}(\hat{\mathbf{i}} + \hat{\mathbf{j}} - \hat{\mathbf{k}})$$

8. A→3, B→2, C→1;

$$\mathbf{a} + \mathbf{b} = 2\hat{\mathbf{i}} + \hat{\mathbf{j}} + 8\hat{\mathbf{k}}$$

$$\mathbf{a} - \mathbf{b} = 6\hat{\mathbf{i}} - \hat{\mathbf{j}} - 2\hat{\mathbf{k}}$$

$$2\mathbf{a} + 5\mathbf{b} = -2\hat{\mathbf{i}} + 5\hat{\mathbf{j}} + 31\hat{\mathbf{k}}$$

9. (i) ✓, (ii) ×, (iii) ✓

10. 90;

Let angle between **P** and **Q** is β, then resultant of **P** and **Q**,

$$|\mathbf{R}| = \sqrt{|\mathbf{P}|^2 + |\mathbf{Q}|^2 + 2|\mathbf{P}||\mathbf{Q}|\cos\beta}$$

As, $|\mathbf{R}| = |\mathbf{P}|$ (given)

So, $|\mathbf{P}|^2 = |\mathbf{P}|^2 + |\mathbf{Q}|^2 + 2|\mathbf{P}||\mathbf{Q}|\cos\beta$

or $|\mathbf{P}|\cos\beta = -\frac{Q}{2}$ .... (i)

If resultant of 2**P** and **Q** makes angle θ with **Q**, then angle θ is given by

$$\tan\theta = \frac{|2\mathbf{P}|\sin\beta}{|\mathbf{Q}| + |2\mathbf{P}|\cos\beta}$$

Substituting the value of $|\mathbf{P}|\cos\beta$ from Eq. (i) in the above equation, we get

$$\tan\theta \to \infty \Rightarrow \theta = \frac{\pi}{2} = 90°$$

11. 20, 30;

Given, $v = (2\hat{\mathbf{i}} + 3\hat{\mathbf{j}})$ m/s

We know that, $v_x = \frac{dx}{dt}$ and $v_y = \frac{dy}{dt}$

Upon integrating both sides, we get

$$x = 2t \text{ and } y = 3t$$

For $t = 10$ s,

$$x = 20 \text{ m and } y = 30 \text{ m}$$

12. 5;

$$v = \sqrt{v_x^2 + v_y^2} = \sqrt{(3t^2)^2 + (4t^3)^2}$$
$$= t^2\sqrt{9 + 16t^2}$$

At $t = 1$ s,

$$v = (1)^2\sqrt{9 + 16(1)^2}$$
$$\Rightarrow v = 5 \text{ m/s}$$

13. II;

$$\mathbf{v} = \left(\frac{dx}{dt}\right)\hat{\mathbf{i}} + \left(\frac{dy}{dt}\right)\hat{\mathbf{j}}$$
$$= p\hat{\mathbf{i}} + p(1 - 2qt)\hat{\mathbf{j}}$$
$$\mathbf{a} = 0\,\hat{\mathbf{i}} + (-2pq)\,\hat{\mathbf{j}}$$

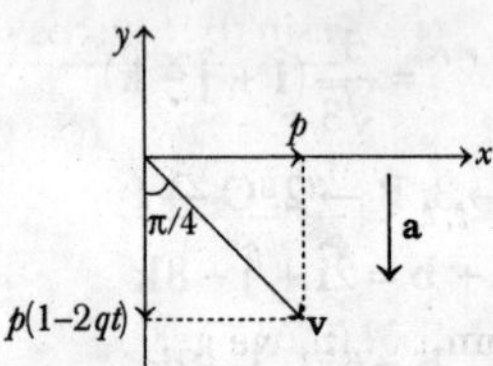

Hence, acceleration **a** is along negative Y-axis. Hence, when **a** and **v** enclose $\frac{\pi}{4}$ between them, the velocity vector makes angle $\frac{\pi}{4}$ with negative Y-axis.

Hence, $\tan\frac{\pi}{4} = \frac{p}{|p(1-2qt)|}$

$$\Rightarrow |1 - 2qt| = 1$$
$$\Rightarrow 1 - 2qt = \pm 1$$
$$\Rightarrow t = \frac{1}{q} \text{ or } 0$$

But when $t = 0$, the y-component of velocity is along positive Y-axis, hence $t = 0$ rejected.

14. 24;

$$\mathbf{v} = v_x\hat{\mathbf{i}} + v_y\hat{\mathbf{j}}$$
$$\Rightarrow |\mathbf{v}| = -\sqrt{v_x^2 + v_y^2}$$
$$\Rightarrow \frac{d}{dt}|\mathbf{v}| = \frac{d}{dt}\left(\sqrt{v_x^2 + v_y^2}\right)$$
$$= \frac{2v_x\frac{dv_x}{dt} + 2v_y\frac{dv_y}{dt}}{2\sqrt{v_x^2 + v_y^2}}$$
$$\Rightarrow \frac{d|\mathbf{v}|}{dt} = \frac{v_x a_x + v_y a_y}{\sqrt{v_x^2 + v_y^2}}$$
$$= \frac{6 \times 24 + 8 \times 12}{\sqrt{6^2 + 8^2}}$$
$$= \frac{240}{10} = 24 \text{ m/s}^2$$

15. 80;

Here, $\mathbf{a} = (6\hat{\mathbf{i}} + 8\hat{\mathbf{j}})$ m/s^2

$$\Rightarrow |\mathbf{a}| = \sqrt{6^2 + 8^2} = 10 \text{ m/s}^2$$
$$\therefore \quad s = ut + \frac{1}{2}at^2$$
$$= 0 \times 4 + \frac{1}{2} \times 10 \times (4)^2$$
$$= 80 \text{ m}$$

16. $7\sqrt{2}$;

$$\therefore \mathbf{v} = \mathbf{u} + \mathbf{a}t$$
$$= (3\hat{\mathbf{i}} + 4\hat{\mathbf{j}}) + (0.4\hat{\mathbf{i}} + 0.3\hat{\mathbf{j}}) \times 10$$
$$= 7\hat{\mathbf{i}} + 7\hat{\mathbf{j}}$$
$$|\mathbf{v}| = \sqrt{7^2 + 7^2} = 7\sqrt{2} \text{ unit}$$

17. 10;

$$|\mathbf{u}| = |\mathbf{v}| \quad \ldots\text{(i)}$$

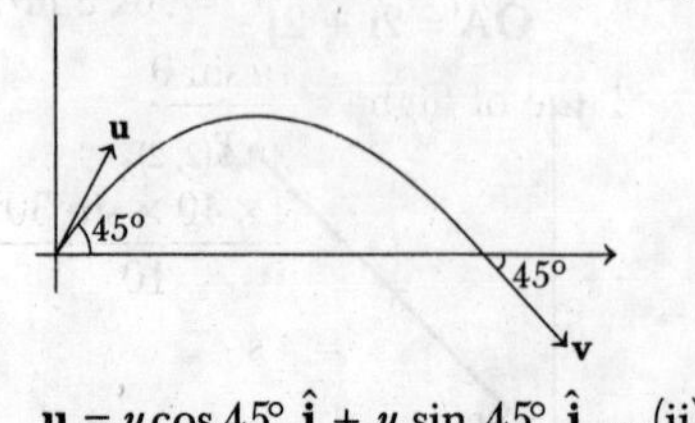

$$\mathbf{u} = u\cos 45°\,\hat{\mathbf{i}} + u\sin 45°\,\hat{\mathbf{j}} \quad \ldots\text{(ii)}$$
$$\mathbf{v} = v\cos 45°\,\hat{\mathbf{i}} - v\sin 45\,\hat{\mathbf{j}} \quad \ldots\text{(iii)}$$
$$|\Delta\mathbf{v}| = |(\mathbf{v} - \mathbf{u})|$$
$$\Delta\mathbf{v} = 2v\sin 45°$$
$$= 2 \times 5\sqrt{2} \times \frac{1}{\sqrt{2}}$$
$$= 10 \text{ ms}^{-1}$$

18. 2, – 3;

In a projectile motion, only velocity of y-component changes, whereas velocity of x-component remains constant. The y-component of velocity reverses because of acceleration due to gravity. So, the velocity at point B becomes $2\hat{\mathbf{i}} - 3\hat{\mathbf{j}}$.

19. False;

Given, $y = \sqrt{3}x - \frac{gx^2}{2}$ ...(i)

The equation of trajectory,

$$y = x\tan\theta - \frac{gx^2}{2v^2\cos^2\theta} \quad \ldots\text{(ii)}$$

Comparing Eqs. (i) and (ii),

$$\sqrt{3}x - \frac{gx^2}{2} = x\tan\theta - \frac{gx^2}{2v^2\cos^2\theta}$$
$$\Rightarrow \tan\theta = \sqrt{3} = \tan 60°$$
$$\theta = 60°$$

20. $2\sqrt{10}$;

Given, $y = \sqrt{3}x - \frac{1}{2}x^2$

Comparing with standard equation of projectile,

$$y = x\tan\theta - \frac{gx^2}{2v^2\cos^2\theta},$$
$$\tan\theta = \sqrt{3} = \tan 60°$$
$$\Rightarrow \theta = 60°$$

Also, $\frac{g}{2v^2\cos^2 60°} = \frac{1}{2}$

$$\Rightarrow v = 2\sqrt{10} \text{ m/s}$$

21. 3;

$$v\cos 30° = u\cos 45°$$
$$\Rightarrow v \cdot \frac{\sqrt{3}}{2} = \frac{10}{\sqrt{2}}$$
$$\Rightarrow v = \frac{10\sqrt{2}}{\sqrt{3}} \text{ m/s}$$

Now, $g\cos 30° = \frac{v^2}{r}$

$$\Rightarrow r = \frac{v^2}{g\cos 30°}$$

$$= \frac{\left(\frac{10\sqrt{2}}{\sqrt{3}}\right)^2}{10 \times \frac{\sqrt{3}}{2}} = \frac{40}{3\sqrt{3}} \text{ m}$$

Comparing with $\frac{40}{(\sqrt{3})x}$, we get

$\therefore \quad x = 3$

22. True;

$$\frac{h_{max}}{T^2} = \frac{u^2 \sin^2 \theta}{2g} \times \frac{g^2}{4u^2 \sin^2 \theta} = \frac{g}{8}$$

23. I;

$$h_1 h_2 = \frac{u^2 \sin^2 \theta}{2g} \cdot \frac{u^2 \sin^2(90° - \theta)}{2g}$$

$$= \frac{1}{16}\left(\frac{u^2 \sin 2\theta}{g}\right)^2 = \frac{1}{16} R^2$$

$$\Rightarrow \quad \sqrt{h_1 h_2} = \frac{R}{4} = \frac{400}{4} = 100 \text{ m}$$

$$t_1 t_2 = \left(\frac{2u \sin \theta}{g}\right)\left[\frac{2u \sin(90° - \theta)}{g}\right]$$

$$= \left(\frac{2}{g}\right) \times \frac{u^2 \sin 2\theta}{g} = \frac{2R}{g} = 80 \text{ m}$$

24. $\tan^{-1}(4)$;

$$H = \frac{u^2 \sin^2 \theta}{2g} \quad \ldots \text{(i)}$$

$$R = \frac{u^2 \sin 2\theta}{g} = \frac{2u^2 \sin \theta \cos \theta}{g} \quad \ldots \text{(ii)}$$

$\because \quad H = R$

$$\frac{u^2 \sin^2 \theta}{2g} = \frac{2u^2 \sin \theta \cos \theta}{g}$$

$\Rightarrow \quad \tan \theta = 4$

$\Rightarrow \quad \theta = \tan^{-1}(4)$

25. 40;

$$R_{max} = \frac{u^2 \sin(2 \times 45°)}{g}$$

$$= \frac{(20)^2}{10} = 40 \text{ m}$$

26. $10\sqrt{10}$;

We know that, $R_{max} = \frac{u^2}{g}$

$$100 = \frac{u^2}{10} \text{ m/s}$$

$$= 10\sqrt{10} \text{ m/s}$$

27. $\left(\frac{R}{2}, \frac{R}{4}\right)$;

Speed is minimum at the highest point, y-coordinate is given by maximum height attained.

$$\text{Height} = \frac{R_{max}}{4}$$

$$y\text{-coordinate} = \frac{R}{4}$$

$$x\text{-coordinate} = \frac{R}{2}$$

28. 1

29. (*b*)

30. (*c*);

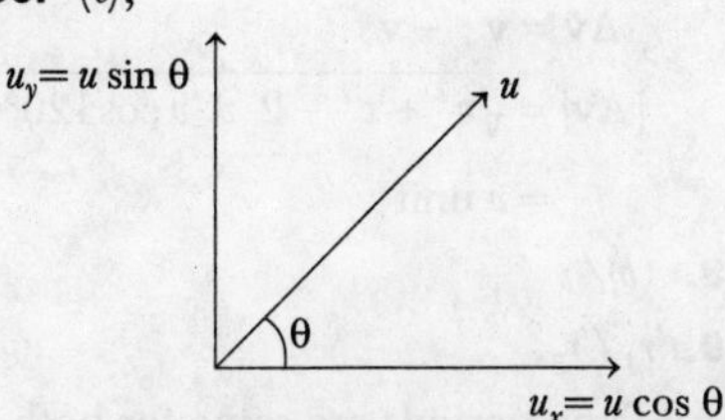

As we know that, for motion along Y-axis,

$$v_y^2 - u_y^2 = 2gh_{max}$$

$$\therefore \quad 0^2 - (25 \sin 45°)^2 = -2 \times 10 \times h_{max}$$

$\Rightarrow \quad -312.5 = -20h_{max}$

$\Rightarrow \quad h_{max} = 15.625 \text{ m}$

$\Rightarrow \quad h_{max} = \frac{1}{2}gt^2$

$$\therefore \quad t = \sqrt{\frac{2h_{max}}{g}} = \sqrt{\frac{2 \times 15.625}{10}}$$

$$= 1.767 \simeq 1.77 \text{ s}$$

31. $\text{I} \to \sqrt{3}, \text{II} \to (20\sqrt{3}\hat{\mathbf{i}} + 10\hat{\mathbf{j}}),$ $\text{III} \to 20\sqrt{3}, \text{IV} \to 4, \text{V} \to 4\sqrt{3}$;

$$\therefore \frac{v_x}{v_y} = \frac{\cos \theta}{\sin \theta} = \cot 30° = \sqrt{3}$$

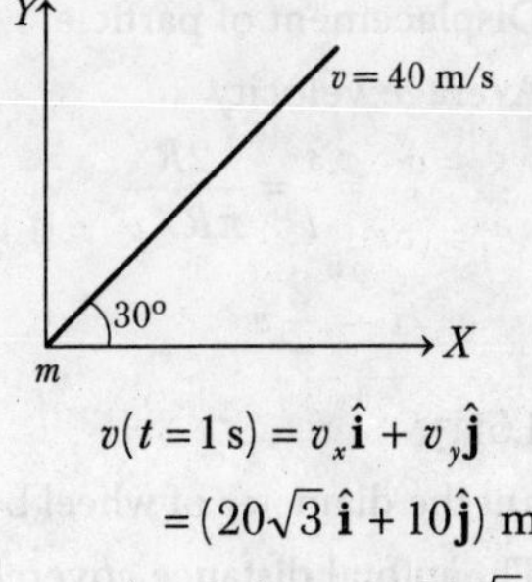

$$v(t = 1 \text{ s}) = v_x \hat{\mathbf{i}} + v_y \hat{\mathbf{j}}$$

$$= (20\sqrt{3}\,\hat{\mathbf{i}} + 10\hat{\mathbf{j}}) \text{ m/s}$$

$$v(t = 2 \text{ s}) = v_x = 20\sqrt{3} \text{ m/s}$$

$$\text{Time of flight} = \frac{2u \sin \theta}{g}$$

$$= \frac{2 \times 40 \times \sin 30°}{10}$$

$$= 4 \text{ s}$$

$$\frac{\text{Range}}{\text{Maximum height}} = 4 \cot \theta$$

$$= 4 \cot 30° = 4\sqrt{3}$$

32. II, III

33. (*d*); $R = \frac{u^2 \sin 2\theta}{g}$

Time of flight is given by

$$t = \frac{2u \sin \theta}{g}$$

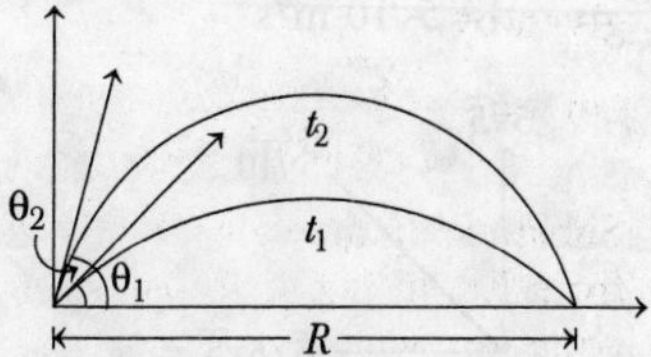

Let θ_1 and θ_2 are the two angles at which shell is fired.

As, range in both cases is same.

i.e. $\quad R_1 = R_2 = R$

$$\Rightarrow \quad R = \frac{u^2 \sin 2\theta_1}{g}$$

$$= \frac{u^2 \sin 2\theta_2}{g} \quad \ldots \text{(i)}$$

$\Rightarrow \quad \sin 2\theta_1 = \sin 2\theta_2$

$\Rightarrow \quad \sin 2\theta_1 = \sin(180° - 2\theta_2)$

$[\because \sin(180° - \theta) = \sin \theta]$

$\Rightarrow \quad 2(\theta_1 + \theta_2) = 180°$

$\Rightarrow \quad \theta_2 = 90° - \theta_1 \quad \ldots \text{(ii)}$

So, time of flight in first case,

$$t_1 = \frac{2u \sin \theta_1}{g} \quad \ldots \text{(iii)}$$

and time of flight in second case,

$$t_2 = \frac{2u \sin \theta_2}{g}$$

$$= \frac{2u \sin(90° - \theta_1)}{g}$$

$$= \frac{2u \cos \theta_1}{g} \quad \ldots \text{(iv)}$$

From Eqs. (iii) and (iv), we get

$$t_1 t_2 = \frac{2u \sin \theta_1}{g} \times \frac{2u \cos \theta_1}{g}$$

$$\Rightarrow \quad t_1 t_2 = \frac{2u^2 \sin 2\theta_1}{g^2}$$

From Eq. (i), we get

$$R = \frac{u^2 \sin 2\theta_1}{g}$$

$$\therefore \quad t_1 t_2 = \frac{2R}{g}$$

34. A → 4, B → 2, C → 5, D → 3
E → 1, F → 6;

Range, $AB = \sqrt{15^2 + 20^2} = 25$

If v be the velocity at point A, then

$$AB = \frac{v^2 \sin 2\theta}{g}$$

$$25 = \frac{v^2 \sin(2 \times 45^\circ)}{10}$$

$$\Rightarrow \quad v = 5\sqrt{10} \text{ m/s}$$

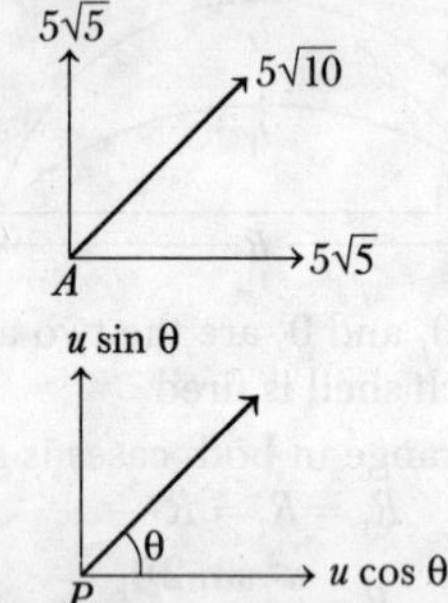

For journey from P to A,

$$u^2 \sin^2 \theta - 2 \times 10 \times 12.5 = (5\sqrt{5})^2$$

$$u \sin \theta = \sqrt{125 + 250} = \sqrt{375}$$

and $u \cos \theta = 5\sqrt{5} = \sqrt{125}$

$$\therefore \quad \tan \theta = \sqrt{\frac{375}{125}} = \sqrt{3}$$

$$\Rightarrow \quad \theta = 60^\circ$$

If u be the speed of particle at point P, then

$$u \cos \theta = 5\sqrt{5} \Rightarrow \theta = 60^\circ$$

$$\Rightarrow \quad u = \frac{5\sqrt{5}}{\frac{1}{2}} = 10\sqrt{5} \text{ m/s}$$

At the top of trajectory, speed $= u \cos \theta = 5\sqrt{5}$ m/s

$$\text{Range} = \frac{u^2 \sin 2\theta}{g}$$

$$= \frac{(10\sqrt{5})^2 \sin 120^\circ}{10}$$

$$= \frac{100 \times 5\sqrt{3}}{2 \times 10} = 25\sqrt{3} \text{ m}$$

$$\text{Time of flight, } T = \frac{2u \sin \theta}{g}$$

$$= \frac{2 \times 10\sqrt{5} \times \sin 60^\circ}{10} = \sqrt{15} \text{ s}$$

35. centre

36. A → 1, B → 2, C → 1, D → 2

37. v;

Let the particle move from A to B.

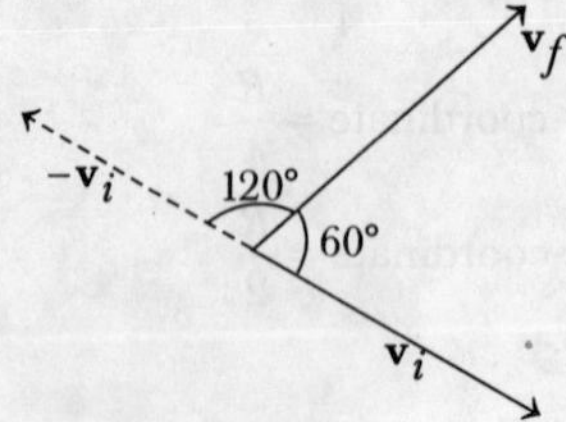

Change in velocity,

$$\Delta \mathbf{v} = \mathbf{v}_f - \mathbf{v}_i$$

$$|\Delta \mathbf{v}| = \sqrt{v^2 + v^2 - 2 \cdot v \cdot v \cos 120^\circ}$$

$$= v \text{ unit}$$

38. (*b*)

39. r_A / r_B;

Time periods are same for both cars,

$$T_A = T_B$$

$$\frac{2\pi}{\omega_A} = \frac{2\pi}{\omega_B}$$

$$\Rightarrow \quad \omega_A = \omega_B$$

$$\frac{v_A}{r_A} = \frac{v_B}{r_B} \qquad \left(\because \omega = \frac{v}{r}\right)$$

$$\Rightarrow \quad \frac{v_A}{v_B} = \frac{r_A}{r_B}$$

40. (*a*); $a_c = \frac{v^2}{r} = \frac{(10)^2}{1000} = 0.1 \text{ m/s}^2$

41. $\frac{2v}{\pi}$;

Time taken in half rotation,

$$t = \frac{\pi R}{v}$$

Displacement of particle, $s = 2R$

Average velocity

$$= \frac{s}{t} = \frac{2R}{\pi R / v}$$

$$= \frac{2}{\pi} v$$

42. 1.51;

Let the diameter of wheel be d m.

Then, total distance covered in one revolution $= \pi d$

In 2000 revolutions $= 2000\pi d$

Also, $\pi d \times 2000 = 9.5 \times 1000$

$$\Rightarrow \quad d = 1.51 \text{ m}$$

43. A → 3, B → 2, C → 1;

Angular speed,

$$\omega = \frac{2\pi}{T} = 2\left(\frac{22/7}{100/7}\right)$$

$$= 0.44 \text{ rad/s}$$

Linear speed, $v = \omega r$

$$= 0.44 \times 12 = 5.3 \text{ cm/s}$$

Magnitude of acceleration,

$$a = \omega^2 r = (0.44)^2 \times 12$$

$$= 2.3 \text{ cm/s}^2$$

44. 1;

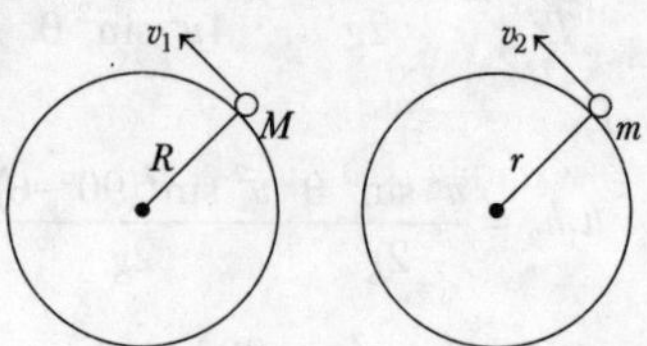

Time period for both the cases can be given as follows

$$T_1 = \frac{2\pi R}{v_1} \text{ and } T_2 = \frac{2\pi r}{v_2}$$

Now, $T_1 = T_2$

$$\frac{2\pi R}{v_1} = \frac{2\pi r}{v_2}$$

$$\Rightarrow \quad \frac{v_2}{v_1} = \frac{r}{R} \qquad \text{...(i)}$$

Using the relation, $v = \omega R$ in Eq. (i), we get

$$\frac{\omega_2 \cdot r}{\omega_1 \cdot R} = \frac{r}{R}$$

$$\Rightarrow \quad \omega_1 = \omega_2$$

45. 5;

$$r = 5 \text{ cm} = 5 \times 10^{-2} \text{ m},$$

$$T = 0.2\pi \text{ s}$$

Acceleration is given by

$$a = r\omega^2 = \frac{4\pi^2}{T^2} r$$

$$= \frac{4 \times \pi^2 \times 5 \times 10^{-2}}{(0.2\pi)^2}$$

$$= 5 \text{ m/s}^2$$

46. (*d*);

$$\mathbf{r}(t) = \cos \omega t \,\hat{\mathbf{i}} + \sin \omega t \,\hat{\mathbf{j}} \qquad \text{...(i)}$$

$$\text{Velocity, } \mathbf{v}(t) = \frac{d\mathbf{r}(t)}{dt}$$

$$= \omega(-\sin \omega t \,\hat{\mathbf{i}} + \cos \omega t \,\hat{\mathbf{j}}) \qquad \text{...(ii)}$$

$$\mathbf{a}(t) = \frac{d\mathbf{v}(t)}{dt}$$

$$= -\omega^2 \cos \omega t \,\hat{\mathbf{i}} - \omega^2 \sin \omega t \,\hat{\mathbf{j}}$$

$$= -\omega^2 (\cos \omega t \,\hat{\mathbf{i}} + \sin \omega t \,\hat{\mathbf{j}})$$

$$\mathbf{a}(t) = -\omega^2 \mathbf{r}(t) \quad ...(iii)$$

From Eqs. (i), (ii) and (iii), it is clear that **v** is perpendicular to **r** and **a** is directed towards the origin.

47. $\frac{r_1}{r_2}$;

$\because \quad T = \frac{2\pi}{\omega}$ and $\omega = v / r$

$\Rightarrow \frac{v_1}{r_1} = \frac{v_2}{r_2}$ or $\frac{v_1}{v_2} = \frac{r_1}{r_2}$

Centripetal acceleration of circular path, $a = \omega^2 r$.

Thus, $\frac{a_1}{a_2} = \frac{\omega^2 r_1}{\omega^2 r_2} = \frac{r_1}{r_2}$

48. I;

For a particle in uniform circular motion,

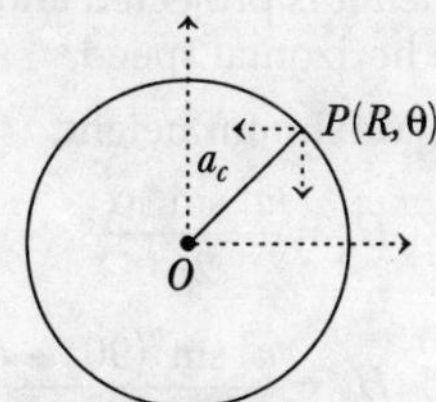

$$a = \frac{v^2}{R}$$

$$\therefore \quad \mathbf{a} = \frac{v^2}{R}(-\cos\theta\,\hat{\mathbf{i}} - \sin\theta\,\hat{\mathbf{j}})$$

or $\mathbf{a} = -\frac{v^2}{R}\cos\theta\,\hat{\mathbf{i}} - \frac{v^2}{R}\sin\theta\,\hat{\mathbf{j}}$

Competition Connect

1. I. $(10\,\hat{\mathbf{i}} - 25\hat{\mathbf{j}})$;

$$v_{AB} = v_A - v_B$$

$$= a_A \cdot t - a_B \cdot t \quad \left(\because \frac{v}{t} = a\right)$$

$$= (3\hat{\mathbf{i}} - 2\hat{\mathbf{j}})(5) - (\hat{\mathbf{i}} + 3\hat{\mathbf{j}})(5)$$

$$= (10\hat{\mathbf{i}} - 25\hat{\mathbf{j}}) \text{ m/s}$$

II. 67.3;

$$r_{AB} = r_A - r_B$$

$$= \frac{1}{2}a_A t^2 - \frac{1}{2}a_B t^2$$

$$= \frac{1}{2}(3\hat{\mathbf{i}} - 2\hat{\mathbf{j}})(5^2) - \frac{1}{2}(\hat{\mathbf{i}} + 3\hat{\mathbf{j}})(5^2)$$

$$= 67.3 \text{ m}$$

III. $(2\hat{\mathbf{i}} - 5\hat{\mathbf{j}})$;

$$a_{AB} = a_A - a_B$$

$$= (3\hat{\mathbf{i}} - 2\hat{\mathbf{j}}) - (\hat{\mathbf{i}} + 3\hat{\mathbf{j}})$$

$$= (2\hat{\mathbf{i}} - 5\hat{\mathbf{j}}) \text{ m/s}^2$$

2. $3\hat{\mathbf{i}}$;

Displacement of A and B in the x-direction must be same.

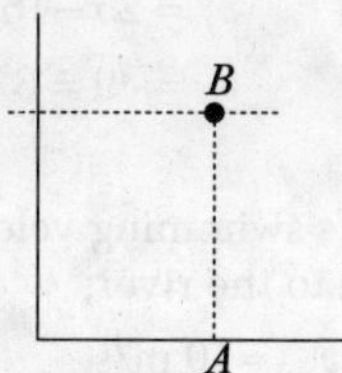

$$v_{B_x} = 3\hat{\mathbf{i}}$$

So, $v_{A_x} = v_{B_x} = 3\hat{\mathbf{i}}$ m/s

3. I. $\mathbf{r}_A - \mathbf{r}_B$

II. $\sqrt{17}$;

$$\mathbf{v}_{AB} = \frac{d}{dt}(r_{AB})$$

$$= \frac{d}{dt}(t\,\hat{\mathbf{i}} + 4t\,\hat{\mathbf{j}})$$

$$= (\hat{\mathbf{i}} + 4\hat{\mathbf{j}}) \text{ m/s}$$

$$|\mathbf{v}_{AB}| = \sqrt{1^2 + 4^2} = \sqrt{17} \text{ m/s}$$

III. $\sqrt{17}$;

$$\mathbf{v}_{BA} = \frac{d}{dt}(r_{BA}) = \frac{d}{dt}(-t\hat{\mathbf{i}} - 4t\hat{\mathbf{j}})$$

$$= (-\hat{\mathbf{i}} - 4\hat{\mathbf{j}}) \text{ m/s}$$

$$\Rightarrow |\mathbf{v}_{BA}| = \sqrt{(-1)^2 + (-4)^2}$$

$$= \sqrt{17} \text{ m/s}$$

4. (*a*); For collision of two particles move with constant velocities, the direction of the relative velocity of one with respect to other should be directed towards the relative position of the other particle.

i.e. $\frac{\mathbf{r}_1 - \mathbf{r}_2}{|\mathbf{r}_1 - \mathbf{r}_2|} \longrightarrow$ direction of relative position of 1 w.r.t. 2.

Similarly, $\frac{\mathbf{v}_1 - \mathbf{v}_2}{|\mathbf{v}_1 - \mathbf{v}_2|} \longrightarrow$ direction of velocity of 1 w.r.t. 2.

So, for collision of A and B, we get

$$\frac{\mathbf{r}_1 - \mathbf{r}_2}{|\mathbf{r}_1 - \mathbf{r}_2|} = \frac{\mathbf{v}_1 - \mathbf{v}_2}{|\mathbf{v}_2 - \mathbf{v}_1|}$$

5. $\omega(R_2 - R_1)\hat{\mathbf{i}}$;

Angle covered by each particle in time duration 0 to $\frac{\pi}{2\omega}$ is

$$\theta = \omega \times t = \omega \times \frac{\pi}{2\omega} = \frac{\pi}{2} \text{ rad}$$

So, positions of particles at $t = \frac{\pi}{2\omega}$ is as shown below.

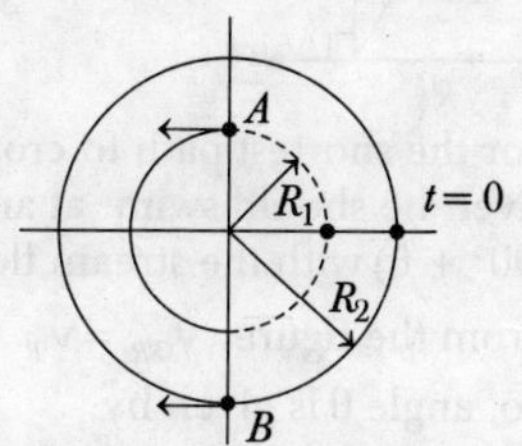

Velocities of particles at $t = \frac{\pi}{2\omega}$ are $\mathbf{v}_A = -\omega R_1\hat{\mathbf{i}}$

and $\mathbf{v}_B = -\omega R_2\hat{\mathbf{i}}$

The relative velocity of particles is

$$\mathbf{v}_A - \mathbf{v}_B = -\omega R_1\hat{\mathbf{i}} - (-\omega R_2\hat{\mathbf{i}})$$

$$= -\omega(R_1 - R_2)\hat{\mathbf{i}}$$

$$= \omega(R_2 - R_1)\hat{\mathbf{i}}$$

6. 5, 127;

$$v_{\text{resultant}} = \sqrt{v_{\text{rain}}^2 + v_{\text{man}}^2}$$

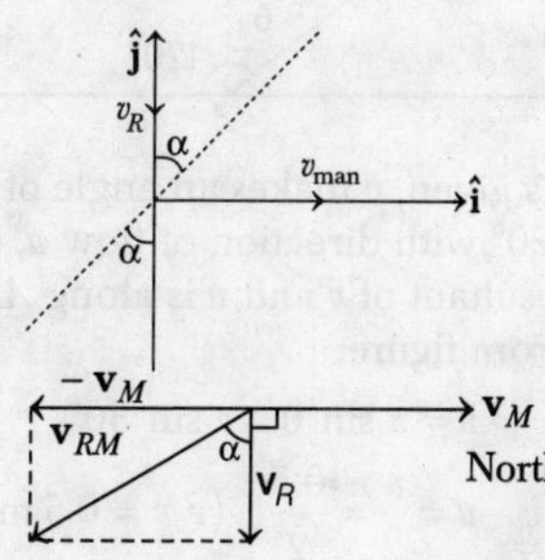

$$v_{\text{rain}} = -4\hat{\mathbf{j}}$$

$$v_{\text{man}} = 3\hat{\mathbf{i}}$$

$$v_{\text{resultant}} = \sqrt{(-4)^2 + (3)^2} = 5 \text{ m/s}$$

$$\tan(90° - \alpha) = \frac{v_{\text{rain}}}{v_{\text{man}}}$$

$$\cot\alpha = \frac{4}{3}$$

$$\therefore \tan\alpha = \frac{3}{4}$$

$$\Rightarrow \quad \alpha = \tan^{-1}(0.75) \approx 37°$$

$\Rightarrow \mathbf{v}_{RM}$ with North

$$= \alpha + 90° = 127°$$

7. A → 4, B → 3, C → 1, D → 3

8. 30;

$$v_{SR} = 20 \text{ m/s}$$

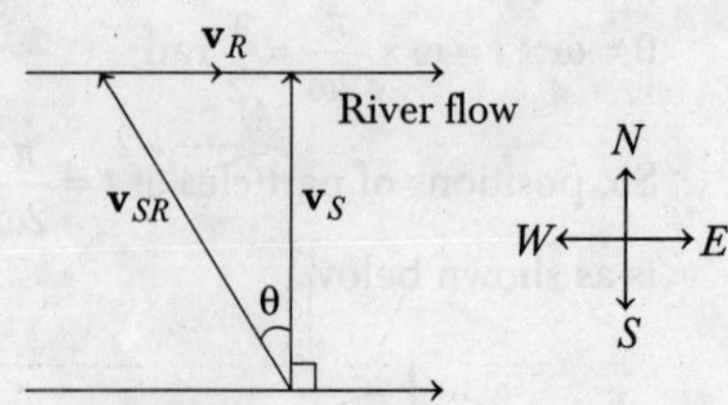

For the shortest path to cross the river, he should swim at an angle $(90° + \theta)$ with the stream flow.

From the figure, $\mathbf{v}_{SR} = \mathbf{v}_R + \mathbf{v}_S$

So, angle θ is given by

$$\sin\theta = \left|\frac{\mathbf{v}_R}{\mathbf{v}_{SR}}\right| = \frac{10}{20} = \frac{1}{2} \Rightarrow \theta = 30°$$

As the river is flowing in East direction, so he should swim towards West.

9. 0.25 m/s;

Let u be the speed of stream and v be the speed of person started from A.

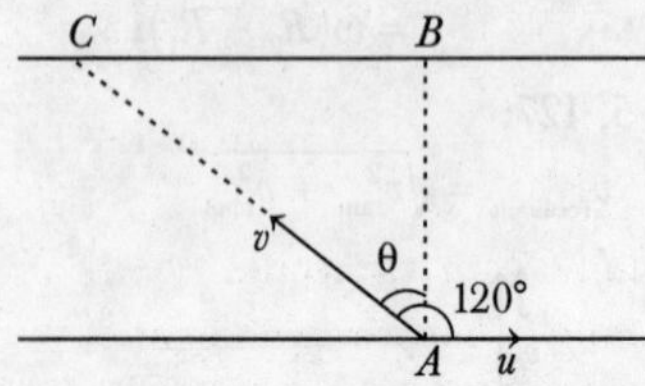

As given, v makes an angle of 120° with direction of flow u, the resultant of v and u is along AB.

From figure,

$$u = v\sin\theta = v\sin 30°$$

$$\therefore \quad u = \frac{v}{2} = \frac{0.5}{2} \quad (\because v = 0.5\,\text{m/s})$$

$$= 0.25\,\text{m/s}$$

10. 3;

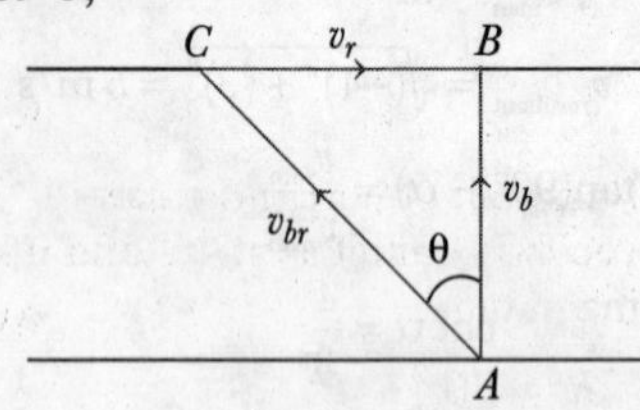

Time taken to cross the river

$$= 15\text{ min}$$

$$= \frac{15}{60}\text{ h} = \frac{1}{4}\text{ h}$$

Shortest path is taken when v_b is along AB.

In this case,

$$v_{br}^2 = v_r^2 + v_b^2$$

Now, $t = \dfrac{w}{v_b} = \dfrac{w}{\sqrt{v_{br}^2 - v_r^2}}$

$$\therefore \quad \frac{1}{4} = \frac{1}{\sqrt{5^2 - v_r^2}}$$

$$\Rightarrow \quad 5^2 - v_r^2 = 16$$

$$\Rightarrow \quad v_r^2 = 25 - 16 = 9$$

$$\therefore \quad v_r = \sqrt{9} = 3\text{ km/h}$$

11. 5;

Person's swimming velocity with respect to the river,

$$v_{mr} = 10\text{ m/s}$$

As shown in the figure,

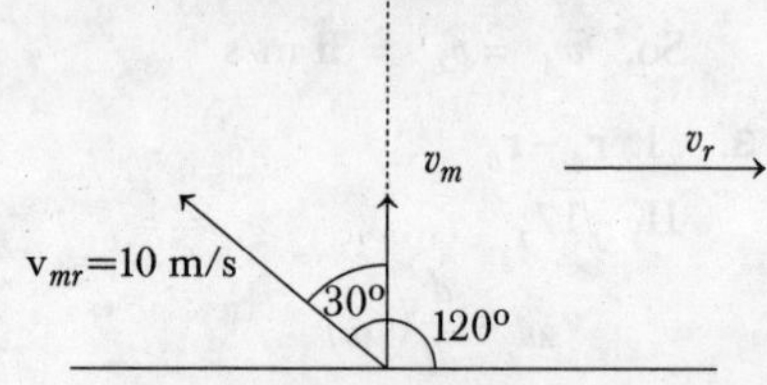

Let the velocity of the river flow is v_r.

In x-direction,

$$v_r = v_{mr}\sin 30° = 10 \times \sin 30°$$

$$\Rightarrow \quad v_r = 5\text{ m/s}$$

12. 120;

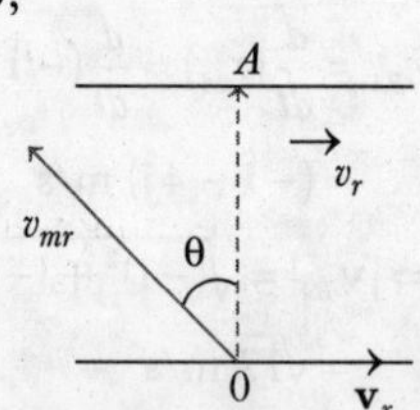

v_{mr} = velocity of man w.r.t. river = 12 km/h

v_r = velocity of water = 6 km/h

To reach A,

$$v_r - v_{mr}\sin\theta = 0$$

$$\Rightarrow \quad 6 - 12\sin\theta = 0$$

$$\Rightarrow \quad \sin\theta = \frac{6}{12}$$

$$\Rightarrow \quad \sin\theta = \frac{1}{2}$$

$$\Rightarrow \quad \theta = 30°$$

$$\therefore \quad \alpha = 90° + \theta = 90° + 30°$$

$$\Rightarrow \quad \alpha = 120°$$

Assertion-Reason Questions

1. (*b*)

2. (*b*); $t_1 = t_2 = \sqrt{\dfrac{2h}{g}}$

(h = height of tower)

$$v_1 = \sqrt{2gh}$$

While $\quad v_2 = \sqrt{v_1^2 + v_0^2}$

(v_0 = initial horizontal velocity)

3. (*b*)

4. (*d*); The equation $x = a\sin\omega t$ and $y = a\cos\omega t$ describes the circular motion.

5. (*d*); $\left|\dfrac{dv}{dt}\right| = |a| = 9.8\text{ ms}^{-2}$ = constant

and it is true that in case of projectile motion, the magnitude of velocity first decreases and then increases during the motion.

6. (*b*); $h_1 = \dfrac{u^2}{2g}$, $h_2 = \dfrac{u^2\sin^2 30°}{2g} = \dfrac{u^2}{8g}$

7. (*d*); The time of flight for a horizontally projected particle depends only on the height from which it is projected and not on the horizontal speed.

8. (*b*); Maximum height,

$$H_1 = \frac{u^2\sin^2\alpha}{2g}$$

and $\quad H_2 = \dfrac{u^2\sin^2(90° - \alpha)}{2g}$

$$= \frac{u^2\cos^2\alpha}{2g}$$

$$\Rightarrow H_1 + H_2 = \frac{u^2}{2g}(\sin^2\alpha + \cos^2\alpha)$$

$$= \frac{u^2}{2g}$$

Thus, the sum of height for angle of projections α and 90° − α is independent of the angle of projection.

As, horizontal range,

$$R = \frac{u^2\sin 2\theta}{g}$$

So, for same value of initial velocity, horizontal range of projectile is same for complementary angles.

9. (*c*); To obtain maximum range, angle of projection must be 45°, i.e. θ = 45°.

So, $\quad R_{\max} = \dfrac{u^2\sin(2\times 45°)}{g}$

$$= \frac{u^2\sin 90°}{g} = \frac{u^2}{g} \quad \ldots\text{(i)}$$

$\therefore H_{max} = \frac{u^2 \sin^2 45°}{2g} = \frac{u^2}{2g}\left(\frac{1}{\sqrt{2}}\right)^2$

$= \frac{u^2}{4g} = \frac{R_{max}}{4}$ [from Eq. (i)]

So, H_{max} is 25% of R_{max}.

10. (*a*)

Case Based Questions

1. (i) (*c*); Since, both balls are at same level, hence for collision, $v_{Ay} = v_{By}$

$\Rightarrow u_{Ay} - gt = u_{By} - gt$ $(\because v = u - gt)$

$\Rightarrow u_{Ay} = u_{By}$

$\Rightarrow 50 \sin 37° = 60 \sin \theta$

$\Rightarrow \sin\theta = \frac{50 \times \frac{3}{5}}{60}$ $\left(\because \sin 37° = \frac{3}{5}\right)$

$= \frac{1}{2}$

$\Rightarrow \theta = 30°$

(ii) (*b*); Time of collision

$= \frac{\text{Initial distance between } A \text{ and } B}{\text{Relative velocity of } A \text{ with respect to } B \text{ in horizontal direction}}$

$t = \frac{91}{50 \cos 37° + 60 \cos 30°}$

$= \frac{91}{50 \times \frac{4}{5} + 60 \times \frac{\sqrt{3}}{2}}$

$= \frac{91}{91} = 1 \text{ s}$

(iii) (*a*); Consider the following equation

$y = u_y t - \frac{1}{2} gt^2$

Substituting the values for the particle *B*,

$y = 60 \sin 30° (1) - \frac{1}{2}(9.8)(1)^2$

$= 25.1$ m

(iv) (*d*)

2. (i) (*a*);

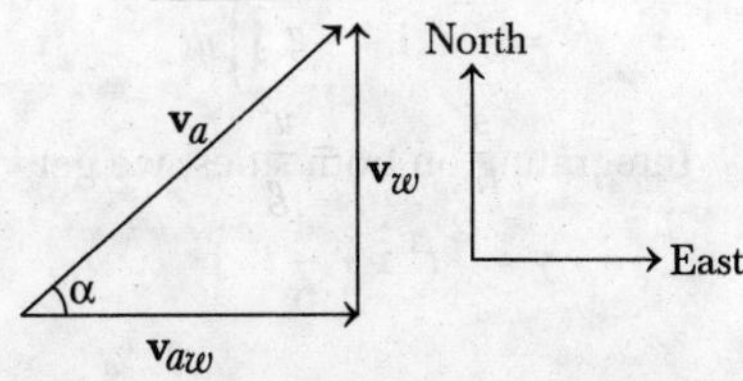

From the above diagram,

$\mathbf{v}_a = \mathbf{v}_{aw} + \mathbf{v}_w$

$\Rightarrow v_a \cos\alpha\hat{i} + v_a \sin\alpha\hat{j} = v_{aw}\hat{i} + v_w\hat{j}$

$\Rightarrow v_a \cos\alpha = v_{aw}$ ...(i)

and $v_a \sin\alpha = v_w$ ...(ii)

$\therefore \frac{v_a \sin\alpha}{v_a \cos\alpha} = \frac{v_w}{v_{aw}}$

$= \frac{20}{100} = 0.2$

$\Rightarrow \tan\alpha = 0.2$

(ii) (*c*); From Eq. (ii),

$v_a \sin\alpha = v_w$

$\Rightarrow v_a = \frac{v_w}{\sin\alpha}$ ...(iii)

$\because \tan\alpha = 0.2 = \frac{1}{5}$

$\Rightarrow \sin\alpha = \frac{1}{\sqrt{26}}$

Hence, from Eq. (iii),

$v_a = \frac{v_w}{\sin\alpha}$

$= \frac{20}{\frac{1}{\sqrt{26}}} = 20\sqrt{26}$ m/s

(iii) (*b*); Relative motion in the context of an airplane refers to its velocity relative to the surrounding air.

(iv) (*c*); Velocity vector indicates the direction in which the plane is travelling relative to a fixed point.

Competition Edge Up

1. (*150*); Given, $|\mathbf{R}| = \frac{|\mathbf{B}|}{2}$

$b\cos\phi = R$

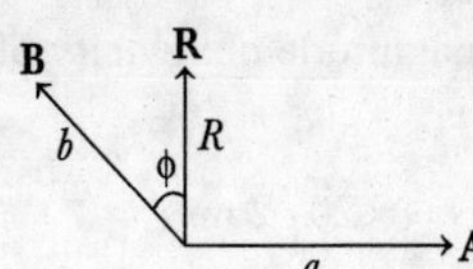

$\Rightarrow b\cos\phi = b/2$

$\Rightarrow \cos\phi = \frac{1}{2} \Rightarrow \phi = 60°$

Thus, angle between A and B

$= 90° + 60° = 150°$

2. (*100*); For ball of mass *M*, time to reach ground

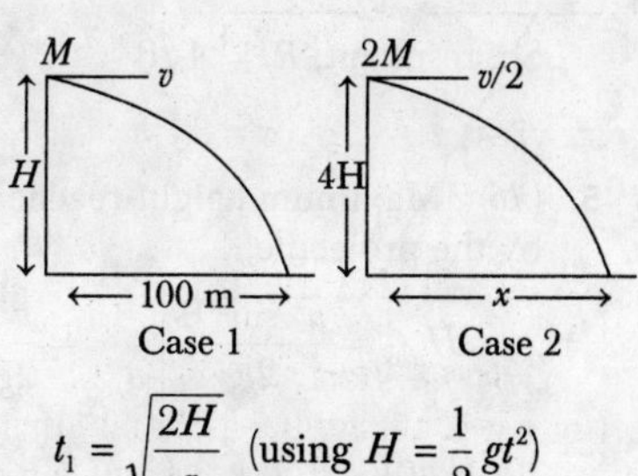

$t_1 = \sqrt{\frac{2H}{g}}$ (using $H = \frac{1}{2}gt^2$)

So, horizontal distance covered

$= 100 = v_x \times t_1$

$\Rightarrow 100 = v \times \sqrt{\frac{2H}{g}}$ ...(i)

For ball of mass 2*M*,

Time to reach ground,

$t_2 = \sqrt{\frac{2(4H)}{g}} = 2\sqrt{\frac{2H}{g}}$

Horizontal distance covers by 2nd ball

$= v_x \times t_2 = \frac{v}{2} \times 2\sqrt{\frac{2H}{g}}$

$= v\sqrt{\frac{2H}{g}} = 100$ m [from Eq. (i)]

3. (*d*); Given, projectile

range = maximum height

$\Rightarrow \frac{u^2 \sin 2\theta}{g} = \frac{u^2 \sin^2\theta}{2g}$

$\Rightarrow \tan\theta = 4 \Rightarrow \theta = \tan^{-1}(4)$

4. (*3*);

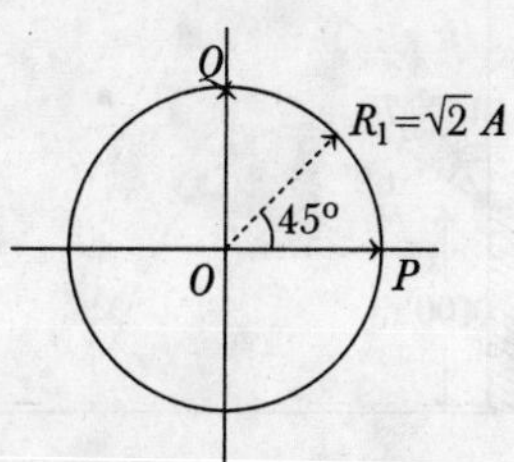

Resultant of perpendicular vectors Q and P is at 45° and it's magnitude,

$R_1 = \sqrt{Q^2 + P^2}$

$= \sqrt{A^2 + A^2} = \sqrt{2}A$

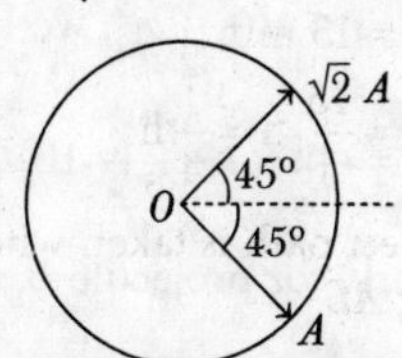

Resultant of A and $\sqrt{2}A$,

$R_2 = \sqrt{A^2 + (\sqrt{2}A)^2}$

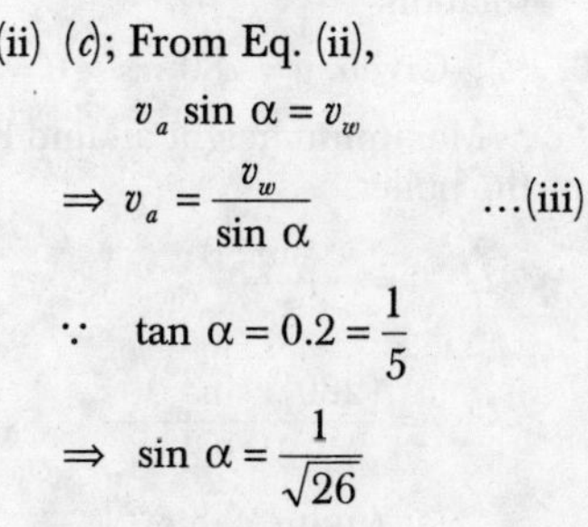

So, resultant, $R_2 = A\sqrt{3}$

$\therefore \quad x = 3$

5. (*16*) ; Maximum height reached by the projectile,

$$H_{max} = \frac{u^2 \sin^2 \theta}{2g}\bigg|_{\theta = 90^\circ} = \frac{u^2}{2g}$$

$$\therefore \frac{(H_{max})_1}{(H_{max})_2} = \left(\frac{u_1}{u_2}\right)^2 = \left(\frac{u}{u/2}\right)^2 = 4$$

$$\therefore (H_{max})_2 = \frac{(H_{max})_1}{4} = \frac{64}{4} = 16 \text{ m}$$

6. (*4*); Magnitude of vector A

$$= \sqrt{3^2 + 4^2} = 5$$

Direction of B

$$= \hat{B} = \frac{B}{|B|} = \frac{4\hat{i} + 3\hat{j}}{\sqrt{4^2 + 3^2}}$$

$$= \frac{4\hat{i} + 3\hat{j}}{5}$$

Required vector has direction of B and magnitude of A, so required vector,

Vector = Magnitude × Direction

$$= 5 \times \left(\frac{4\hat{i} + 3\hat{j}}{5}\right) = 4\hat{i} + 3\hat{j}$$

7. (*d*);

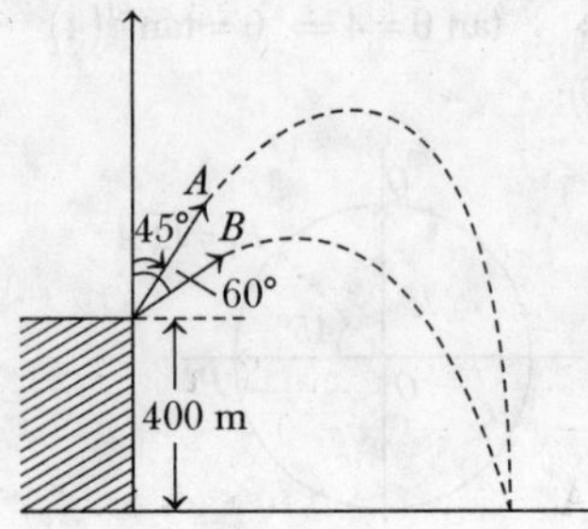

In vertical direction,

For projectile A,

$$u_{yA} = v_A \cdot \cos 45^\circ = \frac{v_A}{\sqrt{2}}$$

$$s_{yA} = -400 \text{ m}, a_{yA} = -10 \text{ m/s}^2$$

Using $s = ut + \frac{1}{2}at^2$, we have

$$-400 = \frac{v_A}{\sqrt{2}} \times t + \frac{1}{2}(-10)t^2 \quad ...(i)$$

Similarly for projectile B,

$$-400 = \frac{v_B}{2} \times t + \frac{1}{2}(-10)t^2 \quad ...(ii)$$

From Eqs. (i) and (ii),

$$\frac{v_A}{\sqrt{2}} t = \frac{v_B}{2} t \text{ or } v_A : v_B = 1 : \sqrt{2}$$

8. (*d*); In uniform circular motion, direction of motion changes continuously motion. So, uniform circular motion have varying velocity and varying acceleration.

9. (*c*); The direction of angular acceleration of a body moving along the circumference of the circular path is perpendicular to the plane in with rotation takes place, i.e. along the axis of rotation.

10. (*b*); Given, $u = 280 \text{ ms}^{-1}$, $\theta = 30^\circ$

$\therefore$ Maximum height attained by the bullet,

$$H_{max} = \frac{u^2 \sin^2 \theta}{2g}$$

$$= \frac{(280)^2 \sin^2 30^\circ}{2 \times 9.8}$$

$$= \frac{(280)^2 \times (0.5)^2}{2 \times 9.8} = 1000 \text{ m}$$

11. (*a*) Given,

Initial velocity, $u = 0$ m/s

Acceleration, $a = 5 \text{ m/s}^2$

Velocity at $t = 4$ s, $v = u + at$

$$\Rightarrow \quad v = 5 \times 4 = 20 \text{ m/s}$$

At this time, a ball is dropped out of a window by a person sitting in the car. The velocity of ball after $t = 6$ s is given by

Vertical velocity of

$$v_y = u_{ball} + a(\Delta t)$$

$$= 0 + 10 \times (6 - 4)$$

$$= 20 \text{ ms}^{-1}$$

Horizontal velocity of ball,

$$v_x = 20 \text{ ms}^{-1}$$

So, magnitude of velocity of ball

$$v_{net} = \sqrt{v_x^2 + v_y^2}$$

$$= 20\sqrt{2} \text{ m/s}$$

Acceleration of the ball will be equal to gravitational acceleration g, i.e. 10 m/s^2

12. (*d*) Maximum height attained it is given as

$$H_{max} = \frac{u^2 \sin^2 \theta}{2g} \quad ...(i)$$

$$H_{max} = 4R \quad \text{(given)}$$

Also, we know that, speed of the particle in circular path,

$$u = \frac{2\pi R}{T}$$

Substituting the values in the Eq. (i), we get

$$4R = \frac{\left(\frac{2\pi R}{T}\right)^2 \sin^2 \theta}{2g}$$

$$\Rightarrow \quad \sin \theta = \left(\frac{2gT^2}{\pi^2 R}\right)^{1/2}$$

$$\Rightarrow \quad \theta = \sin^{-1}\left(\frac{2gT^2}{\pi^2 R}\right)^{1/2}$$

Chapter-4

Laws of Motion

1. inertia of motion

2. True

3. infinite

4. 50 m/s;

5. Yes

6. (*b*)

7. True

8. False;

Momentum is given by the relation

$$p = mv = 10^3 \times 30$$

$$= 0.3 \times 10^5 \text{ kg-m/s}$$

9. 5;

$$|\mathbf{F}| = \sqrt{(3)^2 + (4)^2 + (-5)^2}$$

$$= 5\sqrt{2} \text{ N}$$

According to Newton's second law of motion,

$$5\sqrt{2} = m \times \sqrt{2}$$

$$\Rightarrow \quad m = 5 \text{ kg}$$

10. (*a*); Since, $\mathbf{a} = \frac{\mathbf{F}}{m} = \frac{6t^2\,\hat{\mathbf{i}} + 4t\,\hat{\mathbf{j}}}{3}$

$$\frac{d\mathbf{v}}{dt} = 2t^2\,\hat{\mathbf{i}} + \frac{4}{3}t\,\hat{\mathbf{j}}$$

$$\Rightarrow \quad d\mathbf{v} = \left(2t^2\,\hat{\mathbf{i}} + \frac{4}{3}t\,\hat{\mathbf{j}}\right) dt$$

Integrating on both sides, we get

$$\mathbf{v} = \frac{2}{3}t^3\,\hat{\mathbf{i}} + \frac{4}{6}t^2\,\hat{\mathbf{j}}$$

At $t = 3$ s,

$$\mathbf{v} = \frac{2}{3}(3)^3\,\hat{\mathbf{i}} + \frac{4}{6}(3)^2\,\hat{\mathbf{j}}$$

$$= 18\,\hat{\mathbf{i}} + 6\,\hat{\mathbf{j}}$$

$$|\mathbf{v}| = \sqrt{(18)^2 + (6)^2}$$

$$= 6\sqrt{10} \text{ m/s}$$

11. -270 N;

Using the third equation of motion,

$$2as = v^2 - u^2$$

$$\Rightarrow \quad a = \frac{v^2 - u^2}{2s}$$

$$= \frac{(0)^2 - (90)^2}{2 \times 60 \times 10^{-2}}$$

$$= -6750 \text{ m/s}^2$$

$$\therefore \quad F = ma = -0.04 \times 6750$$

$$= -270 \text{ N}$$

12. mg;

Given, $y = ut + \frac{1}{2}gt^2$

The velocity is given by

$$v = \frac{dy}{dt} = u + \frac{1}{2}g(2t)$$

$$= u + gt$$

Thus, $a = \frac{dv}{dt} = 0 + g$

$$\therefore \quad F = ma = mg$$

13. (*b*); As the three forces are represented by three sides of a triangle taken in order, then they will be in equilibrium.

$$\Rightarrow F_{net} = F_{PQ} + F_{QR} + F_{RP} = 0$$

$$m\frac{dv}{dt} = 0$$

$$\Rightarrow \quad v = \text{constant}$$

14. I, II;

Momentum is given by

$$p = mv$$

When mass m is constant, $p \propto v$

When velocity is constant, $p \propto m$

15. $4mv, mv$;

Momentum is given by

$$p = mv \qquad \ldots\text{(i)}$$

I. When mass and velocity are doubled, using Eq.(i),

$$p = (2m)(2v) = 4mv$$

II. When mass is doubled and velocity is halved, using Eq.(i),

$$p = (2m)\left(\frac{v}{2}\right) = mv$$

16. I, II;

I. The opposing force in first case is the friction which is directly proportional to the normal reaction. The normal force of a loaded truck is obviously larger than that of a car, so much greater force will be needed to push the truck.

II. The opposing force in the second case is the momentum which is again directly proportional to the mass.

So, the mass of truck being larger requires a greater opposing force to stop as compared to the car.

17. True

18. (i) ✓ (ii) ✓ (iii) ✓ (iv) ✓

19. 2000 N;

$$F = \frac{m(v - u)}{t} = \frac{1.5[25 - (-15)]}{0.03}$$

$$= 2000 \text{ N}$$

20. 3;

According to Newton's second law of motion, $F = \frac{dp}{dt}$

Let n be the number of bullets fired, then the total momentum of bullets fired will be given by

$$p = nmv$$

$$\therefore \quad F = \frac{d}{dt}(nmv)$$

$$\Rightarrow \quad \frac{dn}{dt} = \frac{F}{mv}$$

$$= \frac{144}{40 \times 10^{-3} \times 1.2 \times 10^3}$$

$$= 3$$

21. 5;

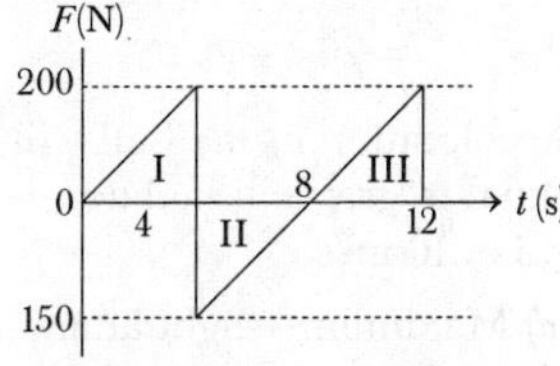

The change in momentum of the particle will be given by the sum of areas of the curves under the force-time graph, so

$$\Delta p = \text{Area (I)} + \text{Area (II)} + \text{Area (III)}$$

$$\Delta p = \frac{1}{2} \times 200 \times 4 - \frac{1}{2} \times 4 \times 150 + \frac{1}{2} \times 4 \times 200$$

$$= 5 \times 10^2 \text{ N-s}$$

[Here, $x \times 10^2 = 5 \times 10^2$ $\therefore x = 5$]

22. -30 N;

As, $F = \frac{m(v - u)}{t}$

$$= \frac{150 \times 10^{-3}(0 - 20)}{0.1}$$

$$= -30 \text{ N}$$

23. 60 kg/s;

$$F_{\text{thrust}} = \frac{dm}{dt} \cdot v_{\text{relative}}$$

F_{thrust} ↑ a ↓ mg

$$\Rightarrow \quad \frac{dm}{dt} v_{\text{relative}} - mg = ma$$

$$\left(\frac{dm}{dt}\right) \times 500 - 10^3 \times 10 = 10^3 \times 20$$

$$\Rightarrow \quad \frac{dm}{dt} = 60 \text{ kg/s}$$

24. $\frac{4F_0T}{3M}$;

Particle is originally at rest

$$\Rightarrow \quad t = 0, u = 0$$

According to Newton's second law of motion,

$$F = Ma$$

$$\Rightarrow \quad a = \frac{F}{M} = \frac{F_0}{M}\left[1 - \left(\frac{t - T}{T}\right)^2\right]$$

$$\frac{dv}{dt} = \frac{F_0}{M} - \frac{F_0}{MT^2}(t - T)^2$$

Integrating both sides, we get

$$\int_0^v dv = \int_{t=0}^{2T}\left[\frac{F_0}{M} - \frac{F_0}{MT^2}(t - T)^2\right]dt$$

$$= \left[\frac{F_0}{M}t\right]_0^{2T} - \frac{F_0}{MT^2}\left[\frac{t^3}{3} - t^2T + T^2t\right]_0^{2T}$$

$$= \frac{4F_0T}{3M}$$

25. $(400\hat{\mathbf{i}}+100\hat{\mathbf{j}})$ m;

According to the Newton's second law of motion,

$$\mathbf{F}=m\mathbf{a}$$

or $$\mathbf{a}=\frac{\mathbf{F}}{m}=\frac{40\,\hat{\mathbf{i}}+10\,\hat{\mathbf{j}}}{5}$$

$$\frac{d\mathbf{v}}{dt}=(8\,\hat{\mathbf{i}}+2\,\hat{\mathbf{j}})\text{ m/s}^2\left(\because a=\frac{d\mathbf{v}}{dt}\right)$$

Integrating both sides, we get

$$\int d\mathbf{v}=\int(8\,\hat{\mathbf{i}}+2\,\hat{\mathbf{j}})\,dt$$

$$\mathbf{v}=(8t\,\hat{\mathbf{i}}+2t\,\hat{\mathbf{j}})\text{ m/s}$$

$$\Rightarrow \frac{d\mathbf{r}}{dt}=(8t\,\hat{\mathbf{i}}+2t\,\hat{\mathbf{j}})\quad\left(\because \mathbf{v}=\frac{d\mathbf{r}}{dt}\right)$$

Similarly, integrating again

$$\mathbf{r}=(4t^2\,\hat{\mathbf{i}}+t^2\,\hat{\mathbf{j}})\text{ m}$$

At $t=10$ s,

$$\mathbf{r}=[4(10)^2\,\hat{\mathbf{i}}+(10)^2\,\hat{\mathbf{j}}]\text{ m}$$

$$=(400\,\hat{\mathbf{i}}+100\,\hat{\mathbf{j}})\text{ m}$$

26. 500;

Since; $$\mathbf{a}=\frac{\mathbf{F}}{m}=\frac{20\,\hat{\mathbf{i}}+10\,\hat{\mathbf{j}}}{2}=10\,\hat{\mathbf{i}}+5\,\hat{\mathbf{j}}$$

Using, $\mathbf{s}=\mathbf{u}\,t+\frac{1}{2}\,\mathbf{a}\,t^2$

$$\mathbf{s}=0+\frac{1}{2}(10\,\hat{\mathbf{i}}+5\,\hat{\mathbf{j}})(10)^2$$

$$=50\,(10\,\hat{\mathbf{i}}+5\,\hat{\mathbf{j}})$$

$\therefore$ Displacement along X-axis

$$=50\times 10=500\text{ m}$$

27. 12;

Since, $$\mathbf{a}=\frac{\mathbf{F}}{m}=\frac{2\,\hat{\mathbf{i}}+3\,\hat{\mathbf{j}}+5\,\hat{\mathbf{k}}}{2}=\hat{\mathbf{i}}+1.5\,\hat{\mathbf{j}}+2.5\,\hat{\mathbf{k}}$$

Using, $\mathbf{s}=\mathbf{u}\,t+\frac{1}{2}\,\mathbf{a}\,t^2$

$$=0+\frac{1}{2}(\hat{\mathbf{i}}+1.5\,\hat{\mathbf{j}}+2.5\,\hat{\mathbf{k}})(4)^2$$

$$=8\,\hat{\mathbf{i}}+12\,\hat{\mathbf{j}}+20\,\hat{\mathbf{k}}$$

On comparing, we get $b=12$

28. 0.707 m/s;

$$a=\frac{F_R}{m}=\frac{-2.5\times 10^{-2}}{20\times 10^{-3}}=-1.25\text{ m/s}^2$$

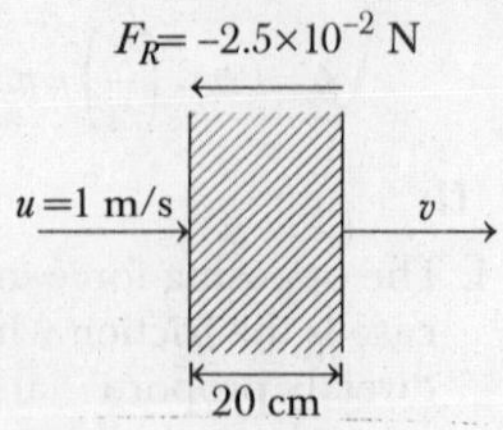

Now, $$v^2=u^2+2as=(1)^2+2(-1.25)\times 0.2$$

$$\therefore\quad v=\frac{1}{\sqrt{2}}=0.707\text{ m/s}$$

29. short, constant

30. $\frac{2ma}{(g+a)}$;

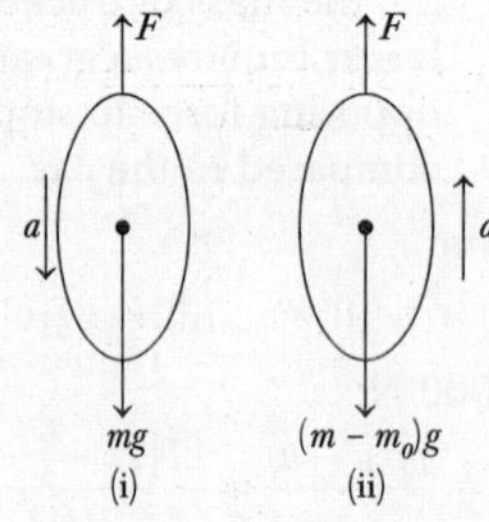

Let $F=$ upthrust on the balloon,

$m_0=$ mass removed

When balloon is descending down, from Newton's second law,

$$F_{\text{net}}=ma$$

$$\Rightarrow\quad mg-F=ma\quad\ldots\text{(i)}$$

When balloon is ascending up,

$$F-(m-m_0)g=(m-m_0)a\quad\ldots\text{(ii)}$$

Adding Eqs. (i) and (ii), we get

$$m_0g=(2m-m_0)\,a$$

$$\therefore\quad m_0=\frac{2ma}{(g+a)}$$

31. (*b*); $F=F_0e^{-bt}$

$$ma=F_0e^{-bt}$$

$$\Rightarrow\quad a=\frac{F_0}{m}e^{-bt}$$

$$\Rightarrow\quad \frac{dv}{dt}=\frac{F_0}{m}e^{-bt}$$

$$\Rightarrow\quad \int_0^v dv=\int_0^t\frac{F_0}{m}e^{-bt}\,dt$$

$$\Rightarrow\quad v=-\frac{F_0}{m}\cdot\frac{1}{b}[e^{-bt}]_0^t$$

$$=-\frac{F_0}{mb}[e^{-bt}-1]$$

$$\therefore\quad v=\frac{F_0}{mb}[1-e^{-bt}]$$

At $t=0$, $v=0$

At $t\to\infty$, $v\to\frac{F_0}{mb}$

$\therefore$ Graph of v *versus* t is given by

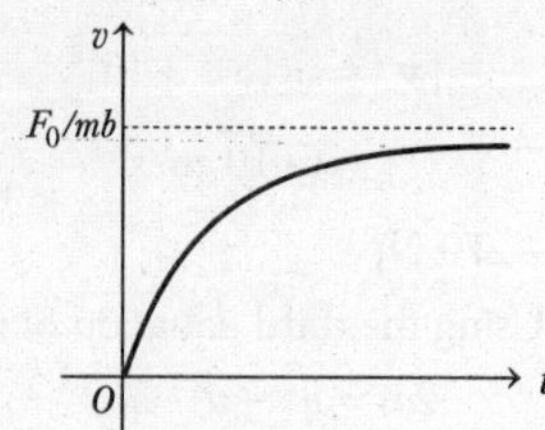

32. Motion up the plane,

$$F-mg\sin\theta=0$$

$\therefore$ $F=mg\sin\theta=$ constant

$\therefore$ F is independent of distance

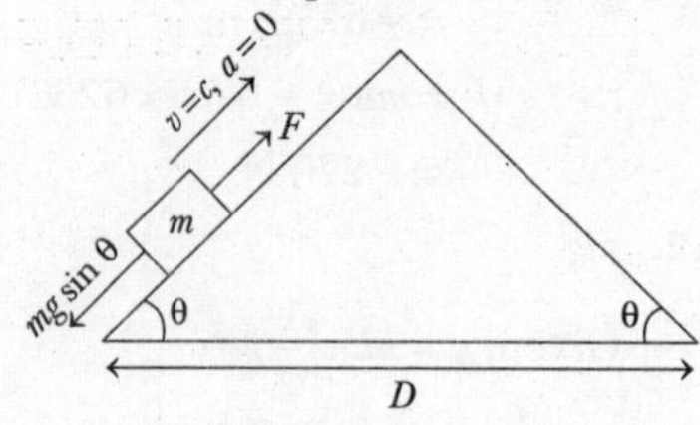

$\therefore$ $F=mg\sin\theta=2$ N

Motion down the plane,

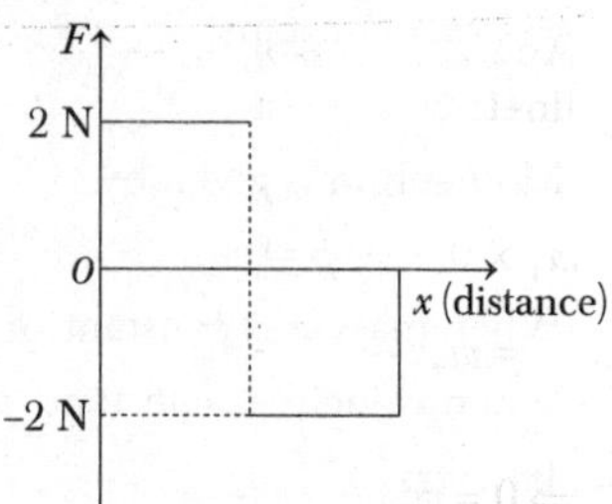

$$F+mg\sin\theta=0$$

$$\therefore\quad F=-mg\sin\theta$$

$$=-2\text{ N}=\text{constant}$$

Hence, graph of F *versus* distance is

F
2 N
O
x (distance)
–2 N

33. (*b*); Impulse

$$=F\cdot\Delta t=\frac{\Delta p}{\Delta t}\cdot\Delta t=\Delta p=p_2-p_1$$

$$=m(v-u)=0.15\,[12-(-12)]$$

$$=3.6\text{ N-s}$$

34. $2:\sqrt{3}$;

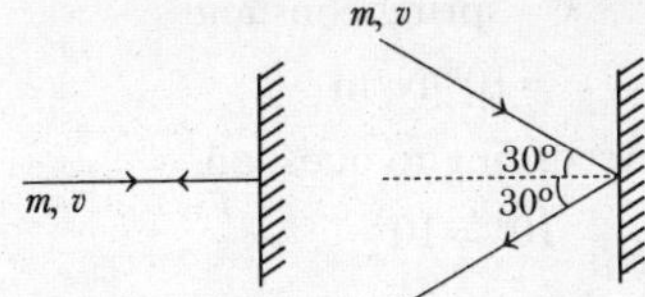

Ratio of impulse, $\frac{\mathbf{I}_1}{\mathbf{I}_2}=\frac{m(\mathbf{v}_1-\mathbf{u}_1)}{m(\mathbf{v}_2-\mathbf{u}_2)}$

$$=\frac{-v\,\hat{\mathbf{i}}-v\,\hat{\mathbf{i}}}{-v\cos 30^\circ\,\hat{\mathbf{i}}-v\cos 30^\circ\,\hat{\mathbf{i}}}=\frac{2}{\sqrt{3}}$$

$=2:\sqrt{3}$

35. 10;

According to second equation of motion,

$$v^2=u^2+2as$$

$$0=(10)^2+2(-a)(0.5)$$

$$\Rightarrow \quad a=100\text{ m/s}^2$$

$$F=ma=(0.1)(100)=10\text{ N}$$

36. (*a*)

37. $\theta=\tan^{-1}\left(\frac{-1}{2}\right)$ to the *X*-axis;

Before collision After collision

As, $F_{\text{ext}}=0$

$\therefore$ Applying law of conservation of linear momentum along *X*-axis,

$$(p_i)_x=(p_f)_x$$

$$m_1\times 0+m_2\times v=m_1v'\cos\theta$$

$$\therefore \quad v'=\frac{m_2v}{m_1\cos\theta} \quad \text{... (i)}$$

Applying law of conservation of linear momentum along *Y*-axis,

$$(p_i)_y=(p_f)_y$$

$$m_1\times 0+m_2\times 0=m_1v'\sin\theta+m_2\cdot\frac{v}{2}$$

$$\Rightarrow 0=m_1\left(\frac{m_2v}{m_1\cos\theta}\right)\cdot\sin\theta+\frac{m_2v}{2}$$

[using Eq. (i)]

$$\Rightarrow \tan\theta=-\frac{1}{2}$$

$$\therefore \quad \theta=\tan^{-1}\left(-\frac{1}{2}\right) \text{ to the } X\text{-axis}$$

38. 100 m/s;

$$v=u+at$$

or $\quad v=u+gt=100-10\times 5 \quad (\because g=10\text{ m/s}^2)$

$$=50\text{ m/s}$$

As, $F_{\text{ext}}=0$

$\therefore$ Applying conservation of linear momentum, $p_i=p_f$

$$1\times 50=-0.4\times 25+0.6\,v$$

[Mass of other part (after collision) = 600 g = 0.6 kg]

$$\therefore \quad v=100\text{ m/s}$$

39. 1000 m/s;

Since, $F_{\text{ext}}=0$

$\therefore$ By conservation of linear momentum, $p_i=p_f$

$$\Rightarrow 0=m\mathbf{v}+M\mathbf{v}'$$

$$\therefore \quad \mathbf{v}=-\frac{M\mathbf{v}'}{m}=-\frac{2\times(-10\,\hat{\mathbf{i}})}{20\times 10^{-3}}$$

$$\therefore \quad v=|\mathbf{v}|=1000\text{ m/s}$$

40. 5 kg;

As $\mathbf{F}_{\text{ext}}=0$

$\therefore$ By conservation of linear momentum,

$$\mathbf{p}_i=\mathbf{p}_f$$

$$0=2\times 8\hat{\mathbf{i}}+1\times 12\hat{\mathbf{j}}+\mathbf{p}_3$$

$$\therefore \quad \mathbf{p}_3=-12\,\hat{\mathbf{i}}-16\,\hat{\mathbf{j}}$$

$$\therefore \quad p_3=\sqrt{(-12)^2+(-16)^2}=20$$

$$\because \quad p_3=m_3v_3$$

$$\therefore \quad m_3=\frac{20}{4}=5\text{ kg}$$

41. -133.25 N, 86.37 N;

$$\Sigma F_H=0$$

$$F\cos 60^\circ+200\cos 45^\circ=300+P\cos 30^\circ$$

$$F=317.16+1.7320P$$

$$\Sigma F_V=0$$

$$F\sin 60^\circ=200\sin 45^\circ+P\sin 30^\circ$$

$$(317.16+1.7320P)\sin 60^\circ=200\sin 45^\circ+P\sin 30^\circ$$

$$274.67+1.5P=141.42+0.5P$$

$$P=-133.25\text{ N}$$

$$F=317.16+1.7320(-133.25)$$

$$F=86.37\text{ N}$$

42. I; For equilibrium of a body,

$$\Sigma F_x=0$$

$$\Sigma F_y=0 \text{ and } \Sigma\tau=0$$

$$\Sigma F_z=0$$

43. No;

Since, direction of two mutual forces are not given.

$F_{\text{resultant}}=14$ N (if 8 N and 6 N acts along same line of action and in same direction)

44. 6;

From parallelogram law of vector addition,

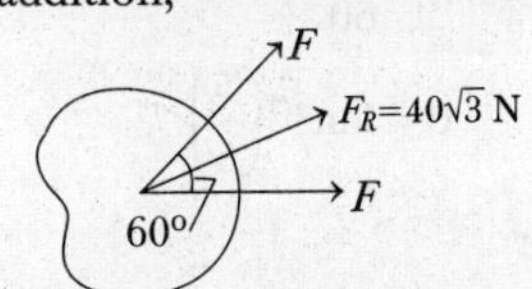

$$F_R=\sqrt{F_1^2+F_2^2+2F_1F_2\cos\theta}$$

$$=\sqrt{F^2+F^2+2F^2\cos\theta}$$

$$\therefore \quad F_R=2F\cos\frac{\theta}{2} \quad \left(\because 1+\cos\theta=2\cos^2\frac{\theta}{2}\right)$$

$$\therefore \quad 40\sqrt{3}=2F\cos\frac{60^\circ}{2}$$

$$\therefore \quad F=40\text{ N}=40\times 10^5\text{ dyne}$$

According to question,

$$4\times 10^x=40\times 10^5$$

$$\therefore \quad x=6$$

45. True;

According to question,

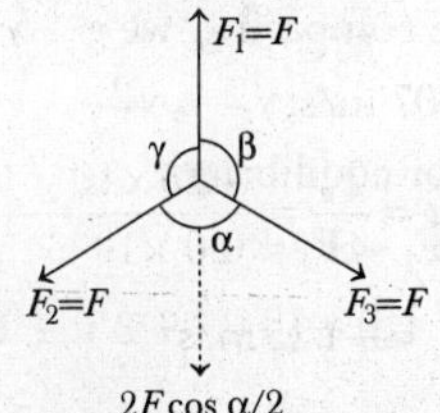

$$F = 2F\cos\frac{\alpha}{2}$$

$\therefore \quad \cos\frac{\alpha}{2} = \frac{1}{2} = \cos 60^\circ$

$\therefore \quad \alpha = 120^\circ$

Similarly, $\beta = \gamma = 120^\circ$

46. $\tan^{-1}\left(\frac{5}{6}\right)$;

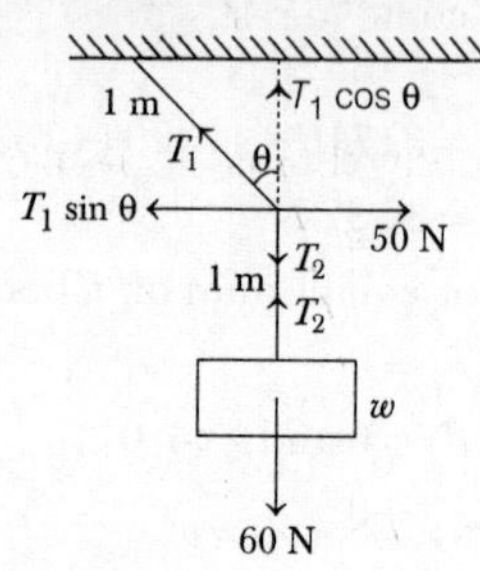

For equilibrium,

$\Sigma F_x = 0$

$T_1 \sin\theta = 50 \quad \dots$ (i)

$\Sigma F_y = 0$

$T_1 \cos\theta = T_2 = 60 \quad \dots$ (ii)

Dividing Eq. (i) by Eq. (ii), we get

$\tan\theta = \frac{50}{60}$

$\therefore \quad \theta = \tan^{-1}\left(\frac{5}{6}\right)$

47. $\sqrt{2}$;

For equilibrium,

$\Sigma F_x = 0,$

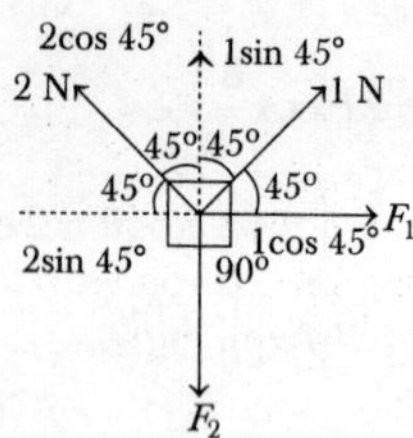

$F_1 + 1\cos 45^\circ = 2\cos 45^\circ$

$\therefore \quad F_1 = \frac{1}{\sqrt{2}}$ N

and $\sin 45^\circ + 2\cos 45^\circ = F_2$

$\therefore \quad F_2 = 3 \times \frac{1}{\sqrt{2}} = \frac{3}{\sqrt{2}}$ N

$\therefore \quad F_2 - F_1 = \frac{3}{\sqrt{2}} - \frac{1}{\sqrt{2}} = \sqrt{2}$ N

48. (*b*); For equilibrium,

$\mathbf{F}_1 + \mathbf{F}_2 + \mathbf{F}_3 = 0$

$\Rightarrow (8\,\hat{\mathbf{i}} - 4\,\hat{\mathbf{j}}) + (-3\,\hat{\mathbf{i}} + 3\,\hat{\mathbf{j}}) + \mathbf{F}_3 = 0$

$\therefore \quad \mathbf{F}_3 = (-5\,\hat{\mathbf{i}} + \hat{\mathbf{j}})$ N

$\therefore \quad F_3 = \sqrt{(-5)^2 + (1)^2} = \sqrt{26}$ N

49. (10, 6);

For equilibrium.

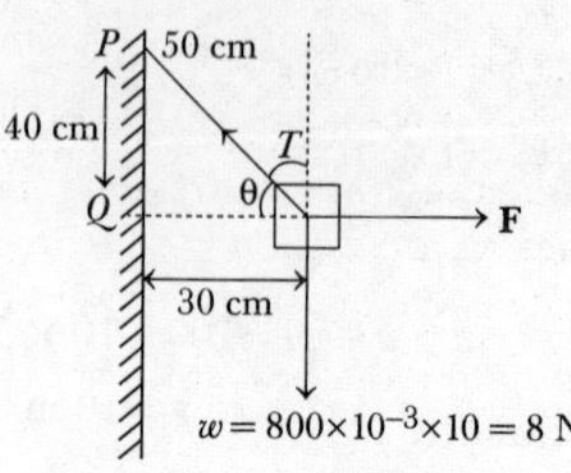

Applying Lami's theorem,

$$\frac{T}{\sin 90^\circ} = \frac{w}{\sin(180^\circ - \theta)} = \frac{F}{\sin(90^\circ + \theta)}$$

$\Rightarrow \quad T = \frac{8}{\sin\theta} = \frac{F}{\cos\theta} \quad \dots$ (i)

From ΔPQR,

$\sin\theta = \frac{4}{5}, \tan\theta = \frac{4}{3}$

$\therefore$ From Eq. (i), we get

$$T = \frac{8}{\sin\theta} = \frac{8}{\frac{4}{5}} = 10 \text{ N},$$

$$F = 8\cot\theta = 8 \times \frac{3}{4} = 6 \text{ N}$$

50. 30°;

For equilibrium,

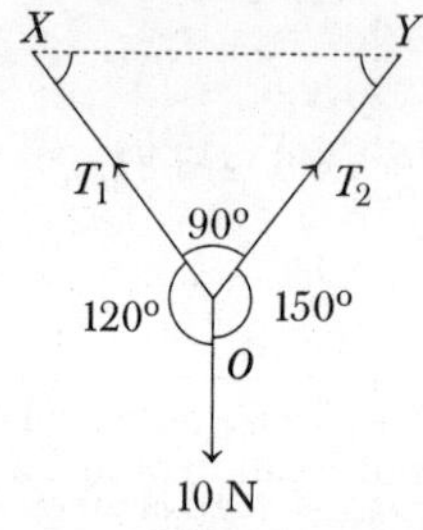

Applying Lami's theorem,

$$\frac{10}{\sin 90^\circ} = \frac{T_1}{\sin 150^\circ} = \frac{T_2}{\sin 120^\circ}$$

$\Rightarrow \tan\alpha = \frac{T_1}{T_2} = \frac{\sin 150^\circ}{\sin 120^\circ}$

$\Rightarrow \tan\alpha = \frac{1/2}{\sqrt{3}/2} = \frac{1}{\sqrt{3}} = \tan 30^\circ$

$\therefore \quad \alpha = 30^\circ$

51. Yes;

F_s = Spring force = kx

$\Rightarrow 50 = k \times 5 \times 10^{-2}$

$\therefore \quad k$ = spring constant

$= 10^3$ N/m

According to question,

$10^x = 10^3$

$\therefore \quad x = 3$

52. $\mu = \frac{F}{R} = \frac{mg\sin\theta}{mg\cos\theta} = \tan\theta$

53. (*a*);

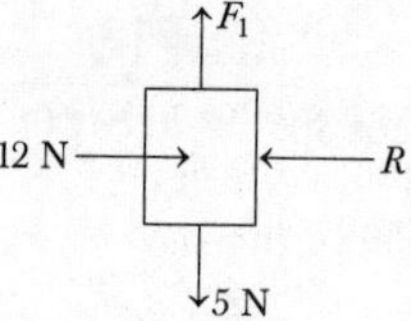

There is no relative motion between the block and the wall, then $R = 12$ N, $F_1 = 5$ N

Hence, the total force acting on wall,

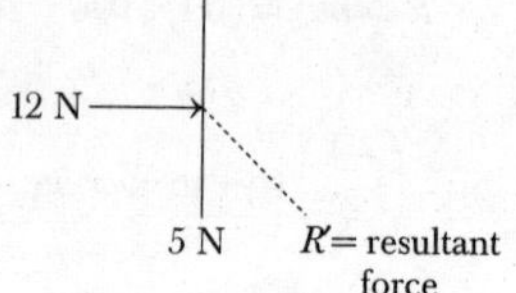

$$R' = \sqrt{(12)^2 + (5)^2} = \sqrt{169} = 13 \text{ N}$$

54. II

55. (*a*); The free body diagram of the system is shown below.

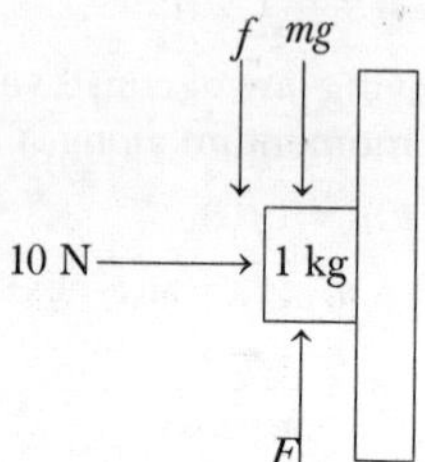

The moment before the block begins to move upward, all vertical forces sum to equal 0.

$\therefore \quad F - f - mg = 0$

$F = f + mg \quad \dots$(i)

$\because \quad f = \mu_s N \quad \dots$(ii)

from Eqs. (i) and (ii), we get

$F = \mu_s N + mg$

$\Rightarrow \quad F = (0.15 \times 10) + (1 \times 10)$

$F = 11.5$ N

56. (i), (ii); The friction acting between the non-moving body (at rest) and the surface is called static friction. And the friction acting between the moving body and the surface is called dynamic friction.

In 1st figure, the object is at rest on the surface, so it is showing static friction. In the second figure, the object is moving and hence, it is showing rolling friction.

57. (i) ✓ (ii) ✓ (iii) ✓;

(iii) As the acceleration of box is due to the static friction,

Therefore, $ma = \delta = \mu_s R$

$= \mu_s mg$

$\Rightarrow a_{\max} = \mu_s g = 0.15 \times 10$

$= 1.5 \text{ m/s}^2$

58.

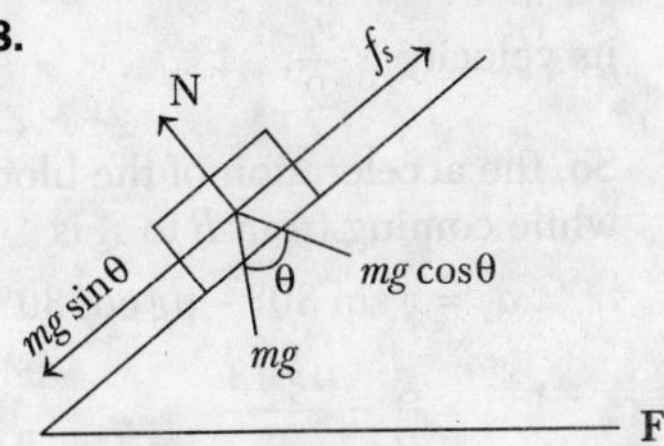

$N = mg\cos\theta$

$mg\sin\theta - f_s = 0$

$f_s = \mu N$

$mg\sin\theta = \mu mg\cos\theta$

$\mu = \tan\theta$

$\mu = \tan 15°$

$= 0.27$

59. (*c*);

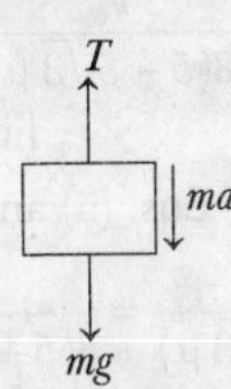

According to the free body diagram of the block,

$ma = T - mg$

$3a = T - 30 \quad \ldots(i)$

According to the free body diagram of the trolley,

$ma = T - f_k = T - \mu_k N$

$20a = T - 0.04 \times 20 \times 10 \quad \ldots(ii)$

Solving Eqs. (i) and (ii) for acceleration and tension, we get

$a = 0.96 \text{ m/s}^2$

and $T = 27.1 \text{ N}$

60. 20 N, 0.14;

Force of friction is given as

$f = T_1 - T_2$

$= 8 \times (10) - 6 \times (10) = 20 \text{ N}$

In equilibrium state, when the masses are about to move, the masses are stationary due to roughness of pulley.

i.e. Force on both sides are balanced. i.e.

$\Rightarrow \mu R = f = 20 \text{ N}$

$\Rightarrow \mu = \dfrac{20}{R} = \dfrac{20}{14 \times 10} = \dfrac{1}{7} = 0.14$

61. A → 2, B → 3, C → 1;

According to question,

$F_{\text{net}} = mg\sin\alpha - \mu mg\cos\alpha$

$= mg(\sin\alpha - \mu_0 xg\cos\alpha)$

$\Rightarrow a = \dfrac{F_{\text{net}}}{m} = g\sin\alpha - \mu_0 xg\cos\alpha$

$\therefore v\dfrac{dv}{dx} = g\sin\alpha - \mu_0 xg\cos\alpha$

or $\int_0^0 v\,dv = \int_0^{x_m} (g\sin\alpha - \mu_0 xg\cos\alpha)\,dx$

$0 = \left[-gx\sin\alpha - \mu_0 \dfrac{x^2}{2} g\cos\alpha\right]_0^{x_m}$

$\Rightarrow x_m = \dfrac{2}{\mu_0}\tan\alpha$

Therefore, maximum distance covered is $\dfrac{2}{\mu_0 \cot\alpha}$

Acceleration of mass at distance x is given as

$a = g(\sin\alpha - \mu_0 x\cos\alpha) = 0$

$\Rightarrow x = \dfrac{\tan\alpha}{\mu_0} = \dfrac{1}{\mu_0\cot\alpha}$

Maximum speed is given, at

$x = \dfrac{\tan\alpha}{\mu_0}$

$v_{\max} = \sqrt{\dfrac{g\sin\alpha\tan\alpha}{\mu_0}}$

62. (3.27);

$f = mg\sin 30° - 4mg\cos 30°$

$ma = mg\sin 30° - \mu mg\cos 30°$

$a = 3.27 \text{ m/s}^2$

$\therefore x = 3.27$

63. (*c*); Acceleration of the block is given by

$a = g(\sin\theta - \mu\cos\theta)$

$= g\left(\dfrac{1}{2} - 0.6 \times 0.866\right)$

$(\because \theta = 30°)$

$= g(0.5 - 0.511) = g(-0.0196)$

Thus, the acceleration is negative, hence the block will slow down and come to rest.

64. 14;

Centrifugal force is given by

$F = \dfrac{mv^2}{r}$

$25 = \dfrac{1}{4} \times \dfrac{v^2}{(1.96)}$

$\Rightarrow 25 \times 4 \times 1.96 = v^2$

$\Rightarrow 196 = v^2$

$\Rightarrow v = 14 \text{ m/s}$

65. 5

66. (*b*); The maximum speed with which a cyclist can take a turn without skidding will be

$v = \sqrt{\mu rg}$

$= \sqrt{(0.1) \times (100) \times (10)}$

$= 10 \text{ m/s}$

67. (*b*); According to question, the optimum speed without slipping,

$v = \sqrt{\mu_s Rg}$

$= \sqrt{(0.1) \times 3 \times 10} = \sqrt{3}$

$= 1.73 \text{ m/s}$

or $= 1.73 \times \dfrac{18}{5} = 6.23 \text{ km/h}$

Since, the possible speed without skidding on this road is 6.23 km/h. The cyclist will slip.

68. 10.15;

Optimum speed of the race car will be

$v_{\text{opt}} = \sqrt{rg\tan\theta}$

$= \sqrt{300 \times 10 \times \tan 15°}$

$\approx 28.35 \text{ m/s}$

Maximum speed permissible to avoid slipping,

$v_m = \sqrt{rg\left(\dfrac{\mu + \tan\theta}{1 - \mu\tan\theta}\right)}$

$= \sqrt{300 \times 10\left(\dfrac{0.2 + \tan 15°}{1 - 0.2\tan 15°}\right)}$

$= 38.5 \text{ m/s}$

Thus, $(v_m - v_{opt}) = (38.5 - 28.35)$
$= 10.15$ m/s

69. I, II

70. (i) ✓ (ii) ✓

71. (*a*); 12N → 3kg | 2kg | 1kg

$$a = \frac{F}{(m_1 + m_2 + m_3)}$$

$$= \frac{12}{3+2+1} = \frac{12}{6} = 2\text{ m/s}^2$$

N_2 = Net force on the 2 kg block by 1 kg block.

12 → [block] ← N_1 N_1 → [2kg] ← N_2

$$12 - N_1 = 3 \times 2$$
$$N_1 = 6\text{ N}$$
$$N_1 - N_2 = 2 \times 2 = 4$$
$$6 - N_2 = 4$$
$$N_2 = 2\text{ N}$$

72. 20 N vertically downward, 267.3 N vertically downward;

From the free body diagram of the block,

$$R = 2 \times 10 = 20\text{ N}$$

Therefore, by Newton's third law, the force exerted on the floor by the block is equal to 20 N directed vertically downwards. Now, the system (block + cylinder) accelerates downwards with 0.1 m/s^2.

Therefore, resultant force of gravity due to earth

$$= (25 + 2) \times 10 = 270\text{ N}$$

and normal reaction R by the floor must be producing this acceleration.

According to Newton's second law,

$$270 - R = 27 \times 0.1$$
$$\Rightarrow \quad R = 270 - 2.7 = 267.3\text{ N}$$

$\therefore$ By Newton's third law, action of the system on the floor is equal to 267.3 N, vertically downwards, the reaction R is vertically upwards.

73. 686;

The collective mass of block and three iron cylinders

$= 10 + 3 \times 20 = 70$ kg

a = acceleration of block = 0.2 ms^{-2}

$g = 10$ ms^{-2}, $\mu = 0.2$

and R = normal reaction

$\therefore$ Force along vertical axis:

The force equation in vertical direction is

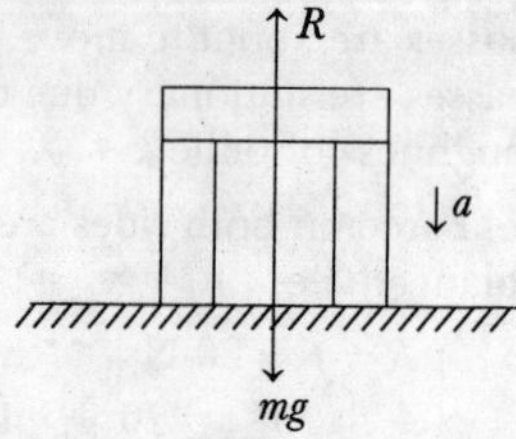

$$mg - R = ma$$

where, m is the collective mass of block and three iron cylinders.

$$\therefore \quad 70g - R = 70 \times 0.2$$
$$\Rightarrow \quad R = 70 \times 10 - 14 = 686\text{ N}$$

74. 3.33;

According to diagram, let f be the friction force applied on the body,

w be the weight $(= mg)$.

N be the normal reaction, thus frictional force will be $f = \mu N$.

$$\therefore \quad N = F\sin 60^\circ + mg$$

$$N = \frac{\sqrt{3}}{2}F + 10\sqrt{3} \quad \text{... (i)}$$

Similarly,

$$F_x = F\cos 60^\circ - \mu N = 0$$

From Eq. (i), we get

$$\Rightarrow \frac{F}{2} - \frac{1}{3\sqrt{3}}\left(\frac{\sqrt{3}}{2}F + 10\sqrt{3}\right) = 0$$

$$\Rightarrow \frac{F}{2} - \frac{F}{6} - \frac{10}{3} = 0$$

$$\Rightarrow \quad F = 10\text{ N}$$

Given, $F = 3x$

$$\Rightarrow \quad x = \frac{10}{3} = 3.33$$

75. 346;

The free body diagram of the given situation is shown below.

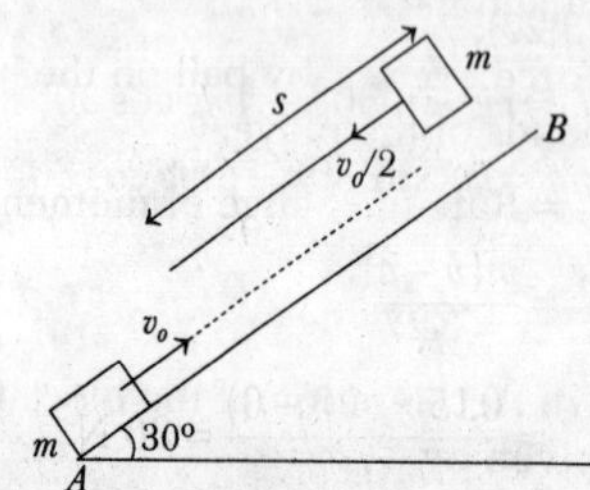

While going from A to B, the acceleration of the block,

$$a_1 = g\sin 30^\circ + \mu g\cos 30^\circ$$

$$\Rightarrow a_1 = \frac{g}{2} + \frac{\mu g\sqrt{3}}{2}$$

$$\Rightarrow a_1 = 5 + 5\sqrt{3}\mu \quad \text{... (i)}$$

Let s be the distance between A and B,

From third equation of motion,

$$v_0^2 - 0 = 2a_1 s$$

$$\Rightarrow \quad s = \frac{v_0^2}{2a_1} = \frac{v_0^2}{2(5 + 5\sqrt{3}\mu)} \quad \text{... (ii)}$$

[using Eq. (i)]

When the block come back to its initial position, i.e. from B to A, its velocity is $\frac{v_0}{2}$.

So, the acceleration of the block while coming from B to A is

$$a_2 = g\sin 30^\circ - \mu g\cos 30^\circ$$

$$= \frac{g}{2} - \frac{\mu g\sqrt{3}}{2}$$

$$= 5 - 5\sqrt{3}\mu \quad \text{... (iii)}$$

Again, using third equation of motion, we have

$$\left(\frac{v_0}{2}\right)^2 - 0 = 2a_2 s$$

$$\Rightarrow \quad \frac{v_0^2}{4} = 2a_2 s \Rightarrow s = \frac{v_0^2}{8a_2}$$

$$\Rightarrow \quad s = \frac{v_0^2}{8(5 - 5\sqrt{3}\mu)} \quad \text{... (iv)}$$

[using Eq. (iii)]

Equating Eqs. (ii) and (iv), we get

$$\frac{v_0^2}{2(5 + 5\sqrt{3}\mu)} = \frac{v_0^2}{8(5 - 5\sqrt{3}\mu)}$$

$$\Rightarrow \quad 4(5 - 5\sqrt{3}) = 5 + 5\sqrt{3}\mu$$

$$\Rightarrow \quad 25\sqrt{3}\mu = 15$$

$$\Rightarrow \quad \mu = \frac{15}{25\sqrt{3}} = \frac{3}{5\sqrt{3}} = \frac{\sqrt{3}}{5}$$

So, $\frac{I}{1000} = \frac{\sqrt{3}}{5} = 0.346$

$$\Rightarrow \quad I = 0.346 \times 1000 = 346$$

Assertion-Reason Questions

1. (*d*) Assertion is incorrect but Reason is correct.

Due to rotation of earth it is non-inertial frame. A frame moving with constant velocity is inertial.

2. (*b*) **3.** (*a*)
4. (*c*) **5.** (*b*)
6. (*b*)
7. (*d*); According to Newton's third law of motion, it is impossible to have a single force out of mutual interaction between two bodies, whether they are moving or at rest.
It means, third law of motion is applicable to all the bodies either at rest or in motion and this law is also applicable to all types of forces.
8. (*d*); Friction opposes the relative motion of the bodies in contact not the motion.
9. (*d*); Tension is non-uniform even if string is not accelerated.

10. (*a*); $(f_2)_{max} = \mu_2 mg$

$(f_1)_{max} = \mu_1(2m)g$

Since $(f_1)_{max} > (f_2)_{max}$

Lower block will not move at all.

Case Based Questions

1. (i) (*b*); Impulse = change in momentum

$= m\Delta V = 0.13\,(26 - (-14))$

$= 5.2$ Ns

(ii) (*c*); Impulse $= F \times t$

$\Rightarrow F = \frac{\text{Impulse}}{t} = \frac{5.2}{0.2} = 26$ N

(iii) (*a*); Force and acceleration are related as follows

$F = ma$

$\Rightarrow a = \frac{F}{m} = \frac{26}{0.13} = 200 \text{ m/s}^2$

(iv) (*d*) *Or* (*b*)

2. (i) (*d*); Given, $m_A = 4$ kg,

$m_B = 2$ kg, $m_C = 1$ kg and

$F = 12$ N

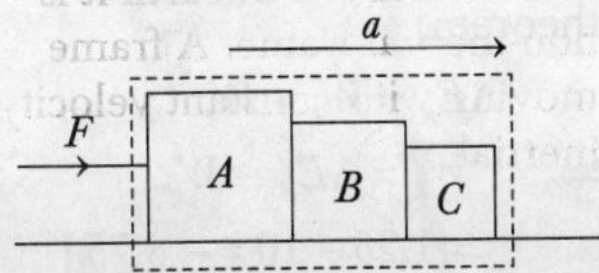

So, total mass,

$M = 4 + 2 + 1 = 7$ kg

Now, $F = Ma$

$\Rightarrow 12 = 7a$

$\Rightarrow a = \frac{12}{7} \text{ ms}^{-2}$

FBD of block *A*,

a
F → [4 kg] → F′

$F - F' = 4a$

$\Rightarrow F' = F - 4a$

$= 12 - \frac{4 \times 12}{7} = \frac{36}{7}$ N

Hence, the contact force between *A* and *B* is $\frac{36}{7}$ N.

(ii) (*b*); Normal force depends on the force acting on the body perpendicular to the ground. If some external force is also acting on the body perpendicular to the ground then normal force will be greater than mg.

Or

(*d*); Frictional force for rough surface is greater than frictional force for smooth surface.

(iii) (*c*); Total force exerted by the spring is

$F = -kx = -500 \times 0.25$

$= -125.0$ N

(iv) (*c*)

Competition Edge Up

1. (*b*); Given, mass of ball = 150 g

$= 0.15$ kg

Initial speed of ball = 20 m/s

Final speed of ball = 0 m/s

Time for process of catching = 0.1 s

Force exerted by ball on the hands of the player

= Rate of change of momentum

$= \frac{m(v-u)}{t}$

$= \frac{0.15 \times (20 - 0)}{0.1} = 30$ N

2. (*d*); The branch pulls the chain by a force given by

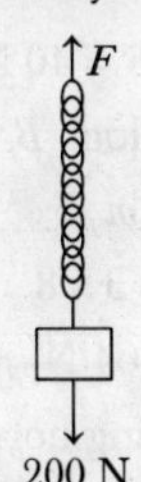

F = weight of body + weight of chain

$= 200 + mg$

$= 200 + (10 \times 10) = 300$ N

3. (*b*); According to given situation

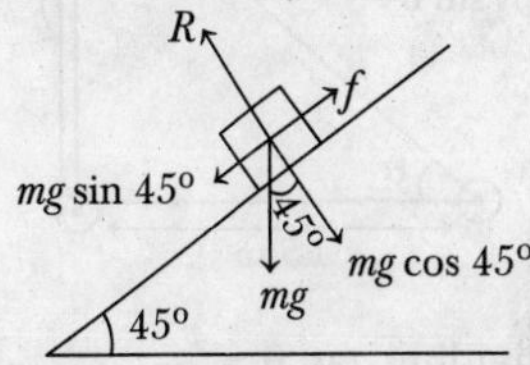

Friction = Component of weight along the plane

i.e. $\mu R = mg \sin 45°$

$\Rightarrow \mu mg \cos 45° = mg \sin 45°$

$\Rightarrow \mu = 1$

4. (*d*);

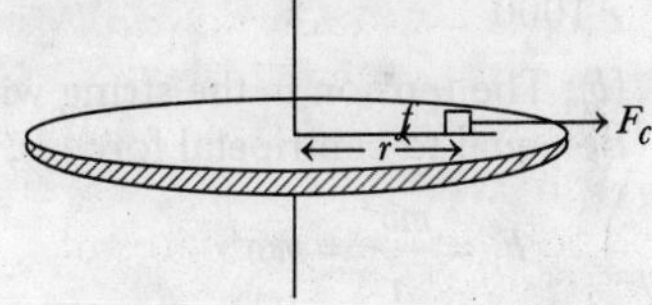

Forces on the coin is centripetal force which is provided by the friction.

So, $f = F_c$

$\mu mg = \frac{mv^2}{r}$, $v = r\omega$

$\mu mg = mr\omega^2$

$\therefore$ Angular speed upto which coin holds is,

$\omega = \sqrt{\mu g / r}$

5. (*c*);

A: 5 kg —T_1— B: 3 kg —T_2— C: 2 kg → $F = 80$ N; $\mu = 0$

Acceleration of system

$= \frac{\text{Net force}}{\text{Total mass}} = \frac{80 \text{ N}}{10 \text{ kg}} = 8 \text{ m/s}^2$

Force on block A,

$T_1 = m_A \times a$

$= 5 \times 8 = 40$ N

Force on block B,

$T_2 - T_1 = m_B a$

$T_2 - 40 = 3 \times 8$

$T_2 = 64$ N

6. (*b*); Resolving normal,

$N \cos\theta = mg$ ...(i)

$N \sin\theta = \dfrac{mv^2}{R}$ ...(ii)

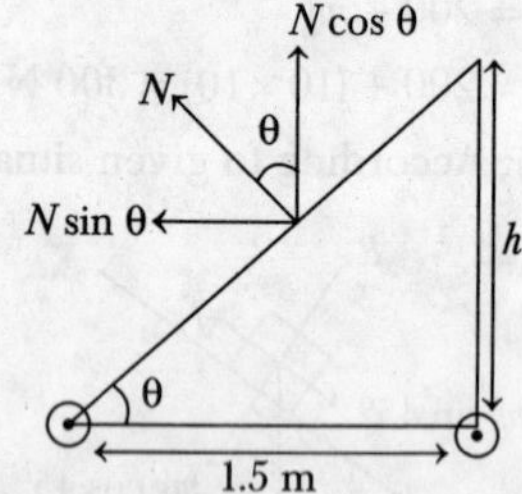

Dividing, $\tan\theta = \dfrac{v^2}{Rg}$

$\dfrac{h}{1.5} = \dfrac{12 \times 12}{400 \times 10}$

$\Rightarrow h = \dfrac{1.5 \times 12 \times 12}{400 \times 10}$

$= \dfrac{54}{1000} = 0.054 \text{ m} = 5.4 \text{ cm}$

7. (*b*); The tension in the string will be equal to centripetal force is,

$F_c = \dfrac{mv^2}{r} = m\omega^2 r$

According to question, $T = m\omega^2 r$

and $T' = m(2\omega)^2 r$

$\dfrac{T'}{T} = \dfrac{m(4\omega^2)r}{m\omega^2 r} \Rightarrow T' = 4T$

8. (*c*); Net force on A and $B = 10$ N

Acceleration of both A and $B = \dfrac{F}{m}$

F=10 N → [A][B]

$a = \dfrac{10}{5} = 2 \text{ ms}^{-2}$

For block A,

F=10 N → [2 kg] ← F_B ($\vec{a}$)

F_B = force exerted by block B on block A.

$F - F_B = 2 \times a$

$\Rightarrow 10 - F_B = 2 \times 2$

$\Rightarrow F_B = 6$ N

[A] → T_1, $m \rightarrow a$

For block B,

F_A → [3 kg] ($\vec{a}$)

T_1 ← [B] → T_2, $m \rightarrow a$

Force exerted by A on B,

$F_A = 3a = 6$ N

9. (*b*); Given, $\mu = 0.15$

For the given situation,

$F = ma = \mu mg$

$\Rightarrow a = \mu g = 0.15 \times 10 = 1.5 \text{ ms}^{-2}$

10. (*b*); We know that,

$|\text{Impulse}| = m\,|\Delta\bar{v}|$

where, $\Delta\bar{v} = v_2 - v_1$

Here, v_2 is velocity reaches to the same height,

v_1 is velocity just before striking to the ground.

For case (1), ball dropped from the 10 m height and strikes to the ground.

Now, the velocity of the ball just before striking to the ground will be

$v_1 = -\sqrt{2gh}$

$\Rightarrow v_1 = -\sqrt{2(10)(10)}$

$\Rightarrow v_1 = -10\sqrt{2}$ m/s

For case (2), ball rebounds to the same height. The velocity with which the ball just reaches to the same height,

$v_2 = \sqrt{2gh}$

$\Rightarrow v_2 = \sqrt{2(10)(10)}$

$\Rightarrow v_2 = 10\sqrt{2}$ m/s

Now, magnitude of the impulse imparted to the ball,

$|\text{Impulse}| = m\,|\Delta\bar{v}|$

$= 0.15\ |10\sqrt{2} - (-10\sqrt{2})|$

$= 0.15\ |2 \times 10\sqrt{2}|$

$= 4.2$ kg-m/s

Chapter-5

Work, Energy and Power

1. No;

$\mathbf{A} \cdot \mathbf{B} = \lambda |\mathbf{A}|^2$

$\Rightarrow AB\cos\theta = \lambda A^2$

$\therefore \cos\theta = \dfrac{\lambda A}{B} \neq 1$

$\therefore$ **A** is not parallel to **B**.

2. (*d*); $\mathbf{A} \cdot \mathbf{B} = AB\cos\theta$

$\therefore \mathbf{A} \cdot \mathbf{B} = 0,$

if (i) $\mathbf{A} = 0$

(ii) $\mathbf{B} = 0$

(iii) $\theta = 90°$ ($\mathbf{A} \perp \mathbf{B}$)

3. 12;

$W_{A \to B} = K_f - K_i$

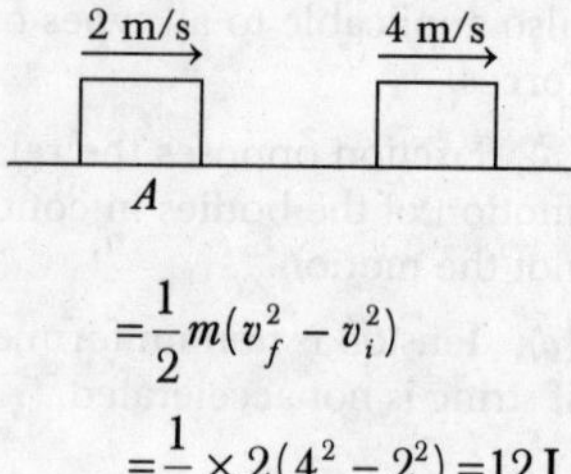

$= \dfrac{1}{2} m(v_f^2 - v_i^2)$

$= \dfrac{1}{2} \times 2(4^2 - 2^2) = 12$ J

4. −146;

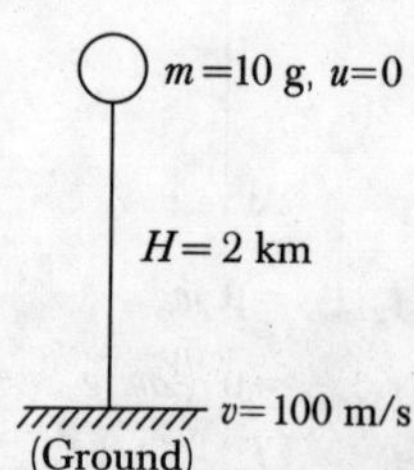

By work-energy theorem,

$\Rightarrow W_{\text{resistance}} = \dfrac{1}{2} m(v^2 - u^2) - mgH$

$= \dfrac{1}{2} \times \dfrac{10}{1000} \times (100^2 - 0^2) - \dfrac{10}{1000} \times 9.8 \times 2 \times 10^3$

$= -146$ J

5. II;

$\Delta E_K = \dfrac{1}{2} mv^2 - 0$

$= \dfrac{1}{2} \times 10^{-3} \times 50^2$

$= 1.25$ J

$W_g = mgh$

$= 10^{-3} \times 10 \times 10^3$

$\Rightarrow W_g = 10$ J

According to work-energy theorem,

$\Delta E_K = W_g + W_r$

$\Rightarrow W_r = \Delta E_K - W_g$

$= 1.25 - 10 = -8.75$ J

6. 0.625;

By work-energy theorem,

$$W_{net} = \Delta K = \frac{1}{2}m(v^2 - u^2) = \frac{1}{2}ma^2t^2$$

$[\because u = 0, v = u + at = at]$

$$= \frac{1}{2} \times 20 \times \left(\frac{5}{20}\right)^2 \times 1^2 = 0.625 \text{ J}$$

7. $-\frac{1}{2}mu^2$;

By work-energy theorem,

$$W_{gravity} = \Delta K = \frac{1}{2}m(v^2 - u^2) = \frac{1}{2}m(0^2 - u^2)$$

$$\therefore W_{gravity} = -\frac{1}{2}mu^2$$

8. 10.19 ms^{-1};

$$W = \frac{1}{2}m(v^2 - u^2) \quad \dots \text{(i)}$$

Putting all values in Eq. (i), we get

$$100 = \frac{1}{2}(2)(v^2 - 2^2)$$

$$\Rightarrow v = 10.19 \text{ ms}^{-1}$$

9. $\cos^{-1}\frac{2}{3}$;

$$\cos\theta = \frac{\mathbf{F}\cdot\mathbf{d}}{|\mathbf{F}|\cdot|\mathbf{d}|} = \frac{(\hat{\mathbf{i}} + 2\hat{\mathbf{j}} - \hat{\mathbf{k}})\cdot(\hat{\mathbf{i}} + 2\hat{\mathbf{j}} + \hat{\mathbf{k}})}{\sqrt{(1)^2 + (2)^2 + (-1)^2}\cdot\sqrt{(1)^2 + (2)^2 + (1)^2}}$$

$$\therefore \cos\theta = \frac{4}{6} = \frac{2}{3} \Rightarrow \theta = \cos^{-1}\frac{2}{3}$$

10. (a); $\mathbf{d} = \mathbf{r}_2 - \mathbf{r}_1 = (4\hat{\mathbf{i}} + 3\hat{\mathbf{k}}) - (-2\hat{\mathbf{i}} + 5\hat{\mathbf{j}}) = 6\hat{\mathbf{i}} - 5\hat{\mathbf{j}} + 3\hat{\mathbf{k}}$

$$\therefore W = \mathbf{F}\cdot\mathbf{d} = (4\hat{\mathbf{i}} + 3\hat{\mathbf{j}})\cdot(6\hat{\mathbf{i}} - 5\hat{\mathbf{j}} + 3\hat{\mathbf{k}}) = 9 \text{ J}$$

11. 0;

$$x = (t-3)^2$$

$$\therefore v(t) = \frac{dx}{dt} = 2(t-3)$$

$$\therefore v_i = v(t=0) = 2(0-3) = -6 \text{ m/s}$$

$$\therefore v_f = v(t = 6\text{s}) = 2(6-3) = 6 \text{ m/s}$$

By work-energy theorem,

Work done, $W = K_f - K_i = \frac{1}{2}m[v_f^2 - v_i^2] = \frac{1}{2}m[(6)^2 - (-6)^2] = 0$

12. −9;

Work done, $W = \int_{r_i}^{r_f} \mathbf{F}\cdot d\mathbf{r}$

$$\int_{(2\text{m}, 3\text{m}, 4\text{m})}^{(1\text{m}, 2\text{m}, 3\text{m})} (2\hat{\mathbf{i}} + 3\hat{\mathbf{j}} + 4\hat{\mathbf{k}})\cdot(dx\hat{\mathbf{i}} + dy\hat{\mathbf{j}} + dz\hat{\mathbf{k}})$$

$$= [2x + 3y + 4z]_{(2\text{m}, 3\text{m}, 4\text{m})}^{(1\text{m}, 2\text{m}, 3\text{m})} = -9 \text{ J} = -9 \times 10^7 \text{ erg}$$

13. 2.88;

Net force on the body,

$$F_{net} = \text{Applied force} - \text{Friction} = 20 - \mu mg = 20 - 0.2 \times 1 \times 10$$

$$\Rightarrow m \cdot a = 18 \text{ N}$$

$$\Rightarrow a = \frac{18}{m} = \frac{18}{1} = 18 \text{ m/s}^2$$

$\therefore$ Distance travelled by the body in 4s, $s = \frac{1}{2}at^2 = \frac{1}{2} \times 18 \times 4^2 = 144$ m

$$\therefore W = F \times s = 20 \times 144 = 2880 \text{ J} = 2.88 \text{ kJ}$$

14. 5 : 4;

We know that, $p = \sqrt{2mE}$

$$\Rightarrow \frac{p_1}{p_2} = \sqrt{\frac{m_1}{m_2}}\cdot\sqrt{\frac{E_1}{E_2}}$$

or $\frac{E_1}{E_2} = \frac{m_2}{m_1} = \frac{5}{4}$ $[\because p_1 = p_2]$

15. $E_K = \frac{p^2}{2m} \Rightarrow p = 2m\sqrt{E_K}$

Graph of $\sqrt{E_K}$ *versus* $\frac{1}{p}$ is

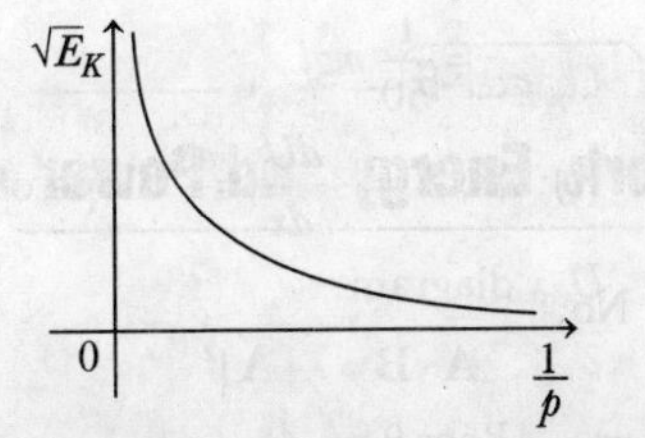

16. True

17. I;

$$E = \frac{1}{2}mv^2$$

$$\therefore v_2 = v_1 + 2$$

$$\therefore \frac{K_1}{K_2} = \left(\frac{v_1}{v_2}\right)^2$$

$$\Rightarrow \frac{1}{2} = \frac{v_1^2}{(v_1 + 2)^2} \quad (\because K_2 = 2K_1)$$

$$\Rightarrow v_1 = 2(\sqrt{2} + 1) \text{ m/s}$$

18. 300;

$$p_2 = (1 + 100\%)\,p_1 = 2p_1$$

$$\frac{K_2}{K_1} = \frac{p_2^2}{2m} \times \frac{2m}{p_1^2} = \left(\frac{p_2}{p_1}\right)^2 = (2)^2 = 4$$

$$\therefore K_2 = 4K_1$$

$\therefore$ % increase in KE

$$= \left(\frac{K_2 - K_1}{K_1}\right) \times 100\% = \left(\frac{4K_1 - K_1}{K_1}\right) \times 100\% = 300\%$$

19. True;

$$(\text{KE})_1 = \frac{1}{2}mu^2$$

$$(\text{KE})_2 = \frac{1}{2}mv^2 = \frac{1}{2}m(2u)^2 \quad [\because v = 2u]$$

$$= 4\left(\frac{1}{2}mu^2\right) = 4(\text{KE})_1$$

Hence, $\text{KE}_2 = 4(\text{KE})_1$

20. $E_1 < E_2$;

As we know, $\text{KE} = \frac{p^2}{2m}$

$$\therefore \frac{E_1}{E_2} = \frac{p_1^2}{2m_1} \times \frac{2m_2}{p_2^2} = \frac{m_2}{m_1} \quad (\because p_1 = p_2)$$

$$\because m_1 > m_2 \Rightarrow E_2 > E_1$$

So, $E_1 < E_2$

21. 15 ;

As, $W = \int_{x_1}^{x_2} F \cdot dx$

= Area of trapezium $OABC$

$$= \frac{1}{2}(2 + 8) \times 3 = 15 \text{ J}$$

22. (*b*); Work done = Area of *F-d* diagram

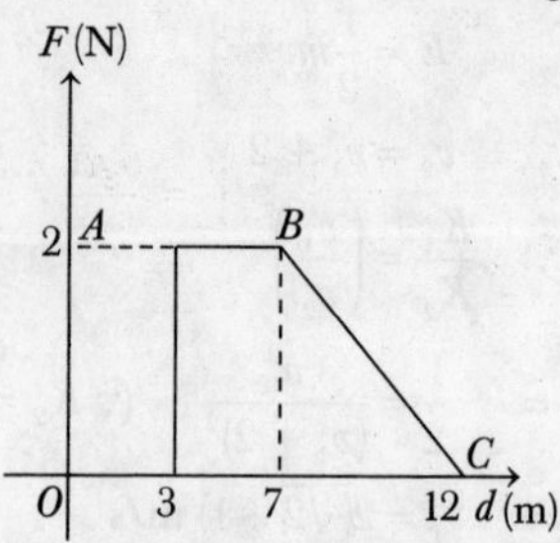

$\therefore$ Work done

$= \text{Area of trapezium } OABC$

$= \frac{1}{2} \times (7 + 12) \times 2 = 19 \text{ J}$

23. (*c*); Work done = Area of *F-x* diagram

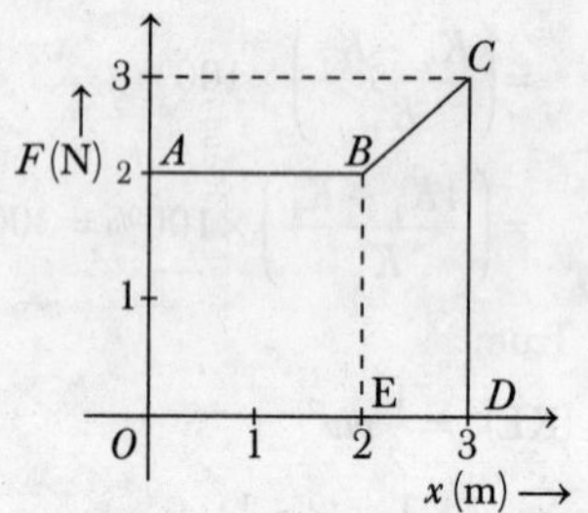

$= \text{Area } (OABE) + \text{Area}(EBCD)$

$= 2 \times 2 + \frac{1}{2}(2 + 3) \times 1$

$= 6.5 \text{ J}$

Initially particle is at rest, hence kinetic energy of the particle at a distance 3 m = 6.5 J

24. 135;

$$W = \int_{x_1}^{x_2} F \cdot dx$$

$$= \int_0^5 (7 - 2x + 3x^2) dx$$

$$= \left[7x - 2 \cdot \frac{x^2}{2} + 3 \cdot \frac{x^3}{3}\right]_0^5$$

$$= 7 \times 5 - (5)^2 + (5)^3 = 135 \text{ J}$$

25. (*a*); $W = \int_{x_1}^{x_2} \mathbf{F} \cdot d\mathbf{x}$

$u = 10 \text{ ms}^{-1}$, $m = 10$ kg, $F = 0.1\, x$ J/m, $x = 20$ m, $x = 30$ m, x-direction

$$= \int_{x_1}^{x_2} F dx \cos 180°$$

$$\therefore W = \int_{20}^{30} (-0.1x) dx$$

$$= \left[-0.1 \cdot \frac{x^2}{2}\right]_{20}^{30} = -25 \text{ J}$$

Now, by work-energy theorem,

$$W = K_f - K_i = K_f - \frac{1}{2} mu^2$$

$$\Rightarrow -25 = K_f - \frac{1}{2} \times 10 \times (10)^2$$

$$\therefore \quad K_f = 475 \text{ J}$$

26. 1;

Since, $K_f - K_i = \int_{x_i}^{x_f} F dx$

$$\Rightarrow \quad K_f = K_i + \int_{0.1}^{2.01} \frac{(-k)}{x} dx$$

$$\Rightarrow \quad \frac{1}{2} mv_f^2 = \frac{1}{2} mv_i^2 - k \ln (x)\Big|_{0.1}^{2.01}$$

$$\Rightarrow \frac{1}{2} mv_f^2 = \frac{1}{2} \times 1 \times 2^2 - k \ln (20.1)$$

$$\Rightarrow \quad \frac{1}{2} mv_f^2 = 2 - 1.5$$

$$\Rightarrow \quad \frac{1}{2} mv_f^2 = 0.5 \text{ J}$$

$$\therefore \quad v_f = \sqrt{\frac{2 \times 0.5}{m}}$$

$$= \sqrt{\frac{1}{1}} = 1 \text{ m/s}$$

27. $\frac{mgl}{50}$;

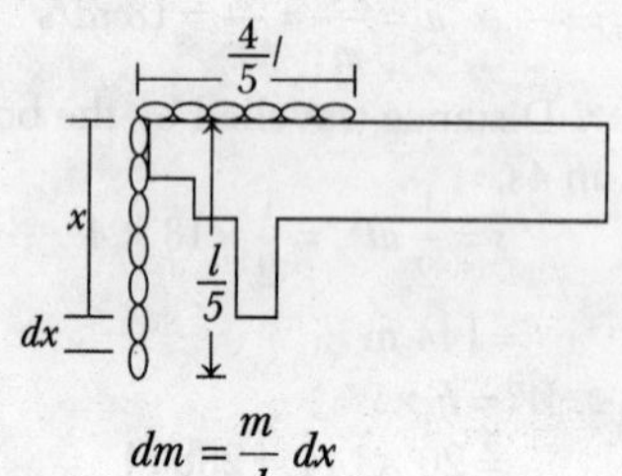

$$dm = \frac{m}{l} dx$$

By work-energy theorem,

$$W_{\text{ext}} + W_{\text{gravity}} = \Delta K = 0$$

$$\therefore \quad W_{\text{ext}} = -W_{\text{gravity}}$$

$$\text{Now, } W_{\text{gravity}} = \int_0^{l/5} -\left(\frac{m}{l} dx\right) g \cdot x$$

$$= -\frac{mg}{l} \int_0^{l/5} x dx = -\frac{1}{50} mgl$$

$$\therefore W_{\text{ext}} = -\left(-\frac{1}{50} mgl\right)$$

$$= \frac{1}{50} mgl$$

28. (*b*); As, $F = -\frac{dU}{dx} = -$ Slope of *U-x* diagram

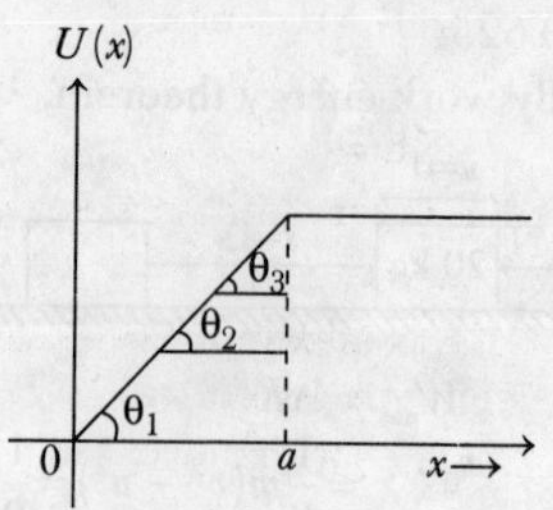

Slope between 0 to a = constant ($\because \theta_1 = \theta_2 = \theta_3 \ldots$)

$\therefore$ Force between 0 to a

$= -\text{(constant)} = -c$

Force between a to ∞

$$= -\frac{d}{dx}\text{(constant)} = 0$$

So, F versus x graph is

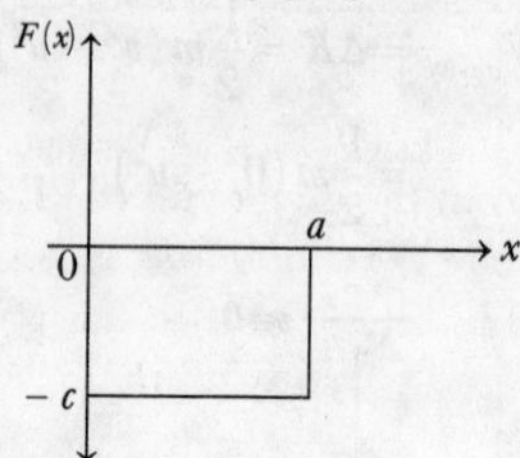

29. $4\sqrt{3}$;

Total energy, $E = \text{KE} + \text{PE}$

At $\quad x = x_1$,

$10 = \text{KE} + (-2)$

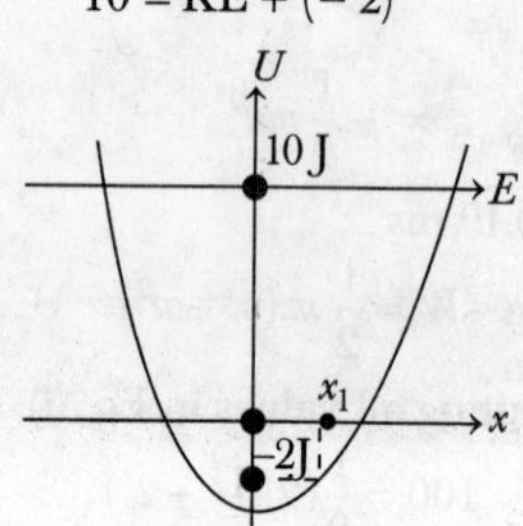

$\Rightarrow \quad \text{KE} = 12 \text{ J}$

Now, $\text{KE} = \frac{1}{2} m(v)^2$

$$\Rightarrow \quad 12 = \frac{1}{2} \times 0.5 \times v^2$$

$$\therefore \quad v(x_1) = 4\sqrt{3} \text{ m/s}$$

30. (*b*); As, $E_{\text{mech}} = \text{KE} + \text{PE}$

At $\quad x > x_4$,

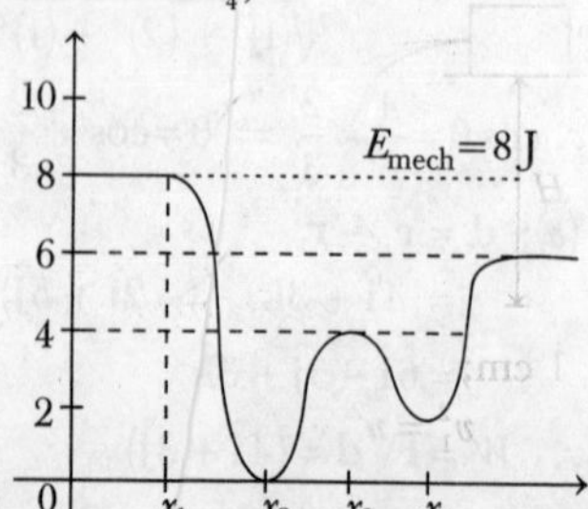

$KE = 8 - 6 = 2\,J$

$\therefore$ KE = constant at $x > x_4$

At $x < x_1$,

$KE = 8 - 8 = 0$

$\therefore$ KE is zero and particle is at rest.

At $x = x_2$, $KE = 8 - 0 = 8\,J$

$\therefore$ KE is maximum and particle is moving at fastest speed.

At $x = x_3$, $KE = 8 - 4 = 4\,J$

31. *A*;

Total energy = KE + PE

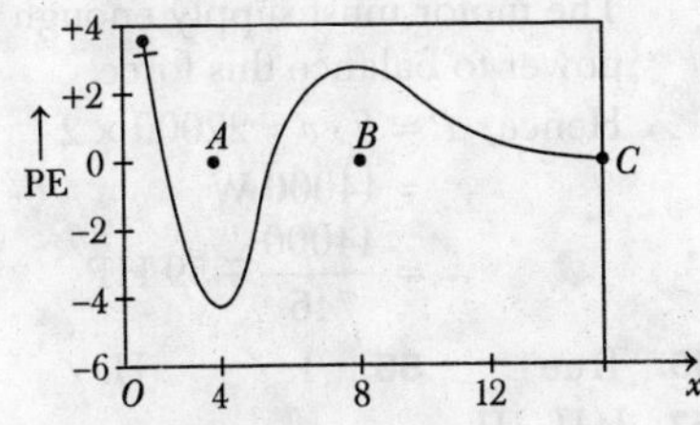

$\therefore$ $KE_{max} = (E)_{max} - (PE)_{min}$

From the given graph, PE at $A = -4\,J$ (minimum)

$\therefore$ On point *A*, kinetic energy of particle is maximum.

32. – 0.5;

As, $F = -\dfrac{dU}{dx}$

$= -\dfrac{d}{dx}\left(\dfrac{1}{2}kx^2\right) = -kx$

$\therefore F|_{x = 1m} = -0.5 \times 1 = -0.5\,N$

Hence, force on particle at $x = 1$ m is – 0.5 N.

33. $10\sqrt{2}$;

By conservation of mechanical energy,

decrease in PE = increase in KE

$\Rightarrow \quad mgh = \dfrac{1}{2}mv^2$

$\Rightarrow 1 \times 10 \times 10 = \dfrac{1}{2} \times 1 \times v^2$

$\therefore \quad v = 10\sqrt{2}$ m/s

34. True;

As height is same for all tracks *A*, *B* and *C*.

$\therefore \quad W_A = W_B = W_C = mgH$

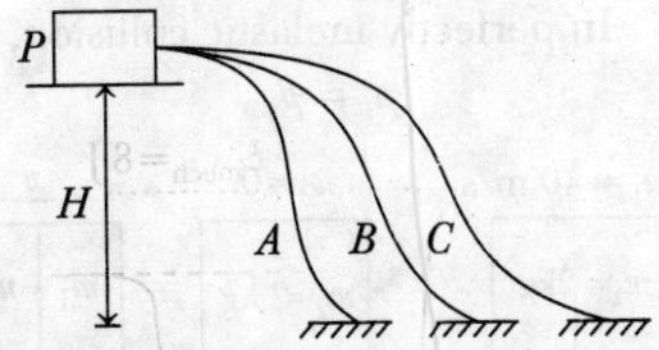

35. 1 cm;

$v_1^2 = u^2 + 2as$

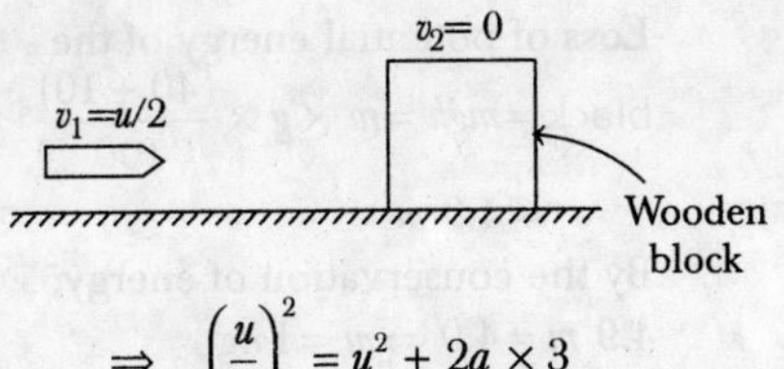

$\Rightarrow \quad \left(\dfrac{u}{2}\right)^2 = u^2 + 2a \times 3$

$\therefore \quad a = -\dfrac{u^2}{8}$

Again, $v_2^2 = u^2 + 2as$

$0^2 = u^2 + 2\left(-\dfrac{u^2}{8}\right) \cdot s$

$\therefore \quad s = 4$ cm

$\therefore$ Change in displacement $= 4 - 3 = 1$ cm

36. (*b*); As, $T_{top} = \dfrac{mv^2}{r} - mg$

and $T_{bottom} = \dfrac{mv^2}{r} + mg$

$\Rightarrow \dfrac{T_{top}}{T_{bottom}} = \dfrac{\dfrac{40 \times 40}{4} - 10}{\dfrac{40 \times 40}{4} + 10} = \dfrac{39}{41}$

37. 4 rad/s;

Maximum tension that string can bear = 3.7 kg-wt = 37 N

Tension at lowest point of vertical loop $= mg + m\omega^2 r$

$\Rightarrow \quad 37 = 0.5 \times 10 + 0.5 \times \omega^2 \times 4$

$= 5 + 2\omega^2$

$\Rightarrow \quad \omega = 4\ \text{rad s}^{-1}$

38. 5 : 1;

According to figure given in question, at point *C*, string is slacked.

$\therefore \quad T_C = 0$

$\therefore \quad T_C + mg = \dfrac{mv_C^2}{R}$

$\therefore \quad v_C = \sqrt{gR}$ ...(i)

$\dfrac{mv_c^2}{R}$ ↑ C • ↓ mg ↓ T_C

$\therefore$ Decrease in KE = Increase in PE

$\Rightarrow \quad \dfrac{1}{2}m(v_A^2 - v_C^2) = mg(2R)$

$\Rightarrow \quad \dfrac{1}{2}m[v_A^2 - (\sqrt{gR})^2] = 2mgR$ [using Eq. (i)]

$\therefore \quad v_A = \sqrt{5gR}$

$\therefore \quad \dfrac{(KE)_A}{(KE)_C} = \dfrac{\dfrac{1}{2}mv_A^2}{\dfrac{1}{2}mv_C^2}$

$= \left(\dfrac{v_A}{v_C}\right)^2 = \dfrac{5gR}{gR} = \dfrac{5}{1}$

39. 2.5 ;

At equilibrium,

$mg = kx$

$g = 10\ m/s^2$, k, k, $x = 20$ cm, $m = 50$ kg, mg, $m = 50$ kg

$\therefore \quad 50 \times 10 = k \times 0.2$

$\Rightarrow \quad k = 2.5$ kN/m

40. 50;

U = PE of spring

$= \dfrac{1}{2}kx^2 = \dfrac{1}{2}\left(\dfrac{mg}{x}\right) \cdot x^2$

$\therefore U = \dfrac{1}{2}mgx = \dfrac{1}{2} \times 50 \times 10 \times 0.2$

$(\because g = 10\ m/s^2)$

$\Rightarrow \quad U = 50\,J$

41. (*a*)

42. 2;

At maximum compression, the kinetic energy of the car is converted entirely into the potential energy of the spring.

The kinetic energy of the moving car,

$E_K = \dfrac{1}{2}mv^2 = \dfrac{1}{2} \times 1000 \times 5^2$

$= 1.25 \times 10^4\,J$

$(\because v = 18\ \text{km/h} = 5\ \text{m/s})$

According to principle of conservation of energy,

$U = E_K$

$\dfrac{1}{2}kx_m^2 = 1.25 \times 10^4$

$\Rightarrow \frac{1}{2} \times 6.25 \times 10^3 \times x_m^2$

$= 1.25 \times 10^4$

$\Rightarrow \quad x_m = 2\text{ m}$

43. I;

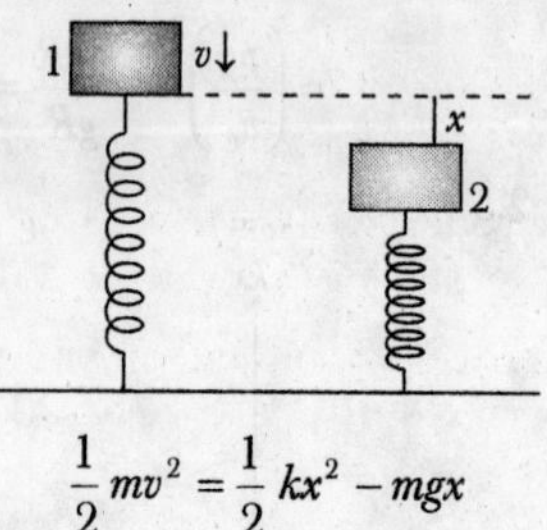

$$\frac{1}{2} mv^2 = \frac{1}{2} kx^2 - mgx$$

44. False;

It is not given in question that out of k_1 and k_2 which one is greater.

45. 16;

By work-energy theorem,

$$(\text{WD})_{\text{total}} = K_f - K_i = \frac{1}{2} m(v^2 - u^2)$$

$$= \frac{1}{2} \times 40000 \left[0^2 - \left(72 \times \frac{5}{18} \right)^2 \right]$$

$$= -800 \times 10^4 \text{ J}$$

Now, because 90% of total energy is lost.

$\therefore \ (\text{WD})_{\text{net}} = (1 - 0.9) \times (\text{WD})_{\text{total}}$

$\therefore \ (\text{WD})_{\text{net}} = -0.1 \times 800 \times 10^4 \text{ J}$

As, $\text{WD} = \int F dx = -\int k \cdot x dx$

$$= -\frac{1}{2} kx^2$$

$$\therefore -0.1 \times 800 \times 10^4 = \frac{k \cdot (1)^2}{2}$$

$\Rightarrow \quad k = 16 \times 10^5 \text{ N/m}$

46. True;

We know that, potential energy of the spring,

$$U = \frac{1}{2} kx^2$$

$\Rightarrow \quad U \propto x^2$

$$\Rightarrow \quad \frac{U_2}{U_1} = \left(\frac{x_2}{x_1} \right)^2$$

$$\Rightarrow U_2 = U_1 \left(\frac{x_2}{x_1} \right)^2 = 20 \left(\frac{5}{4} \right)^2$$

$$= 31.25 \text{ J}$$

47. I;

Energy stored in compressed spring

$$= \frac{1}{2} kx^2 = \frac{1}{2} \times 980 \times \left(\frac{10}{100} \right)^2$$

$$= 4.9 \text{ J}$$

Loss of potential energy of the block $= mgh = m \times g \times \frac{(40 + 10)}{100}$

$$= 4.9\, m$$

By the conservation of energy,

$4.9\, m = 4.9 \Rightarrow m = 1 \text{ kg}$

48. *(a)*

49. True;

$$\text{Power, } P = \frac{W}{t} = \frac{mgh}{t}$$

$$= \frac{100 \times 10 \times 100}{1} = 100 \text{ kW}$$

50. 2.05;

By work-energy theorem,

$$\text{Work done} = \frac{1}{2} m (v^2 - u^2)$$

$$= \frac{1}{2} \times 2.05 \times 10^6 \times (25^2 - 5^2)$$

$$= 615 \text{ MJ}$$

$$\therefore \text{Power} = \frac{\text{Work done}}{\text{Time}} = \frac{615}{5 \times 60}$$

$$= 2.05 \text{ MW}$$

51. 28000;

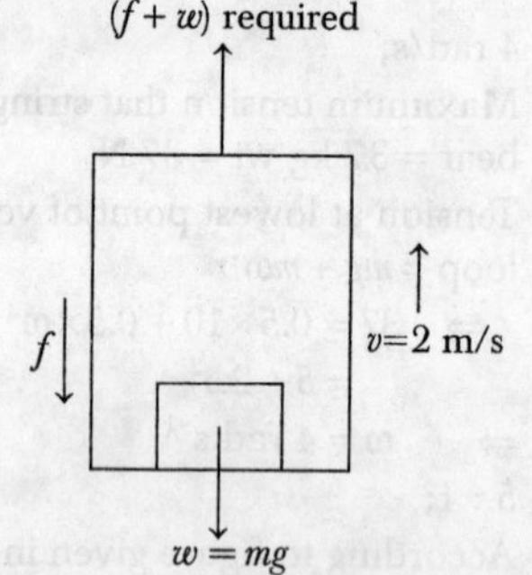

Power = Force × Velocity

$\therefore \quad P = (w + f) \cdot v$

$= (1200 \times 10 + 2000) \times 2$

$= 28000 \text{ W}$

52. *(a)* ;

$$\text{Rate of KE} = \frac{\text{KE}}{\text{Time}} = \frac{1}{2} \left(\frac{M}{t} \right) v^2$$

$$= \frac{1}{2} \cdot \frac{ml}{t} v^2 = \frac{1}{2} mv^3 \quad \left(\because v = \frac{l}{t} \right)$$

53. *(d)*; By work-energy theorem,

Work done, W

$$= \Delta K = \frac{1}{2} m(v^2 - u^2)$$

$$= \frac{1}{2} mv^2 \qquad (\because u = 0)$$

$$\text{Now, } P = \frac{W}{t} = \frac{\frac{1}{2} mv^2}{t}$$

$$\Rightarrow \quad v = \left(\frac{2P}{m} \right)^{\frac{1}{2}} \cdot t^{\frac{1}{2}} = \frac{dx}{dt}$$

$$\Rightarrow \quad x = \int dx = \left(\frac{2P}{m} \right)^{\frac{1}{2}} \int t^{\frac{1}{2}} dt$$

$$\therefore \quad x = \left(\frac{8P}{9m} \right)^{\frac{1}{2}} \cdot t^{\frac{3}{2}}$$

54. I, II;

The net downward force on the elevator,

$F = mg + F_f$

$= (1800 \times 10) + 4000$

$= 22000 \text{ N}$

The motor must supply enough power to balance this force.

Hence, $P = F \cdot v = 22000 \times 2$

$= 44000 \text{ W}$

$$= \frac{44000}{746} \simeq 59 \text{ HP}$$

55. True **56.** I. ✓ II. ✓

57. I, II, III

58. $\frac{1}{2} \left(\frac{Mm}{M + m} \right) v^2$;

v → m; v = 0 M; = ; v′ → M+m

Since, $F_{\text{ext}} = 0$

$\therefore$ By conservation of linear momentum,

$p_i = p_f$

$\Rightarrow \quad mv + 0 = (M + m)v'$

$$\therefore \quad v' = \left(\frac{mv}{M + m} \right) \qquad \dots(\text{i})$$

Now, heat generated

$= \text{Loss of KE} = K_i - K_f$

$$= \frac{1}{2} mv^2 - \frac{1}{2} (M + m) v'^2$$

$$= \frac{1}{2} mv^2 - \frac{1}{2} (M + m) \left(\frac{mv}{M + m} \right)^2$$

[using Eq. (i)]

$$= \frac{1}{2} mv^2 \left(\frac{M}{M + m} \right)$$

$$\therefore \text{Heat generated} = \frac{1}{2} \left(\frac{Mm}{M + m} \right) v^2$$

59. 5;

In perfectly inelastic collision,

$p_i = p_f$

$u_1 = 10$ m/s, $m_1 = 2$ kg; $u_2 = 0$, $m_2 = 2$ kg; ≡ m_1 m_2 → v

$m_1 u_1 + m_2 u_2 = (m_1 + m_2)\, v$

$\Rightarrow \quad 2 \times 10 + 0 = (2 + 2)\, v$

$\therefore \quad v = 5 \text{ m/s}$

60. True;

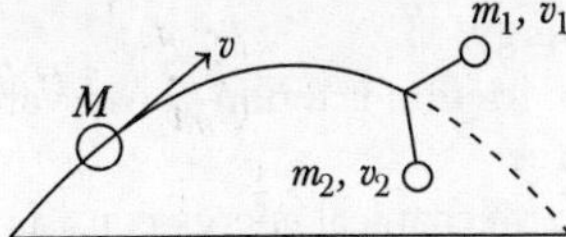

When a body explodes in mid-air, it gets separated into small pieces which has higher velocity than previous one. Hence, total kinetic energy is increased during explosion.

61. $4m$;

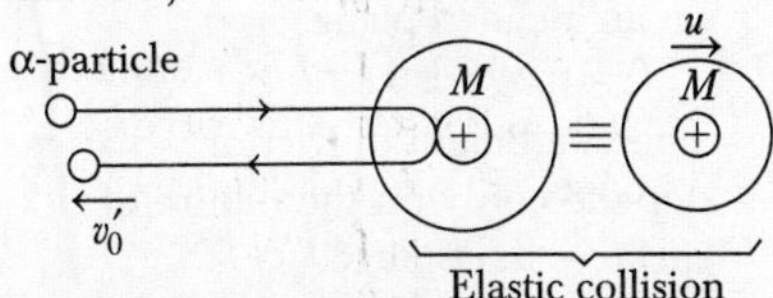

According to question,

$$\frac{1}{2}mv_0'^2 = (1-0.64)\frac{1}{2}mv_0^2$$

$$\therefore \quad v_0' = 0.6v_0 \quad \ldots\text{(i)}$$

Now, by conservation of linear momentum, $p_i = p_f$

$$mv_0 = Mu - mv_0'$$

$$= Mu - m(0.6v_0) \quad \text{[from Eq. (i)]}$$

$$\therefore \quad \frac{M}{m} = 1.6\left(\frac{v_0}{u}\right) \quad \ldots\text{(ii)}$$

By conservation of KE,

$$\frac{1}{2}mv_0^2 = \frac{1}{2}Mu^2 + \frac{1}{2}mv_0'^2$$

$$\therefore \quad \frac{M}{m} = \frac{0.4v_0^2}{u^2} \quad \ldots\text{(iii)}$$

$$(\because v_0' = 0.6\, v_0)$$

From Eqs.(ii) and (iii), we get

$$u = 0.4v_0$$

$\therefore$ From Eq. (ii), $M = 4\,m$

62. False;

Since, collision is elastic,

$$\therefore v_1 = \left(\frac{m_1 - m_2}{m_1 + m_2}\right)u_1 + \left(\frac{2m_2}{m_1 + m_2}\right)u_2$$

$$\therefore \quad v_1 = \left(\frac{4m - 2m}{4m + 2m}\right)u_1 = \frac{u_1}{3}$$

Now, ΔK = Loss of KE of body A

$$= \frac{1}{2}m_1u_1^2 - \frac{1}{2}m_1v_1^2$$

$$= \frac{1}{2}(4m)u_1^2 - \frac{1}{2}(4m)\left(\frac{u_1}{3}\right)^2$$

$$\Delta K = \frac{16}{9}mu_1^2 \quad \ldots\text{(i)}$$

$\therefore$ Fraction of KE lost by body

$$A = \frac{\Delta K}{\frac{1}{2}m_1u_1^2}$$

$$= \frac{16mu_1^2}{9} \times \frac{2}{m_1u_1^2} \quad (\because m_1 = 4\,m)$$

[using Eq. (i)]

$$= \frac{8}{9}$$

63. (*d*);

Since, collision is elastic.

$$\therefore \quad v_1 = \left(\frac{m_1 - m_2}{m_1 + m_2}\right)u_1 + \left(\frac{2m_2}{m_1 + m_2}\right)u_2$$

$$= \left(\frac{2m}{2m}\right)(-0.3)$$

$$\therefore \quad v_1 = -0.3\text{ m/s}$$

$$v_2 = \left(\frac{2m_1}{m_1 + m_2}\right)u_1 - \left(\frac{m_1 - m_2}{m_1 + m_2}\right)u_2$$

$$= \left(\frac{2m}{2m}\right)(0.5) = 0.5\text{ m/s}$$

$$\therefore v_2 = 0.5\text{ m/s}$$

64. (i) (✓) (ii) (✓) (iii) (✓) (iv) (✓)

65. $\frac{8}{9}$;

When two bodies of mass m_1 and m_2 collides elastically, then fraction of kinetic energy transferred from body first to body second

$$= \frac{4m_1m_2}{(m_1 + m_2)^2} = \frac{4 \times 1 \times 2}{(1+2)^2} = \frac{8}{9}$$

66. 1; When collision is elastic

$$v_1 = \left(\frac{m_1 - m_2}{m_1 + m_2}\right)u_1 + \left(\frac{2m_2}{m_1 + m_2}\right)u_2$$

$$v_2 = \left(\frac{2m_1}{m_1 + m_2}\right)u_1 - \left(\frac{m_1 - m_2}{m_1 + m_2}\right)u_2$$

$\therefore$ $v_1 = u_2$ and $v_2 = u_1$, if $m_1 = m_2$

$$\therefore \frac{m_a}{m_b} = 1$$

67. (*a*);

$$15m + 10m = mv_1 + mv_2$$

$$\Rightarrow \quad 25 = v_1 + v_2 \quad \ldots\text{(i)}$$

and $\quad \frac{v_2 - v_1}{u_1 - u_2} = 1$

$$\Rightarrow \quad \frac{v_2 - v_1}{15 - 10} = 1$$

$$\Rightarrow \quad v_2 - v_1 = 5 \quad \ldots\text{(ii)}$$

Solving Eqs. (i) and (ii), we get

$v_2 = 15\text{ ms}^{-1}$, $v_1 = 10\text{ ms}^{-1}$

68. 60 J ;

According to question, $F_{ext} = 0$

Applying conservation of linear momentum,

$$p_i = p_f$$

$$\therefore \quad m_1u_1 + m_2u_2 = (m_1 + m_2)v$$

$$\Rightarrow 2 \times 36 \times \frac{5}{18} + 3 \times 0 = (2+3)\,v$$

$$\Rightarrow \quad v = 4\text{ m/s}$$

$\therefore$ Loss in KE

$$= \frac{1}{2}\left(\frac{m_1m_2}{m_1 + m_2}\right)(u_1 - u_2)^2$$

$$= \frac{1}{2}\left(\frac{2 \times 3}{2 + 3}\right)(10 - 0)^2 = 60\text{ J}$$

69. 400;

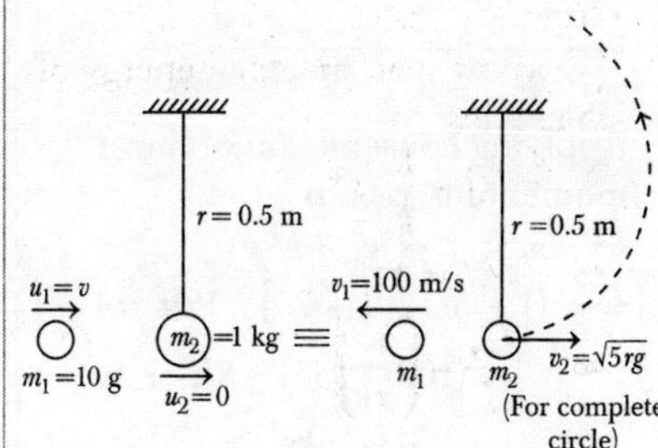

Minimum velocity of bob at bottom of a pendulum for complete circle, $v_2 = \sqrt{5rg}$

$$= \sqrt{5 \times 0.5 \times 10}$$

$$\Rightarrow \quad v_2 = 5\text{ m/s}$$

As, $\quad F_{ext} = 0$

So, applying conservation of linear momentum,

$p_i = p_f$

$\Rightarrow \quad m_1u_1 + m_2u_2 = m_1v_1 + m_2v_2$

$\Rightarrow \quad \frac{10}{1000} \times v + 1 \times 0$

$= \frac{10}{1000} \times (-100) + 1 \times 5$

$\therefore \quad v = 400 \text{ m/s}$

70. (*d*);

For elastic collision of *A* and *B*,

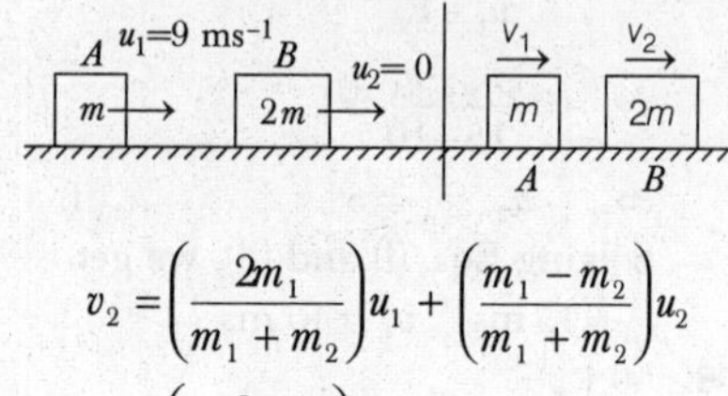

$$v_2 = \left(\frac{2m_1}{m_1 + m_2}\right)u_1 + \left(\frac{m_1 - m_2}{m_1 + m_2}\right)u_2$$

$$= \left(\frac{2m}{m + 2m}\right) \times 9 + 0$$

$\Rightarrow v_2 = 6 \text{ m/s}$

For completely inelastic collision of *B* and *C*,

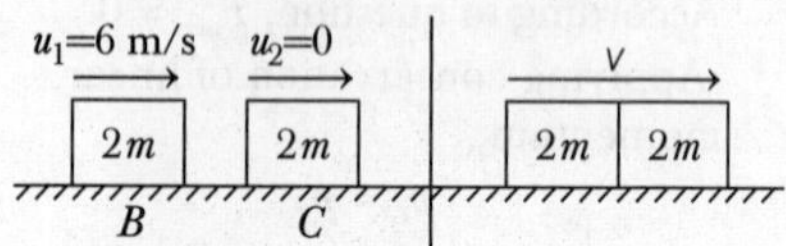

Applying conservation of linear momentum, $p_i = p_f$

$m_1u_1 + m_2u_2 = (m_1 + m_2)\, v$

$\Rightarrow 2m(6) + m_2(0) = (2m + 2m)\, v$

$\therefore \quad v$ = velocity of *B* after collision = velocity of *C* after collision = 3 m/s

71. (*a*);

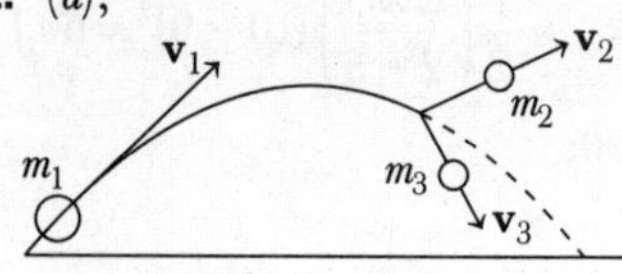

$\because \quad F_{\text{ext}} = 0$

Applying conservation of linear momentum, $\mathbf{p}_i = \mathbf{p}_f$

$\Rightarrow \quad m_1\mathbf{v}_1 = m_2\mathbf{v}_2 + m_3\mathbf{v}_3$

$\Rightarrow \quad (1 + 5)\,(20\hat{\mathbf{i}} + 25\hat{\mathbf{j}} - 12\hat{\mathbf{k}}) = 1$

$(100\hat{\mathbf{i}} + 35\hat{\mathbf{j}} + 8\hat{\mathbf{k}}) + 5\mathbf{v}_3$

$\therefore \ \mathbf{v}_3 = 4\hat{\mathbf{i}} + 23\hat{\mathbf{j}} - 16\hat{\mathbf{k}}$

72. $\frac{4}{3}$;

As, $F_{\text{ext}} = 0$

u=0   5m $mv\hat{i}$ $mv\hat{j}$ 3m   v′

Applying conservation of linear momentum, $\mathbf{p}_i = \mathbf{p}_f$

$\Rightarrow 5m \times \mathbf{u} = mv\hat{\mathbf{i}} + mv\hat{\mathbf{j}} + 3m\mathbf{v}'$

$\therefore \quad v' = +\frac{\sqrt{2}v}{3}$

$\therefore \ \Delta K$ = Increase in KE $= K_f - K_i$

$= \frac{1}{2}mv^2 + \frac{1}{2}mv^2 + \frac{1}{2}(3m)(v')^2$

$= \frac{4}{3}mv^2$

According to question, energy released

$$= xmv^2 = \frac{4}{3}mv^2$$

$$\therefore \quad x = \frac{4}{3}$$

Assertion-Reason Questions

1. (*b*); $W = \mathbf{F} \cdot \mathbf{d} = Fd\cos\theta$

$= mgd\cos 90° = 0$

$\therefore \quad W = 0$

2. (*c*); For work to be done by a force, point of application of force must not be stationary. If a body is moving, its point of application may not move in a frame.

3. (*a*)

4. (*b*)

5. (*c*); **Assertion** Change in PE is same.

Reason Acceleration is different. Hence, net force is different.

6. (*c*); Coefficient of friction is the mutual property of two surfaces. It does not depend on angle of inclination.

7. (*a*); As we know that, spring force,

$$F_s = kx$$

Given, $F = k_1x_1 = k_2x_2\,;\ \frac{k_1}{k_2} = \frac{x_2}{x_1}$

The work done in stretching is equal to elastic potential energy, i.e. $W = E = \frac{1}{2}kx^2$

$$\Rightarrow \quad \frac{W_1}{W_2} = \frac{E_1}{E_2} = \frac{k_1x_1^2}{k_2x_2^2}$$

$$= \frac{k_1}{k_2}\cdot\left(\frac{k_2}{k_1}\right)^2 = \frac{k_2}{k_1}\left(\because \frac{x_1}{x_2} = \frac{k_2}{k_1}\right)$$

$\Rightarrow$ Since, $k_1 > k_2$, so $W_2 > W_1$.

8. (*a*); In case of friction, work done in moving a body over a closed path is never zero. It is because some work is converted into heat energy.

So, friction is a non-conservative force.

9. (*c*); Mechanical energy consists of both PE and KE. In the given cases, some of the mechanical energy is converted into heat energy and it is more in the case when inclination is less due to increased (as θ decreases, value of $\cos\theta$ will increases) friction force on an inclined plane.

$$f_r = \mu mg\cos\theta$$

The coefficient of friction depends only on the nature of surfaces in contact.

10. (*c*); Work done by friction on *A* is positive and on *B* is negative. If there is no slipping between the two blocks, then $s_A = s_B$. Therefore, net work done will be zero, otherwise not.

Case Based Questions

1. (i) (*b*)

(ii) (*c*); When work done by the conservative force is negative, then change in potential energy will be positive i.e. potential energy of the system will increase.

(iii) (*c*); Weight
$= mg = (2)\,(10) = 20$ N

Work done by the applied force, $W_F = Fh\cos 0°$

As the angle between force and displacement is 0°

or $W_F = (40)\,(2)\,(1) = 80$ J

(iv) (*d*); $W = \int_0^5 F dx$

$= \int_0^5 (7 - 2x + 3x^2)dx$

$= [7x - x^2 + x^3]_0^5$

$= 7\,(5 - 0) - (5^2 - 0) + (5^3 - 0)$

$= (35 - 25 + 125) = 135$ units

Or

(*b*); $W = \mathbf{F}\cdot\mathbf{S} = \mathbf{F}\cdot(\mathbf{r}_2 - \mathbf{r}_1)$

$= (\hat{\mathbf{i}} + 2\hat{\mathbf{j}} + 3\hat{\mathbf{k}})\cdot[(\hat{\mathbf{i}} - \hat{\mathbf{j}} + 2\hat{\mathbf{k}}) - (\hat{\mathbf{i}} + \hat{\mathbf{j}} + \hat{\mathbf{k}})]$

$= (\hat{\mathbf{i}} + 2\hat{\mathbf{j}} + 3\hat{\mathbf{k}})\cdot(-2\hat{\mathbf{j}} + \hat{\mathbf{k}})$

$= -4 + 3 = -1$ J

2. (i) (*a*); From $x = 0$ to $x = 2$ m, displacement of particle and force acting on the particle both are along positive x-direction. Therefore, work done is positive and given by the area under F-x graph, or

$$W = \frac{1}{2}(2)(10) = 10 \text{ J}$$

$$\therefore \quad P = \frac{W}{t} = \frac{10}{1} = 10\text{W}$$

(ii) (*b*); Since, centripetal force is perpendicular to velocity in uniform circular motion.

$$\therefore \quad P = \mathbf{F} \cdot \mathbf{v} = Fv\cos 90° = 0$$

(iii) (*c*); $P = \frac{W}{t}$

$$\therefore \quad t = \frac{W}{P} = \frac{mgh}{P}$$

$$= \frac{200 \times 10 \times 40}{10 \times 10^3} = 8 \text{ s}$$

Or

(*b*); $\quad P = F \cdot v$

$$\therefore \quad F = \frac{P}{v} = \frac{7500}{20} = 375\text{N}$$

(iv) (*c*); Two forces are acting on bob, i.e. tension and weight. Power of tension will be zero and that of weight is,

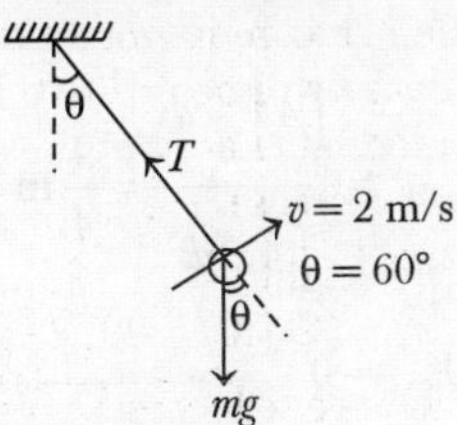

$$P = mgv\cos(90° + \theta)$$

$$= -mgv\sin 60°$$

$$= -50 \times 9.8 \times 2 \times \frac{\sqrt{3}}{2}$$

$$= -490\sqrt{3}\text{ W}$$

$\therefore$ Power delivered is $490\sqrt{3}$ W.

Competition Edge Up

1. (*a*); Given, $v = \alpha\sqrt{x}$, at $x = 0, v = 0$

at $\quad x = d, v = \alpha\sqrt{d}$

$$\text{WD} = K_f - K_i = \frac{1}{2}mv_f^2 - \frac{1}{2}mv_i^2$$

$$\Rightarrow \frac{1}{2}m(v_f^2 - v_i^2)$$

$$= \frac{1}{2}m[(\alpha\sqrt{d})^2 - \frac{1}{2}m(0)^2]$$

$$= \frac{1}{2}m\alpha^2 d$$

2. (*d*); $mgh = \mu mg(2 + x) + \frac{1}{2}kx^2$

$$5 \times 10 \times 5 = 0.5 \times 5 \times 10 \times (2 + x) + \frac{1}{2} \times 100 \times x^2$$

$$250 = 25 \times (2 + x) + 50x^2$$

$$50x^2 + 25x - 200 = 0$$

$$x \approx 1.77 \text{ m}$$

$$x = 2 \text{ m}$$

3. (*c*); Given,

$$K_A = K_B = K_C$$

$$\Rightarrow \frac{1}{2}m_A v_A^2 = \frac{1}{2}m_B v_B^2 = \frac{1}{2}m_C v_C^2$$

$$\Rightarrow \frac{m_A^2 v_A^2}{m_A} = \frac{m_B^2 v_B^2}{m_B} = \frac{m_C^2 v_C^2}{m_C}$$

$$\Rightarrow \frac{p_A^2}{m_A} = \frac{p_B^2}{m_B} = \frac{p_C^2}{m_C}$$

$$\Rightarrow \frac{p_A}{\sqrt{m_A}} = \frac{p_B}{\sqrt{m_B}} = \frac{p_C}{\sqrt{m_C}}$$

$$\Rightarrow p_A : p_B : p_C = \sqrt{m_A} : \sqrt{m_B} : \sqrt{m_C}$$

$$= \sqrt{400} : \sqrt{1200} : \sqrt{1600}$$

$$= 2 : 2\sqrt{3} : 4$$

$$= 1 : \sqrt{3} : 2$$

4. (*b*); According to given situation,

$$K_i = \frac{1}{2}mv_i^2$$

$$= \frac{1}{2}m(100)^2$$

and $\quad K_f = \frac{1}{2}mv_f^2 = \frac{1}{2}m(40)^2$

$\therefore$ Percentage loss (in KE)

$$= \left(\frac{K_i - K_f}{K_i}\right) \times 100$$

$$= \frac{\frac{1}{2}m(100)^2 - \frac{1}{2}m(40)^2}{\frac{1}{2}m(100)^2} \times 100$$

$$= \frac{10000 - 1600}{10000} \times 100 = 84\%$$

5. (*a*); Kinetic energy K and momentum p are related as

$$K = \frac{p^2}{2m}$$

For same mometnum, $K \propto \frac{1}{m}$

Particle A has least mass.

$\therefore$ Particle A has maximum kinetic energy.

6. (*d*); Since, $P = Fv = mav$ $\quad [\because F = ma]$

$$= ma \cdot at$$

$$P = ma^2 t \quad [\because v = at]$$

$$\Rightarrow a = \sqrt{\frac{P}{mt}}$$

We know that, $s = ut + \frac{1}{2}at^2$

$$= \frac{1}{2}at^2 = \frac{1}{2}\sqrt{\frac{P}{mt}} \cdot t^2 \quad [\because u = 0]$$

$$s = \frac{1}{2}\sqrt{\frac{P}{m}} \cdot t^{3/2} \Rightarrow s \propto t^{3/2}$$

7. (*c*); Given force, $\mathbf{F} = 6t\,\hat{i} + 6t^2\hat{j}$

and mass, $m = 2$ kg

Acceleration $\mathbf{a} = \frac{\mathbf{F}}{m} = 3t\,\hat{i} + 3t^2\hat{j}$

So, velocity at time t is,

$$\mathbf{v} = \int \mathbf{a} \cdot dt = \int (3t\hat{i} + 3t^2\hat{j})\,dt$$

$$= \frac{3}{2}t^2\,\hat{i} + t^3\hat{j}$$

$$\text{Power} = \mathbf{F} \cdot \mathbf{v}$$

$$= (6t\hat{i} + 6t^2\hat{j}) \cdot \left(\frac{3}{2}t^2\hat{i} + t^3\hat{j}\right)$$

$$= (9t^3 + 6t^5)\text{ W}$$

8. (*a*); Given,

$$x = 2t - 1 \text{ unit}$$

Force, $F = 5$ N

Instantaneous power, $P = F.v$

Thus, $P = F\frac{dx}{dt}$

$$= 5 \times \frac{d(2t-1)}{dt}$$

$$= 5 \times 2 = 10 \text{ unit}$$

9. (*b*); Let both masses be m

A →v_1 B (Before) AB →v_2 (After)

Thus, applying conservation of momentum, we get

$$m_1u_1 + m_2u_2 = m_1v_1 + m_2v_2$$

Both masses A and B stick together as a system.

So, $\quad mv_1 = 2mv_2 \quad [\because u_2 = 0]$

$$v_1 = 2v_2$$

$$\Rightarrow \frac{v_1}{v_2} = \frac{2}{1}$$

10. (*c*); $\quad U = \frac{1}{2}kx^2$

$$\frac{U_1}{U_2} = \frac{x_1^2}{x_2^2}$$

$$\frac{U_1}{U_2} = \frac{(2)^2}{(8)^2}$$

$$U_2 = \frac{64}{4}U = 16U$$

Chapter-6

System of Particles and Rotational Motion

1. True **2.** I, II

3. P_1, Translational motion

4. $\left(\frac{7}{12}\text{ m}, \frac{\sqrt{3}}{4}\text{ m}\right)$

From the given diagram,

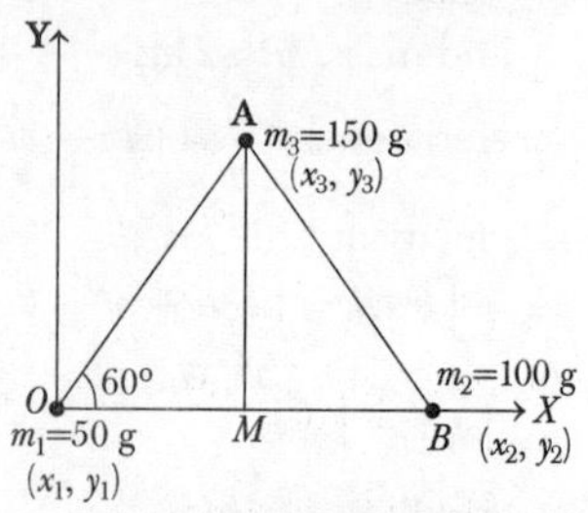

$$x_1 = 0, y_1 = 0$$
$$x_2 = 1\text{ m}, y_2 = 0$$
$$x_3 = \frac{1}{2}\text{ m} = 0.5\text{ m}$$
$$y_3 = AM = \sqrt{OA^2 - OM^2}$$
$$= \sqrt{1^2 - (0.5)^2} = \frac{\sqrt{3}}{2}\text{ m}$$
$$\therefore \quad X_{CM} = \frac{m_1x_1 + m_2x_2 + m_3x_3}{m_1 + m_2 + m_3}$$
$$= \frac{50 \times 0 + 100 \times 1 + 150 \times 0.5}{50 + 100 + 150}$$
$$= \frac{7}{12}\text{ m}$$

Similarly,

$$Y_{CM} = \frac{m_1y_1 + m_2y_2 + m_3y_3}{m_1 + m_2 + m_3}$$
$$= \frac{50 \times 0 + 100 \times 0 + 150 \times \frac{\sqrt{3}}{2}}{50 + 100 + 150}$$
$$= \frac{\sqrt{3}}{4}\text{ m}$$

5. (0, 0);

$$X_{CM} = \frac{m_1x_1 + m_2x_2}{m_1 + m_2}$$
$$= \frac{m(-4) + m(4)}{m + m} = 0$$
$$(\because m_1 = m_2 = m)$$
$$Y_{CM} = \frac{m \times 0 + m \times 0}{m + m} = 0$$

6. $\left(\frac{-3}{2}, \frac{-3}{2}, \frac{-3}{2}\right)$;

Let x_1, x_2 and x_3 be the initial centre of mass of particles of mass 10 g, 20 g and 30 g, respectively.

Then, the coordinate of centre of mass in this case is given by

$$\frac{10x_1 + 20x_2 + 30x_3}{10 + 20 + 30} = 1$$
$$10x_1 + 20x_2 + 30x_3 = 60 \quad \text{...(i)}$$

New centre of mass when 40 g mass is added to the system is given by

$$10x_1 + 20x_2 + 30x_3 + 40x_4 = 0 \quad \text{...(ii)}$$

From Eqs. (i) and (ii), we can write

$$60 + 40x_4 = 0$$
$$\Rightarrow \quad x_4 = \frac{-3}{2}$$

The coordinates will be $\left(\frac{-3}{2}, \frac{-3}{2}, \frac{-3}{2}\right)$.

7. $\left(\frac{5}{12}, \frac{2}{3}\right)$;

Let the coordinates of the centre of mass be (x, y).

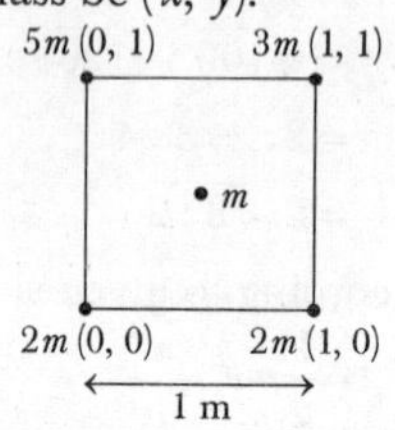

$$X_{CM} = \frac{m_1x_1 + m_2x_2 + m_3x_3 + m_4x_4}{m_1 + m_2 + m_3 + m_4}$$
$$= \frac{2m(0) + 2m(1) + 3m(1) + 5m(0)}{12m}$$
$$= \frac{5}{12}$$
$$Y_{CM} = \frac{m_1y_1 + m_2y_2 + m_3y_3 + m_4y_4}{m_1 + m_2 + m_3 + m_4}$$
$$= \frac{2m(0) + 2m(0) + 3m(1) + 5m(1)}{12m} = \frac{2}{3}$$

So, the coordinates of CM is $\left(\frac{5}{12}, \frac{2}{3}\right)$.

8. (i) × (ii) × (iii) ✓ (iv) ✓

Coordinates of mass, $m_1 = (0, 0)$

Coordinates of mass, $m_2 = (1.4, 0)$

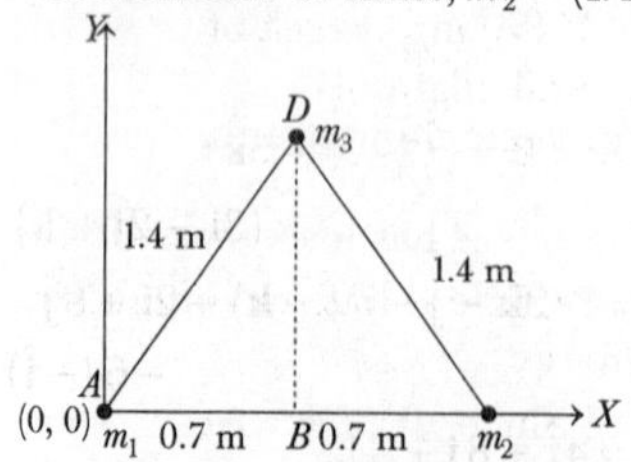

In ΔABD, by Pythagoras theorem,

$$AD^2 = AB^2 + BD^2$$
$$(1.4)^2 = (0.7)^2 + BD^2$$
$$\Rightarrow \quad BD = 1.21\text{ m}$$

Coordinates of mass,

$$m_3 = (0.7\text{m}, 1.21\text{ m})$$
$$\therefore X_{CM} = \frac{m_1x_1 + m_2x_2 + m_3x_3}{m_1 + m_2 + m_3}$$
$$= \frac{12(0) + 25(1.4) + 38(0.7)}{12 + 25 + 38}$$
$$= 82.1\text{ cm}$$

Similarly,

$$Y_{CM} = \frac{m_1y_1 + m_2y_2 + m_3y_3}{m_1 + m_2 + m_3}$$
$$= 61.3\text{ cm}$$

9. $\left(4x^2 \cdot dx, \frac{32}{3}, \frac{9}{4}, 0\right)$;

A. $\lambda(x) = \frac{dm}{dx} = 4x^2$

$$dm = 4x^2 \cdot dx$$

B. $m = \int_0^2 dm = \int_0^2 4x^2 \cdot dx$

$$= \frac{4}{3}[x^3]_0^2 = \frac{32}{3}\text{ kg}$$

C. $X_{CM} = \frac{\int_0^3 x \cdot dm}{\int_0^3 dm}$

$$= \frac{\int_0^3 4x^3 \cdot dx}{\int_0^3 4x^2 dx} = \frac{9}{4}\text{ m}$$
$$Y_{CM} = 0$$

10. (b)

11. $\frac{b}{2}, \frac{h}{3}$

12. A → 2, B → 3, C → 4, D → 4

13. II

14. Yes

15. B

16. $\frac{11}{8}$;

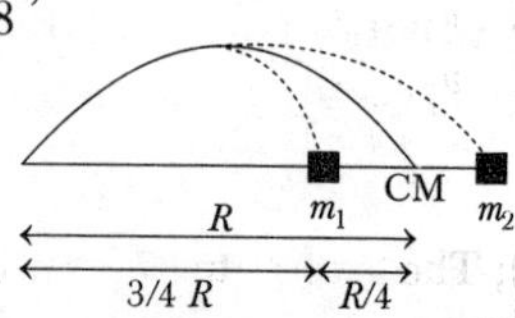

This is an example of explosion which has no external influence. After the explosion, the centre of mass will continue to follow the parabolic path regardless, where the fragments fall.

The centre of mass will rest at a distance R from the point of projection.

$$m_1x_1 = m_2x_2$$
$$3\times\frac{R}{4} = 2\times x_2$$
$$\Rightarrow \quad x_2 = \frac{3}{8}R$$

So, the other fragment will fall at distance $R + x_2$ from the point of projection.

$$R + x_2 = R + \frac{3}{8}R = \frac{11}{8}R$$

17. (i) $2(\hat{\mathbf{i}} + \hat{\mathbf{j}})$;

$$\mathbf{v}_{CM} = \frac{m_1v_1 + m_2v_2}{m_1 + m_2}$$
$$= \frac{v_1 + v_2}{2} \quad [\because m_1 = m_2]$$
$$= \frac{4\hat{\mathbf{i}} + 4\hat{\mathbf{j}}}{2}$$
$$= 2(\hat{\mathbf{i}} + \hat{\mathbf{j}})\ \text{m/s}$$

(ii) $\hat{\mathbf{i}} + \hat{\mathbf{j}}$;

$$\mathbf{a}_{CM} = \frac{\mathbf{a}_1 + \mathbf{a}_2}{2}$$
$$= \frac{2\hat{\mathbf{i}} + 2\hat{\mathbf{j}} + 0}{2}$$
$$= (\hat{\mathbf{i}} + \hat{\mathbf{j}})\ \text{m/s}^2$$

(iii) (straight line);
Since, v_{CM} is parallel to a_{CM}, hence path will be a straight line.

18. Yes;

$$v_{CM} = \frac{m_1v_1 + m_2v_2}{m_1 + m_2}$$
$$3\hat{\mathbf{i}} = \frac{4\times 1.5\hat{\mathbf{i}} + 2\times v_2}{4+2}$$
$$\Rightarrow \quad v_2 = 6\hat{\mathbf{i}}\ \text{m/s}$$

19. 0;

$\therefore \quad F_{ext} = 0$

So, there is no acceleration of centre of mass.

As, $\quad v_{i\,CM} = 0$

$\Rightarrow \quad v_{f\,CM} = 0$

$\therefore \quad nv = 0$

$\Rightarrow \quad n = 0$

20. (II); The given situation is shown below.

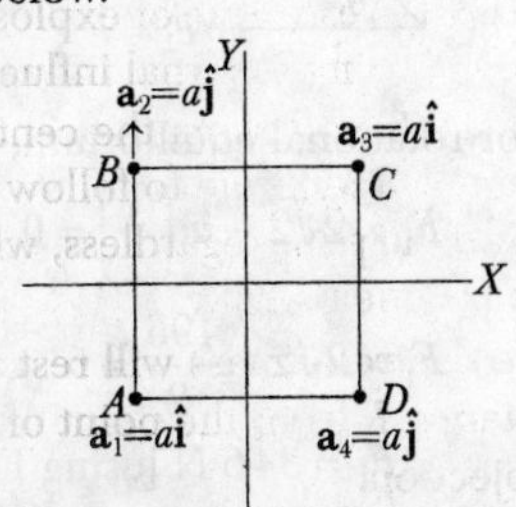

$$a_{CM} = \frac{m_Aa_1 + m_Ba_2 + m_Ca_3 + m_Da_4}{m_A + m_B + m_C + m_D}$$
$$= \frac{-ma\,\hat{\mathbf{i}} + 2ma\,\hat{\mathbf{j}} + 3ma\,\hat{\mathbf{i}} - 4ma\,\hat{\mathbf{j}}}{m + 2m + 3m + 4m}$$
$$= \frac{2a\,\hat{\mathbf{i}} - 2a\,\hat{\mathbf{j}}}{10} = \frac{a}{5}(\hat{\mathbf{i}} - \hat{\mathbf{j}})\ \text{m/s}^2$$

This only possible when

$$|a_1| = |a_2| = |a_3| = |a_4| = 0.$$

21. $\sqrt{75}$;

$$\mathbf{a}\times\mathbf{b} = \begin{vmatrix} \hat{\mathbf{i}} & \hat{\mathbf{j}} & \hat{\mathbf{k}} \\ 3 & -4 & 5 \\ -2 & 1 & -3 \end{vmatrix}$$
$$= \hat{\mathbf{i}}(12 - 5) - \hat{\mathbf{j}}(-9 + 10) + \hat{\mathbf{k}}(3 - 8)$$
$$= 7\hat{\mathbf{i}} - \hat{\mathbf{j}} - 5\hat{\mathbf{k}}$$
$$|\mathbf{a}\times\mathbf{b}| = \sqrt{75}$$

22. (i) × (ii) ✓ (iii) ✓

$$v_{CM} = \frac{m_1v_1 + m_2v_2}{m_1 + m_2}$$
$$= \frac{85(6.4)\hat{\mathbf{i}} + 200(-6.7\hat{\mathbf{i}} - 2\hat{\mathbf{j}})}{85 + 200}$$
$$= (-2.8\hat{\mathbf{i}} - 1.4\hat{\mathbf{j}})\ \text{cm s}^{-1} \quad \text{...(i)}$$

Linear momentum,

$$p = m_1v_1 + m_2v_2$$
$$= 85(6.4\hat{\mathbf{i}}) + 200(-6.7\hat{\mathbf{i}} - 2\hat{\mathbf{j}})$$
$$= (-796\hat{\mathbf{i}} - 400\hat{\mathbf{j}})\ \text{g cm s}^{-1}$$
$$v_1 = -6.4\hat{\mathbf{i}}\ \text{cm s}^{-1}$$

From Eq. (i), the velocity of m_1 with respect to centre of mass is

$$= 6.4\hat{\mathbf{i}} + (-2.8\hat{\mathbf{i}} - 1.4\hat{\mathbf{j}})$$
$$= (-9.2\hat{\mathbf{i}} - 1.4\hat{\mathbf{j}})\ \text{cm s}^{-1}$$

23. $-10, -5, 10$;

$$\mathbf{a}\times\mathbf{b} = \begin{vmatrix} \hat{\mathbf{i}} & \hat{\mathbf{j}} & \hat{\mathbf{k}} \\ 3 & -2 & 2 \\ 2 & 2 & 3 \end{vmatrix}$$
$$= \hat{\mathbf{i}}(-6 - 4) - \hat{\mathbf{j}}(9 - 4) + \hat{\mathbf{k}}(6 + 4)$$
$$= -10\hat{\mathbf{i}} - 5\hat{\mathbf{j}} + 10\hat{\mathbf{k}}$$
$$x = -10,\ y = -5,\ z = 10$$

24. (*d*); Required area of parallelogram,

$$\mathbf{A}\times\mathbf{B} = (\hat{\mathbf{i}} - 2\hat{\mathbf{j}} + 3\hat{\mathbf{k}}) \times (3\hat{\mathbf{i}} - 2\hat{\mathbf{j}} + \hat{\mathbf{k}})$$
$$= -2\hat{\mathbf{k}} - \hat{\mathbf{j}} - 6(-\hat{\mathbf{k}}) - 2\hat{\mathbf{i}} + 9\hat{\mathbf{j}} - 6(-\hat{\mathbf{i}})$$
$$= 4\hat{\mathbf{i}} + 8\hat{\mathbf{j}} + 4\hat{\mathbf{k}}$$
$$|\mathbf{A}\times\mathbf{B}| = \sqrt{4^2 + 8^2 + 4^2}$$
$$= \sqrt{32 + 64}$$
$$= \sqrt{96} = 4\sqrt{6}\ \text{units}$$

25. $(-2\hat{\mathbf{i}} + \hat{\mathbf{j}} + \hat{\mathbf{k}})$; We have, $\mathbf{A}\times\mathbf{B} = (\hat{\mathbf{i}} + 2\hat{\mathbf{k}})\times(\hat{\mathbf{j}} - \hat{\mathbf{k}})$

$$= \begin{vmatrix} \hat{\mathbf{i}} & \hat{\mathbf{j}} & \hat{\mathbf{k}} \\ 1 & 0 & 2 \\ 0 & 1 & -1 \end{vmatrix}$$
$$= \hat{\mathbf{i}}(0 - 2) + \hat{\mathbf{j}}(0 + 1) + \hat{\mathbf{k}}(1 - 0)$$
$$= -2\hat{\mathbf{i}} + \hat{\mathbf{j}} + \hat{\mathbf{k}}$$

26. (*d*); Velocity

$$\mathbf{v} = \omega\times\mathbf{r} = \begin{vmatrix} \hat{\mathbf{i}} & \hat{\mathbf{j}} & \hat{\mathbf{k}} \\ 3 & -4 & 1 \\ 5 & -6 & 6 \end{vmatrix}$$
$$= -18\hat{\mathbf{i}} - 13\hat{\mathbf{j}} + 2\hat{\mathbf{k}}$$

27. (a) 4 rad/s (b) 3.2 ms^{-2} (c) 1.6 ms^{-1} (d) 0;

(a) ∵Rotational speed,

$$\omega = \frac{v}{R} = \frac{80}{20} = 4\ \text{rad s}^{-1}$$

(b) Since, there is no acceleration for cylinder, $\alpha = 0$ and here it is radial acceleration.

$$a_r = \omega^2 r = 3.2\ \text{ms}^{-2}$$

(c) Velocity at the top will be given as

$$v_T = v + \omega r = 1.6\ \text{ms}^{-1}$$

(d) Velocity of the point of the cylinder which is in contact with floor at any moment will be 0 ms^{-1}

28. 3 : 2;

Using the relation,

$$\omega = \frac{v}{r}$$
$$\because \quad \frac{\omega_A}{\omega_B} = \frac{\left(\frac{v}{r_A}\right)}{\left(\frac{v}{r_B}\right)} \quad (\because v_A = v_B = v)$$
$$\Rightarrow \quad \frac{\omega_A}{\omega_B} = \frac{6}{4} = \frac{3}{2}$$

29. equals to 1, more than 1;

Case I In pure translational motion, all the particles of the body have same velocity at any instant of the time.

So, $\quad \dfrac{v_{P_1}}{v_{P_2}} = 1$

Case II $\quad v = \omega r$

This implies that, v is directly proportional to r.

As, $\dfrac{OP_1}{OP_2} = 2$

So, $\dfrac{v_{P_1}}{v_{P_2}} = 2$

30. All the statement are correct I, II, III

31. X-axis;
Direction of angular velocity is always perpendicular to the plane of rotation.

32. A. ✓ B. ✓

33. $\dfrac{\pi}{6}$;

$$\tau = r \cdot F \cdot \sin\theta$$
$$2.5 = 5 \times 1 \cdot \sin\theta$$
$$\Rightarrow \sin\theta = \frac{1}{2}$$
$$\Rightarrow \theta = \frac{\pi}{6}$$

34. (*c*); Torque, $\tau = \mathbf{r} \times \mathbf{F}$
$$= (\hat{\mathbf{i}} - \hat{\mathbf{j}}) \times (-f\,\hat{\mathbf{k}})$$
$$= f\,\hat{\mathbf{i}} + f\,\hat{\mathbf{j}}$$
$$= f(\hat{\mathbf{j}} + \hat{\mathbf{i}}) = f(\hat{\mathbf{i}} + \hat{\mathbf{j}})$$

35. $14\hat{\mathbf{i}} - 43\hat{\mathbf{j}} - 37\hat{\mathbf{k}}$ N-m;

$$\tau = \mathbf{r} \times \mathbf{F} = \begin{vmatrix} \mathbf{i} & \mathbf{j} & \mathbf{k} \\ 7 & 4 & -2 \\ 4 & -3 & 5 \end{vmatrix}$$
$$= \hat{\mathbf{i}}(20-6) - \hat{\mathbf{j}}(35+8) + (-21-16)\hat{\mathbf{k}}$$
$$= 14\hat{\mathbf{i}} - 43\hat{\mathbf{j}} - 37\hat{\mathbf{k}} \text{ N-m}$$

36. C and D

37. Anti-clockwise

38. i. (×) ii. (✓) iii. (✓)

39. (*a*);

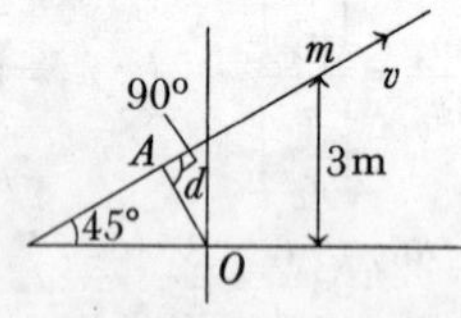

By geometry, the distance $OA = d$ is given by
$$OA = d = 3\sin 45^\circ$$
$$\Rightarrow \quad d = \frac{3}{\sqrt{2}} \text{ m}$$

Angular momentum $= p \cdot d_1$
$$= mv \times \frac{3}{\sqrt{2}} = \frac{3mv}{\sqrt{2}}$$

40. Yes

41. (i) ✓ (ii) ✓ (iii) ×;

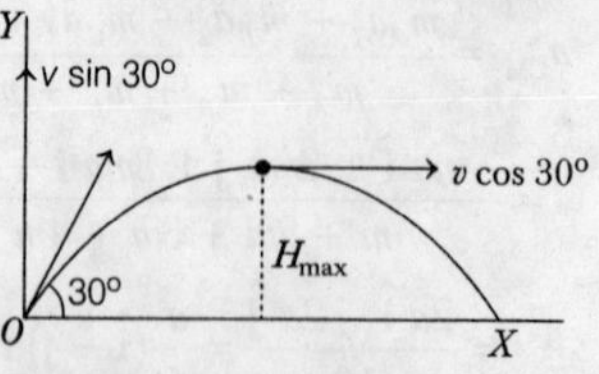

Maximum height,
$$H_{max} = \frac{v^2 \sin^2 30^\circ}{2g} = \frac{v^2}{8g}$$

Linear momentum,
$$p = mv\cos 30^\circ$$
$$= \frac{\sqrt{3}}{2} mv$$

Angular momentum = Linear momentum × H_{max}
$$= \frac{\sqrt{3}}{2} mv \times \frac{v^2}{8g} = \frac{\sqrt{3}\,mv^3}{16g}$$

42. (i) $2v$, (ii) $\dfrac{3}{2}mv^2$, (iii) $mv'\,r$, $\dfrac{mv'r}{2}$;

(i) According to the conservation of angular momentum,
$$mvr = mv'\frac{r}{2} \Rightarrow v' = 2v$$

(ii) Change in kinetic energy
$$= \frac{1}{2}mv'^2 - \frac{1}{2}mv^2$$
$$= \frac{1}{2}m[(2v)^2 - v^2]$$
$$= 3 \cdot \frac{1}{2}mv^2 = \frac{3}{2}mv^2$$

(iii) Initial angular momentum,
$$L_i = mvr$$
Final angular momentum,
$$L_f = m\,(2v)\frac{r}{2} = mv'\frac{r}{2}$$

43. $\dfrac{1}{4}$;

As, $\tau = I\omega \Rightarrow \omega \propto \dfrac{1}{I}$

$$\therefore \frac{\omega'}{\omega} = \frac{I}{I'} = \frac{\frac{2}{5}m(R)^2}{\frac{2}{5}m(2R)^2} = \frac{1}{4}$$
$$\therefore \frac{\omega'}{\omega} = \frac{1}{4}$$

44. (*c*)

45. (i) ✓ (ii) ✓ (iii) × (iv) ×;
Let the normal reactions for k_1 and k_2 be N_1 and N_2, respectively. For bar to be in equilibrium,
$$N_1 + N_2 = mg = (4+6) \times 9.8$$
$$= 98 \text{ N} \quad \text{...(i)}$$

Since, the system is in rotational equilibrium, the net torque about the centre of the rod must be zero.

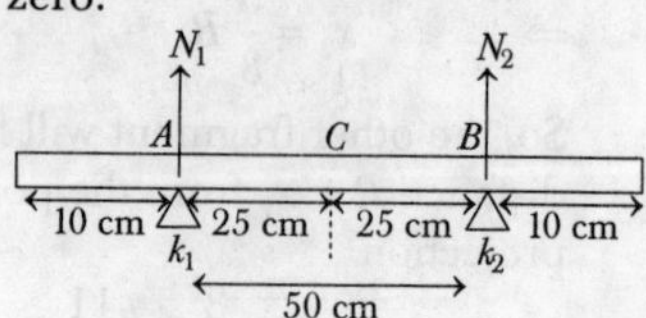

$$\Rightarrow N_1(AC) = (6 \times 9.8)5 + N_2(BC)$$
$$N_1(25) = 294 + N_2(25) \quad \text{...(ii)}$$

Solving Eqs. (i) and (ii) for N_1 and N_2, we get
$$N_1 = 55 \text{ N}$$
$$N_2 = 43 \text{ N}$$

46. 199 N;

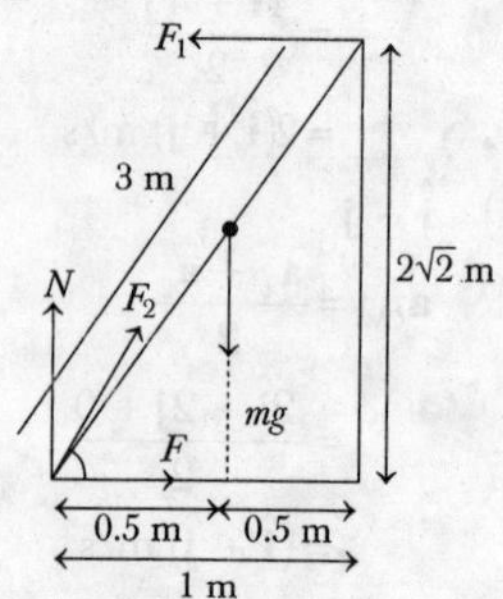

Forces acting on the ladder are
(i) Weight (w) of the ladder acting downwards.
(ii) Force (F_1) reaction of wall on ladder acting perpendicular.
(iii) Force (F_2) reaction of the floor on the wall.

For translational equilibrium in horizontal direction,
$$F - F_1 = 0 \Rightarrow F = F_1$$
For translational equilibrium in vertical direction,
$$N - w = 0$$
$$\Rightarrow N = w = 20 \text{ kg} \times 9.8 \text{ m/s}^2$$
$$N = w = 196 \text{ N} \quad \text{...(i)}$$

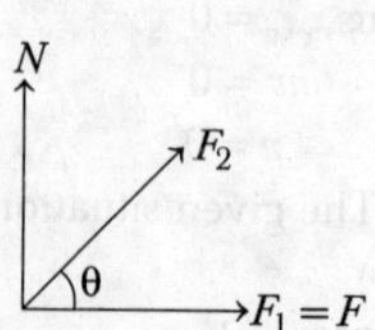

For rotational equilibrium,
$$F_1 \times 2\sqrt{2} - w\left(\frac{1}{2}\right) = 0$$
$$F_1 \times 2\sqrt{2} - \frac{196}{2} = 0$$
$$F_1 = 34.6 \text{ N [using Eq. (i)]}$$

Now, $F_2 = \sqrt{N^2 + F^2}$

$$= \sqrt{(196)^2 + (34.6)^2}$$

$$\approx 199 \text{ N}$$

47. $F_1 + F_2 = R$

48. 1.5 m;

2.5 m x

15 kg 25 kg

At equilibrium,

$$(m_1 g) x_1 = (m_2 g) x$$

$$15 \times 2.5 = 25 \times x$$

$$\Rightarrow \quad x = 1.5 \text{ m}$$

49. $\frac{g}{13}$;

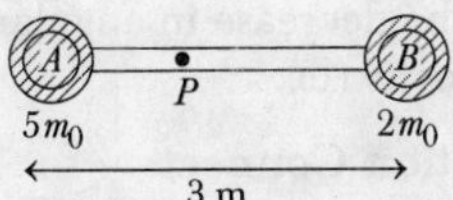

Let P be any point on the rod such that, $AP = 1$ m and $BP = 2$ m. Then, the moment of inertia of rod,

$$I = 5m_0 I^2 + 2m_0(2)^2$$

$$= 13 m_0 \quad \text{...(i)}$$

Suppose that, when the rod is released from some height, it gets rotated in the anti-clockwise direction. Applying torque equation,

$$5m_0 g - 2m_0 g(2) = I\alpha \quad \text{...(ii)}$$

From Eqs. (i) and (ii), we get

$$\Rightarrow \quad \alpha = \frac{g}{13} \text{ rad/s}^2$$

50. Rod I is in rotation and Rod II is in translation.

51. (*d*)

52. $\frac{R}{\sqrt{2}}$;

In case of a circular disc, $I = \frac{mR^2}{2}$

Radius of gyration, $K = \sqrt{\frac{I}{m}}$

$$= \sqrt{\frac{mR^2}{2m}} = \frac{R}{\sqrt{2}}$$

53. B, C

54. increases

55. A → 3, B → 2, C → 4, D → 1;

For solid sphere, $I = \frac{2}{5} ml^2$

For thin shell, $I = \frac{2}{3} ml^2$

For rod, $I = \frac{ml^2}{12}$

For thin disc, $I = \frac{ml^2}{2}$

56. $\frac{mL^2}{12}$;

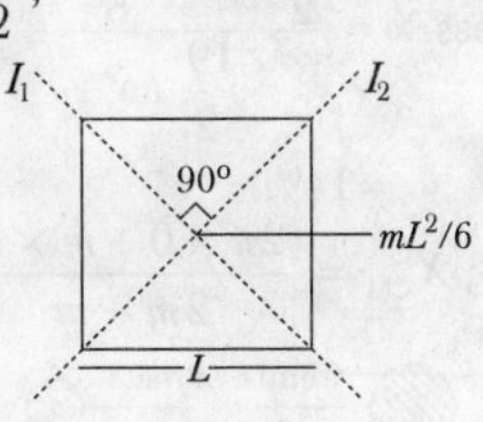

$$\therefore \quad I_1 + I_2 = \frac{mL^2}{6}$$

$$\because \quad I_1 = I_2 = \frac{mL^2}{12}$$

57. True;

The moment of inertia of a thin rod about an axis passing through one of its end and perpendicular to the length is given by

$$I = \frac{ML^2}{3} \quad \text{...(i)}$$

Comparing Eq. (i) with the general equation for the moment of inertia, we get

$I = MK^2$, where K is the radius of gyration.

$$\therefore \quad K = \frac{L}{\sqrt{3}}$$

58. (*d*); Moment of inertia of the system about rod is shown in the following figure.

x z y

$$I = I_x + I_y + I_z$$

$$= 0 + \left[\frac{Ml^2}{12} + \frac{Ml^2}{4}\right] + Ml^2$$

$$= \frac{4}{3} Ml^2$$

59. A → 2, B → 4, C → 3, D → 1;

For uniform solid sphere,

$$K = \sqrt{\frac{2}{5}} R$$

$$\Rightarrow \quad \frac{K^2}{R^2} = \frac{2}{5} = 0.4$$

For solid circular disc,

$$K = \frac{R}{\sqrt{2}}$$

$$\frac{K^2}{R^2} = \frac{1}{2} = 0.5$$

For hollow sphere,

$$K = \sqrt{\frac{2}{3}} R$$

$$\frac{K^2}{R^2} = \frac{2}{3} = 0.67$$

For uniform ring, $K = R$

$$\frac{K^2}{R^2} = \frac{R^2}{R^2} = 1$$

60. (12) ;Using $\omega_2^2 - \omega_1^2 = 2\alpha\theta$, we get

$$\left(\frac{\omega}{2}\right)^2 - \omega^2 = 2\alpha(36 \times 2\pi)$$

$$\Rightarrow -\frac{3}{4}\omega^2 = 144\pi\alpha \quad \text{...(i)}$$

Similarly, $0 - \left(\frac{\omega}{2}\right)^2 = 2\alpha(n \times 2\pi)$

$$-\frac{\omega^2}{4} = 4n\pi\alpha \quad \text{...(ii)}$$

Dividing Eq. (ii) by Eq. (i), we get

$$\frac{-\frac{\omega^2}{4}}{-\frac{3}{4}\omega^2} = \frac{4n\pi\alpha}{144\pi\alpha}$$

$$\Rightarrow \quad \frac{1}{3} = \frac{n}{36}$$

$$\Rightarrow \quad n = 12$$

61. $\omega t + \frac{1}{2}\alpha t^2$

62. 11;

Angular acceleration,

$$\alpha = \frac{2\pi(n_2 - n_1)}{t} = \frac{2\pi(75 - 20)}{10}$$

$$= 11\pi \text{ rad/s}^2$$

$$\therefore \quad p = 11$$

63. (i) (40π rad/s);

$$\omega_1 = \frac{1200 \times 2\pi}{60} = 40\pi \text{ rad/s}$$

(ii) (104π rad/s);

$$\omega_2 = \frac{3120 \times 2\pi}{60} = 104\pi \text{ rad/s}$$

(iii) (4π rad/s^2)

$$\alpha = \frac{\omega_2 - \omega_1}{t}$$

$$= \frac{(104 - 40)\pi}{16} = 4\pi \text{ rad/s}^2$$

(iv) (576);

Using, $\theta = \omega_0 t + \frac{1}{2}\alpha t^2$

$$= \left(40\pi \times 16 + \frac{1}{2} \times 4\pi \times 16^2\right) \text{ rad}$$

$$= 1152\pi \text{ rad}$$

Number of revolution

$$= \frac{1152\pi}{2\pi} = 576 \quad [\because = 2n\pi]$$

64. (*a*); $\omega = \alpha - \beta t$

Comparing with $\omega = \omega_0 - \alpha t$

Initial angular velocity = α

Angular retardation = β

$\therefore$ Angle rotated before it stops α^2.

$0 = \alpha^2 - 2\beta\theta \Rightarrow \theta = \dfrac{\alpha^2}{2\beta}$

65. (12.5); From the equation,

$0 = \omega_0 - \alpha t$

$\therefore\ \alpha = \dfrac{\omega_0}{t} = \dfrac{(100 \times 2\pi)/60}{15}$

$= 0.7\ \text{rads}^2$

Now angle rotated before coming to rest, $\theta = \dfrac{\omega_0^2}{2\alpha}$

or $\theta = \dfrac{(100 \times 2\pi / 60)^2}{2 \times 0.7} = 78.33\ \text{rad}$

or number of rotations,

$n = \dfrac{\theta}{2\pi} = 12.5$

66. (5.5);

Work done by gravity from initial to final position is

$W = \dfrac{mgl}{2} \sin 30° = \dfrac{mgl}{4}$ ...(i)

Making use of the work-energy theorem,

$W = \dfrac{1}{2} I\omega^2 = \dfrac{ml^2\omega^2}{6}$ ...(ii)

From Eqs. (i) and (ii), we get

$\dfrac{ml^2\omega^2}{6} = \dfrac{mgl}{4}$

$\Rightarrow \omega = \sqrt{\dfrac{3g}{2l}} = \sqrt{\dfrac{3 \times 10}{2 \times 0.5}} = 5.5\ \text{rad/s}$

67. A. $\dfrac{7\omega}{3}$, B. 14%;

$\tau_{ext} = 0$

This implies that angular momentum is conserved.

$L_i = L_f$

$I_1\omega_1 + I_2\omega_2 = (I_1 + I_2)\omega_f$

$I\omega + (2I)(3\omega) = (I + 2I)\omega_f$

$\Rightarrow \omega_f = \dfrac{7}{3}\omega$

$\text{KE}_{\text{initial}} = \dfrac{I_1\omega_1^2}{2} + \dfrac{I_2\omega_2^2}{2}$

$= \dfrac{I\omega^2}{2} + 9I\omega^2$

$= \dfrac{19I\omega^2}{2}$

$\text{KE}_{\text{final}} = \dfrac{1}{2}(I_1 + I_2)\omega_f^2$

$= \dfrac{1}{2}(3I) \times \dfrac{49}{9}\omega^2 = \dfrac{49I\omega^2}{6}$

$\text{Loss \%} = \dfrac{\dfrac{19}{2}I\omega^2 - \dfrac{49}{6}I\omega^2}{\dfrac{19}{2}I\omega^2} \times 100\%$

$= 14\%$

68. (*b*); $X_{\text{CM}} = \dfrac{(2m \times 0 + m \times L)}{2m + m} = \dfrac{L}{3}$

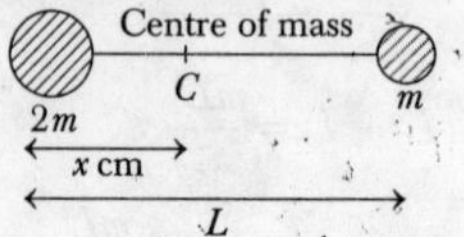

Velocity of stone A with respect to the centre of mass C is

$v_A = \omega \cdot X_{\text{CM}} = \dfrac{\omega L}{3}$

Similarly,

$v_B = \omega(L - X_{\text{CM}}) = \dfrac{2\omega L}{3}$

Angular momentum about C becomes

$L = 2mv_A X_{\text{CM}} + mv_B(L - X_{\text{CM}})$

$= 2m \times \dfrac{\omega L}{3} \times \dfrac{L}{3} + m \times \dfrac{2\omega L}{3} \times \dfrac{L}{3}$

$= \dfrac{4m\omega L^2}{9}$

69. Yes;

Torque, $\tau = F \times R$

$= 25 \times 0.20 = 5\ \text{N-m}$

Moment of inertia of flywheel about its axis,

$I = \dfrac{1}{2}mR^2$

$= \dfrac{1}{2} \times 20 \times (0.20)^2$

$\Rightarrow\ I = 0.4\ \text{kg-m}^2$

Now, $\alpha = \dfrac{\tau}{I} = \dfrac{5}{0.4} = 12.5\ \text{rad/s}^2$

As, the wheel starts from rest, $\omega_1 = 0$. Then, the angular displacement of wheel when 2m cord is unwound.

$\theta = \dfrac{l}{R} = \dfrac{2}{0.2} = 10\ \text{rad}$

If ω_2 is the final angular velocity of the wheel, then by equation of motion,

$\omega_2^2 = \omega_1^2 + 2\alpha\theta = 0 + 2(12.5) \times 10$

$= 250\ \text{rad/s}$

So, kinetic energy $= \dfrac{1}{2}I\omega_2^2$

$= \dfrac{1}{2} \times 0.4 \times 250 = 50\ \text{J}$

70. 0;

$\tau_{\text{net}} = \Sigma \mathbf{r}_1 \times \mathbf{F}_1$

$- Fr \sin 90° - Fr \sin 30°$

$- Fr \sin 30° + Fr \sin 0°$

$= Fr - \left(\dfrac{1}{2}Fr + \dfrac{1}{2}Fr\right)$

$= Fr - Fr = 0$

$\therefore$ Angular acceleration,

$\alpha = \dfrac{\tau}{I} = \dfrac{0}{I} = 0$

71. (*b*);

Stretching of arms while spinning increases the moment of inertia (I) about the rotation. This results in the decrease in angular velocity (ω).

Competition Connect

1. (*a*);

m $3m$

L $3L$

$X_{\text{CM}} = \dfrac{m \times \dfrac{L}{2} + 3m \times \left(L + \dfrac{3L}{2}\right)}{m + 3m}$

$= 2L$

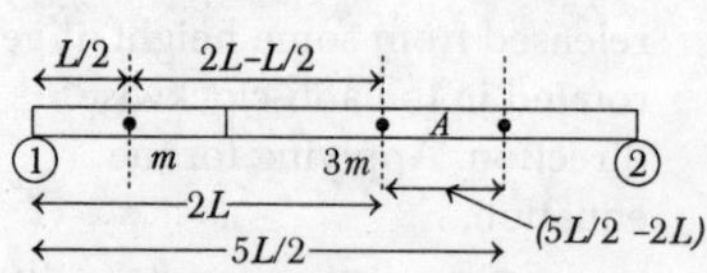

A is the centre of mass of system of rods.

$I_A = I_1 + I_2$

$= \left[\dfrac{mL^2}{12} + m\left(2L - \dfrac{L}{2}\right)^2\right]$

$+ \left[\dfrac{3m(3L)^2}{12} + 3m\left(\dfrac{5L}{2} - 2L\right)^2\right]$

$= \dfrac{16mL^2}{3}$

2. (*b*); $I_{CD} = I_{AB} + mR^2$

$\Rightarrow\ I_{AB} = I_{CD} - mR^2$

A C B D

$= \dfrac{3}{2}mR^2 - mR^2 = \dfrac{1}{2}mR^2$

3. $\dfrac{3}{2}$; $I_{AB}(\text{tangent}) = I_{XY} + MR^2$

$= \dfrac{1}{2}MR^2 + MR^2$

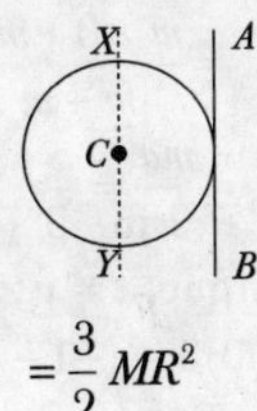

$= \frac{3}{2}MR^2$

4. Yes;

For cylinder, total kinetic energy is

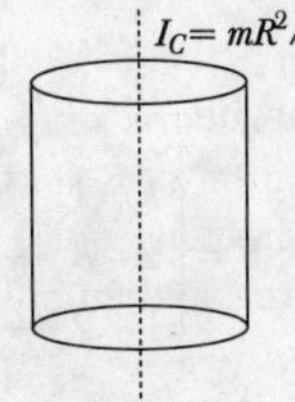

$$KE_{cylinder} = \frac{1}{2}mv^2 + \frac{1}{2}I_C\omega^2$$

$$75 = \frac{3}{4}mv^2$$

$$\Rightarrow \quad mv^2 = 100 \quad \ldots(i)$$

For sphere, total kinetic energy is

$$KE_{sphere} = \frac{1}{2}mv^2 + \frac{1}{2}I\omega^2$$

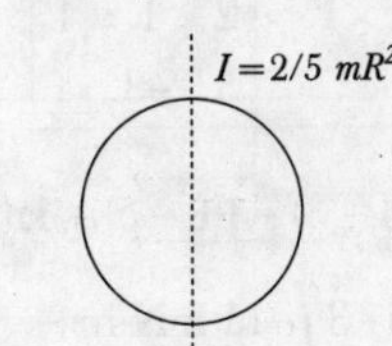

$$= \frac{1}{2}mv^2 + \frac{1}{2}\left(\frac{2}{5}mR^2\right)\left(\frac{v^2}{R^2}\right)$$

$$= \frac{7}{10}mv^2 = \frac{7}{10} \times 100 \text{ [from Eq. (i)]}$$

$= 70$ J

5. $\frac{4}{3}$;

This is the case of pure rolling motion. Angular acceleration (α) can be obtained about the bottom most point about which torque of function is zero.

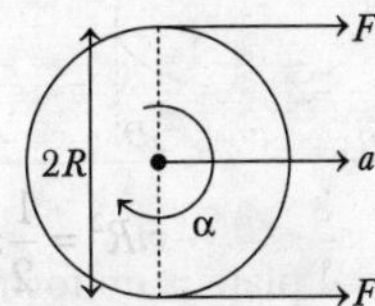

$$\alpha = \frac{F(2R)}{\frac{3}{2}mR^2} = \frac{4F}{3mR}$$

$$\therefore \quad a = R\alpha = \frac{4F}{3m}$$

6. 1 : 2;

$$\frac{v_1}{v_2} = \frac{r\omega}{2r\omega}$$

7. (*b*); In case of pure rolling, total mechanical energy remains conserved.

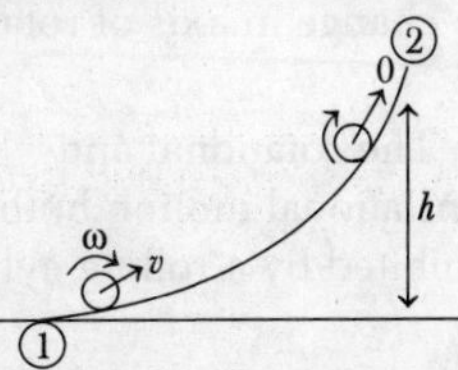

$\Rightarrow (v = \omega r)$, and $v = v_{CM}$ for pure rolling.

$\therefore$ Applying the mechanical energy conservation between position (1) and postion (2),

$$KE_1 + PE_1 = KE_2 + PE_2$$

$$\frac{1}{2}mv_{CM}^2 + \frac{1}{2}I_{CM}\omega^2 = 0 + mgh$$

PE = 0 at position (1).

$$\Rightarrow \frac{1}{2}mv^2 + \left[\frac{1}{2} \times \frac{2}{3} \times mr^2\left(\frac{v}{r}\right)^2\right]$$

$$= mgh$$

$$\Rightarrow \quad \frac{5}{6}mv^2 = mgh \Rightarrow h = \frac{5v^2}{6g}$$

Hence, h is maximum height attained when its slope finally on the inclined surface is

$$v = 0, \omega = 0$$

8. 2 : 7;

$$I_{solid\ sphere} = \frac{2}{5}mR^2$$

Rotational kinetic energy,

$$K_R = \frac{1}{2}I\omega^2$$

$$= \frac{1}{2} \times \frac{2}{5}mR^2 \times \left(\frac{v^2}{R^2}\right)\left(\because \omega = \frac{v}{R}\right)$$

$$K_R = \frac{2}{10}mv^2$$

Total kinetic energy,

$$K_T = K_R + K_t$$

$$= \frac{2}{10}mv^2 + \frac{1}{2}mv^2 = \frac{7}{10}mv^2$$

$$\text{So, } \frac{K_R}{K_T} = \frac{\frac{2}{10}mv^2}{\frac{7}{10}mv^2} = \frac{2}{7}$$

9. True;

Translational kinetic energy,

$$K_T = \frac{1}{2}mv_{CM}^2$$

Rotational kinetic energy,

$$K_R = \frac{1}{2}I\omega^2$$

We know that, total kinetic energy $= K_T + K_R$

$$= \frac{1}{2}mv_{CM}^2 + \frac{1}{2}I\omega^2$$

10. Solid sphere;

Rotational kinetic energy is given by

$$K_R = \frac{1}{2}I\omega^2 = \frac{1}{2}mK^2\left(\frac{v}{r}\right)^2$$

$$(\because I = mK^2 \text{ and } v = \omega R)$$

$$K_R = \frac{1}{2}mv^2\left(\frac{K^2}{R^2}\right)$$

Translational kinetic energy is

$$K_T = \frac{1}{2}mv^2$$

According to the question,

$$K_R = 40\% K_T$$

$$\therefore \quad \frac{1}{2}mv^2\left(\frac{K^2}{R^2}\right) = 40\% \times \frac{1}{2}mv^2$$

$$\Rightarrow \quad \frac{K^2}{R^2} = \frac{40}{100} = \frac{2}{5}$$

$\Rightarrow$ For solid sphere,

$$\frac{K^2}{R^2} = \frac{2}{5}$$

Hence, the shape of the body will be solid sphere.

11. 216 J;

Given, $m = 8$ kg, $r = 40$ cm $= \frac{2}{5}$ m.

$\omega = 15$ rad s^{-1}, $L = 0.64$ kgm^{-2}

$$\therefore \text{Total KE} = \frac{1}{2}I\omega^2 + \frac{1}{2}mv^2$$

$$= \frac{1}{2}I\omega^2 + \frac{1}{2}mr^2\omega^2 \quad [\because v = \omega r]$$

$$= \frac{1}{2} \times 0.64 \times (15)^2 +$$

$$\frac{1}{2} \times 8 \times \left(\frac{2}{5}\right)^2 \times (15)^2$$

KE = 216 J

12. $\frac{7}{5}mvR$;

Angular momentum of the sphere at a point P (point of contact) is given by

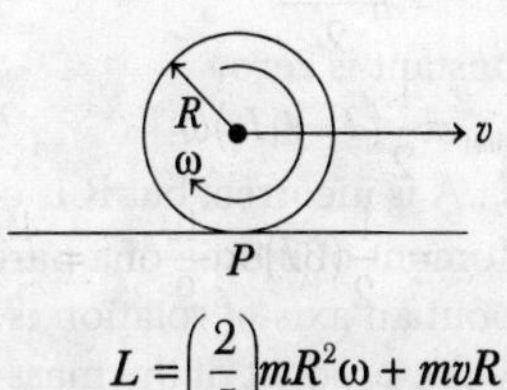

$$L = \left(\frac{2}{5}\right)mR^2\omega + mvR$$

$$= \frac{2}{5} mR^2 \times \frac{v}{R} + mvR$$
$$(\because v = \omega R)$$
$$= \frac{7}{5} mvR$$

13. (*a*); $I_{ring} = MR^2$

$$I_{disc} = \frac{1}{2} MR^2$$
$$I_{sphere} = \frac{2}{5} MR^2$$
$$\because \quad I_{sphere} < I_{disc} < I_{ring}$$

Hence, $v_{sphere} > v_{disc} > v_{ring}$

Assertion-Reason Questions

1. (*a*); The body explodes somewhere during the flight and splits into a number of particles. When the body explodes only internal forces act on the body and we know that the internal forces contribute nothing to the motion of centre of mass. Therefore, the centre of mass will follow the same parabolic path after the explosion.

2. (*c*); The position of centre of mass of a body depends on shape, size and distribution of mass of the body. The centre of mass does not lie necessarily at the centre of the body.

3. (*a*); If no external forces are applied, then acceleration, velocity and displacement of centre of mass is zero. Hence, the linear momentum of the system remains the same.

4. (*b*); $L = mvr \sin\theta$ or $mvr_\perp$
In case of constant velocity m, v and $r_\perp$ all are constant. Therefore, angular momentum is constant. It is a vector quantity.

5. (*a*); Angular momentum about centre is mvR and in circular motion, angular momentum about centre is always constant.

6. (*c*); L about centre

$$= mvR = \text{constant}$$

$\because \tau = \frac{dL}{dt}$ and derivative of any constant is zero.

$$\tau_{centre} = 0$$

7. (*d*); A is incorrect but R is correct. Moment of inertia of a particle about an axis of rotation is given by the product of the mass of the particle and the square of the perpendicular distance of the particle from the axis of rotation. For different axis, distance would be different, therefore moment of inertia of a particle changes with the change in axis of rotation.

8. (*a*)

9. (*a*); The rotational and translational motion both are exhibited by a rolling cylinder.

10. (*a*)

Case Based Questions

1. (i) (*a*); Let the coordinates of mass be (x, y).

$$x = \left(\frac{m_1x_1 + m_2x_2}{m_1 + m_2}\right)$$
$$= \frac{1 \times (-1) + 2 \times 2}{1 + 2} = \frac{-1 + 4}{3} = 1$$
$$y = \left(\frac{m_1y_1 + m_2y_2}{m_1 + m_2}\right)$$
$$= \frac{1 \times 2 + 2 \times 4}{1 + 2}$$
$$= \frac{2 + 8}{3} = \frac{10}{3}$$

Therefore, the coordinates of centre of mass are $\left(1, \frac{10}{3}\right)$.

(ii) (*b*); The point mass can be any where as shown in figure. So, COM can lie at R or at less than R.

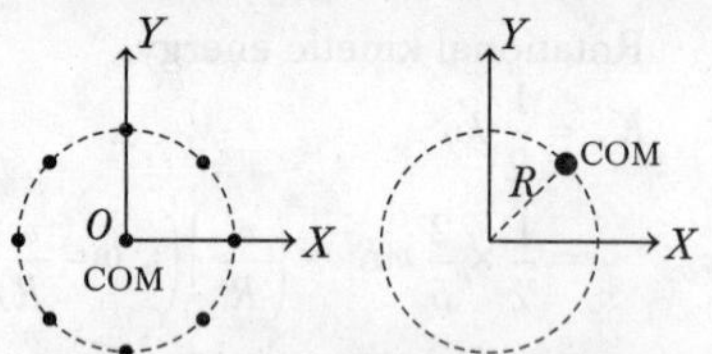

(iii) (*a*); They will meet at $\frac{L}{2}$ from the first ball because the first position of centre of mass and final position of centre of mass is same here.

(iv) (*b*) Given, $a_1 = 0$

$$a_2 = a$$

Both particles are identical, so mass will be the same.
Let it is m.
Acceleration of the centre of mass,

$$a_{com} = \frac{m_1a_1 + m_2a_2}{m_1 + m_2}$$
$$a_{com} = \frac{m \times 0 + ma}{m + m}$$
$$a_{com} = \frac{ma}{2m} = \frac{a}{2}$$

2. (i) (*a*); Torque, $\tau = \mathbf{r} \times \mathbf{F}$

$$= [(1-0)\,\hat{\mathbf{i}} + (-1-0)\,\hat{\mathbf{j}} + (0-0)\,\hat{\mathbf{k}}] \times (-10)\,\hat{\mathbf{k}}$$
$$= 10\,(\hat{\mathbf{i}} - \hat{\mathbf{j}}) \times (-\hat{\mathbf{k}})$$
$$= 10\,(\hat{\mathbf{i}} + \hat{\mathbf{j}}) \text{ N-m.}$$

(ii) (*b*)

(iii) (*d*); Torque,

$$\tau = \mathbf{r} \times \mathbf{F} = \begin{vmatrix} \hat{\mathbf{i}} & \hat{\mathbf{j}} & \hat{\mathbf{k}} \\ 2 & 3 & -1 \\ 1 & 2 & -3 \end{vmatrix}$$
$$= \hat{\mathbf{i}}\,(-9+2) + \hat{\mathbf{j}}\,(-1+6) + \hat{\mathbf{k}}\,(4-3)$$
$$= (-7\hat{\mathbf{i}} + 5\hat{\mathbf{j}} + \hat{\mathbf{k}}) \text{ N-m}$$

(iv) (*d*); Given, $\mathbf{F} = 5\,\hat{\mathbf{i}} - 3\,\hat{\mathbf{j}} + 4\,\hat{\mathbf{k}}$

$$\mathbf{r} = 2\,\hat{\mathbf{i}} + \hat{\mathbf{j}} + \hat{\mathbf{k}}$$
$$\tau = \mathbf{r} \times \mathbf{F} = \begin{vmatrix} \hat{\mathbf{i}} & \hat{\mathbf{j}} & \hat{\mathbf{k}} \\ 2 & 1 & 1 \\ 5 & -3 & 4 \end{vmatrix}$$
$$= \hat{\mathbf{i}}(4+3) - \hat{\mathbf{j}}(8-5) + \hat{\mathbf{k}}(-6-5)$$
$$= 7\,\hat{\mathbf{i}} - 3\,\hat{\mathbf{j}} - 11\,\hat{\mathbf{k}} \text{ N-m}$$

Competition Edge Up

1. (100); Given, $\tau = 40R$

$$\Rightarrow \alpha = \frac{\tau}{I} \quad \Rightarrow \alpha = \frac{40R}{I}$$
$$\therefore \quad \omega = \alpha t = \frac{400R}{I} = \frac{400 \times 0.1}{0.4}$$
$$= 100 \text{ rad/s}$$

2. (15);

As metal plate is uniform,
mass $\propto$ area
By symmetry along X-axis
$x_{cm} = 3/2 = 1.5$ units

$$y_{cm} = \frac{3 \times \frac{1}{2} + 1 \times \frac{3}{2} + 1 \times \frac{3}{2}}{3 + 1 + 1}$$

$$= \frac{9}{5 \times 2} = \frac{9}{10} \text{ units}$$

Ratio $\frac{x_{cm}}{y_{cm}} = \frac{15}{9}$

So, $n = 15$

3. (3); Given, system of masses is,

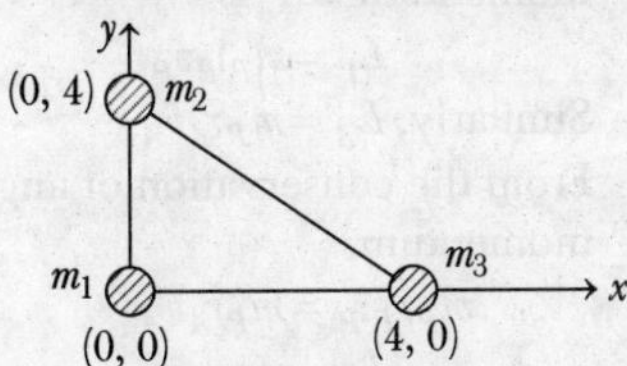

x-coordinate of COM,

$$x = \frac{m_1x_1 + m_2x_2 + m_3x_3}{m_1 + m_2 + m_3}$$

$$= \frac{2m \times 0 + 2m \times 0 + 2m \times 4}{2m + 2m + 2m}$$

$$= \frac{8}{6} = \frac{4}{3}$$

y-coordinate of COM,

$$y = \frac{m_1y_1 + m_2y_2 + m_3y_3}{m_1 + m_2 + m_3}$$

$$= \frac{2m \times 0 + 2m \times 4 + 2m \times 0}{2m + 2m + 2m}$$

$$= \frac{4}{3}$$

$$\therefore \quad \mathbf{r} = x\hat{\mathbf{i}} + y\hat{\mathbf{j}} = \frac{4}{3}\hat{\mathbf{i}} + \frac{4}{3}\hat{\mathbf{j}}$$

Magnitude of position vector,

$$|\mathbf{r}| = \sqrt{\left(\frac{4}{3}\right)^2 + \left(\frac{4}{3}\right)^2} = \frac{4\sqrt{2}}{3}$$

4. (60);

Since, $y = x + 4$

$x - y + 4 = 0$

Perpendicular difference on the line from origin,

$$OP = \frac{4}{\sqrt{1^2 + 1^2}} = 2\sqrt{2}$$

$\therefore$ Angular momentum

$$L = mv \times OP$$

$$= 5 \times 3\sqrt{2} \times 2\sqrt{2}$$

$$= 60 \text{ kg m}^2\text{s}^{-1}$$

5. (*a*);

Since, $I = \frac{ml^2}{12}$

$$\Rightarrow \frac{12 \times I}{m} = l^2$$

$$\Rightarrow l^2 = \frac{12 \times 2400}{400} \Rightarrow l^2 = 12 \times 6$$

$$\Rightarrow l = \sqrt{72} = 8.48 \simeq 8.5 \text{ cm}$$

6. (*); Radius of gyration of solid sphere and hollow sphere are K_1 and K_2 respectively, then

$$MK_1^2 = \frac{2}{5}MR^2$$

$$\Rightarrow K_1 = \sqrt{\frac{2}{5}}R$$

and $MK_2^2 = \frac{2}{3}MR^2$

$$\Rightarrow K_2 = \sqrt{\frac{2}{3}}R$$

$$\therefore \quad \frac{K_1}{K_2} = \frac{\sqrt{2/5R}}{\sqrt{2/3R}} = \sqrt{\frac{3}{5}}$$

7. (*a*); The given situation is shown below.

Let X_{CM} be the position of centre of mass from 10 kg mass.

$$\therefore X_{CM} = \frac{m_1x_1 + m_2x_2}{m_1 + m_2}$$

$$= \frac{10 \times 0 + 20 \times 10}{10 + 20} = \frac{200}{30} = \frac{20}{3} \text{ m}$$

8. (*a*); $\omega_0 = 2\pi \text{ rad} \times 1200 \text{ rpm}$

$$= 2\pi \text{ rad} \times \frac{1200}{60} \text{ rps}$$

$$= 40\,\pi \text{ rad/s}$$

$$\omega = 2\pi \text{ rad} \times 3120 \text{ rpm}$$

$$= 2\pi \text{ rad} \times \frac{3120}{60} \text{ rps}$$

$$= 104\,\pi \text{ rad/s}$$

Time, $t = 16$ s

$$\therefore \quad \omega = \omega_0 + \alpha t$$

$$\Rightarrow \quad 104\pi = 40\pi + \alpha \times 16$$

$$\Rightarrow \quad \alpha = \frac{104\,\pi - 40\,\pi}{16} = \frac{64\,\pi}{16}$$

$$= 4\pi \text{ rad/s}^2$$

9. (*a*); An arc corresponding to a 90° sector in the circular ring is removed, means one-fourth part of circular ring is removed. Then, the mass of the removed circular ring,

$$M' = \frac{M}{4}$$

Now, the moment of inertia of the remaining part,

$$I'' = I - I' = MR^2 - \frac{MR^2}{4}$$

$$\Rightarrow \quad I'' = \frac{3MR^2}{4}$$

Comparing with $I'' = KMR^2$

The value of $K = 3/4$.

10. (*a*); Initial angular speed of wheel,

$$\omega_0 = 2\pi f_0 = 2\pi \times \frac{360}{60} \text{ rad/s}$$

$$= 12\pi \text{ rad/s}$$

Final angular speed of wheel,

$$\omega = 2\pi f = 2\pi \times \frac{1200}{60} \text{ rad/s}$$

$$= 40\pi \text{ rad/s}$$

$$t = 14 \text{ s}$$

From the equation of rotational motion, $\omega = \omega_0 + \alpha t$

$$\Rightarrow \quad \alpha = \frac{\omega - \omega_0}{t}$$

$$= \frac{40\pi - 12\pi}{14} = \frac{28\pi}{14}$$

$$= 2\pi \text{ rad/s}^2$$

11. (*b*); Let the centre of mass lies at origin *O*.

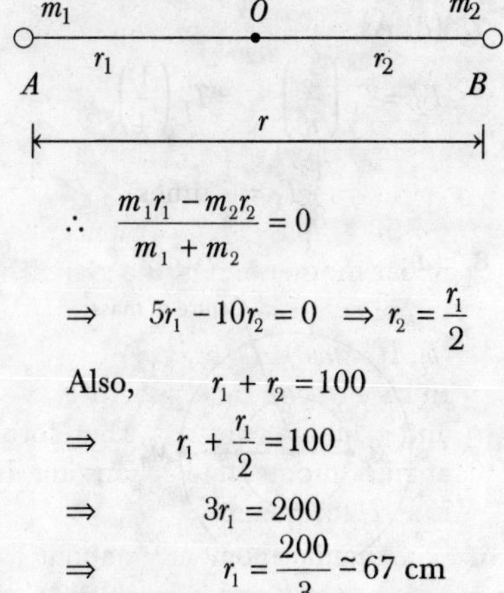

$$\therefore \quad \frac{m_1r_1 - m_2r_2}{m_1 + m_2} = 0$$

$$\Rightarrow \quad 5r_1 - 10r_2 = 0 \Rightarrow r_2 = \frac{r_1}{2}$$

Also, $r_1 + r_2 = 100$

$$\Rightarrow \quad r_1 + \frac{r_1}{2} = 100$$

$$\Rightarrow \quad 3r_1 = 200$$

$$\Rightarrow \quad r_1 = \frac{200}{3} \simeq 67 \text{ cm}$$

Chapter-7

Gravitation

1. $C \rightarrow$ Perihelion

$A \rightarrow$ Aphelion

2. (26.7 AU)

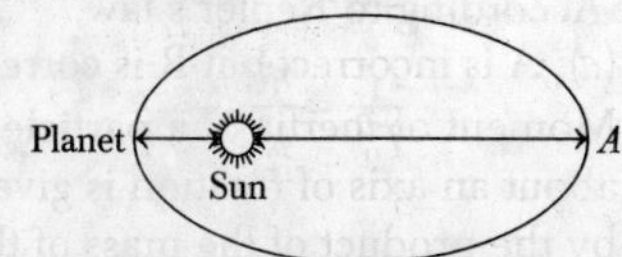

From the above diagram, it is clear that

Perihelion + Aphelion
= Major axis

$\Rightarrow$ Aphelion = 27 − 0.3
= 26.7 AU

3. (*b*); Since, mvr = constant

4. $(\frac{4}{3}\times10^3$ km);

Since, $L = mvr$ = constant

Thus, $mv_{max}r_{min} = mv_{min}r_{max}$ $[\because m_1 = m_2 = m]$

$$\therefore r_{min} = \frac{1\times10^3\times4\times10^4}{3\times10^4} = \frac{4}{3}\times10^3 \text{ km}$$

5. $\left(\frac{7A}{31}\right)$;

Total days in January = 31

Total area swept by the mars in January = A

Therefore, area swept by mars in 1 day $= \frac{A}{31}$.

$\Rightarrow$ Area swept by mars in second week of January $= \frac{7}{31}\times A$

6. (*c*); Since, $T^2 \propto R^3$

7. (*c*); As,

$$T_2 = T_1\left(\frac{r_2}{r_1}\right)^{3/2} = T_1\left(\frac{1}{4}\right)^{3/2} = \frac{1}{8}T_1 = \frac{1}{8} \text{ times}$$

8. (*d*);

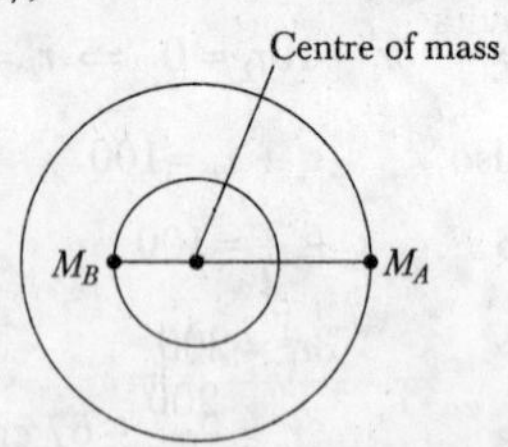

Both stars will revolve around the centre of mass. The gravitational force of attraction will provide the necessary centripetal force. Therefore, the angular velocity of both stars is the same. Hence, $T_A = T_B$.

9. (129);

According to Kepler's law,

$$\frac{T_1^2}{T_2^2} = \frac{r_1^3}{r_2^3}$$

Given, $r_2 = \frac{r_1}{2}$

$$\therefore \left(\frac{T_1}{T_2}\right)^2 = \frac{r_1^3}{\left(\frac{r_1}{2}\right)^3} = 8$$

$$\Rightarrow \frac{T_1}{T_2} = 2\sqrt{2}$$

$$\Rightarrow T_2 = \frac{T_1}{2\sqrt{2}} = \frac{365}{2\sqrt{2}} = 129.05 \text{ days} \simeq 129 \text{ days}$$

10. (670);

From Kepler's law

$$T_1^2 \propto R_1^3 \text{ and } T_2^2 \propto R_2^3$$

$$\Rightarrow \frac{T_1^2}{T_2^2} = \left(\frac{R_1}{R_2}\right)^3$$

$$\left(\frac{1}{T_2}\right)^2 = \left(\frac{1}{1.52}\right)^3$$

$$\Rightarrow T_2 = (1.52)^{\frac{3}{2}} \approx 1.837 \text{ year} \approx 670 \text{ days}$$

11. (True);

From the Kepler's law, we have

$$T^2 \propto R^3$$

Therefore, $T_2^2 \propto (9R)^3$

$$\therefore \frac{T_2}{T} = \left(\frac{9R}{R}\right)^{\frac{3}{2}} \Rightarrow T_2 = 27T$$

12. $(6.94\times10^{22}\text{ m}^2)$;

Areal velocity of a planet around the sun is given by

$$\frac{dA}{dt} = \frac{L}{2m} \text{ or } \int dA = \frac{L}{2m}\int dt$$

$$\Rightarrow A = \frac{L}{2m}\cdot t$$

where, t is the time in year.

$$\Rightarrow \text{Area, } A = \frac{1}{2}\times4.4\times10^{15} \times365\times24\times3600 \quad \left(\because \frac{L}{m} = 4.4\times10^{15}\right)$$

$$= 6.94\times10^{22}\text{ m}^2$$

13. Yes

14. $(t_1 = 2t_2)$;

According to Kepler's second law,

$$\frac{dA}{dt} = \text{constant.}$$

$$\therefore \frac{A_1}{t_1} = \frac{A_2}{t_2} \text{ or } \frac{A_1}{A_2} = \frac{t_1}{t_2}$$

$$\Rightarrow \frac{2}{1} = \frac{t_1}{t_2}$$

$$\Rightarrow t_1 = 2t_2$$

15. (*d*);

16. (False);

The magnitude of the angular momentum at P is

$$L_P = m_P r_P v_P$$

Similarly, $L_A = m_P r_A v_A$

From the conservation of angular momentum,

$$m_P v_P r_P = m_P r_A v_A$$

or $$\frac{v_P}{v_A} = \frac{r_A}{r_P}$$

Since, $r_A > r_P$, therefore $v_P > v_A$. Thus, the area *SBAC* bounded by the ellipse and radius vectors *SB* and *SC* is larger than *SBPC*. According to Kepler's second law, equal areas are swept in equal times. Hence, the planet will take longer time to traverse *BAC* than *CPB*.

17. True

18. (*b*); From conservation of angular momentum, mvr = constant

$$\Rightarrow v_A r_A = v_B r_B = v_C r_C$$

$$\because v_A > v_B > v_C$$

$$\Rightarrow K_A > K_B > K_C$$

19. (*a*); According to Newton's law of gravitation combined with Kepler's planetary motion, acceleration due to gravity,

$$g = \frac{GM}{R^n}$$

$$\Rightarrow \frac{GM}{R^n} = \omega^2 R$$

$$\Rightarrow \frac{GM}{R^n} = \frac{4\pi^2}{T^2}R$$

$$\Rightarrow T^2 = \left(\frac{4\pi^2}{GM}\right)R^{n+1}$$

$$\Rightarrow T \propto R^{\frac{n+1}{2}}$$

20. $\left(\frac{7}{2}\right)$;

From Kepler's law, we can deduce

$$T \propto R^{\frac{n+1}{2}} \quad \left(\because \frac{GM}{R^n} = \frac{4\pi^2 R}{T^2}\right)$$

$$\therefore T \propto R^{\frac{6+1}{2}} \text{ or } T \propto R^{\frac{7}{2}}$$

$$\therefore n = \frac{7}{2}$$

21. ($GMk = 4\pi^2$);

Time period of planet,

$$T = \frac{2\pi r}{v}$$

Since, $v = \sqrt{\frac{GM}{r}}$

$$\therefore \quad T^2 = \frac{4\pi^2 r^2}{\frac{GM}{r}}$$

$$\text{or} \quad T^2 = \frac{4\pi^2}{GM} r^3 \quad \text{...(i)}$$

From Kepler's third law, we have

$$T^2 = kr^3 \quad \text{...(ii)}$$

Thus, from eqs. (i) and (ii), we get

$$k = \frac{4\pi^2}{GM}$$

or $GMk = 4\pi^2$

22. (15);

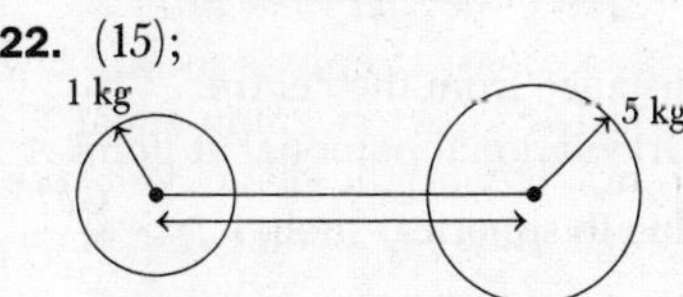

Total distance covered by both bodies before collision

$$= 24 - 4 - 2 = 18 \text{ m}$$

The bodies are moving under the action of central forces, therefore centre of mass will remain stationary, so

$$m_1 x_1 = m_2 x_2$$

$$\Rightarrow \quad mx = 5m(18 - x)$$

$$\text{or} \quad x = 15 \text{ m}$$

23. (2.6×10^8 m);

As the rocket is fired from the earth E towards sun S. At point P, the distance from the centre x of earth will balance each other.

Therefore, $\frac{GM_e M}{x^2} = \frac{GM_s M}{(r-x)^2}$

$$\frac{6 \times 10^{24}}{x^2} = \frac{2 \times 10^{30}}{(r-x)^2}$$

$$\Rightarrow \left(\frac{r-x}{x}\right)^2 = \frac{2 \times 10^{30}}{6 \times 10^{24}}$$

$$\Rightarrow \frac{r-x}{x} = \frac{10^3}{1.732}$$

On solving this equation, we get

$$x = (2.6 \times 10^8) \text{ m}$$

24. (Yes);

Net force on C, due to A and B is given by

$$F_{net} = \sqrt{F_A^2 + F_B^2 + 2F_A F_B \cos 60°}$$

$$= F_A\sqrt{3}$$

$$= \sqrt{3} \times \frac{Gm^2}{l^2} \quad \left(\because F = \frac{Gmm}{l^2}\right)$$

25. (III);

I. Gravitational force on m due to M and $2M$,

$$F_{\text{I}} = \frac{GMm}{4r^2} + \frac{G2Mm}{r^2}$$

$$= \frac{9}{4}\frac{GMm}{r^2}$$

II. Gravitational force on M due to m and $64\,M$ is

$$F_{\text{II}} = \sqrt{\left(\frac{G64Mm}{64r^2}\right)^2 + \left(\frac{GMm}{36r^2}\right)^2}$$

$$= \frac{GmM}{r^2}$$

III. Gravitational force on m due to different positions of M,

$$F_{\text{III}} = \left[\frac{\sqrt{3}GmM}{r^2} + \frac{4}{5}\frac{GmM}{r^2}\right]$$

$$= \frac{GmM}{r^2}\left(\frac{4}{5} + \sqrt{3}\right)$$

$$\therefore F_{\text{III}} > F_{\text{I}} > F_{\text{II}}$$

26. $v = \sqrt{\frac{Gm}{r}\left(\frac{2\sqrt{2}+1}{4}\right)}$;

Gravitational force between two masses $= \frac{Gm_1m_2}{r^2}$

So, $F_{12} = F_{14} = \frac{Gm^2}{(\sqrt{2}r)^2} = \frac{Gm^2}{2r^2}$

The resultant of these two forces is given by $\frac{\sqrt{2}\,Gm^2}{2r^2}$.

Also, $F_{13} = \frac{Gm^2}{4r^2}$

Thus, $F_{net} = \frac{\sqrt{2}\,Gm^2}{2r^2} + \frac{Gm^2}{4r^2}$

$$= \frac{Gm^2}{r^2}\left(\frac{\sqrt{2}}{2} + \frac{1}{4}\right)$$

Equating this force with centripetal force, we get

$$\frac{mv^2}{r} = \frac{Gm^2}{r^2}\left(\frac{2\sqrt{2}+1}{4}\right)$$

$$\text{or} \quad v = \sqrt{\frac{Gm}{r}\left(\frac{2\sqrt{2}+1}{4}\right)}$$

27. True

28. Yes

29. $\left(\frac{GMm}{R^2} \times \frac{\sqrt{8}}{27}\right)$;

Magnitude of the gravitational field of ring on the axis

$$E_{\text{ring}} = \frac{Gmx}{(R^2 + x^2)^{\frac{3}{2}}}$$

Force between sphere and ring is given by

$$F = \frac{GmM(\sqrt{8}R)}{(R^2 + 8R^2)^{\frac{3}{2}}}$$

($\because$ force = mass $\times$ gravitational field)

$$= \frac{GmM}{(9R^2)^{\frac{3}{2}}}(\sqrt{8}R)$$

$$= \frac{GMm}{R^2} \times \frac{\sqrt{8}}{27}$$

30. (*a*)

31. (*c*); Let mass of the sphere be M and mass of spherical cavity be M'.

Thus, $M' = \rho\frac{4\pi}{3}\left(\frac{R}{2}\right)^3 = \frac{M}{8}$

$$(\because M = \rho V)$$

By using the concept of gravitational force,

$$F_1 = \frac{GMm}{(3R)^2} = \frac{GMm}{9R^2} \quad \text{...(i)}$$

and $F_{\text{cavity}} = \frac{GM'm}{(AB)^2}$

$$= \frac{G\left(\frac{M}{8}\right)m}{\left(2R + \frac{R}{2}\right)^2}$$

$$= \frac{1}{50}\frac{GMm}{R^2} \quad \text{...(ii)}$$

$$\therefore \quad F_2 = F_1 - F_{\text{cavity}}$$

$$= \frac{GMm}{9R^2} - \frac{1}{50}\frac{GMm}{R^2}$$

$$= \frac{41}{50 \times 9}\frac{GMm}{R^2}$$

$$\therefore \quad \frac{F_1}{F_2} = \frac{50}{41}$$

32. I; Force of attraction between mass m and an elemental mass dm of rod is

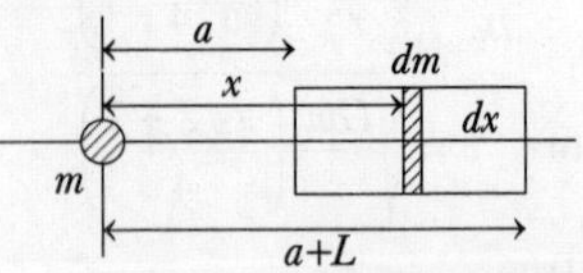

$$dF = \frac{Gmdm}{x^2} = \frac{Gm(A + Bx^2)}{x^2}dx$$

Total attraction force is sum of all the differential forces produced by elemental parts of rod from $x = a$ to $x = a + L$.

$$\therefore \quad F = \int dF$$

$$= \int_{x=a}^{x=a+L} \frac{GM(A + Bx^2)dx}{x^2}$$

$$= GM \int_{x=a}^{x=a+L} \left(\frac{A}{x^2} + B\right)dx$$

$$= GM\left[\frac{-A}{a+L} + B(a+L) + \frac{A}{a} - Ba\right]$$

$$= GM\left[A\left(\frac{1}{a} - \frac{1}{a+L}\right) + BL\right]$$

33. (2.6);

Acceleration due to gravity at a height h from earth's surface is given by

$$g_h = g\left(1 + \frac{h}{R_e}\right)^{-2}$$

$$\Rightarrow \quad 4.9 = 9.8\left(1 + \frac{h}{R_e}\right)^{-2}$$

$$\Rightarrow \quad \left(\frac{1}{2}\right)^{\frac{1}{2}} = \left(1 + \frac{h}{R_e}\right)^{-1}$$

(using binomial) [as $h << R_e$]

$$\left(1 + \frac{h}{R_e}\right) = \sqrt{2}$$

$$\Rightarrow \quad \frac{h}{R_e} = \sqrt{2} - 1$$

$$\Rightarrow \quad h = R_e(\sqrt{2} - 1)$$

$$\Rightarrow \quad h = 2.6 \times 10^6 \text{ m}$$

$$(\because R_e = 6.4 \times 10^6 \text{ m})$$

34. (1000 N);

The value of g at the depth d from the earth's surface is given by

$$g' = g\left(1 - \frac{d}{R_e}\right)$$

$$\Rightarrow \quad g' = 10\left(1 - \frac{R}{2R}\right)$$

$$= 10\left(1 - \frac{1}{2}\right)$$

$$g' = \frac{10}{2} = 5 \text{ m/s}^2$$

$\therefore$ Weight of rock

$$= mg' = 200 \times 5 = 1000 \text{ N}$$

35. (*c*)

36. (2);

$$\sqrt{h} = 1 \text{ km} = 1000 \text{ m}$$

According to question,

$$g\left(1 - \frac{2h}{R}\right) = g\left(1 - \frac{d}{R}\right)$$

$$\Rightarrow \quad 1 - \frac{2 \times 100}{R} = 1 - \frac{d}{R}$$

$$\Rightarrow \quad d = 2000 \text{ m} = 2 \text{ km}$$

37. (No);

The gravitational acceleration becomes half at a height equal to half of radius of earth. Therefore, the body will weight 20 kg -wt.

38. (*a*);

39. (3.8×10^8 m);

$$U = -\frac{GM_m M_e}{r_{\text{mean}}}$$

$$\therefore \quad r_{\text{mean}} = \frac{6.67 \times 10^{-11} \times 7.4 \times 10^{22} \times 6 \times 10^{24}}{7.79 \times 10^{28}}$$

$$\Rightarrow \quad r_{\text{mean}} = 384.4 \times 10^6 \text{ m}$$

$$\text{or} \quad r_{\text{mean}} = 3.8 \times 10^8 \text{ m}$$

40. (2600 km);

Gravitational potential

$$V = \frac{-GM}{R+h} = -5.4 \times 10^7 \quad \text{...(i)}$$

$$\text{and } g = \frac{GM}{(R+h)^2} = 6 \quad \text{...(ii)}$$

Dividing Eq. (i) by Eq. (ii), we get

$$\frac{\frac{GM}{(R+h)}}{\frac{GM}{(R+h)^2}} = \frac{5.4 \times 10^7}{6}$$

(negative sign is omitted as distance cannot be negative)

$$\Rightarrow \quad (R+h) = \frac{5.4 \times 10^7}{6}$$

$$\Rightarrow \quad R + h = 9000 \text{ km}$$

$$\Rightarrow \quad h = 2600 \text{ km}$$

$$(\because R = 6400 \text{ km for earth})$$

41. (*d*);

Gravitational potential

$$V = -\frac{GM}{x}$$

Gravitational potential at origin,

$$V = -\frac{2G}{1} - \frac{2G}{2} - \frac{2G}{4} - \frac{2G}{8} \ldots \infty$$

$$\Rightarrow V = -2G\left(\frac{1}{1} + \frac{1}{2} + \frac{1}{4} + \ldots \infty\right)$$

Since, $\frac{1}{1} + \frac{1}{2} + \frac{1}{4} + \frac{1}{8} \ldots$ is a GP series, where $a = 1$, $r = \frac{1}{2}$.

$\Rightarrow$ Sum of GP series,

$$S = \frac{a}{1-r} \quad (\because r < 1)$$

Therefore, potential,

$$V = -2G \times \frac{1}{1 - \frac{1}{2}} = -4G$$

42. (3);

Let point A be situated at $\frac{a}{2}$ distance from the centre.

Gravitational potential at point A due to spherical shell, $V_1 = -\frac{GM}{a}$

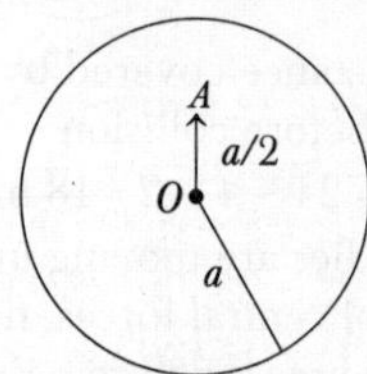

Gravitational potential at point A due to mass M at point O,

$$V_2 = \frac{-GM}{\frac{a}{2}} = -\frac{2GM}{a}$$

$\therefore$ Total gravitational potential,

$$V = V_1 + V_2$$

$$= -\frac{GM}{a} - \frac{2GM}{a} = -\frac{3GM}{a}$$

43. (No);

By the superposition principle, potential at centre of mass is given as

$$V = -\frac{GM}{2R^3}(3R^2 - r^2) \quad \text{...(i)}$$

For $r = \frac{R}{2}$, $V_1 = -\frac{11GM}{8R}$

Subtracting potential due to cavity of mass $M_C = \frac{M}{8}$

and $R_C = \frac{R}{2}$, we get

$$V_2 = -\frac{3GM_C}{2R_C}$$

$$(\because \text{mass} = \text{density} \times \text{volume})$$

Therefore, net potential at CM is given by $V = V_1 - V_2$

$$\Rightarrow \quad V = -\frac{11GM}{8R} - \left(-\frac{3GM_C}{2R_C}\right)$$

$$= \frac{-11GM}{8R} + \frac{\frac{3GM}{8}}{\frac{2R}{2}} \Rightarrow V = -\frac{GM}{R}$$

44. (17,100);

Let r be the distance of the given point from the centre of earth. Thus, gravitational potential energy,

$$U = -9.4 \times 10^7 = -\frac{Gm}{r} \quad ...(i)$$

Acceleration due to gravity at this point, $g = 4 = \frac{Gm}{r^2}$ ...(ii)

From Eqs. (i) and (ii), we get

$$\frac{Gm \times r^2}{Gm \times r} = \frac{9.4 \times 10^7}{4}$$

$$= 2.35 \times 10^7 \text{m}$$

or $r = 23500$ km

Now, height of the point from earth's surface,

$$H = r - R_e$$

$$\Rightarrow \quad H = 23500 - 6400 = 17100 \text{ km}$$

45. $\left(\frac{1}{2}\right)$;

Since, $U = -\frac{Gm_1m_2}{r}$

$$\therefore \quad U_1 = -\frac{Gm_1m_2}{6} \quad (\because r = 6 \text{ m})$$

and $U_2 = -\frac{Gm_1m_2}{12}$

(since, new separation is $r = 12$ cm)

Therefore, $\frac{U_1}{U_2} = \frac{2}{1}$

$$\Rightarrow \quad x = \frac{1}{2}$$

46. (*a*);

The gravitational potential energy at the centre of the square,

$$U = -\frac{4Gm}{r}$$

where, $r = \frac{\sqrt{2}l}{2}$ (from geometry)

Thus, $U = -\frac{4Gm}{\left(\frac{\sqrt{2}l}{2}\right)}$

$$\Rightarrow \quad U = -4\sqrt{2}\frac{Gm}{l}$$

47. (– 240 J);

Since, $E = -\frac{V}{r}$

i.e. $V = -\mathbf{E} \cdot \mathbf{r}$

$$= -(5\hat{\mathbf{i}} + 12\hat{\mathbf{j}}) \cdot (12\hat{\mathbf{i}} + 5\hat{\mathbf{j}})$$

$$= -(60 + 60) = -120 \text{ J/kg}$$

Gravitational potential energy,

$$U = V \times m = -120 \times 2 = -240 \text{ J}$$

48. A → 2, B → 1, C → 3;

A. Gravitational potential at point P due to M,

$$V = -\frac{GM}{r}$$

B. Gravitational potential due to a solid sphere at point P is given as

$$V = -\frac{GM}{2R^3}(3R^2 - r^2)$$

[for $r << R$]

$$= -\frac{GM}{2R^3} \times 3R^2 = -\frac{3GM}{2R}$$

C. Gravitational potential due to a circular ring at point P is given by $V = -\frac{GM}{\sqrt{R^2 + r^2}}$

49. $\frac{GMmh}{R(R+h)}$;

50. (2); For the given system, the potential energy will be

$$U_T = -\frac{Gm(M-m)}{d} - \frac{Gm(M-m)}{d}$$

$$-\frac{Gm(M-m)}{d} - \frac{Gm(M-m)}{d}$$

$$-\frac{Gmm}{(\sqrt{2}d)} - \frac{G(M-m)(M-m)}{(\sqrt{2}d)}$$

$$\Rightarrow U_T = -\frac{4Gm(M-m)}{d}$$

$$-\frac{Gm^2}{\sqrt{2}d} - \frac{G(M-m)^2}{\sqrt{2}d}$$

For maximum potential energy,

Using, $\frac{dU_T}{dm} = 0$, we get

$$\Rightarrow \frac{M}{m} = \frac{2(4-\sqrt{2})}{4-\sqrt{2}} = 2$$

Thus, $x = 2$.

51. (*d*); At the height h, its kinetic energy will be equal to potential energy,

i.e. $\frac{1}{2}mv^2 = \frac{GMm}{h}$

$$\Rightarrow \quad v = \sqrt{\frac{2GM}{h}}$$

Since, $v = \frac{dh}{dt}$

$$\Rightarrow \quad \frac{dh}{dt} = \sqrt{\frac{2GM}{h}}$$

$$\Rightarrow \int_{R_e}^{R_e+h} h^{\frac{1}{2}} dh = \int_0^t \sqrt{2GM}\, dt$$

$$\Rightarrow \frac{2}{3}\left[h^{\frac{3}{2}}\right]_{R_e}^{R_e+h} = \sqrt{2GM} \cdot t$$

$$\Rightarrow \frac{2}{3}\left[(R_e + h)^{\frac{3}{2}} - R_e^{\frac{3}{2}}\right] = \sqrt{2GM} \cdot t$$

$$\Rightarrow t = \frac{2}{3}\left[\frac{(R_e + h)^{\frac{3}{2}} - R_e^{\frac{3}{2}}}{\sqrt{2GM}}\right] \quad ...(i)$$

Now, acceleration due to gravity g is given by

$$g = \frac{GM}{R_e^2}$$

$$\Rightarrow \quad 2GM = 2gR_e^2 \quad ...(ii)$$

Putting the value of Eq. (ii) in Eq. (i) we get

$$t = \frac{2}{3}\left[\frac{(R_e + h)^{\frac{3}{2}} - R_e^{\frac{3}{2}}}{(2gR_e^2)^{\frac{1}{2}}}\right]$$

$$= \frac{1}{3}\sqrt{\frac{2R_e}{g}}\left[\left(1 + \frac{h}{R_e}\right)^{\frac{3}{2}} - 1\right] \text{s}$$

52. ($v_A = v_B = v_C$);

Escape velocity of a particle or an object is given by

$$v_e = \sqrt{\frac{2GM_e}{R_e}}$$

It does not depend on the individual masses of the particle or object.

53. (increases);

Let radius of earth be R_e and mass be M_e. Thus, escape velocity,

$$v_e = \sqrt{\frac{2GM_e}{R_e}}$$

$$\Rightarrow \quad v_e \propto \frac{1}{\sqrt{R_e}}$$

As, the radius R_e decreases (keeping M_e constant), the escape velocity increases.

54. (52.7);

$$\frac{v_s}{v_e} = \frac{\sqrt{\frac{2GM_s}{R_s}}}{\sqrt{\frac{2GM_e}{R_e}}}$$

$$= \sqrt{\frac{M_s}{M_e} \times \frac{R_e}{R_s}} = \sqrt{\frac{3 \times 10^5}{108}}$$

(take, $\frac{M_s}{M_e} = 3 \times 10^5$ and $\frac{R_s}{R_e} = 108$)

$$\approx 52.704 \simeq 52.7$$

55. (i) ✓ (ii) ✓ (iii) × (iv) ×

56. (*c*);

According to question,
let mass of planet $P = M$
Radius of planet $P = R$
Surface area of planet $P = A$
$\therefore$ Surface area of Q = 4(Surface area of P)

$$\Rightarrow 4\pi(R_Q)^2 = (4\pi R^2) \times 4$$

$$\Rightarrow \quad R_Q = 2R$$

Also, $M \propto V \propto R^3 \Rightarrow M_Q = 8M$

Now, mass of R is

$$(M_P + M_Q) = 9M$$

Therefore, radius of R is $(9)^{\frac{1}{3}}$ or $3\sqrt{9}R$.

Escape velocity of planet P is given by

$$v_P = \sqrt{\frac{2GM}{R}}$$

$$\Rightarrow \quad v_Q = \sqrt{\frac{2G(8M)}{2R}}$$

and $v_R = \sqrt{\frac{2G(9M)}{(9^{1/3})R}}$

$$\therefore \quad \frac{v_P}{v_Q} = \frac{1}{2}$$

and $v_R > v_Q > v_P$

57. (4.24);

Let the acceleration due to gravity at that planet be g', such that

$$\frac{g'}{g} = \frac{\sqrt{6}}{11} \quad \text{(given)}$$

and the density of ρ', such that

$$\frac{\rho'}{\rho} = \frac{1}{3}$$

$$\because \quad g = \frac{GM}{R^2}$$

$$\Rightarrow \quad g \propto \frac{M}{R^2}$$

and $\rho \propto \frac{M}{V}$

Also, $V \propto R^3$

Hence, $\frac{R'}{R} = \frac{\sqrt{6}}{11} \times \frac{3}{1} \Rightarrow \frac{3\sqrt{6}}{11}$

The ratio of escape velocities will be

$$\frac{v'_e}{v_e} \propto \sqrt{\frac{R'^2 \rho'}{R^2 \rho}} = \sqrt{\left(\frac{3\sqrt{6}}{11}\right)^2 \times \frac{1}{3}}$$

$$= \sqrt{\frac{9 \times 6 \times 1}{121 \times 3}}$$

$$\Rightarrow \quad \frac{v'_e}{v_e} = \frac{3}{11}\sqrt{2}$$

$$\Rightarrow \quad v'_e = \frac{3}{11}\sqrt{2} \times \sqrt{11}$$

$$= 3\sqrt{2} = 4.24 \text{ km/s}$$

58. (4);

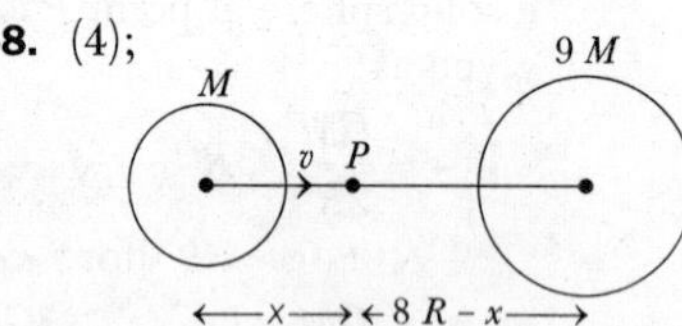

Acceleration due to gravity will be zero at P, therefore

$$\frac{GM}{x^2} = \frac{G9M}{(8R - x)^2}$$

$$\Rightarrow \quad 8R - x = 3x$$

$$\Rightarrow \quad x = 2R$$

Applying conservation of energy and consider velocity at P is zero.

$$\frac{1}{2}mv^2 - \frac{GMm}{R} - \frac{G9Mm}{7R}$$

$$= -\frac{GMm}{2R} - \frac{G9Mm}{6R}$$

$$\therefore \quad v = \sqrt{\frac{4}{7}\frac{GM}{R}}$$

59. ($4v$);

The escape velocity,

$$v_e = \sqrt{\frac{2GM}{R}} \quad \dots \text{(i)}$$

According to the question,
i.e. $R' = 4R$

$$\rho' = \rho$$

Thus, mass of another planet,

$$M' = \rho \times \frac{4}{3}\pi(R')^3$$

$$= \frac{4\rho}{3} \times \pi(4R)^3 = 64 \times M$$

Therefore, escape velocity of the planet,

$$v'_e = \sqrt{\frac{2G \times 64 \times M}{4 \times R}}$$

[from Eq. (i)]

$$= v_e\sqrt{16} = 4v_e$$

60. True;

$\therefore$ Escape velocity of another planet,

$$v' = \sqrt{\frac{2GM'}{R'}} \quad \dots \text{(i)}$$

Now, mass of another planet,
M' = volume × density

$$= \frac{4}{3}\pi(R')^3 \times (2\rho)$$

$$= \frac{4}{3}\pi(2R)^3 \times 2\rho$$

$$= \frac{4}{3}\pi R^3 \times \rho \times 16$$

$$= M \times 16$$

where, M is the mass of earth.

$$\therefore \quad v' = \sqrt{\frac{2GM \times 16}{2R}} \quad \text{[from Eq. (i)]}$$

$$= v\sqrt{8} \text{ or } 2\sqrt{2}\, v_e$$

$$\left(\because \sqrt{\frac{2GM}{R}} = v_e \text{ for earth}\right)$$

Thus, ratio of escape velocity at earth v_e to escape velocity at a planet v_p will be

$$\frac{v_e}{v_p} = \frac{v_e}{2\sqrt{2}v_e} = \frac{1}{2\sqrt{2}}$$

61. (9 mm);

Since, the black hole's gravitational field is so strong that even light cannot escape from it, the escape velocity at event horizon (outer surface of black hole) must be equal to the speed of light. i.e.

$$v_e = c = 3 \times 10^8 \text{ m/s}$$

Now, from the relation of escape velocity at the surface of earth,

$$v_e = \sqrt{\frac{2GM}{R}}$$

$$\therefore \quad 3 \times 10^8 = \sqrt{\frac{2 \times 6.67 \times 10^{-11} \times 5.98 \times 10^{24}}{R}}$$

$$\Rightarrow 9 \times 10^{16} = \frac{79.7732 \times 10^{13}}{R}$$

$$\Rightarrow \quad R = \frac{79.7732 \times 10^{13}}{9 \times 10^{16}}$$

$$\Rightarrow \quad R = 8.86 \times 10^{-3} \text{ m}$$

or $\quad R = 8.86 \text{ mm} \simeq 9 \text{ mm}$

62. True;

Escape velocity of earth,

$$v_e = \sqrt{\frac{2GM}{R}}$$

New escape velocity,

$$10v_e = \sqrt{\frac{2GM}{R'}}$$

$$\Rightarrow \quad \frac{10v_e}{v_e} = \frac{\sqrt{\frac{2GM}{R'}}}{\sqrt{\frac{2GM}{R}}}$$

$$\Rightarrow \quad 10 = \sqrt{\frac{R}{R'}}$$

$$\Rightarrow \quad R' = \frac{R}{100}$$

or $\quad R' = \frac{6400}{100} = 64$ km

63. (False);

The projectile is acted by two opposing forces which cancel out each other at N (called as neutral point), therefore

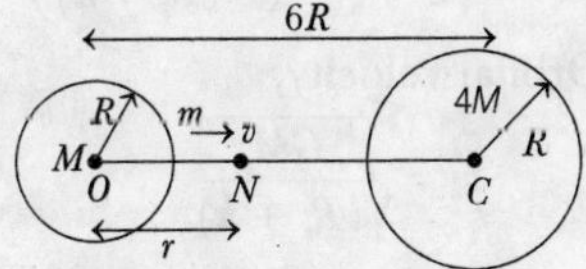

$\frac{GMm}{r^2} = \frac{4GMm}{(6R-r)^2}$ (on solving the quadratic equation)

$\Rightarrow \quad r = 2R$ or $-6R$

Since, distance cannot be negative. Thus, $ON = r = 2R$.

The mechanical energy at the surface of M,

$$E_M = \frac{1}{2}mv^2 - \frac{GMm}{R} - \frac{4GMm}{5R}$$

At neutral point N, the speed approaches zero. The mechanical energy at N is purely potential.

$$E_M = -\frac{GMm}{\cdot 2R} - \frac{4GMm}{4R}$$

From the principle of conservation of energy,

$$\frac{1}{2}v^2 - \frac{GM}{R} - \frac{4GM}{5R} = -\frac{GM}{2R} - \frac{GM}{R}$$

or $\quad v^2 = \frac{2GM}{R}\left(\frac{4}{5} - \frac{1}{2}\right)$

$$\Rightarrow \quad v = \sqrt{\frac{3}{5}\frac{GM}{R}}$$

64. $\left(\frac{1}{\sqrt{2}}\right)$;

Since, kinetic energy = potential energy

$$\Rightarrow \quad \frac{1}{2}m(v_e')^2 = \frac{GMm}{(R+h)}$$

$$\Rightarrow \quad v_e' = \sqrt{\frac{2GM}{(R+h)}}$$

$$= \sqrt{\frac{2GM}{2R}} = \sqrt{\frac{GM}{R}}$$

At the surface of earth,

$$v_e = \sqrt{\frac{2GM}{R}}$$

$$\therefore \quad \frac{v_e}{v_e'} = \frac{\sqrt{\frac{2GM}{R}}}{\sqrt{\frac{GM}{R}}}$$

$$\Rightarrow \quad \frac{v_e}{fv_e} = \frac{\sqrt{2}}{1} \Rightarrow f = \frac{1}{\sqrt{2}}$$

65. (10);

$$\therefore \quad E_i = \frac{1}{2}mv_i^2 - \frac{GMm}{R}$$

and $\quad E_f = \frac{1}{2}m(v)^2 - \frac{GMm}{(10R+R)}$

$$E_f = -\frac{GMm}{11R}$$

$[\because v = 0$ at height of $10R]$

From the conservation of energy,

$$E_i = E_f$$

$$\Rightarrow \frac{1}{2}mv_i^2 - \frac{GMm}{R} = -\frac{GMm}{11R}$$

$$\Rightarrow \quad \frac{1}{2}v_i^2 = \frac{-GM}{11R} + \frac{GM}{R}$$

$$\Rightarrow \quad v_i^2 = \frac{20GM}{11R}$$

$$\Rightarrow \quad v_i = \sqrt{\frac{10}{11} \times \frac{2GM}{R}}$$

Taking $v_e = \sqrt{\frac{2GM}{R}}$, we get

$$v_i = \sqrt{\frac{10}{11}}v_e$$

$$= \sqrt{\frac{x}{y}}v_e \quad \text{(given)}$$

$$\therefore \quad x = 10$$

66. (3);

Binding energy of earth is given by

$$\text{BE} = -\frac{3}{5}\frac{GM^2}{R}$$

$\therefore$ Energy required to break earth into pieces

$$= -\text{BE} = \frac{3}{5}\frac{GM^2}{R}$$

According to the question, the amount of energy that needs to be supplied,

$$E = \frac{x}{5}\frac{GM^2}{R}$$

Therefore, $x = 3$

67. (8×10^6 m);

At the surface, the rocket has potential energy and kinetic energy. As it goes up, its kinetic energy decreases and potential energy increases. At point where its kinetic energy becomes zero, it returns to the earth surface.

Therefore,

$$\frac{1}{2}mv^2 - \frac{GM_em}{R_e} = -\frac{GM_em}{R_e + h}$$

where, h is the height or the distance it travels vertically.

$$\therefore \quad \frac{v^2}{2} = \frac{GM_eh}{R_e(R_e+h)}$$

Put $g = \frac{GM_e}{R_e^2}$ and rearrange

$$h = \frac{R_ev^2}{2g\,R_e - v^2}$$

$$= \frac{6.4 \times 10^6 \times (5 \times 10^3)^2}{2 \times 9.8 \times 6.4 \times 10^6 - (5 \times 10^3)^2}$$

$$= 1.6 \times 10^6 \text{ m}$$

Therefore, height achieved by the rocket w.r.t. earth is

$$R_e + h = 6.4 \times 10^6 + 1.6 \times 10^6$$

$$= 8.00 \times 10^6 \text{ m}$$

68. (1 : 1);

The kinetic energy needed to escape from the surface is given as

$$E = \frac{1}{2}mv_e^2$$

$$= \frac{1}{2}m\left(\sqrt{\frac{2GM}{R_e}}\right)^2 = \frac{GMm}{R_e}$$

Since, the potential energy at the maximum height will be equal to the sum of half kinetic energy and the potential energy at the surface of earth.

Therefore, we can write,

$$-\frac{GMm}{R_e} + \frac{1}{2}\frac{GMm}{R_e} = -\frac{GMm}{R_e + h}$$

$$\Rightarrow \quad \frac{1}{2R_e} = \frac{1}{R_e + h}$$

$$\Rightarrow \quad h = R_e$$

$$\therefore \quad \frac{h}{R_e} = \frac{1}{1}$$

69. (d);

Initial energy of the particle at the time of projection = KE + PE

$$= \frac{1}{2}mv^2 + \left(-\frac{GMm}{R}\right)$$

Final energy at the maximum height h from the surface of the earth

$$= \text{KE} + \text{PE}$$

$$= \frac{1}{2}mv^2 - \frac{GMm}{R+h} = \frac{-GMm}{R+h}$$

($\because$ final velocity is zero at height h from the surface of earth)

According to law of conservation of energy,

$$\Rightarrow \frac{1}{2}mv^2 - \frac{GMm}{R} = -\frac{GMm}{R+h}$$

$$\Rightarrow v^2 = \frac{2GMh}{R(R+h)}$$

Substituting the value of $v = kv_e$ and $v_e^2 = \frac{GM}{R}$, we get

$$(kv_e)^2 = \frac{v_e^2 h}{(R+h)}$$

$$k^2 = \frac{h}{R+h}$$

$$\text{or} \quad h = \left(\frac{k^2}{1-k^2}\right)R$$

70. $\left(\frac{1}{2\sqrt{2}}\right)$;

Orbital velocity is given by

$$v = \sqrt{\frac{GM}{R}}$$

According to the question

$$\frac{v_1}{v_2} = \frac{\sqrt{\frac{GM}{R_1}}}{\sqrt{\frac{GM}{R_2}}}$$

$$\Rightarrow \frac{v_1}{v_2} = \sqrt{\frac{R_2}{R_1}} = \sqrt{2}$$

Now, time period of a satellite is given by

$$T = \frac{\text{path length in circular orbit}}{\text{velocity}}$$

$$\therefore \quad T_1 = \frac{2\pi R_1}{v_1}$$

$$\text{and} \quad T_2 = \frac{2\pi R_2}{v_2}$$

$$\Rightarrow \frac{T_1}{T_2} = \frac{\frac{2\pi R_1}{v_1}}{\frac{2\pi R_2}{v_2}}$$

$$\Rightarrow \frac{T_1}{T_2} = \frac{R_1}{R_2} \times \frac{v_2}{v_1}$$

$$= \frac{1}{2} \times \frac{1}{\sqrt{2}} = \frac{1}{2\sqrt{2}}$$

71. (*a*); $v_o = \sqrt{\frac{GM}{R+h}} = \sqrt{\frac{gR^2}{(R+h)}}$

$$= \sqrt{\frac{9.8 \times (6.4 \times 10^6)^2}{10^6(6.4+2)}}$$

$$\approx 6.9 \times 10^3 \text{ m/s}$$

72. (False);

$$v_o = \sqrt{\frac{GM}{(R+h)}} \quad \text{...(i)}$$

According to the question, orbital speed $= \frac{1}{2} \times$ escape speed

$$v_o = \frac{1}{2} \times \sqrt{\frac{2GM}{R}}$$

$$v_o = \sqrt{\frac{GM}{2R}} \quad \text{...(ii)}$$

Thus, from Eqs. (i) and (ii), we have

$$\sqrt{\frac{GM}{(R+h)}} = \sqrt{\frac{GM}{2R}}$$

$$\Rightarrow \quad 2R = R + h \text{ or } h = R$$

73. (*c*); Force on star is provided by the mass enclosed inside region ρ, radius R as shown below.

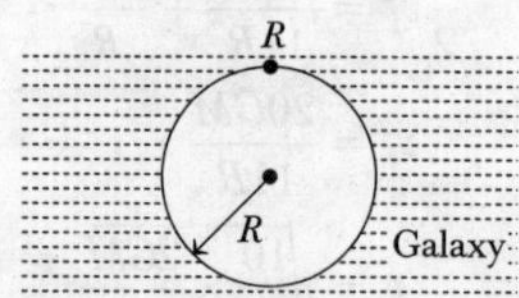

where, R = orbital radius of star. Lets consider a spherical region of radius r and thickness dr as shown below.

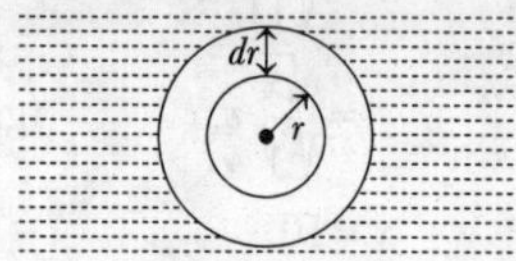

Mass enclosed in that region,

$$dm = \rho \times dv$$

$$= \frac{k}{r} \times 4\pi r^2 \cdot dr$$

$\therefore$ Total mass

$$= \int dm = \int_0^R \frac{k}{r} \cdot 4\pi r^2 \cdot dr$$

$$\Rightarrow \quad M = 4\pi k\left[\frac{r^2}{2}\right]_0^R$$

$$= 2\,k\pi R^2$$

Gravitational pull of this mass provides necessary centripetal force for rotation to start.

$$\text{So,} \quad \frac{GMm}{R^2} = \frac{mv^2}{R}$$

$$\Rightarrow \quad v^2 = \frac{GM}{R}$$

$$= \frac{G2k\pi R^2}{R}$$

$$\Rightarrow \quad v^2 = 2Gk\pi R$$

$$\Rightarrow \quad v = \sqrt{2kG\pi R}$$

Time period of rotation

$$= \frac{2\pi R}{v} = \frac{2\pi R}{\sqrt{2Gk\pi R}}$$

$$\Rightarrow \quad T \propto \sqrt{R} \quad \text{or} \quad T^2 \propto R$$

74. (2.65×10^{11} J);

Total energy of the mass at height h (400 km)

$$= \frac{1}{2}mv^2 + \left(-\frac{GM_e m}{(R_e + h)}\right)$$

Orbital velocity,

$$v_o = \sqrt{\frac{GM_e}{(R_e + h)}}$$

$\therefore$ Total energy at height h

$$= \frac{1}{2}\frac{GM_e m}{(R_e + h)} - \frac{GM_e m}{(R_e + h)}$$

$$= -\frac{1}{2}\frac{GM_e m}{(R_e + h)}$$

Energy required to throw the mass into the orbit

$$= -\text{ Binding energy}$$

$$= \frac{GM_e m}{2(R_e + h)}$$

$$= \frac{6.67 \times 10^{-11} \times 6 \times 10^{24} \times 9000}{2(6.4 \times 10^6 + 4 \times 10^5)}$$

$$= 2.65 \times 10^{11} \text{ J}$$

75. False;

Total energy of a satellite orbiting in a circular orbit,

$$E = -\frac{GM_e m}{2(R_e + h)}$$

Potential energy of the satellite,

$$\text{PE} = \frac{-GM_e m}{(R_e + h)}$$

$$\frac{E}{\text{PE}} = \frac{1}{2}$$

[$\because$ total energy = – kinetic energy and $\text{KE} = \frac{|\text{PE}|}{2}$

$$\text{As,} \quad \text{KE} = \frac{1}{2}mv^2$$

$\Rightarrow$ Total energy $= -\frac{1}{2}mv^2$]

76. (3.13×10^9);

Energy of a satellite in an orbit is given by $E = -\frac{GMm}{2R_e}$

Thus, $E_i = -\frac{GM_e m}{4R_e}$

$E_f = -\frac{GM_e m}{8R_e}$

Energy required

$= E_f - E_i$

$= -\frac{GM_e m}{8R_e} - \left(-\frac{GM_e m}{4R_e}\right)$

$= \frac{GM_e m}{8R_e} = \frac{g \cdot mR_e}{8}$

$(\because GM_e = gR_e^2)$

$= \frac{9.8 \times 400 \times 6.4 \times 10^6}{8}$

$= 3.13 \times 10^9$ J

77. (i) × (ii) × (iii) ✓ (iv) ×

78. (No);

$\text{TE} = -\text{KE} = -\frac{1}{2}mv^2$

79. $(2R_e)$;

Using law of conservation of energy for position I and position II of satellite, we have

$(\text{PE} + \text{KE})_{\text{position I}} = (\text{PE} + \text{KE})_{\text{position II}}$

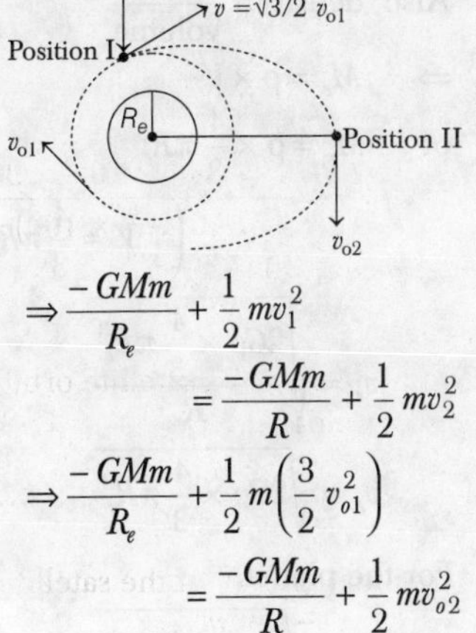

$\Rightarrow \frac{-GMm}{R_e} + \frac{1}{2}mv_1^2 = \frac{-GMm}{R} + \frac{1}{2}mv_2^2$

$\Rightarrow \frac{-GMm}{R_e} + \frac{1}{2}m\left(\frac{3}{2}v_{o1}^2\right) = \frac{-GMm}{R} + \frac{1}{2}mv_{o2}^2$

As, orbital speed, $v_o' = \sqrt{\frac{GM}{Re}}$

Therefore,

$-\frac{GMm}{R_e} + \frac{1}{2}m\left(\frac{3}{2}\frac{GM}{R_e}\right) = -\frac{GMm}{R} + \frac{1}{2}m\left(\frac{GM}{R}\right)$

$\Rightarrow -\frac{1}{4}\left(\frac{GMm}{R_e}\right) = -\frac{1}{2}\left(\frac{GMm}{R}\right)$

$\Rightarrow R = 2R_e$

Assertion-Reason Questions

1. (*d*); $\frac{dA}{dt} = \frac{L}{2m}$ = constant

$= \frac{mvr \sin\theta}{2m} = \frac{vr \sin\theta}{2}$

i.e. $\frac{dA}{dt}$ is independent of m.

2. (*b*); Square of time period is proportional to the cube of the mean distance from the sun.

$T^2 \propto a^3$

So, we can conclude that longer distance takes longer time to complete a revolution.

3. (*d*); Angular momentum is constant about the centre of sun and the force acting on the planet is a central force.

4. (*d*); Field strengths due to masses at 1 and 2 are acting at 60°.

Therefore, resultant is $\frac{\sqrt{3}Gm}{a^2}$.

5. (*a*)

6. (*d*); Principle of superposition is valid for gravitational forces. According to principle of superposition in gravitation, net gravitational field at a point is the vector sum of the gravitational fields at that point due to different sources.

7. (*b*); Potential energy of an object is the always defined with respect to a reference point. If location of the reference point changes, the potential energy at that point would also change.

8. (*c*); At the surface of moon

$V_{\text{rms}} > V_{\text{escape}}$

Hence, molecules escape out before reaching their rms velocity that's why there is no atmosphere present.

9. (*a*); The gravitational of force provides the necessary centripetal acceleration to keep the satellite in circular orbit. The speed of the satellite is constant but its velocity keeps changing in circular motion.

10. (*d*); $W_2 = \frac{1}{2}mv^2 = \frac{1}{2}m\left(\sqrt{\frac{GM}{r}}\right)^2$

$= \frac{GMm}{2r} = \frac{GMm}{4R}$

$W_1 = \Delta U = \frac{mgh}{1 + \frac{h}{R}} = \frac{mgRh}{R + h}$

$= \frac{m\left(\frac{GM}{R^2}\right)Rh}{r} = \left(\frac{GMm}{rR}\right)h = \frac{GMm}{r}$

Case Based Questions

1. (i) (*a*); $[\text{ML}^1\text{T}^{-2}]$

(ii) (*b*); Using $w = mg$

$= 25 \times 9.8 = 245$ N

(iii) (*c*); Using $w = mg$

$m = \frac{w}{g}$

$m = \frac{500}{1.62} = 308.64$ kg

(iv) (*b*); Weight at height $h = 3R$

$w' = mg'$

$= m\frac{g}{\left(1 + \frac{3R}{R}\right)^2} = \frac{mg}{16}$

$= \frac{w}{16}$ $[\because w = mg]$

Or

(*c*);

2. (i) (*a*); The potential energy of the system = Sum of potential energies of all the three possible distinct pairs.

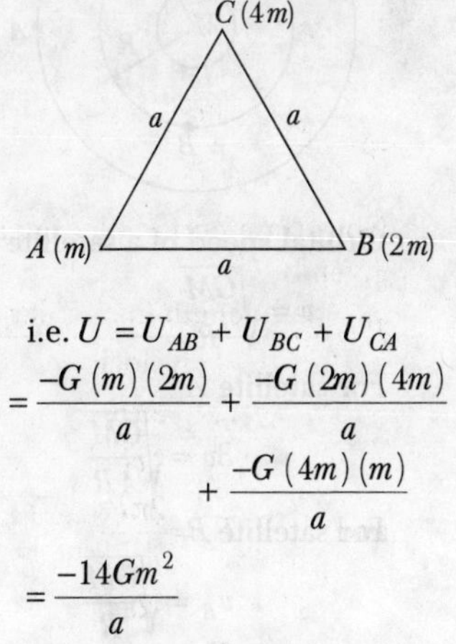

i.e. $U = U_{AB} + U_{BC} + U_{CA}$

$= \frac{-G(m)(2m)}{a} + \frac{-G(2m)(4m)}{a} + \frac{-G(4m)(m)}{a}$

$= \frac{-14Gm^2}{a}$

(ii) (a); The resulting gravitational potential

$V = -2G\left(\frac{1}{1} + \frac{1}{2} + \frac{1}{4} + \frac{1}{8} + \ldots\right)$

$$= -2G\left(1+\frac{1}{2}+\frac{1}{2^2}+\frac{1}{2^3}+\ldots\right)$$

$$\Rightarrow \quad V = \frac{-2G}{\left(1-\frac{1}{2}\right)}$$

$$= \frac{-2G}{\frac{1}{2}} = -4G$$

(iii) (*b*); $[ML^2T^{-2}]$

(iv) (*a*);

Or (*a*)

Competition Edge Up

1. (*b*); Total energy on the earth's surface

$$E_i = \frac{-GM_em}{R_e}$$

Total energy at altitude h

$$E_f = -\frac{GM_em}{2(R_e+h)}$$

$$E_f = -\frac{GM_em}{2(R_e+h)} = \frac{-GM_em}{2\left(R_e+\frac{R_e}{20}\right)}$$

$$= \frac{-10\,GM_em}{21R_e}$$

$\therefore$ Change in energy $= E_f - E_i$

$$= \frac{11}{21}\frac{GM_em}{R_e}$$

$\therefore \quad x = 11$

2. (*c*);

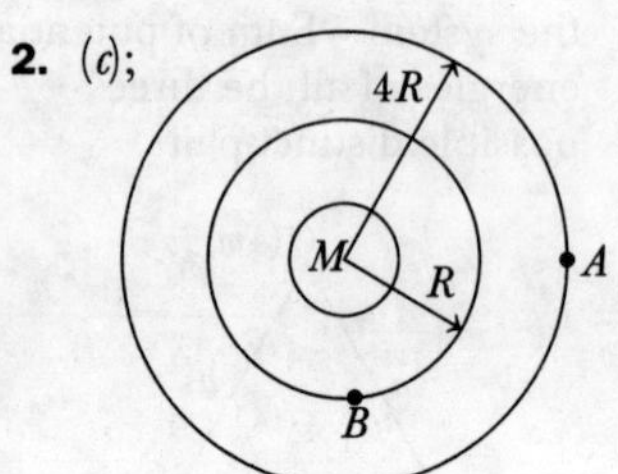

Orbital speed of a satellite is,

$$v = \sqrt{\frac{GM}{R}}$$

For satellite *A*,

$$3v = \sqrt{\frac{GM}{4R}}$$

For satellite *B*,

$$v_B = \sqrt{\frac{GM}{R}}$$

So, $\quad \dfrac{v_B}{3v} = \dfrac{\sqrt{(GM/R)}}{\sqrt{(GM/4R)}} = 2$

$$\Rightarrow \quad v_B = 6v$$

3. (*a*); $g_d = g\left(1-\dfrac{d}{R}\right)$

At the depth, $d = R/4$

$$= g\left(1-\frac{R/4}{R}\right) = \frac{3g}{4}$$

Weight on the surface of earth,

$$w = mg = 300 \text{ N}$$

Weight of body at depth, $d = \dfrac{R}{4}$

$$w' = mg_d$$

$$= m \times \frac{3g}{4} = \frac{3}{4}mg$$

$$= \frac{3}{4}\times 300 = 225 \text{ N}$$

4. (*b*); According to conservation of energy,

$$\frac{1}{2}mv_E^2 = \frac{GM_Em}{R_E}$$

$$\Rightarrow \quad K = \frac{GM_Em}{R_E}$$

$$= \frac{gR_E^2\cdot m}{R_E} \quad [\because GM_E = gR_E^2]$$

$$\Rightarrow \quad K = gmR_E$$

5. (*d*); We know that,

Time period of revolving satellite,

$$T = \frac{2\pi r^{3/2}}{\sqrt{GM}}$$

$$\therefore \quad \frac{T_1}{T_2} = \left(\frac{r_1}{r_2}\right)^{3/2}\cdot\left(\frac{M_2}{M_1}\right)^{1/2}$$

$$\Rightarrow \quad \frac{6}{24} = \frac{r_1^{3/2}}{(4.2\times10^4)^{3/2}} \times \left(\frac{M}{M/4}\right)^{1/2}$$

$$\Rightarrow \quad r_1 = 1.05\times10^4 \text{ km}$$

6. (*d*); $g = \dfrac{GM}{R^2}$

According to question,

$$g = \frac{G\left(\frac{M}{10}\right)}{\left(\frac{R}{2}\right)^2} = \frac{GM\times4}{R^2\times10} = \frac{GM}{R^2}\times\frac{2}{5}$$

Hence, $\quad \dfrac{g'}{g} = \dfrac{\frac{GM}{R^2}\times\frac{2}{5}}{\frac{GM}{R^2}}$

$$\Rightarrow g' = \frac{2}{5}\times g = \frac{2}{5}\times 9.8 = 3.92 \text{ ms}^{-2}$$

7. (*b*); The given situation is shown below.

(m) ←— x —→ O ←— R−x —→ (9m)

Since, gravitational field at point *O* is zero, hence

$$\frac{Gm}{x^2} = \frac{G(9m)}{(R-x)^2}$$

$$\Rightarrow \quad \left(\frac{1}{x}\right)^2 = \left(\frac{3}{R-x}\right)^2$$

$$\Rightarrow \quad \frac{1}{x} = \frac{3}{R-x}$$

$$\Rightarrow \quad 3x = R - x$$

$$\Rightarrow \quad x = \frac{R}{4}$$

$\therefore$ Gravitational potential at point *O*

$$V = \frac{-Gm}{x} + \left[\frac{-G(9m)}{R-x}\right]$$

$$= \frac{-Gm}{\frac{R}{4}} - \frac{9Gm}{R-\frac{R}{4}}$$

$$= -\frac{4Gm}{R} - \frac{12Gm}{R} = -\frac{16Gm}{R}$$

8. (*a*); Magnitude of gravitational field intensity,

$$I = \frac{F}{m} = \frac{3}{6\times10^{-2}}$$

$$= 50 \text{ N/kg}$$

9. (*d*); We know that,

escape velocity from earth's surface, $v_e = \sqrt{\dfrac{2GM_e}{R_e}}$

Also, density $= \dfrac{\text{mass}}{\text{volume}}$

$$\Rightarrow \quad M_e = \rho\times V$$

or $\quad M_e = \rho\times\dfrac{4}{3}\pi R_e^3$

$$\left(\because V = \frac{4}{3}\pi R_e^3\right)$$

$$v_e = \sqrt{\frac{2G\rho\times\frac{4}{3}\pi R_e^3}{R_e}}$$

$$v_e = \sqrt{2G\rho\times\frac{4}{3}\pi R_e^2} \quad \ldots\text{(i)}$$

For the planet,

$$v_p = \sqrt{2G\rho\times\frac{4}{3}\pi R_p^2}$$

$$v_p = \sqrt{2G\rho\times\frac{4}{3}\pi(4R_e)^2}$$

$$(\because R_p = 4R_e)$$

$$v_p = 4\sqrt{2G\rho\times\frac{4}{3}\pi(R_e)^2} \quad \ldots\text{(ii)}$$

On dividing Eq. (ii) by Eq. (i), we get

$$\frac{v_p}{v_e} = \frac{4\sqrt{2G\rho \times \frac{4}{3}\pi (R_e)^2}}{\sqrt{2G\rho \times \frac{4}{3}\pi R_e^2}}$$

$$\Rightarrow \quad v_p = 4v_e = 4v$$

10. (*b*); $\quad g_d = \frac{g}{n}$

$$\Rightarrow g\left(1 - \frac{d}{R}\right) = \frac{g}{n}$$

$$\Rightarrow \quad 1 - \frac{d}{R} = \frac{1}{n} \Rightarrow 1 - \frac{1}{n} = \frac{d}{R}$$

$$\Rightarrow \quad \frac{n-1}{n} = \frac{d}{R}$$

$$\Rightarrow \quad d = \left(\frac{n-1}{n}\right)R$$

Chapter-8

Mechanical Properties of Solids

1. III

2. compression, tension

3. r_1

4. equal to

5. (*a*); Instantaneous stress $= \frac{\text{Force}}{\text{Area}}$

$$= \frac{5}{0.5} \quad (\because \text{Weight} = \text{Force})$$

$$= 10 \text{ Pa}$$

6. A → 2, B → 3, C → 1

7. (*b*); Let original length be l.

New length $= 2l$

Change in length $= 2l - l = l$

$$\therefore \text{Strain} = \frac{\text{Change in length}}{\text{Original length}}$$

$$= \frac{l}{l} = 1$$

8. (3.12)

Tensile stress, $\sigma = \frac{\text{Force}}{\text{Area}}$

$$= \frac{4 \times 9.8}{\pi(2 \times 10^{-3})^2}$$

$$= 3.12 \times 10^6 \text{ Nm}^{-2}$$

9. (*d*); Force at a height $\left(\frac{3L}{4}\right)$ from its lower end, F = weight suspended + weight of $\frac{3}{4}$ of the chain

Since, the wire is uniform, therefore weight of the lower portion,

$$w_L = \frac{3}{4}L \times \frac{w}{L} = \frac{3}{4}w$$

$\therefore$ Force, $\quad F = w_1 + \frac{3}{4}w$

$$\text{Stress}(\sigma) = \frac{\text{Force}}{\text{Area}} = \frac{w_1 + \frac{3}{4}w}{A}$$

10. $\frac{1}{4}$;

$$\text{Stress} = \frac{\text{Force}}{\text{Area}} = \frac{F}{\pi r^2}$$

Therefore, $\frac{S_1}{S_2} = \frac{F}{\pi r_1^2} \times \frac{\pi r_2^2}{F}$

$$\Rightarrow \frac{S_1}{S_2} = \left(\frac{r_2}{r_1}\right)^2 = \left(\frac{1}{2}\right)^2 \quad \left(\because \frac{r_1}{r_2} = \frac{2}{1}\right)$$

$$= \frac{1}{4}$$

11. I;

I.

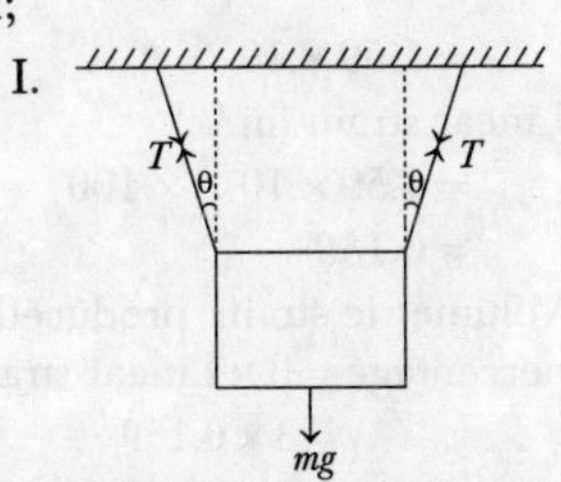

In the equilibrium, both forces will balance each other, therefore

$$2T\cos\theta = Mg$$

$$\Rightarrow T\cos\theta = \frac{Mg}{2}$$

$$\Rightarrow \quad T = \frac{Mg}{2\cos\theta}$$

II.

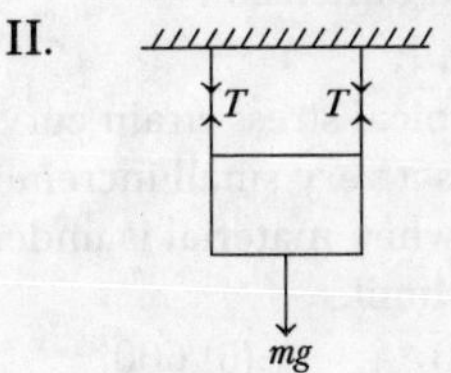

Let mass of the frame be m.

In equilibrium, both forces will balance each other, therefore

$$2T = mg \text{ or } T = \frac{mg}{2} \text{ N}$$

III.

In equilibrium, both forces will balance each other, therefore

$$2T\sin\theta = Mg$$

$$\Rightarrow \quad T = \frac{Mg}{2\sin\theta}$$

The value of $\cos\theta$ and $\sin\theta$ lies between -1 to 1.

Therefore, $T > \frac{Mg}{2}$ for any value of $\cos\theta$ or $\sin\theta < 1$.

Hence, tension will be minimum in Fig. II.

Hence, stress will be least in the string shown in Fig. I.

12. No

13. False;

$$\text{Stress} = \frac{\text{Force (weight)}}{\text{Area}}$$

$$10^5 = \frac{mg}{A}$$

$$\Rightarrow 10^5 = \frac{AL\rho g}{A}$$

$$(\because m = \text{Volume} \times \text{Density})$$

$$\Rightarrow \quad L = \frac{10^5}{\rho g} = 5 \text{ m}$$

14. 1.69 m/s^2;

When elevator is accelerating upwards, total weight

$$= mg + ma = m(g + a)$$

Maximum allowed stress

$$= \frac{\text{Force (Weight)}}{\text{Area}}$$

$$= \frac{m(g+a)}{\pi r^2}$$

$$\Rightarrow 1.15 \times 10^8 = \frac{900(9.8 + a)}{\pi(0.535 \times 10^{-2})^2}$$

$$\Rightarrow \frac{22}{7} \times \frac{0.286 \times 10^{-4} \times 1.15 \times 10^8}{900}$$

$$= 9.8 + a$$

$$\Rightarrow \quad a = 1.69 \text{ ms}^{-2}$$

15. 80 N;

We know that, $F = YA \times \frac{\Delta l}{l}$

$$\Rightarrow \quad F \propto \pi r^2$$

Hence, $\quad F_1 \propto \pi r_1^2$

and $F_2 \propto \pi r_2^2$

$$\Rightarrow \quad \frac{F_1}{F_2} = \frac{\pi r_1^2}{\pi r_2^2}$$

$$\Rightarrow \quad F_2 = F_1 \times \frac{\pi r_2^2}{\pi r_1^2} = 20 \times \frac{(0.02)^2}{(0.01)^2}$$

$$= 20 \times 4 = 80 \text{ N}$$

16. (*a*) Shearing strain,

$$\phi = \frac{x}{L} = \frac{0.02\,\text{cm}}{10\,\text{cm}} = 0.002$$

17. A $\to$ 2, B $\to$ 3, C $\to$ 1, D $\to$ 4;

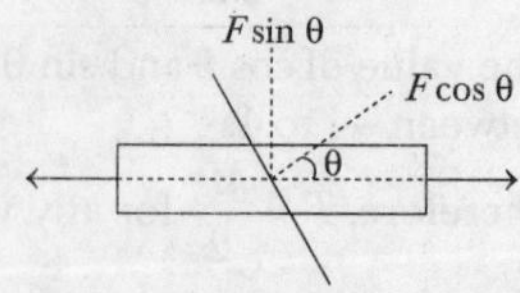

B. Shearing stress

$$= \frac{\text{Force}}{\text{Area}} = \frac{F\sin\theta}{A\sec\theta}$$

$A\sec\theta$ is the area of plane section perpendicular to the force.

Shearing stress

$$= \frac{F\sin\theta\cos\theta}{A}$$

$$= \frac{F}{2A}\sin 2\theta$$

A. Tensile stress

$$= \frac{\text{Force}}{\text{Area}} = \frac{F\cos\theta}{A\sec\theta}$$

$$= \frac{F}{A}\cos^2\theta$$

C. Tensile stress will be maximum when $\cos^2\theta$ will be maximum.

$$\Rightarrow \cos\theta^\circ = 1$$

$$\Rightarrow \theta = 0^\circ$$

D. Shearing stress will be maximum for maximum value of sin 2θ.

$$\Rightarrow \sin 2\theta = 1$$

$$\Rightarrow \theta = 45^\circ$$

18. I, II;

I. Change in volume, ΔV

$$= 1000 - 996 = 4\text{ mL}$$

II. Strain $= \dfrac{\Delta V}{V} = \dfrac{4}{1000} = 0.004$

$$= 0.004 \times 100\% = 0.4\%$$

III. The object is subjected to volumetric strain. As the volume of the object decreases due to compression when it is taken 5 km below the surface of Indian ocean.

19. (*c*);

I. Final length,

$$l' = l + \frac{1}{100}l = (1.01)l$$

$$\text{Strain} = \frac{\Delta l}{l} = \frac{l'-l}{l} = \frac{(1.01)l - l}{l}$$

$$= 0.01$$

II. Let the side of the cube be *a*.

Volume, $V = a^3$

Volumetric strain (Bulk strain)

$$= \frac{\Delta V}{V}$$

% decrease in each side = 1%

Therefore, change in volume

$$= 3 \times \%\text{ change in length}$$

$$= 3 \times 1\% = 3\%$$

Hence, Bulk strain

$$= \frac{\Delta V}{V} = 0.03$$

20. 0.48%;

$$\text{Linear strain} = \frac{\Delta l}{l} = \frac{1.59\times10^{-3}}{1}$$

$$= 1.59 \times 10^{-3}$$

Linear strain (in %)

$$= 1.59 \times 10^{-3} \times 100$$

$$= 0.159\%$$

Volumetric strain produced in percentage = 3 × Linear strain

$$= 3 \times 0.159$$

$$= 0.477\%$$

21. (*c*)

22. *B*

23. 25;

$$\text{Ratio, } \frac{a}{b} = \frac{5\times10^{-10}}{2\times10^{-11}}$$

$$= 2.5 \times 10^1$$

$$= 25\text{ m}^2/\text{N}$$

24. original dimension

25. Region I;

In a typical stress-strain curve, there is a very small increment in strain when material is under elastic limit.

26. (i) 500 (ii) 600

(iii) 550 (iv) *B*, 600

(v) 800 (vi) 700

(vii) *OAB*, *BCD*

(viii) more than or equals to

(ix) less than or equals to

27. A $\to$ 4, B $\to$ 3, C $\to$ 1, D $\to$ 2.

28. 1.67;

Since, $K = \dfrac{\text{Stress}}{\text{Strain}} = \dfrac{1}{\tan\theta}$

$$\therefore \frac{K_A}{K_B} = \frac{\tan\theta_B}{\tan\theta_A} = \frac{\tan 53^\circ}{\tan 37^\circ} = 1.67$$

29. I, II;

If *A* and *B* are prepared for identical wires of two different materials, then

$$Y = \frac{Fl}{A\Delta l}$$

$$\Rightarrow F = \frac{YA}{l}\cdot\Delta l$$

So, slope of load extension graph

$$= \frac{YA}{l}$$

As wires are identical

$$\frac{(\text{Slope})_A}{(\text{Slope})_A} = \frac{\tan\theta_A}{\tan\theta_B}$$

$$= \frac{\tan 60^\circ}{\tan 30^\circ} = \frac{Y_A}{Y_B}$$

$$\Rightarrow Y_A : Y_B = 3:1$$

As, $\Delta l = \dfrac{Fl}{AY} \Rightarrow \Delta l \propto \dfrac{1}{A}$

and extension for wire *A* is less. Hence, *A* is thicker.

30. I. $\to$ *A*, II. $\to$ *B*;

I. In the two graphs, the slope of graph in Fig. (i) is greater than the slope of graph in Fig. (ii). So material *A* has greater Young's modulus.

II. Material *B* is stronger than material *A*, because it can withstand more load without breaking. For material *B*, the ultimate stress is higher.

31. Material *A*;

As, Young's modulus,

$$Y = \frac{F}{A} \times \frac{l}{\Delta l}$$

or $$Y = \frac{F \times l^2}{\Delta l \times V} \quad \text{...(i)}$$

Since, $$V = \frac{m}{\rho} \quad \text{...(ii)}$$

From Eqs. (i) and (ii), we get

$$Y = \frac{F \times l^2 \times \rho}{\Delta l \times m}$$

Hence, $Y \propto \rho$

32. 1.59;

Young's modulus of elasticity is given by

$$Y = \frac{F}{A} \times \frac{l}{\Delta l}$$

where, $\dfrac{F}{A}$ (= stress)

$$= 3.18 \times 10^8\text{ Nm}^{-2}$$

and $Y = 2 \times 10^{11}\text{ Nm}^{-2}$

Therefore,

$$2\times 10^{11} = 3.18\times 10^{8}\times\frac{1}{\Delta l}$$

$$\Rightarrow \Delta l = \frac{3.18\times 10^{8}}{2\times 10^{11}} = 1.59\times 10^{-3}\text{ m} = 1.59\text{ mm}$$

33. False;

Since, $Y = \frac{\text{Stress}}{\text{Strain}}$

$$\Rightarrow 2\times 10^{10} = \frac{\text{Stress}}{0.15}$$

$$\Rightarrow 0.15\times 2\times 10^{10} = \text{Stress}$$

or $\text{Stress} = 3\times 10^{9}\text{ N/m}^2$

34. 2×10^{9};

The ratio $\frac{1}{2}$ implies that the length of wire is doubled, therefore

$$\text{Strain} = \frac{\text{Change in length}}{\text{Original length}} = \frac{2L-L}{L} = 1$$

$$\text{Young's modulus} = \frac{\text{Stress}}{\text{Strain}} = 20\times 10^{8}\text{ N/m}^2 = 2\times 10^{9}\text{ N/m}^2$$

35. 10;

Young's modulus for steel,

$$Y = 2\times 10^{11}\text{ Nm}^{-2}$$

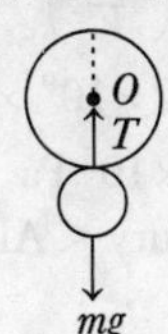

At lowest point of the vertical circle,

$$T - mg = ml\omega^2$$

$$\Rightarrow T = mg + ml\omega^2$$

$$= (14.5\times 9.8) + [14.5\times 1\times (4\pi)^2]$$

$$= 2431.94\text{ N}$$

Young's modulus,

$$Y = \frac{\text{Stress}}{\text{Strain}} = \frac{(T/A)}{\Delta l/l} = \frac{Tl}{A\Delta l}$$

$$\Rightarrow A = \frac{Tl}{Y\Delta l} = \frac{2431.94\times 1}{2\times 10^{11}\times 1.87\times 10^{-3}} = 6.5\times 10^{-2}\times 10^{-8}\text{ m}^2 = 6.5\times 10^{-10}\text{ m}^2$$

$\therefore x = 10$

36. 91.04×10^{-6};

Young's modulus of elasticity is given as

$$Y = \frac{F}{A}\times\frac{l}{\Delta l}$$

$$\Rightarrow \frac{\Delta l}{l} = \frac{F}{A}\times\frac{1}{Y} = \frac{1078}{1.26\times 10^{-3}}\times\frac{1}{9.4\times 10^{9}} = 91.04\times 10^{-6}$$

37. 177 ;

Young's modulus of elasticity,

$$Y = \frac{F}{A}\frac{l}{\Delta l}$$

$$\Rightarrow Y\times\frac{\Delta l}{l} = \frac{F}{A}$$

Since, both wires will experience same stress, therefore

$$Y_{\text{Cu}}\times\frac{\Delta l_{\text{Cu}}}{l_{\text{Cu}}} = Y_{\text{steel}}\times\frac{\Delta l_{\text{steel}}}{l_{\text{steel}}}$$

$$\Rightarrow 1.1\times 10^{11}\times\frac{\Delta l_{\text{Cu}}}{2.2} = 2\times 10^{11}\times\frac{\Delta l_{\text{steel}}}{1.6}$$

$[\because Y_{\text{Cu}} = 1.1\times 10^{11}\text{ N/m}^2$ and $Y_{\text{steel}} = 2.0\times 10^{11}\text{ N/m}^2]$

$$\Rightarrow \frac{\Delta l_{\text{Cu}}}{\Delta l_{\text{steel}}} = \frac{40}{16} = 2.5 \quad\text{...(i)}$$

According to the question,

elongation = 0.70 mm $= 0.7\times 10^{-3}$ m

$$\Rightarrow \Delta l_{\text{Cu}} + \Delta l_{\text{steel}} = 0.7\times 10^{-3}\text{ m} \quad\text{...(ii)}$$

From Eqs. (i) and (ii), we get

$$(\Delta l)_{\text{steel}} = 2\times 10^{-4}\text{ m}$$

$$(\Delta l)_{\text{Cu}} = 5\times 10^{-4}\text{ m}$$

Now, Young's modulus,

$$Y = \frac{F}{A}\times\frac{l}{\Delta l}$$

$$\Rightarrow F = YA\frac{\Delta l}{l}$$

$$\Rightarrow F = \frac{1.1\times 10^{11}\times\pi\times(1.5\times 10^{-3})^2\times 5\times 10^{-4}}{2.2} = 176.78\text{ N}\approx 177\text{ N}$$

38. 10^{-5}

39. 4 ;

O ω T_{max} mv^2/l

In space station, $g_{\text{eff}} = 0$

$$T = \frac{mv^2}{l}$$

$$\sigma_{\max}\times A = \frac{mv^2}{l} = m\omega^2 l$$

$$\Rightarrow \omega_{\max} = \sqrt{\frac{\sigma_{\max}\times A}{ml}} = \sqrt{\frac{4.8\times 10^{7}\times 10^{-2}\times(10^{-2})^2}{10\times 0.3}} = \sqrt{16} = 4\text{ rad/s}$$

40. Yes;

Total elongation,

$$\Delta l = \Delta l_1 + \Delta l_2 \quad\text{...(i)}$$

Using the relation,

$$Y = \frac{\frac{F}{\pi r^2}}{\frac{\Delta l}{l}}$$

Eq.(i) can be rewritten as

$$\frac{F\cdot 2l}{Y\pi r^2} = \frac{Fl}{Y_1\pi r^2} + \frac{Fl}{Y_2\pi r^2}$$

$$\frac{F\,2l}{Y\cdot\pi r^2} = \frac{Fl}{\pi r^2}\left(\frac{1}{Y_1} + \frac{1}{Y_2}\right)$$

Upon comparing, we get

$$Y = \frac{2Y_1Y_2}{Y_1 + Y_2}$$

41. 12.5;

Tension for system,

$$T = \frac{2m_1m_2g}{m_1 + m_2} = \frac{2\times 3\times 5\times 10}{3+5} = \frac{300}{8}\text{ N}$$

Using the relation, $\sigma = \frac{T}{\pi r^2}$

$$\Rightarrow r = \sqrt{\frac{T}{\sigma\pi}} = \sqrt{\frac{300}{8\times\frac{24}{\pi}\times 10^2\times\pi}} = 12.5\text{ cm}$$

$$\Rightarrow r_{\min} = 12.5\text{ cm}$$

42. 2.5×10^{9}

43. 1;

$$Y = \frac{\frac{F}{A}}{\frac{\Delta l}{l}}$$

$$\Rightarrow F = \frac{Y\Delta l\cdot A}{l} \quad\text{...(i)}$$

$$\because \frac{A_1}{A_2} = \frac{\pi r_1^2}{\pi r_2^2} = \left(\frac{r_1}{r_2}\right)^2 = \left(\frac{1}{\sqrt{2}}\right)^2 = \frac{1}{2} \quad\text{...(ii)}$$

Using Eq.(i), we get

$$\frac{F_1}{F_2} = \frac{\Delta l_1 \cdot A_1}{l_1} \times \frac{l_2}{\Delta l_2 \cdot A_2}$$

$$= \left(\frac{\Delta l_1}{\Delta l_2}\right) \cdot \left(\frac{l_2}{l_1}\right) \cdot \left(\frac{A_1}{A_2}\right)$$

Substituting known values, we get

$$1 = \left(\frac{\Delta l_1}{\Delta l_2}\right) \cdot \left(\frac{2}{1}\right)\left(\frac{1}{2}\right)$$

[using Eq. (ii)]

$$\Rightarrow \frac{\Delta l_1}{\Delta l_2} = 1$$

44. 0.2;

Net elongation in the system can be given by

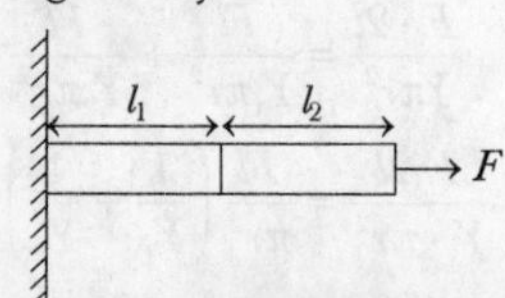

$$\Delta l_{net} = \Delta l_1 + \Delta l_2$$

$$= \frac{Fl}{AY_1} + \frac{Fl}{AY_2}$$

$$= \frac{F}{A} \times l\left(\frac{1}{Y_1} + \frac{1}{Y_2}\right)$$

$$\left(\because \text{Stress} = \frac{F}{A}\right)$$

$$= 8 \times 10^6 \times 1 \left(\frac{1}{120 \times 10^9} + \frac{1}{60 \times 10^9}\right)$$

$$= 0.2 \times 10^{-3} \text{ m}$$

45. I. Case $A \rightarrow 2L\,\Delta T$, Case $B \rightarrow 0$

II. Case $A = \alpha \Delta T$, Case $B =$ Zero

46. 2.2×10^8 N/m^2

47. 0.16;

The area of the face parallel to which the force is applied, is

$$A = 50 \text{ cm} \times 10 \text{ cm}$$

$$= 5 \times 10^{-2} \text{ m}^2$$

Therefore, the stress applied

$$= 9.0 \times 10^4 / 5 \times 10^{-2}$$

$$= 1.8 \times 10^6 \text{ N/m}^2$$

Shearing strain

$$= \frac{\Delta x}{L} = \frac{\text{Stress}}{\text{Shear modulus } (G)}$$

$$\Rightarrow \Delta x = \frac{L \times \text{Stress}}{G}$$

$$= \frac{0.5 \times 1.8 \times 10^6}{5.6 \times 10^9}$$

$$= 0.16 \times 10^{-3} \text{ m}$$

$$= 0.16 \text{ mm}$$

48. (i) 1.5×10^{-3};

Shearing strain,

$$\theta = \frac{x}{h} = \frac{15 \times 10^{-6}}{10^{-2}}$$

$$= 1.5 \times 10^{-3}$$

(ii) 6.75×10^7 N/m^2;

Modulus of rigidity,

$$\eta = \frac{\text{Shearing stress}}{\text{Shearing strain}}$$

$$4.5 \times 10^{10} = \frac{\text{Shearing stress}}{1.5 \times 10^{-3}}$$

$\Rightarrow$ Shearing stress

$$= 6.75 \times 10^7 \text{ N/m}^2$$

(iii) 1.688×10^7 N;

Shearing force, $F = \eta A\theta$

$$= 4.5 \times 10^{10} \times (0.5)^2 \times 1.5 \times 10^{-3}$$

$$= 1.688 \times 10^7 \text{ N}$$

49. I ;

I. $G = \frac{FL}{Al} = \frac{FL}{L^2 l}$ $\quad (\because A = L^2)$

$$= \frac{F}{Ll} = \frac{0.25}{5 \times 10^{-2} \times 0.65 \times 10^{-2}}$$

$$= 770 \text{ N/m}^2$$

II. Similarly, for second case,

$$G = \frac{5}{5 \times 10^{-2} \times 0.65 \times 10^{-2}}$$

$$= 15384 \text{ N/m}^2$$

50. 0.12°;

According to relation, $r\theta = l\phi$

$$\Rightarrow \phi = \frac{r\theta}{l} = \frac{0.4 \times 30°}{10} = 0.12°$$

51. 10^6;

Bulk modulus is given as

$$B = \frac{-\text{Volume}}{\text{Change in volume}} \times \text{Pressure}$$

Let volume be V such that volumetric strain is 0.01%.

or $\frac{\Delta V}{V} = 0.01\% = 10^{-4}$

$$\therefore \quad B = \frac{1}{10^{-4}} \times 100 = 10^6 \text{ atm}$$

$$= 10^6 \text{ N/m}^2$$

52. (d)

53. (c)

54. 1.36×10^{-2};

The pressure exerted by 3000 m column of water on the bottom layer,

$$p = h\rho g = 3000 \times 1000 \times 10$$

$$= 3 \times 10^7 \text{ kg m}^{-1}\text{s}^{-2}$$

$$= 3 \times 10^7 \text{ Nm}^{-2}$$

Fractional compression,

$$\frac{\Delta V}{V} = \frac{\text{Stress}}{\text{Bulk modulus}}$$

$$= \frac{3 \times 10^7}{2.2 \times 10^9} = 1.36 \times 10^{-2}$$

55. False;

The fractional decrement is given by

$$\frac{\Delta V}{V} = \frac{\text{Force}}{\text{Area}} \times \frac{1}{\text{Bulk modulus}}$$

$$= \frac{50}{10^{-2}} \times \frac{1}{(12 \times 10^9)}$$

$$= 4.17 \times 10^{-7}$$

56. (i) 2×10^9 N/m^2

(ii) 5×10^{-10} m^2/N

57. 2.2×10^5 Pa;

Given, fractional decrease in volume, $\frac{\Delta V}{V} = -0.01\%$

$$= \frac{-0.01}{100} = -10^{-4}$$

Bulk modulus,

$$B = \frac{-p}{\left(\frac{\Delta V}{V}\right)}$$

$$\Rightarrow p = -B\left(\frac{\Delta V}{V}\right)$$

$$= -2.2 \times 10^9 \times (-10^{-4})$$

$$= 2.2 \times 10^5 \text{ Pa}$$

58. Air < Mercury < Aluminium

59. 10^5 ;

Bulk modulus,

$$B = \frac{p}{\frac{\Delta V}{V}}$$

$$= \frac{1.45 \times 10^4}{\frac{14.5}{100}} = 10^5 \text{ N/m}^2$$

60. A $\rightarrow$ 3 $\rightarrow$ R, B $\rightarrow$ 1 $\rightarrow$ Q, C $\rightarrow$ 2 $\rightarrow$ P

61. III

62. increase

63. A. $\frac{Fx}{AL}$

B. $dW = \frac{YAxdx}{L}$

C. $\left[\frac{YAx^2}{2L}\right]$

D. potential

E. $\frac{1}{2}Fl$

F. $\frac{1}{2}\times$ stress $\times$ strain

64. 0.025 J

Elastic potential energy,

$$E = \frac{1}{2}kx^2$$
$$= \frac{1}{2}\times 5\times(10^{-1})^2$$
$$= 0.5\times 5\times 10^{-2}$$
$$\Rightarrow \quad E = 25\times 10^{-3}$$
$$= 0.025\,\text{J}$$

65. $\sqrt{2}:1$;

$$\frac{u_A}{u_B} = \frac{1}{4}$$

$$\Rightarrow \frac{\frac{1}{2Y}\cdot\frac{F^2}{A_A^2}}{\frac{1}{2Y}\cdot\frac{F^2}{A_B^2}} = \frac{1}{4} \Rightarrow \frac{A_B^2}{A_A^2} = \frac{1}{4}$$

$$\Rightarrow \frac{A_B}{A_A} = \frac{1}{2} \Rightarrow \frac{\pi r_A^2}{\pi r_B^2} = \frac{1}{2}$$

$$\Rightarrow \frac{r_A}{r_B} = \frac{1}{\sqrt{2}} \Rightarrow \frac{\frac{d_A}{2}}{\frac{d_B}{2}} = \frac{1}{\sqrt{2}}$$

$$\Rightarrow \frac{d_B}{d_A} = \frac{\sqrt{2}}{1}$$

66. 5;

$\therefore$ Strain, $\frac{\Delta L}{L} = \alpha\Delta T$

$$= 10^{-5}\times 10 = 10^{-4}$$

Now, energy

$$= \frac{1}{2}\text{(strain) (stress) (volume)}$$
$$= \frac{1}{2}\text{(strain)}\,(Y\times\text{strain})\,(Al)$$

or $\frac{E}{l} = \frac{1}{2}\times YA\,(\text{strain})^2$

$$= \frac{1}{2}\times 10^{11}\times 0.01\times(10^{-4})^2$$
$$= 5\,\text{J}$$

67. (*a*); Torsional constant is given by

$$C = \frac{\eta\pi r^4}{2L}$$
$$= \frac{5.9\times 10^{11}\times 3.14\times(2\times 10^{-3})^4}{2\times 5\times 10^{-2}}$$
$$= 2.9\times 10^{-6}$$

Potential energy of the wire

$$= \frac{1}{2}C\theta^2 = \frac{1}{2}\times 2.9\times 10^{-6}\times(0.0029)^2$$
$$= 1.253\times 10^{-11}\,\text{J}\ (10' = 0.0029\text{ rad})$$

68. 2 : 1

69. True

Assertion-Reason Questions

1. (*a*)

2. (*c*)

3. (*c*) Hooke's law states that

Stress $\propto$ Strain

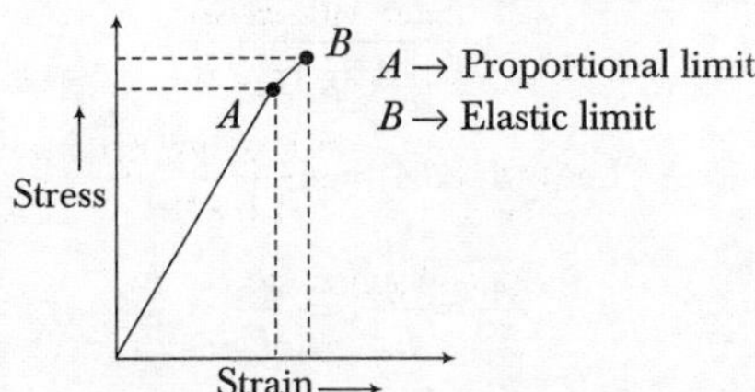

It is obeyed upto proportional limit.

4. (*a*); Spring balance shows incorrect reading after using it for a long time as with time the spring in it loses its elastic strength.

5. (*a*)

6. (*a*)

7. (*d*); Bulk modulus, $B = \frac{-\Delta p}{\Delta V/V}$

For incompressible fluids,

$$\Delta V = 0$$
$$\therefore \quad B = \infty$$

Apart form this, it is true to say that compressibility is inverse of bulk modulus of elasticity.

8. (*c*)

9. (*a*)

10. (*a*); If a solid sphere placed in the fluid under high pressure, then it is compressed uniformly on all sides.

The force applied by the fluids acts in perpendicular direction at each point of the surface and the body is said to be under hydraulic compression.

This leads to decrease in its volume without any change of its geometrical shape.

Case Based Questions

1. (i) (*c*);The curve will be stress-strain proportional upto the proportionality limit. After this, the elastic limit will occur.

(ii) (*a*); The elastic modulus is the ratio of stress and strain. So, in the stress-strain curve, it is the slope.

(iii) (*c*); Necking in a ductile material is observed after the body crosses the point of ultimate strength on the stress-strain curve.

(iv) (*c*)

Or

(*a*)

2. (i) (*c*); Young's modulus is given as

$$Y = 3K(1-2\sigma)$$
$$\Rightarrow \quad \sigma = \frac{1}{2}\left(1-\frac{Y}{3K}\right) \quad \ldots(\text{i})$$

Also, $Y = 3G(1+\sigma)$

$$\Rightarrow \quad \sigma = \left(\frac{Y}{2G}-1\right) \quad \ldots(\text{ii})$$

From Eqs. (i) and (ii), we have

$$\frac{1}{2}\left(1-\frac{Y}{3K}\right) = \left(\frac{Y}{2G}-1\right)$$
$$\Rightarrow \quad 1-\frac{Y}{3K} = \frac{Y}{G}-2$$
$$\Rightarrow \quad \frac{Y}{3K} = 3-\frac{Y}{G}$$
$$\Rightarrow \quad K = \frac{GY}{9G-3Y}\,\text{N/m}$$

(ii) (*a*); Given,

$$A = 1\text{ cm}^2 = 10^{-4}\text{ m}^2,$$
$$L_1 = l$$
$$L_2 = 2l$$
$$\because \quad \Delta l = L_2 - L_1 = l$$

We know that, Young's modulus is

$$Y = \frac{Fl}{A\Delta l}$$
$$\Rightarrow \quad F = \frac{YA\Delta l}{l}$$
$$\Rightarrow \quad F = 2\times 10^7\text{ N}$$

(iii) (*a*); The value of Young's modulus depends upon the nature of the material of the body and the manner in which the body is deformed.

Or

(*c*); Young's modulus of a body does not depend on length of wire.

(iv) (*c*); Given, $A = 4\text{ mm}^2$

$$= 4\times 10^{-6}\text{ m}^2$$
$$F = 10^8\text{ N}$$
$$Y = 10^{15}\text{N/m}^2$$

Young's modulus can be written as

$$Y = \frac{F}{A\varepsilon}$$

$$\Rightarrow \quad \varepsilon = \frac{F}{AY}$$

$$\Rightarrow \quad \varepsilon = 0.025$$

Competition Edge Up

1. (20); According to question,

200N ← → 200N

$$\frac{F}{A} = Y\frac{\Delta l}{l}$$

$$\Rightarrow \quad \Delta l = \frac{Fl}{YA} = \frac{200\times 2}{10^{11}\times 2\times 10^{-4}}$$

$$= 2\times 10^{-5} = 20\,\mu\text{m}$$

2. (*c*); Given,

$$Y = 49000\times\frac{M}{l}\frac{\text{dyne}}{\text{m}^2}$$

$\therefore$ Percentage error in Y is,

$$\frac{\Delta Y}{Y}\times 100 = \frac{\Delta M}{M}\times 100 + \frac{\Delta l}{l}\times 100$$

$\Rightarrow$ Percentage error in Y

$$= \frac{\Delta M}{M}\times 100 + \frac{\Delta l}{l}\times 100$$

$$= \frac{5}{500}\times 100 + \frac{0.02}{2}\times 100$$

$$= 1 + 1 = 2\%$$

3. (600); Given,

Density, $\rho = 6\times 10^4\ \text{kg/m}^3$

Breaking stress,

$$\sigma = 1.2\times 10^8\ \text{N/m}^2$$

$$g_{\text{planet}} = \frac{g_{\text{earth}}}{3}$$

T, l, A, mg

Now, $\quad T = mg_{\text{planet}} \quad \ldots(\text{i})$

$$\text{Stress} = \frac{T}{A} = \frac{mg_{\text{planet}}}{A}$$

$$\sigma = \frac{(\rho Al)}{A}g_{\text{planet}}$$

$$\Rightarrow \quad l = \frac{\sigma}{\rho g_{\text{planet}}} \quad \ldots(\text{ii})$$

$$= \frac{1.2\times 10^8\times 3}{6\times 10^4\times 10} = 600\ \text{m}$$

4. (3); Wires are similar, so $Y_{\text{I}} = Y_{\text{II}}$

Since, wires are similar, then area of both wires

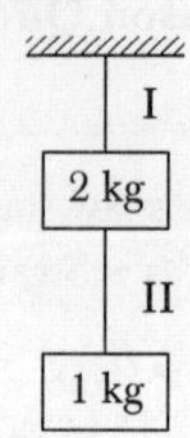

Let, $A_1 = A_2 = A$

$$\frac{\frac{F_{\text{I}}}{A}}{E_{\text{I}}} = \frac{\frac{F_{\text{II}}}{A}}{E_{\text{II}}} \Rightarrow \frac{F_{\text{I}}}{F_{\text{II}}} = \frac{E_{\text{I}}}{E_{\text{II}}}$$

Ratio of strains in wire is

$$\frac{E_{\text{I}}}{E_{\text{II}}} = \frac{F_{\text{I}}}{F_{\text{II}}} = \frac{3}{1}$$

5. (*c*); On increasing temperature, change in length will be more for same load.

$\therefore$ Strain will be more, so Young's modulus value decreases.

$$\because \quad Y \propto \frac{1}{\Delta L}$$

6. (*b*); Young's modulus describe the relation between stress and strain,

$$Y = \frac{\text{Stress}}{\text{Strain}}$$

It is independent of geometrical factor.

7. (16); Given,

$$V_1 = V_2 \Rightarrow A_1l_1 = A_2l_2$$

$$\Rightarrow \quad \frac{A_1}{A_2} = \frac{l_2}{l_1} \quad \ldots(\text{i})$$

We know that,

$$Y = \frac{F/A}{\Delta l/l} = \frac{Fl}{A\Delta l} \Rightarrow F = \frac{YA\Delta l}{l}$$

$$\Rightarrow F \propto \frac{A\Delta l}{l} \Rightarrow \frac{F_1}{F_2} = \frac{A_1}{A_2}\cdot\frac{l_2}{l_1}\cdot\frac{\Delta l_1}{\Delta l_2}$$

$$= \frac{A_1}{A_2}\cdot\frac{A_1}{A_2}$$

[$\because \Delta l_1 = \Delta l_2$ and using Eq. (i)]

$$= \left(\frac{A_1}{A_2}\right)^2 = \left(\frac{4}{1}\right)^2 = 16$$

8. (*c*); We know that,

$$Y = \frac{F/A}{\Delta l/l} = \frac{Fl}{A\Delta l}$$

$$\Rightarrow \quad Y = \frac{Fl}{\pi r^2\Delta l}$$

$$\Rightarrow \quad \Delta l = \frac{Fl}{\pi r^2 Y}$$

$$\Rightarrow \quad \Delta l \propto \frac{F}{r^2}$$

$$\therefore \quad \frac{\Delta l_2}{\Delta l_1} = \frac{F_2}{F_1}\times\left(\frac{r_1}{r_2}\right)^2$$

$$= \frac{F_1/2}{F_1}\times\left(\frac{r_1}{r_1/2}\right)^2$$

$$= \frac{1}{2}\times 4 = 2$$

$$\therefore \quad \Delta l_2 = 2\Delta l_1$$

9. (*a*); We know that,

$$Y = \frac{F}{A}\frac{l}{\Delta l}$$

Here, $\frac{F}{A}$ = Elastic limit E

$$\Rightarrow \quad Y = E\frac{l}{\Delta l}$$

$$\Rightarrow \quad \Delta l = \frac{E}{Y}l$$

$$\Rightarrow \quad \Delta l = \frac{8\times 10^8}{2\times 10^{11}}\times 1$$

$$= 4\times 10^{-3}\ \text{m}$$

$$= 4\ \text{mm}$$

10. (*b*); Stress $= Y\cdot\frac{\Delta l}{l}$

Here, $\Delta l = l\alpha\Delta T$

$$= 1\times 10^{-5}\times 100 = 10^{-3}$$

$$\Rightarrow \quad \frac{F}{A} = Y\cdot\frac{10^{-3}}{1}$$

Compressive force,

$$F = 0.5\times 10^{11}\times 10^{-3}\times 10^{-3}$$

$$= 0.5\times 10^5 = 50\times 10^3\ \text{N}$$

11. (*a*); Longitudinal

$$\text{stress} = \frac{\text{Weight}}{\text{Area}} = \frac{w}{A}$$

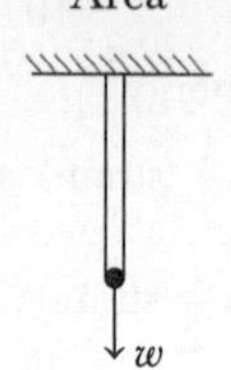

12. (*c*); Here, change in length of wire,

$$\Delta L = (L_1 - L)$$

Area of cross-section $= A$

Force, $F = Mg$

Young's modulus,

$$Y = \frac{\text{Normal stress}}{\text{Longitudinal strain}}$$

$$\Rightarrow \quad Y = \frac{(F/A)}{\left(\frac{\Delta L}{L}\right)} = \frac{\left(\frac{Mg}{A}\right)}{\left(\frac{L_1 - L}{L}\right)}$$

$$= \frac{MgL}{A(L_1 - L)}$$

Chapter-9

Mechanical Properties of Fluids

1. 1.96×10^5 Pa;

$$\text{Pressure} = \frac{\text{Force}}{2\times\text{Area}} = \frac{mg}{2A} = \frac{40\times9.8}{2\times10\times10^{-4}} = 1.96\times10^5\text{ Pa}$$

2. I, II;

Let the fluid exerts pressure p_a, p_b and p_c on the faces *BEFC*, *ADFC* and *ADEB* of area denoted by A_a, A_b and A_c corresponding to the normal forces F_a, F_b and F_c, respectively. Then, at equilibrium

$F_b\sin\theta = F_c,\ F_b\cos\theta = F_a$ (by equilibrium)

$A_b\sin\theta = A_c,\ A_b\cos\theta = A_a$ (by geometry)

Thus, $\frac{F_b}{A_b} = \frac{F_c}{A_c} = \frac{F_a}{A_a}$

3. (*c*); Pressure at the top is the atmospheric pressure itself,

so $p_1 = p_A$

At the base of beaker of height h and density of liquid ρ, the pressure,

$p_2 = p_A + \rho gh$

Therefore, $p_1 + p_2 = \rho gh$

$p_1 - p_2 = \rho gh$

$p_1 - p_2$ is equal to the weight of fluid per unit area.

4. 1:1:1:1;

The pressure increases with depth according to the formula, $p = \rho gh$, since all the beakers contain water up to same height.

Hence, $p_1 = p_2 = p_3 = p_4$ or 1 : 1 : 1 : 1.

5. ρgh, $p_a + \rho gh$;

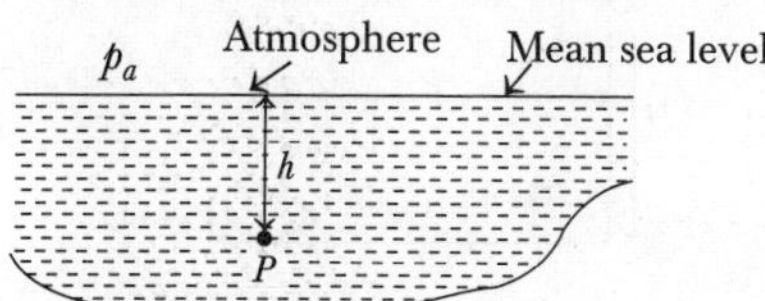

At point P, gauge pressure $= \rho gh$

The absolute pressure $= p_a + \rho gh$

where, p_a is the atmospheric pressure.

6. 1; Absolute pressure,

$$p_A = p_a + \rho gh$$

$$= 1.01\times10^5 + 1.03\times10^3\times10\times1000$$

$$= 104.01\times10^5\text{ Pa}$$

Gauge pressure,

$$p_G = \rho gh = 1.03\times10^3\times10\times1000 = 103\times10^5\text{ Pa}$$

The ratio becomes

$$\frac{p_A}{p_G} = \frac{104.01\times10^5}{103\times10^5} \approx 1$$

7. 13.6 m;

$$p_{\text{liquid}} = p_{\text{mercury}}$$

$$h_l\rho_l g = h_m\rho_m g$$

$$h_l = h_m\times\frac{\rho_m}{\rho_l} = 76\times\frac{13600}{760} = 13.6\text{ m}$$

8. (*b*); According to Pascal's law, pressure due to water column of height 15 cm is equal to the pressure due to oil column of height 20 cm. So,

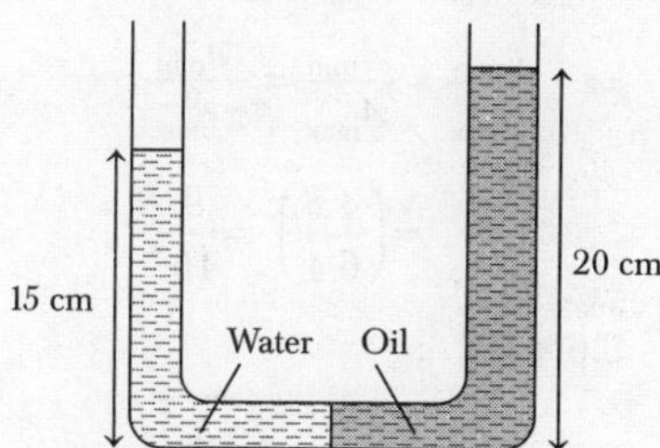

$$h_w\rho_w g = h_o\rho_o g$$

$$15\rho_w = 20\rho_o$$

$$\Rightarrow\ \rho_o = \frac{15}{20}\times1000 = 750\text{ kg m}^{-3}$$

9. (*a*); Initial pressure,

$$p_1 = \rho gd + p_0 = 3\times10^5\text{ Pa}$$

$$\therefore\ \rho gd + 1\times10^5 = 3\times10^5$$

$$\rho gd = 2\times10^5\text{ Pa}$$

When the depth is doubled,

$$p_2 = 2\rho gd + p_0 = 2\times2\times10^5 + 1\times10^5 = 5\times10^5\text{Pa}$$

Percentage increase

$$= \frac{p_2 - p_1}{p_1}\times100 = \frac{(5-3)\times10^5}{3\times10^5}\times100 = \frac{200}{3}\ \%$$

10. (*c*);

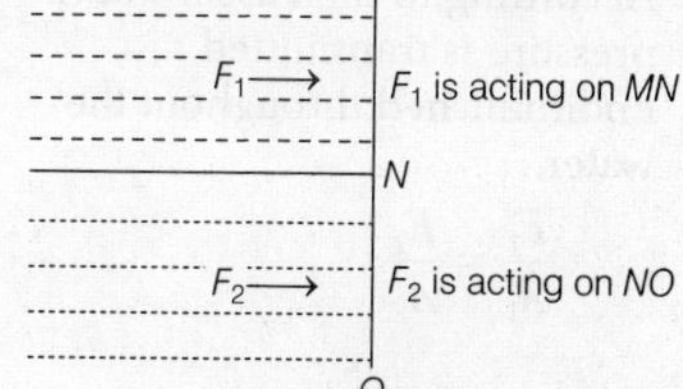

Force F_1 is acting on MN. It is given by

$$F_1 = \frac{\rho gh}{2}\times A$$

Force F_2 is acting on NO. It is given by

$$F_2 = \rho ghA + \frac{2\rho ghA}{2} = 2\rho ghA$$

The ratio of force on $MN(F_1)$ and force on $NO(F_2)$ is given by

$$\frac{F_1}{F_2} = \frac{\rho gh}{2}\times A\times\frac{1}{2\rho ghA}$$

$$\frac{F_1}{F_2} = \frac{1}{4}$$

11. False;

In a car brake system, piston connected with brake padel is smaller, whereas piston connected with the brake shoe is of larger area.

12. IV

13. $F_1 = 3F_2$;

According to the Pascal's law,

$$\frac{F_1}{A_1} = \frac{F_2}{A_2}$$

$$\frac{F_1}{3A_2} = \frac{F_2}{A_2}\quad(\text{given, } A_1 = 3A_2)$$

$$\Rightarrow\ F_1 = 3F_2$$

14. (i) 10, (ii) 20;

(i) Volume covered by movement of piston 1 inwards is equal to the volume covered by movement of piston 2 outwards.

Therefore, $V_1 = V_2$

$$A_1x_1 = A_2x_2$$

$$(3A_2)x_1 = A_2\ (30)\quad(\text{given } A_1 = 3A_2)$$

$$\Rightarrow\ x_1 = 10\text{ cm}$$

(ii) Work done by piston 1 will be equal to the work done by P_2, i.e. 20 J.

15. 90 N;

According to the Pascal's law, pressure is transmitted undiminished throughout the water.

$$\therefore \quad \frac{F_1}{A_1} = \frac{F_2}{A_2}$$

$$\frac{F_1}{\pi\left(\frac{D_1}{2}\right)^2} = \frac{F_2}{\pi\left(\frac{D_2}{2}\right)^2}$$

$$= \frac{10}{\pi\left(\frac{10^{-2}}{2}\right)^2} = \frac{F_2}{\pi\left(\frac{3\times10^{-2}}{2}\right)^2}$$

$$\Rightarrow \quad F_2 = 90 \text{ N}$$

16. 25600;

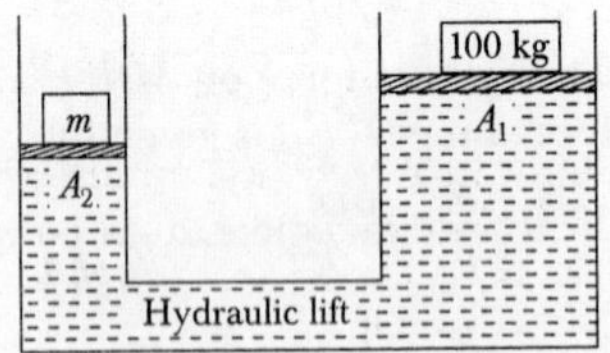

According to the Pascal's law,

$$\frac{F_2}{A_2} = \frac{F_1}{A_1}$$

$$\frac{100\times g}{A_1} = \frac{mg}{A_2} \quad \text{...(i)}$$

In the second case, let the mass lifted by m_0 kg, then

$$\frac{m_0 g}{16A_1} = \frac{mg}{\frac{A_2}{16}} \quad \text{...(ii)}$$

$$\left(\because A = \frac{\pi d^2}{4}\right)$$

From Eqs. (i) and (ii), we get

$$\frac{m_0}{16\times100} = 16$$

$$\Rightarrow \quad m_0 = 25600 \text{ kg}$$

17. $A \rightarrow$ Turbulent, $B \rightarrow$ Laminar

18. $v_1 > v_2 > v_3$, $A_1v_1 = A_2v_2 = A_3v_3$;

Since, at narrower portions where the streamlines are closely spaced, velocity increases and *vice-versa.*

$$\because \quad A_3 > A_2 > A_1$$

$$\therefore \quad v_1 > v_2 > v_3$$

According to the equation of continuity flow,

$$A_1v_1 = A_2v_2 = A_3v_3$$

So, volume flow rates would be equal through A_1, A_2 and A_3.

19. 4; $r_A = \frac{2}{2} = 1$ cm

$$r_B = \frac{4}{2} = 2 \text{ cm}$$

According to the equation of continuity of flow,

$$A_Av_A = A_Bv_B$$

$$\pi r_A^2 \cdot v_A = \pi r_B^2 \cdot v_B$$

$$\frac{v_A}{v_B} = \left(\frac{r_B}{r_A}\right)^2 \Rightarrow \frac{v_A}{v_B} = 4$$

20. 1; According to equation of continuity,

$$A_Av_A = A_Bv_B + A_Cv_C$$

$$A\times3 = A\times1.5 + 1.5A\times v_C$$

$$\Rightarrow \quad v_C = 1 \text{ ms}^{-1}$$

21. I, IV

22. 9, 16;

According to the equation of continuity of flow,

$$A_{\text{max}}v_{\text{min}} = A_{\text{min}}v_{\text{max}}$$

$$\Rightarrow \quad \frac{v_{\text{min}}}{v_{\text{max}}} = \frac{A_{\text{min}}}{A_{\text{max}}} = \frac{\pi r_{\text{min}}^2}{\pi r_{\text{max}}^2}$$

$$= \left(\frac{4.8}{6.4}\right)^2 = \frac{9}{16}$$

23. 3.6×10^{-3};

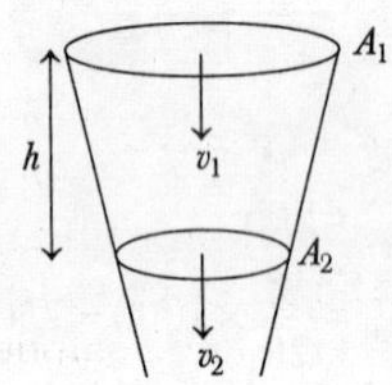

According to the equation of motion,

$$v_2 = \sqrt{v_1^2 + 2gh}$$

$$= \sqrt{(0.4)^2 + 2\times10\times0.2}$$

$$= 2 \text{ m/s}$$

Applying the equation of continuity of flow,

$$A_1v_1 = A_2v_2$$

$$\pi\left(\frac{8\times10^{-3}}{2}\right)^2 \times 0.4 = \pi\left(\frac{d_2}{2}\right)^2 \times 2$$

$$\Rightarrow d_2 = 3.6\times10^{-3} \text{ m}$$

24. (*a*)

25. $(p_A - p_B)V, mg(h_B - h_A), \frac{1}{2}m(v_B^2 - v_A^2)$;

I. Work done in terms of pressure and volume is given by

$$\Rightarrow W = pV = (p_A - p_B)V$$

II. Potential energy $= \text{PE}_f - \text{PE}_i$

$$= mgh_B - mgh_A$$

$$= mg(h_B - h_A)$$

III. Change in kinetic energy

$$= \text{KE}_f - \text{KE}_i$$

$$= \frac{1}{2}mv_B^2 - \frac{1}{2}mv_A^2$$

$$= \frac{1}{2}m(v_B^2 - v_A^2)$$

26. (*a*); Applying Bernoulli's principle, we have

$$p_1 + \frac{1}{2}\rho v_1^2 = p_2 + \frac{1}{2}\rho v_2^2$$

$$\Rightarrow p_2 - p_1 = \frac{1}{2}\rho(v_1^2 - v_2^2)$$

$$= \frac{1}{2}\times1.2(120^2 - 80^2)$$

$$= 4800 \text{ Pa}$$

27. 2.4×10^5 N, upwards;

Applying Bernoulli's theorem just above and below the roof, we get

$$p + \frac{1}{2}\rho v^2 = p_a$$

or $$\Delta p = (p_a - p) = \frac{1}{2}\rho v^2$$

Force required for the lift of roof to happen

$$F = \Delta p \cdot A = \frac{1}{2}\rho A v^2$$

$$= \frac{1}{2}\times1.2\times250\times(40)^2$$

$$= 2.4\times10^5 \text{ N}$$

28. 3 m/s;

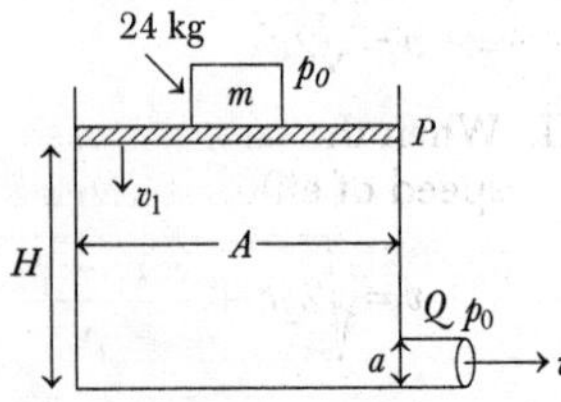

According to the Bernoulli's principle, for points P and Q, we can write

$$p_0 + \frac{mg}{A} + \rho gh + \frac{1}{2}\rho v_1^2$$

$$= p_0 + \frac{1}{2}\rho v^2$$

At point P, $v_1 = 0$, so the equation simplifies to

$$\frac{mg}{A} + \rho gh = \frac{1}{2}\rho v^2$$

$$\frac{24 \times 10}{0.4} + 10^3 \times 10 \times 0.4$$

$$= \frac{1}{2} \times 10^3 \times v^2 \Rightarrow v = 3 \text{ m/s}$$

29. 2720 cm^3/s;

Rate of low of water is given by

$$A_P v_P = A_Q v_Q$$

$$(40) v_p = (20) v_Q$$

$$\Rightarrow \quad v_Q = 2v_p \quad ...(i)$$

Applying Bernoulli's theorem at points A and B, we get

$$p_P + \frac{1}{2}\rho v_P^2 = p_Q + \frac{1}{2}\rho v_Q^2$$

$$p_P - p_Q = \frac{1}{2}\rho(v_Q^2 - v_P^2)$$

From Eq. (i), we get

$$700 = \frac{1}{2} \times 1000\,(4v_P^2 - v_P^2)$$

$$\Rightarrow \quad v_P = 68 \text{ cm/s}$$

Rate of flow of water $= A_P v_P$

$$= (40)(68) = 2720 \text{ cm}^3/\text{s}$$

30. I;

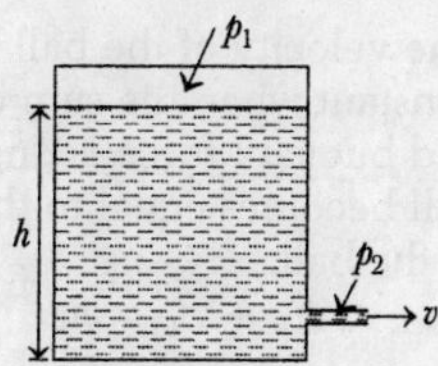

I. When the tank is open,

$$p_1 = p_2 \quad ...(i)$$

Using the relation,

$$v = \sqrt{2gh + \frac{2(p_1 - p_2)}{\rho}}$$

Substituting Eq. (i),

$$\Rightarrow v = \sqrt{2gh}$$

II. When the tank is closed, the speed of efflux is given by

$$v = \sqrt{2gh + \frac{2(p_1 - p_2)}{\rho}} \quad (p_1 >> p_2)$$

31. True;

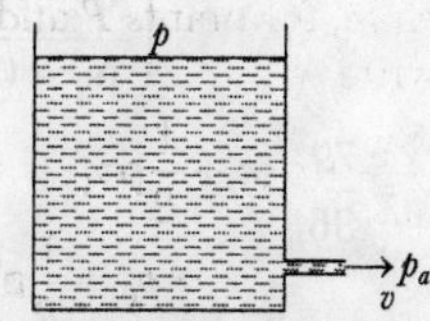

In case of an open tank,

$$p = p_a \quad ...(i)$$

Using the relation,

$$v = \sqrt{2gh + \frac{2(p - p_a)}{\rho}}$$

From Eq. (i), we get

$$v = \sqrt{2gh}$$

This is equal to the speed of freely falling body. This is known as Torricelli's law.

32. (*d*);

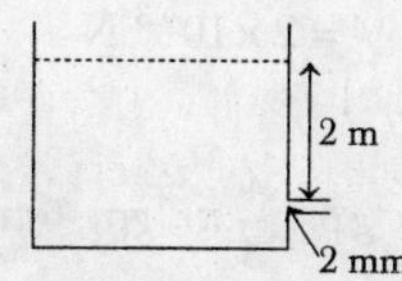

The rate of flow of the liquid is given by

$$Q = Av = A\sqrt{2gh}$$

Since, the tank is open, so the pressure at the hole is equal to the pressure above.

So, $Q = 2 \times 10^{-6} \times \sqrt{2 \times 10 \times 2}$

$$\simeq 12.6 \times 10^{-6} \text{ m}^3/\text{s}$$

33. 7.07;

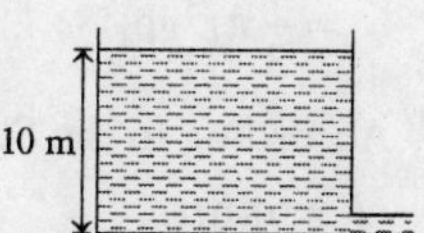

Let the area of the hole at the bottom be A_0 and the area of the vessel be A. Thus, the time taken for the tank to be emptied is given by

$$t = \frac{A}{A_0}\sqrt{\frac{2H}{g}} \quad ...(i)$$

When the tank is fully filled, $H = 10$ m, using Eq. (i), we get

$$10 = \frac{A}{A_0}\sqrt{\frac{2 \times 10}{g}} \quad ...(ii)$$

When the tank is half filled, $H = 5$ m, using Eq. (i), we get

$$t = \frac{A}{A_0}\sqrt{\frac{2 \times 5}{g}} \quad ...(iii)$$

Dividing Eq. (iii) by Eq. (ii), we get

$$\frac{t}{10} = \frac{1}{\sqrt{2}}$$

$$\Rightarrow \quad t = 7.07 \text{ min}$$

34. 6;

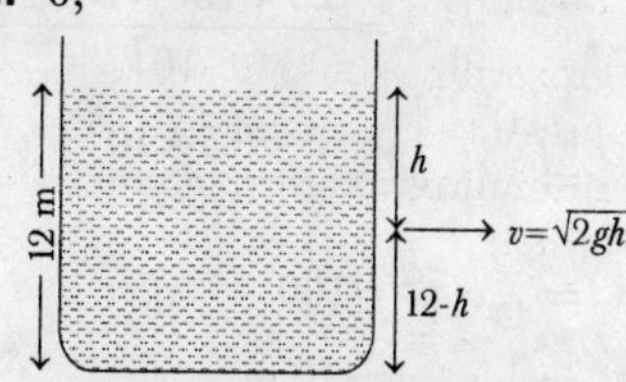

Velocity of efflux $= \sqrt{2gh}$

Time taken to reach the ground

$$= \sqrt{\frac{2(12 - h)}{g}}$$

The horizontal range is simply the product of velocity and time. So,

$$\text{Range, } R = \sqrt{2gh} \times \sqrt{\frac{2(12 - h)}{g}}$$

$$= \sqrt{4h(12 - h)}$$

For range to be maximum, we will find the equilibrium point

$$\frac{dR}{dh} = 0$$

$$\Rightarrow \quad h = 6 \text{ m}$$

35. II

36. (*c*);

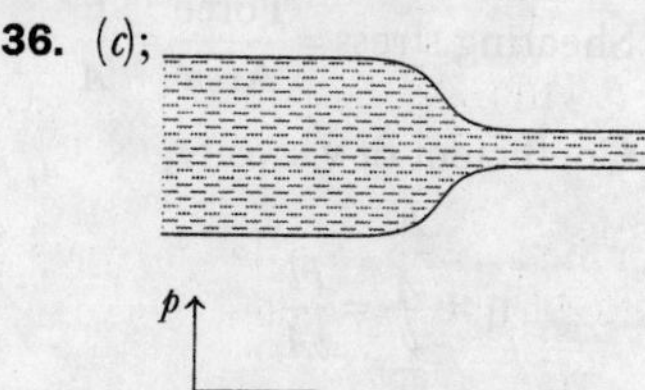

In the given case, the pressure remains constant initially and then decrease as the area of cross-section of the tube decreases and remains constant after that.

37. (*a*)

38. 10 m/s;

The Bernoulli's theorem for unit mass of liquid can be written as

$$\frac{p}{\rho} + \frac{1}{2}v^2 = \text{constant}$$

The pressure energy of the liquid starts decreasing as the liquid starts flowing. So,

$$\frac{1}{2}v^2 = \frac{p_1 - p_2}{\rho}$$

$$= \frac{3.5\times 10^5 - 3\times 10^5}{10^3}$$

$$\Rightarrow \quad v^2 = \frac{2\times 0.5\times 10^5}{10^3}$$

$$\Rightarrow \quad v^2 = 100$$

$$\Rightarrow \quad v = 10 \text{ m/s}$$

39. (*b*)

40. minimum, maximum

41. (*c*)

42. True

43. $A \to \frac{v\Delta t}{l}$, $B \to \frac{v}{l}$, $C \to \frac{F}{A}$, $D \to \frac{Fl}{vA}$;

For instantaneous time Δt, topmost layer moves with a velocity v. So, change in length is $\Delta l = v \cdot \Delta t$

So, shear strain $= \frac{v\cdot \Delta t}{l}$

Similarly, Strain rate

$$= \frac{\text{Shear strain}}{\Delta t} = \frac{v}{l}$$

Shearing stress $= \frac{\text{Force}}{\text{Area}} = \frac{F}{A}$

Coefficient of viscosity,

$$\eta = \frac{\frac{F}{A}}{\frac{v}{l}} = \frac{Fl}{vA}$$

44. Blood < Glycerine < Machine oil < Honey;

Honey is the most viscous, whereas blood is the least.

45. $A \to 1\ \text{N/m}^2$, $B \to 283$, $C \to 3.5\times 10^{-3}$ Pa-s;

The metal block moves to the right due to the tension T of the string which is equal to the weight of the mass suspended at the end of the string.

So, $F = T = mg$

$$= 0.01\times 10 = 0.1 \text{ N}$$

Shear stress on fluid

$$= \frac{F}{A} = \frac{0.1}{0.1} = 1\ \text{N/m}^2$$

Strain rate of fluid

$$= \frac{v}{l} = \frac{0.085}{0.3\times 10^{-3}} = 283$$

Coefficient of viscosity of fluid,

$$\eta = \frac{\text{Stress}}{\text{Strain rate}} = \frac{1}{283}$$

$$= 3.5\times 10^{-3} \text{ Pa-s}$$

46. 2, 3;

We know that, the viscosity is given by

$$\eta = \frac{\frac{F}{A}}{\frac{v}{l}} \quad \text{or} \quad F = \frac{\eta A v}{l}$$

$$= \frac{10^{-3}\times 10^{-2}\times 0.1}{5\times 10^{-4}}$$

$$= 2\times 10^{-3} \text{ N}$$

47. (*c*)

48. $\frac{4}{3}\pi r^3 g\rho_2$, $\frac{4}{3}\pi r^3 g\rho_1$, $6\pi\eta r v$;

A. Force of gravity on ball $= mg$

$$= \rho V g \quad (\because m = \rho V)$$

$$= \rho_2 \times \frac{4}{3}\pi r^3 g$$

$$= \frac{4}{3}\pi r^3 g\rho_2$$

B. Upward force of buoyancy

$$= \rho_1 \times \frac{4}{3}\pi r^3 \times g$$

$$= \frac{4}{3}\pi r^3 g\rho_1$$

C. According to the Stokes' law,

$$F = 6\pi\eta r v$$

49. (*c*)

50. (*c*); In the first 100 m, the body starts from rest and its velocity goes on increasing and after 100 m, it acquires the terminal velocity.

Further, the viscous force is low in the beginning as it is directly proportional to the velocity.

It becomes maximum at $v = v_T$.

So, work done against air friction is more for the second 100 m.

51. 7.94 cm/s;

Let R be the radius of bigger drop formed, then

$$\frac{4}{3}\pi R^3 = 2\times\frac{4}{3}\pi r^3 \Rightarrow R = (2)^{\frac{1}{3}} r$$

We know that, the terminal speed, $v_T \propto r^2$

If v_T and $v_{T'}$ are terminal speeds of bigger drop and smaller drops respectively, then

So, $$\frac{v_T}{v'_T} = \frac{R^2}{r^2} = \frac{(2)^{\frac{2}{3}} r^2}{r^2}$$

$$\Rightarrow \quad v_T = 5(4)^{\frac{1}{3}}$$

$$= 7.94 \text{ cm/s}$$

52. False;

Rate of production of heat is simply the power. So,

$$p = F v_T \quad \text{...(i)}$$

By Stokes' law, we have

$$F = 6\pi\eta v_T r \quad \text{...(ii)}$$

From Eqs. (i) and (ii), we get

$$p = 6\pi\eta r v_T^2 \quad \text{...(iii)}$$

Terminal velocity,

$$v_T = \frac{2r^2(\rho - 6)}{9\eta} \quad \text{...(iv)}$$

From Eqs. (iii) and (iv), we get

$$p \propto r^5$$

53. (*a*);

F_B, F_V, mg

The velocity of the ball becomes constant when the sum of viscous and buoyant force acting on the ball becomes equal to the weight of the ball.

So, $$F_B + F_V = mg$$

$$V_s \rho_g\ g + F_V = mg$$

$$V\times\frac{d}{2}\times g + F_V = Vdg$$

$$\Rightarrow \quad F_V = \frac{Vdg}{2} = \frac{mg}{2}$$

54. $\frac{79}{36}$; The terminal velocity is given by

$$v = \frac{2r^2(\rho - \sigma)g}{9\eta}$$

Using this relation, we can write for two cases

$$\frac{v_1}{v_2} = \left(\frac{r_1}{r_2}\right)^2 \frac{(\rho_1 - \sigma)}{(\rho_2 - \sigma)} = \left(\frac{1}{2}\right)^2 \left(\frac{8\rho_2 - 0.1\rho_2}{\rho_2 - 0.1\rho_2}\right)$$

$$= \frac{79}{36}$$

55. 0.025 N/m;

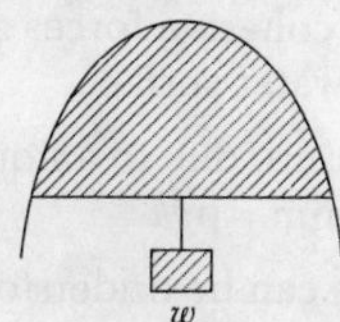

The force due to the surface tension balances the weight suspended. So,

$$F_S = w$$
$$2SL = w$$
$$\Rightarrow \quad S = \frac{w}{2L} = \frac{1.5 \times 10^{-2}}{2 \times 30 \times 10^{-2}}$$
$$= 0.025 \text{ N/m}$$

56. $2(\Delta A)S, \frac{F}{2a}$;

Initial area $= ab$

Final area $= (a + x)\,b$

Then, $\Delta A = (a + x)b - ab = ax$

Work done = Force × Displacement $= Fx$

Surface energy

$$= \frac{\text{Work done}}{A} = \frac{Fx}{a}$$

Work done $= (2\Delta A)S$

$$\Rightarrow S \times \frac{W}{2ax} = \frac{Fx}{2ax} = \frac{F}{2a}$$

57. I. ×, II. ×;

Perimeter of square plate $= 4a$

Tension, $S = \frac{F}{l}$ (l = total length)

$\Rightarrow F = S \cdot (4a) = 4aS$

But two surfaces are involve. So,

$$F = 2 \times 4aS = 8aS$$

For needle, $F = 2LS$ (for two surfaces)

$$mg = 2LS$$
$$\Rightarrow \quad m = \frac{2LS}{g}$$

58. (*b*); Work done per unit surface area is given by

$$\frac{W}{A} = S$$

Since, surface tension remains the same, we can write

$$\frac{w_1}{A_1} = \frac{w_2}{A_2}$$
$$\frac{w_1}{A_1} = \frac{w_2}{2A_1} \quad (\because A_2 = 2A_1)$$
$$\Rightarrow \quad w_2 = 2w_1$$

59. $mg + S[2\pi(r_1 + r_2)]$;

Ring's own weight is acting in the downward direction when we lift the ring. Also, the force due to surface tension points in direction opposite to the motion, in downward direction. Hence, minimum force required to lift the ring will be $F = w + S$ (circumference of ring)

$$= mg + S[2\pi(r_1 + r_2)]$$

60. $8\pi r \cdot \Delta r \cdot S$;

Extra surface energy required is given by

$$\Delta E = [4\pi(r + \Delta r)^2 - 4\pi r^2]S$$
$$= (4\pi r^2 + 4\pi\Delta r^2 + 8\pi r\,\Delta r - 4\pi r^2)\,S$$
$$= 8\pi r\Delta r \cdot S$$

(neglect $4\pi\Delta r^2$ as Δr^2 is very small)

61. $\Delta p \cdot 4\pi r^2 \cdot \Delta r$;

The work done by an excess of pressure in displacing the surface,

dW = Force × Displacement

= Excess of pressure × Surface area × Displacement

$$= (\Delta p \times 4\pi r^2)\Delta r$$
$$= \Delta p \cdot 4\pi r^2 \cdot \Delta r$$

62. 7.5×10^{-3};

Work done is given by

$$W = 2 \times 4\pi r^2 \times S$$
$$= 2 \times 4\pi(10 \times 10^{-2})^2 \times 0.03$$
$$= 75.36 \times 10^{-4}\text{ J}$$
$$= 7.5 \times 10^{-3}\text{ J}$$

63. 2.4×10^{-4} J;

The surface tension acts on both faces of the film. Thus, the change in area of both surfaces is to be considered

$$\Delta A = 2 \times (100 - 60)$$
$$= 80 \text{ cm}^2$$
$$= 80 \times 10^{-4}\text{ m}^2$$

Work done $= S\Delta A$

$$= 3 \times 10^{-2} \times 80 \times 10^{-4}$$
$$= 2.4 \times 10^{-4}\text{ J}$$

64. $24\pi r^2 S$;

Initial outer surface area of bubble, $A_0 = 4\pi r^2$

Final outer surface area of bubble,

$$A_0' = 4\pi(2r)^2 = 16\pi r^2$$

Change in outer surface area,

$$\Delta A = 16\pi r^2 - 4\pi r^2 = 12\pi r^2$$

As the bubble has two surfaces (inner and outer), thus total change in surface area gets doubled.

$$\Rightarrow \Delta A = 24\pi r^2$$

$$\therefore \text{Energy} = \Delta A \times S = 24\pi r^2 S$$

65. $2^{\frac{1}{3}}:1$;

Let the radius of the large drop formed be R', so

Volume of large drop

= 2 × Volume of small drops

$$\frac{4}{3}\pi R'^3 = 2 \times \frac{4}{3}\pi R^3$$
$$R' = (2)^{\frac{1}{3}} R \quad \text{... (i)}$$

Surface area (total) of two drops

$$= 2 \times 4\pi R^2 = 8\pi R^2$$

Surface area of resultant drop

$$= 4\pi R'^2 = 4\pi(2)^{\frac{2}{3}} R^2$$

[using Eq. (i)]

Therefore, surface energy of two drops before coalescing is given by

$$U_1 = (8\pi R^2)S$$

Similarly, surface energy of drop after coalescing,

$$U_2 = \left(4\pi(2)^{\frac{2}{3}} R^2\right) S$$
$$\therefore \quad \frac{U_1}{U_2} = \frac{8\pi R^2 S}{2^{\frac{2}{3}} \times 4\pi R^2 S} = \frac{2}{2^{\frac{2}{3}}}$$
$$= 2^{\frac{1}{3}}:1$$

66. (*b*); Initial area of the film,

$$A_i = 4 \times 2 = 8 \text{ cm}^2$$
$$= 8 \times 10^{-4}\text{ m}^2$$

Final area, $A_f = 5 \times 4 = 20 \text{ cm}^2$

$= 20 \times 10^{-4}\ \text{m}^2$

Change in area,

$\Delta A = A_f - A_i$

$= 12 \times 10^{-4}\ \text{m}^2$

Work done $= S(2\Delta A)$

$3 \times 10^{-4} = S(2 \times 12 \times 10^{-4})$

$\Rightarrow \quad S = 0.125\ \text{N/m}$

67. $\frac{8}{3}$;

Volume of the bigger drop = Sum of volumes of 2 smaller drops

$\frac{4}{3}\pi R^3 = 2 \times \frac{4}{3}\pi r^3$

$\Rightarrow \quad R = 2^{\frac{1}{3}} r \quad \ldots \text{(i)}$

Surface energy $= T \cdot 4\pi R^2$

$= T \cdot 4\pi (2)^{\frac{2}{3}} r^2$ [using Eq. (i)]

$= 2^{\frac{8}{3}}\ \pi r^2 T$

68. No

69. acute, obtuse

70. False

71. decrease, increase

72. False;

Excess pressure inside a layer of liquid with radius of curvature R is $\frac{2S}{R}$.

Since, a soap has two spherical surfaces, the excess pressure inside the soap bubble

$= 2 \times \frac{2S}{R} = \frac{4S}{R}$.

73. 2;

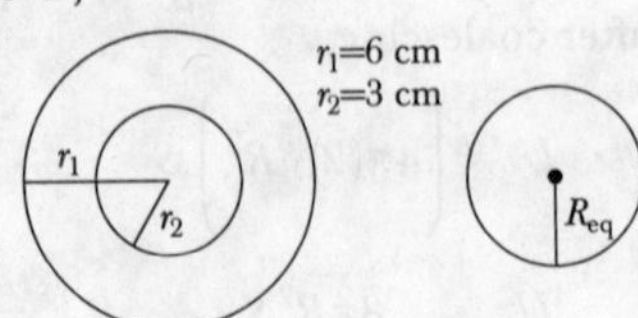

Excess pressure inside the smaller soap bubble,

$\Delta p = \frac{4S}{r_1} + \frac{4S}{r_2} \quad \ldots \text{(i)}$

Excess pressure inside equivalent soap bubble,

$\Delta p = \frac{4S}{R_{eq}} \quad \ldots \text{(ii)}$

From Eqs. (i) and (ii), we get

$\frac{4S}{R_{eq}} = \frac{4S}{r_1} + \frac{4S}{r_2}$

$\frac{1}{R_{eq}} = \frac{1}{r_1} + \frac{1}{r_2} = \frac{1}{6} + \frac{1}{3}$

$\Rightarrow \quad R_{eq} = 2\ \text{cm}$

74. 10 g;

Using the relation, rh = constant

$r_2 h_2 = r_1 h_1$

$(2r) h_2 = rh$

$\Rightarrow \quad h_2 = \frac{h}{2}$

Mass of the water that rises in the first capillary = 5 g

Mass of water that will rise in second capillary, $M_2 = \rho(\pi r_2^2 h_2)$

Similarly, for first case, we can write

$\rho \pi r^2 h = 5\ \text{g} \quad \ldots \text{(i)}$

Now, $M_2 = \rho\pi(2r)^2 \frac{h}{2} = 2 \times \rho \pi r^2 h$

$M_2 = 2 \times 5 = 10\ \text{g}$ [from Eq. (i)]

75. (i) ✓ (ii) × (iii) ✓ (iv) ✓ (v) ✓;

(i) For a soap bubble,

$\Delta p = \frac{4T}{r}$

Using the above relation, we can write,

$\frac{r_1}{r_2} = \frac{\Delta\rho_2}{\Delta\rho_1} = \frac{1.02 - 1}{1.01 - 1}$

(Excess pressure = Pressure inside – Outside)

$= \frac{2}{1}$

Since, $V = \frac{4}{3}\pi r^3$

$\therefore \quad \frac{V_1}{V_2} = \left(\frac{r_1}{r_2}\right)^3 = \frac{8}{1}$

(ii) The pressure inside the bubble having smaller radius will be more, thus air will flow from smaller to bigger bubble.

(iii) If the meniscus is concave, η will be positive. It means that liquid level will rise in capillary.

(iv) It is due to the surface tension and cohesive forces acting on the water surface.

(v) Pressure due to a liquid column $= \rho g h$

This can be understood on the basis of Pascal's law.

76. 9:10;

According to Ascent formula,

$h = \frac{2S\cos\theta}{rdg}$

Using the above relation

$\Rightarrow \quad \frac{h_1}{h_2} = \frac{S_1}{S_2} \times \frac{d_2}{d_1} = \frac{60}{50} \times \frac{0.6}{0.8} = \frac{9}{10}$

77. (*b*); Capillary rise is given by

$h = \frac{2T\cos\theta}{r\rho g}$

Since, $h_1 = h_2 = h_3$ and T and r are constant values, we get the relation

$h_1 = h_2 = h_3$

$\frac{\cos\theta_1}{\rho_1} = \frac{\cos\theta_2}{\rho_2} = \frac{\cos\theta_3}{\rho_3}$

Since, $\rho_1 > \rho_2 > \rho_3$

$\Rightarrow \cos\theta_1 > \cos\theta_2 > \cos\theta_3$

For $\quad 0 \le \theta < \frac{\pi}{2}$, we get

$\Rightarrow \quad 0 \le \theta_1 < \theta_2 < \theta_3 < \frac{\pi}{2}$

Competition Connect

1. (*c*)

2. $\rho_A < \rho_B < \rho_C$

3. True

4. $\frac{5}{4}$;

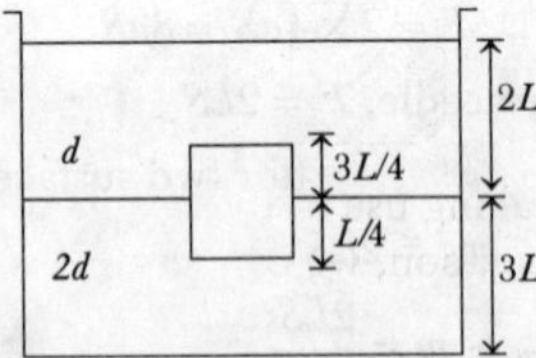

According to the law of floatation, Weight of the block = Weight of the two liquids displaced

$(L)\ ADg = \left(\frac{3L}{4}\right) Adg + \left(\frac{L}{4}\right) A(2d)g$

$$D \times ALg = \frac{5ALdg}{4}$$

$$\Rightarrow \quad \frac{D}{d} = \frac{5}{4}$$

5. 89; Let V be the volume of iceberg and let x be the volume of submerged part of iceberg. According to the Archimedes principle, weight of the iceberg is equal to the weight of the water displaced. So,

$$V\rho_{\text{iceberg}}\, g = x\rho_{\text{water}}\, g$$

$$V \times 0.92 \times g = x \times 1.03 \times g$$

$$\Rightarrow \quad \frac{x}{V} = \frac{92}{103}$$

Percentage of volume of iceberg submerged in sea water

$$= \frac{92}{103} \times 100 = 89.32\% \simeq 89\%$$

6. (*c*);

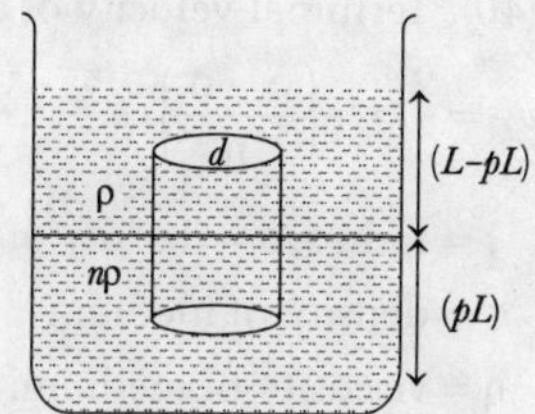

According to the law of floatation, weight of cylinder is equal to the upthrust by two liquids.

$$LAdg = n\rho(pLA)g + \rho(L - pL)Ag$$

$$d = np\rho + \rho(1 - p)$$

$$\Rightarrow \quad d = \{1 + (n-1)p\}\rho$$

7. 19;

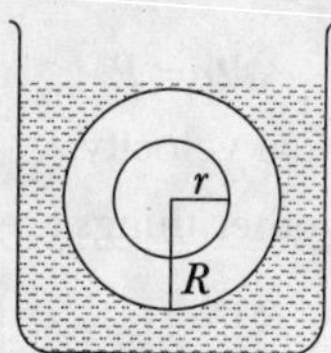

Making use of the law of floatation, we can write

$$\frac{4}{3}\pi R^3 \times \rho_w \times g = \frac{4}{3}\pi(R^3 - r^3) \times \rho_m \times g$$

$$\Rightarrow \quad R^3 = (R^3 - r^3) \times \frac{27}{8}$$

$$\Rightarrow r = \left(\frac{19}{27}\right)^{\frac{1}{3}} R = \left(\frac{x}{27}\right)^{\frac{1}{3}} R \text{ (given)}$$

$$\therefore\ x = 19$$

8. 1.01;

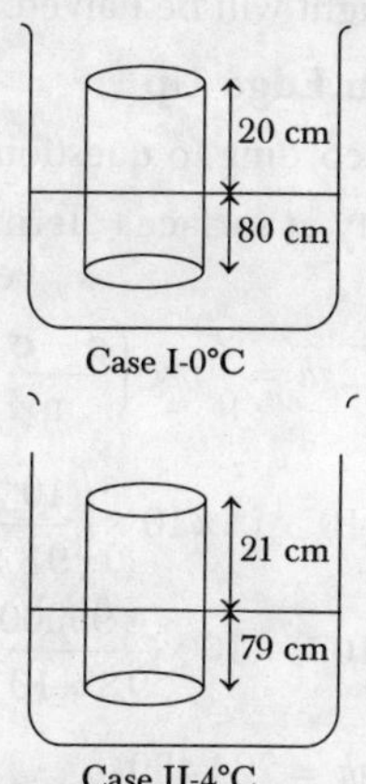

At 0°C, the weight of the cylinder is balanced by the buoyant force, given by

$$\rho_{0°C} A(0.8)g = mg \quad \text{...(i)}$$

Similarly at 4°C, the weight of cylinder is equal to buoyant force, given by

$$\rho_{4°C} A(0.79)\, g = mg \quad \text{...(ii)}$$

Dividing Eq. (ii) by Eq. (i), we get

$$\frac{\rho_{4°C}}{\rho_{0°C}} = \frac{80}{79} = 1.01$$

9. $\frac{3}{5}$; In case 1, Buoyant force,

$$F_b = mg$$

$$\rho_w \frac{4}{5} \cdot V \cdot g = \rho_b \cdot V \cdot g$$

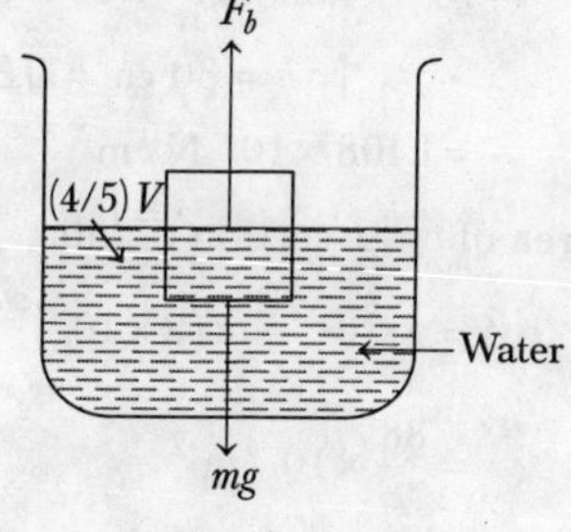

$$\Rightarrow \quad \frac{\rho_b}{\rho_w} = \frac{4}{5} \quad \text{...(i)}$$

Similarly in case 2,

$$\rho_w \cdot \frac{V}{2} \cdot g + \rho_o \cdot \frac{V}{2} \cdot g = \rho_b \cdot V \cdot g$$

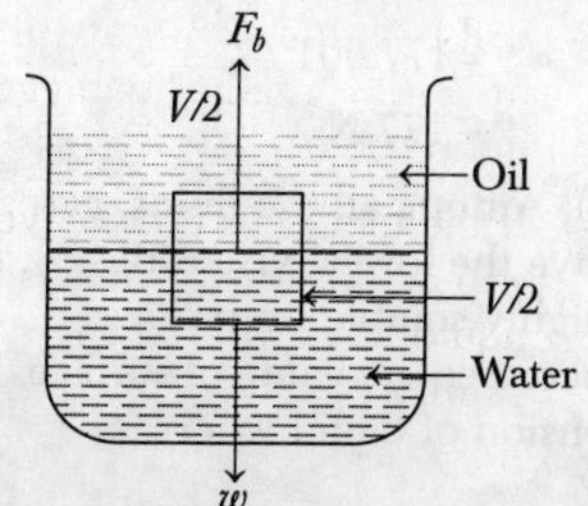

$$\Rightarrow \quad \rho_w + \rho_o = 2\rho_b$$

$$\Rightarrow \quad \frac{\rho_o}{\rho_w} + 1 = 2 \cdot \frac{\rho_b}{\rho_w} = \frac{2 \times 4}{5}$$

$$= \frac{8}{5} \quad \text{[from Eq. (i)]}$$

$$\Rightarrow \quad \frac{\rho_o}{\rho_w} = \frac{8}{5} - 1 = \frac{3}{5}$$

Assertion-Reason Questions

1. (*a*); Fluid pressure at a depth h is given by

$$p = p_0 + \rho g h$$

where, p_0 is the atmospheric pressure.

$\rho g h$ is gauge pressure at a depth h due to weight of the fluid.

2. (*a*); Both liquids and gases are called fluid. Fluid have tendency to flow and Pascal's law is applicable for all fluids.

3. (*b*); According to Pascal's law pressure applied to an enclosed fluid will be transmitted to every point of the fluid and to the walls of the container in equal magnitude. The pressure at any point in the fluid is equal in all directions.

4. (*b*)

5. (*d*)

6. (*a*)

7. (*a*)

8. (*b*); The internal forces decrease due to increase in temperature and therefore, viscosity of liquid decreases on increasing temperature.

9. (*c*)

10. (*c*); As lower surface energy generally indicates a more stable liquid interface.

Case Based Questions

1. (i) (*d*); Pressure, $P = \frac{F_1}{A_1}$

$$= \frac{200 \text{ N}}{0.02 \text{ m}^2}$$

$$= 10000 \text{ Pa}$$

(ii) (*b*); Force exerted by the large piston,

$$F_2 = P \times A_2$$

$$= 10000 \times 1 = 10000 \text{ N}$$

(iii) (*b*); Work done by the hydraulic lift,

$W = F_2 \times \text{Height}$

$= 10000 \text{ N} \times 0.5 \text{ m}$

$= 5000 \text{ J}$

(iv) (*c*); Displacement volume for the large piston will be the same due to principle of incompressibility of fluids.

Or

(*c*); Actual work output

$= \text{Efficiency} \times \text{Input work}$

$= 0.8 \times 25000$

$= 20000 \text{ J}$

2. (i) (*d*); Pressure difference inside and outside the water column,

$$\Delta p = \frac{2T}{r}$$

$$= \frac{2 \times 0.0728}{0.0005}$$

$$= 291.2 \text{ Pa}$$

(ii) (*c*); Surface energy = Surface tension × Area

$$= T \times 2\pi rh$$

$$\therefore\ h = \frac{2T\cos\theta}{\rho g r}$$

$$= \frac{2 \times 0.0728 \times \cos 0°}{1000 \times 9.8 \times 0.0005}$$

$$= 0.02971 \text{ m}$$

$$\simeq 0.03 \text{ m}$$

Thus, surface energy

$$= 0.0728 \times 2 \times \frac{22}{7} \times 0.0005 \times 0.03$$

$$= 0.00000685 \text{ J}$$

$$\simeq 7\ \mu\text{J}$$

(iii) (*b*); $\therefore\ W = \Delta p \times v$

$$= \Delta p \times \pi r^2 h$$

$$= 291.2 \times \frac{22}{7} \times (0.0005)^2 \times 0.03$$

$$= 0.000006857 \text{ J}$$

$$\simeq 7 \times 10^{-6} \text{ J}$$

(iv) (*a*); $\therefore\ h = \dfrac{2T\cos\theta}{r\rho}$

$$= \frac{2 \times 0.0728 \times \cos 0°}{0.0005 \times 1000 \times 9.8}$$

$$\simeq 0.03 \text{ m}$$

Or

(*c*); We know that $h \propto \dfrac{1}{r}$

Hence, if the radius is doubled, the height will be halved.

Competition Edge Up

1. (*b*); According to question,

Velocity at surface = Terminal velocity

$$\sqrt{2gh} = \frac{2}{9} r^2 g \left(\frac{\rho - \sigma}{\eta}\right)$$

$$= \frac{2}{9} \times (10^{-4})^2 \times 10 \times \left(\frac{10^5 - 10^3}{9.8 \times 10^{-6}}\right)$$

$$= \frac{2}{9} \times 10^{-8} \times 10 \times \frac{99000}{9.8 \times 10^{-6}}$$

$$\Rightarrow \sqrt{2gh} = 224.489$$

$$\Rightarrow\ h = \frac{224.49 \times 224.49}{2 \times 10}$$

$$\simeq 2518 \text{ m}$$

2. (*c*)

3. (*b*); For the given situation,

$$mg - F_{\text{upthrust}} - F_{\text{viscous}} = ma$$

For constant velocity, $a = 0$

$$\therefore\ mg = F_{\text{upthrust}} + F_{\text{viscous}}$$

$$F_{\text{viscous}} = mg - F_{\text{upthrust}}$$

$$= mg - \frac{m}{\rho} \cdot \rho_0 g$$

$$= mg\left(1 - \frac{\rho_0}{\rho}\right)$$

4. (177); Since, $p = p_0 + \rho g h$

$$= 10^5 + 1.36 \times 10^4 \times 10 \times 0.3$$

$$[\because h = 30 \text{ cm} = 0.3 \text{ m}]$$

$$= 1.408 \times 10^5 \text{ N/m}^2$$

Area of cross-section of tube,

$$A = \pi r^2 = \frac{22}{7} \times (2 \times 10^{-2})^2$$

$$= \frac{88}{7} \times 10^{-4} \text{ m}^2$$

$\therefore$ Force exerted by the mercury on the bottom of the tube,

$$\therefore\quad F = pA$$

$$= 1.408 \times 10^5 \times \frac{88}{7} \times 10^{-4}$$

$$= 177.001$$

$$\simeq 177 \text{ N}$$

5. (*b*); Among all the fluids, gases have the lowest viscosities. Highly soluble impurities increases the value of surface tension of liquid whereas insoluble impurities decreases the surface tension of liquid.

6. (*c*); Weight, $W = \dfrac{4}{3}\pi\left(\dfrac{D^3 - d^3}{8}\right)\sigma g$

Buoyant force $= 1 \times \dfrac{4}{3}\pi \dfrac{D^3}{8} \cdot g$

For just float $\Rightarrow W = F_1$

$$(D^3 - d^3)\sigma = D^3$$

$$1 - \frac{d^3}{D^3} = \frac{1}{\sigma} \Rightarrow \frac{-d^3}{D^3} = \frac{1}{\sigma} - 1$$

$$\frac{d^3}{D^3} = 1 - \frac{1}{\sigma} \Rightarrow \frac{d^3}{D^3} = \frac{\sigma - 1}{\sigma}$$

$$\frac{D^3}{d^3} = \frac{\sigma}{\sigma - 1}$$

$$\Rightarrow\quad \frac{D}{d} = \left(\frac{\sigma}{\sigma - 1}\right)^{\frac{1}{3}}$$

7. (40); Terminal velocity of a ball is

$$v_T = \frac{2}{9} \cdot r^2 \cdot \left(\frac{\rho - \sigma}{\eta}\right) \cdot g$$

r = radius, ρ = density of ball

σ = density of medium

η = viscosity of medium.

It is given 8 balls of radius 0.01 mm combined to form a large drop.

As volume of water remains same.

$$\therefore\ 8 \times V_{\text{small drop}} = V_{\text{large drop}}$$

$$\Rightarrow\quad 8 \times \frac{4}{3}\pi r^3 = \frac{4}{3}\pi R^3$$

$$\text{or}\qquad 8r^3 = R^3$$

$$\Rightarrow\qquad 2r = R$$

As terminal velocity,

$v_T \propto r^2$ (other things are same)

$$\Rightarrow \frac{v_{T_2}}{v_{T_1}} = \left(\frac{R}{r}\right)^2 = (2)^2$$

$$\Rightarrow v_{T_2} = 4 \times v_{T_1}$$

$$= 4 \times 10 = 40 \text{ cm/s}$$

8. (1000); If F_1 be the force required to applied on the thicker arm, then by using Pascal's law

$$\frac{F_1}{A_1} = \frac{F_2}{A_2} \Rightarrow F_2 = \frac{F_1 A_2}{A_1}$$

$$= \frac{10 \times \pi r_2^2}{\pi r_1^2}$$

$$=10\cdot\left(\frac{r_2}{r_1}\right)^2=10\times\left(\frac{7}{0.7}\right)^2$$
$$=1000\text{ N}$$

9. (*a*); $F = S\times 2\pi r$
$$=0.07\times 2\times 3.14\times 4.5\times 10^{-2}$$
$$=1.9782\times 10^{-2}\text{ N}=19.8\text{ mN}$$

10. (*a*)

11. (*b*); $\therefore$ Amount of energy required,
$$E=2TA=2\times 0.03\times 4\pi(2\times 10^{-2})^2$$
$$=3.01\times 10^{-4}\text{ J}$$

12. (*d*); We know that, pressure inside the soap bubble of radius r is given as,
$$p=\frac{4T}{r}\Rightarrow p\propto\frac{1}{r}\quad\dots\text{(i)}$$
Therefore, when soap bubble expands, then its radius increases, hence from Eq. (i), pressure inside it will decrease.

13. (*a*); When a spherical ball is dropped in a long column of a highly viscous liquid, then its velocity first increases and after sometime, it moves with constant velocity, known as terminal velocity (v). Hence, correct variation of speed of ball in liquid column with time is given as

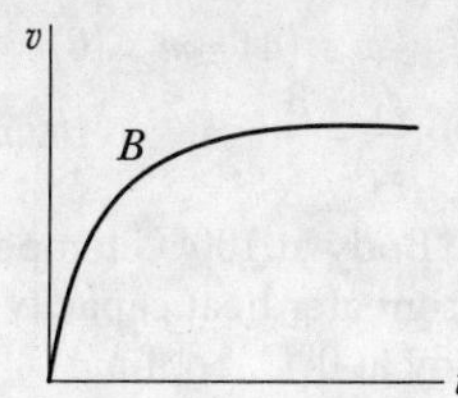

14. (*b*); Since,
$$h=\frac{2T\cos\theta}{\rho gr}\Rightarrow h\propto\frac{1}{r}$$
$$\Rightarrow\quad \frac{h_1}{h_2}=\frac{r_2}{r_1}=\frac{2r}{r}=2$$
As $\quad m=A\cdot h\cdot\rho$
$$\therefore\quad \frac{m_2}{m_1}=\frac{A_2h_2\rho}{A_1h_1\rho}=\frac{\pi(r_2)^2}{\pi(r_1)^2}\frac{h_2}{h_1}=\frac{4}{2}=2$$
$$\Rightarrow\quad m_2=2\times m_1=2\times 5=10\text{ g}$$

15. (*c*); A liquid does not wet the solid surface, if the angle of contact is obtuse i.e., $\theta>90°$.

16. (*b*); Let height of liquid in liquid column be h_l, then $p_{\text{liquid}}=p_{\text{mercury}}$
$$\Rightarrow\quad h_l\rho_l g=h_m\rho_m g$$
$$\Rightarrow\quad h_l=\frac{h_m\rho_m}{\rho_l}=\frac{0.76\times 13600}{760}$$
$$=13.6\text{ m}$$

Chapter-10
Thermal Properties of Matter

1. (*b*)
2. Joule (J)
3. form of energy
4. A–1, B–2, C–1, D–2
5. True
6. False
7. – 40, 233.15;

For different temperature scales, we have
$$C=(F-32)\times\frac{5}{9}$$
$$=(-40-32)\times\frac{5}{9}$$
$$=-72\times\frac{5}{9}=-40°\text{C}$$
$$\Rightarrow\quad K=-40+273.15$$
$$=233.15\text{ K}$$

8. $T_B=\frac{2}{3}(T_A-30)$;

We can write a relationship to convert these temperature scales,
$$\frac{T_A-30}{150}=\frac{T_B}{100}$$
$$\Rightarrow\quad T_B=\frac{2}{3}(T_A-30)$$

9. 90°C;

Change in temperature
$$=0-10°\text{C}=-10°\text{C}$$
Also, $\Delta T=50°\text{C}-60°\text{C}$
$$=-10°\text{C}$$
Thus, thermometer will read, boiling point
$$=100°\text{C}-10°\text{C}=90°\text{C}$$

10. 117°W;

The relation between these scales is given by
$$\left(\frac{t-\text{LFP}}{\text{UFP}-\text{LFP}}\right)_{\text{celsius scale}}=\left(\frac{t-\text{LFP}}{\text{UFP}-\text{LFP}}\right)_{\text{new scale}}$$
$$\Rightarrow\quad\left(\frac{39-0}{100-0}\right)=\frac{t-39}{239-39}$$
$$\Rightarrow\quad\frac{39}{100}=\frac{t-39}{200}$$
$$\Rightarrow\quad t=117°\text{ W}$$

11. (*d*); By principle of thermometry, for any linear temperature scale
$$\frac{T-T_{\text{LFP}}}{T_{\text{UFP}}-T_{\text{LFP}}}=a\text{ (constant)}$$
$$\Rightarrow\quad\frac{T-0}{100-0}=\frac{\frac{x_0}{2}-\frac{x_0}{3}}{x_0-\frac{x_0}{3}}$$
$$\Rightarrow\quad\frac{T}{100}=\frac{1}{4}$$
$$\Rightarrow\quad T=25°\text{C}$$

12. equal to 1

13. –273.15;

At – 273.15° C, the pressure is zero.

14. I and IV;

Statements I and IV are correct but Statements II and III are incorrect and these can be corrected as,

y-intercept of all graphs are different.

All graphs are linear.

15. True **16.** False **17.** (*d*)

18. (*c*); Since, for both the metals, expansion is same.
$$\therefore\quad\Delta l_1=\Delta l_2$$
$$\Rightarrow\quad l_1\alpha_1\Delta T=l_2\alpha_2\Delta T$$
$$\Rightarrow\quad l_1\alpha_1=l_2\alpha_2$$

19. 68 cm;

Since, the elongation produced in both rods are same,
$$(\Delta l)_{\text{Cu}}=(\Delta l)_{\text{Al}}$$
$$l_{\text{Cu}}\alpha_{\text{Cu}}\Delta T=l_{\text{Al}}\alpha_{\text{Al}}\Delta T$$
$$\Rightarrow 88\times 1.7\times 10^{-5}=l_{\text{Al}}\times 2.2\times 10^{-5}$$
$$\Rightarrow\quad l_{\text{Al}}=68\text{ cm}$$

20. (*d*); The coefficient of expansion of metal A is greater than that of B, i.e.
$$\alpha_A>\alpha_B$$
If bimetallic strip is placed in a cold bath, then the length of both strips will decrease.

So, $\quad\Delta l_A>\Delta l_B$

Therefore, the bimetallic strip will bend towards the left.

21. 1: 4 : 12;
$$\Delta l:\Delta A:\Delta V=l\alpha_1\Delta T:2A\alpha_1\Delta T:3V\alpha_1\Delta T$$
$$=2:2\times(4):3\times(8)$$
$$=1:4:12$$

22. 0.996 ω_0;

Increase in diameter of the sphere,
$$\Delta d=d\times\alpha\times\Delta T$$
$$=d\times 2\times 10^{-5}\times 100$$
$$=d\times 2\times 10^{-3}$$

Therefore, initial radius, $R_1 = R$

Final radius,

$$R_2 = R \times 2 \times 10^{-3} + R = R(1 + 2 \times 10^{-3})$$

According to conservation of angular momentum,

$$I_1\omega_1 = I_2\omega_2$$

$$\frac{2}{5}MR_1^2\omega_1 = \frac{2}{5}MR_2^2\omega_2$$

$$R_1 = R_2 = R$$

$$\Rightarrow R^2\omega_0 = R^2(1 + 2 \times 10^{-3})^2\,\omega_2$$

$$\Rightarrow \omega_2 = \frac{\omega_0}{(1 + 2 \times 10^{-3})^2} = 0.996\,\omega_0$$

23. $3a^3\alpha\Delta T$;

The volume expansion is given as

$$\frac{\Delta V}{V} = \gamma\,\Delta T$$

$$\Rightarrow \Delta V = V(3\alpha)\Delta T \quad (\because \gamma = 3\alpha)$$

$$\Rightarrow \Delta V = 3a^3\alpha\Delta T$$

$(\because$ volume of metal box $= a^3)$

24. 15.2;

Coefficient of volume expansion of glass will be

$$\gamma = 3\,\alpha = 0.3 \times 10^{-4}\,{}^\circ C^{-1}$$

$\therefore$ Expansion in glass will be

$$\Delta V_2 = (0.3 \times 10^{-4}) \times 1000 \times (100) = 3\text{ cc}$$

Expansion in mercury will be

$$\Delta V_1 = (1.82 \times 10^{-4}) \times 1000 \times 100 = 18.2\text{ cc}$$

Thus, the amount of mercury spilled out $= \Delta V_1 - \Delta V_2 = 18.2 - 3 = 15.2$ cc

25. 20;

As, change in volume of beaker = change in volume of mercury

$$\Rightarrow V_b\gamma_b\Delta T = V_m\gamma_m\Delta T$$

$$\Rightarrow V_b\gamma_b = V_m\gamma_m$$

$$\Rightarrow V_m = \frac{V_b\gamma_b}{\gamma_m} = \frac{500 \times 6 \times 10^{-6}}{1.5 \times 10^{-4}} = 20\text{ cm}^3 = 20\text{ cc}$$

26. 0.020;

Due to thermal expansion, density as a function of temperature is given by

$$\rho = \frac{\rho_0}{(1 + \gamma\Delta T)}$$

$$\Rightarrow \rho(1 + \gamma\Delta T) = \rho_0$$

$$\Rightarrow \frac{\rho - \rho_0}{\rho} = -\gamma\Delta T = -5 \times 10^{-4} \times 40 = -0.020$$

Negative sign indicates that density decrease with increase in temperature.

27. 0.06%;

We have, $\alpha = \dfrac{\Delta l}{l\,\Delta T} = \dfrac{0.02}{100 \times 10} = 2 \times 10^{-5}$

$\therefore$ Coefficient of volume expansion, $\gamma = 3\alpha = 6 \times 10^{-5}$

We know that, $\rho = \dfrac{m}{V}$

$$\therefore \frac{\Delta\rho}{\rho} = \frac{\Delta m}{m} - \frac{\Delta V}{V}$$

Here, $\dfrac{\Delta m}{m} = 0$

Thus, $\dfrac{\Delta\rho}{\rho} \times 100 = \gamma\Delta T \times 100 \quad \left(\because \dfrac{\Delta V}{V} = \gamma\Delta T\right)$

$$= 6 \times 10^{-5} \times 10 \times 100 = 0.06\%$$

28. 5, 1;

Heat capacity of water,

$$S = \frac{\Delta Q}{\Delta T} = \frac{500\text{ cal}}{100^\circ C} = 5\text{ cal/}^\circ C$$

Specific heat capacity of water,

$$s = \frac{1}{m}\frac{\Delta Q}{\Delta T} = \frac{500}{5 \times 100} = 1\text{ cal / g}^\circ C$$

29. 15,600 ;

$$\text{Thermal capacity} = \frac{\Delta Q}{\Delta T} = \frac{300}{45 - 25} = 15\text{ J/}^\circ C$$

Specific heat,

$$s = \frac{1}{m}\frac{\Delta Q}{\Delta T} = \frac{300 \times 1000}{25 \times (45 - 25)} = 600\text{ J/kg}^\circ C$$

30. 81;

Heat required = Mass × Specific heat × Temperature

$$= m \times \int_{t_1}^{t_2} c\,dt$$

$$= 2 \times \int_5^{15} (0.2 + 0.14t + 0.023t^2)\,dt$$

$$= 2 \times \left[0.2\,(t) + \frac{0.14}{2}\,t^2 + \frac{0.023}{3}\,t^3\right]_5^{15}$$

$$= 2 \times [0.2(15 - 5) + 0.07\,(15^2 - 5^2) + 0.0076(15^3 - 5^3)]$$

$$= 2 \times 40.7 \approx 81\text{ cal}$$

31. 3/8;

According to the question,

$$\left(\frac{\Delta Q}{\Delta t}\right)_A = \left(\frac{\Delta Q}{\Delta t}\right)_B$$

$$ms_A\left(\frac{\Delta T}{\Delta t}\right)_A = ms_B\left(\frac{\Delta T}{\Delta t}\right)_B$$

$$\Rightarrow \frac{s_A}{s_B} = \frac{\left(\frac{\Delta T}{\Delta t}\right)_B}{\left(\frac{\Delta T}{\Delta t}\right)_A} = \frac{90/6}{120/3} = \frac{3}{8}$$

32. (*a*);

According to the question, one- half of kinetic energy of bullet is converted into heat.

So, $ms\Delta T = \dfrac{1}{2}\left(\dfrac{1}{2}mv^2\right)$

$$\Rightarrow \Delta T = \frac{v^2}{4s} = \frac{(21000)^2}{4 \times 0.030 \times 4.2 \times 10^7}$$

$(\because 1\text{ cal} = 4.2 \times 10^7$ ergs)

$$= 87.5^\circ C$$

33. False

34. 3 : 2;

According to principle of calorimetry,

$$m_1s_1(30 - 26) = m_2s_2(26 - 20)$$

$$m_1s_1(4) = m_2s_2(6)$$

$$\Rightarrow \frac{s_1}{s_2} = \frac{3}{2} \quad (\because m_1 = m_2)$$

35. (*b*); Body at 100°C temperature has greater heat capacity than body at 0°C. So, final temperature will be closer to 100°C.

So, $T_C > 50^\circ C$

36. 0.0628 g;

Heat absorbed by ice (to melt),

$$Q_1 = m \times L = m_1(3.34 \times 10^5\text{ J kg}^{-1})$$

The heat absorbed by ice to bring it to melting point from − 20° C,

$$Q_2 = m_1c \times \Delta T = m_1(2000) \times [0 - (-20)] = m_1(40000)$$

Total heat absorbed by ice

$$= Q_1 + Q_2 = m_1(3.74 \times 10^5) + m_1(40000)$$

Heat lost by cola, $Q = m_2c \times \Delta T$

$$= (0.25) \times (4160) \times (25 - 0) = 26000\text{ J}$$

Using principle of calorimetry, we get

$m_1(3.74\times10^5+40000)=26000$

$\Rightarrow \quad m_1 = 0.0628$ g

37. (*d*);

Heat gained by water = Heat lost by steam

$m_w s_w \Delta T_1 = mL + m s_w \Delta T_2$

$20\times1\times(80-10)$

$= m\times540 + m\times1\times(100-80)$

$\Rightarrow \quad m = 2.5$ g

Therefore, total mass of water

$= 20 + 2.5 = 22.5$ g

38. 50°;

Applying the law of calorimetry to the table values,

$1T_1 + 2T_2 = (1+2)60° = 180$ ... (i)

$1T_2 + 2T_3 = (1+2)30° = 90$ ... (ii)

$2T_1 + 1T_3 = (1+2)60° = 180$ .. (iii)

Adding Eqs. (i), (ii) and (iii), we get

$3(T_1+T_2+T_3) = 450$

$(1+1+1)\,\theta = 150$

$\Rightarrow \quad \theta = 50°$ C

39. time

40. (i) ✓ (ii) ✓ (iii) × (iv) ✓;

For (iii) The curve *BC* represents heating of water.

41. (*c*);

The dry ice sublimates very quickly when a small amount of heat is supplied. The graph (c) represents the quick change in temperature for a small change in heat.

42. (*a*);

In this case, the variation of temperature with time is best explained by (a). In the graph,

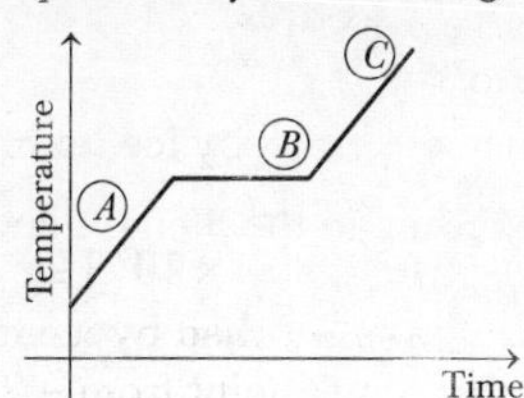

Region *A* Corresponds to the increase in temperature of liquid oxygen in the same phase initially.

Region *B* Liquid oxygen changes to gaseous phase during which, the temperature will remain constant.

Region *C* Corresponds to the increase in temperature of oxygen in the gaseous state.

43. lowering

44. No;

During sublimation, both solid and vapour states come in thermal equilibrium.

45. *A* = Pressure

B = Temperature

C = Solid region

D = Liquid region

E = Vapour region

F = Triple point

G = Sublimation curve

H = Fusion curve

I = Vaporisation curve

46. 80 cal/g;

Amount of heat absorbed

$= m\times L$

Therefore, $8000 = 100\times L$

$\Rightarrow \quad L = 80$ cal/g

47. (*a*) ;

Heat required to melt ice $= mL_f$

$= 5\times(80) = 400$ cal

Heat released by steam $= mL_v$

$= 1\times540 = 540$ cal

Therefore, amount of heat released by steam is more than the heat required by ice to melt. Thus, the ice will completely melt and mixture will contain only water.

48. 40;

Heat released = Heat released during condensation + Heat released by water ($100°\text{C}\rightarrow40°\text{C}$)

$= M\times540 + M\times C_p$ (water) $\times(100-40)$...(i)

Heat absorbed = Heat absorbed by ice during melting + Heat absorbed by water (0°C – 40°C).

$= 200\times80 + 200\times C_p$ (water) $\times(40-0)$ ...(ii)

Condition of heat balance gives out [i.e. on equating Eqs. (i) and (ii), we get]

$M(540+60) = 200(80+40)$

$\{\because C_p(\text{water}) = 1\text{ cal/g}°\text{C}\}$

$\Rightarrow \quad M = 40$ g

49. 100;

Heat required to melt 5 g ice

$= mL_f = 5\times80$

$= 400$ cal

Heat required to raise 1 g ice to 100°C = 100 cal

$\therefore$ Heat required to raise 5 g ice to 100°C will be

$= 5\times100 = 500$ cal

Therefore, total heat required,

$Q_1 = 400 + 500 = 900$ cal

Now, heat liberated by 1 kg steam $= mL_v$

$Q_2 = 1000\times540 = 540000$ cal

Now, $Q_2 >> Q_1$, therefore the ice will melt and come into thermal equilibrium at 100°C.

50. 136 km ;

As given, only one-quarter of its energy is absorbed by the ice.

So, $\dfrac{mgh}{4} = mL_f$

$\Rightarrow \quad h = \dfrac{L_f\times4}{g} = \dfrac{3.4\times10^5\times4}{10}$

$= 136000$ m $= 136$ km

51. I, III;

Temperature gradient $= \dfrac{\theta_1-\theta_2}{l}$

$= \dfrac{50-10}{0.5} = 80°\text{C m}^{-1}$

52. (*b*) ; The heat equation is

$H = \dfrac{Q}{t} = \dfrac{KA}{l}\Delta\theta$ or $H \propto \dfrac{1}{l}$

It suggests that *H versus x* graph will have a negative slope as shown in option (b).

53. 1728;

Using the heat equation,

$\dfrac{Q}{t} = \dfrac{KA}{l}\Delta\theta$

$\dfrac{Q}{24\times60\times60}$

$= \dfrac{2\times10^{-4}\times400\times10^{-4}}{4\times10^{-2}}(100-0)$

$Q = 1728$ kcal

54. 40°C ;

Let the temperature of junction be θ, then

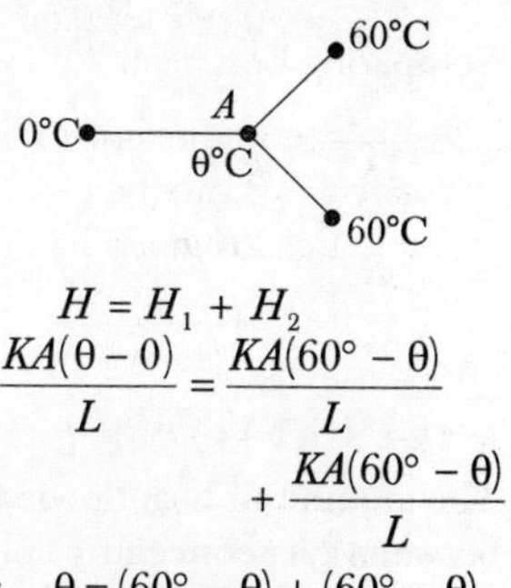

$H = H_1 + H_2$

$\dfrac{KA(\theta-0)}{L} = \dfrac{KA(60°-\theta)}{L} + \dfrac{KA(60°-\theta)}{L}$

or $\quad \theta = (60°-\theta) + (60°-\theta)$

$\Rightarrow \quad \theta = 40°$ C

55. 45;

Let the temperature of junction be θ, then

0°C, 30°C, P, θ°C, 90°C, 60°C

$$H = H_1 + H_2 + H_3$$

$$\frac{KA(\theta - 0)}{L} = \frac{KA(30° - \theta)}{L} + \frac{KA(90° - \theta)}{L} + \frac{KA(60° - \theta)}{L}$$

or $\theta = (30° - \theta) + (90° - \theta) + (60° - \theta)$

$\Rightarrow \quad \theta = 45° \text{ C}$

56. 58/37;

The rate of flow of heat through each bar would be same, so

$$\frac{Q}{t} = \frac{K_{AB} A \Delta T}{L_{AB}} = \frac{K_{BC} A\Delta T}{L_{BC}} = \frac{K_{CD} A \Delta T}{L_{CD}}$$

$$\Rightarrow \frac{2KA(200 - T_1)}{L} = \frac{4KA(T_1 - T_2)}{L} = \frac{3KA(T_2 - 18)}{L}$$

$$\Rightarrow 2(200 - T_1) = 4(T_1 - T_2) = 3(T_2 - 18)$$

Solving above equation, we get

$T_1 = 116° \text{C}$ and $T_2 = 74° \text{C}$

$$\therefore \frac{T_1}{T_2} = \frac{116}{74} = \frac{58}{37}$$

57. (*a*);

$$R_{\text{eff}} = \frac{l}{K_1 A} + \frac{l}{K_2 A} = \frac{l}{A}\left(\frac{1}{K_1} + \frac{1}{K_2}\right) \quad \ldots \text{(i)}$$

For the combination,

$$R_{\text{eff}} = \frac{2l}{K_{\text{eq}} A} \quad \ldots \text{(ii)}$$

Comparing Eqs. (i) and (ii), we get

$$\frac{2}{K_{\text{eq}}} = \frac{1}{K_1} + \frac{1}{K_2}$$

$$\Rightarrow K_{\text{eq}} = \frac{2K_1 K_2}{K_1 + K_2}$$

58. $\frac{r_1 r_2}{r_2 - r_1}$;

The amount of heat flowing between two concentric spheres can be given by

$$\frac{dQ}{dt} = \frac{KAdT}{dx} = \frac{K 4\pi x^2 dT}{dx}$$

or $K \cdot 4\pi dT = \frac{dQ}{dt} \cdot \frac{dx}{x^2}$

Integrating both sides, we get

$$K \cdot 4\pi \int_{T_1}^{T_2} dT = \frac{dQ}{dt} \int_{r_1}^{r_2} \frac{dx}{x^2}$$

Solving it, we get

$$\frac{dQ}{dt} = \frac{4\pi K r_1 r_2 (T_2 - T_1)}{r_1 - r_2}$$

Therefore, $\frac{dQ}{dt} \propto \frac{r_1 r_2}{(r_2 - r_1)}$

59. Yes

60. $T_1 > T_2 > T_3$;

According to Wien's law,

$$\lambda_m \propto \frac{1}{T}$$

and from the figure,

$$(\lambda_m)_1 < (\lambda_m)_2 < (\lambda_m)_3$$

Therefore, $T_1 > T_2 > T_3$

61. (*c*); According to Wien's law, we get

$$\lambda_m T = b$$

$$\Rightarrow \lambda_m = \frac{b}{T} = \frac{2.88 \times 10^6 \text{ nm-K}}{5760 \text{ K}}$$

$\Rightarrow \quad \lambda_m = 500 \text{ nm}$

$\because \lambda_m =$ wavelength corresponding to maximum energy, so $U_2 > U_1$.

62. 2750 K;

According to Wien's displacement law,

$$\lambda_m T = b \text{ or } \lambda_m \propto \frac{1}{T}$$

$$\Rightarrow \frac{(\lambda_m)_s}{(\lambda_m)_f} = \frac{T_f}{T_s}$$

or $T_f = T_s \times \frac{(\lambda_m)_s}{(\lambda_m)_f}$

$$= 5500 \text{ K} \times \frac{(5.5 \times 10^{-7} \text{m})}{(11 \times 10^{-7} \text{m})} = 2750 \text{ K}$$

63. 0.69;

From Wien's displacement law,

$\Rightarrow \quad \lambda_m T = \text{constant}$

$$\frac{T_1}{T_2} = \frac{\lambda_{m_2}}{\lambda_{m_1}} = \frac{350}{510}$$

$$\Rightarrow \frac{T_1}{T_2} = \frac{35}{51} = 0.69$$

64. 1

65. 3/2;

$$a + r + t = 1$$

$$\Rightarrow a + \frac{1}{3} + \frac{1}{6} = 1$$

$$\Rightarrow a = \frac{1}{2}$$

Now, $\frac{a}{r} = \frac{1/2}{1/3} = \frac{3}{2}$

66. 1

67. I, IV;

The rate of emission of heat by a body of emissivity e is $= \sigma e A T^4$

When $T_0 = T$, the bodies are in thermal equilibrium.

So, no heat exchange takes place.

Clearly, rate $\propto A$ (surface area of body).

Hence, rate depends upon the shape of the body.

68. 1: 1 ;

Using the relation, $H = \sigma A T^4$

$$\frac{H_1}{H_2} = \frac{A_1 T_1^4}{A_2 T_2^4} = \frac{\pi r_1^2 T_1^4}{\pi r_2^2 T_2^4} = \frac{(4)^2 \times (2000)^4}{(1)^2 \times (4000)^4} = \frac{1}{1}$$

69. $(\pi/6)^{1/3} : 1$;

$$\frac{Q_{\text{sphere}}}{Q_{\text{cube}}} = \frac{4\pi r^2}{6a^2}$$

$$\frac{4}{3}\pi r^3 = a^3 \text{ (Given)}$$

$$a = \left(\frac{4\pi}{3}\right)^{1/3} r$$

$$\frac{Q_{\text{sphere}}}{Q_{\text{cube}}} = \frac{4\pi r^2}{6\left[\left(\frac{4}{3}\pi\right)^{1/3} r\right]^2} = \left(\frac{\pi}{6}\right)^{1/3} : 1$$

70. $\frac{625}{81}$;

According to the Stefan's law,

$$E \propto T^4$$

$$T_1 = 27° \text{C} = (27 + 273) \text{ K} = 300 \text{ K}$$

$$T_2 = 227° \text{C} = (227 + 273) \text{ K} = 500 \text{ K}$$

$$\frac{E_1}{E_2} = \frac{T_1^4}{T_2^4} = \left(\frac{300}{500}\right)^4 = \frac{81}{625}$$

or $\frac{E_2}{E_1} = \frac{625}{81}$

71. 64;

From Stefan's law, the energy radiated by sun is given by

$$P = \sigma e A T^4$$

Case I $T = T,\ R = R$

$$P_1 = \sigma e(4\pi R^2)\,T^4 \quad \ldots \text{(i)}$$

Case II $T = 2T,\ R = 2R$

$$P_2 = \sigma e[4\pi(2R)^2](2T)^4 \quad \ldots \text{(ii)}$$

Dividing Eq. (ii) by Eq. (i), we get

$$\frac{P_2}{P_1} = \frac{\sigma e[4\pi(4R^2)](16T^4)}{\sigma e(4\pi R^2)T^4} = 64$$

72. $\left[\frac{\theta_1 + \theta_2}{2} - \theta_0\right]$;

From Newton's law of cooling,

$$\frac{\theta_1 - \theta_2}{t} = K\left[\frac{\theta_1 + \theta_2}{2} - \theta_0\right]$$

$$\Rightarrow \frac{\theta_1 - \theta_2}{t} \propto \frac{\theta_1 + \theta_2}{2} - \theta_0$$

73. $35°$;

According to Newton's law of cooling, when body cools from 52.5°C to 47.5°C

$$\frac{52.5 - 47.5}{5} = K\left(\frac{52.5 + 47.5}{2} - T_0\right)$$

$$\Rightarrow 1 = K(50 - T_0) \quad \ldots \text{(i)}$$

When body further cools from 47.5°C to 42.5°C.

$$\frac{47.5 - 42.5}{7.5} = K\left(\frac{47.5 + 42.5}{2} - T_0\right)$$

$$\Rightarrow \frac{2}{3} = K(45 - T_0) \quad \ldots \text{(ii)}$$

Dividing Eq. (i) by Eq. (ii), we get

$$T_0 = 35°\text{ C}$$

74. (*c*);

According to Newton's law of cooling,

$$\frac{T_1 - T_2}{t} = K\left(\frac{T_1 + T_2}{2} - T_0\right)$$

In this case, $T_1 - T_2 = 10$ (same for all). So, time taken will be determined by $(T_1 + T_2)$ value

Time taken will be more for lower value of $(T_1 + T_2)$. Hence, the correct relation will be

$t_1 < t_2 < t_3$

75. 10°C;

From Newton's law of cooling, when body cools from 60°C to 50°C in 10 min,

$$\frac{60° - 50°}{10} = K\left[\frac{60° + 50°}{2} - \theta_0\right] \quad \ldots \text{(i)}$$

When body cools from 50°C to 42°C in 10 min,

$$\frac{50° - 42°}{10} = K\left[\frac{50° + 42°}{2} - \theta_0\right] \quad \ldots \text{(ii)}$$

Dividing Eq. (i) by Eq. (ii), we get

$$\frac{10}{8} = \frac{55° - \theta_0}{46° - \theta_0}$$

$$\Rightarrow \theta_0 = 10°\text{ C}$$

76. 2;

According to Newton's law of cooling, when metal cools from 62°C to 61°C in 2 min,

$$\frac{62° - 61°}{2} = K\left[\frac{62° + 61°}{2} - 30°\right]$$

$$\Rightarrow K = \frac{1}{63}$$

When metal cools from 46°C to 45.5°C

$$\frac{46° - 45.5°}{t} = \frac{1}{63}\left[\frac{46° + 45.5°}{2} - 30°\right]$$

$$\Rightarrow t = 2\text{ min}$$

77. 15 min;

According to Newton's law of cooling, when object takes 12 min to cool from 80° to 70°C

$$\frac{80° - 70°}{12} = K\left[\frac{80° + 70°}{2} - 25°\right]$$

$$\Rightarrow K = \frac{1}{60} \quad \ldots \text{(i)}$$

When object cools from 70°C to 60°C,

$$\frac{70° - 60°}{t} = K\left[\frac{70° + 60°}{2} - 25°\right]$$

$$\Rightarrow K = \frac{1}{4t} \quad \ldots \text{(ii)}$$

From Eqs. (i) and (ii), we get

$$\frac{1}{4t} = \frac{1}{60} \Rightarrow t = 15\text{ min}$$

78. 6 min;

According to Newton's law of cooling, when body cools from 61°C to 59°C,

$$\frac{61° - 59°}{4} = K\left[\frac{61° + 59°}{2} - 30°\right] \ldots \text{(i)}$$

When body cools from 51°C to 49°C,

$$\frac{51° - 49°}{t} = K\left[\frac{51° + 49°}{2} - 30°\right] \ldots \text{(ii)}$$

Dividing Eq. (i) by Eq. (ii), we get

$$\frac{t}{4} = \frac{60° - 30°}{50° - 30°} = \frac{30°}{20°}$$

$$\Rightarrow t = 6\text{ min}$$

79. 57 ;

According to the Newton's law of cooling, when body cools from 75°C to 65°C,

$$\frac{75° - 65°}{5} = K\left(\frac{75° + 65°}{2} - 25°\right)$$

$$\Rightarrow K = \frac{2}{45}$$

When body cools from 65°C to T°C,

$$\frac{65° - T}{5} = \frac{2}{45}\left(\frac{65° + T}{2} - 25°\right)$$

$$\Rightarrow T = 57°\text{ C}$$

Assertion-Reason Questions

1. (*c*)

2. (*c*); It is true that temperature can be perceived by touch but our skin is not reliable measurement organ as it can only sense relative hotness or coldness and also in a very subjective way.

3. (*b*); Celsius scale has 100 divisions and this scale is more intritive and user friendly. Thus, celsius scale is more practical for everyday.

4. (*a*)

5. (*b*); According to ideal gas law $pV = nRT$ the volume of the gas tends to zero at absolute zero.

6. (*c*); A is correct but R is incorrect.

7. (*c*)

8. (*d*); Due to strong intermolecular forces, it is easy to distribute heat evently in the bulk of material which in turn require less heat energy to raise its temperature.

9. (*a*)

10. (*a*)

Case Based Questions

1. (i) (*b*) ; Initial temperature $(t_1) = 30°$C

Final temperature $(t_2) = 40°$C

Coefficient of linear thermal expansion

$(\alpha) = 11 \times 10^{-6}$ per °C

length $(l) = 1$ km $= 1000$ m

Change in length

$(\Delta l) = l\alpha\,(t_2 - t_1)$

$= 1000 \times 11 \times 10^{-6}\,(40 - 30)$

$= 0.110$ m $= 110$ mm

(ii) (*b*)

(iii) (*d*)

(iv) (*a*)

Or

(*b*); Using the formula for thermal expansion,

$$\Delta l = l\alpha\,(t_2 - t_1)$$
$$= 1000 \times 11 \times 10^{-6}\,(5 - 30)$$
$$= 1000 \times 11 \times 10^{-6}\,(-25)$$
$$= -0.275 \text{ m}$$
$$= -275 \text{ mm}$$

Contraction in length = 275 mm

2. (i) (*a*); Given, latent heat of fusion, $L = 334$ J/g

Mass of ice cube, $m = 20$ g

Heat required,

$$Q = m \cdot L = 20 \times 334 = 6680 \text{ J}$$

(ii) (*b*); Given, the specific heat capacity of water,

$$c = 4.18 \text{ J/g °C}$$
$$Q = mc \cdot \Delta T = 20 \times 4.18\,(90 - 0) = 7524 \text{ J}$$

(iii) (*b*); At equilibrium condition

Heat loss by coffee = Heat gained by ice and water

$$200 \times 4.18\,(90 - T) = 6680 + 2 \times 20 \times 4.18 \times T$$
$$\Rightarrow 75240 - 836T = 6680 + 167.2T$$
$$\Rightarrow 167.2T + 836T = 75240 - 6680$$
$$\Rightarrow 1003.2T = 68560$$
$$\simeq 68°\text{C}$$

(iv) (*a*); Heat, $Q = m \times c \times \Delta T$

$$= 200 \times 4.18\,(90 - 25) = 54340 \text{ J}$$

Or

(*d*); Heat lost by coffee,

$$Q_{\text{lost}} = 200 \times 4.18\,(80 - 30) = 41800 \text{ J}$$

Heat gained by melted ice

$$Q_{\text{melt}} = 20 \times 334 = 6680 \text{ J}$$

Heat gained by melted ice to reach 30°C,

$$Q_{\text{heat}} = 20 \times 4.18 \times 30 = 2508 \text{ J}$$

Number of ice cubes

$$\frac{41800}{6680 + 2508} = \frac{41800}{9188} = 4.55 \simeq 5 \text{ ice cubes}$$

Competition Edge Up

1. (*a*); $\therefore \dfrac{F - 32}{9} = \dfrac{C}{5}$

Change in celsius and fahrenheit is related as,

$$\Delta C = \frac{5}{9}\Delta F$$

Now, $\Delta C = 40°$ C (given)

$$40 = \frac{5}{9}\Delta F \Rightarrow \Delta F = 72° \text{ F}$$

2. (*b*);

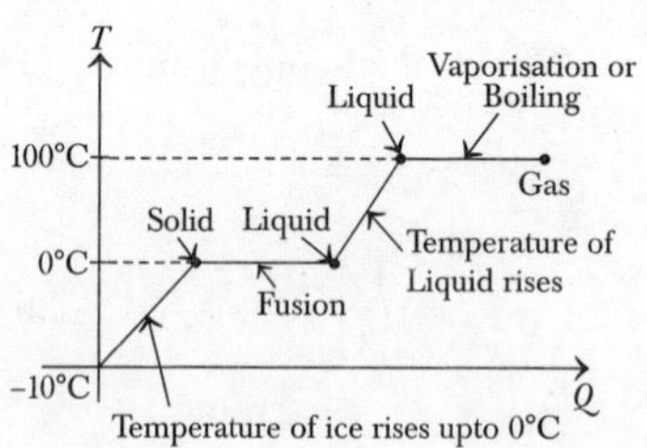

3. (*d*); Change in internal energy is,

$$\Delta U = mS_V \Delta T$$
$$\Delta U = 0.08 \times 0.17 \times 10^3 \times 5$$
$$\Delta U = 68 \text{ cal} \Rightarrow 68 \times 4.184 \text{ J}$$
$$\Delta U = 284.512 \text{ J} \simeq 284 \text{ J}$$

4. (*b*); We know that, stress $= Y \cdot \dfrac{\Delta l}{l}$

Here, $\Delta l = l\alpha\Delta T = 1 \times 10^{-5} \times 100 = 10^{-3}$

$$\Rightarrow \frac{F}{A} = Y \cdot \frac{10^{-3}}{1}$$
$$F = 0.5 \times 10^{11} \times 10^{-3} \times 10^{-3} = 0.5 \times 10^5 = 50 \times 10^3 \text{ N}$$

5. (*b*); Using the Newton's law of cooling,

rate of cooling

$$= \frac{dT}{dt} = K\left[\frac{T_i + T_f}{2} - T_0\right]$$
$$\Rightarrow \frac{90 - 80}{t} = K\left[\frac{90 + 80}{2} - 20\right]$$
$$\Rightarrow \frac{10}{t} = K\,[65]$$
$$\Rightarrow K = \frac{2}{13t}$$

In second conditions;

$$T_i' = 80°\text{C}$$
$$T_f' = 60° \text{ C.}$$

Using the Newton's law of cooling, rate of cooling

$$\frac{dT}{dt} = K\left[\frac{T'_i + T'_f}{2} - T_0\right]$$
$$\Rightarrow \frac{80 - 60}{t_1} = \frac{2}{13t}\left[\frac{60 + 80}{2} - 20\right]$$
$$\frac{20}{t_1} = \frac{2}{13t}[50] \Rightarrow t_1 = \frac{13}{5}t$$

6. (*d*); According to Wein's displacement law,

$$\lambda_{\text{max}} = \frac{b}{T}$$

i.e., $\lambda_{\text{max}} \propto \dfrac{1}{T}$ ... (i)

We know that,

$$\lambda_{\text{bluish}} < \lambda_{\text{yellowish}} < \lambda_{\text{reddish}}$$

Hence, using Eq. (i), we have

$$T_A > T_C > T_B$$

7. (*d*) ; Since, heat required,

$$Q = mc\Delta T = \left(\frac{4}{3}\pi r^3 \cdot \rho\right) c\Delta T$$

$[\because m = V_{\text{sphere}}\,\rho]$

Since, π, ρ, c and T are constants.

$$\Rightarrow Q \propto r^3 \text{ or } \frac{Q_1}{Q_2} = \frac{r_1^3}{r_2^3}$$
$$= \left(\frac{r_1}{r_2}\right)^3 = \left(\frac{1.5r_2}{r_2}\right)^3 = \frac{27}{8}$$

Chapter-11
Thermodynamics

1. (*c*); Adiabatic or insulating walls do not allow the flow of energy (heat) from one system to another.

So, the thermodynamic states (pressure and temperature) of *A* and *B* will not change with time.

2. $p_1(V_1 - nb) = \dfrac{p_2V_2}{1 - \left(\dfrac{nb'}{V_2}\right)}$;

For systems 1 and 3, we have

$$p_1V_1 - nbp_1 - p_3V_3 = 0 \quad \text{... (i)}$$

For systems 2 and 3, we have

$$p_2V_2 - p_3V_3 + \frac{nb'\,p_3V_3}{V_2} = 0 \quad \text{... (ii)}$$

From Eq. (i), we have

$$p_3V_3 = p_1V_1 - nbp_1 = p_1(V_1 - nb)$$

Putting the value of p_3V_3 into Eq. (ii), we get

$$p_2V_2 - [p_1(V_1 - nb)] + \frac{nb'}{V_2}$$

$$[p_1(V_1 - nb)] = 0$$

$$\Rightarrow \quad p_2V_2 = p_1(V_1 - nb)\left(1 - \frac{nb'}{V_2}\right)$$

$$\Rightarrow \quad p_1(V_1 - nb) = \frac{p_2V_2}{1 - \frac{nb'}{V_2}}$$

which is the required relationship between systems 1 and 2 to be in thermal equilibrium.

3. (*d*)

4. (i) ✓ (ii) × (iii) ✓ (iv) ✓ (v) ✓ (vi) ✓;

All statements are correct, except (ii). It can be corrected as "Internal energy of a gas is not path dependent.

5. Internal energy of the ideal monoatomic gas would be same in all three ways taken by it to go from A to B because internal energy is independent of path.

6. $\Delta U = Q - W$;

From the first law of thermodynamics,

$$\Delta Q = \Delta U + \Delta W$$

Therefore, change in internal energy, $\Delta U = Q - W$

7. 20;

Change in internal energy,

ΔU = Heat supplied − Work done

$$\Delta U = 35 - 15 = 20\text{ J}$$

8. 654;

Change in internal energy,

$$\Delta U = \Delta Q - \Delta W$$

$\therefore$ Heat, $\Delta Q = 300$ cal

$$= 300 \times 4.18$$

$$= 1254\text{ J}$$

Work, $W = 600$ J

$$\therefore \quad \Delta U = 1254 - 600 = 654\text{ J}$$

9. False;

From first law of thermodynamics, we have

$$\Delta Q = \Delta U + \Delta W$$

$$110 = 40 + \Delta W$$

$$\Rightarrow \Delta W = 70\text{ J}$$

10. 500;

From first law of thermodynamics, we have

$$\Delta Q = \Delta U + \Delta W$$

$$= 167 + 333$$

$$= 500\text{ cal}$$

11. 13.5 J;

According to the first law of thermodynamics,

Heat loss/gain = Change in internal energy + Work done

$$= 3.5 + 10 = 13.5\text{ J}$$

12. According to the question,

I. 50 J;

Change in internal energy,

$$\Delta U = \Delta Q - \Delta W$$

$$= 80 - 30 = 50\text{ J}$$

II. 60 J;

$$\Delta Q = \Delta U + \Delta W$$

$$= 50 + 10$$

$$= 60\text{ J}$$

III. −70 J;

$$\Delta W = -20\text{ J}, \Delta U = -50\text{ J}$$

$$\because \Delta Q = \Delta U + \Delta W$$

$$\Rightarrow \Delta Q = (-50) + (-20)$$

$$\Rightarrow \Delta Q = -70\text{ J}$$

13. I. 4 J/°C;

Heat capacity

$$= \frac{\text{Heat supplied}}{\text{Change in temperature}}$$

$$= \frac{40}{33 - 23} = 4\text{ J/°C}$$

II. 0.2 J/g°C;

Specific heat capacity

$$= \frac{\text{Heat supplied}}{\text{Mass} \times \text{Change in temperature}}$$

$$= \frac{40}{20 \times 10} = 0.2\text{ J/g°C}$$

III. 0.4 J/mol°C;

Molar mass (mass of 1 mole) = 2 g

Total sample mass = 20 g

Number of moles in the sample $= \frac{20}{2} = 10$ mol

Molar specific heat capacity of substance

$$= \frac{40}{10 \times 10} = 0.4\text{ J/mol°C}$$

14. True;

As, $U = 3k_BT \times N_A = 3RT$

and $C = \frac{\Delta Q}{\Delta T} = \frac{\Delta U}{\Delta T} = 3R$

15. $\frac{5}{2}R$;

Since, $C_p - C_V = R$

$$\Rightarrow \quad C_p = C_V + R$$

$$= \frac{3}{2}R + R = \frac{5}{2}R$$

16. 300 R;

From the molar specific heat capacity, we have

$$C = \frac{\Delta Q}{n\Delta T}$$

$$\Rightarrow \Delta Q = nC\Delta T \quad [\text{Here, } C = \frac{3}{2}R]$$

$$= \frac{3}{2}R(373 - 273) \times 2$$

$$= \frac{3}{2}R \times 100 \times 2$$

$$= 300\,R$$

17. (*b*)

18. True;

From an ideal gas equation, we have $pV = nRT$ ... (i)

The change in internal energy,

$$\Delta U = n \times C_V \times dT \quad \text{... (ii)}$$

By using Eqs. (i) and (ii), we have

$$\Delta U = C_V \times \frac{p \times V}{R} = \frac{C_V \times p \times V}{C_p - C_V}$$

$$\{\because C_p - C_V = R\}$$

$$= \frac{p \times V}{\frac{C_p}{C_V} - 1} = \frac{pV}{\gamma - 1} \quad (\because C_p / C_V = \gamma)$$

19. I, III; Statements I and III are correct but II is incorrect and it can be corrected as,

In isothermal process, heat transferred from the reservoir or source to the system does not affect the temperature of the reservoir or source.

20. 1.37×10^3;

Work done in isothermal process is given as $W = nRT \ln \frac{V_2}{V_1}$

$$= 0.5 \times R \times 300 \times \ln\left(\frac{6}{2}\right)$$

$$= 0.5 \times 8.314 \times 300 \times 1.0986$$

$$= 1370.06$$

$$= 1.37 \times 10^3\text{ J}$$

21. (*a*); Using $pV = nRT$, we see the higher value of pV, higher will be T. Since, pV is higher for T_1. Thus, $T_1 > T_2$.

22. 5.19 kJ;
Work done in isothermal expansion, $W = nRT \ln \frac{V_2}{V_1}$

$$= \frac{M}{M_0} \times R \times (273 + 27) \ln\left(\frac{140}{70}\right)$$

$$\left(\because n = \frac{M}{M_0}\right)$$

$$= \frac{96}{32} \times 8.314 \times (300)\,(0.693)$$

$$= 3 \times 8.314 \times 300 \times 0.693$$

$$= 5185.44\,\text{J} = 5.19\,\text{kJ}$$

23 negative;
Work done in isothermal process,

$$W = nRT \ln \frac{V_2}{V_1}$$

Since, volume is halved, i.e.

$$V_2 = \frac{1}{2} V_1$$

$$\Rightarrow \quad W = nRT \ln\left(\frac{1}{2}\right)$$

$$\Rightarrow \quad W = -0.693\,nRT = -\text{ve}$$

24. I, II;

I. If an ideal gas is compressed isothermally, then heat is released.
According to first law of thermodynamics,
$\Delta Q = \Delta W + \Delta U$
Since, $\Delta U = 0$ in isothermal process, the work done in compression is converted into heat, which is given by the gas.

II. According to the first law of thermodynamics,
$$\Delta Q = \Delta W + \Delta U$$
Since, $\Delta U = 0$ in isothermal process, all the heat given to the system is converted into work done.

25. 10 J;
We know,
Area under p-V graph is equal to work done.

26. Process (b) $\rightarrow$ isothermal expansion
Process (d) $\rightarrow$ isothermal compression

27. $W = \frac{\mu R}{\gamma - 1}(T_1 - T_2)$;
If an ideal gas undergoes from (p_1, V_1) to (p_2, V_2) adiabatically, then work done is given by

$$W = \int_{V_1}^{V_2} p\,dV$$

$$= \int_{V_1}^{V_2} \frac{dV}{V^{\gamma}} \quad (\because pV^{\gamma} = \text{constant})$$

$$= \left.\frac{V^{-\gamma+1}}{1-\gamma}\right|_{V_1}^{V_2}$$

$$= \frac{1}{1-\gamma}(p_2V_2 - p_1V_1)$$

$$= \frac{\mu R(T_1 - T_2)}{\gamma - 1}$$

[using $pV = nRT$]

28. Yes;
We know that, for an adiabatic process,

$$pV^{\gamma} = \text{constant} \quad \ldots \text{(i)}$$

For an ideal gas,

$$pV = nRT$$

$$\Rightarrow \quad p = \frac{C \cdot T}{V} \quad (\text{where, } C = nR)$$

Now, putting the value of p in Eq. (i), we get

$$\left(\frac{C \cdot T}{V}\right) V^{\gamma} = \text{constant}$$

$$\Rightarrow \quad TV^{\gamma - 1} = \text{constant}$$

$$\therefore \quad T_1V_1^{\gamma-1} = T_2V_2^{\gamma-1}$$

29. 20.18 K;
In adiabatic process,

$$\frac{T^{\gamma}}{p^{\gamma-1}} = \text{constant}$$

Thus, $\left(\frac{T_2}{T_1}\right) = \left(\frac{p_1}{p_2}\right)^{\frac{1-\gamma}{\gamma}}$

According to question,

$$T_2 = T_1\left(\frac{4}{1}\right)^{\frac{1-1.4}{1.4}}$$

$$= 300(4)^{\frac{-0.4}{1.4}}$$

$$= 300(4)^{\frac{-2}{7}}$$

$$= 300\left(\frac{1}{4}\right)^{\frac{2}{7}}$$

$$= 300\left(\frac{1}{16}\right)^{\frac{1}{7}}$$

$$= 300(0.6729)$$

$$= 20.18\,\text{K}$$

30. -2077.5;

$$T_1 = 27°\,\text{C} = 300\,\text{K}$$

$$T_2 = 127°\,\text{C} = 400\,\text{K}$$

$$\therefore \quad W = \frac{\mu R}{\gamma - 1}(T_1 - T_2)$$

$$= \frac{1 \times 8.31\,(300 - 400)}{(1.4 - 1)}$$

$$= -2077.5\,\text{J}$$

31. γ;
Slope of isothermal curve,

$$pV = \text{constant}$$

$$\Rightarrow \quad \frac{Vdp}{dV} + p\frac{dV}{dV} = 0$$

$$\Rightarrow \quad \frac{dp}{dV} = \frac{-p}{V} \quad \ldots \text{(i)}$$

Slope of adiabatic curve,

$$pV^{\gamma} = \text{Constant}$$

$$\Rightarrow \quad p\frac{d(V^{\gamma})}{dV} + V^{\gamma}\frac{dp}{dV} = 0$$

$$\Rightarrow \quad \frac{dp}{dV} = \frac{-p\gamma V^{\gamma-1}}{V^{\gamma}} = -p\gamma V^{-1}$$

$$\Rightarrow \quad \frac{dp}{dV} = -\gamma\frac{p}{V} \quad \ldots \text{(ii)}$$

From Eqs. (i) and (ii), we get

$$\frac{\text{Slope of adiabatic curve}}{\text{Slope of isothermal curve}} = \frac{\left(-\gamma\frac{dp}{dV}\right)_{\text{adi}}}{\left(\frac{-dp}{dV}\right)_{\text{iso}}} = +\gamma$$

32. I, III;
For an adiabatic process,

$$W > 0 \text{ if } T_2 < T_1$$

and $W < 0$ if $T_2 > T_1$

According to first law of thermodynamics,

$$\Delta Q = \Delta U + \Delta W$$

Change in heat in an adiabatic process is zero.
Thus, $\quad \Delta Q = 0$

$$\Rightarrow \quad \Delta U + \Delta W = 0$$

33. (a);

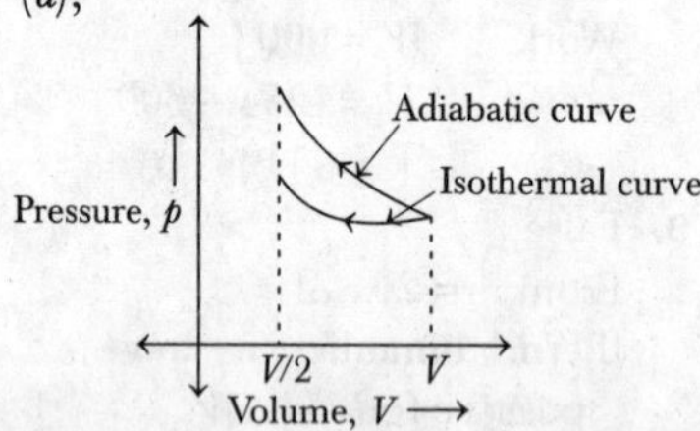

Since, the isothermal curve is less steeper than the adiabatic curve. So, area under the (p-V) curve for adiabatic process has more magnitude than isothermal curve. Hence, work done in adiabatic process will be more than in isothermal process.

34. $A \rightarrow 3$, $B \rightarrow 1$, $C \rightarrow 4$, $D \rightarrow 2$.

35. Here, $CB \rightarrow$ isothermal process
$AB \rightarrow$ isobaric process
Thus,

Path	dp	dV	dT	dV	dQ	dW
BA	0	–	–	–	–	–
AC	+	0	+	+	+	0
CB	–	+	0	0	+	+

36. 831 J;
Work done at constant pressure is
$$W = p\Delta V = \mu R \,\Delta T$$
Given, $\mu = 1$, $T_1 = 27°\,C = 300\,K$
and $T_2 = 127°\,C = 400\,K$
$$R = 8.31\ J/mol\text{-}K$$
$$\therefore \quad W = 1 \times 8.31 \times (400 - 300)$$
$$= 831\ J$$

37. (*a*); Work done, $W = nR\,\Delta T$ ...(i)
At constant pressure, heat given to gas is given by
$$Q = nC_p \Delta T \quad ...(ii)$$
On dividing Eq. (i) by Eq. (ii), we get
$$\frac{W}{Q} = \frac{nR\,\Delta T}{nC_p\,\Delta T} = \frac{R}{C_p}$$
$$\Rightarrow \frac{W}{Q} = \frac{R}{(7/2)R} = \frac{2}{7}$$
$$\Rightarrow \frac{10}{Q} = \frac{2}{7}$$
$$\Rightarrow Q = 35\,J$$

38. III,IV;
Work done in an anti-clockwise process is negative.
Therefore, $\Delta U = \Delta Q - \Delta W$
Total work done in cyclic process
$$= \text{Area under the curve}$$
$$= \frac{1}{2} \times (V_1 - V_2)(p_2 - p_1)$$
$$= -20\,J$$
$$W_{A \rightarrow B} = \int_2^4 p dV = 20 \int_2^4 dV$$
$$= 20 \times 2 = 40J$$
Work done by the system is positive for $A \rightarrow B$.
$\therefore$ The internal energy is positive.

39. (*b*) **40.** entropy

41. False **42.** (*c*)

43. II;

I. Combustion reaction of mixture of air and petrol is an irreversible process.

II. Cooking gas leaking from a gas cylinder cannot on its own go back into the gas cylinder. This is an irreversible process.

III. Processes involving increase or decrease in internal energy are always irreversible in nature.

44. (*a*)

45. (*b*)

46. True; $\eta = 1 - \frac{T_2}{T_1}$
$$\frac{70}{100} = 1 - \frac{T_2}{1000}$$
$$\Rightarrow \quad T_2 = 300\,K = 27°\,C$$

47. 273/473;
$$\eta_1 = 1 - \frac{273}{473} = \frac{200}{473}$$
$$\eta_2 = 1 - \frac{73}{273} = \frac{200}{273}$$
$$\therefore \frac{\eta_1}{\eta_2} = \frac{273}{473}$$

48 50%;
$$\eta = 1 - \frac{150}{300} = \frac{1}{2} \text{ or } 50\%$$

49. 40%;
$$\eta = 1 - \frac{300}{500} = \frac{2}{5} \text{ or } 40\%$$

50. True

51. 27.64;
We know that,
$$\eta = 1 - \frac{T_2}{T_1} = 1 - \frac{(273 + 15)}{(273 + 125)}$$
$$= \frac{110}{398} = 27.64\%$$

52. 120;
$$\frac{Q_1}{Q_2} = \frac{T_1}{T_2} \Rightarrow Q_2 = Q_1 \times \frac{T_2}{T_1}$$
$$= 200 \times \frac{300}{500} = 120\,J$$
$$\therefore \quad x = 120$$

53. 2000;
$$\eta_A = \eta_B$$
$$1 - \frac{500}{1000} = 1 - \frac{1000}{x}$$
$$\Rightarrow \quad \frac{1000}{x} = \frac{1}{2} \Rightarrow x = 2000$$

54. 219, 137;
Initially, the efficiency of the engine,
$$\eta = 1 - \frac{T_2}{T_1}$$
$$\frac{1}{6} = 1 - \frac{T_2}{T_1} \quad ...(i)$$
$$\frac{1}{6} - 1 = -\frac{T_2}{T_1};\ -\frac{5}{6} = -\frac{T_2}{T_1}$$
$$\Rightarrow \quad \frac{T_1}{T_2} = \frac{6}{5}$$
$$\Rightarrow \quad T_1 = \frac{6}{5} T_2 \quad ...(ii)$$
Finally the sink temperature is reduced by 82°C.
$$\therefore \quad T_2' = T_2 - 82$$
$$\text{Thus, } \eta' = 1 - \frac{T_2'}{T_1} = 1 - \left(\frac{T_2 - 82}{T_1}\right)$$
$$\text{Given, } \eta' = 2\eta$$
$$= 2 \times \left(\frac{1}{6}\right) \quad \left(\because \eta = \frac{1}{6}\right)$$
$$= \frac{1}{3}$$
$$\Rightarrow \quad \frac{1}{3} = 1 - \left(\frac{T_2 - 82}{\frac{6}{5} T_2}\right)$$
[using Eq. (ii)]
$$\Rightarrow \quad \left(\frac{T_2 - 82}{\frac{6}{5} T_2}\right) = 1 - \frac{1}{3}$$
$$\Rightarrow \quad T_2 - 82 = \frac{2}{3} \times \frac{6}{5} T_2$$
$$\Rightarrow \quad \frac{1}{5} T_2 = 82$$
$$\Rightarrow \quad T_2 = 410\,K$$
$$\text{Thus,} \quad T_2 = 137°\,C$$
$$\text{and} \quad \frac{1}{6} = 1 - \frac{410}{T_1} K$$
[from Eq. (i)]
$$\Rightarrow \quad T_1 = 492\,K \text{ or } 219°C$$

55. I. 650;
Work done by heat engine
$$= Q_1 - Q_2$$
If $W_1 = W_2$, then
$$900 - T = T - 400$$
$$\Rightarrow \quad 2T = 1300$$
$$\Rightarrow \quad T = 650\,K$$

II. 600;
Efficiency,
$$\eta = 1 - \frac{T_2}{T_1}$$
If $\eta_1 = \eta_2$, then
$$1 - \frac{T}{900} = 1 - \frac{400}{T}$$
$$\Rightarrow \quad T^2 = 360000$$
$$\Rightarrow \quad T = 600\,K$$

Assertion-Reason Questions

1. (*a*)
2. (*b*); Heat can be completely converted into work, if change in internal energy is zero.
3. (*c*); First law of thermodynamics explains energy conversion. It does not put any condition as the heat flow from lower temperature to higher temperature.
According to first law of thermodynamics, $\Delta U = Q - W$. Here, ΔU is the change in internal energy of system, Q is net heat transfer.
4. (*b*)
5. (*c*); In a quasi-static process, at every stage, the difference between the system and the external pressure is infinitesimally small. The same is true for the temperature difference between the system and its surroundings.
6. (*b*);For isochoric process,
$$\Delta V = 0$$
and $\Delta W = p\Delta V \Rightarrow \Delta W = 0$
From 1st law,
$$\Delta Q = \Delta U + \Delta W \Rightarrow \Delta Q = \Delta U$$
7. (*a*); A quasi-static isothermal expansion of an ideal gas in a cylinder fitted with a frictionless movable piston stays in equilibrium with its surrounding at each step. Thus, it is a reversible process.
8. (*b*) In an unisolated system, heat may enter into or escape from the system due to which entropy may increase or decrease but for the isolated system, we do not consider an exchange of heat. So in this case, entropy will always increase as the process is spontaneous.
As $\Delta Q = 0$, so the process is adibatic.
9. (*a*); Energy spent in working agains dissipative force is not recovered back due to this processes in nature are irreversible.
10. (*a*)

Case Based Questions

1. (i) (*a*)
(ii) (*a*)
(iii) (*b*); Work done in isothermal process,
$$W = nRT \ln\left(\frac{V_2}{V_1}\right)$$
$$= 1 \times 8.314 \times 300 \times \ln\left(\frac{4}{2}\right)$$
$$= 8.314 \times 300 \times \ln 2$$
$$\simeq 1728\text{ J} \simeq 1.7\text{ kJ}$$
(iv) (*c*); For adiabatic process,
$$\Delta U = W$$
Or
(*a*); For isochoric process,
$$Q = nC_V\Delta T$$
$$= 1 \times \frac{3}{2}R \times (600 - 300)$$
$$= \frac{3}{2} \times 8.314 \times 300 = 3741.3\text{ J}$$
$$\simeq 3.7\text{ kJ}$$
2. (i) (*a*); Heat added, $Q = mC\Delta T$
$$= 2 \times 385 \times (350 - 300)$$
$$= 38500\text{ J}$$
$$= 38.5\text{ kJ}$$
(ii) (*a*); For copper, at constant pressure, $\Delta U = \Delta Q$
i.e. $\Delta U = 38.5$ kJ
(iii) (*a*); Heat added, $Q = mC\Delta T$
$$= 2 \times 385 \times (400 - 350)$$
$$= 38.5\text{ kJ}$$
(iv) (*b*); Total change in internal energy
$$\Delta U_{\text{total}} = 38.5 + 38.5\text{ kJ}$$
$$= 77\text{ kJ}$$
Or
(*b*); For copper, at constant pressure and volume,
$$\Delta U = \Delta Q$$
i.e. $\Delta Q = 77.0$ kJ

Competition Edge Up

1. (*c*); $W_{AB} = \int p dV$
(Assuming T to be constant)
$$= \int \frac{RT}{V^3} dV \quad [\because pV^3 = RT]$$
$$= RT\int_2^4 V^{-3} dV$$
$$= 8 \times 300 \times \left[-\frac{1}{2}\left(\frac{1}{4^2} - \frac{1}{2^2}\right)\right]$$
$$= 225\text{ J}$$
$$W_{BC} = p\int_4^2 dV = 10(2-4) = -20\text{ J}$$
$$W_{CA} = 0$$
$$\therefore \quad W_{\text{cycle}} = 205\text{ J}$$
2. (*a*); For adiabatic process,
$$p_i V_i^\gamma = p_f V_f^\gamma$$
$$p_i (5)^{1.5} = p_f (4)^{1.5}$$
$$\frac{p_i}{p_f} = \left(\frac{4}{5}\right)^{1.5}$$
$$\frac{p_i}{p_f} = \left(\frac{4}{5}\right)^{3/2} = \frac{4}{5}\left(\frac{4}{5}\right)^{1/2}$$
$$\frac{p_i}{p_f} = \frac{8}{5\sqrt{5}}$$
3. (*d*); We know that, $TV^{\gamma-1}$ = constant
$$T_i V^{\frac{3}{2}-1} = T_f (2V)^{\frac{3}{2}-1}$$
$$TV^{1/2} = T_f 2^{1/2} \cdot V^{1/2}$$
$$T_f = \frac{T}{\sqrt{2}}$$
$$\text{Now, } W = \frac{nR\Delta T}{1-\gamma} = \frac{1R\left(\frac{T}{\sqrt{2}} - T\right)}{1 - \frac{3}{2}}$$
$$= 2RT\left(1 - \frac{1}{\sqrt{2}}\right)$$
$$W = RT(2 - \sqrt{2})$$
4. (*c*); Since, $\Delta Q = \Delta U + W$
$$\Rightarrow \Delta Q = nC_V\Delta T + W$$
$$\Rightarrow 48 = 1\left(\frac{3R}{2}\right)(2) + W$$
$$\Rightarrow W = 48 - 3R$$
$$= 48 - 3 \times 8.3 = 23.1\text{ J}$$
5. (*d*); From thermodynamic equation,
$$W = \Delta U + \Delta Q$$

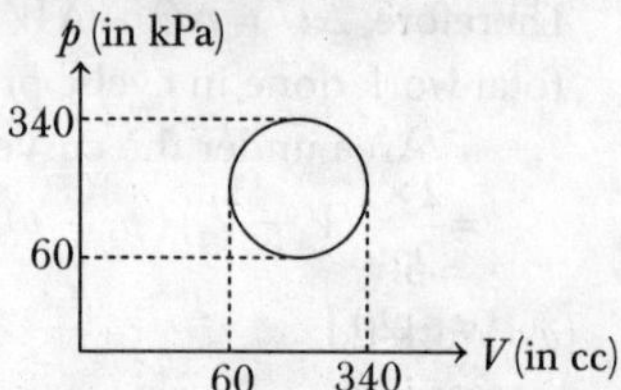

$\Delta U = 0$ for cyclic process
$$\therefore \Delta Q = W = \text{Area of } p\text{-}V \text{ curve}$$
$$= \pi \times (140 \times 10^3\text{ Pa}) \times (140 \times 10^{-6}\text{ m}^3)$$
$$\Delta Q = 61.6\text{ J}$$
The heat absorb is 61.6 J.
6. (*d*); For isobaric process,
$$p = \text{constant}$$
So, from gas equation, we get
$$\frac{V}{T} = \frac{nR}{p}$$

or $\quad V = \dfrac{nR}{p} \cdot T$

So, slope of V-T curve is proportional to $\dfrac{1}{p}$ value.

As slope of line 2 is more,

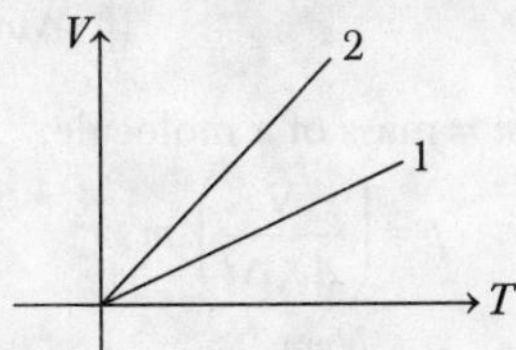

$$\frac{1}{p_2} > \frac{1}{p_1}$$

or $\quad p_2 < p_1$

7. (*); For thermodynamic process A,

$$\log p = \gamma \log V$$
$$p = V^{\gamma}, (\gamma > 1)$$
$$pV^{\gamma - 1} = \text{constant}$$
$$C_A = C_V + \frac{R}{1+\gamma} \quad \ldots\text{(i)}$$

Now for process B,

$$pV^{-1} = \text{constant}$$
$$C_B = C_V + \frac{R}{1+1}$$
$$C_B = C_V + \frac{R}{2} \quad \ldots\text{(ii)}$$
$$C_p = C_V + R \quad \ldots\text{(iii)}$$

From Eqs. (i), (ii) and (iii), we get

$$C_p > C_B > C_A > C_V$$

8. (c); We know that,

$$pV = nkT \Rightarrow T = \frac{pV}{nK}$$
$$= \frac{1.38 \times 10^5 \times 1}{2 \times 10^{25} \times 1.38 \times 10^{-23}}$$
$$= 500 \text{ K}$$

9. (a); Work done in an isochoric process is always zero.

10. (d); Efficiency of Carnot engine,

$$\eta = 50\% = 0.5$$

Temperature of source,

$$T_1 = 327°\text{C}$$
$$= (327 + 273) \text{ K} = 600 \text{ K}$$

If T_2 be the temperature of sink, then

$$\eta = 1 - \frac{T_2}{T_1} \Rightarrow 0.5 = 1 - \frac{T_2}{600}$$
$$\Rightarrow \frac{T_2}{600} = 0.5 \Rightarrow T_2 = 300 \text{ K}$$
$$= (300 - 273)°\text{C} = 27°\text{C}$$

11. (a); Curve 1 is isochoric process because volume is constant. In curve 2 and 3, curve 3 has smaller slope than curve 2. Hence, curve 3 represents isothermal process and curve 2 represents adiabatic process.

12. (c); From the p-V diagram, it is clear that pressure of ideal gas in the piston cylinder is constant during thermodynamic process. Hence, this process is isobaric.

Chapter-12

Kinetic Theory

1. (c)

2. 10^{-10} m

3. definite, multiple

4. 6.023×10^5;

By ideal gas equation, $pV = \mu RT$

$$\Rightarrow \quad 8.31 \times 10^{-10} \times 1 \times 10^{-6}$$
$$= \mu \times 8.31 \times 100$$
$$\therefore \quad \mu = 10^{-18}$$

$\therefore$ Number of molecules,

$$N = \mu N_A = 10^{-18} \times 6.023 \times 10^{23}$$
$$\Rightarrow N = 6.023 \times 10^5$$

5. II;

By ideal gas equation,

$$pV = \mu RT$$
$$\Rightarrow \quad pV = \frac{m}{M} RT$$

As, V, m and T are constants.

$$\therefore \quad \frac{p_A}{p_B} = \frac{\mu_A}{\mu_B} = \frac{m_{H_2}}{M_{H_2}} \times \frac{M_{He}}{m_{He}}$$
$$= \frac{M_{He}}{M_{H_2}} \quad (\because m_{H_2} = m_{He})$$
$$= \frac{4}{2} = 2$$

6. (d); From diagram,

$$T_1 > T_2 > T_3$$

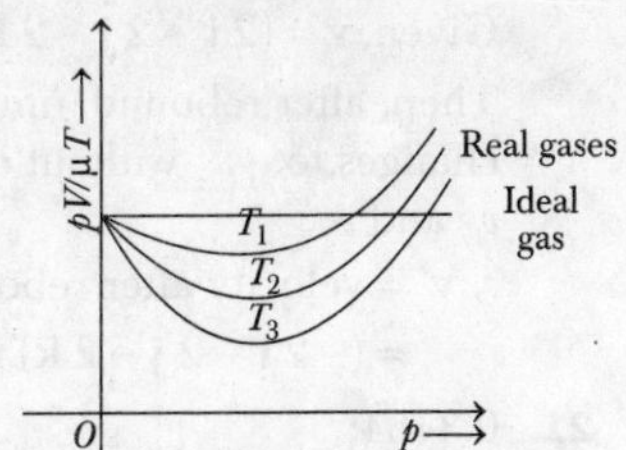

7. I, II, III;

I. The dotted line in the diagram shows that, there is no deviation in the value of $\dfrac{pV}{nT}$ for different temperatures T_1 and T_2 for increasing pressure, so this gas behaves ideally.

Hence, dotted line corresponds to ideal gas behaviour.

II. At high temperature, the deviation of the gas is less and at low temperature, the deviation of gas is more.

In the graph, deviation for T_2 is greater than that for T_1. Thus,

$$T_1 > T_2$$

III. Since, the two curves intersect at dotted line, so the value of $\dfrac{pV}{nT}$ at that point on the Y-axis is same for all gases.

8. (b); As, $pV = \mu RT$

$$= m\left(\frac{RT}{M}\right)$$

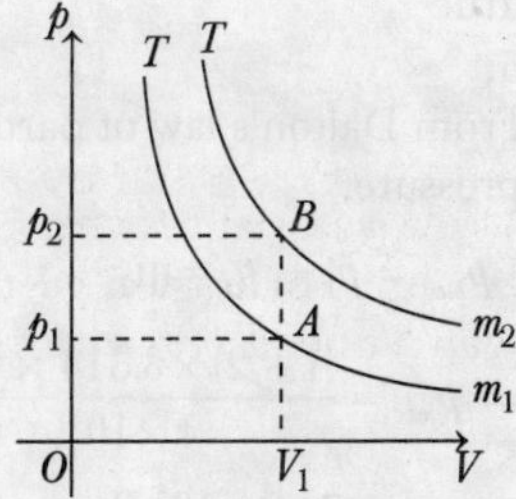

At point A,

$$p_1 V_1 = m_1 \left(\frac{RT}{M}\right) \quad \ldots\text{(i)}$$

At point B,

$$p_2 V_2 = m_2 \left(\frac{RT}{M}\right) \quad \ldots\text{(ii)}$$

Dividing Eq. (i) by Eq. (ii), we get

$$\Rightarrow \quad \frac{p_1}{p_2} = \frac{m_1}{m_2} \quad \ldots\text{(iii)}$$

From diagram, we can write

$$p_2 > p_1 \quad \ldots\text{(iv)}$$

From Eqs. (iii) & (iv), we get

$$\Rightarrow \quad m_2 > m_1$$

9. 546 K;

As, $\quad pV = \mu RT$

$$\Rightarrow \quad \frac{pV}{T} = \text{constant}$$

As, $\quad p = \text{constant}$

$$\Rightarrow \quad \frac{V}{T} = \text{constant}$$

$$\therefore \quad \frac{V_1}{T_1} = \frac{V_2}{T_2}$$

$$\Rightarrow \quad \frac{V_1}{273} = \frac{2V_1}{T_2} \quad (\because V_2 = 2V_1)$$

$$\therefore \quad T_2 = 546 \text{ K}$$

10. (*a*)

11. $p_1 > p_2 > p_3$;

As, $pV = \mu RT$

$\therefore$ At V = constant,

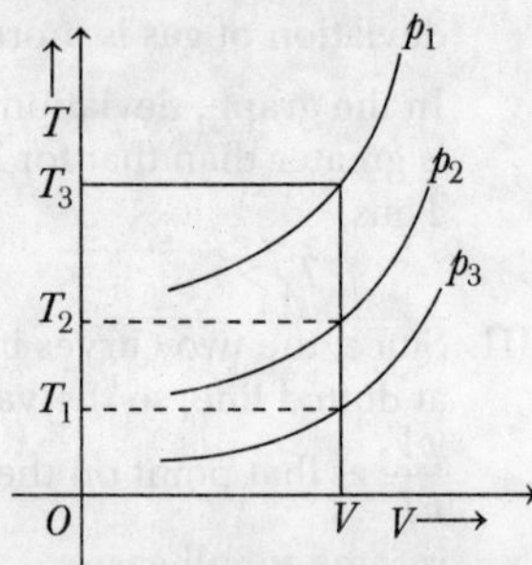

$$p \propto T$$

As, $\quad T_3 > T_2 > T_1$

So, $\quad p_1 > p_2 > p_3$

12. True

13. 5;

From Dalton's law of partial pressure,

$$p_{mix} = p_1 + p_2 = (\mu_{\text{H}} + \mu_{\text{CO}_2}) \frac{RT}{V}$$

$$\Rightarrow p_{mix} = \frac{(1+2) \times 8.314 \times 400}{4 \times 10^3}$$

$$= 24.9 \times 10^5 \text{ Pa}$$

Now, according to the question,

$$p_{\text{mix}} = 24.9 \times 10^x = 24.9 \times 10^5$$

$$\therefore \quad x = 5$$

14. 0.2 kg/m^3;

We know that,

$$pV = nRT$$

$$\Rightarrow pV = \left(\frac{m}{M}\right) RT \quad \left(\because n = \frac{m}{M}\right)$$

$$\Rightarrow \rho = \frac{pM}{RT} \quad \left(\because \rho = \frac{m}{V}\right)$$

$$= \frac{249 \times 10^3 \times 2 \times 10^{-3}}{8.3 \times 300}$$

$$= 0.2 \text{ kg/m}^3$$

15. (*b*); As, $pV = \mu RT = \mu kT$

$\therefore$ Using $pV = NkT \quad \ldots$(i)

Using RHS of Eq. (i), we get

$$= \mu N_A \cdot kT = \frac{m}{M_0} \cdot N_A \cdot kT$$

$$\left(\because \mu = \frac{m}{M_0}\right)$$

$$\Rightarrow \quad V = \frac{m}{pM_0} N_A kT \quad \ldots \text{(ii)}$$

$$\Rightarrow \quad \rho = \frac{m}{V} = \frac{pM_0}{N_A kT} \text{ [using Eq. (ii)]}$$

$$= \frac{pM_0}{N_A kT} = \frac{p \cdot mN_A}{N_A kT}$$

$$\therefore \quad \rho = \frac{pm}{kT}$$

16. Yes;

As, $\rho = \dfrac{pM_0}{RT}$

$\therefore$ At T = constant, $\rho \propto pM_0$

$$\therefore \frac{(M_0)_A}{(M_0)_B} = \frac{(\rho / p)_A}{(\rho / p)_B} = \frac{\rho_A}{\rho_B} \times \frac{p_B}{p_A}$$

$$= \frac{1.5 \rho_B}{\rho_B} \times \frac{p_B}{2p_B} = \frac{3}{4}$$

$$(\because \rho_A = 1.5 \rho_B)$$

Hence, $\dfrac{(M_0)_A}{(M_0)_B} = \dfrac{x}{y} = \dfrac{3}{4}$

17. 126.42 kg ;

As, $pV = \mu RT = \dfrac{m}{M_0} RT$

At $\quad V$ = constant, $p \propto mT$

$$\Rightarrow \quad \frac{p_2}{p_1} = \frac{m_2 T_2}{m_1 T_1}$$

$$p_2 = 45 \text{ cm of Hg}$$

$$= 45 \times 10^{-2} \times 13.6 \times 10^3 \times 10$$

$$= 612 \times 10^2 \text{ Pa}$$

$$\therefore \quad \frac{612 \times 10^2}{1.01 \times 10^5} = \frac{m_2 \times 266}{185 \times 300}$$

$$\therefore \quad m_2 = 126.42 \text{ kg}$$

18. I, II

19. II, III;

If $\mathbf{v} = v_x \hat{\mathbf{i}} + v_y \hat{\mathbf{j}} + v_z \hat{\mathbf{k}}$, then after elastic collision on shaded wall, molecule rebounds with velocity without v_y and v_Z change.

$$\mathbf{v}' = -v_x \hat{\mathbf{i}} + v_y \hat{\mathbf{j}} + v_z \hat{\mathbf{k}}$$

20. $(-2\hat{\mathbf{i}} - 2\hat{\mathbf{j}} - 2\hat{\mathbf{k}})$;

Given, $\mathbf{v} = (2\hat{\mathbf{i}} - 2\hat{\mathbf{j}} - 2\hat{\mathbf{k}})$ m/s

Then, after rebound, only v_x changes to $-v_x$ without change of v_y and v_z.

$\therefore \mathbf{v}'$ = velocity after rebound

$$= (-2\hat{\mathbf{i}} - 2\hat{\mathbf{j}} - 2\hat{\mathbf{k}}) \text{ m/s}$$

21. 0.3464;

Pressure, $p = nmv_x^2$

where, n = number of molecules per unit volume $= \left(\dfrac{N}{Av_x \Delta t}\right)$

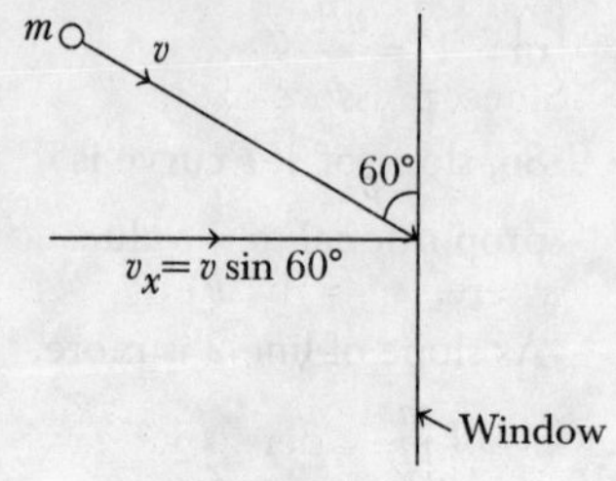

m = mass of a molecule.

$$\therefore \quad p = \left(\frac{N}{Av_x \Delta t}\right) \cdot m \cdot v_x^2$$

$$= \frac{Nmv_x}{A \cdot \Delta t}$$

$$= \frac{200 \times 5 \times 10^{-3} \times 6 \times \frac{\sqrt{3}}{2}}{0.5 \times 30}$$

$$(v_x = v \sin 90°)$$

$$= 0.3464 \text{ Pa}$$

22. 46.66;

Speed	Number of particles	v^2
v	2	v^2
$2v$	3	$4v^2$
$3v$	5	$9v^2$
$4v$	4	$16v^2$
$5v$	3	$25v^2$
$6v$	2	$36v^2$
$7v$	1	$49v^2$
	$N = 20$	$\Sigma v^2 = 140v^2$

$$\therefore \bar{v}^2 = \text{Mean squared speed} = \frac{\Sigma v^2}{N}$$

$$= \frac{140 \, v^2}{20} = 7 \, v^2$$

Now, $pV = \dfrac{1}{3} nVm \, \bar{v}^2$

$$\therefore \quad N = nV = \frac{1}{3} Nm\bar{v}^2$$

$$= \frac{140}{3} mv^2 \quad \ldots \text{(i)}$$

According to the question,

$$pV = xmv^2 \quad \ldots \text{(ii)}$$

From Eqs. (i) and (ii), we get

$$x = \frac{140}{3} = 46.66$$

23. False;

Since, $pV = \dfrac{2}{3} E$,

$\therefore \quad$ At $p = c$ (isobaric condition),

$$E \propto V$$

24. I, II;
Since, pressure of gas,
$$p = \frac{1}{3}\frac{mn}{V}v^2$$
where, nm = mass of the gas,
V = volume of gas
and $\frac{mn}{V}$ = density of gas.
Thus, $p = \frac{1}{3}\rho v^2$
$$\Rightarrow \quad p = \frac{1}{3}\rho \cdot \frac{3RT}{M_0} = \frac{\rho RT}{M_0}$$
$$\Rightarrow \quad \rho = \frac{pM_0}{RT} = \frac{pmN_A}{kN_AT}$$
$[\because R = N_Ak \text{ and } M_0 = mN_A]$
$$\Rightarrow \quad \rho \propto p \text{ and } \rho \propto \frac{1}{T}$$

25. 7729;
Kinetic energy per molecule
$$= \frac{3}{2}k_BT$$
$$= \frac{3}{2} \times 1.38 \times 10^{-23} \times T$$
$$\therefore \quad T = 7729 \text{ K}$$

26. A → 2, B → 1, C → 1.

27. A → 3, B → 2, C → 1.

28. doubled;
As, kinetic energy of gas, $E \propto T$

29. (*a*)

30. (*c*); Mean KE per molecule
$$= \frac{3}{2} \cdot \frac{pV}{N}$$
where, N = number of molecules.
$$\Rightarrow 2 \times 10^{-9} = \frac{3}{2} \times \frac{2 \times 1.01 \times 10^5 \times 1 \times 10^{-3}}{N}$$
$$\therefore \quad N = 1.5 \times 10^{11} \text{ molecules}$$

31. 78.77×10^3 K;
Escape velocity is given by
$$v_e = 11.2 \text{ km/s}$$
Now, $v = \sqrt{\frac{3RT}{M_0}} = \sqrt{\frac{3k_BT}{M}}$
$$\therefore 11.2 \times 10^3 = \sqrt{\frac{3 \times 1.38 \times 10^{-23} \times T}{2.6 \times 10^{-26}}}$$
$$\therefore \quad T = 78.77 \times 10^3 \text{ K}$$

32. A → 3, B → 1, C → 2

33. $v_{mp} < v_{av} < v_{rms}$;
$$v = \sqrt{\frac{2RT}{M_0}}$$
$$v_{av} = \sqrt{\frac{5RT}{\pi M_0}}$$
$$v = \sqrt{\frac{3RT}{M_0}}$$
$$\therefore v_{mp} : v_{av} : v_{rms} = 1 : 1.28 : 1.224$$
Hence, $v_{mp} < v_{av} < v_{rms}$

34. 1.33:1;
As, $v_{rms} = \sqrt{\frac{3RT}{M_0}}$
$\therefore$ At T = constant, $v_{rms} \propto \frac{1}{\sqrt{M_0}}$
$$\therefore \quad \frac{(v_{rms})_{Ar}}{(v_{rms})_{Cl_2}} = \sqrt{\frac{(M_0)_{Cl_2}}{(M_0)_{Ar}}}$$
$$= \sqrt{\frac{70.9}{39.9}} = 1.33$$

35. 0.707 : 1 ;
As, $v_{rms} = \sqrt{\frac{3RT}{M_0}}$
$$\therefore \quad \frac{(v_{rms})_1}{(v_{rms})_2} = \sqrt{\frac{T_1}{T_2}} = \sqrt{\frac{T}{2T}} = 0.707$$

36. (a) 5;
Mean speed, $v = \frac{\Sigma v}{N}$
$$= \frac{6 \times 3 + 4 \times 2 + 2 + 1 + 8 \times 2 + 5 + 3 + 7}{12}$$
$$= 5 \text{ cm/s}$$
(b) 5.44;
$$v = \sqrt{< v^2 >}$$
$$= \sqrt{\frac{6^2 \times 3 + 4^2 \times 2 + 2^2 + 1^2 + 8^2 \times 2 + 5^2 + 3^2 + 7^2}{12}}$$
$$= 5.44 \text{ cm/s}$$
(c) 3.9;
$$\frac{v}{v} = \frac{1}{1.28}$$
$$\Rightarrow v = \frac{5}{1.28} = 3.9 \text{ cm/s}$$
(d) 10;
Number of collisions per second $= \frac{\Sigma v}{6L}$
$$= \frac{6 \times 3 + 4 \times 2 + 2 + 1 + 8 \times 2 + 5 + 3 + 7}{6 \times 1} = 10$$

37. number of molecules;
The area of n_v *versus* v graph will give number of molecules.

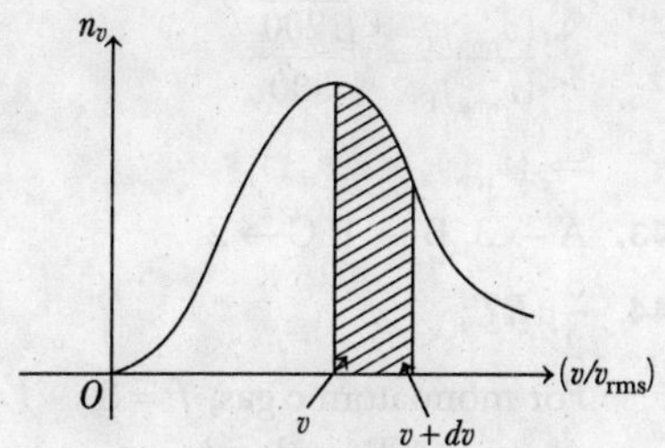

Hence, area of strip indicates number of molecules between speed v and $v + dv$.

38. 640 m/s;
$$v_{rms} = \sqrt{\frac{3RT}{M_0}}$$
$$\therefore \quad \frac{(v_{rms})_{H_2}}{(v_{rms})_{O_2}} = \sqrt{\frac{(M_0)_{O_2}}{(M_0)_{H_2}}}$$
$$\therefore \quad (v_{rms})_{H_2} = \sqrt{\frac{32}{2}} \times 160$$
$$= 640 \text{ m/s}$$

39. (*d*) ; By kinetic theory of gases,
$$pV = \frac{1}{3}Nmv^2$$
$$\therefore \quad v \propto \frac{1}{\sqrt{m}}$$
As, $m_A < m_B < m_C$
$$\Rightarrow \quad \frac{1}{v_A} < \frac{1}{v_B} < \frac{1}{v_C}$$

40. 400;
As, $v_{rms} = \sqrt{\frac{3RT}{M_0}}$
$\therefore \quad v \propto \sqrt{T}$ and it is independent of pressure.
$$\therefore \quad \frac{(v_{rms})_2}{(v_{rms})_1} = \sqrt{\frac{T_2}{T_1}}$$
$$\Rightarrow (v_{rms})_2 = \sqrt{\frac{400}{300}} \times 200$$
$$= \frac{400}{\sqrt{3}} \text{ m/s}$$
$$\therefore \quad x = 400$$

41. $\sqrt{\frac{3\pi}{8}}$;
$$v_{rms} = \sqrt{\frac{3RT}{M_0}}, v_{av} = \sqrt{\frac{8RT}{\pi M_0}}$$
$$\therefore \quad \frac{v_{rms}}{v_{av}} = \frac{\sqrt{3}}{\sqrt{\frac{8}{\pi}}} = \sqrt{\frac{3\pi}{8}}$$

42. (*d*); $v_{rms} = \sqrt{\frac{3RT}{M_0}}$
$$\because \quad v_{rms} \propto \sqrt{T}$$

$\therefore \frac{(v_{rms})_2}{(v_{rms})_1} = \sqrt{\frac{1200}{300}}$

$\Rightarrow (v_{rms})_2 = 2(v_{rms})_1$

43. A → 3, B → 1, C → 2

44. $\frac{3}{2}\mu RT$;

For monoatomic gas, $f = 3$

Average KE/molecule

$= \frac{f}{2}k_BT = \frac{3}{2}k_BT$

$\therefore$ Average KE

$= \left(\frac{3}{2}k_BT\right)N = \frac{3}{2}\mu RT$

45. $\frac{1}{2}k_BNT$;

Average KE $= \left(\frac{f}{2}k_BT\right)N$

For single degree of freedom,

Average KE $= \frac{1}{2}k_BNT$

46. (*d*)

47. True

48. 5 (3 translational + 2 rotational)

49. A→ 2, B → 1, C → 4, D → 3

50. I;

I. As, $\Delta Q = \Delta U + \Delta W$

$\therefore$ Fraction of heat that increases internal energy

$= \frac{\Delta U}{\Delta Q} = \frac{nC_V\Delta T}{nC_p\Delta T} = \frac{C_V}{C_p} = \frac{1}{\gamma}$

II. Fraction of heat that can be converted into work

$= \frac{\Delta W}{\Delta Q} = 1 - \frac{\Delta U}{\Delta Q} = \left(1 - \frac{1}{\gamma}\right)$

51. 100;

$C_V = \frac{f}{2}R = \frac{6}{2}R = 3R$

$\therefore \quad C_p = C_V + R$

$= 3R + R = 4R$

Now, $\Delta W = \Delta Q - \Delta U$

$\Rightarrow \quad \Delta W = nC_p\Delta T - nC_V\Delta T$

$\Rightarrow \quad \Delta W = n(4R)\Delta T - n(3R)\Delta T$ $[\because n = 1]$

$25 = R\Delta T$ ...(i)

$\therefore \quad \Delta Q = nC_p\Delta T$

$\Rightarrow \quad \Delta Q = 4R\Delta T$

$\Rightarrow \quad \Delta Q = 4 \times 25$ [using Eq. (i)]

$= 100$ J

Hence, $\Delta Q = 100$ J

52. A → 2 → Q, B → 3 → P

C → 1 → R

53. (i) ✓ (ii) × (iii) ✓ (iv) ×

(ii) For monoatomic gas,

f = degree of freedom = 3

$\therefore U$ = Internal energy per mole

$= \frac{f}{2}RT = \frac{3}{2}RT$

$C_V = \frac{dU}{dT} = \frac{3}{2}R$

$C_p = C_V + R = \frac{3}{2}R + R = \frac{5}{2}R$

(iii) For diatomic gases, $f = 5$

$\therefore \quad U = \frac{f}{2}RT = \frac{5}{2}RT$

$\therefore \quad C_V = \frac{dU}{dT} = \frac{5}{2}R$

$C_p = C_V + R = \frac{7}{2}R$

(iv) For polyatomic gases, mean energy per molecule

$= \frac{n}{2}kT$

54. $\frac{5}{4}$;

Degree of freedom,

f = Translational + Rotational + Vibrational

For polyatomic gases,

$f = 3 + 3 + 2 = 8$

Now, $C_V = \frac{f}{2}R = \frac{8}{2}R = 4R$

$\therefore \quad C_p = C_V + R = 5R$

$\therefore \quad \beta = \frac{C_p}{C_V} = \frac{5R}{4R} \Rightarrow \beta = \frac{5}{4}$

55. 25;

As, gas is diatomic (only rotate but do not oscillate)

$\therefore \quad f$ = Translational + Rotational

$= 3 + 2 = 5$

Now, $\Delta U = \frac{f}{2}nR\Delta T$

$= \frac{5}{2} \times 3R \times (40) = 300R$

$\therefore \quad \Delta W = p\Delta V = nR\Delta T$

$= 3 \times R \times 40 = 120R$

$\therefore \quad \frac{\Delta U}{\Delta W} = \frac{300R}{120R} = \frac{25}{10}$

$\therefore \quad x = 25$

56. (*a*)

57. 15;

Total internal energy,

$U_{mix} = U_1 + U_2$

$= \frac{f_1}{2}n_1RT + \frac{f_2}{2}n_2RT$

$= \frac{5}{2} \times 3 \times RT + \frac{3}{2} \times 5 \times RT$

$= 15RT$

58. 6;

$(Q)_{p=c} = nC_p\Delta T$

$160 = nC_p(50)$ ... (i)

$(Q)_{V=c} = nC_V(\Delta T)$

$\Rightarrow -240 = nC_V(-100)$ ... (ii)

Dividing Eq. (i) by Eq.(ii), we get

$\frac{160}{240} = \frac{nC_p \times 50}{nC_V \times 100}$

$\therefore \quad \frac{C_p}{C_V} = \gamma = \frac{4}{3}$

Now, $\quad \gamma = 1 + \frac{2}{f} \Rightarrow \frac{4}{3} = 1 + \frac{2}{f}$

$\therefore \quad f = 6$

59. (*a*); As $\gamma = \frac{C_p}{C_V} = 1 + \frac{2}{f}$, where

For hydrogen (H_2), diatomic

$f = 5$

$\therefore \quad \gamma = 1 + \frac{2}{5} = \frac{7}{5}$

For helium (He), monoatomic

$f = 3$

$\therefore \quad \gamma = 1 + \frac{2}{3} = \frac{5}{3}$

For *X*-diatomic with one vibrational mode

$\therefore f = 5 + 2 = 7$

($\because$ for 1 vibration, $f = 2$)

$\therefore \quad \gamma_X = 1 + \frac{2}{7} = \frac{9}{7}$

Hence, $\gamma = \frac{7}{5}, \gamma_{He} = \frac{5}{3}, \gamma_X = \frac{9}{7}$

60. 11;

Total internal energy,

$U = U_1 + U_2$

$= \frac{f_1}{2}\mu_1RT + \frac{f_2}{2}\mu_2RT$

$= \left(\frac{5}{2} \times 2 + \frac{3}{2} \times 4\right)RT = 11RT$

$\therefore n = 11$

61. (i) ✓ (ii) × ;

(i) For mixing of gases, $\Delta U = 0$

$\Rightarrow \quad U_1 + U_2 = U$

$\Rightarrow n_1C_{V_1}T + n_2C_{V_2}T$

$= (n_1 + n_2)C_V T$

$\therefore C_V = \frac{n_1C_{V_1} + n_2C_{V_2}}{n_1 + n_2}$

(ii) As, $U_1 + U_2 = U$

$$\therefore \frac{f_1}{2} n_1 RT + \frac{f_2}{2} n_2 RT = \frac{f}{2}(n_1 + n_2)RT$$

$$\therefore f = \frac{n_1 f_1 + n_2 f_2}{n_1 + n_2}$$

62. (*b*); As mixing is such that there is no loss of energy.

$$\therefore \Delta U = 0$$

$$\therefore (\Delta U)_1 + (\Delta U)_2 = 0$$

$$\Rightarrow \frac{f_1}{2} n_1 R\Delta T_1 + \frac{f_2}{2} n_2 R\Delta T_2 = 0$$

$$\Rightarrow \frac{f_1}{2} n_1 (T_1 - T) + \frac{f_2}{2} n_2 (T_2 - T) = 0$$

$$\therefore T = \frac{n_1 f_1 T_1 + n_2 f_2 T_2}{n_1 f_1 + n_2 f_2}$$

63. True;

For mixing process, $\Delta U = 0$

$$\Rightarrow n_1 C_{V_1} T + n_2 C_{V_2} T = (n_1 + n_2) C_V T$$

$$\Rightarrow \frac{n_1 R}{\gamma_1 - 1} + \frac{n_2 R}{\gamma_2 - 1} = \frac{(n_1 + n_2)R}{\gamma - 1}$$

$$\Rightarrow \frac{2}{\frac{5}{3} - 1} + \frac{3}{\frac{4}{3} - 1} = \frac{(2+3)R}{\gamma - 1}$$

$$\therefore \gamma = \frac{17}{12} = 1.42$$

64. $\frac{n_1 T_1 + n_2 T_2 + n_3 T_3}{n_1 + n_2 + n_3}$;

For mixing of gases, $\Delta U = 0$

$$\therefore U_i = U_f$$

$$\Rightarrow n_1\left(\frac{1}{2}k_B T_1\right) + n_2\left(\frac{1}{2}k_B T_2\right) + n_3\left(\frac{1}{2}k_B T_3\right) = (n_1 + n_2 + n_3)\left(\frac{1}{2}k_B T\right)$$

$$\therefore T = \frac{n_1 T_1 + n_2 T_2 + n_3 T_3}{n_1 + n_2 + n_3}$$

65. $\bar{v}\Delta t, n\pi d^2 \bar{v}\Delta t, \frac{1}{n\pi d^2}$;

From diagram

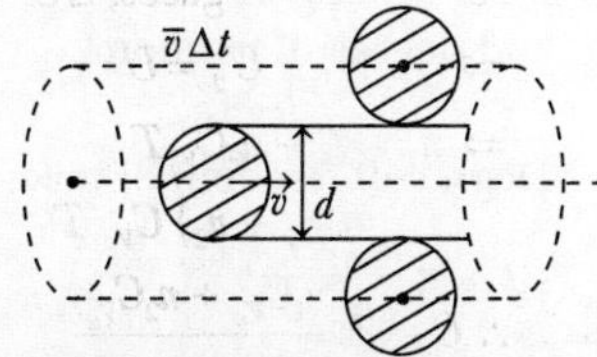

Distance moved by molecule in time interval $\Delta t = v\,\Delta t$.

Number of collisions made by molecule in the interval $\Delta t = n\pi d^2 \bar{v} \cdot \Delta t$

Mean free path, $l = \bar{v} \cdot \tau = \frac{1}{n\pi d^2}$

66. 1 : 2;

As, mean free path,

$$\lambda = \frac{1}{\sqrt{2}n\pi d^2}$$

$$\lambda = \frac{1}{\sqrt{2} \cdot \frac{N}{V} \pi d^2} \quad \text{... (i)}$$

$$\because V = \frac{\mu RT}{p} \quad \text{... (ii)}$$

From Eqs. (i) and (ii), we get

$$\therefore \lambda = \frac{\mu RT}{\sqrt{2}\pi d^2 Np}$$

$$\because \lambda \propto T$$

$$\therefore \frac{\lambda_2}{\lambda_1} = \frac{T_2}{T_1}$$

$$\therefore \frac{\lambda_1}{\lambda_2} = \frac{200}{400} = \frac{1}{2}$$

67. (*a*); Mean free path, $\lambda = \frac{1}{\sqrt{2}n\pi d^2}$

$$\therefore \lambda \propto \frac{1}{d^2}$$

68. 102.5 nm;

Mean free path,

$$\lambda = \frac{1}{\sqrt{2}n\pi d^2}$$

where, $n = \frac{N}{V} = \frac{p}{k_B T}$

$$\therefore \lambda = \frac{1}{\sqrt{2}\left(\frac{p}{k_B T}\right)\pi d^2}$$

$$= \frac{1.38 \times 10^{-23} \times 300}{\sqrt{2} \times 1.01 \times 10^5 \times \pi \times (0.3 \times 10^{-9})^2}$$

$$= 102.5 \text{ nm}$$

69. 25;

As, mean free path,

$$\lambda = \frac{1}{\sqrt{2}n\pi d^2}$$

$$\because \lambda \propto \frac{1}{d^2}$$

$$\therefore \frac{\lambda_A}{\lambda_B} = \left(\frac{d_B}{d_A}\right)^2$$

$$= \left(\frac{5}{10}\right)^2 = 25 \times 10^{-2}$$

70. (*d*); As, $\lambda = \frac{1}{\sqrt{2}n\pi d^2}$

Now, mean free time,

$$\tau = \frac{\lambda}{<v>} = \frac{\frac{1}{\sqrt{2}n\pi d^2}}{\sqrt{\frac{8RT}{\pi M_0}}}$$

$$\therefore \tau \propto \frac{\sqrt{M_0}}{d^2}$$

$$\therefore \frac{\tau_1}{\tau_2} = \frac{\sqrt{(M_0)_1}}{d_1^2} \times \frac{d_2^2}{\sqrt{(M_0)_2}}$$

$$= \left(\frac{r_2}{r_1}\right)^2 \times \sqrt{\frac{(M_0)_1}{(M_0)_2}}$$

$$= \left(\frac{0.1}{0.07}\right)^2 \sqrt{\frac{40}{140}} = 1.83$$

71. $2^{\frac{\gamma+1}{2}}$;

As, $\tau = \frac{\lambda}{V} = \frac{1}{\sqrt{2} \cdot \frac{N}{V} \pi d^2} \times \frac{\sqrt{\pi M_0}}{8RT}$

$$\therefore \tau \propto \frac{V}{\sqrt{T}} \quad \text{... (i)}$$

Now, for adiabatic process,

$TV^{\gamma-1}$ = constant

$$\therefore \frac{1}{\sqrt{T}} \propto V^{\frac{\gamma-1}{2}} \quad \text{... (ii)}$$

From Eqs. (i) and (ii), we get

$$\tau \propto V \cdot V^{\frac{\gamma-1}{2}} \Rightarrow \tau \propto V^{\frac{\gamma+1}{2}}$$

$$\therefore \frac{\tau_2}{\tau_1} = \left(\frac{V_2}{V_1}\right)^{\frac{\gamma+1}{2}}$$

$$= \left(\frac{2V_1}{V_1}\right)^{\frac{\gamma+1}{2}} = 2^{\frac{\gamma+1}{2}}$$

72. Mean free time,

$$\tau = \frac{\lambda}{<v>} = \frac{1}{\sqrt{2}n\pi d^2} \times \sqrt{\frac{\pi M_0}{8RT}}$$

$$\therefore \tau \propto \frac{1}{\sqrt{T}}$$

$\therefore$ Graph of τ *versus* $\frac{1}{\sqrt{T}}$ is given by

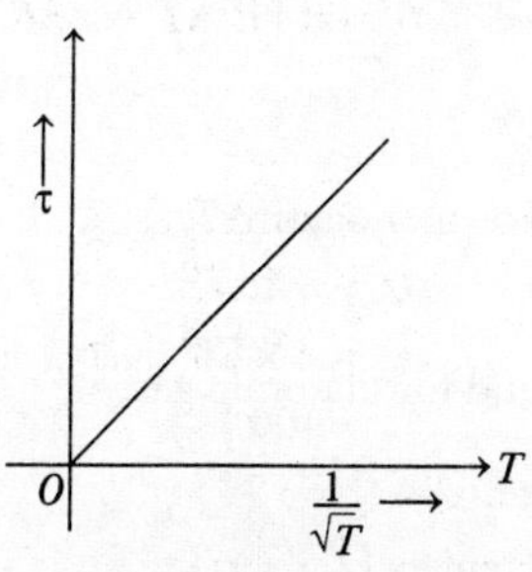

Assertion-Reason Questions

1. (*b*); During driving the temperature of the tyre increases which increases the pressure in the tyre.

2. (*a*); The motion of the gases in container is known as the ordered motion of the gas and *zig-zag* motion of gas molecules with container is called disordered motion.

3. (*b*);

4. (*a*); All collisions between molecules among themselves or between molecules and walls are elastic. This implies that total kinetic energy is conserved.

5. (*d*); $V_{\text{rms}} = \sqrt{\dfrac{3RT}{M}}$

$$V_{\text{mp}} = \sqrt{\frac{2RT}{M}}$$

$\therefore\ V_{\text{rms}} > V_{\text{mp}}$

6. (*c*); By law of equipartition of energy, the energy for each degree of freedom in thermal equilibrium is $\frac{1}{2}k_BT$.

Each vibrational mode gives 2 degrees of freedom is,

$$E = f\left(\frac{1}{2}k_BT\right) = k_BT$$

Hence, Reason is false.

7. (*b*); The degree of freedom depends upon

(i) the number of atoms forming a molecule

(ii) the structure of the molecule

(iii) temperature of the gas

Hence, Reason is false, and for linear triatomic molecule it has 3 translational, 3 rotational and 1 vibrational degree of freedom.

8. (*a*)

9. (*d*); $\gamma = \dfrac{C_p}{C_V}$

For monoatomic gas;

$$\gamma = 1 + \frac{2}{3} = \frac{5}{3}$$

and for diatomic gas;

$$\gamma_D = 1 + \frac{2}{5} = \frac{7}{5}$$

Hence, $\gamma_D > \gamma_m$.

10. (*a*)

Case Based Questions

1. (i) (*c*)

(ii) (*a*); The rms speed,

$$V_{\text{rms}} = \sqrt{\frac{3k_BT}{m}}$$

When temperature becomes $4T$,

$$V_{\text{rms}} = \sqrt{\frac{3k_B \times 4T}{4}}$$

$$= 2\,V_{\text{rms}}$$

(iii) (*c*); $V_{\text{rms},\,A} = \sqrt{\dfrac{3k_BT}{M_A}}$

and $V_{\text{rms},\,B} = \sqrt{\dfrac{3k_BT}{M_B}}$

Since, k_BRT are constant then,

$$V_{\text{rms},A} \times \sqrt{M_A} = V_{\text{rms},B} \times \sqrt{M_B}$$

(iv) (*b*)

Or

(*c*); Since, $pV = nRT$

If n is doubled, the pressure must also be doubled.

2. (i) (*b*); For monoatomic gas,

$$C_V = \frac{3}{2}R$$

$$C_p = C_V + R \quad \text{(Mayer's relation)}$$

$$\Rightarrow\ C_p = \frac{3}{2}R + R = \frac{5}{2}R$$

(ii) (*d*); For diatomic gas,

$$C_V = \frac{5}{2}R$$

$$C_p = C_V + R = \frac{5}{2}R + R = \frac{7}{2}R$$

(iii) (*d*); $\lambda \propto \dfrac{1}{d^2}$

(iv) (*b*)

Or

(*b*); At constant pressure, the energy required is proportional to C_p. For Gas A (monoatomic), $C_p = \frac{5}{2}R$ and for Gas B (diatomic), $C_p = \frac{7}{2}R$.

Therefore, Gas B require more energy to raise the temperature by one degree celsius.

Competition Edge Up

1. (*b*); Given,

Temperature, $T = 27°\text{C} = 300\text{ K}$

We know that, $(C_V)_{\text{monoatomic}} = \frac{3}{2}R$

and $(C_V)_{\text{diatomic}} = \frac{5}{2}R$

$$\therefore\ \frac{(C_V)_{\text{monoatomic}}}{(C_V)_{\text{diatomic}}} = \frac{3}{5}$$

2. (*c*); Degree of freedom of non-rigid diatomic molecules,

$$= 5 + 2(3N - 5)$$
$$= 5 + 2(3 \times 2 - 5)$$
$$= 5 + 2 = 7$$
$$f = 7$$

Energy of one molecule $= \frac{f}{2}k_BT$

$\therefore$ Energy of 10 molecule

$$= 10\left(\frac{f}{2}k_BT\right)$$

$$= 10 \times \frac{7}{2}k_BT = 35k_BT$$

3. (*b*); We know that, $v_{\text{rms}} = \sqrt{\dfrac{3RT}{M}}$

$$\therefore\ \frac{(v_{\text{rms}})_{O_2}}{(v_{\text{rms}})_{\text{He}}} = \sqrt{\frac{M_{\text{He}}}{M_{O_2}}} = \sqrt{\frac{4}{32}} = \frac{1}{2\sqrt{2}}$$

$$\therefore\ \frac{(v_{\text{rms}})_{\text{He}}}{(v_{\text{rms}})_{O_2}} = \frac{2\sqrt{2}}{1}$$

4. (*c*); For CH_4 molecule, there are 3 rotational degree of freedom and 3 translational degree of freedom. i.e. $f_t = 3$ and $f_r = 3$

5. (*c*); Argon is monoatomic, its degree of freedom is 3.

Oxygen is diatomic with 5 degree of freedom.

Total internal energy of mixture = Internal energy of Ar + Internal energy of O_2

$$= 8 \times \frac{3}{2}RT + 6 \times \frac{5}{2}RT$$

$$= (12 + 15)\,RT = 27\,RT$$

6. (*b*); For monoatomic gas, number of moles, $n_1 = 3$

and degree of freedom,

$$f_1 = 3$$

For diatomic gas, number of moles,

$$n_2 = 2$$

and degree of freedom,

$$f_2 = 5$$

Degree of freedom of mixed gas,

$$f_{\text{mix}} = \frac{n_1f_1 + n_2f_2}{n_1 + n_2}$$

$$= \frac{3 \times 3 + 2 \times 5}{3 + 2} = \frac{19}{5}$$

$$\therefore \gamma_{\text{mixture}} = 1 + \frac{2}{f_{\text{mix}}} = 1 + \frac{2}{(19/5)}$$

$$= 1 + \frac{10}{19} = \frac{29}{19} = 1.52$$

7. (*d*); Average KE = 0.414 eV, for monoatomic $f = 3$

$$\frac{f}{2} k_B T = \frac{3}{2} k_B T$$

$$= 0.414 \times 1.6 \times 10^{-19} \text{ J}$$

$$T = 3200 \text{ K}$$

8. (*d*); Charle's law states that volume of a gas is proportional to its temperature on Kelvin scale at constant pressure.
It is clear for p_1, T is higher.
Thus, $p_1 > p_2 > p_3$.

Alternate Solution

We know that,

$$pV = nRT$$

$$\frac{T}{V} = \frac{p}{nR}$$

$$\text{Slope} = \frac{p}{nR}$$

i.e., slope $\propto p$
Hence, $p_1 > p_2 > p_3$

9. (*c*); We know that,

$$v_{\text{rms}} = \sqrt{3RT/M}$$

Pressure exerted by an ideal gas,

$$p = \frac{1}{3} nm\bar{v}^2$$

$\bar{v}$ is the average speed of the gas molecules. The average kinetic energy of a molecule,

$$\text{KE}_{\text{av}} = \frac{3}{2} k_B T$$

For diatomic gas, degree of freedom, $f = 5$
As, total internal energy of 1 mole of diatomic gas,

$$\Delta U = \frac{nfRT}{2}$$

$$\Rightarrow \Delta U = \frac{1(5)RT}{2} \Rightarrow \Delta U = \frac{5RT}{2}$$

The correct match is A $\to$ 2, B $\to$ 1, C $\to$ 4 and D $\to$ 3.

10. (*a*); Given,
pressure, $p = 249$ kPa

$$= 249 \times 10^3 \text{ Pa}$$

Temperature, $T = 27°\text{C}$

$$= 273 + 27 \text{ K} = 300 \text{ K}$$

As, from ideal gas equation,

$$pV = nRT$$

$$\Rightarrow pV = \frac{m}{M} RT \quad \left[\text{as } n = \frac{m}{M}\right]$$

$$\Rightarrow pVM = mRT$$

$$\Rightarrow pM = \frac{m}{V} RT = \rho RT \quad \left[\text{as } \frac{m}{V} = \rho\right]$$

$$\Rightarrow \rho = \frac{pM}{RT} = \frac{249 \times 10^3 \times 2 \times 10^{-3}}{8.3 \times 300}$$

[$\because$ for hydrogen gas, $M = 2$ g $= 2 \times 10^{-3}$ kg]

$$\rho = 0.2 \text{ kg/m}^3$$

11. (*a*); The average thermal energy of a system with degree of freedom f is equals to its average energy, which is given as

$$= \frac{f}{2} k_B \cdot T$$

For monoatomic gas, $f = 3$
$\therefore$ Average thermal energy

$$= \frac{3}{2} k_B \cdot T$$

12. (*a*); The mean free path λ for a gas, with molecular diameter d and number density n is given by the relation $\lambda = \frac{1}{\sqrt{2} n\pi d^2}$

13. (*a*); The mean free path l for a gas molecule is given as

$$l = \frac{1}{\sqrt{2}\pi nd^2} \Rightarrow l \propto \frac{1}{d^2}$$

where, d = diameter of molecule of gas.

Chapter-13

Oscillations

1. (*a*) The rotation of earth about its axis is periodic because it repeats after a regular interval of time. However, it is obviously not a to and fro type of motion about a fixed point, hence its motion is not simple harmonic motion.

2. (*a*)A periodic function repeats itself after a time period T.
Given, $f(t) = A \sin \omega t$
If the argument of this function ωt, is increased by an integral multiple of 2π radians. Then, the value of the function remains the same. The given function $f(t)$ is then periodic and repeats itself after every 2π radians.

$$\Rightarrow \quad f(t) = f(t + T)$$

3. (*b*) The function $\log \omega t$ increases monotonically with time t. Therefore, it cannot repeat its value and is a non-periodic function. It may be noted that as $t \to \infty$, $\log \omega t$ diverges to ∞. Therefore, it cannot represents any kind of physical displacement.

4. (*b*) In option (b),
$(\sin \omega t + \cos \omega t)$

$$= \sqrt{2}\left(\frac{1}{\sqrt{2}} \sin \omega t + \frac{1}{\sqrt{2}} \cos \omega t\right)$$

$$= \sqrt{2}\left(\cos \frac{\pi}{4} \sin \omega t + \sin \frac{\pi}{4} \cos \omega t\right)$$

$$= \sqrt{2}\left[\sin\left\{\omega t + \frac{\pi}{4}\right\}\right]$$

[$\because$ using trigonometric identity, $\sin(A + B) = \sin A \cos B + \cos A \sin B$]

Comparing the above equation with the standard equation of periodic function $f(t) = A \sin(\omega t + \phi)$, we can say that, the above function has amplitude $\sqrt{2}$ with phase constant $\pi/4$. Also, it represents a periodic function with period $2\pi/\omega$.

5. (*a*) In the given x-t graph, for

(a) No repetition of motion takes place rather it represents a unidirectional, linear but non-uniform motion of the particle, hence motion is non-periodic.

(b) Motion repeats after every 2 s. Hence, it is periodic with time period 2 s.

(c) Motion repeats after every 4s, hence it is periodic with time period of 4 s.

(d) Clearly, the motion repeats itself after 2 s. Hence, periodic having a time period of 2 s.

6. (*d*); The graph (a) and (c) represent periodic motion as the motion repeats itself after a certain interval of time.

7. Yes

8. $A \cos(\omega t + \phi)$

9. II;

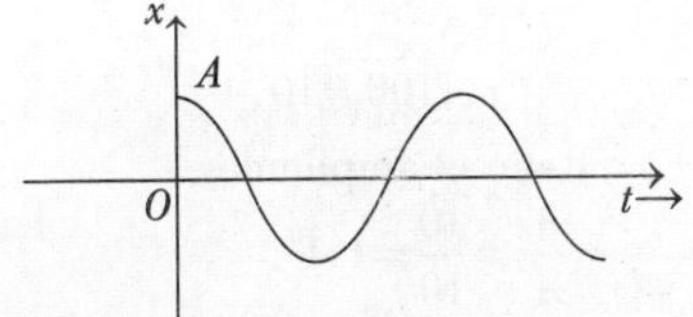

10. $A \sin(2\omega t)$

11. I, III;

For a simple harmonic motion,

$$\frac{d^2x}{dt^2} \propto -x$$

Hence, equations

$$y = \sin \omega t - \cos \omega t$$

and $y = 5\cos\left(\frac{3\pi}{4} - 3\omega t\right)$

are satisfying this condition and equation $y = 1 + \omega t + \omega^2 t^2$ is not periodic and $y = \sin^3 \omega t$ is periodic but not SHM.

12. $\frac{1}{50}$ s;

$x = 0.01 \sin(100\pi t + 5)$

Comparing the given equation with displacement (x) of SHM, we get

$100\pi t = \omega t \Rightarrow \omega = 100\pi$

Time period,

$$T = \frac{2\pi}{\omega} = \frac{2\pi}{100\pi} = \frac{1}{50} \text{ s}$$

13. half and twice;

From the graph, it is clear that the curve b completes its revolution within half time interval of a.

Thus, it has twice the frequency of a.

14. I, II;

Since, A is the maximum amplitude, therefore both equations have same amplitude.

As, $x(t) = A\cos(\omega t + \phi)$

$y(t) = A \sin(\omega t + \phi)$

Since, $\sin(90° - \theta) = \cos\theta$

Therefore, both $x(t)$ and $y(t)$ have a phase difference of $\frac{\pi}{2}$.

15. 1;

As, $y_1 = 10 \sin\left(3\pi t + \frac{\pi}{3}\right)$

$A_1 = 10$

$y_2 = 5(\sin 3\pi t + \sqrt{3}\cos 3\pi t)$

$= 5\sin 3\pi t + 5\sqrt{3}\cos 3\pi t$

Amplitude of SHM y_2 is

$$A_2 = \sqrt{5^2 + (5\sqrt{3})^2}$$

$$= \sqrt{25 + 75}$$

$$= \sqrt{100} = 10$$

$\therefore$ Ratio of amplitudes,

$$\frac{A_1}{A_2} = \frac{10}{10} = 1:1$$

According to question, ratio of amplitude of y_1 to y_2 is $x:1$.

On comparing, we get $x = 1$

16. No;

The time period of the simple harmonic motion, $T = 2$ s

Displacement covered by the particle,

$$x = A/2$$

Here, A is the amplitude of the particle.

The general equation of the simple harmonic motion,

$$x = A \sin \omega t$$

$$\Rightarrow \frac{A}{2} = A \sin\left(\frac{2\pi}{T}t\right)$$

$$\Rightarrow \frac{1}{2} = \sin\left(\frac{2\pi}{2}t\right)$$

$$\Rightarrow \sin\frac{\pi}{6} = \sin(\pi t)$$

$$\Rightarrow \frac{\pi}{6} = \pi t$$

$$\Rightarrow t = \frac{1}{6}$$

17. $\frac{\pi}{6}$;

The general equation is given as

$$y = A\sin(\omega t + \phi_0)$$

At $t = 0$, $y = \frac{A}{2}$, then

$$\frac{A}{2} = A\sin(0 + \phi_0) = A \sin\phi_0$$

$$\Rightarrow \sin\phi_0 = \frac{1}{2}$$

$$\Rightarrow \phi_0 = \frac{\pi}{6}$$

18. True;

Equation for SHM is given as

$y = 5(\sin 3\pi t + \sqrt{3}\cos 3\pi t)$

$= 5 \times 2\left(\frac{1}{2} \times \sin 3\pi t + \frac{\sqrt{3}}{2}\cos 3\pi t\right)$

$= 5 \times 2\left(\cos\frac{\pi}{3} . \sin 3\pi t + \sin\frac{\pi}{3} . \cos 3\pi t\right)$

$= 5 \times 2 \sin\left(3\pi t + \frac{\pi}{3}\right)$

[using, $\sin(a + b) = \sin a \cos b + \cos a \sin b$]

or $y = 10 \sin\left(3\pi t + \frac{\pi}{3}\right)$

Comparing this equation with the general equation of SHM,

i.e. $y = A\sin\left(\frac{2\pi t}{T} + \phi\right)$

We get, amplitude, $A = 10$ cm

and $2\pi / T = 3\pi$

or Time period, $T = \frac{2}{3}$ s

19. (c)

20. $\sqrt{A^2 + B^2}$;

Displacement,

$y = A_0 + A\sin\omega t + B\cos\omega t$ ...(i)

The general equation of SHM can be given as

$x = a \sin\omega t + b\cos\omega t$ ...(ii)

From Eqs. (i) and (ii), we can say that A_0 is the value of mean position, at which $y = 0$

$\therefore$ Amplitude,

$$R = \sqrt{A^2 + B^2 + 2AB\cos\theta}$$

As two functions sine and cosine has phase difference of 90°.

$\therefore$ $R = \sqrt{A^2 + B^2}$ ($\because \cos 90° = 0$)

21. II;

According to question,

$y_1 = a\sin\omega t$

$y_2 = b\cos\omega t$

$= b\sin\left(\omega t + \frac{\pi}{2}\right)$

$\therefore$ The resultant displacement is given by

$y = y_1 + y_2$

$= \sqrt{a^2 + b^2}\sin(\omega t + \phi)$

22. $A\sin(\omega t + \phi)$

23. (c); Let O be the centre of circle, then at $t = 0$, the displacement y is maximum and have value 3 m.

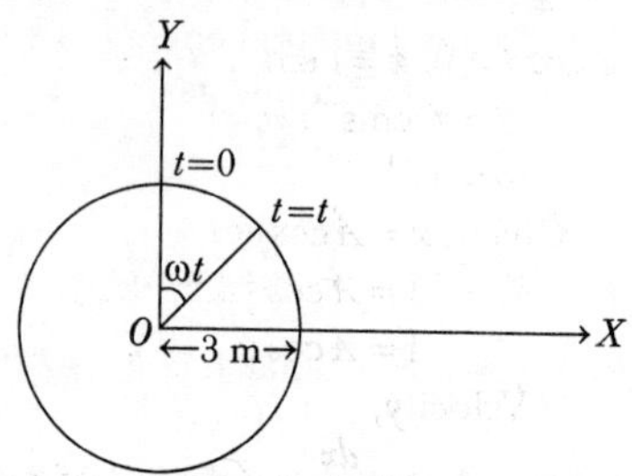

As the general equation of displacement of a particle will be in the form,

$y = A\cos\omega t$ ...(i)

Here, $A = 3$ m

Then, $\omega = \frac{2\pi}{T} = \frac{2\pi}{4}$ (given, $T = 4$ s)

$= \frac{\pi}{2}$

Putting the value of A and ω in Eq. (i), we get

$$y = 3\cos\left(\frac{\pi}{2}t\right) \text{ m}$$

24. (*b*);

Angular distance,

$\theta = 30° = \pi/6$ rad

Let l be the arc length, then

$l = R\theta$

$\Rightarrow \quad l = \frac{36}{100} \times \frac{\pi}{6} = \frac{6\pi}{100}$ m

As, speed on circular track (v) = Arc length (l) / Time (t)

$\Rightarrow \quad v = \frac{6\pi}{100 \times 0.1} = \frac{6\pi}{10}$ ms^{-1}

If F be the restoration force and a be the radial acceleration ($= v^2/R$), then

$F = ma_r$

$\Rightarrow \quad a_r = \frac{F}{m} = \frac{v^2}{R} = \left(\frac{6\pi}{10}\right)^2 \times \frac{100}{36}$

$= \frac{36 \times 9.87}{100} \times \frac{100}{36}$

$= 9.87$ N

25. II ;

All SHM follow the condition, acceleration $\propto$ – displacement

acceleration = – constant × displacement

This condition is followed by option II as acceleration $= -k(x + a)$.

26. $\frac{3\pi}{4}$;

At $t = 0$, $x = 1$ cm

$v = \pi$ cms^{-1}, $\phi = ?$

$\omega = \pi$s^{-1}

Given, $x = A\cos(\omega t + \phi)$

$1 = A\cos(\pi \times 0 + \phi)$

$1 = A\cos\phi \quad$ ...(i)

$\because$ Velocity,

$v = \frac{dx}{dt} = -A\omega\sin(\omega t + \phi)$

$\pi = -A\pi\sin(\pi \times 0 + \phi)$

$= -A\pi\sin\phi$

$\Rightarrow \quad 1 = -A\sin\phi$

or $\quad A\sin\phi = -1 \quad$ ...(ii)

Dividing Eq. (ii) by Eq. (i), we get

$\tan\phi = -1 = -\tan\frac{\pi}{4}$

$= \tan\left(\pi - \frac{\pi}{4}\right) = \tan\frac{3\pi}{4}$

$\Rightarrow \quad \phi = \frac{3\pi}{4}$

27. (*c*);

For a particle executing SHM, acceleration, $a \propto -\omega^2$ displacement (x) ...(i)

Given, $x = a\sin^2\omega t$ ...(ii)

Differentiating the above equation w.r.t. t, we get

$\frac{dx}{dt} = 2a\omega(\sin\omega t)(\cos\omega t)$

Again, differentiating, we get

$\frac{d^2x}{dt^2} = a = 2a\omega^2[\cos^2\omega t - \sin^2\omega t]$

$= 2a\omega^2\cos 2\omega t$

The given equation does not satisfy the condition for SHM [Eq. (i)]. Therefore, motion is not simple harmonic.

28. $\frac{2\pi}{3}$;

Equation of SHM, $x(t) = A\sin\omega t$

Thus, $v_{max} = A\omega$

$\Rightarrow \quad 12 = 4\omega$

$\Rightarrow \quad \omega = 3$ rad/s

Time period, $T = \frac{2\pi}{\omega}$

$\Rightarrow \quad T = \frac{2\pi}{3}$ s

29. 10π cms^{-1};

We know that, $\omega = 2\pi\nu$

$\Rightarrow \quad \omega = 2\pi \times 1 = 2\pi$

Maximum speed, $v_{max} = A\omega$

$= 5 \times 2\pi = 10\pi$ cms^{-1}

30. False;

Maximum velocity,

$v_{max} = A\omega$

$= 0.01 \times (\pi) = \frac{\pi}{100}$ ms^{-1}

31. $2\sqrt{2}$ cm;

A particle executes simple harmonic motion represented by displacement function,

$x(t) = A\sin(\omega t + \phi) \quad$ ...(i)

Differentiating equation w.r.t. t, we get

$v(t) = A\omega\cos(\omega t + \phi) \quad$ ...(ii)

As per question, position of particle at $t = 0$ is 2 cm.

Using Eq. (i), we get

$2 = A\sin[\omega(0) + \phi]$

$\Rightarrow \quad A\sin\phi = 2 \quad$ ...(iii)

and velocity of particle at $t = 0$ is 2ω cms^{-1}.

Using Eq. (ii), we get

$2\omega = A\omega\cos[\omega(0) + \phi]$

$\Rightarrow \quad A\cos\phi = 2 \quad$ ...(iv)

Dividing Eq. (iii) by Eq. (iv), we get

$\frac{A\sin\phi}{A\cos\phi} = \frac{2}{2}$

$\Rightarrow \quad \tan\phi = 1$

$\Rightarrow \quad \tan\phi = \tan 45° \quad [\because \tan 45° = 1]$

$\Rightarrow \quad \phi = 45°$

Putting the value of ϕ in Eq. (iii), we get

$A\sin 45° = 2$

$\Rightarrow \quad A\left(\frac{1}{\sqrt{2}}\right) = 2 \quad \left[\because \sin 45° = \frac{1}{\sqrt{2}}\right]$

$\Rightarrow \quad A = 2\sqrt{2}$ cm

32. $2\pi\sqrt{\frac{x_2^2 - x_1^2}{v_1^2 - v_2^2}}$;

Velocity of particle performing SHM is given by

$v = \pm\omega\sqrt{(A^2 - x^2)} \quad$ ...(i)

According to given situation,

$v_1 = \omega\sqrt{A^2 - x_1^2} \quad$ ...(ii)

and $\quad v_2 = \omega\sqrt{A^2 - x_2^2} \quad$ ...(iii)

On squaring Eq. (ii), we get

$v_1^2 = \omega^2(A^2 - x_1^2) \quad$ ...(iv)

On squaring Eq. (iii), we get

$v_2^2 = \omega^2(A^2 - x_2^2) \quad$ ...(v)

Subtracting Eq. (iv) from Eq. (v), we get

$v_1^2 - v_2^2 = \omega^2(x_2^2 - x_1^2)$

$\Rightarrow \quad v_1^2 - v_2^2 = \left(\frac{2\pi}{T}\right)^2(x_2^2 - x_1^2)$

$\Rightarrow \quad T = 2\pi\sqrt{\frac{(x_2^2 - x_1^2)}{(v_1^2 - v_2^2)}}$

33. True;

Velocity of particle in SHM in terms of displacement x is given as

$v = \omega\sqrt{A^2 - x^2}$

$\Rightarrow \quad v = A\omega\sqrt{1 - x^2/A^2}$

$$\Rightarrow \frac{v}{A\omega} = \sqrt{1 - x^2 / A^2}$$

$$\Rightarrow \frac{v^2}{A^2\omega^2} = 1 - \frac{x^2}{A^2}$$

$$\Rightarrow \frac{v^2}{A^2\omega^2} + \frac{x^2}{A^2} = 1 \quad \text{... (i)}$$

As equation of ellipse is

$$\frac{x^2}{a^2} + \frac{y^2}{b^2} = 1$$

Eq. (i) is similar to the equation of ellipse. So, the graph between velocity and displacement is an ellipse.

34. 3;

Maximum velocity, $v = A\omega$

Let displacement be y when

speed, $v_2 = v/2 = \frac{A\omega}{2}$ ...(i)

By using equation of wave velocity,

$$v_2^2 = \omega^2(A^2 - y^2)$$

$$\therefore \left(\frac{\omega A}{2}\right)^2 = \omega^2(A^2 - y^2)$$

[using Eq. (i)]

$$\Rightarrow \frac{\omega^2 A^2}{4} = \omega^2(A^2 - y^2)$$

$$\Rightarrow \frac{A^2}{4} = A^2 - y^2$$

$$\Rightarrow y = \frac{\sqrt{3}}{2} A = \frac{A\sqrt{x}}{2}$$

Hence, $x = 3$

35. 0.5;

Displacement is given as

$x = (2 \times 10^{-2}) \cos \pi t$

Here, $a = 2 \times 10^{-2}$ m $= 2$ cm

At $t = 0$, $x = 2$ cm, i.e. the object is at positive extreme, so to acquire maximum speed (i.e. to reach mean position), it takes $\frac{1}{4}$th of time period.

$\therefore$ Required time $= \frac{T}{4}$

As $x = a \cos \omega t$

where, $\omega = \frac{2\pi}{T} = \pi$

$\Rightarrow T = 2$ s

So, required time $= \frac{T}{4} = \frac{2}{4} = 0.5$ s

36. No;

For particle 1, displacement is given as

$$y_1 = 0.1 \sin\left(100\pi t + \frac{\pi}{3}\right)$$

$\Rightarrow$ Velocity of particle 1, $\frac{dy_1}{dt} = v_1$

$$= 0.1 \times 100\pi \cos\left(100\pi t + \frac{\pi}{3}\right)$$

$$\text{or } v_1 = 10\pi \sin\left(100\pi t + \frac{\pi}{3} + \frac{\pi}{2}\right)$$

$$\text{or } v_1 = 10\pi \sin\left(100\pi t + \frac{5\pi}{6}\right)$$

For particle 2, $y_2 = 0.1 \cos 100\pi t$

$\Rightarrow$ Velocity of particle 2,

$$\frac{dy_2}{dt} = v_2 = -0.1 \sin 100\pi t$$

or $v_2 = 0.1 \sin(100\pi t + \pi)$

Hence, phase difference,

$$\Delta\phi = \phi_1 - \phi_2$$

$$= \left(100\pi t + \frac{5\pi}{6}\right) - (100\pi t + \pi)$$

$$= \frac{5\pi}{6} - \pi \quad [\text{at } t = 0]$$

$$= \frac{\pi}{6}$$

37. $\frac{T}{12}$;

According to question, equation of SHM is

$$x = a \sin\left(\omega t + \frac{\pi}{6}\right)$$

$$v = \frac{dx}{dt} = a\omega \cos\left(\omega t + \frac{\pi}{6}\right)$$

$$\Rightarrow \frac{a\omega}{2} = a\,\omega \cos\left(\omega t + \frac{\pi}{6}\right)$$

$$\frac{1}{2} = \cos\left(\omega t + \frac{\pi}{6}\right)$$

$$\Rightarrow \omega t + \frac{\pi}{6} = \frac{\pi}{3}$$

$$\Rightarrow \omega t = \frac{\pi}{6}$$

$$\Rightarrow \frac{2\pi}{T} t = \frac{\pi}{6}$$

$$\Rightarrow t = \frac{T}{12}$$

38. I, II;

As, we know,

$$u = A \sin \omega t$$
$$v = A\omega \cos \omega t$$
$$a = -A\omega^2 \sin \omega t$$

Thus, with respect to displacement plot, velocity plot has a phase difference $\frac{\pi}{2}$ and acceleration plot has a phase difference of π.

39. (*b*);

Displacement is given as

$$x = a \sin \omega t \quad \text{...(i)}$$

$$\text{Velocity, } v = \frac{dx}{dt} = a\omega \cos \omega t \quad \text{...(ii)}$$

$$\Rightarrow v = a\omega\sqrt{1 - \sin^2 \omega t}$$

$$= \omega\sqrt{a^2 - x^2} \quad \text{...(iii)}$$

[using Eq. (i)]

Acceleration,

$$\alpha = \frac{dv}{dt} = \frac{d}{dt}(a\omega \cos \omega t)$$

[using Eq. (ii)]

$$= -a\omega^2 \sin \omega t \quad [\text{using Eq. (i)}]$$

$$= -\omega^2 x$$

When $x = 0$, $v = a\omega = v_{max}$ and $\alpha = 0$

When $x = a$, $v = 0 = v_{min}$

$\Rightarrow \alpha = -\omega^2 a = \alpha_{max}$

40. π second;

Acceleration, $\alpha = -\omega^2 x$

$\Rightarrow 12 \text{ cm/s}^2 = -\omega^2 (3 \text{ cm})$

$\Rightarrow \omega^2 = 4$

$\Rightarrow \omega = \pm 2$

Here, −ve sign shows that acceleration is towards the centre.

Thus, time period,

$$T = \frac{2\pi}{\omega} = \frac{2\pi}{\pm 2} = \pm \pi \text{ second}$$

Since, time cannot be negative, therefore time period will be π second.

41. 5, 4;

Equation of SHM,

$$y = 5 \sin \pi (t + 4)$$
$$y = 5 \sin (\pi t + 4\pi)$$

$$\text{Velocity, } v = \frac{dy}{dt} = 5\pi \cos(\pi t + 4\pi)$$

Acceleration,

$$\alpha = \frac{d^2y}{dt^2} = -5\pi^2 \sin(\pi t + 4\pi)$$

On comparing the equation given as

$$\alpha = -a\pi^2 \sin(\pi t + b\pi),$$

we get $a = 5$

$b = 4$

42. False;

Acceleration, $\alpha = -\omega^2 x$

$$2.0 = -\omega^2(0.02)$$

$$\Rightarrow \omega^2 = \frac{2}{0.02}$$

$$\Rightarrow \omega^2 = 100$$

$$\Rightarrow \omega = 10 \text{ rad/s}$$

43. $\frac{8\pi}{3}$;

In simple harmonic motion, position (x), velocity (v) and acceleration (a) of the particle are given by

$$x = A\sin\omega t$$
$$v = \omega\sqrt{A^2 - x^2}$$

or $v = A\omega\cos\omega t$ and $a = -\omega^2 x$

or $a = -\omega^2 A\sin\omega t$

Given, amplitude, $A = 5$ cm and displacement, $x = 4$ cm.

At this time (when $x = 4$ cm), velocity and acceleration have same magnitude.

$$\Rightarrow \quad |v_{x=4}| = |a_{x=4}|$$

or $|\omega\sqrt{5^2 - 4^2}| = |-4\omega^2|$

$$\Rightarrow \quad 3\omega = +4\omega^2$$

$$\Rightarrow \quad \omega = (3/4)\text{ rad/s} \quad \ldots\text{(i)}$$

So, time period, $T = \frac{2\pi}{\omega}$

$$= \frac{2\pi}{3}\times 4 \quad \text{[using Eq. (i)]}$$

$$= \frac{8\pi}{3}\text{ s}$$

44. 1 : 100;

As we know that, $\alpha_{max} = \omega^2 a$

So, for two different cases,

$$\frac{\alpha_{max_1}}{\alpha_{max_2}} = \frac{\omega_1^2}{\omega_2^2} \quad (\because a \text{ is same})$$

$$= \frac{(100)^2}{(1000)^2} = \frac{1}{100}$$

45. False;

The phase difference between acceleration and displacement is π rad.

46. $\frac{4\pi}{\sqrt{5}}$;

Magnitude of velocity of particle when it is at displacement x from mean position

$$= \omega\sqrt{A^2 - x^2}$$

Also, magnitude of acceleration of particle in SHM $= \omega^2 x$

Given, when $x = 2$ cm

$$|\mathbf{v}| = |\mathbf{a}|$$

$$\Rightarrow \quad \omega\sqrt{A^2 - x^2} = \omega^2 x$$

$$\Rightarrow \quad \omega = \frac{\sqrt{A^2 - x^2}}{x} = \frac{\sqrt{9-4}}{2}$$

$\Rightarrow$ Angular velocity,

$$\omega = \frac{\sqrt{5}}{2}$$

$\therefore$ Time period of motion,

$$T = \frac{2\pi}{\omega} = \frac{4\pi}{\sqrt{5}}\text{ s}$$

47. $\frac{\beta}{\alpha}$;

For a particle executing SHM, we have maximum acceleration,

$$\alpha = A\omega^2 \quad \ldots\text{(i)}$$

where, A is maximum amplitude and ω is angular velocity of a particle.

Maximum velocity,

$$\beta = A\omega \quad \ldots\text{(ii)}$$

Dividing Eq. (i) by Eq. (ii), we get

$$\frac{\alpha}{\beta} = \frac{A\omega^2}{A\omega}$$

$$\Rightarrow \quad \frac{\alpha}{\beta} = \omega = \frac{2\pi}{T}$$

i.e. $\quad T = \frac{2\pi\beta}{\alpha}$

Thus, its time period of vibration, $T = \frac{2\pi\beta}{\alpha}$

48. $2\pi\sqrt{\frac{m}{2k}}$;

Equation of motion of the spring is given by

$$F_1 = -2kx \text{ and } F_2 = -2kx$$
(from both sides)

Thus, $F = F_1 + F_2 = -4kx$

or $\quad a = \frac{F}{m} = \frac{-4kx}{2m}$

$$= \frac{-2kx}{m} \quad \ldots\text{(i)}$$

Acceleration of a body in SHM is given by

$$\alpha = -\omega^2 x \quad \ldots\text{(ii)}$$

From Eqs. (i) and (ii), we get

$$\omega^2 x = 2\frac{k}{m}x$$

or $\quad \omega^2 = \frac{2k}{m}$

$$\Rightarrow \quad \omega = \sqrt{\frac{2k}{m}}$$

Time period,

$$T = 2\pi\sqrt{\frac{m}{2k}}$$

49. 0.63 ms^{-1};

Angular frequency of spring-block system is given by

$$\omega = \sqrt{\frac{k}{m}}$$

Maximum speed in oscillation,

$$v_{max} = A\omega = A\sqrt{\frac{k}{m}}$$

$$= 0.1\sqrt{\frac{400}{10}}$$

$$v_{max} = 0.1\sqrt{40} = 0.63\text{ ms}^{-1}$$

50. False;

Time period in SHM is given by

$$T = 2\pi\sqrt{\frac{m}{k}} \quad \ldots\text{(i)}$$

When the spring is cut into two equal parts, the spring constant of one part will become $2k$, when spring is connected in parallel

$$k_{eff} = 2k + 2k$$

therefore new time period will become $T' = 2\pi\sqrt{\frac{m}{4k}} = \frac{T}{2}$

51. I. True, II. True;

I. When both springs are joined together, we have

$$x_1 = \frac{F}{k_1}$$

and $x_2 = \frac{F}{k_2}$

Therefore, $x_1 + x_2$

$$= \frac{F}{k_1} + \frac{F}{k_2}$$

$$= F\left(\frac{1}{k_1} + \frac{1}{k_2}\right)$$

II. When both springs are joined parallel to each other with the same load,

then $F = -k_1 x - k_2 x$

$$= -x(k_1 + k_2)$$

52. 0.628 s;

According to question,

$$F = -kx$$
$$10 = -k(5\times 10^{-2})$$

Here, – ve sign shows that displacment will be in opposite dirction of force.

$$\Rightarrow \quad k = \frac{10}{5\times 10^{-2}} = 200\text{ N/m}$$

Time period of oscillation,

$$T = 2\pi\sqrt{\frac{m}{k}} = 2\pi\sqrt{\frac{2}{200}}$$

$$= 2\pi\sqrt{\frac{1}{100}} = \frac{2\pi}{10} = 0.628\text{ s}$$

53. $\left(\frac{9}{16}\right)$;

As we know that,

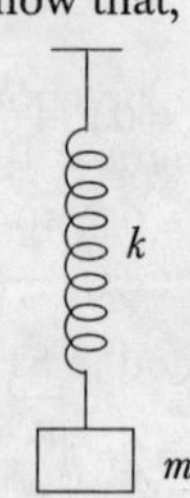

Time period, $T = 2\pi\sqrt{\frac{m}{k}}$

Case I $T_1 = 2\pi\sqrt{\frac{m}{k}}$ ...(i)

Case II When the mass m is increased by 1 kg, then $= m + 1$

$$\Rightarrow \quad T_2 = \sqrt{\frac{m+1}{k}} \quad \text{...(ii)}$$

On dividing Eq. (ii) by Eq. (i), we get

$$\frac{T_2}{T_1} = \sqrt{\frac{m+1}{m}}$$

$$\Rightarrow \quad \frac{5}{3} = \sqrt{\frac{m+1}{m}}$$

$$\Rightarrow \quad \frac{25}{9} = \frac{m+1}{m}$$

$$\Rightarrow \quad \frac{25}{9} = 1 + \frac{1}{m}$$

$$\Rightarrow \quad \frac{1}{m} = \frac{16}{9}$$

$$\therefore \quad m = \frac{9}{16}\text{ kg}$$

54. II;

According to question,

$$T_1 = 2\pi\sqrt{\frac{m}{k_1}} = 3$$

$$\Rightarrow \quad 9 = \frac{4\pi^2 m}{k_1}$$

$$\Rightarrow \quad k_1 = \frac{4\pi^2 m}{9} \quad \text{...(i)}$$

and $\quad T_2 = 2\pi\sqrt{\frac{m}{k_2}} = 4$

$$\Rightarrow \quad 16 = 4\pi^2\frac{m}{k_2}$$

$$\Rightarrow \quad k_2 = \frac{4\pi^2 m}{16}$$

I. When springs are in series,

$$F = -k_1 x_1$$

$$\Rightarrow \quad x_1 = \frac{F}{k_1}$$

Here, –ve sign shows that displacement will be in the opposite direction of force.

Thus, net displacement,

$$x_1 + x_2 = F\left(\frac{1}{k_1} + \frac{1}{k_2}\right)$$

or $\quad k_{\text{eff}} = \frac{k_1 + k_2}{k_1 k_2}$

Hence, time period,

$$T = 2\pi\sqrt{\frac{m}{k_{\text{eff}}}}$$

$$= 2\pi\sqrt{\frac{m}{\frac{k_1 + k_2}{k_1 k_2}}}$$

$$= 2\pi\sqrt{\frac{m}{4\pi^2 m\left(\frac{\frac{1}{9}+\frac{1}{16}}{\frac{1}{9}\times\frac{1}{16}}\right)}}$$

$$= 5\text{ s}$$

II. When springs are in parallel,

$$k_{\text{eff}} = k_1 + k_2$$

Time period,

$$T = 2\pi\sqrt{\frac{m}{k}}$$

$$= 2\pi\sqrt{\frac{m}{4\pi^2\left(\frac{1}{9}+\frac{1}{16}\right)m}}$$

$$= \frac{12}{5}\text{ s}$$

55. 3 : 9 : 1;

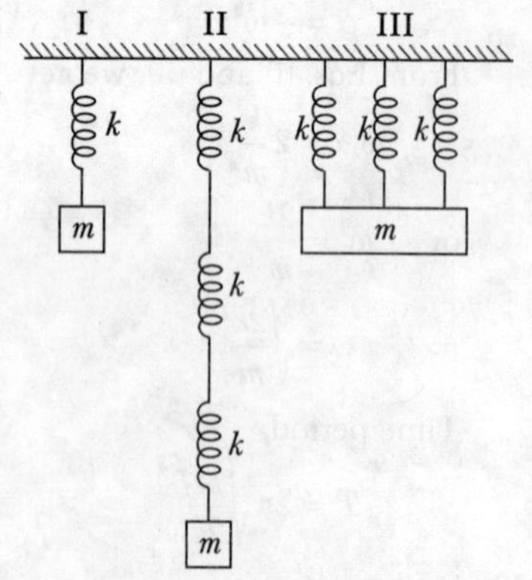

Case I Time period,

$$T_1 = 2\pi\sqrt{\frac{m}{k}}$$

Case II Time period,

$$T_2 = 2\pi\sqrt{\frac{m}{\frac{k}{3}}} = 2\pi\sqrt{\frac{3m}{k}}$$

Case III Time period,

$$T_3 = 2\pi\sqrt{\frac{m}{3k}}$$

$$\therefore \quad T_1 : T_2 : T_3 = 2\pi\sqrt{\frac{m}{k}} : 2\pi\sqrt{\frac{3m}{k}} : 2\pi\sqrt{\frac{m}{3k}}$$

$$= 1 : \sqrt{3} : \frac{1}{\sqrt{3}} = \sqrt{3} : 3 : 1$$

or $\quad 3 : 9 : 1$

56. $\sqrt{2} : 1$;

Time period of Fig. 1 can be given as

$$T_a = 2\pi\sqrt{\frac{m}{k}}$$

In Fig. 2, both springs are in series combination, therefore its time period can be given as

$$T_b = 2\pi\sqrt{\frac{m}{k_{\text{eff}}}} = 2\pi\sqrt{\frac{m}{k/2}}$$

$$\left(\because k_{\text{eff}} = \frac{k \times k}{k + k}\right)$$

Now, $\frac{T_a}{T_b} = \frac{2\pi\sqrt{\frac{m}{k}}}{2\pi\sqrt{\frac{2m}{k}}} \Rightarrow \frac{T_b}{T_a} = \frac{\sqrt{2}}{1}$

57. (*c*); Let spring constants of two springs be k_1 and k_2. Since, two springs are connected in parallel connection, k_{eff} is given by

$$k_{\text{eff}} = k_1 + k_2$$
$$= 2 + 2 = 4\text{ N/m}$$

As, time period, $T = 2\pi\sqrt{\frac{m}{k_{\text{eff}}}}$

$$\Rightarrow \quad T = 2\pi\sqrt{\frac{400}{4}} = 20\pi$$

58. $\frac{1}{2\pi}\sqrt{\frac{2k}{m}}$;

Let T be the time period of oscillation, then $T = 2\pi\sqrt{\frac{m}{k_{\text{eff}}}}$

$$\therefore \quad T = 2\pi\sqrt{\frac{m}{2k}} \quad (\because k_{\text{eff}} = k + k)$$

and frequency $(f) = \frac{1}{T} = \frac{1}{2\pi}\sqrt{\frac{2k}{m}}$

59. 10;

Given, spring constants of springs k_1 and k_2 are k and $4k$.

where, $k = 20$ N/m

$m_A = 200\text{ g} = 200\times10^{-3}$ kg

$m_B = 800\text{ g} = 800\times10^{-3}$ kg

As we know that,

$$T = 2\pi\sqrt{\frac{m_{eq}}{k_{eq}}} \quad \ldots(i)$$

where, equivalent or reduced mass,

$$m_{eq} = \frac{m_A m_B}{m_A + m_B}$$

$$\Rightarrow m_{eq} = \frac{(200\times10^{-3})(800\times10^{-3})}{200\times10^{-3} + 800\times10^{-3}}$$

$$= \frac{16\times10^4\times10^{-6}}{1000\times10^{-3}}$$

$$= 16\times10^{-2}\text{ kg}$$

and equivalent spring constant,

$$k_{eq} = \frac{k_1k_2}{k_1 + k_2} = \frac{k\times4k}{k+4k} = \frac{4k}{5}$$

$$= \frac{4}{5}\times20 = 16\text{ N/m}$$

Putting the value of m_{eq} ank_{eq}d in Eq. (i), we get

$$T = 2\pi\sqrt{\frac{16\times10^{-2}}{16}}$$

$$= 2\pi\times10^{-1} = \frac{2\pi}{10}$$

As, $\omega = \frac{2\pi}{T} = \frac{2\pi}{2\pi}\times10$

$= 10\text{ rads}^{-1}$

60. A (✓) B (✓) C (✓) D (×);

From the graph, we can conclude that

at $t = \frac{3T}{4}$, particle is at mean position. At mean position of SHM, acceleration of particle is zero, i.e. force is zero.

Statement (A) is correct.

At $t = T$, particle is at extreme position. As direction is changing, so its acceleration is maximum.

Statement (B) is correct.

At $t = \frac{T}{4}$, particle is at mean position, so whole of energy is kinetic, i.e. its speed is maximum.

Statement (C) is correct.

PE = KE at $t = \frac{T}{8}$, so statement (D) is incorrect.

61. Yes;

The kinetic energy of the particle executing SHM is given by

$$\text{KE} = \frac{1}{2}m\omega^2(A^2 - y^2)$$

$$\Rightarrow 16 = \frac{1}{2}\times5.12\times\omega^2 [(25\times10^{-2})^2 - 0]$$

$$\Rightarrow \omega^2 = 100$$

or $\omega = 10$ rad/s

Time period is given by

$$T = \frac{2\pi}{\omega} = \frac{2\pi}{10} = \frac{\pi}{5}\text{ s}$$

62. $\frac{E}{4}$;

Total energy of the particle executing SHM at an instant t is given by

$$E = \frac{1}{2}m\omega^2a^2 \quad \ldots(i)$$

and kinetic energy of the particle at an instant t is given by

$$E_K = \frac{1}{2}m\omega^2(a^2 - x^2) \ldots(ii)$$

When $x = \frac{a}{2}$,

$$E_K = \frac{1}{2}m\omega^2\left(a^2 - \frac{a^2}{4}\right)$$

$$= \frac{1}{2}m\omega^2\times\frac{3}{4}a^2$$

or $E_K = \frac{1}{2}\times\frac{3}{4}m\omega^2a^2 \quad \ldots(iii)$

On dividing Eq. (iii) by Eq. (i), we get

$$\frac{E_K}{E} = \frac{3}{4}$$

$$\Rightarrow E_K = \frac{3}{4}E$$

$$\therefore \text{PE} = E - \frac{3}{4}E = \frac{E}{4}$$

63. (*b*); In SHM, at mean position, i.e. at $x = 0$, kientic energy (KE) will be maximum and potential energy (PE) will be minimum. Total energy (TE) is always constant.

64. False;

Total energy, TE

$= 1/2m\,\omega^2A^2 = \text{constant}$

Hence, total energy of a particle remains constant or the total energy in simple harmonic motion does not depend on displacement x.

65. No;

Potential energy (PE) $= \frac{1}{2}m\omega^2x^2$

x^2 will be maximum at $\pm A$.

Therefore, potential energy will be maximum at $\pm A$.

66. False;

Average kinetic energy of particle

$$= \frac{1}{4}mA^2\omega^2$$

$$= \frac{1}{2}mA^2(2\pi\nu)^2 \quad (\because \omega = 2\pi\nu)$$

$$= \pi^2\nu^2ma^2$$

67. $\pm\frac{A}{2}$;

Potential energy of the body executing SHM is given by

$$U = \frac{1}{2}m\omega^2x^2$$

Total energy of the body executing SHM is given by

$$E = \frac{1}{2}m\omega^2A^2$$

According to question,

$$U = \frac{1}{4}E$$

$$\therefore \frac{1}{2}m\omega^2x^2 = \frac{1}{4}\times\frac{1}{2}m\omega^2A^2$$

$$\Rightarrow x^2 = \frac{A^2}{4} \text{ or } x = \pm\frac{A}{2}$$

68. False;

In first scenario, a particle is executing SHM of amplitude a and energy E.

$$\therefore \text{Energy, } E = \frac{1}{2}KA^2 \quad \ldots(i)$$

In second scenario, it is given that the kinetic energy of particle becomes $\frac{3E}{4}$.

∴ Energy,

$$\frac{3E}{4} = \frac{1}{2}K(a^2 - y^2) \quad \ldots(ii)$$

where, y is the displacement.

On dividing Eq. (i) by Eq. (ii), we get

$$\frac{E}{\frac{3E}{4}} = \frac{\frac{1}{2}KA^2}{\frac{1}{2}K(A^2 - y^2)}$$

$$\Rightarrow \frac{4}{3} = \frac{A^2}{A^2 - y^2}$$

$$\Rightarrow 4A^2 - 4y^2 = 3A^2 \Rightarrow -4y^2 = -A^2$$

$$\Rightarrow y^2 = \frac{A^2}{4} \Rightarrow y = \pm\frac{A}{2}$$

69. $\left(\frac{3}{4}\right)$;

Let total mechanical energy be ME, kinetic energy be KE and potential energy be PE.

Put wave displacement, $x = \frac{A}{2}$

In SHM, $KE = \frac{1}{2}m\omega^2(A^2 - x^2)$

where, m is mass of particle, ω is angular frequency and A is amplitude.

$$= \frac{1}{2}m\omega^2\left(A^2 - \frac{A^2}{4}\right)$$

$$\Rightarrow KE = \frac{3}{8}m\omega^2A^2 \quad \ldots(i)$$

$$PE = \frac{1}{2}kx^2$$

As, $\omega = \sqrt{\frac{k}{m}} \Rightarrow k = m\omega^2$

$$\therefore \quad PE = \frac{1}{2}m\omega^2\frac{A^2}{4}$$

$$= \frac{1}{8}m\omega^2A^2$$

Now, ME = KE + PE

$$= \frac{3}{8}m\omega^2A^2 + \frac{1}{8}m\omega^2A^2$$

$$= \frac{4m\omega^2A^2}{8} = \frac{m\omega^2A^2}{2} \quad \ldots(ii)$$

Dividing Eq. (i) by Eq. (ii), we get

$$\frac{KE}{ME} = \frac{\frac{3}{8}m\omega^2A^2}{\frac{1}{2}m\omega^2A^2} = \frac{3}{4}$$

70. Yes;

Kinetic energy in SHM

$$KE = \frac{1}{2}m\omega^2(A^2 - x^2)$$

Potential energy in SHM

$$PE = \frac{1}{2}m\omega^2x^2$$

According to question,

$$\frac{1}{2}m\omega^2(A^2 - x^2) = \frac{1}{2}m\omega^2x^2$$

$$\Rightarrow \quad x^2 = A^2 - x^2$$

$$\Rightarrow \quad 2x^2 = A^2$$

$$\Rightarrow \quad x = \pm\frac{A}{\sqrt{2}}$$

71. 1, 3;

Given, displacement,

$$x(t) = A\sin\left(\frac{\pi t}{90}\right)$$

Standard equation of simple harmonic motion, $x(t) = A\sin\omega t$

So, $\quad \omega = \frac{\pi}{90} \quad \ldots(i)$

We know that,

$$KE = \frac{1}{2}m\omega^2A^2\cos^2\omega t$$

and $PE = \frac{1}{2}m\omega^2A^2\sin^2\omega t$

Ratio of kinetic energy to potential energy is

$$\frac{KE}{PE} = \frac{\frac{1}{2}m\omega^2A^2\cos^2\omega t}{\frac{1}{2}m\omega^2A^2\sin^2\omega t}$$

$$\Rightarrow \frac{KE}{PE} = \cot^2\omega t$$

$$= \cot^2\left(\frac{\pi}{90}\times t\right)$$

[from Eq. (i)]

$$= \cot^2\left(\frac{\pi}{90}\times 210\right)$$

$$= \cot^2\left(\frac{7\pi}{3}\right)$$

$$= \cot^2\left(2\pi + \frac{\pi}{3}\right)$$

$$= \cot^2\left(\frac{\pi}{3}\right) = \frac{1}{3} = \frac{x}{y}$$

$$\therefore \quad x = 1, y = 3$$

72. 6 cm;

At $x = 0.04$ m,

Total energy = KE + PE

$= 0.5 + 0.4 = 0.9$ J

We know that, total energy of SHM

$$= \frac{1}{2}m\omega^2A^2$$

$$0.9 = \frac{1}{2}m\omega^2A^2$$

$$\Rightarrow \quad 0.9 = \frac{1}{2}\times 0.2\times(50)^2A^2$$

$$\Rightarrow \quad A = 0.06 \text{ m} = 6 \text{ cm}$$

73. True;

Particle is executing SHM, therefore total energy is given as

$$TE = \frac{1}{2}m\omega^2A^2 = \frac{1}{2}m\left(\frac{2\pi}{T}\right)^2A^2$$

Since, mass is constant, therefore total energy depends on amplitude and time period.

74. (*d*)

75. Displacement of mass is given as

$$x = x_0\sin\omega t$$

The potential energy is given as

$$PE = \frac{1}{2}kx^2$$

Substituting the value of x, we get

$$PE = \frac{1}{2}kx_0^2\sin^2\omega t$$

or $\quad PE = C\sin^2\omega t \quad \left(\because C = \frac{1}{2}kx_0^2\right)$

Simplify the value of $\sin^2\omega t$, we get

$$PE = C\left[\frac{1-\cos 2\omega t}{2}\right]$$

The value of function $\cos 2\omega t$ will always lies between −1 and 1.

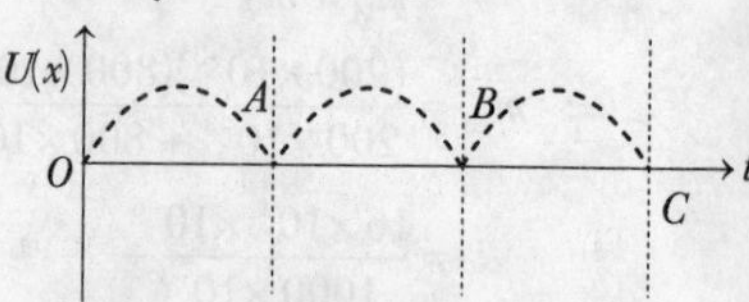

76. 0.25 J ;

Angular frequency of SHM is given as

$$\omega = \sqrt{\frac{k}{m}} = 5\sqrt{2}$$

Here, the body is displaced to maximum at $x = 10$ cm = 0.1 m

Total energy of the body executing SHM is given as

$$TE = \frac{1}{2}m\omega^2A^2$$

$$= \frac{1}{2}\times 1\times(5\sqrt{2})^2\times(0.1)^2$$

$$= \frac{1}{2}\times 25\times 2\times 0.01$$

$$= 0.25 \text{ J}$$

77. KE is maximum at mean position and minimum at extreme position $\left(\text{at } t = \frac{T}{4}\right)$

Therefore, the graph is as given below.

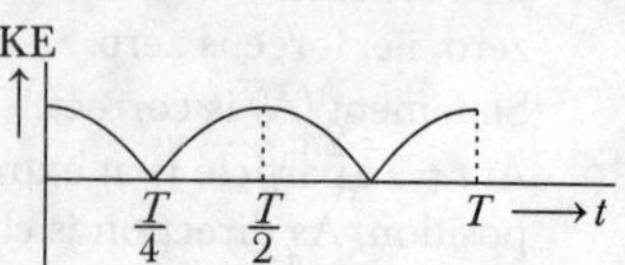

78. (π);

The acceleration of particle/body executing SHM at any instant (at position x) is given as

$$a = -\omega^2x$$

where, ω is the angular frequency of the body.

$\Rightarrow \quad |a| = \omega^2 x \quad \ldots(i)$

Here, $x = 5\,m, |a| = 20\ ms^{-2}$

Substituting the given values in Eq. (i), we get

$$20 = \omega^2 \times 5$$

$$\Rightarrow \quad \omega^2 = \frac{20}{5} = 4$$

or $\quad \omega = 2\ rad\ s^{-1}$

As we know that,

Time period, $T = \frac{2\pi}{\omega} \quad \ldots(ii)$

$\therefore$ Substituting the value of ω in Eq. (ii), we get

$$T = \frac{2\pi}{2} = \pi\ s$$

79. increase, decrease;

The time period of the pendulum,

$$T = 2\pi\sqrt{\frac{l}{g}} \rightarrow T \propto \sqrt{l}$$

Initially, the centre of mass of the sphere is at the centre of sphere. As the water slowly flows out of the hole at the bottom, the centre of mass of the liquid (hollow sphere) first goes downwards and then upwards. Hence, the effective length of the pendulum first increases and then decreases. Therefore, the time period also first increases and then decreases.

80. Yes;

Time period of shorter pendulum,

$$T_1 = 2\pi\sqrt{\frac{l}{g}} = 2\pi\sqrt{\frac{0.5}{10}}$$

$$= 2\pi\sqrt{\frac{1}{20}} = \sqrt{\frac{4\pi^2}{20}}\ s$$

Time period of bigger pendulum,

$$T_2 = 2\pi\sqrt{\frac{l}{g}}$$

$$= 2\pi\sqrt{\frac{2.0}{10}} = 2\pi\sqrt{\frac{1}{5}}$$

$$= \sqrt{\frac{4\pi^2}{5}}\ s$$

Suppose the time when both pendulum will be in same phase is t, then $\frac{1}{t} = \frac{1}{T_1} - \frac{1}{T_2}$

$$\Rightarrow \frac{1}{t} = \frac{1}{\sqrt{\frac{4\pi^2}{20}}} - \frac{1}{\sqrt{\frac{4\pi^2}{5}}}$$

$$= \frac{\sqrt{20} - \sqrt{5}}{\sqrt{4\pi^2}}$$

$$\frac{1}{t} = \frac{2\sqrt{5} - \sqrt{5}}{\sqrt{4\pi^2}} = \frac{\sqrt{5}}{\sqrt{4\pi^2}}$$

$$\Rightarrow t = \sqrt{\frac{4\pi^2}{5}}\ s \text{ or } 2\sqrt{\frac{4\pi^2}{20}}\ s$$

Therefore, shorter pendulum will complete $= \frac{t}{T_1}$ oscillations $= 2$

81. (*c*); Given, density of bob,

$$\rho = \frac{4}{3} \times 10^3\ kgm^{-3}$$

density of water, $\sigma = 1000\ kgm^{-3}$

$\therefore$ In air, $t_0 = 2\pi\sqrt{l/g}$

and in water,

$$t = 2\pi\sqrt{\frac{l}{g\left(1 - \frac{\sigma}{\rho}\right)}}$$

$$= 2\pi\sqrt{\frac{l}{g\left(1 - \frac{3}{4}\right)}}$$

$$t = 2 \times 2\pi\sqrt{l/g} = 2t_0$$

Assertion-Reason Questions

1. (*c*)

2. (*b*); Both statements are true but velocity of particle does not explain about the periodic motion.

3. (*b*); Velocity is $v = \omega\sqrt{A^2 - x^2}$

$\frac{v^2}{\omega^2} + x^2 = A^2 \rightarrow$ equation of ellipse.

Reason does not explain Assertion.

4. (*a*); $g_{eff} = 0$

$\Rightarrow \quad T \propto \frac{1}{\sqrt{g_{eff}}}$

$\Rightarrow T$ is infinite

5. (*b*); Here, swing is like a simple pendulum.

$$T = 2\pi\sqrt{\frac{l_{CM}}{g}}$$

$l_{CM} \rightarrow$ length of COM

when a girl stands up, the COM moves up and l_{CM} decreases.

$T = 2\pi\sqrt{\frac{l_{CM}}{g}}$, T also decreases.

When girl stands up, angular momentum, L = constant.

$$I\omega' = L \Rightarrow \omega' = \frac{L}{I}$$

According to Newton's law

$$T - mg = m\omega'^2 l_{CM}$$

$$T = mg + mL^2 / I^2$$

$$T = mg + \frac{mL^2}{Kl_{CM}^4} l_{CM} = \frac{mg + mL^2}{Kl_{CM}^3}$$

6. (*b*); $KE = \frac{1}{2}m\omega^2(A^2 - x^2)$

$$= \frac{1}{2}K(A^2 - x^2)$$

$$PE = \frac{1}{2}Kx^2$$

Here, both KE and PE are functions of x^2 which means w.r.t. position is a parabola.

Also, PE and KE do not vary linearly with position.

7. (*c*); $KE = \frac{1}{2}m\omega^2(a^2 - x^2)$

$$PE = \frac{1}{2}m\omega^2 x^2$$

Since, square of displacement is always positive, therefore potential energy and kinetic energy in SHM will always be positive.

Both energies peak four times during each period of SHM.

8. (*a*); $K = \frac{1}{2}m\omega^2(A^2 - x^2)$

where, $x = A\sin\omega t$

$$x^2 = A^2\sin^2\omega t$$

Since, $\sin^2\omega t$ varies from 0 to 1.

Kinetic energy in SHM also varies from 0 to max.

9. (*b*); For free fall

$$a = g$$

$$g_{eff} = 0$$

$$\Rightarrow |\mathbf{g} - \mathbf{a}| = 0$$

$$T = 2\pi\sqrt{\frac{l}{0}} = \infty$$

Case Based Questions

1. (i) (*d*); The acceleration of the particle is directed towards the extreme position.

(ii) (*a*); $\frac{d^2x}{dt^2} = -\omega^2 x$

(iii) (*d*); $x = A\sin\omega t\cos^2\omega t$

(iv) (*d*); mass

Or

(*a*); $\sqrt{\frac{k}{m}}$

2. (i) (*c*); Kinetic energy

$= K_0 \cos^2 \omega t$

Since, total energy is conserved in the motion.

Total energy = Maximum KE = Maximum PE

Maximum KE = K_0

$\Rightarrow$ Total energy and Maximum PE = K_0

(ii) (*c*); $-A$ —— O —— A

Extreme position	Mean position	Extreme position
KE = 0	KE = maximum	KE = 0
PE = maximum	PE = 0	PE = maximum

(iii) (*b*); Energy $= \frac{1}{2} m\omega^2 A^2 = \frac{1}{2} KA^2$

(iv) (*b*); When $x = \frac{A}{2}$,

then $\text{KE} = \frac{1}{2} m\omega^2 (A^2 - x^2)$

$$= \frac{1}{2} m\omega^2 \left(A^2 - \frac{A^2}{4}\right)$$

$$= \frac{3}{4}\left(\frac{1}{2} m\omega^2 A^2\right)$$

$$= \frac{3}{4} \times \text{Total energy}$$

Or

(*d*); Kinetic energy in SHM,

$$\text{KE} = \frac{1}{2} m\omega^2 (A^2 - x^2)$$

Potential energy in SHM,

$$\text{PE} = \frac{1}{2} m\omega^2 x^2$$

According to question,

$$\frac{1}{2} m\omega^2 (A^2 - x^2) = \frac{1}{2} m\omega^2 x^2$$

$\Rightarrow \quad x^2 = A^2 - x^2$

$\Rightarrow \quad 2x^2 = A^2$

$$x = \pm \frac{A}{\sqrt{2}}$$

Competition Edge Up

1. (22) ; Given, mass = 0.50 kg

Force, $F = (-50x \text{ Nm}^{-1})$

Time period, $T = \frac{x}{35}$ s

We know that, $F = -kx$

$F = -50x \text{ Nm}^{-1}$

$\Rightarrow k = -50 \text{ Nm}^{-1}$

Time period,

$$\tau = 2\pi\sqrt{\frac{m}{k}} = 2\pi\sqrt{\frac{0.50}{50}}$$

$$= \frac{2\pi}{10} = \frac{2 \times 22}{10 \times 7} = \frac{22}{35} \Rightarrow 22 \times \frac{1}{35} \text{ s}$$

Hence, $x = 22$

2. (17) ; We know that,

$$a = \omega^2 x$$

$$16 = \omega^2(4)$$

$$\omega^2 = 4 \Rightarrow \text{rad/s}$$

$$v = \omega\sqrt{A^2 - x^2}$$

$$A = \sqrt{\frac{v^2}{\omega^2} + x^2}$$

$\Rightarrow \quad A = \sqrt{\frac{4}{4} + 16}$

$$A = \sqrt{17} \text{ m}$$

$\therefore \quad x = 17$

3. (*d*) ; The time period of simple pendulum is given by

$$T = 2\pi\sqrt{\frac{l}{g}}$$

and acceleration due to gravity is given by

$$g = \frac{GM}{R^2}$$

$$T = 2\pi\sqrt{\frac{lR^2}{GM}} \text{ or } T \propto R \quad \text{...(i)}$$

Now, for height R above

$$T_1 \propto (R + R) \quad \text{...(ii)}$$

For height $2R$ above

$$T_2 \propto (R + 2R) \quad \text{...(iii)}$$

From Eqs. (ii) and (iii),

$$\frac{T_1}{T_2} = \frac{R + R}{R + 2R} = \frac{2}{3}$$

$\Rightarrow \quad 3T_1 = 2T_2$

4. (*d*); Since, E does not depend on mass of oscillating particle, hence New energy, $E' = E$

5. (3) ; Frequency of oscillation of a string-mass system

$$f = \frac{1}{T} = \frac{1}{2\pi}\sqrt{\frac{k}{m}}$$

So, $f_1 = \frac{1}{2\pi}\sqrt{\frac{k}{m}}$

and $f_2 = \frac{1}{2\pi}\sqrt{\frac{k}{9m}}$

$$= \frac{1}{3} \cdot \frac{1}{2\pi}\sqrt{\frac{k}{m}}$$

$$= \frac{1}{3} f_1$$

So, $f_1 / f_2 = 3$

6. (12) ;

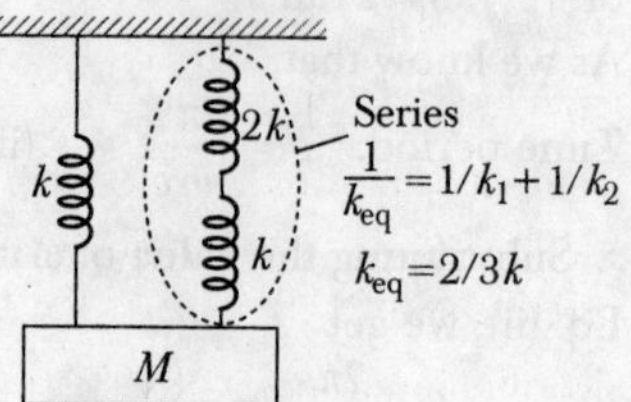

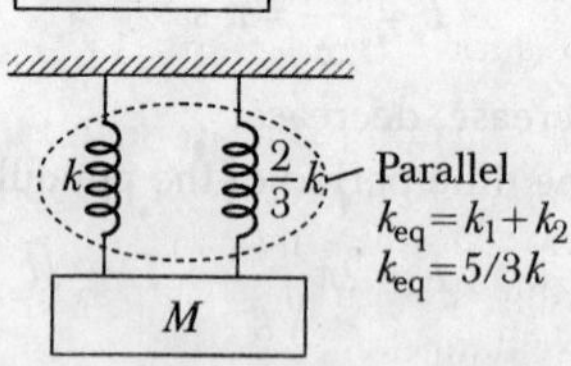

k — $\frac{2}{3}k$ — Parallel

$k_{eq} = k_1 + k_2$

$k_{eq} = 5/3k$

M

Time period,

$$T = 2\pi\sqrt{\frac{m}{k_{eq}}} = 2\pi\sqrt{\frac{3m}{5k}}$$

$$= \pi\sqrt{\frac{12m}{5k}}$$

$$= \pi\sqrt{\frac{\alpha m}{5k}} \quad \text{(given)}$$

$\therefore \quad \alpha = 12$

7. (*b*) ; Given,

$$x = 5\sin\left(\pi t + \frac{\pi}{3}\right) \text{m} \quad \text{...(i)}$$

The standard Eq. for SHM is

$$x = A\sin(\omega t + \phi) \quad \text{...(ii)}$$

Thus, comparing Eqs. (i) and (ii), we get

$$A = 5 \text{ m and } \omega = \pi$$

$\Rightarrow \quad \frac{2\pi}{T} = \pi \Rightarrow T = 2\text{s}$

Hence, option (b) is correct.

8. (*b*) ; Time period of a bob is given by,

$$T = 2\pi\sqrt{\frac{l}{g}}$$

According to question,

$$T' = 2\pi\sqrt{\frac{l}{2g}}$$

$$= \frac{2\pi\sqrt{l}}{\sqrt{2g}}$$

Thus, $\frac{T'}{T} = \frac{T}{\sqrt{2}} = \frac{x}{2}T$

Hence, $x = \sqrt{2}$

9. (*d*) Given, $l_1 = 121$ cm $= 1.21$ m

$l_2 = 100$ cm $= 1$ m

Let T_1 and T_2 be the time periods of longer and shorter pendulum, respectively.

Since, $T = 2\pi\sqrt{l/g}$

$$\Rightarrow \frac{T_1}{T_2} = \sqrt{\frac{l_1}{l_2}} = \sqrt{\frac{1.21}{1}} = 1.1 = \frac{11}{10}$$

$\Rightarrow \quad 10\,T_1 = 11\,T_2$

$\therefore$ 10 vibrations of longer pendulum $= 11$ vibrations of shorter pendulum

$\therefore$ Minimum number of vibrations of shorter pendulum $= 11$

10. (*b*) ; In simple harmonic motion, both kinetic energy and potential energy attain their maximum value two times in one complete oscillation.

Hence, frequency of kinetic energy and potential energy is 2 for one complete oscillation.

So, the frequency of the potential energy of a body executing SHM with frequency n is $2n$.

11. (*d*) ; In SHM, equation of displacement of a particle is $y = a \sin \omega t$ and equation of acceleration of a particle is

$A = a\omega^2 \sin \omega t = a\omega^2 \sin(\omega t + \pi)$

$\therefore$ Phase difference between displacement and acceleration of a particle is

$= (\omega t + \pi) - \omega t = \pi$ rad

Chapter-14
Waves

1. (*a*); In a mobile phone, initially sound waves are converted into an electric current signal which in turn generate electromagnetic waves (radio waves).

2. (*d*); Light waves, radiowaves, X-rays, are all electromagnetic waves which do not necessarily require a medium for their propagation.

While seismic waves are mechanical waves and hence require a material medium for their propagation.

3. (*d*); The wave generated from up and down jerk given to the string or by up and down motion of the piston at the end of the pipe will be transverse or longitudinal waves, respectively.

These transverse and longitudinal waves are also called progressive waves, as they travel from one part of the medium to another.

4. (*c*) In a water wave, it is the disturbance that moves, not water as a whole.

However, a stream constitutes motion of water as a whole.

Likewise a wind (motion of air as a whole) should not be confused with a sound wave which is a propagation of distrurbance (in pressure density) in air, without the motion of air medium as a whole.

5. I;

I. For transverse wave, motion of particle is perpendicular to the motion of wave direction. i.e. $\theta = 90°$

$\therefore \quad \mathbf{y} \cdot \mathbf{v} = yv \cos 90° = 0$

II. For longitudinal waves, motion of particle is parallel to motion of wave direction. i.e. $\theta = 0°$

$\therefore \quad \mathbf{y} \times \mathbf{v} = yv \sin 0° \cdot \hat{\mathbf{n}} = 0$

$\Rightarrow \mathbf{y} \times \mathbf{v} = 0$

6. I, IV

7. $y = A \sin(kx - \omega t + \phi)$;

The general progressive wave equation in positive x-direction is $y = A \sin(kx - \omega t + \phi)$

At $x = 0$, $t = 0$

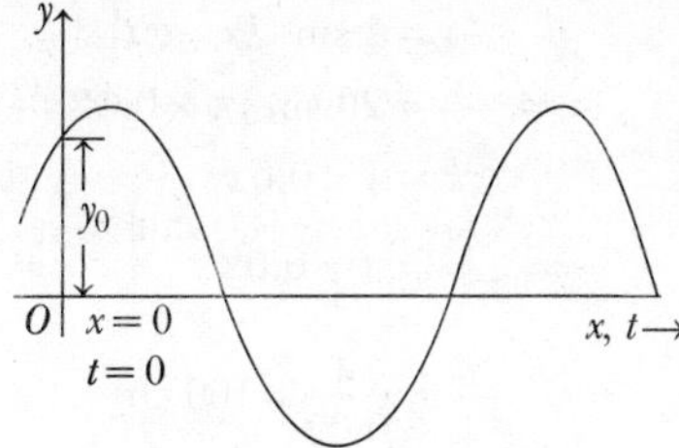

$y = y_0$

$\therefore y_0 = A \sin(\phi)$

$\Rightarrow \phi = \sin^{-1}\left(\frac{y_0}{A}\right) \neq 0$

Hence, wave equation is

$y = A \sin(kx - \omega t + \phi)$

8. No;

From the given diagram,

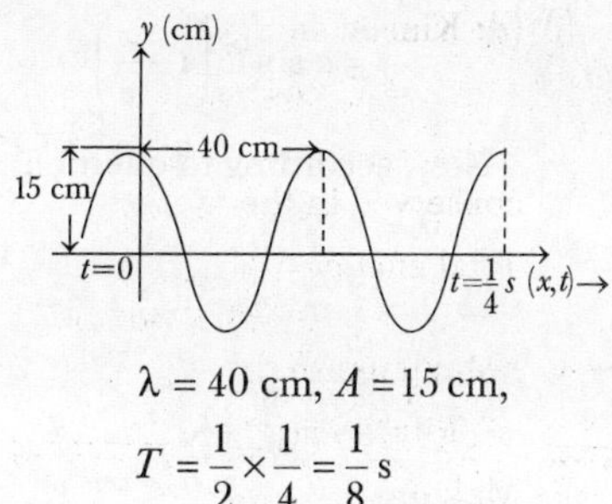

$\lambda = 40$ cm, $A = 15$ cm,

$$T = \frac{1}{2} \times \frac{1}{4} = \frac{1}{8}\text{ s}$$

$\therefore$ General equation of wave,

$$y = A \sin 2\pi\left(\frac{x}{\lambda} - \frac{t}{T}\right)$$

$$= 15 \sin 2\pi\left(\frac{x}{40} - \frac{t}{1/8}\right)$$

$$= 15 \sin\left(\frac{2\pi}{40}x - 16\pi t\right)$$

9. (4); $y = 4 \sin\left[\frac{\pi}{2}\left(2t + \frac{x}{8}\right)\right]$

$\therefore y(x = 8\text{ cm}, t = 1\text{ s})$

$$= 4 \sin\left[\frac{\pi}{2}\left(2\times1 + \frac{8}{8}\right)\right]$$

$$= 4 \sin\frac{3\pi}{2} = 4 \sin\left(\pi + \frac{\pi}{2}\right)$$

$$= -4 \sin\frac{\pi}{2}$$

$\therefore y(8, 1) = -4$ cm $\left\{\because \sin\frac{\pi}{2} = 1\right\}$

$= 4$ cm downward

10. I. $y = a \sin \omega\left(t - \frac{x}{v}\right)$

$\omega = 2\pi n = 2\pi \times 50$

$= 100\pi$ rad/s

$\therefore y = 0.002 \sin\left[100\pi\left(t - \frac{x}{300}\right)\right]$

II. Wave equation which is travelling in +ve x-direction is

$$y = a \sin 2\pi\left(\frac{t}{T} - \frac{x}{\lambda}\right)$$

$$n = \frac{1}{\pi}\text{Hz}$$

$$\Rightarrow \quad T = \frac{1}{n} = \pi\text{ s}$$

$$\therefore \quad y = 1 \sin 2\pi\left(\frac{t}{\pi} - \frac{x}{2\pi}\right)$$

$$= \sin(2t - x)$$

III. Wave equation in positive X-axis direction is

$$y = a\sin\omega\left(t - \frac{x}{v}\right)$$

Now, according to question,

$5\lambda = 4$

$\Rightarrow \lambda = \frac{4}{5}$ m

$\therefore\ v = n\lambda = \frac{\omega}{2\pi}\cdot\lambda$

$\Rightarrow \omega = \dfrac{2\pi \times 128}{\frac{4}{5}}$

$= 320\pi$ rad/s

$\therefore\ y = 0.02\sin\left[320\pi\left(t - \frac{x}{128}\right)\right]$

IV. $y = a\sin\frac{2\pi}{\lambda}(vt - x)$

$\therefore\ y = 0.2\sin\frac{2\pi}{60}(360t - x)$

$y = 0.2\sin\left(12\pi t - \frac{\pi}{30}x\right)$

11. Given, $y = A\sin 2\pi\left(\frac{x}{\lambda} - \frac{t}{T}\right)$

$= A\sin\left(\frac{2\pi}{\lambda}x - \frac{2\pi}{T}t\right)$

$= A\sin(kx - \omega t)$

A. Angular frequency, $\omega = \frac{2\pi}{T}$

B. Wave number, $k = \frac{2\pi}{\lambda}$

C. At $t = 0$, $y = A\sin kx$ ...(i)

Since, sine repeats at an internal 2π.

$\therefore$ $\sin kx = \sin(kx + 2n\pi)$, $n = 0, 1, 2, \ldots$

$\sin kx = \sin k\left(x + \frac{2n\pi}{k}\right)$

Hence, $y_x = y_{\left(x + \frac{2n\pi}{k}\right)}$

So, y has same value at position x and $\left(x + \frac{2n\pi}{k}\right)$

where $n = 1, 2, \ldots$

or $(x + n\lambda)$ $\left(\because \lambda - \frac{2\pi}{k}\right)$

D. At $x = 0$, $y = -A\sin\omega t$ ...(i)

$\therefore$ $\sin\omega t = \sin(\omega t + 2n\pi)$

$= \sin\omega\left(t + \frac{2n\pi}{\omega}\right)$

$n = 1, 2, \ldots$

$\therefore$ From Eq. (i), we get

$y_t = y_{\left(t + \frac{2n\pi}{\omega}\right)} = y_{(t+nT)}$ $\left[\because T = \frac{2\pi}{\omega}\right]$

So, y has same value at time t and $t + nT$.

12. $y(x, t) = 0.1\sin(\pi x - \pi t)$;

Equation of wave is

$y(x, t) = A\sin k(x - vt)$

$k = \frac{2\pi}{\lambda} = \frac{2\pi}{2} = \pi$

$\therefore\ y(x, t) = 0.1\sin(\pi x - \pi t)$

13. (*b*); Points are said to be in same phase, if they have equal displacement in same direction at different locations.

14. (*b*); When five particles which are separated by n number of wavelengths are in same phase.

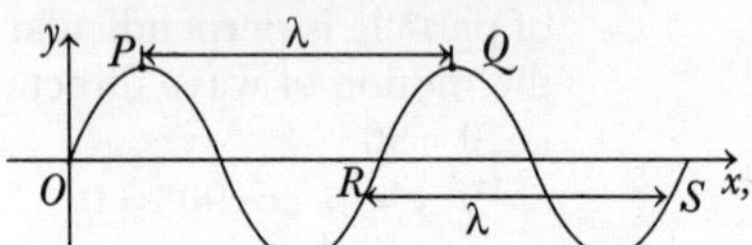

Hence, they have same displacement in same direction.

15. 0.57;

$y_1 = a\sin(\omega t + kx + 0.57)$

$y_2 = a\cos(\omega t + kx)$

Phase difference $= \phi_1 - \phi_2$

$= (\omega t + kx + 0.57) - (\omega t + kx)$

$= 0.57$

16. (100); $y = 20\sin\pi(0.02x - 2t)$

General equation,

$y = a\sin(kx - \omega t)$

$\Rightarrow\ y = 20\sin(\pi \times 0.02x - 2\pi t)$

$\therefore\ k = \pi \times 0.02$

$\Rightarrow\ \frac{2\pi}{\lambda} = \pi \times 0.02$ $\left[\because k = \frac{2\pi}{\lambda}\right]$

$\lambda = \frac{2}{0.02} = 100$ cm

17. (*d*); $y(x, t) = 0.00327\sin(72.1x - 2.72t)$

$\therefore$ Amplitude,

$A = 0.00327$ m $= 3.27$ mm

Wave number, $k = 72.1$ rad/m

18. $y = 0.03\sin\left(490\pi t - \frac{49\pi}{30}x\right)$;

Travelling wave equation in positive X-axis direction is given by

$y = a\sin\frac{2\pi}{\lambda}(vt - x)$

Now, $2a = 6$

$\Rightarrow a = 3$ cm

$\Rightarrow a = 0.03$ m

$\because\ v = n\lambda$

$\Rightarrow \lambda = \frac{300}{245}$ m

$\therefore\ y = 0.03\sin\frac{2\pi \times 245}{300}(300t - x)$

$= 0.03\sin\left(490\pi t - \frac{49\pi}{30}x\right)$

19. 16;

Frequency = 3600 waves/min

$= \frac{3600}{60}$ Hz $= 60$ Hz

Now, $v = n\lambda$

$\Rightarrow\ 960 = 60 \times \lambda$

$\therefore\ \lambda = 16$ m

20. A. 0.075, B. 1.256, C. 0;

$y(x, t) = 0.1\sin\left(\frac{\pi}{8}x + 4\pi t\right)$

$\therefore y(1.6, t) = 0.1\sin\left(\frac{\pi}{8} \times 1.6 + 4\pi t\right)$

$= 0.1\sin(0.2\pi + 4\pi t)$

A. For maximum displacement,

$y(1.6, t) = 0.1$

$\therefore\ 0.1 = 0.1\sin(0.2\pi + 4\pi t)$

$\Rightarrow\ \sin(0.2\pi + 4\pi t)$

$= 1 = \sin\frac{\pi}{2}$

$\Rightarrow\ 0.2\pi + 4\pi t = \frac{\pi}{2}$

$\therefore t = 0.075$ s

B. v_p = Particle speed $= \frac{dy}{dt}$

$= \frac{d}{dt}[0.1\sin(0.2\pi + 4\pi t)]$

$= 4\pi \times 0.1\cos(0.2\pi + 4\pi t)$

$= 4\pi \times 0.1\cos(0.2\pi + 4\pi \times 0.2)$

$\therefore (v_p)_{\text{at } t = 0.2\text{s}}$

$= -0.4\pi = -1.256$ m/s

$= 1.256$ m/s (towards left)

C. a_p = Particle acceleration

$$= \frac{d^2y}{dt^2} = \frac{d}{dt}(v_p)$$

$$= \frac{d}{dt}[0.4\pi \cos(0.2\pi + 4\pi t)]$$

$$= -4\pi \times 0.4\pi \sin(0.2\pi + 4\pi t)$$

$$= -1.6\pi^2 \sin(0.2\pi + 4\pi \times 0.2)$$

$$\therefore (a_p)_{\text{at } t=0.25} = 0 \text{ m/s}^2$$

21. A → 4, B → 3, C → 1, D → 2;

$$y = 0.25 \sin(0.3x - 40t)$$

$$\therefore \omega = 40 \text{ rad/s}$$

$$k = 0.3 \text{ rad/m}$$

$$v = \frac{\omega}{k} = \frac{40}{0.3} = 133 \text{ m/s}$$

$$\lambda = \frac{2\pi}{k} = \frac{2\pi}{0.3} = 20.9 \text{ m}$$

22. (*d*); $y = a \sin\left(100t - \frac{x}{10}\right)$

Wave velocity,

$$v = \frac{\omega}{k} = \frac{100}{\frac{1}{10}} = 1000 \text{ m/s}$$

23. 40 m/s;

$$y = 0.2\sin(1.5x + 60t)$$

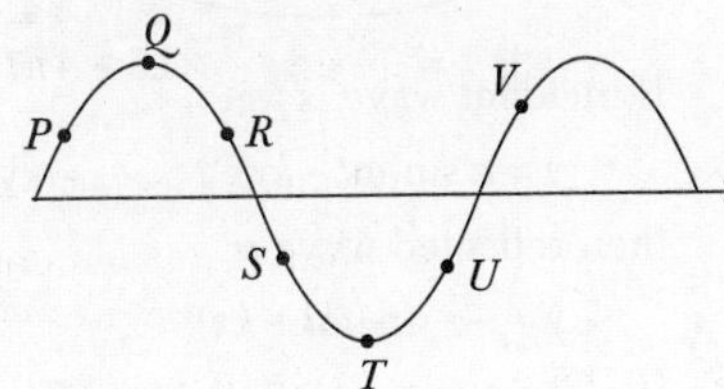

Wave velocity,

$$v = \frac{\omega}{k} = \frac{60}{1.5} = 40 \text{ m/s}$$

24. 2 m/s;

$y(x, t) = 0.002 \sin [(0.2 \text{ m}^{-1})\, x - (0.4 \text{ s}^{-1})\, t]$

Speed of wave,

$$v = \frac{\omega}{k} = \frac{0.4}{0.2} = 2 \text{ m/s}$$

25. I, III;

$$y = 0.001 \sin(60t + 2x)$$

I. Wave velocity,

$$v = \frac{\omega}{k} = \frac{60}{2}$$

= 30 m/s in positive *X*-axis direction

III. As, $\omega = 2\pi n$

∴ Frequency,

$$n = \frac{60}{2\pi} = \left(\frac{30}{\pi}\right) \text{Hz}$$

26. $2\pi A$;

Wave equation,

$$y = A \sin(\omega t - kx)$$

$$\therefore v_p = \text{Particle velocity}$$

$$= \frac{d}{dt} = A\omega \cos(\omega t - kx)$$

$$\therefore (v_p)_{max} = A\omega$$

According to the question,

Wave velocity $= (v_p)_{max}$

$$\Rightarrow \frac{\omega}{k} = A\omega \Rightarrow \frac{\lambda}{2\pi} = A$$

$$\therefore \lambda = 2\pi A$$

27. πy_0;

Wave equation is

$$y = y_0 \sin \frac{2\pi}{\lambda}(vt - x)$$

$$\therefore v_p = \text{Particle velocity} = \frac{dy}{dt}$$

$$= \left(\frac{2\pi}{\lambda}\right) \cdot y_0 \cdot v \cos \frac{2\pi}{\lambda}(vt - x)$$

According to the question,

$(v_p)_{max} = 2$ (Wave velocity)

$$\Rightarrow \frac{2\pi}{\lambda} y_0 \cdot v = 2v$$

$$\therefore \lambda = \pi y_0$$

28. (*d*);

$$y(x, t) = 8 \sin\left(0.5\pi x - 4\pi t - \frac{\pi}{4}\right)$$

Wave speed,

$$v = \frac{\omega}{k} = \frac{4\pi}{0.5\pi} = 8 \text{ m/s}$$

29. 100;

μ = Mass per unit length

$$= \frac{80 \times 10^{-3}}{10}$$

$$= 8 \times 10^{-3} \text{ kg/m}$$

∴ Speed of transverse wave,

$$v = \sqrt{\frac{T}{\mu}} = \sqrt{\frac{80}{8 \times 10^{-3}}} = 100 \text{ m/s}$$

30. 1215;

$$y = -\ 0.21 \sin(x + 30t)$$

∴ Wave velocity,

$$v = \frac{\omega}{k} = \frac{30}{1} = 30 \text{ m/s}$$

Now, wave speed in string,

$$v = \sqrt{\frac{T}{\mu}} \Rightarrow 30 = \sqrt{\frac{T}{0.0135}}$$

[∵ μ = mass per unit length

$$= 0.135 \text{ g/cm}$$

$$= \frac{0.135 \times 10^{-3}}{10^{-2}} \text{ kg/m}$$

$$= 0.0135 \text{ kg/m}]$$

$$\therefore T = 1215 \times 10^{-2} \text{ N}$$

31. A → 4, B → 3, C → 2, D → 1

32. 60.06;

$$\mu = \frac{m}{L} = \frac{5 \times 10^{-3}}{0.72}$$

$$= \frac{1}{144} \text{ kg/m}$$

Tension in string, $T = \mu v^2$

$$= \frac{1}{144} \times 93 \times 93$$

$$= 60.06 \text{ N}$$

33. 5000 m/s;

Speed of longitudinal wave,

$$v = \sqrt{\frac{Y}{\rho}} = \sqrt{\frac{3 \times 10^{10}}{1.2 \times 10^3}} = 5000 \text{ m/s}$$

34. Hydrogen < Water < Rubber < Aluminium;

As we know, $v_{solid} > v_{liquid} > v_{gas}$ where, v = speed of sound in a medium.

35. 330.6 m/s;

Speed of sound in air,

$$v = \sqrt{\frac{\gamma p}{\rho}} = \sqrt{\frac{1.41 \times 10^5}{1.29}}$$

$$= 330.6 \text{ m/s}$$

36. 51;

By Newton's formula, speed of sound,

$$v = \sqrt{\frac{B_{in}}{\rho}} = \sqrt{\frac{p}{\rho}}$$

$$= \sqrt{\frac{1.01 \times 10^5}{1.293}} = 280 \text{ m/s}$$

By Laplace modified formula, speed of sound,

$$v = \sqrt{\frac{B_{ad}}{\rho}} = \sqrt{\frac{\gamma p}{\rho}}$$

$= \sqrt{\dfrac{1.4 \times 1.01 \times 10^5}{1.293}}$

$= 331 \text{ m/s}$

Hence, difference

$= (331 - 280) = 51 \text{ m/s}$

37.

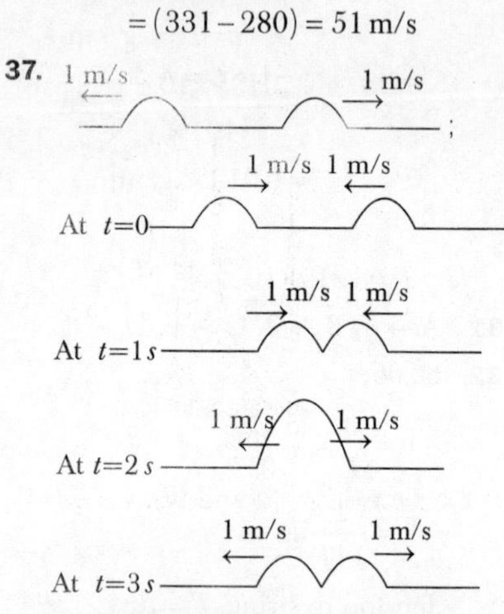

38. I, II;

Since, relative speed of pulses

$= 1 - 1 = 0$

At $t = 1$ s,

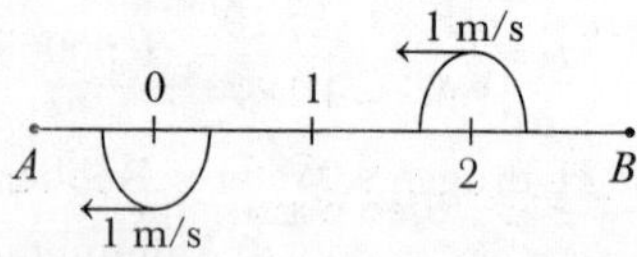

At $t = 2$ s,

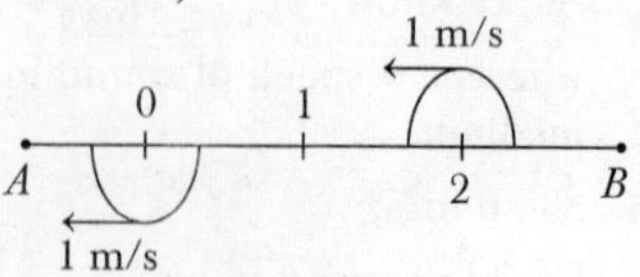

39. be zero and same

40. B;

For reflection, $\alpha = \beta$

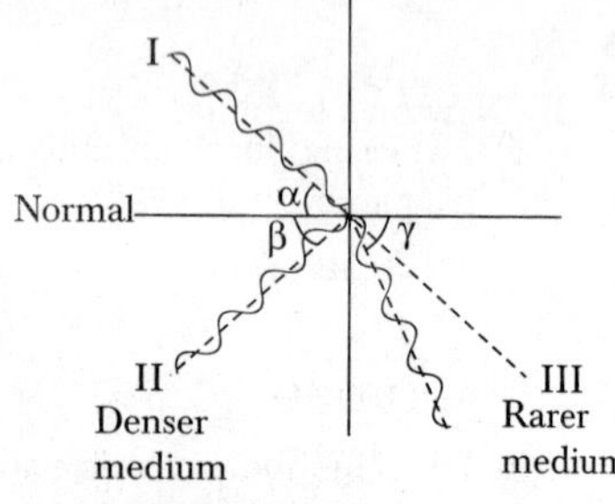

For refraction, $\gamma > \alpha$

$\therefore \quad \alpha = \beta$ and $\beta < \gamma$

Now, as frequency of wave is independent of medium.

$\therefore \quad f_{\text{I}} = f_{\text{II}} = f_{\text{III}}$

41. I, II;

When incident wave from hard boundary is

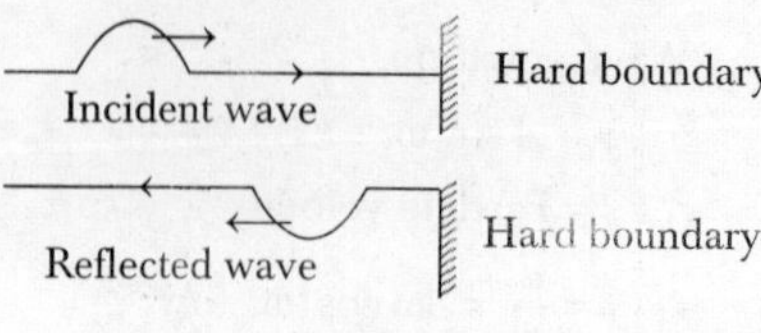

$y = A \sin (kx - \omega t)$

Then for reflected wave,

p = phase difference $= \pi$

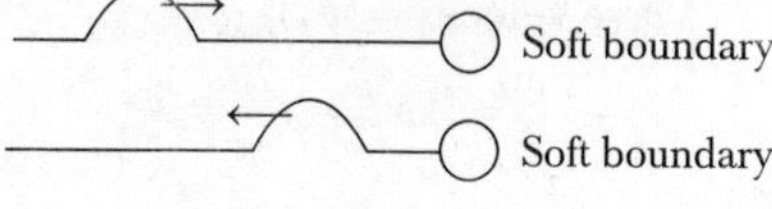

$\therefore \; y_R = A \sin(kx - \omega t + \pi)$

$= -A \sin (kx - \omega t)$

When incident wave from soft boundary is $y_{\text{I}} = A \sin (\omega t - kx)$

$\therefore$ For reflected wave, phase difference, $\phi = 0$

$\therefore \quad y_R = A \sin (\omega t - kx)$

42. (*d*);

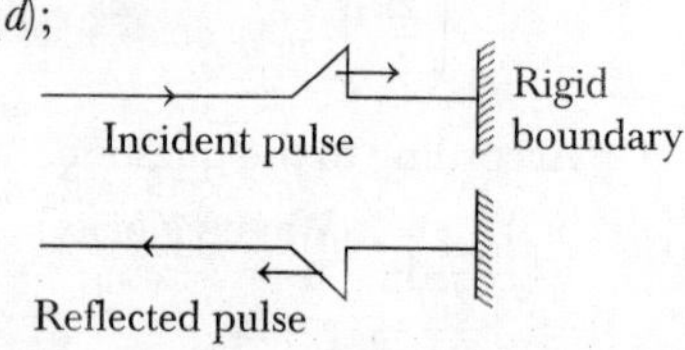

43. $y_R = -0.3 \sin(200x - 0.5t)$;

$y_{\text{I}}(x, t) = 0.3 \sin (200x - 0.5t)$

When it is reflected by a rigid boundary.

$\therefore \quad y_R = -0.3 \sin (200x - 0.5t)$

When it is reflected by a free end.

$\therefore \quad y_R = 0.3 \sin (200x - 0.5t)$

44. I;

When two progressive waves move in opposite direction with same frequency and amplitude, then

I. resultant wave is stationary wave or standing wave.

II. at nodes, energy is only kinetic.

III. at anti-nodes, energy is only potential.

45. A $\rightarrow$ 2, 3; B $\rightarrow$ 1, 4

46. $\left(\dfrac{\lambda}{4}, \dfrac{\lambda}{2}\right)$;

Stationary wave in stretched string;

Distance between any two successive nodes $= \dfrac{\lambda}{2}$

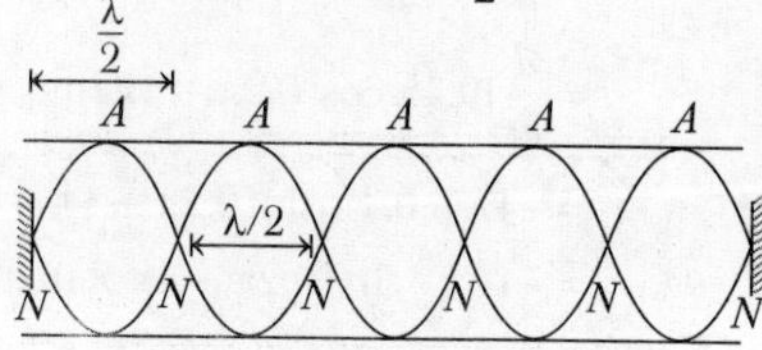

Distance between any two successive anti-nodes $= \dfrac{\lambda}{2}$

Distance between consecutive node and anti-node $= \dfrac{\lambda}{4}$

47. Yes;

For producing node at one end, the wave should be standing or stationary wave.

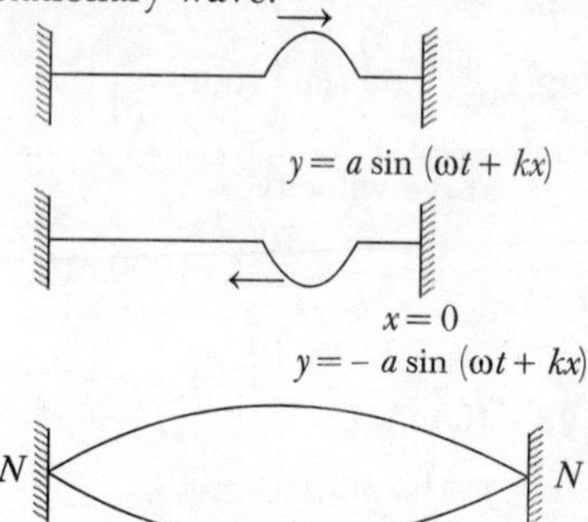

If incident wave is

$y = a \sin(\omega t - kx)$,

then reflected wave is

$y = -a \sin (\omega t + kx)$

48. (*b*); The wave equation,

$y = A \cos kx \sin \omega t$ has separate kx and ωx. Hence, it is an equation of standing wave or stationary wave with amplitude $A \cos kx$.

49. No

50. 50 mm;

The equation of stationary wave is

$$y = 10 \cos \pi (0.02x) \sin \pi (4.0)t \quad \ldots\text{(i)}$$

Also, $y = (2a \cos kx) \sin \omega t \quad \ldots\text{(ii)}$

$\therefore \quad \lambda = \dfrac{2\pi}{k} = \dfrac{2\pi}{0.02\pi} = 100 \text{ mm}$

$\therefore$ Distance between two nearest nodes $= \dfrac{\lambda}{2}$

$= \dfrac{100}{2} = 50 \text{ mm}$

51. 5 Hz;

Distance of one segment $= \dfrac{\lambda}{2}$

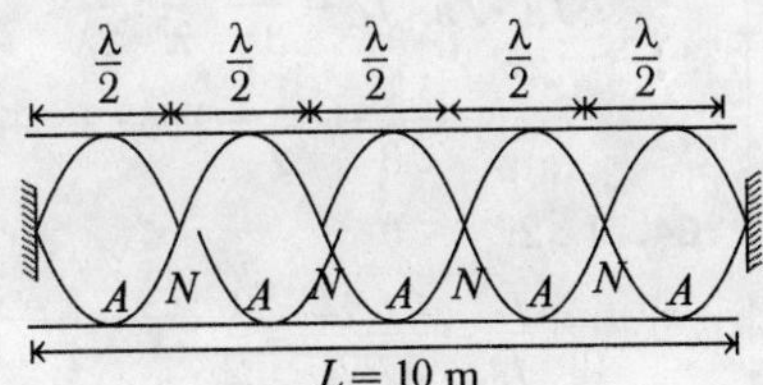

$\therefore$ According to the question,

$$5\frac{\lambda}{2} = 10 \Rightarrow \lambda = 4 \text{ m}$$

Now, $v = n\lambda \Rightarrow 20 = n \times 4$

$\therefore \quad n = 5 \text{ Hz}$

Hence, frequency of standing wave is 5 Hz.

52. 1;

From figure

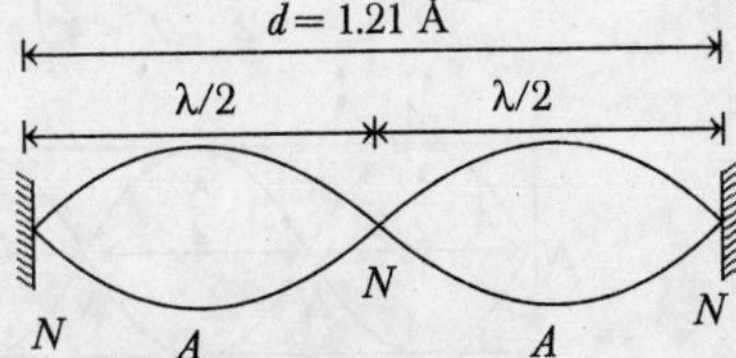

$$d = \frac{\lambda}{2} + \frac{\lambda}{2} = \lambda$$

$\Rightarrow \quad \lambda = 1.21 \text{ Å}$

According to the question,

$$\lambda = 1.21 \text{ Å} = x.2x \text{ Å}$$

$\therefore \quad x = 1$

53. increases;

Empty vessel behaves like closed organ pipe.

$\therefore$ Frequency, $f = \dfrac{v}{4L}$

i.e. $\quad f \propto \dfrac{1}{L}$

$\therefore$ When some water is poured, its length decreases.

Hence, frequency increases.

54. False;

Sound produced by an open organ pipe is richer because it contains all harmonics and, frequency of a fundamental note in an open organ pipe is twice the fundamental frequency in a closed organ pipe of same length.

55. (*a*); For pipe fill with air and both ends open,

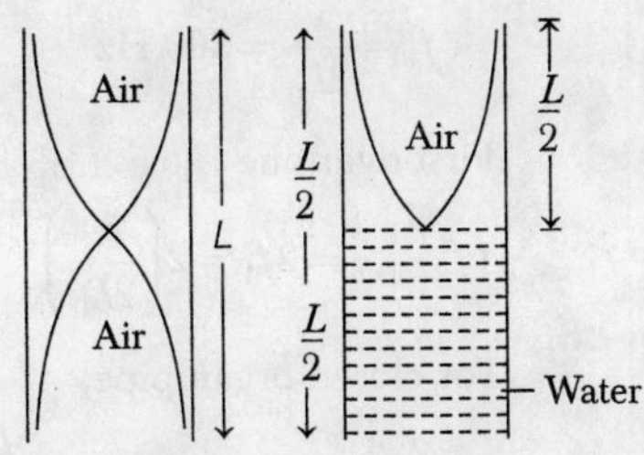

f_1 = fundamental frequency

$$= \frac{v}{2L} = v$$

For pipe dipped in water,

f_1 = fundamental frequency

$$= \frac{v}{4\left(\dfrac{L}{2}\right)} = \frac{v}{2L} = \nu$$

56. 13.33;

For an open organ pipe,

$$(f_1)_{\text{open}} = \frac{v}{2L_0}$$

(fundamental frequency)

For a closed organ pipe,

$$(f_3)_{\text{closed}} = 3\left(\frac{v}{4L_C}\right)$$

[3rd harmonic]

According to question,

$$(f_1)_{\text{open}} = (f_3)_{\text{closed}}$$

$$\Rightarrow \frac{v}{2L_0} = 3\left(\frac{v}{4L_C}\right)$$

$$\Rightarrow \frac{1}{L_0} = \frac{3}{2 \times 20}$$

$$\Rightarrow L_0 = 13.33 \text{ cm}$$

Hence, length of open organ pipe is 13.33 cm.

57. (*b*); For a closed organ pipe,

$$f_1 = \frac{v}{4l_1} = f$$

(where, f = frequency of tuning fork)

$\therefore \quad v = 4f\,l_1 \quad \ldots\text{(i)}$

Now, next frequency

$$(f_3) = 3\left(\frac{v}{4l_2}\right) = f$$

$$\Rightarrow \frac{3 \times 4f\,l_1}{4l_2} = f \quad \text{[using Eq. (i)]}$$

$$\Rightarrow l_2 = 3l_1 = 3 \times 50$$

$$= 150 \text{ cm}$$

58. 66.4;

For a closed organ pipe, fundamental frequency,

$$v = \frac{v}{\lambda} \quad \ldots\text{(i)}$$

Now, $L = \dfrac{\lambda}{4} \Rightarrow \lambda = 4\,L \quad \ldots\text{(ii)}$

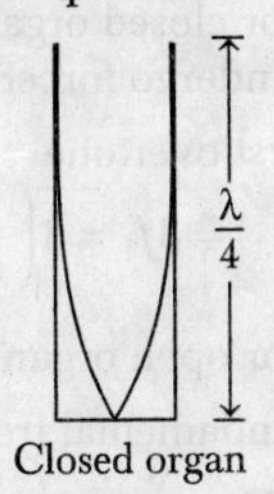

Closed organ pipe

From Eqs. (i) and (ii), we get

$$\therefore \quad \nu = \frac{v}{4L}$$

$$\Rightarrow \quad 125 = \frac{332}{4 \times L}$$

$\therefore \quad L = 66.4 \text{ cm}$

59. 5,6;

For open organ pipe, second overtone,

$$(f_3)_{\text{open}} = 3f_1 = 3\left(\frac{\nu}{2L_1}\right)$$

For closed organ pipe, second overtone,

$$(f_5)_{\text{closed}} = 5f_1 = 5\left(\frac{\nu}{4L_2}\right)$$

According to the question,

$$(f_3)_{\text{open}} = (f_5)_{\text{closed}}$$

$$\Rightarrow 3\left(\frac{\nu}{2L_1}\right) = 5\left(\frac{\nu}{4L_2}\right)$$

$$\Rightarrow \frac{L_2}{L_1} = \frac{x}{y} = \frac{5}{4} \times \frac{2}{3} = \frac{5}{6}$$

60. (i) ✓ (ii) × (iii) ×;

(i) For string, fundamental frequency $(f_1) = 220$ cycle/s

$\therefore$ 5th harmonic

$$= f_5 = 5f_1 = 5 \times 220$$

$$= 1100 \text{ Hz}$$

(ii) For pipe open at both ends, fundamental frequency $(f_1) = 200$ Hz

$$\therefore \quad \frac{\nu}{2L} = 200$$

$\therefore$ For pipe closed at one end, fundamental frequency

$$(f_1) = \frac{v}{4L} = \frac{1}{2}\left(\frac{v}{2L}\right)$$

$$= \frac{1}{2} \times 200 = 100 \text{ Hz}$$

(iii) For closed organ pipe (undergo forced oscillation), first overtone

$$(f_3) = 3f_1 = 3\left(\frac{v}{4L}\right) = 384$$

For open organ pipe, fundamental frequency

$$(f_1) = \frac{v}{2L} = 2\left(\frac{v}{4L}\right)$$

$$= 2 \times \frac{384}{3} = 256 \text{ Hz}$$

61. 9 : 7;

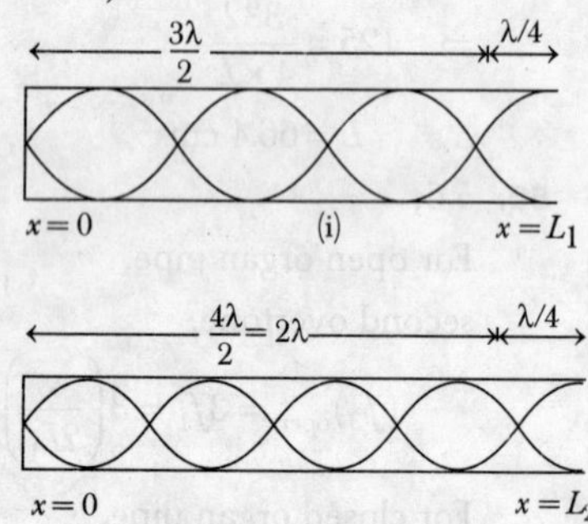

For vibrating air column (i)

$$L_1 = \frac{3\lambda}{2} + \frac{\lambda}{4} = \frac{7\lambda}{4}$$

$$f_1 = \frac{v}{4L_1} = \frac{v \times 4}{4 \times 7\lambda} = \frac{v}{7\lambda} \quad \left(\because L_1 = \frac{7\lambda}{4}\right)$$

For vibrating air column (ii),

$$L_2 = 2\lambda + \frac{\lambda}{4} = \frac{9\lambda}{4}$$

$$f_2 = \frac{v}{4L_2} = \frac{v \times 4}{4 \times 9\lambda} = \frac{v}{9\lambda} \quad \left(\because L_2 = \frac{9\lambda}{4}\right)$$

$$\therefore \frac{f_1}{f_2} = \frac{v/7\lambda}{v/9\lambda} = \frac{9}{7}$$

Hence, ratio of frequency = 9 : 7

62. 0.375 m;

For open organ pipe,

$$f_1 = \frac{v}{2L_0} = 300 \text{ Hz} \quad \ldots \text{(i)}$$

First overtone

$$(f_2)_{\text{open}} = 2f_1 = 2\left(\frac{v}{2L_0}\right)$$

For closed organ pipe,

$$\text{first overtone } (f_3)_{\text{closed}} = 3\left(\frac{v}{4L_C}\right)$$

According to question,

$$(f_2)_{\text{open}} = (f_3)_{\text{closed}}$$

$$\Rightarrow \frac{v}{2L_0} \times 2 = 3\left(\frac{v}{4L_C}\right)$$

$$\therefore \quad L_C = \frac{3}{4} L_0 \quad \ldots \text{(ii)}$$

Now, from Eq. (i), we get

$$\frac{v}{2L_0} = 300$$

$$\Rightarrow L_0 = \frac{300}{2 \times 300} = \frac{1}{2} \text{ m}$$

$\therefore$ From Eq. (ii), we get

$$L_C = \frac{3}{4} L_0$$

$$= \frac{3}{4} \times \frac{1}{2} = \frac{3}{8}$$

$$= 0.375 \text{ m}$$

$$L_C = 0.375 \text{ m}$$

63. 2 : 6 : 3;

Pipe (A) is a closed organ pipe.

$$\therefore \quad f_A = \frac{v}{4L_A} = \frac{v \times 4}{4 \times 3\lambda} = \frac{v}{3\lambda}$$

$$L_A = \frac{\lambda}{2} + \frac{\lambda}{4} = \frac{3\lambda}{4}$$

(A)

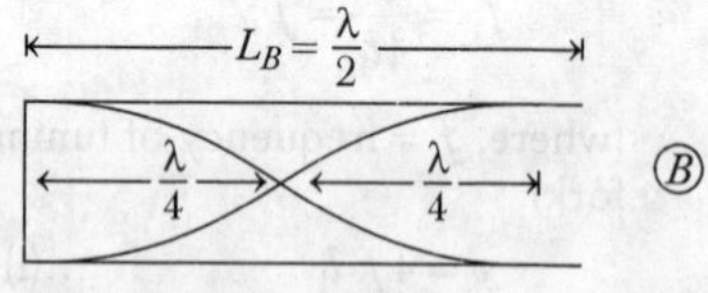

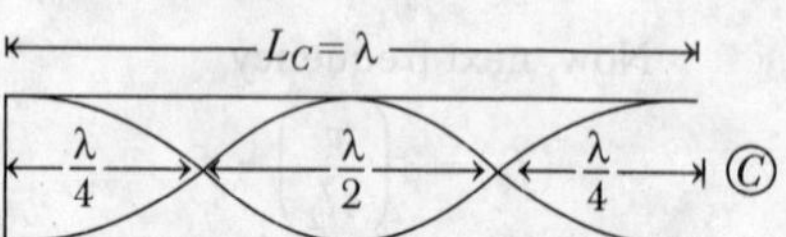

Pipe (B) is open organ pipe.

$$\therefore \quad f_B = \frac{v}{2L_B} = \frac{v \times 2}{2 \times \lambda} = \frac{v}{\lambda}$$

Pipe (C) is open organ pipe.

$$\therefore \quad f_C = \frac{v}{2L_c} = \frac{v}{2 \times \lambda} = \frac{v}{2\lambda}$$

$$\therefore f_A : f_B : f_C = \frac{v}{3\lambda} : \frac{v}{\lambda} : \frac{v}{2\lambda}$$

$$= \frac{1}{3} : 1 : \frac{1}{2} = 2 : 6 : 3$$

64. 1 : 2;

$$\frac{f_c}{f_0} = \frac{v/4L}{v/2L} = \frac{1}{2}$$

65. 3, 3;

In a closed organ pipe,

second overtone = $f_5 = 5f_1$ = fifth harmonic

$$= 5\left(\frac{v}{4L}\right) = \frac{v}{\frac{4L}{5}} = \frac{v}{\lambda}$$

$$\therefore \quad \lambda = \frac{4L}{5}$$

$$\Rightarrow \quad L = \frac{5\lambda}{4} = \left(\frac{\lambda}{2} + \frac{\lambda}{2} + \frac{\lambda}{4}\right)$$

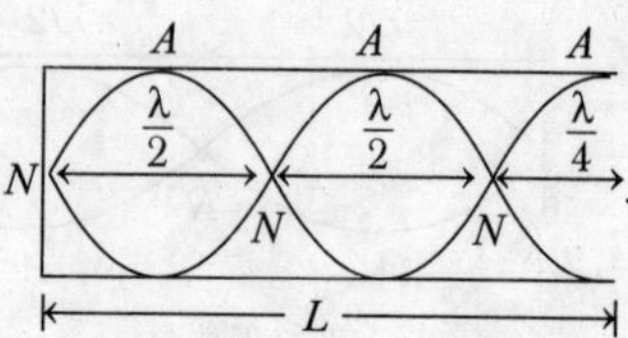

$\therefore$ 3 nodes and 3 anti-nodes are produced.

66. (c); In closed organ pipe,

$$f_1 = \frac{v}{4L}$$

(fundamental frequency or first harmonic)

$$f_3 = 3f_1$$

(first overtone or third harmonic)

$$f_{(2P+1)} = (2P+1)f_P$$

(Pth overtone or $(2P+1)$th harmonic)

67. I, III;

For closed organ pipe,

$$f_1 = \frac{v}{4L} = \frac{320}{4 \times 2} = 40 \text{ Hz}$$

$$f_3 = 3f_1 = 3 \times 40 = 120 \text{ Hz}$$

$$f_5 = 5f_1 = 5 \times 40 = 200 \text{ Hz}$$

From given options, only 40 Hz and 200 Hz can resonate with tuning fork frequency.

68. Yes;

For open organ pipe,

$$f_1 = \frac{v}{2L} = \frac{350}{2 \times 0.5} = 350 \text{ Hz}$$

For closed organ pipe,

$$f_1 = \frac{v}{4L} = \frac{350}{2} = 175 \text{ Hz}$$

69. 127.98;

If you jam one end of pipe with ear, then it behaves as closed organ pipe.

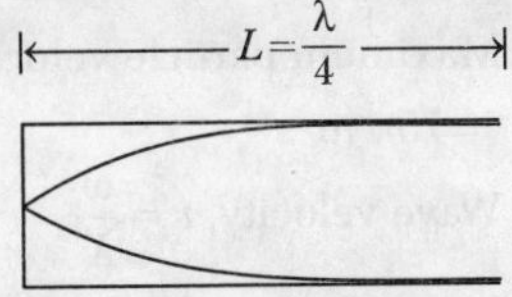

$\therefore$ Fundamental frequency

$$(f_1) = \frac{v}{4L} = \frac{343}{4 \times 0.67} = 127.98 \text{ Hz}$$

70. (*c*); For a closed organ pipe,

$$f_1 = \frac{v}{4l_1} = f \; \therefore \; l_1 = \frac{v}{4f}$$

(where, f = tuning fork frequency)

Now, $f_3 = 3\left(\frac{v}{4l_2}\right) = f$

$$\therefore \quad l_2 = \frac{3v}{4f}$$

Now, $f_5 = 5\left(\frac{v}{4l_3}\right) = f$

$$\therefore \quad l_3 = \frac{5v}{4f}$$

$$\therefore \quad l_3 - l_2 = l_2 - l_1 = \frac{2v}{4f}$$

$$\Rightarrow (52.75 - 31.25) \times 10^{-2} = \frac{v}{800 \times 2}$$

$$\therefore \quad v = 344 \text{ m/s}$$

71. 106.06;

For open organ pipe, $v = \sqrt{\frac{r p}{\rho}}$

$$\therefore \quad v \propto \frac{1}{\sqrt{\rho}}$$

(assuming same bulk modulus)

$$\therefore \quad \frac{v_{gas}}{v_{air}} = \sqrt{\frac{\rho_{air}}{\rho_{gas}}} = \frac{1}{\sqrt{2}}$$

$$\therefore \quad v_{gas} = v_{pipe} = \frac{300}{\sqrt{2}}$$

$$= 212.132 \text{ m/s}$$

Now, second harmonic frequency – fundamental frequency

$$= 2f_1 - f_1 = f_1 = \frac{v}{2L}$$

$$= \frac{212.132}{2 \times 1} = 106.06 \text{ Hz}$$

72. 384 m/s;

Resonant tube behaves like an organ pipe.

$$\therefore \quad l_2 - l_1 = \frac{v}{2f}$$

where, f = frequency of tuning fork.

$$\Rightarrow \quad (70 - 30) \times 10^{-2} = \frac{v}{2 \times 480}$$

$$\therefore \quad v = 384 \text{ m/s}$$

Hence, speed of sound in air by resonance tube method is 384 m/s.

73. (i) (✓), (ii) (✓), (iii) (✓), (iv) (×), (v) (✓);

(i) For an open organ pipe, first overtone

$$(f_2)_{open} = 2\left(\frac{v}{2L_0}\right)$$

for a closed organ pipe, first overtone

$$(f_3)_{closed} = 3\left(\frac{v}{4L_C}\right)$$

For resonance,

$$(f_2)_{open} = (f_3)_{closed}$$

$$\Rightarrow \quad 2\left(\frac{v}{2L_0}\right) = 3\left(\frac{v}{4L_C}\right)$$

$$\therefore \quad \frac{L_0}{L_C} = \frac{4}{3}$$

(ii) For producing beats, the two sources have slightly different frequencies, $f_{beat} = f_1 - f_2$

(iii) For producing beats, frequencies should be slightly different, $f_{beat} = (f_1 - f_2)$

(iv) f_{beat} = Number of beats heard per second

$$= (f_1 - f_2)$$

(v) $f_{beat} = (f_1 - f_2)$

74. equal to;

As beats are form of sound.

Hence, beats velocity = velocity of sound.

75. (*a*); Given, two waves are of frequencies, $f_1 = 9$ Hz and $f_2 = 11$ Hz

Beat frequency, f_{beat} = Difference in frequencies of two waves,

$$f_{beat} = |f_1 - f_2| = |11 - 9| = 2 \text{ Hz}$$

i.e. 2 beats are produced per second.

Time period of oscillation of amplitude is given by

$$T = \frac{1}{f_{beat}} = \frac{1}{2} = 0.5 \text{ s}$$

Although, the graph of oscillation is not given, the equation of envelope is given by option (a).

76. 368 Hz;

Frequency of first tuning fork,

$$f_1 = 364 \pm 4 = 368 \text{ Hz}$$

or 360 Hz

At $f_1 = 368$ Hz;

After loading with little wax, its frequency decreases and $(f_1 \sim f_2)$ decreases which is 2.

So, condition satisfied.

$$\therefore \quad f_1 = 368 \text{ Hz}$$

77. I. 6 Hz, II. 60 Hz, III. $\frac{v\Delta x}{2x^2}$

IV. 1 Hz, V. 2 Hz;

I. f_{beat} $f_1 \cdot f_2$

$$= 458 - 452 = 6 \text{ Hz}$$

II. $f_{beat} = f_1 - f_2 = \left(\frac{v}{\lambda_1} - \frac{v}{\lambda_2}\right)$

$$= \left(\frac{440}{88} - \frac{440}{100}\right) \times 10^2$$

$$= 60 \text{ Hz}$$

III. $f_{beat} = f_1 - f_2$

$$= \frac{v}{2x} - \frac{v}{2(x + \Delta x)}$$

$$= \frac{v}{2} \cdot \frac{\Delta x}{x(x + \Delta x)}$$

As $x >> \Delta x$

$\therefore$ Δx is very small and can be neglected.

$$\therefore \quad f_{beat} = \frac{v\Delta x}{2x^2}$$

IV. Beat produced by f_1 and f_2 is

$$f_{B_1} = f_1 \sim f_2$$

$$= 412 - 411 = 1 \text{ Hz}$$

Beat produced by f_1 and f_3 is

$$f_{B_2} = f_1 \sim f_3$$

$$= 413 - 411 = 2 \text{ Hz}$$

$\therefore$ Beat produced by f_{B_1} and f_{B_2} is $f_B = 2 - 1 = 1$ Hz

V. $f_B = f_1 - f_2 = \frac{\omega_1}{2\pi} - \frac{\omega_2}{2\pi}$

$$= \frac{330\pi - 326\pi}{2\pi} = 2 \text{ Hz}$$

78. (*a*); $T = \frac{1}{f_1 - f_2} = \frac{1}{507 - 502}$

$\therefore \quad T = 0.2\text{ s}$

79. increases

80. 371.95;

$f_{\text{beat}} = f_1 - f_2 = \frac{v}{2L_1} - \frac{v}{2L_2}$

$\Rightarrow \quad \frac{28}{10} = \frac{v}{2}\left(\frac{1}{81} - \frac{1}{82}\right) \times 10^2$

$\Rightarrow \quad v = 371.95\text{ m/s}$

Hence, the velocity of sound in air is 371.95 m/s.

81. I. (✓), II. (×), III. (×);

I. Number of beats per second

$= f_1 - f_2 = \frac{v}{\lambda_1} - \frac{v}{\lambda_2}$

$= \left(\frac{330}{500} - \frac{330}{550}\right) \times 10^2 = 6$

II. For producing beats, there is slightly different frequencies is required.

$f_{\text{beat}} = f_1 - f_2$

III. $f_1 = f = 255 \pm 5 = 260$ Hz

or 250 Hz

Now, at $f_1 = 250\text{ Hz} < f_2$;

As f_1 increases to $2f$ and f_2 decreases.

So, $(f_2 - f_1)$ decreases which does not satisfy the condition.

Hence, $f = 260$ Hz

82. 2;

$f_{\text{beat}} = f_1 - f_2 = (v+1) - (v-1) = 2$

83. 335 Hz;

$f_A = 340 \pm 5 = 345\text{ Hz}$

or 335 Hz

At $f_A = 345\text{ Hz} > f_B = 340\text{ Hz}$

As f_A is filled. So, its frequency increases.

Hence, $(f_A - f_B)$ increases, which does not satisfy the given condition.

$\therefore \quad f_A = 335\text{ Hz}$

Assertion-Reason Questions

1. (*b*) Wavelength

$(\lambda) = \frac{\text{Velocity of wave } (v)}{\text{Frequency } (f)}$

2. (*b*) Transverse wave can be produced in liquid like water.

3. (*c*) A is correct but R is incorrect.

The distance between two successive nodes and antinodes in stationary wave is $\frac{\lambda}{2}$.

4. (*c*) A is correct but R is incorrect.

Wavelength depends on two things i.e., frequency and propagation speed.

5. (*b*) Both A and R are correct but R is not is not the correct explanation of A.

On pressing the stem against a desk top, sound becomes, louder because area of vibration increases.

6. (*c*) A is correct but R is incorrect.

We know that, at anti-node displacement of particles is maximum and pressure difference is minimum while at node, the displacement of particles is minimum and pressure change is maximum. Hence, person will heat the loud sound at node than at anti-nodes. In stationary waves, particles in two different segment vibrates in opposite phase.

7. (*d*) A is incorrect but R is correct.

The particle velocity is a function of time but on the other hand, the wave velocity is independent of time.

8. (*a*)

9. (*b*) Both A and R are correct but R is not the correct explanation of A.

For beats to be heard, the beat frequency should be less than 10 Hz

$f_b = |f_1 - f_2|$

$= |524 - 510|$

$= 14\text{ Hz} > 10\text{ Hz}$

Therefore, the beats cannot be recognized by humar ear.

10. (*c*)

Case Based Questions

1. (i) (*b*); $K = \frac{2\pi}{\lambda} = \frac{2\pi}{2\pi} = 1,$

$w = 2\pi f = 2\pi\left(\frac{1}{\pi}\right) = 2$

equation of wave,

$y = \sin(kx - \omega t) = \sin(x - 2t)$

(ii) (*b*); $y = 3\sin\frac{\pi}{2}(50t - x)$

Particle velocity $= \frac{dy}{dt}$

$= 3\left(\frac{\pi}{2} \times 50\right)\cos\frac{\pi}{2}(50t - x)$

Maximum particle velocity

$= 75\pi$ m/s

Wave velocity, $v = \frac{\omega}{K}$

$= \frac{50}{1} = 50$ m/s

Required ratio $= \frac{75\pi}{50} = \frac{3}{2}\pi$

(iii) (*a*); $y_1 = a\sin(\omega t + kx + 0.57)$

$\phi_1 = \omega t + kx + 0.57$

$y_2 = a\cos(\omega t + kx)$

$= a\sin\left(\omega t + kx + \frac{\pi}{2}\right)$

$\phi_2 = \omega t + kx + \frac{\pi}{2}$

Phase difference,

$\Delta\phi = \phi_2 - \phi_1$

$= (\omega t + kx + \frac{\pi}{2})$

$- (\omega t + kx + 0.57)$

$= \frac{\pi}{2} - 0.57$

$= (1.57 - 0.57) = 1$ rad

(iv) (*a*); Standard wave equation

$y = a\sin\left(\frac{2\pi x}{\lambda} - \frac{2\pi t}{T} + \phi\right)$

$\frac{2\pi}{\lambda} = 0.5\pi$

$\Rightarrow \lambda = \frac{2\pi}{0.5\pi} = 4$ m

So, $\frac{2\pi}{T} = 4\pi$

$\Rightarrow \quad T = \frac{1}{2}$ s

$\nu = \frac{1}{T} = 2$ Hz

Wave velocity $v = \lambda\nu$

$= 4 \times 2 = 8$ m/s

Or (*a*)

2. (i) (*b*);

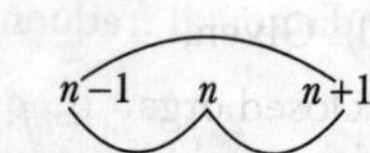

Beats → Maximum difference between two wave frequency.

$\therefore \ (n+1)-(n-1)=2$

(ii) (*d*); Number of beats

$= \nu_1 - \nu_2$

$= \frac{330}{5} - \frac{330}{5.5}$

$= 66 - 60 = 6$

(iii) (*d*); $\omega_1 = 500\pi$

$\Rightarrow \ \nu_1 = 250$

$\Rightarrow \omega_2 = 506\pi$

$\Rightarrow \ \nu_2 = 253$

Number of beats per min

$= \nu_2 - \nu_1$

$= 253 - 250 = 3$

Number of beats per sec

$= 3 \times 60 = 180$

(iv) (*c*); Frequency of beats will be

$\frac{1}{3} - \frac{1}{4} = \frac{1}{12}$

Time period = 12 s

Or

(*c*); Given, $f_A = f$

and $f_B = 260$ Hz

Since, it produces 8 beats

$b = |f_A - f_B| = |f - 260|$

$\pm 8 = f - 260$

$\Rightarrow f = 268$ Hz or 252 Hz.

Competition Edge Up

1. (60); $(f_O)_1 l_1 = (f_O)_2 l_2$

$\Rightarrow \ 400 \times 90 = 600 \times l_2$

$\Rightarrow \ l_2 = \frac{400 \times 90}{600} = 60$ cm

2. (6); Frequency of tuning fork

= Frequency of string

$= f_1 = \frac{1}{2L}\sqrt{\frac{T}{\mu}} = \frac{1}{2}\sqrt{\frac{6}{\mu}}$

When tension is made 54 N, then 12 beats are produced.

Now, frequency of string is,

$f_2 = \frac{1}{2}\sqrt{\frac{54}{\mu}} = \frac{3}{2}\sqrt{\frac{6}{\mu}} = 3f_1$

Also, $3f_1 - f_1 = 12$

$\Rightarrow \quad 2f_1 = 12$ or $f_1 = 6$ Hz

3. (400); Given,

For closed organ pipe fundamental frequency,

$f = 30$ Hz

($v = 330$ m/s given)

Let, length of closed organ pipe

$= L$

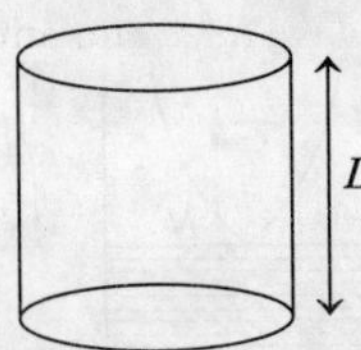

We know that,

Fundamental frequency,

$$f = \frac{v}{4L} \quad \ldots \text{(i)}$$

$30 = \frac{330}{4L}$

$L = \frac{330}{30 \times 4} = \frac{11}{4} = 2.75$ m

Now, *x* g of water is added

Water filled upto height *h*.

New frequency $f' = 110$ Hz

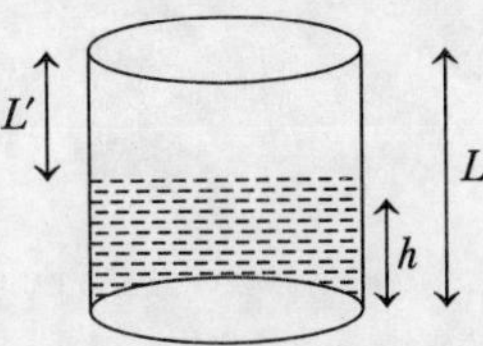

Again using formula Eq.(i)

$f' = \frac{v}{4L'} \qquad [L' = L - h]$

$110 = \frac{330}{4L'}$

$\Rightarrow \quad L' = \frac{330}{110 \times 4} = 0.75$ cm

$h = L - L'$

$\Rightarrow \quad h = 2.75 - 0.75 = 2$ m

Volume of liquid (water) filled

= Area × Height

$V = 2 \times 200 \text{ cm}^3 (a = 2 \text{ cm}^2$ given)

$= 400 \text{ cm}^3$

Amount of water (mass) = Volume × Density of water

$= 400 \times 1 = 400$ g

4. (3); As intensity of sound is inversely proportional to square of distance;

$I \propto \frac{1}{r^2}$

or $I_1 r_1^2 = I_2 r_2^2$

So, Intensity at 2m distance

$I_1 = \frac{16 \times 10^{-8}}{2^2} = 4 \times 10^{-8} \frac{\text{W}}{\text{m}^2}$

Intensity at 4 m distance

$I_2 = \frac{16 \times 10^{-8}}{4^2} = 1 \times 10^{-8} \frac{\text{W}}{\text{m}^2}$

So, difference is,

$I_1 - I_2 = (4-1) \times 10^{-8} \frac{\text{W}}{\text{m}^2}$

$= 3 \times 10^{-8} \frac{\text{W}}{\text{m}^2}$

5. (*16*); Given, length of closed organ pipe (L_1) = Length of open organ pipe (L_2) = L (say);

Now, for closed organ pipe,

*n*th overtone, $f_n = (2n+1)\frac{v}{4l}$

For open organ pipe

*n*th overtone,

$f_n = (n+1)\frac{v}{2l}$

$\therefore \ \frac{(f_n)_{\text{closed}}}{(f_n)_{\text{open}}} = \frac{\frac{15v}{4l}}{\frac{8v}{2l}}$

$= \frac{15}{4} \times \frac{2}{8} = \frac{15}{16}$

6. (*740*); The difference in frequency in open organ pipe,

$\Delta f = \frac{6v}{2 \times 0.6} - \frac{5v}{2 \times 0.9} \left[\because f = \frac{nv}{2L}\right]$

$= \frac{6 \times 333}{2 \times 0.6} - \frac{5 \times 333}{2 \times 0.9}$

$= 740$ Hz

7. (*b*); Velocity of transverse wave in the string, $v \propto \sqrt{T}$

$\therefore \ \frac{v_1}{v_2} = \sqrt{\frac{T_1}{T_2}} = \sqrt{\frac{T_1}{2T_1}} \quad [\because T_2 = 2T_1]$

$= \frac{1}{\sqrt{2}}$

$v_1 : v_2 = 1 : \sqrt{2}$

8. (*b*); Length of string of musical instrument, $l = 90$ cm $= 0.9$ m

Fundamental frequency,

$f_1 = 120$ Hz

$f_2 = 180$ Hz

$\therefore$ We know that, $f \propto \frac{1}{l}$

$\Rightarrow \frac{f_1}{f_2} = \frac{l_2}{l_1}$

$$\Rightarrow l_2 = \frac{f_1 l_1}{f_2} = \frac{120 \times 0.9}{180}$$

$$= \frac{2}{3} \times 0.9 = 0.6 \text{ m}$$

$$= 60 \text{ cm}$$

9. (*a*); In case of beats formation unknown frequency $(\nu_B) = \nu_A \pm$ beats

where, $\nu_A = 530$ Hz and beats $= 6$ Hz.

$\Rightarrow \quad \nu_B = 530 \pm 6 = 536$

or 524 Hz

When tension in B is slightly decreased, then beats frequency increases to 7 Hz. This is possible if we take original frequency of B as 524 Hz.

10. (*c*); For vibrating tunning fork over a resonance tube, the first resonance is obtained at the length

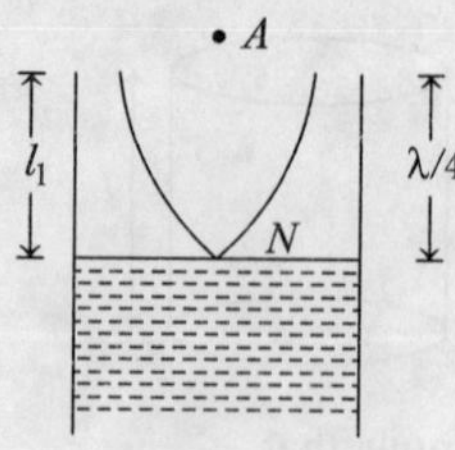

and for second resonance,

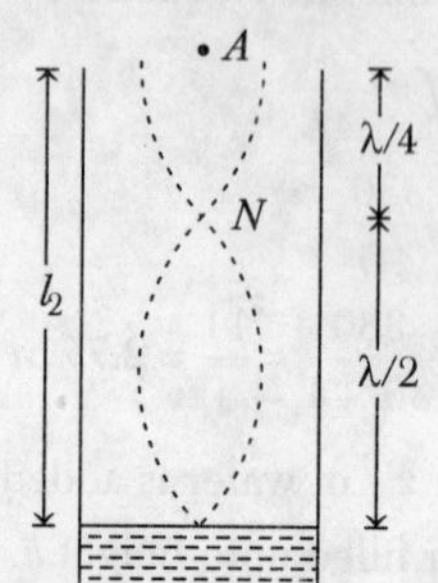

$$l_2 = \frac{\lambda}{4} + \frac{\lambda}{2} = \frac{3\lambda}{4} \quad \ldots \text{(ii)}$$

From Eq. (i) and (ii), we get

$$l_2 - l_1 = \frac{3\lambda}{4} - \frac{\lambda}{4} = \frac{\lambda}{2}$$

$$\Rightarrow \quad \lambda = 2(l_2 - l_1)$$

$$\Rightarrow \quad v = 2f(l_2 - l_1) \quad \ldots \text{(iii)}$$

$$\left(\because \lambda = \frac{v}{f}\right)$$

Here, $f = 800$ Hz, $l_1 = 9.75$ cm, $l_2 = 31.25$ cm

On substituting the given values in Eq. (iii), we get

$$\Rightarrow \quad v = 2 \times 800(31.25 - 9.75)$$

$$= 34400 \text{ cm/s}$$

$$= 344 \text{ m/s}$$